Hungarian Yearbook 2021

eleven

Hungarian Yearbook of International Law and European Law
Volume 9 HYIEL 2021

Aim and scope
Hungarian Yearbook of International Law and European Law is a collection of articles written mostly by Hungarian authors covering developments in the field of international law and European law, and progress in domestic implementation and application of these fields of law. The online archives consist of all the articles published in the book series since 2013. The Yearbook articles analyse well-known Hungary-related cases and their assessment from the perspective of Hungarian legal experts. Moreover, the articles offer a comprehensive picture of the state of application and implementation of EU law and international law in Hungary.

Submission of articles
Manuscripts should be submitted by email to the editorial team at editors@hungarianyearbook.com. The instructions for authors are available from www.hungarianyearbook.com.

Publisher
Eleven International Publishing, Hofweg 9D, P.O. Box 85576, 2508 CG The Hague, info@elevenpub.com, www.elevenpub.com.

Subscriptions
The East European Yearbook on Human Rights is published once a year. Individual annual subscription rates for 2021 are € 125 (online) and € 175 (access via IP). Prices exclude VAT. For more information or to request a quote, please contact info@elevenpub.com.

Open access policy
The Author has the right six months after publication to upload the Contribution in the repository of his university (green open access), under a Creative Commons BY-NC-SA license. For more information, visit www.elevenjournals.com. Eleven International Publishing assumes that the author agrees to the license which can be found on the website. Subscription queries and requests for sample copies should be addressed to the Publisher.

The publication of this volume was supported by Pallas Athéné Domus Meriti Alapítvány.

ISSN 2666-2701

Hungarian Yearbook of International Law and European Law
2021 (9) 1

Table of Contents

EDITORIAL

Editorial Comments: COVID-19 – EU Citizenship and the Right to Free Movement in a Public Health Crisis

Foreword to Vol. 9 (2021) of the Hungarian Yearbook of International Law and European Law

*Laura Gyeney**

1. Introduction

It is still a prevailing view in legal literature,[1] that the legal instrument of Union citizenship is in its "regressive phase".[2] So far, the *Zambrano* doctrine,[3] developed by the CJEU just a decade ago to ensure respect for the substance of Union citizenship, has played merely a marginal role in the life of the EU citizens.[4] This statement is particularly true when considered from the perspective of Article 21 TFEU guaranteeing the primary right of free movement.[5] However, the CJEU's

* Laura Gyeney: editor; associate professor of law, Pázmány Péter Catholic University, Budapest.

1 On future challenges of the institution of EU citizenship *see* Daniel Thym (ed.), *Questioning EU Citizenship*, Hart Publishing, Oxford, 2017; Nathan Cambien *et al.* (eds.), *European Citizenship Under Stress: Social Justice, Brexit and Other Challenges*, Brill, Nijhoff, Leiden, 2020.

2 Stephen Coutts, 'The Absence of Integration and the Responsibilisation of Union Citizenship', *European Papers*, Vol. 3, Issue 2, 2018, p. 761.

3 The CJEU declared in connection with the status of EU citizenship in *Zambrano* that "Article 20 TFEU precludes national measures which have the effect of depriving citizens of the Union of the genuine enjoyment of the substance of the right conferred by virtue of their status as citizens of the Union." Judgment of 8 March 2011, *Case C-34/09, Ruiz Zambrano*, ECLI:EU:C:2011:124, para. 42.

4 It is mostly due to the fact that the doctrine based on Article 20 TFEU may be applied only in extraordinary cases.

5 While van Eijken acknowledges the narrow scope of the doctrine but highlights its role in promoting certain fundamental rights, such as respect for family life and children's rights, Van der Brink questions its *raison d'etre*. He concludes as the Zambrano doctrine is also rooted in free movement, the differentiation between legal status enshrined in Articles 20 and 21 TFEU is artificial, moreover, it results in conceptual confusion. *See* Hanneke van Eijken, 'Connecting the Dots Backwards, What Did Ruiz Zambrano Mean for EU Citizenship and Fundamental Rights in EU Law?', *European Journal of Migration and Law*, Vol. 23, Issue 1, 2021, p. 67; Martijn van den Brink, 'Is It Time to Abolish the Substance of EU Citizenship Rights Test?', *European Journal of Migration and Law*, Vol. 23, Issue 1, 2021, pp. 13-28.

doi: 10.5553/HYIEL/266627012021009001001

case-law, which shows sensitivity to Member States fears' of social tourism,[6] and significantly curtails the right to free movement of economically inactive citizens,[7] pushes more and more Union citizens to struggle with the sense of being expelled from the 'elite club' of those enjoying the advantages of free movement.[8]

This situation is exacerbated by the global public health crisis triggered by the COVID-19 pandemic, which is doing unprecedented harm to European mobility. The Member States' travel restrictions / bans and the reintroduction of internal border controls to control the spread of the pandemic have a direct effect on the personal life of thousands of Union citizens and their family members besides the fact that they may also lead to economic collapse and threaten the operation of the internal market.[9] As a result, at the time of the writing of this Editorial (May 2021), the question is not who benefits from free movement, but rather, who is affected by the limitation of this right and to what extent.

The first, rather hectic reactions of the Member States to the crisis did not only restrict individual rights, but also seemed to shake belief in the European project. The lack of delivering quick and efficient EU response made sceptic voices grow stronger: "Europe may not be as united as people would like to believe."[10] Apparently, it cannot be considered otherwise as the rise of Euroscepticism. What else could underlie the fact that Member States are introducing measures restricting the export of individual protective equipment and later certain drugs and drug substances with the aim of mitigating the pressure on their respective health care systems, than the lack of solidarity.[11] And as if this were not enough,

6 The exact reasons for the austerity measures are still disputable. Representatives of legal literature cite here the crisis process having inflicted Europe over the last one and half decades, the prolonged economic crisis of 2008, the global migration crisis, and Brexit. They also attach high importance to some internal factors, such as the restoration of federal bargaining processes related to the institution of EU citizenship.

7 This restrictive approach was realized mostly in connection with the social benefits of EU citizens and the practice of expelling them from the territory of the host country.

8 According to Davies, the members of the elite club of those enjoying the right of free movement are the people who are brave enough to improve their life by their own actions. *See* Gareth Davies, 'How Citizenship Divides: The New Legal Class of Transnational Europeans', *European Papers*, Vol. 4, Issue 3, 2019, p. 678.

9 "The spread of the virus is causing disruption of global supply chains, volatility in financial markets, consumer demand shocks and negative impact in key sectors like travel and tourism." Communication from the Commission to the European Parliament, the European Council, the Council, the European Central Bank, the European Investment Bank and the Eurogroup, *Coordinated Economic Response to the COVID-19 Outbreak*, COM(2020) 112 final.

10 Saila Heinikoski, 'COVID-19 Bends the Rules on Border Controls – Yet Another Crisis Undermining the Schengen Acquis?' *FIIA Briefing Paper*, Issue 281, April 2020, p. 7.

11 Restrictive measures greatly varied: whiles export of safety glasses, medical masks or FFP2/FFP3 masks required merely a prior notification in Poland, there was an export ban on heart monitors. Likewise, Germany introduced a total export ban on protective gear, while Hungary banned exports of a pharma raw material called hidroxi chloroquine sulfat. On compliance of export bans with EU law *see* Tomislav Sokol, 'Public Health Emergencies and Export Restrictions: Solidarity and A Common Approach or Disintegration of the Internal Market?', *Common Market Law Review*, Vol. 57, Issue 6, 2020, pp. 1819-1842.

doi: 10.5553/HYIEL/266627012021009001001

governments convey a symbolic message to their citizens by imposing travel bans: We have taken the fight to coronavirus, we are protecting our citizens."

However, it would be premature to conclude that the quick and drastic Member State reactions should be regarded as a sign of dissatisfaction with the EU or, *ad absurdum*, a violation of the principle of loyalty, stigmatizing the EU as an IGO with an inability to react. It is worth bearing in mind that the EU is a multi-level system with overlapping competences of the Member States and the EU, in which public health issues, including crises, still belong under Member State competences. In the course of an unprecedented public health crisis, the excessive use of political symbolism does not come as a surprise,[12] for citizens, in these critical situations expect first and foremost that the national governments provide them with protection.[13]

The proper (and lawful) EU conduct is to take a side role and let the Member State governments use their power to manage public health emergencies to fulfil their duty of 'serving the public good'. In this respect, one may conclude that the COVID-19 pandemic has managed to highlight interdependence and reciprocity in a completely new field: Member States are required to exercise their exclusive powers concerning public health while still abiding by EU rules. In the same way, the EU is also required to adjust to the Member States' exercise of powers concerning public health matters. According to Coutts, the above must be carried out under Commission surveillance, monitoring available exemptions and safeguards, which the author refers to as 'managed flexibility'. However, Coutts' way of thinking must be slightly adjusted, for in this case, it is not only one or few Member States' public health situation that is at stake, but that of all Member States.

Nevertheless, there is no doubt that the Member States' restrictions on free movement described below are well-founded from the point of view of both public international law and European law. As to how they should be put into practice: that is another issue. Still, it is the preferential role of free movement as a part of integration that requires a deeper examination of controversial measures whether to ascertain whether these are in compliance with EU legal principles. Among the elements to be reviewed are proportionality and the prohibition on discrimination. Due to the limitations of the Editorial, this article focuses on travel restrictions and bans and the temporary reintroduction of internal border controls. It concentrates in particular on Member States'

12 On symbolic power of borders in crisis situation *see* Daniel Thym & Jonas Bornemann,'Schengen and Free Movement Law During the First Phase of the COVID-19 Pandemic: Of Symbolism, Law and Politics', *European Papers*, Vol. 5, Issue 3, 2020, p. 1144. The authors take the example of President Donald Trump's campaign on constructing a border wall between Mexico and the USA. President Joe Biden, the successor of former President Donald Trump, revoked the declaration of emergency situation right on the first day of his presidency, which allowed for a restructuring defense funds to finance the wall on the Mexican border.

13 It is hardly a coincidence that even the WHO refrained from raising its voice against the austerity measures.

doi: 10.5553/HYIEL/266627012021009001001

measures introduced concerning one another, without addressing measures regarding the closing of the EU's external borders.[14]

2. National Restrictions to Prevent the Spread of the Pandemic, with Special Regard to Hungarian Legislation

Early 2020, COVID-19 spread quickly throughout Europe. Italy was the first Member State to announce a high concentration of coronavirus cases, followed by a growing number of states. By March 2020, coronavirus could be detected in every Member State. The WHO declared a pandemic, albeit after some hesitation.[15]

Member States gave a surprisingly quick response, taking unilateral restrictive measures affecting the operation of the internal market in an unprecedented way. In order to contain the spread of this contagious illness, most Member States[16] reintroduced border controls for air and road transport.[17] Simultaneously, Member States launched travel bans and restrictions for both entry and exit travels.[18] These restrictions and prohibitions were adopted in various legal forms and with different content, but generally it can be said that entry travel restrictions did not apply to own citizens[19] and non-citizens residing in the Member State.

Individual entry travel restrictions predominantly applied to foreign citizens who had COVID-19 symptoms, and the medical check / COVID-19 test showed a positive result upon entry. Currently, there is an individual entry travel restriction in force under the existing Hungarian law.[20] Accordingly, a person may not enter Hungary if the medical check results in a suspicion of contagion. Meanwhile, in certain cases, some Member States opted for introducing general prohibition measures that go beyond individual safety precautions against

14 On closing external borders *see* Luisa Marin, 'The COVID-19 Crisis and the Closure of External Borders: Another Stress-test for the Challenging Construction of Solidarity Within the EU?', *European Papers*, Vol. 5, 2020, Issue 2, pp. 1071-1086.

15 The WHO was harshly criticized for underestimating the virulence of COVID-19 and hereby contributing to the accumulation of global delay in imposing safety precautions.

16 *See* at https://ec.europa.eu/home-affairs/what-we-do/policies/borders-and-visas/schengen/reintroduction-border-control_en.

17 By the second half of March 2020, 16 states had reintroduced border controls. The first Schengen country to take this step by specifically referring to COVID-19, was Austria at its common border with Italy, extending it out to its other borders as well.

18 The principle of free movement does not only ensure the right to entry, but also the exit right which has been supported several times in the legal practice of the CJEU. *See e.g.* Judgment of 10 July 2008, Case C-33/07, *Jipa*, ECLI:EU:C:2008:396; Judgment of 17 November 2011, *Case C-434/10, Aladzhov*, ECLI:EU:C:2011:750; Judgment of 17 November 2011, *Case C-430/10, Gaydarov*, ECLI:EU:C:2011:749.

19 This consideration is completely understandable in view of the fact that the constitutions of the European States expressly stipulate that their own citizens are entitled to return home from abroad at any time. *See e.g.* Article XIV(2) of the Fundamental Law of Hungary: "Hungarian nationals [...] may return from abroad at any time."

20 Government Decree No. 408/2020. (VIII. 30.) on travel restrictions during pandemic times, which entered into force on 1 September 2020.

doi: 10.5553/HYIEL/266627012021009001001

entrants from high-risk countries. An example would be the rules in force in Hungary since March 2020, which precluded the entry of citizens arriving from Italy, that is, the center of the pandemic in Europe. In practice, this meant the suspension of passenger transport: no train, bus or civil air flight transporting citizens internationally was allowed to enter the State, with the exception of transiting vehicles.[21] The Romanian rules bear resemblance to the legislation described above. Here, the mass return of Romanian citizens was curbed by the suspension of air transport and later train transport between Italy and Romania, forcing Hungary to open a humanitarian corridor.[22] Lastly, Sweden launched a similar prohibition against entrants from Norway upon the emergence of the new UK strain.[23]

It is essential to distinguish between complete entry prohibition and the case when the Member States concerned formally provide for an entry prohibition, but the *high number of exceptions* imply entry restrictions (in terms of substance). The Hungarian rules in force can be mentioned here as an example, according to which "Non-Hungarian citizens are barred from entering the State, unless otherwise stipulated by laws or government decrees."[24] Upon request, official exemption may be granted on the condition that the applicant substantiates that the reason of entry falls under one of the listed exemptions.

In most cases, *the Member States made rules on merely entry restrictions* (irrespective of its official denomination). Under these rules, with the exception of their own citizens and those residing there, EU citizens from other Member States are allowed to enter their territory only if the reason for the entry is listed as an exemption in the provision restricting entry. Engagement in business-economic related activity is widely regarded as a compelling reason in most Member States, yet there was no complete agreement between the Member States even on such a basic issue. Denmark refrained banned entry in general without regard to business-economic related activities for a long time. Finland allowed for entry on work or business reasons from the onset of the crisis in respect of those whose activity is essential to ensure supply and the functioning of society. Germany followed a similar route; the State turned back thousands of EU entrants at its border shared with Tirol and the Czech Republic once the UK strain had appeared. The official reasoning of the German Interior Ministry is

21 Government Decree No. 41/2020. (III. 11.) on the measures to be taken during the state of danger declared for the prevention of the human epidemic endangering life and property and causing massive disease outbreaks, for the elimination of its consequences, and for the protection of the health and lives of Hungarian citizens.

22 On effect of Romanian regulations on free movement imposed in connection with COVID-19 *see* Sandra Mantu, 'EU Citizenship, Free Movement, and Covid-19 in Romania', *Frontiers in Human Dynamics*, 2:594987, December 2020, at www.frontiersin.org/articles/10.3389/fhumd.2020.594987/full.

23 Concerns over the British coronavirus variant prompted a lot of countries to enact entry bans on those arriving from the UK. Thus, many countries suspended air travel from this state. However, considering the fact that the UK has not been a member of the EU since 1 January 2021, discussing the said regulation here is unnecessary.

24 Government Decree No. 408/2020. (VIII. 30.), Section 5.

doi: 10.5553/HYIEL/266627012021009001001

that only essential workers were entitled to enter the State.[25] In the Member States' practice, exemptions to entry restrictions include study obligations based on students' status, important family or private reasons, *e.g.* marriage, baptism, funeral ceremony, or medical treatment, or exceptionally, the aversion of imminent damage to property.[26]

Measures rendering entry contingent on prior or posterior conditions *can also be regarded as travel restrictions to prevent further spread of the pandemic.*[27] Most Member States require a negative (PCR or antigen) COVID-19 test done within a maximum of 72 hours[28] before the commencement of the travel from those arriving from high-risk regions. This requirement is complemented by a compulsory quarantine following entry,[29] mostly in the form of domestic quarantine.[30] The period of compulsory quarantine was predominantly stipulated as 14 days during the first wave and 10 days during the second and third wave. Most States allow for a substitution of the quarantine with one or typically two negative tests (two-test strategy), the conditions of which diverge.[31] In addition, several Member States introduced a 'passenger locator form' for entrants, mostly arriving from high-risk regions. This form focuses on information on the method of travel (flight, car) and areas the entrants have visited in the two weeks preceding entry.[32]

Last but not least, it is also worth mentioning national restrictions in the Member States generally referred to as *'lockdown'*. This expression covers any internal restriction within the Member State's boundaries that is not essential. Examples include general curfew or domestic regional travel restrictions. Although these measures played a significant role in curbing the spread of the virus, due to their internal, non-essential nature their relevance under international or EU law is marginal.

25 *See* at www.euronews.com/2021/02/16/eu-concerned-as-germany-partially-closes-border-with-austria-and-czech-republic.

26 Entry bans implicitly apply to transit travel, which is allowed, subject to strict conditions in most Member States. This option is normally available for a compelling reason, without stop in case of road travel, without leaving the transit zone in case of air travel, and always within a set time limit. The Member States normally provide 6-12 hours for crossing their territory.

27 The scope of measure generally depends on whether the entrant arrives from a low or high-risk area from pandemic point of view. Currently, the States uniformly apply the ECDC color ranking in contrast with the former routine when it was different country by country, furthermore, some States like Cyprus used a letter code. *See* at www.schengenvisainfo.com/news/cyprus-introduces-new-categorization-of-entry-restrictions/.

28 It is maximum 24 or 48 hours in some Member States.

29 Compulsory quarantine is applied by Austria, Belgium, Czech Republic, Estonia, Germany, Hungary, Ireland, Italy, Latvia, Lithuania, Romania, Slovakia and Slovenia.

30 At the same time, Denmark was one of the few Member States that did not apply quarantine measures, self-quarantine was only a recommendation made by health care authorities. In other countries, for example in Finland, quarantine was obligatory but without official control.

31 Thus, exemption from quarantine is granted in Hungary if the person who is to undertake quarantine presents two negative PCR tests within 5 days following entry into the country's territory, with 48 hours difference.

32 Belgium, Cyprus, Germany, Greece, Malta, Romania, Spain and Slovakia.

doi: 10.5553/HYIEL/266627012021009001001

3. Legal Assessment of Member States' Actions in Terms of EU Law

The EU is founded on open borders and free movement guaranteed by the Schengen System on the one hand, and, on the other hand, by the legal status of EU citizenship and concomitant rights of free movement. Pandemic-related safety precautions affected every area in a radical way. Meanwhile, some provisions of EU law (even if within limits) enabled the Member States to reintroduce temporary border controls and to put entry bans and restrictions into place. In the following, we will discuss their compliance with the principles of EU law.[33]

3.1. Measures of the Member States to Reintroduce Border Controls

First and foremost, it is essential to distinguish between Member State actions to reintroduce border controls and travel bans / restrictions launched for the first time in EU history. While the former measures may cause some inconveniences for travelers but do not curb mobility between the Member States *per se* (they may merely make it more burdensome in practice), travel bans, and restrictions completely exclude or at least restrict travel.

Under the *Schengen Borders Code*,[34] Member States are entitled to temporarily reintroduce internal border controls in case of a significant danger to public policy or internal security.[35] Article 25 of the Code expressly provides for a reintroduction of border controls in case of foreseeable events. By contrast, Article 28 is applicable for unexpected, that is, unforeseeable events, where the imminent threat requires prompt action from the Member States. Thus, the two provisions complement one another and involve different procedural rules. Article 25 requires the Commission's prior written notification of the reintroduction of internal border controls, whereas Article 28 stipulates that notification shall take place simultaneously with the action. These actions may be extended for 6 months in case of foreseeable events,[36] and for a maximum of 2 months when introducing immediate action. Respect for time limits, the unique nature of the reintroduction of controls and compliance with the principle of proportionality[37] ensure lawfulness of the action. At least, in an ideal case.

During the first wave of the pandemic, altogether 17 Schengen States sent notifications regarding the reintroduction of border controls. Initially, these

33 Thym & Bornemann 2020, p. 1146.

34 Regulation (EU) 2016/399 of the European Parliament and of the Council of 9 March 2016 on a Union Code on the rules governing the movement of persons across borders (Schengen Borders Code).

35 The Schengen Borders Code provides for the reintroduction of border control in three cases. The specific procedure enshrined in Article 29 does not need to be closely analyzed as this applies to cases when the overall functioning of the area without internal border control becomes jeopardized due to persistent and serious deficiencies related to external border control.

36 As the main rule, the border control can be reintroduced for a maximum 30 days, or for the expected duration of the serious threat if it exceeds 30 days. If needed, this period can be extended by a further 30 days, however, it cannot exceed 6 months in total.

37 The scope and duration of the temporary reintroduction of border control shall not exceed what is strictly necessary to respond to the serious threat.

doi: 10.5553/HYIEL/266627012021009001001

States referred to Article 28 regulating actions under unexpected circumstances.[38] Next, they invoked Article 25 allowing for the maximum 6 months ban after the expiry of the 2-month period. In 6 States, however, the formerly introduced border control measure was extended. Austria, Denmark, France, Germany, Norway and Sweden have maintained border controls since the commencement of the migration crisis with reference to the terror threat or danger provoked by the secondary movement of illegal migrants.[39]

The legitimacy of the Schengen legal order can, however, be easily undermined by shifting from one legal basis to another[40] for the reintroduction of border controls and ignoring the maximum time periods, *ad absurdum* the lapse of time for exercising border control.[41] This is particularly true as EU lawmakers[42] have failed to make a decision on the amendment of the Commission proposal on extending the time limit to temporarily reintroduce border controls.[43] As Thym and Bornemann put it, the Member States keep treating border control as their '*quasi* sovereign domain' regardless of the fact whether their actions are in line with the Code or not.[44] Despite the fact that the European Parliament expressed its concern about the Member State actions described above several times,[45] the

38 With the exception of Denmark, Finland, and France that referred to Article 25 and the clause of foreseeable event, the former did so exclusively and purely as a means to curb the pandemic, whereas the latter two relied on a new justification ground for the formerly introduced measures.

39 *See* at www.infomigrants.net/en/post/20754/border-checks-in-eu-countries-challenge-schengen-agreement.

40 According to Montaldo, the change in justification is highly problematic as the justifying reasons do not meet necessity and proportionality requirements in many cases. To give an example, although the number of migrants arriving in EU territory has been dramatically declining since 2016, the Member States repetitively and generally refer to a threat posed by secondary migration movement. *See* Stefano Montaldo,'The COVID-19 Emergency and the Reintroduction of Internal Border Controls in the Schengen Area: Never Let a Serious Crisis Go to Waste', *European Papers*, Vol 5, Issue 1, 2020, p. 528.

41 "These serious threats compelled some Member States to prolong reintroduced border control several times, sometimes until the exhaustion of the current legal time frames." *See* Proposal for a Regulation of the European Parliament and of the Council amending Regulation (EU) 2016/399 as regards the rules applicable to the temporary reintroduction of border control at internal borders. COM(2017) 571 final.

42 As the Member States were unable to broker an agreement about the 2017 proposal, it has been suggested that a new Commission proposal shall be discussed as part of the Schengen strategy. *See* at www.europarl.europa.eu/RegData/etudes/BRIE/2021/662622/EPRS_BRI(2021)662622_EN.pdf.

43 The cited Commission proposal would extend the maximum time frame of border controls from 6 months to 1 year in the case of foreseeable events. Moreover, to make the length of renewable periods more proportionate with the maximum time frame of border controls, the latter ones would be extended from 30 days to 6 months.

44 Thym and Bornemann 2020, p. 1148.

45 In May 2018, the European Parliament called upon the Commission to launch an infringement procedure, however, the Commission seems not to have attached importance to the infringement of the Code, in spite of the fact that the Commission encourages the Member States to lift internal border controls. *See* European Parliament resolution of 30 May 2018 on the annual report on the functioning of the Schengen area, at www.europarl.europa.eu/doceo/document/TA-8-2018-0228_EN.html.

doi: 10.5553/HYIEL/266627012021009001001

Commission failed to launch infringement procedures[46] and call the Member States to lift permanent border control.[47] Furthermore, it did not even request on-the-spot inspections or hear relevant Member State authorities (notwithstanding the fact that the Schengen Evaluation Mechanism expressly provides for this possibility).

The measures introduced doubtlessly proved to be a justifiable reaction to the danger to public policy and internal security triggered by the COVID-19 pandemic. This cannot be called into question even by the fact that the Code itself does not explicitly refer to public health threat as a reason for reintroducing border control. The wide interpretation of public health in this particular case includes serious public health risk. It is underlined *expressis verbis* by the Commission Guidelines of March 2020 on "Guidelines for border management measures to protect public health and ensure the availability of goods and essential service" that *"In an extremely critical situation, a Member State can identify a need to reintroduce border controls as a reaction to the risk posed by a contagious disease."*[48] Furthermore, the high threshold set by EU jurisdiction regarding public policy and public security exceptions[49] seems to be applied in light of the serious social and economic consequences of the COVID-19 pandemic.[50]

3.2. Measures Hindering the Free Movement of EU Citizens

The right to free movement, as the crux of economic integration,[51] *has become a constitutional right* after being expanded to EU citizens and enshrined in the EU Charter of Fundamental Rights.[52] Its limitation[53] requires judicial review in every single case. On the other hand, EU law counterbalances, as Király put it, rules which materially affect the sovereignty of the Member States' right to make and

46 Implementation of the Schengen Borders Code in this specific field, parallel to the Commission's general competence, is regulated by a *lex specialis*, that is, a regulation on the Schengen Evaluation Mechanism. *See* Council Regulation (EU) No 1053/2013 of 7 October 2013 establishing an evaluation and monitoring mechanism to verify the application of the Schengen acquis and repealing the Decision of the Executive Committee of 16 September 1998 setting up a Standing Committee on the evaluation and implementation of Schengen.

47 Since the entry into force of the Schengen Evaluation and Monitoring Mechanism in 2015, a single infringement procedure was launched against Estonia, related to the Schengen rules on external borders. *See* at https://ec.europa.eu/commission/presscorner/detail/hu/inf_20_1687.

48 *See* COVID-19: Guidelines for border management measures to protect health and ensure the availability of goods and essential services, COM(2020) 1753 final, especially para. 18.

49 In the case-law of the CJEU public order allows for restrictions against persons directly and seriously threatening one of the society's fundamental values.

50 Less serious epidemics may trigger travel restrictions only on individuals.

51 The development of the facet of free movement of persons has remained unbroken for the past 60 years, a stable edifice has gradually been built upon the axis of equal treatment. *See e.g.* Éva Gellérné Lukács, 'From Equal Treatment to Positive Actions Through Non-Discriminative Obstacles – Regarding the Free Movement of Persons', *ELTE Law Journal*, 2018/2, pp. 101-125.

52 *See* Article 45 of the Charter.

53 The Treaties have contained provisions on the Member States' right to restrict free movement based on public order, public security and public health since the very beginning. These provisions cover every restriction on EU citizens residing in the Member States including entry and exit bans, the refusal to renew/issue residence permits and the adoption of expulsion decisions against them.

doi: 10.5553/HYIEL/266627012021009001001

apply laws by offering a generous set of exceptions.[54] One of the exceptions enshrined in primary law is the justification of public health, which also appears in secondary law as part of the Free Movement Directive.[55] Article 29 of the directive explicitly empowers the Member States to take measures that restrict free movement if the protection of public health is at stake.

It is beyond doubt that COVID-19 can definitely be regarded as a 'disease with epidemic potential' that can justify restrictions on free movement. It is also obvious that public health, as a derogation from the economic freedom, must be interpreted strictly. However, the circumstances that can justify reference to public health can vary from one State to another. Thus, in this respect, the discretional power of the Member States must be recognized or admitted.[56] Evidently, the question can be posed whether Article 29 provides for the introduction of public health restrictions with general effect. In other words, does it allow for restrictions not based on individual assessment, as opposed to individual threats to public policy and public security. I am convinced that the answer is in the affirmative: *in lack of opposing, expressly directive-type provisions, no individual assessment can be required in case of a public health threat.*[57] On the other hand, even if we accept that generalized restrictions can be justified on public health grounds, and the Member States have wide discretion in terms of how they may react to crisis, it is inevitable to examine their compliance with EU law.

When examining the *legality of travel bans and restrictions*, the concordance between the measures taken by the Member State must be assessed, that is, the internal coherence of the relevant policy of the Member State.[58] If there is no coherence, there are solid grounds to suspect arbitrary discrimination and the disproportionality of the measures. Lang questions the proportionality of measures due to concerns about opening humanitarian corridors from the point

54 Miklós Király, *A diszkrimináció tilalma az Európai Bíróság joggyakorlatában*, Akadémiai, Budapest, 1998, p. 208.

55 Directive 2004/38/EC of the European Parliament and of the Council of 29 April 2004 on the right of citizens of the Union and their family members to move and reside freely within the territory of the Member States amending Regulation (EEC) No 1612/68 and repealing Directives 64/221/EEC, 68/360/EEC, 72/194/EEC, 73/148/EEC, 75/34/EEC, 75/35/EEC, 90/364/EEC, 90/365/EEC and 93/96/EEC.

56 *See* Judgment of 4 December 1974, *Case C-41/74, Van Duyn*, ECLI:EU:C:1974:133, para. 18.

57 This viewpoint is supported by the latest CJEU case-law which does not require the examination of the individual circumstances in every case regarding equal treatment in connection with the Member States' restriction on social benefits based on the principle of free movement. Thus, in *Alimanovic* and *Garcia Nieto* regarding social provision of economically inactive citizens, the CJEU found that a Member State is entitled to refuse the provision applied for automatically in the first 3 months of the residence and during the period of job seeking exceeding three months, even if no individual examination is carried out, as the Free Movement Directive per se takes into account the special circumstances of the claimant. *See* Strumia Francesca, 'European Citizenship and Transnational Rights: Chronicles of a Troubled Narrative', *in* Thym (ed.) 2017, pp. 149-168.

58 Thym & Bornemann 2020, p. 1168.

doi: 10.5553/HYIEL/266627012021009001001

of view of public health, in respect of their suitability and necessity.[59] As far as Hungary is concerned, the issue of compliance with EU law can be raised in connection with opening humanitarian corridors to facilitate the return of Romanian and Bulgarian migrant workers.[60] Since the Hungarian authorities permitted the return of Romanian and Bulgarian citizens merely on one single occasion, moreover by transfer at night, *via* Hungary, one can conclude that this measure completely complies with the generally restrictive set of rules related to COVID-19.[61]

A similar question may be raised in connection with *'travel bubbles'*, which allows Member States to open their borders for travelers from one given country, while their bans or restrictions on travelers arriving from other countries are still in force. The first countries to open such a bubble were Estonia, Latvia, and Lithuania to ensure free movement of their citizens and simultaneously, they maintained quarantine requirements for other entrants.[62] Indeed, this practice may pose a problem from the perspective of non-discrimination and proportionality; nevertheless, it can be justified if the member states' incidence rate shows similar numbers. The Commission underlined:

> "Where a Member State decides to allow travel into its territory or to specific regions and areas within its territory, it should do so in a non-discriminatory manner – allowing travel from all regions or countries in the EU with similar epidemiological situations."[63]

Obviously, the procedures for lifting restrictions must comply with the non-discrimination principle. It is clear that reference to the public health exception may not result in an arbitrary discrimination against citizens of other Member States. However, equal treatment cannot be required, either.[64]

Those applying these rules are faced with a much more difficult challenge related to the fulfilment of the third element of the *proportionality test*, that is, proportionality *stricto sensu*. This test requires Member States to implement laws

59 In her opinion, the public health risk generated by opening the corridor may undermine the efficiency of other precautions, that is, the suitability of the regulation is controversial. On the other hand, one may also raise the question why the same public health aim is not attainable (necessity) with less restrictive measures if the corridor can be operated by meeting public health standards. *See* Iris Goldner Lang, 'Laws of Fear in the EU: The Precautionary Principle and Public Health Restrictions to Free Movement of Persons in the Time of COVID-19', *European Journal of Risk Regulation*, First View, 2021, p. 20, at www.cambridge.org/core/journals/european-journal-of-risk-regulation/article/laws-of-fear-in-the-eu-the-precautionary-principle-and-public-health-restrictions-to-free-movement-of-persons-in-the-time-of-covid19/56741AF86D63D0465EC1AA364CA136CB#article.

60 International law does not obligate the states to provide entry for other citizens.

61 *See* at https://hungarytoday.hu/coronavirus-hungary-austria-border-transit-romania-bulgaria/.

62 *See* at www.bbc.com/news/world-europe-52673373.

63 Communication from the Commission, 'Towards a phased and coordinated approach for restoring freedom of movement and lifting internal border controls – COVID-19', C/2020/3250.

64 Judgment of 17 February 2005, *Case C-215/03, Oulane*, ECLI:EU:C:2005:95, para. 34; Judgment of 18 May 1982, *Joined Cases C-115/81 and C-116/81, Adoui and Cornuaille*, ECLI:EU:C:1982:183, para. 8.

doi: 10.5553/HYIEL/266627012021009001001

that can prevent free movement within the EU at a significantly lower level, notwithstanding the fact that they result in a less effective protection of their rights.[65] To put it differently, this is the requirement of reasonability, where the right to free movement shall be weighed against the opposing social interests of the Member States. In some cases, it is obvious what can be qualified as 'reasonable'. It is beyond doubt that *the interest of employees working in essential positions must be exempt from strict travel restrictions*. This exemption is quoted in a Council recommendation adopted in October 2020,[66] which was passed to determine the common criteria and framework of travel regulations in light of the COVID-19 pandemic, and which obliges the Member States to frequently provide data. On this basis, the European Centre for Disease Prevention and Control (ECDC) published the weekly map of EU Member States categorized into regions shown in different colors.

The Council recommendation specifies that Member States are not allowed to curb free movement of persons into or out of green territories, however, travelers from other, non-green areas can be placed under quarantine or required to undergo a coronavirus test. It is apparent that this recommendation takes a regional approach, in other words, it does not concentrate on the Member States respectively when making a safe or less safe qualification. This way, it facilitates the fulfillment of the proportionality principle.[67] However, in most cases, due to the epidemic dragging out and its serious nature and its unpredictable social and economic consequences, it is hardly an easy task to decide what complies with the 'reasonability' requirement. The lawmaker must take into consideration several factors in addition to public health issues in the course of introducing or lifting restrictive measures. One of them is ensuring the continuous operation of the health care system, or the wider social effect of the implemented precautions on more vulnerable social layers.[68] In the same way, 'tolerance' of the society must also be taken into account, mostly if the restrictions are expected to be in force over a longer period of time, even for months. In case these different, often non-legal (and even more often expressly political) interests cannot be held in a balance, they can easily lead to government crisis.[69]

65 Opinion of Advocate General Poiares Maduro delivered on 13 July 2006, *Case C-434/04, Ahokainen and Leppik*, ECLI:EU:C:2006:462, paras. 23-26.

66 Council Recommendation (EU) 2020/1475 of 13 October 2020 on a coordinated approach to the restriction of free movement in response to the COVID-19 pandemic.

67 Due to the appearance of different and more infectious virus mutations, the Council amended the previous proposal on 28 January 2021, and introduced a dark red code to designate areas with a high-level spreading rate.

68 To name but a few: social alienation of old people, risk arising from postponement of elective health services which mainly concerns old people, or the high unemployment rate of predominantly women.

69 This situation is made worse by the fact that the different social groups prioritize different values.

doi: 10.5553/HYIEL/266627012021009001001

I am of the opinion that *the restrictions introduced during the first wave of the pandemic met political rather than legal requirements*.[70] Most governments[71] put the emphasis on the protection of public health by citing the principle of precaution. By contrast, safety precautions adopted over the course of the second and the third wave followed a more balanced practice.[72] As a result, I am of the view that *the legality of travel bans and restrictions adopted in the course of the second and third wave must be approached from a different angle*. When assessing the Member States' reactions during the first wave, it is crucial to take into consideration the high level of scientific uncertainty surrounding the pandemic (which was mainly dominant during the first wave).[73] But also the tight time limit to make decisions resulting in a wider than average latitude for Member States to implement restrictions in the public interest. We cannot ignore the fact, either, that the social value system of the Member States regarding their inclination to assume risk or the individual responsibility differs greatly.[74] To give an example, trust in public institutions and a high level of individual responsibility are characteristic of Scandinavian countries, whereas it is less ubiquitous in the post-socialist countries due to historical experiences of state paternalism over its citizens. It is clear that these were all factors that resulted in a significantly different meaning of 'reasonability' during the first wave.

The Member States refrained from introducing more drastic travel restrictions during the second and the third wave in spite of the emergence of the much more contagious British coronavirus variant. Furthermore, it can be generally said that the precautions introduced are less strict (albeit more differentiated) than the ones launched during the first wave. In compliance with the abovementioned Council recommendations, the Member States' authorities still oblige entrants arriving from non-green areas to undergo quarantine or present a negative test before or after the travel, however, as a main rule, travel restrictions do not apply to those who travel on business or for pressing family reasons.[75] It stems from the reasonability principle however, that the restrictions introduced during the second and third wave are significantly more

70 On restrictive measures introduced during the first wave of the pandemic *see* Daniel Thym,' Travel Bans in Europe: A Legal Appraisal (Part I.)', *EU Immigation and Asylum Law and Policy Blog*, at https://eumigrationlawblog.eu/travel-bans-in-europe-a-legal-appraisal-part-i/.

71 An exception was the Swedish model introduced initially in the Northern states which later proved to be inadequate, thus, these countries later introduced at least as strict measures as countries in other parts of Europe.

72 The stricter measures introduced in reaction to the British variant are exceptions, the proportionality of which is undisputable. The Council recommendation no. 2020/1475 on enhancing coordination, which was accepted in the meantime, must have had a role in this balanced practice.

73 Lang opines that due to scientific uncertainty, the principle of precaution transforms the traditional proportionality test and obviously sets less strict standards regarding national restrictions. Lang 2021, p. 19.

74 The Member States greatly differ not only in their social value systems, but also in their economic plight. The economically less powerful Member States may be pressed to lift restrictions too early to avoid collapse.

75 *See* Council Recommendation (EU) 2020/1475, para. 19.

doi: 10.5553/HYIEL/266627012021009001001

differentiated: the Member States did not have to solely rely on their public health experience gained in the first wave. Rather, they could take into account real social habits and the social tolerance levels besides foreseeable proximity to the vaccine. On the other hand, differentiated Member State reactions in the second and third wave have posed new, in the first wave unprecedented problems. These are mostly related to the documentation needed for travel, *e.g.* a valid employment agreement, a document evidencing family relations, chiefly the marriage certificate.[76] In this respect, it is the CJEU's practice that is authoritative: the mobile citizen is entitled to verify the legitimacy of his/her travel in any unambiguous way.[77]

The same issue arose in connection with the acceptance of tests allowing for entry into a country. It is hardly a coincidence that the Council made a recommendation on a mutual framework for applying antigen quick tests and the mutual recognition of COVID-19 test results all around Europe on 21 January 2021, which remarkably facilitates free movement between the Member States.[78]

However, the difficulties in ensuring mutual recognition have cast light on a much more significant, prospective problem, notably, the issue of recognizing one another's vaccine passports. The European Commission made a recommendation on creating a *digital green certificate* on 17 March 2021, to foster the citizens' safe and free movement during the COVID-19 pandemic within the EU.[79] The recommendation stipulates that every EU citizen (or foreign citizen residing legally in the EU) having a digital green certificate shall be exempt from any restriction on free movement similarly to the citizens of the visited Member States' citizens.[80] It has already been stated several times that the digital green certificate will not be a precondition for free movement, it will only facilitate it. In fact, it cannot even become a precondition as the former is a fundamental right of every EU citizen which can be directly traced back to the provisions of TFEU.

76 In practice, the situation of those living in a *de facto* partnership is even more complicated regarding free movement between the Member States, which is exacerbated by the relevant directive that obliges Member States 'authorities only to ease entry for them. In addition, it is still to clarify whether this easement restriction applies to same-sex partners. *See* Alina Tryfonidou & Robert Wintemute, 'Obstacles to the Free Movement of Rainbow Families in the EU', European Union, 2021, at www.europarl.europa.eu/RegData/etudes/STUD/2021/671505/IPOL_STU(2021)671505_EN.pdf, p. 61.

77 In *Oulane* it has been stated that the Dutch law runs counter to EU law which compels citizens from other Member States to present a valid identity card or passport, whereas the country's citizens are exempt from this obligation and allows them to identify themselves in any other way set forth in their national law. *Case C-215/03, Oulane*, para. 34.

78 *See* at https://data.consilium.europa.eu/doc/document/ST-5451-2021-INIT/hu/pdf.

79 Proposal for a Regulation of the European Parliament and of the Council on a framework for the issuance, verification and acceptance of interoperable certificates on vaccination, testing and recovery to facilitate free movement during the COVID-19 pandemic (Digital Green Certificate). COM(2021) 130 final.

80 It is necessary to emphasize here that according to the proposal, public health restrictions could be maintained concerning both domestic citizens and EU citizens. The center of gravity is whether equal treatment can be guaranteed within certain personal categories of the green card depending on the fact it is based on vaccination, recovery or test.

doi: 10.5553/HYIEL/266627012021009001001

However, the question arises if it is in compliance with EU principles that Member States are only obliged to recognize those green cards which certify inoculation with vaccines that have an EU marketing authorization, whereas Member States enjoy discretion concerning all other vaccines. A special weight is given to this issue in connection with Hungary owing to the fact that Hungary was the first EU country to approve the Russian Sputnik-V and the Chinese Sinopharm vaccines.

As a result, other EU Member States are entitled to *not issue travel permits from citizens having been inoculated with these vaccines*, or rather, almost exclusively the Hungarian citizens in the whole EU. Meanwhile, the Sputnik-V vaccine has been undergoing an authorization process at the European Medicines Agency (EMA),[81] whereas the manufacturer of the Chinese vaccine does not even consider filing for an authorization on the European market.[82] Nevertheless, the fact that a pharma manufacturer does not consider applying for an authorization of one of their products (a vaccine, in this particular case) on the European market *does not necessarily prove lack of effectivity*. It is a common practice that business (and sometimes political) reasons drive a pharmaceutical company to determine the region where they would wish to market a product after taken into account supply and demand, and the expected costs and authorization time, too. All this seems to indicate that the Union legislator chose to take *a slightly unorthodox solution, taking a shortcut in the assessment of proportionality by not reviewing the effectiveness of the vaccine* based on available health data, but instead tying the recognition of vaccines to the EMA license. Of course, in such an uncertain situation where most of the EMA licensed vaccines are basically still being tested, this somewhat simplified solution of the legislator may appear to be acceptable.

At the same time we need to see that if the said proposal is accepted, Hungarian citizens will be unambiguously in a disadvantageous situation compared to other EU citizens, in terms of hindering their free movement. This primarily lies in the fact that they could not escape quarantine and test requirement upon entry with a COVID passport, incurring for example extra costs (costs of testing, missed working day due to quarantine, *etc*.).

Taking a look at the CJEU jurisprudence in cases related to free movement of EU citizens, it is obvious that the CJEU strives to enforce *the principle of mutual recognition* so that free movement rights could be exercised in the most effective way possible. In *Coman*,[83] the issue was whether a Union citizen can require the State of destination to admit within its territory his same-sex spouse, irrespective of whether that State has opened marriage to same-sex couples within its territory. The CJEU gave an expressly affirmative answer and reasoned that the refusal of recognizing a marriage would generate a situation whereby the free movement right would vary from one Member State to another depending on

81 Although Germany ordered vaccines in bulk from Russia, authorization is a precondition.

82 On the contrary, the Chinese vaccine has already been granted WHO approval.

83 Judgment of 5 June 2018 *Case C-673/16, Coman and others*, ECLI:EU:C:2018:385.

marriage regulations on same-sex couples.[84] Analogously, it can be inferred that *an authorization issued by a Member State*, notably by the Hungarian National Institute of Pharmacy and Nutrition, *shall be recognized by the authorities of the other Member States to enforce the right of free movement*. I am of the opinion that the only possible exception can be when it is proven that *the vaccine at issue fails to provide as effective protection as other vaccines authorized by EMA*. It does not indicate, however, that free movement cannot be curbed based on objective reasons in the public interest, or, on public health reasons in this particular case.[85]

The issue at hand is compliance with the principle of proportionality, in other words, whether the restriction can be suitable for achieving the previously set objective, mainly with view to the fact that Hungary boasted the highest vaccination rate regarding the adult EU population late April 2021.[86] It is beyond doubt that people having been administered any type of vaccine (either Russian, or Chinese) pose a significantly lesser risk of spreading the virus than those who have not been inoculated. Here, the question arises whether it has any relevance that the EU citizens concerned were deprived of the possibility of choosing between the vaccines. Their only discretion was to decide if they wished to register for the vaccination or not. If the provisions of the EU Charter of Fundamental Rights (especially Article 35) are taken into consideration, the answer is undisputable. As the EU Member States' citizens exercised their right to preserve their health without being granted the right to make a decision between the vaccines, it can be stated that the EU proposal on the legal effect of vaccine certificates having no EU market authorization is able to undermine free movement and questions the EU citizens' right to high level health protection enshrined in the Charter. The question is whether the requirement of proportionality is correctly applied by the Union legislator where recognition is tied exclusively to the EMA license.

4. Conclusion

Whereas the legal literature seems unified in regarding the reintroduction of internal border controls as a reaction of the Member States to the COVID-19 pandemic as one being in compliance with EU legal principles, the standpoints vary when it comes to travel restrictions and bans. This does not mean that the operation of Schengen system is without questions, far from it, the COVID-19 pandemic has pinpointed the system's weak points and the need for an immediate reform.

As for travel restrictions, it is obvious that their long-term 'side effects' will be visible later. In case the issue of the legality of the measures introduced by the

84 Moreover, it can prevent an EU citizen from exercising the right to free movement.

85 In *Coman*, the CJEU stipulated that the said recognition obligation does not undermine the concerned Member State's national identity and does not threaten its public policy.

86 *See* at https://ourworldindata.org/covid-vaccinations and https://coronavirus.jhu.edu/vaccines/international.

doi: 10.5553/HYIEL/266627012021009001001

Member States is raised, either before national or international forums, the assessment will be based upon their necessity and proportionality and on the requirement of non-discrimination. In this respect, the Member States are in a safe position as necessity / proportionality is a vague point due to the unprecedented gravity of the health care crisis and the scientific uncertainties surrounding its treatment. There are only some areas where the infringement of EU legal standards may be contentious. One of them is discriminatory measures based on citizenship if supported by an incoherent Member State policy.

However, it cannot be overstated that the citizens expect concrete measures in crisis situations, predominantly from their own Member State. In turbulent times, such as the last decade of integration, the nation-state's framework has become the fundamental pillar of safety, increasing the importance of national allegiance and identification. This can be substantiated by the fact that masses of citizens residing in another State returned to their countries upon breakout of the pandemic in spite of the travel restrictions. Return can be triggered by the loss of the workplace in the host State in many cases. Still, it can be generally stated that the wish for a safe environment meaning predominantly the country of citizenship seems to be the priority during pandemic times.

The first, exaggerated Member State reactions to COVID-19 and the delayed EU reactions seemed to question the legitimacy of free movement. Moreover, the pandemic worsened the financial and migration-related woes that hurt the EU's integrity.[87] However, it should not be treated as a debacle of Union citizenship or a collective attack on the legal institute of free movement. Rather, it is an adequate Member State reaction to a public health issue arising in a multi-layered governmental system, where the EU must give a wide leeway for Member State activity. In return, Member States have to respect the implementation and enforcement of EU principles, among them, the principle of solidarity. In this respect, it is a sign of hope that the pandemic affects Member States in a more symmetric way than earlier crises. As a result, it is much more realistic that an attitude of common problem-solving and solidarity between the Member States will prevail.

In addition, the experience that we as EU citizens cannot exercise our free movement rights can easily reverse the former trend and inspire us to exploit our possibilities afforded by this freedom,[88] by "improving our life by our own actions".[89]

87 This is evidenced by the debates over bonds issued to mitigate the grave social, economic effects arising from the financial crisis triggered by the corona virus, which highlighted the EU's Northern / Southern division similarly to the former financial crisis. Heinikoski 2020, p. 7.

88 It inevitably requires the reform of the Schengen system which would enable the Member States to implement the provisions of the Code in a more flexible way by avoiding the infringement of EU law.

89 Davies 2019, p. 680.

5. Lessons from COVID-19 in Vol. 9 (2021) of the Hungarian Yearbook

The thematic chapter of Vol. 9 (2021) of the Hungarian Yearbook of International Law and European Law tackles different aspects related to dealing with the consequences of COVID-19.

In his piece on the new offence of scaremongering at the time of special legal order, *András Koltay* argues that the novel provision of the Hungarian Criminal Code in combination with the Constitutional Court's decision on the interpretation of the statutory elements of scaremongering guarantees the constitutional right to free speech. It is now up to the ordinary courts to develop their respective jurisprudence and refine the concrete application of this COVID-19 inspired provision. *Lóránt Csink* examines the leeway for restricting fundamental rights in Hungary at the time of the special legal order, putting the issue into the broader context of legal history and comparative law. He argues that while the Hungarian Fundamental Law allows for the restriction of most fundamental rights during the special legal order, this does not mean that such restriction should be exempt from the necessity and proportionality requirement laid down in the jurisprudence of the Constitutional Court. Through an overview of the Commission's Temporary Framework and the CJEU's rulings in the *Ryanair* cases, *Mónika Papp*'s piece on state aid granted to airlines at the time of the pandemic highlights that there is no entitlement to state aid, indeed, it is an instrument in the hands of the Member States to pursue industrial policy objectives within a certain margin of discretion subject only to binding secondary law. *Katalin Gombos and Anikó Edit Szűcs* also focus on the Temporary Framework and in particular, present specific examples of state aid that had been approved in order to mitigate the effects of COVID-19. In her contribution on the development of family benefits at the time of the pandemic, *Éva Gellérné Lukács* provides insight into the European legal and policy context of combating social exclusion from the Porto Declaration to the emergency measures introduced, arriving at the conclusion that Hungary largely followed other Member States in its efforts to mitigate crisis effects, introducing the additional element of housing benefit. Finally, *Lilla Nóra Kiss and Orsolya Johanna Sziebig* look into the opportunities for reinforcing European identity in the light of the pandemic, through enhancing the participatory and free movement rights of Union citizens that produce our unique, European way of life.

***

On behalf of the entire Editorial Team, I wish you a good read and hope you enjoy the current Volume of our Yearbook. I also hope to welcome you among the authors of Vol. 10 (2022) of the Hungarian Yearbook of International Law and European Law. We plan to dedicate the thematic chapter of the 25th anniversary of the *Gabcikovo-Nagymaros Project Case* judgment of the ICJ. Please feel free to submit your contribution (to be published in any of our chapters) with us no later than 15 April 2022, in accordance with our Style Guide and Call for papers (available at our website, www.hungarianyearbook.com).

Hungarian Yearbook of International Law and European Law 2021 (9) 1
doi: 10.5553/HYIEL/266627012021009001001

PUBLIC HEALTH EMERGENCY: NATIONAL, EUROPEAN AND INTERNATIONAL LAW RESPONSES

On the Constitutionality of the Punishment of Scaremongering in the Hungarian Legal System

András Koltay[*]

Abstract

Scaremongering criminalized as a limitation to freedom of speech in Hungarian law. In lack of relevant case-law, free speech commentators rarely discussed the provision until the Government took action to step up the fight against the COVID-19 pandemic, and the ensuing amendment of the Criminal Code in Spring 2020 brought the subject back to the forefront of public debate. The article analyses the constitutional issues related to the criminalization of scaremongering, taking the two available Constitutional Court decisions rendered in this subject as guideline. Though the newly introduced legislation attracted widespread criticism in Hungary and elsewhere in Europe, a thorough examination of the new statutory elements makes it clear that public debate and critical opinions may not be stifled by prosecuting individuals for scaremongering. Although the applicable standard cannot yet be determined with full accuracy, the Constitutional Court's decisions and relevant academic analysis resolve the main issues in order to protect freedom of expression, while the clarification of further details remains a matter for the case-law.

Keywords: scaremongering, clear and present danger, COVID-19 pandemic, freedom of expression, Constitutional Court of Hungary.

1. Introduction: On the Protection of Untrue Statements

The issue of false allegations, including the possibility of prohibiting deliberate lies or their inclusion under the scope of freedom of expression, is one which concerns European, and among them the Hungarian legal system. Nevertheless, it can be stated with some certainty that lies cannot be prohibited in a general sense, given the widespread constitutional protection of freedom of expression. It is possible to take legal action against untruths if they violate certain specific statutory provisions, such as those governing the protection of reputation,[1] or

* András Koltay: rector and professor of law, University of Public Service, Budapest; professor of law, Pázmány Péter Catholic University, Budapest.

1 Section 2:45(2) of the Civil Code (in this article I refer to only Hungarian pieces of legislation).

doi: 10.5553/HYIEL/266627012021009001002

false allegations made during the election campaign that disregard the requirements of good faith and the proper exercise of rights,[2] or rules on the scope of misleading commercial practices,[3] and finally, provisions in connection with the denial of genocides (primarily, the Holocaust).[4] Scaremongering is another activity which may be prohibited, *i.e.* if the relevant criminal law statutory elements exist: a false statement may be punishable. The individual statutory elements of the crime have been interpreted by established case-law related to other crimes, but in the absence of significant case-law regarding scaremongering itself, these statutory elements, altogether avoided the scrutiny of analysts of freedom of expression. With the Hungarian Government's actions to control the COVID-19 pandemic and the resulting amendment to the Criminal Code in the spring of 2020 the issues related to statutory regulation of scaremongering came under the public eye. This article will discuss the constitutional issues related to the prohibition of scaremongering in light of the two decisions of the Hungarian Constitutional Court delivered on this subject.

2. A Brief Overview of the Ban on Scaremongering in the Hungarian Legal System

The first Hungarian Criminal Code, the so-called *Csemegi Code* of 1878, was supplemented by Act XL of 1879 on Petty Offences, Article 40 of which regulated "scaremongering" as follows:

> "Whoever, by setting off bells or any other alarm, knowing that there is no cause, disturbs the peace of the inhabitants; or who intentionally misleads the authority by reporting false news of distress or riot shall be punished by imprisonment for up to eight days. And if, as a result of reporting a false rumor, the police or the armed forces are called out: the perpetrator shall be punished by imprisonment for up to fifteen days."

Article 80 of Act III of 1930 on the Entry into Force of the Military Criminal Code and on the Amendment and Supplementation of Certain Provisions of the Ordinary Criminal Code prescribed capital punishment for anyone who "fabricates or spreads false news in war-time or in connection with warfare." Section 68 of the same Act set forth a serious penalty for any person who communicated a false or forged document or drawing or other untrue document, which, if authentic would be a state secret, to a foreign state authority, foreign organization or their agent, if the communication is capable of compromising the military or other important interests of the state. The model of this regulation

2 Section 2(1) of Act XXXVI of 2013 on Electoral Procedure (obligation to exercise rights in good faith and for their intended purpose).

3 Sections 6 and 7 of Act XLVII of 2008 on the Prohibition of Unfair Commercial Practices against Consumers.

4 Section 333 of the Criminal Code.

Hungarian Yearbook of International Law and European Law 2021 (9) 1
doi: 10.5553/HYIEL/266627012021009001002

was German legislation, dating from 1927.[5] This provision foresaw punishment for deception by using a non-existent state secret. Act X of 1937, on the other hand, set out the general statutory elements of scaremongering, on the basis of which the offence is committed by "fabricating news or spreading untrue news that may disturb public order or peace of mind or endanger the country's foreign policy or adversely affect its economic situation or its lending practice."

After World War II, it was Decree No. 8800/1946. (VII. 28.) of the Prime Minister on the criminal protection of the economic order that regulated scaremongering, followed by general statutory elements on the dissemination of economic rumors, set out in Section 26 of Act XXXIV of 1947 on certain provisions relating to the people's justice:

> "in the presence of two or more persons, [to] state or spread rumors of any untrue fact or allegation that is capable of disturbing public order or public peace, or endangering the country's foreign policy interests or adversely affecting the economic situation."

The latter Act prescribed punishment for scaremongering primarily for the reason that it was capable of disturbing the public peace and endangering certain named state interests.

Despite the new statutory elements, the comprehensive compendium of Criminal Substantive Law, the *'Hatályos Anyagi Büntetőjogi Szabályok Hivatalos Összeállítása'*, which in principle contained the full body of legislation in force on 31 August 1951, also uphold the above-mentioned statutory elements of 1930 and 1937. Finally, the Criminal Code of 1961 brought order into the overlapping rules; Section 218(1) of which re-regulated scaremongering:

> "Whoever claims or spreads rumors, in front of others, of a false fact or fact distorted in such a way as to disturb the public peace or adversely affect the economic situation shall be punished by imprisonment for a term not exceeding two years."

Section 270(1) of the Criminal Code of 1978 only penalized scaremongering that was capable of disturbing the public peace, and Paragraph (2) of the code defined scaremongering committed in a place of public danger or during war as an aggravated case. The statutory elements contained in the 1978 Criminal Code were amended by Act XXV of 1989 at the time of the transition from Communism to the rule of law, which established a requirement that the offence be committed before a large audience as a mandatory statutory element, narrowing thereby the scope of the punishable acts:

> "270(1) A person who, before a large audience, states or disseminates any untrue fact or any misrepresented true fact that is capable of causing

5 Gyula Isaák, 'Az államtitok büntetőjogi védelméhez', *Magyar Jogi Szemle*, 1931/2, p. 58.

doi: 10.5553/HYIEL/266627012021009001002

> disturbance is guilty of a misdemeanor and shall be punished by imprisonment for up to one year, community service or a fine.
>
> (2) The punishment shall be imprisonment for a term not exceeding three years for a criminal offence if the scaremongering is committed in a place of public danger or during a war."

The statutory elements of scaremongering were already free of ideologized content by then, so no major changes had to made to the provision at the time of the democratic transition.[6]

3. The Constitutionality of the Prohibition of Scaremongering: *Decision No. 18/2000. (VI. 6.) AB*

The constitutionality of the prohibition set forth in Section 270 of the Criminal Code was considered in *Decision No. 18/2000. (VI. 6.) AB*, which annulled the provision in its entirety. The decision (by then based on several years of Constitutional Court's case-law on free expression) established the constitutional significance of freely-formed public opinion:

> "the expression of individual opinion, public opinion formed in accordance with its own laws, and the possibility of individual opinion-forming based on the widest possible information in interaction with them are what enjoy constitutional protection."[7]

In assessing the constitutionality of the statutory elements of scaremongering, the decision recalled the Constitutional Court's 1992 decision regarding the statutory elements of hate speech; more precisely, 'incitement to hatred against a community', enshrined in the Criminal Code. The cited decision, *Decision No. 30/1992. (V. 26.) AB* is one of the early and most influential decisions of the Constitutional Court related to the freedom of speech, which has been frequently referred to ever since and whose exact interpretation has been disputed since its adoption.

According to the relevant part of the reasoning of *Decision No. 18/2000. (VI. 6.) AB*,

> "[w]ith regard to 'incitement to hatred' the Constitutional Court has recognized the restriction of the freedom of expression as constitutional, the protected legal object of which is also the public peace, following from its location in the Criminal Code. According to the Constitutional Court, behind such a disturbance of public peace, there is also a danger of violating a large

6 For more information on the history of the scaremongering, *see* Szabolcs Hornyák, *A köznyugalom elleni bűncselekmények*, doctoral dissertation, PTE, Pécs, 2010, pp. 37-42, 47-48, and 154-157.

7 Decision No. 18/2000. (VI. 6.) AB, Reasoning III/2., ABH 2000, 117, 121.

Hungarian Yearbook of International Law and European Law 2021 (9) 1
doi: 10.5553/HYIEL/266627012021009001002

> number of individual rights: the violence against the group threatens the honor and dignity (in extreme cases, life) of those belonging to the group, and restricts them from exercising other rights (including free expression) by intimidation. Incitement to hatred also poses a threat to individual rights that give such weight to the public peace as its direct object that a restriction on freedom of expression is considered necessary and proportionate. Although the practical result of the deliberations is similar, this line of reasoning is not just about the intensity of the disturbance of public peace (clear and present danger), which justifies a restriction on the right to the freedom of expression if it exceeds a certain level. What is decisive here is that which has been endangered: incitement also endangers the rights of individuals, which are very highly positioned in the constitutional order of values."[8]

The above text, from the sentence beginning with "Although…", is a literal quote from the statement of reasons for *Decision No. 30/1992. (V. 26.) AB*, which was also included in the statement of reasons for *Decision No. 18/2000. (VI. 6.) AB*. The reasoning of *Decision No. 30/1992. (V. 26.) AB* seeks to separate the public peace and individual rights, which are both protected legal objects as set out in the criminal offence. The logic of the reasoning is based on the fact that public peace is not a specific right or interest that can, in general, justify a restriction of the freedom of expression. Such a restriction is only constitutional if the intensity of the disturbance of the public peace reaches the level of a *clear and present danger*; that is, there is a manifest and imminent danger to the public peace.

In my opinion, the text of the statement of reasons for *Decision No. 30/1992. (V. 26.) AB* quoted means, if interpreted correctly, that while the protection of the public peace provides a constitutional basis for restricting the freedom of speech only *if the risk of its violation is manifest and imminent, the standards for restricting freedom of speech may be lower in the case of individual rights*. Nevertheless, their endangerment is a condition for the commission of a criminal offence. The nature of this danger, however, and the extent to which it is punishable remains an open question.

In any case, in the application of the law, when assessing a specific real-life situation (incitement against a community before a large audience), it is not possible to separate acts that violate or endanger the public peace and those which threaten individual rights from each other. The endangerment of individual rights also entails the endangerment of the public peace and, conversely, the public peace may be endangered in such a way that the exercise of the freedom of expression threatens individual rights. In other words, the protection of the public peace and the protection of individual rights are inseparable, which also means that it is unnecessary to apply a different standard in practice for these two protected legal objects. This is because, due to their inseparability, the lower of the two rather restrictive standards, *i.e.* the one that

8 Id. III.3.3., ABH 2000, 117, 127.

allows for the restriction of freedom of speech to a greater extent, should be applied to establish whether a criminal offence has been committed. Individual rights (because they are specific) may be constitutionally defended from violation arising from an expressed opinion by using a lower standard. Therefore, the standard of clear and present danger to the public peace which a violation would have to meet (if it were, in itself, the protected legal object of the criminal offence) for the Constitutional Court to consider it as worthy of protection is immaterial. The latter should therefore not be taken into account in the application of the law.

It is worth considering the relevant sentence from *Decision No. 30/1992. (V. 26.) AB*:

> "[t]he conduct sanctioned in Paragraph (1) also constitutes a threat to individual rights, which gives such weight to the public peace as the direct object that [...] a restriction on the freedom of expression is considered necessary and proportionate."

This sentence also underlines the close connection and inseparability of the public peace and individual rights. According to the text, the threat to individual rights affects the public peace ("giving it weight", *i.e.* justifying its protection); and as such the two protected legal objects are inseparable. The quote continues thus:

> "[a]lthough the practical result of the deliberations is similar, this line of reasoning is not merely about the intensity of the disturbance of the public peace, which justifies a restriction on the right to the freedom of expression above a certain degree (clear and present danger). What is decisive here is what has been endangered: incitement also endangers the rights of individuals, which are very highly positioned in the constitutional order of values."[9]

This can be interpreted as follows: *if there is 'merely' a disturbance of the public peace then clear and present danger should be used to restrict the freedom of expression*. However, this is not enough: *decisive is that subjective (individual) rights are also in danger (but not necessarily in clear and present danger)*. Thus, an independent examination of the danger to the public peace is unnecessary, and the sentence in which the clear and present danger doctrine is mentioned does not help establish an applicable standard of 'incitement to hatred'.

The scholars interpreting the statement of reasons of the 1992 decision may be divided into three groups. The first includes authors who see it as an application of the US' clear and present danger standard[10] on the basis of which incitement to hatred may only be punished if there is a manifest and imminent

9 Decision No. 30/1992. (V. 26.) AB, Reasoning V.2., ABH 1992, 167, 179.

10 For more information on this standard, *see* András Koltay, *Freedom of Speech – A Mirage out of Reach*, Wolters Kluwer, Budapest, 2013, pp. 127-132.

doi: 10.5553/HYIEL/266627012021009001002

danger caused by speech of acts of violence against the community concerned.[11] The inception of the *clear and present danger doctrine* may be attributed essentially to two US Supreme Court Justices, Oliver Wendell Holmes and Louis D. Brandeis. It first appeared in *Schenk v United States*,[12] drafted by Holmes:

> "The question in each case is whether the words used were disclosed in circumstances and were of such a nature as to create a manifest and imminent danger of significant harm, which the Congress is entitled to prevent."

Later, Holmes expressed the view, in the dissenting opinion attached to the *Abrams v United States* judgment,[13] that although stricter restrictions on freedom of expression were permissible in certain cases in conditions of war, the directness of the danger posed by communication was the standard requirement in all cases. The new formulation of the clear and present danger doctrine, which is still valid today, was made in 1969 in *Brandenburg v Ohio*.[14] According to the new test set out in the statement of reasons, communications that call for violence or other offences may only be restricted if they are specifically aimed at inciting imminent violence or law-breaking, expressly call for it and this is likely to occur. The original test was thus thoroughly narrowed down to a new standard, called the *Brandenburg* test: in addition to the likelihood of danger, the intention to cause a breach of the law and an express call for an infringement are also required for the restriction of speech. (It should also be noted that the imminent danger concept used in Hungarian criminal dogmatics cannot be definitively equated with the US clear and present danger, given that in the legal literature the Hungarian version of the latter is generally referred to as a "manifest and imminent danger". Nevertheless, we shall disregard these differences for the sake of simplicity, as it does not interfere with the process of finding a constitutional standard.)

In the other group are those who believe that although the Constitutional Court did not introduce the US standard mentioned, in order for "incitement to hatred" to take place, *some kind of (real, actual, genuine, etc.) state of danger must*

11 Gábor Halmai, '"Az előző vizsgálat eltöröltetvén örökre..."?', *Fundamentum*, 1997/1, p. 63; Gábor Halmai, 'Hátramenetben az alapjogvédelem?', *Fundamentum*, 2000/3, p. 69. *See also* Gábor Halmai, '"Gyűlöletbeszéd" és uniós csatlakozás', *Fundamentum*, 2003/2, p. 112; Gábor Halmai, 'Túl kevés és túl sok szólásszabadság – egy utilitarista megközelítés', *Fundamentum*, 2005/3, p. 190; Péter Molnár, 'Uszítás vagy gyalázkodás?', *Fundamentum*, 2001/4, p. 114; Péter Molnár, 'Az alkotmányos mérce világosabb értelmezése felé', *Fundamentum*, 2004/1, p. 144; János Kis, 'A szólásszabadság próbája', *Magyar Narancs*, 7 February 2002. *See* confirmation in János Kis, 'A bírói döntéstől a törvény fölötti döntésig', *Élet és Irodalom*, 2003/47; János Kis & László Sólyom, 'Az alkotmány és a szólásszabadság', *Népszabadság*, 11 October 2003.

12 249 U.S. 47 (1919).

13 250 U.S. 616 (1919).

14 395 U.S. 444 (1969).

doi: 10.5553/HYIEL/266627012021009001002

arise in the wake of the opinion expressed.[15] The President of the Hungarian Republic, Ferenc Mádl, in his motion to the Constitutional Court, which served as the basis of *Decision No. 18/2004. (V. 25.) AB*, put it as follows:

> "[t]he Constitutional Court has not precisely defined the extent of the threat required for the restriction – although it referred to the famous US Supreme Court test of clear and present danger. In my interpretation, however, it is clear that although the Constitutional Court does not set, as a standard of constitutionality, that incitement to hatred is to cause a manifest and imminent danger, the threat to specific fundamental rights must however be realistic and genuine."[16]

The third group is comprised of traditionalist proponents of criminal law, who argue that *the objectivity of a communication to incite hatred is sufficient for the statutory elements* to exist and that its effect need not be assessed in order to establish criminal liability.[17]

When interpreting *Decision No. 18/2000. (VI. 6.) AB*, the question is not just what the reference in the 1992 decision to clear and present danger means, but, regardless of what it means, what its role is in the constitutional review of the statutory elements of scaremongering. The statement of reasons does not provide a definitive answer to this question. Recalling the decision on incitement to hatred, it states:

> "As a result of the examination of the constitutionality of Section 270 of the Criminal Code, the Constitutional Court reached the same position in the case of scaremongering. The criminalization of conduct defined by the law is an unconstitutional restriction on the freedom of communication."[18]

But what is meant by "same position" here? As we have seen, there are at least three possible answers to this.

The statement of reasons no longer applies the clear and present danger (in Hungarian criminal law, manifest and imminent danger) test, but there is no doubt that, in order to establish the constitutionality of scaremongering, it expects special circumstances to prevail that would justify a serious violation of interests and a restriction on speech:

15 László Sólyom, *Az alkotmánybíráskodás kezdetei Magyarországon*. Osiris, Budapest, 2001, pp. 477-478; László Sólyom, 'Szeretetbeszéd, tiszteletbeszéd', *Népszabadság*, 24 December 2001; Bernát Török, 'A gyűlöletbeszéd tilalmának médiajogi mércéi', *Jogtudományi Közlöny*, Vol. 68, Issue 2, 2013, p. 67.

16 'A gyűlöletbeszéd büntethetősége. Motion of the President of the Republic to the Constitutional Court', *Fundamentum*, 2004/1, p. 132.

17 Gyula Szeder, 'A társadalom békéjének büntetőjogi védelméről', *Magyar Jog*, 2002/1, p. 7; Ervin Belovics *et al.*, *Büntetőjog. Különös rész*. HVG-ORAC, Budapest, 2001, p. 331; Endre Bócz & Kálmán Györgyi, 'Hol az alkotmányosság határa?', *Népszabadság*, 30 October 2003; András Szabó, 'Eső után köpönyeg?', *Népszabadság*, 6 November 2003; Gergely Bárándy, *A gyűlöletbeszéd Magyarországon*, Scolar, Budapest, 2009, p. 84.

18 Decision No. 18/2000. (VI. 6.) AB, Reasoning III/4., ABH 2000, 117, 130.

doi: 10.5553/HYIEL/266627012021009001002

> "It follows from the high value of [the] fundamental constitutional right to the freedom of expression that the damage to the interests on which the restriction is based must be particularly serious."[19]

The assertion of untrue facts cannot in itself be prohibited, even if it is objectively capable of disturbing the public peace:

> "The assertion or rumor of untrue facts, or the distortion of facts, even if the person asserting the fact is aware of the detrimental effect of his act on the public peace accepts it, or even so desires it, is within the realm of freedom of expression not limited by criminal law."[20]

Although, of the statutory elements examined, the one in Paragraph (1) is unconstitutional, this does not mean that scaremongering could not be prohibited more narrowly than by the statutory elements which were annulled.

> "At the same time, the Constitutional Court has ruled that the Constitution does not preclude the legislature from using criminal law in certain cases to protect the public peace against scaremongering. As it follows from Section 8(4) of the Constitution, it is possible to suspend or restrict freedom of expression during a state of national crisis, state of emergency or state of danger."[21]

Furthermore:

> "[N]o constitutional obstacle exists to prevent the legislature from prescribing the punishment of knowingly false allegations (rumors, distortions of facts) made before a large audience, if committed in a state of danger, *e.g.* committed in a place of public danger or in time of war and which may lead to disturbances in the public peace."[22]

The Constitutional Court did not find the other statutory elements specified in Paragraph (2) to be unconstitutional *per se*. However, in view of the fact that the elements of the legal statutory elements of scaremongering had already been set out in Section 270(1) of the Criminal Code, [Paragraph (2) merely referred back to them and used the term 'scaremongering'], and due to the applied codification technique, the Constitutional Court also annulled Section 270(2) of the Criminal Code.

In a later part of the statement of reasons, the Constitutional Court referred to *"a realistic possibility of disturbing the public peace" as a condition for the criminality for scaremongering*. That is, it would be an unconstitutional restriction

19 Id.
20 Id.
21 Id.
22 Id.

doi: 10.5553/HYIEL/266627012021009001002

if the legislator were satisfied with the objective capability of the communication to disturb the public peace, it is the real risk of disturbing the public peace that reaches the level of criminality:

> "Public peace is itself a precarious social phenomenon that requires interpretation, and the assessment of whether a statement of fact or rumor is indeed capable of disturbing the public peace explicitly provides an opportunity for possible and, where appropriate, arbitrary interpretation and application of the law. The condition for establishing criminal liability is, in principle, a realistic possibility of disturbing the public peace, but in certain specific cases it is for the criminal authorities, and ultimately the criminal court, to assess it as a conclusion drawn from the comparison of the content of the statement of facts, the perpetrator and the circumstances of the offence."[23]

Although, according to the Constitutional Court, the statutory elements allow such an interpretation, due to the lack of clarity, annulment was the only constitutional route:

> "[From S]ection 270 of the Criminal Code, judged in terms of the definiteness, accuracy and clarity required from the statutory elements in the Criminal Law, it may be concluded that, in deciding on criminal liability, those applying the law must take into account an impermissible number of circumstances from the point of view of constitutionality that are not formulated by the law but by the justification of the law, decisions in individual cases and legal commentaries. All this leaves too much room for error on the part of law enforcement, as some aspects may not be taken into account, even with the most careful consideration, but also for arbitrary selection (what is taken and not taken into account), reaching a level of legal uncertainty."[24]

The decision also lays down the *ultima ratio* nature of criminal law, which allows for penal intervention only in the most necessary cases.[25] The Constitutional Court put it very clearly:

> "In the system of legal liability, criminal law is the *ultima ratio*. It is its social purpose to be a sanctioning keystone for the legal system as a whole. Criminal sanctions and the role and purpose of punishment are to maintain the integrity of legal and moral norms when sanctions from other branches of law are no longer successful."[26]

23 Id. Reasoning III.5., ABH 2000, 117, 131.
24 Id.
25 Id. Reasoning III.4., ABH 2000, 117, 129.
26 Decision No. 30/1992. (V. 26.) AB, Reasoning IV.4., ABH 1992, 167, 176.

Hungarian Yearbook of International Law and European Law 2021 (9) 1
doi: 10.5553/HYIEL/266627012021009001002

At the same time, threatening behavior may be punishable, *i.e.* the protection of the freedom of expression does not require that criminal law only react to events that have already caused harm, *i.e.* scaremongering does not have to be a crime of strict liability.[27]

The place of the reasoning of the decision in the fabric of Constitutional Court jurisprudence depends on what we think about the standard of scaremongering set by it. If it is assumed that the standard is the same as that set by *Decision No. 30/1992. (V. 26.) AB* then the two decisions are in line, and it only needs to be clarified how the 1992 decision may be interpreted. According to Bernát Török, however, the reasoning of the 2000 decision differs from that of the 1992 decision. In his view, the decision on hate speech only required a manifest and imminent danger of criminality in connection with the disturbance of the public peace (but in the event of a violation of individual rights it considered a lesser effect sufficient), by contrast, the subsequent decision actually established *a Hungarian version of the clear and present danger standard* for scaremongering, with general validity.

> "The 1992 decision also indicates the nature of the stricter conditions: the risk of a breach of the public peace in this case must be manifest and imminent. The Constitutional Court applied this test later in *Decision No. 18/2000. (VI. 6.) AB*, when it considered the prohibition of scaremongering to be constitutional only at the scene of public danger or in times of war, in which cases there is undoubtedly an imminent and manifest danger of harm to the public peace. In other cases, a restriction on scaremongering cannot be considered an 'overriding social need', an 'overriding public interest' that would justify a criminal law prohibition. It is not about the Constitutional Court not recognizing the public peace as a constitutional value, but about the fact that its theoretical violation, independent from individual rights, does not constitute a 'particularly serious harm', essential for the criminal law restriction of the right to the freedom of expression. In that case, the standard of criminal law intervention must be set as high as possible, limiting official action to manifest and imminent states of danger."[28]

According to Török, therefore, *Decision No. 18/2000. (VI. 6.) AB* is the first decision in the case-law of the Constitutional Court that actually requires the existence of a manifest and imminent danger to establish criminality.[29] However, it is also possible to interpret the decision as meaning that it did not in fact apply the test of manifest and imminent (clear and present) danger itself. This

27 Decision No. 18/2000. (VI. 6.) AB, Reasoning III.5., ABH 2000, 117, 131.

28 Bernát Török, *Szabadon szólni, demokráciában*, HVG-ORAC, Budapest, 2018, pp. 100-101.

29 In connection with incitement to hatred, Decisions No. 18/2004. (V. 25.) AB and 95/2008. (VII. 3.) AB also applied this standard, choosing the first of the possible interpretations of Decision No. 30/1992. (V. 26.) AB, cited above. *See* for more András Koltay, 'A nagy magyar gyűlöletbeszéd-vita: a "gyűlöletre uszítás" alkotmányos mércéjének azonosítása felé', *Állam- és Jogtudomány*, Vol. 53, Issue 1-2, 2013, pp. 91-123.

doi: 10.5553/HYIEL/266627012021009001002

interpretation is supported by the ambiguous reference to the statement of reasons of the 1992 decision and by the criterion of a "realistic possibility of disturbing the public peace" for establishing criminal liability, set out later in the text. In Török's view, there is no doubt that there is a manifest and imminent danger of harm to the public peace at the scene of public danger or in times of war. That is to say, the Constitutional Court narrowed the criminality of scaremongering to a period covered by the special legal order,[30] at the scene of public danger, thus implicitly stating that a manifest and imminent danger was also necessary. It may also be argued, however, that in principle, a situation is conceivable in which someone intentionally makes a false statement at the time of a special legal order or in a situation of war, but which is not capable of causing a manifest and imminent danger. In such cases, the occurrence of danger may be presumed, since it is easier to cause, yet it should not be accepted automatically. A diverging interpretation of the 2000 decision states that the 'realistic' occurrence of the danger is sufficient to allow law enforcement authorities to accept this kind of automatism, due to the causal link between speech and the danger it poses.

The statutory elements of scaremongering present in the old Criminal Code were re-codified by the legislator in Act CXXV of 2000. The new rule took into account the Constitutional Court's intentions and only penalized communications at a scene of public danger which could cause confusion or unrest in a larger group of people:

> "Section 270: A person who, at a site of public danger, states or disseminates any untrue fact or any misrepresented true fact that is capable of causing disturbance or unrest in a larger group of persons is guilty of a felony and shall be punished by imprisonment for up to three years."

According to the Criminal Code commentary, public danger should be understood as a situation:

> "When there is a realistic risk of damage to an unspecified or larger number of specified persons or material assets of significant value. The concept of a place of public danger also includes the actual place and time of the public danger, and here the conduct must be exerted before a large audience."[31]

According to the commentary, this public danger is caused by human behavior, rather than, for example, a natural disaster,[32] but this is at least an arguable interpretation. In my view, this interpretation may be due to the fact that the notion of public danger is mostly interpreted in the commentaries in relation to

30 In the Fundamental Law, these are: state of national crisis, state of emergency, state of preventive defence, state of terrorist threat, unexpected attack and state of danger (Articles 48-53 of the Fundamental Law).

31 Wolters Kluwer Commentary to the Criminal Code (explanation to Section 337 of the Criminal Code, which is essentially the same text as Section 270 of the old Criminal Code).

32 Id.

doi: 10.5553/HYIEL/266627012021009001002

the criminal offence of 'causing public danger', where the state of danger is manifestly caused by human behavior. This is also typical in practice, but it cannot be ruled out that, with regard to other crimes, public danger may also be caused by a natural phenomenon, the definition of which was left undetermined by criminal law, so in recent decades it has been shaped by case-law.

> "Although the law in force does not define the concept of public danger, it is settled case-law that a danger becomes a public danger if it threatens not only one or more (but in any event, a small number of) predetermined persons, but one or more unspecified or a larger number of specified persons."[33]

In addition, it can be considered a public danger if assets of significant value become endangered. An additional condition, in line with the decision of the Constitutional Court, is that the communication should be capable of causing confusion or anxiety in a larger group of people. The statutory elements are of an endangering nature; they are not concerned with the degree of danger (imminent or real), but the actual occurrence of the disturbance or unrest certainly does not have to be examined in criminal proceedings; the credible possibility of this is sufficient.[34]

The *statutory elements of scaremongering* set out in the Criminal Code (Act C of 2012) were supplemented by a single element clarifying the conditions of criminality: under Section 337, a false statement of facts must be capable of causing confusion or unrest in a larger group of people "at the site of public danger". The criminal offence may also be committed if the perpetrator is not personally present at the site of the public danger, but the communication of the rumor is perceived by those present (*e.g.* through the media).[35] No substantive case-law related to these statutory elements has been developed, and at the time of the writing the official database (the birosag.hu website) does not contain any decisions made in criminal proceedings initiated due to scaremongering.

4. Amendments to the Statutory Elements of Scaremongering and *Decision No. 15/2020. (VII. 8.) AB*

In the spring of 2020, following the adoption of the bill on the 'defense against the coronavirus', the Criminal Code was also amended, and a second scaremongering statutory element was introduced into the act:

> "Section 337(1): A person who, at a site of public danger and before a large audience, states or disseminates any untrue fact or any misrepresented true fact with regard to the public danger that is capable of causing disturbance or unrest in a larger group of persons at the site of public danger is guilty of a felony and shall be punished by imprisonment for up to three years.

33 BH 1970.8.6461.
34 István Ambrus, 'A koronavírus-járvány és a büntetőjog', *MTA Law Working Papers*, 2020/5, p. 13.
35 Id.

doi: 10.5553/HYIEL/266627012021009001002

> (2) A person who, during the period of a special legal order and before a large audience, states or disseminates any untrue fact or any misrepresented true fact that is capable of hindering or preventing the efficiency of protection is guilty of a felony and shall be punished by imprisonment for one to five years."

The statement of reasons for the bill argued that the statutory elements in Paragraph (1), which are the same as the earlier elements, were not suitable for sanctioning scaremongering related to the pandemic, because they only allowed for action to be taken against communications made at the scene of a public danger. By contrast, "the state of danger declared during the coronavirus pandemic affects the entire country". It is therefore justified to enact the statutory elements set out in Paragraph (2) without any geographical restriction.

There was a fierce public debate about the bill. Critics of the new provision have most often criticized the disregard for the requirement of normative clarity.[36] By contrast, the Constitutional Court, in *Decision No. 15/2020. (VII. 8.) AB* found that when applying the law, each of the terms enshrined in the provision may be vested with a meaning that is in accordance with constitutional requirements.

> "In this case, with regard to the new statutory elements of the Criminal Code, there are insufficient grounds to conclude that certain definitions contained therein (fact, statement of fact, statement of untrue fact, distortion of fact, distinction of statement and rumor, special legal order, general public, *etc.*) are incomprehensible from the outset and therefore inapplicable. Other statutory elements in the Criminal Code contain elements identical or similar to them. The related case-law may provide a basis for judging what qualifies as scaremongering specified in Section 337(2) of the Criminal Code. The court of general jurisdiction may conclude that the subject of this criminal offence may not be the criticism of certain measures taken by the government during the special legal order, nor of forecasting future events, nor of speculating on data not disclosed in the context of the special legal order. It is also for the case-law to determine the manner of commission, *i.e.* the kind of act that is capable of "hindering or frustrating the effectiveness of defense". Neither the effectiveness of defense, nor the obstruction, nor the failure are an indecipherable statutory element to begin with. In respect of several statutory elements, the Criminal Code requires that the act be capable

36 László Bodolai, 'Rémhírek és vélemények', *Élet és Irodalom*, Vol. LXIV, Issue 13, 27 March 2020; Mátyás Bencze & Krisztina Ficsor, 'A koronavírus kihívásai és a jogtudomány: a rémhírterjesztés tényállásának jogalkalmazási kérdései', *TK JTI Blog*, 2 April 2020, at https://jog.tk.mta.hu/blog/2020/04/a-remhirterjesztes-tenyallasanak-jogalkalmazasi-kerdesei; *Még egyszer a koronavírus elleni védekezésről szóló törvénytervezetről (állásfoglalás)*, EKINT, 22 March 2020, at www.ekint.org/alkotmanyossag/2020-03-22/meg-egyszer-a-koronavirus-elleni-vedekezesrol-szolo-torvenytervezetrol-allasfoglalas; *Dermesztő hatással járhat a rémhírterjesztés tényállásának módosítása*, TASZ, 24 March 2020, at https://tasz.hu/cikkek/dermeszto-hatassal-jarhat-a-remhirterjesztes-tenyallasanak-modositasa.

doi: 10.5553/HYIEL/266627012021009001002

> of producing a consequence. This suitability indicates the objective effectiveness and direction of the act."[37]

Legal concepts may indeed be misleading if the interpreter starts from the general grammatical meaning of the words. Thus, for example, the expression 'untrue fact' may appear to be a contradiction in terms in the eyes of non-lawyers.[38] However, it is clear from the text of the Civil Code and from decades of case-law that *a statement of 'untrue fact' implies false statements purporting to be facts, i.e. the communication of untruths.*[39]

The decision analyses in detail the requirement of intentional conduct; in other words, *what exactly the offender's intention must be* when disclosing the untrue fact.

> "Scaremongering may only be committed intentionally. Consequently, the perpetrator must be aware that he is committing his act at a time of a special legal order; that the fact he alleges is untrue or has significantly distorted the true fact, and that the communication of his allegation is (objectively) capable of hindering or frustrating the effectiveness of defense. Furthermore, the intent of the perpetrator must include committing the above-mentioned conscious communication in front of a large audience. If his consciousness or intention does not extend to any of these elements, or if the allegation is not objectively capable of hindering or frustrating the effectiveness of the defense, the offence is not committed according to the rules of criminal law."[40]

The statement of reasons addresses the issues of the freedom of public debate in detail. According to the strongest criticisms of the new statutory elements, the aim of the regulation is to silence critical voices against government action. The statement of reasons thoroughly explores the differences between statements of fact and the restriction of opinions.

> "Section 337(2) of the Criminal Code [...] is not generally applicable to the content of public debates on the basis of criminal dogmatics. The measures of public authorities can be criticized and censored. The Criminal Code's rule restricts prohibited communication to (untrue) information that may hinder or frustrate the effectiveness of defense, during a special legal order. The same follows from the provisions of the Fundamental Law."[41]

> "Section 337(2) of the Criminal Code does not generally cover all published statements of fact related to the pandemic, which gave rise to its adoption.

37 Decision No. 15/2020. (VII. 8.) AB, Reasoning [43].
38 Krisztián Ungváry, 'Valós tény és a büntethetőség', *Index*, 25 March 2020, at https://index.hu/velemeny/2020/03/25/szolasszabadsag_remhirterjesztes_ungvary_krisztian.
39 Section 2:45(2) of the Civil Code, Violation of good reputation.
40 Decision No. 15/2020. (VII. 8.) AB, Reasoning [46].
41 Id. Reasoning [47].

doi: 10.5553/HYIEL/266627012021009001002

> Nor shall it cover statements of fact that are disputed at the time of their communication or whose falsehood comes to light after their disclosure, where the perpetrator is not aware of their falsehood, since his conduct does not fully satisfy the statutory elements."[42]
>
> "The prohibition, then, applies only to knowingly untrue (or distorted) statements of fact, not to critical opinions. There is a well-established case-law that the latter should be included in the circle of protected opinions and, as epidemiology is currently one of our most important public affairs, the strictest protection should be given to public debates on this subject within the framework of legal norms affecting this subject."[43]

The prohibition set out in the statutory elements *applies only to false statements of fact, not to opinions; nor can any strong criticism of the actions of the government or any other public body be prohibited.* The statement of reasons also analyses the issue of the impact of scaremongering:

> "[S]ection 337(2) of the Criminal Code [...] prohibits the expression of an opinion based on knowingly false (or distorted) facts that, taking into account the place and time of the commission, and in particular the manner of its commission, may impede defense due to its effect on the audience. In this case, the restriction is set out in an act."[44]
>
> "The danger or harm that the restriction seeks to remedy in this case does not relate solely to the communication but to the effect of the communication. According to the guidelines of the General Prosecutor's Office, issued on 25 May 2020 with a view to ensuring the unity of law enforcement practice, the conduct specified in Section 337(2) of the Criminal Code is a statement or rumor of a false fact or a distorted assertion of a true fact that is capable of hindering or frustrating the effectiveness of defense. According to the guidelines, such conduct means the assertion or rumor of an untrue or distorted true fact that goes beyond the critique of each measure and is capable of triggering a human action, omission or related consequences, that may be contrary to epidemiological measures or other provisions laid down to prevent the spread of the pandemic or to prevent or eliminate its adverse effects."[45]

The prohibition only applies to a certain set of statements of fact. The range of (untrue) information that is capable of hindering the effectiveness of defense is relatively narrow; at least, it is much narrower than the range of all published statements of fact about the danger which justified the introduction of a special legal order. The prohibited act must be objectively capable of hindering or

42 Id. Reasoning [48].
43 Id. Reasoning [49].
44 Id. Reasoning [52].
45 Id. Reasoning [53].

doi: 10.5553/HYIEL/266627012021009001002

frustrating the effectiveness of defense, whether it is an act of government or of other state, municipal or even private effort.

However, this ability to cause harmful consequences, as required by the statement of reasons, may be a less strict standard than the manifest and imminent danger of such activities (clear and present danger). Although the 2020 decision does not refer to the 2000 decision, the relationship between the two may nevertheless be examined, on the basis of which the decisions may be in two kinds of relationship with each other. As this is the most sensitive issue, determining the standard of criminality, a lot is at stake when deciding which interpretation to follow.

Judging this issue essentially depends on whether we agree with Török. To be precise, if the mere fact that the rumor is communicated while under a special legal order also means that the communication poses a manifest and imminent danger then that must also be taken into account when applying the new 2020 statutory elements. All this would not represent a separate difficulty for the courts because, in Török's view, under the special legal order, communications meeting the statutory elements automatically pose a manifest and imminent danger. Thus, the two decisions, which are twenty years apart, may be considered compatible. There may also be consistency between them if we dispute Török's position and hold instead that the test of "real" rather than "manifest and imminent" danger may be read from the 2000 decision, as we may consider that, at the time of the special legal order, the real danger arises in itself when an act meeting the statutory elements is committed.

Of course, it is also possible to imagine an approach that does not seek to reconcile the two decisions. In this case, whatever the interpretation of the 2000 decision, we may consider the mere capability of causing harm as the standard in the 2020 decision (the capability of triggering a human action, omission or related consequences, which may be contrary to epidemiological measures or other provisions laid down to prevent the spread of the pandemic or to prevent or eliminate its adverse effects). This does not require the justification of any danger (either manifest and imminent nor real) for criminality to be found but links it only to the standard of objective capability.

In any case, *the silence of the 2020 decision on the criterion of danger* does not allow us to definitively determine which of the above possible options is the right choice, so the decision rests with the law enforcement in this regard, too. At the same time, it may be stated with general validity that scaremongering may only be constitutionally restricted by means of criminal law in very narrow cases since each possible interpretation sets a high standard for speech to be punished.

As an aid to law enforcement, the decision lays down a constitutional requirement for a range of relevant statutory elements and strengthens the protection of the freedom of expression. This is the case, for instance, where the veracity of the statement of fact in the communication cannot yet be established at the time of the communication but may later turn out to be false. The criterion of willful conduct already answers this question quite adequately, but the

doi: 10.5553/HYIEL/266627012021009001002

constitutional requirement leaves no doubt as to the correctness of *the interpretation in favor of the freedom of expression*.[46]

> "The motion assumes that the challenged provisions of the Criminal Code may be interpreted (from a grammatical point of view) and applied in such a way as to cover cases within public debate, in which the act is a communication where its capability to hinder or frustrate protection is not expected to be definite but doubtful."[47]
>
> "When the criminal offence is committed, falsehood in the subjective sense is also relevant; that is, whether the perpetrator was aware of the falsehood himself. This is examined by criminal law within the framework of guilt. Because it is an intentional criminal offence, criminal liability may only be established if the perpetrator has been shown to be aware of the untruthfulness (distortion) of the statement of facts. it is the perpetrator's consciousness at the time of his act that is relevant from the perspective of criminal prosecution. Communication of facts disputed at the time of the commission (meaning that the perpetrator was aware of neither their falsehood, nor their veracity at that time), and only proved to be false later cannot be included under the scope of Section 337(2) of the Criminal Code."[48]

However, the Constitutional Court still considered it necessary to confirm its interpretation in the form of a constitutional requirement:

> "[T]he Constitutional Court, acting *ex officio*, finds that, in the interpretation and application of Section 337(2) of Act C of 2012 on the Criminal Code, under Articles IX(1) and XXVIII(1) of the Fundamental Law, it is a constitutional requirement that only the communication of a fact of which the perpetrator should have known at the time the act was committed that it was false or which he himself distorted and which is capable of obstructing or frustrating protection at the time of the special legal order is threatened by punishment."[49]

It is important to point out that *the Constitutional Court did not impose any new requirement that would deviate from the well-established application of criminal law in judicial practice*. Following the entry into force of these statutory elements, the police initiated proceedings in several cases on the grounds of speech having

46 However, according to the correct legal interpretation, a statement of fact may only concern a "phenomenon that existed in the past or exists in the present", *cf.* Hornyák 2010, p. 157.

47 Decision No. 15/2020. (VII. 8.) AB, Reasoning [55], 2.

48 Id. Reasoning [58].

49 Id. Operative part, 1.

doi: 10.5553/HYIEL/266627012021009001002

threatened public danger, in addition to scaremongering.[50] According to information from the National Police Headquarters, by 15 May 2020, the police had initiated 90 proceedings for scaremongering, of which 61 were closed by 10 June while two had reached a motion for indictment, according to information provided to the daily *Népszava*.[51] In some cases, a substantive decision will presumably be delivered, such as in a case which was brought in the city of Pécs.[52] The Pécs District Court reprimanded the accused person for the criminal offence of scaremongering. The accused had posted comments on social media that denied the existence of the new COVID-19 pandemic, and its adverse health consequences. The case highlights that law enforcement agencies recognize the danger to society of fake news and rumors spread on social media.

Where exactly the new boundaries of free speech lie will emerge once the final and binding judgments are available. The first examples include two high-profile cases (in the towns of Gyula and Szerencs) that were launched following communications through Facebook posts. In the Gyula case, the commenter criticized the release of hospital beds, which he said meant "sending dying patients [...] home", according to reports.[53] In Szerencs, in addition to several strong opinions, the author of the post expressed the opinion that Prime Minister Viktor Orbán is deliberately allowing security measures to be relaxed at the peak of the pandemic in order to reduce the budget burden by allowing large numbers of retirees to become infected and "sending thousands to their deaths".[54] The two proceedings were quickly terminated without indictment. According to a statement by the Minister of Justice, Judit Varga, "unfortunately sometimes the authority is wrong";[55] Gergely Gulyás, the Minister of the Prime Minister's Office, stated that "the strength of the rule of law is shown by the fact

50 Criminal Code, Section 338(1): "A person who states or disseminates any untrue fact, which is capable of disturbing the public peace, or pretends that an event resulting in public danger is about to happen, is guilty of a felony and shall be punished by imprisonment for up to three years. (2) The punishment shall be imprisonment for one to five years if the criminal offence of threatening public danger resulted in any serious disturbance of public peace."

51 Tamás Koncz, 'Érthető, miért hallgatott a rendőrség: megszereztük a rémhírterjesztés miatt indított eljárások adatait', *Népszava*, 10 June 2020, at https://nepszava.hu/3081120_ertheto-miert-hallgatott-a-rendorseg-megszereztuk-a-remhirterjesztes-miatt-inditott-eljarasok-adatait.

52 'Jogerősen megrovásban részesítette a Pécsi Járásbíróság a rémhírterjesztőt', *Birosag.hu*, 6 October 2020, at https://birosag.hu/aktualis-kozlemenyek/pecsi-torvenyszek-jogerosen-megrovasban-reszesitette-pecsi-jarasbirosag.

53 Árpád Németh & Ádám Magyar, 'Nem zárult le a rémhírterjesztés miatt előállított momentumos büntetőeljárása', *Euronews*, 14 May 2020, at https://hu.euronews.com/2020/05/14/nem-zarult-le-az-eljarasa-a-remhirterjesztes-miatt-eloallitott-momentumosnak.

54 Dániel Szalay, 'A TASZ jogásza szerint rémisztő, hogy a rendőrség bevitte a kormányfőt bíráló szerencsi férfit rémhírterjesztés vádjával – a hatóság furcsa magyarázatot adott a történtekre', *Media1*, 12 May 2020, at https://media1.hu/2020/05/12/a-tasz-jogasza-szerint-remiszto-hogy-a-rendorseg-bevitte-a-kormanyfot-biralo-szerencsi-ferfit-remhirterjesztes-vadjaval-a-hatosag-furcsa-magyarazatot-adott-a-tortentekre.

55 Judit Varga, 'Előfordul, hogy a hatóság téved', *Mandiner*, 16 May 2020, at https://mandiner.hu/cikk/20200516_varga_judit_elofordul_hogy_a_hatosag_teved.

doi: 10.5553/HYIEL/266627012021009001002

that the prosecutor's office changed the wrong decision within a few hours".[56] The conclusion in the two cases is that opinions that are harshly critical of the Government and the Prime Minister, accusing decision-makers of indirectly taking human lives, may be freely aired. According to the police and the Government, all of this falls within the framework of the freedom of expression, and in any case is not considered to be scaremongering.

5. Conclusion

Until now, in the absence of substantive case-law, it was only possible to engage in abstract exchanges of views on the crime of scaremongering at the level of principles. It may well be that the COVID-19 pandemic will change this situation, and the publication of untrue allegations, primarily in online social media, could have criminal consequences in cases provided for by the law. It is therefore not futile to prepare for such situations and to clarify what interpretations of the criminal statutory elements emerge from the reasoning of the two related Constitutional Court decisions. In general, it is timely for the case-law to establish specific standards for social media opinions, whether published by non-professional opinion-leaders or by public actors.

It is also important that the case-law on the new statutory elements make it clear from the outset that *public debates and critical opinions may not be stifled* by the prosecution of individuals for scaremongering. This basic premise is clear from the decisions of the Constitutional Court, as is the fact that, in contrast to the situation in the past, scaremongering may now only be punished in special situations, in particularly justified and narrow cases. Although the applicable standard cannot be determined with full accuracy from the decisions analyzed here, it is sufficient to establish these starting points in order to protect the freedom of expression, while the clarification of further details remains a matter for the case-law.

56 Lénárd Sándor, 'Rémhírterjesztésről, alkotmányosan', *Mandiner*, 17 June 2020, at https://precedens.mandiner.hu/cikk/20200617_remhirterjesztesrol_alkotmanyosan.

doi: 10.5553/HYIEL/266627012021009001002

Constitutional Rights in the Time of Pandemic

The Experience of Hungary

Lóránt Csink[*]

Abstract

Special circumstances may require special measures. This article is to highlight the importance of constitutional rights, also in the time of a pandemic. Its hypothesis is that constitutional rights are not luxuries one can only afford in peacetime, they are much rather at the core of civilization and democracy. History shows that a world without rights may easily turn into a nightmare. The article first focuses on the Hungarian constitutional basis of the state of emergency (Section 2). Next, it analyses the text of the constitution with respect to the limitation of fundamental rights and elaborates on the various interpretations through the lens of the case-law of the Constitutional Court (Sections 3-4). Finally, the article concludes that despite the rigid wording of the Hungarian Fundamental Law, constitutional rights can be restricted only if the restriction meets the necessity-proportionality test (Section 5)

Keywords: state of emergency, emergency powers, restriction of fundamental rights, Fundamental Law, Constitutional Court of Hungary.

1. Introduction

On 28 February 1933, the day after the German Parliament, the *Reichstag* burnt down, Paul von Hindenburg, president of the German Empire, issued a decree to protect the People and the State.[1] Referring to Article 48 of the Weimar Constitution, he authorized the Government to restrict constitutional rights. On 23 March 1933 the German Parliament confirmed the decree in an Act of Parliament and suspended fundamental rights for four years; the expiry date of the Act was prolonged both in 1937 and in 1941. It is noteworthy that in 1933 the Nazi party did not have majority in the Parliament, nevertheless, the act was adopted with a qualified (two-thirds) majority.

We all know what followed. 1933 was the year of the Nazi takeover and the start of brutal infringements on constitutional rights. The Weimar Constitution, which otherwise served German society well in the mid-war period, earned a bad

* Lóránt Csink: associate professor of law, Pázmány Péter Catholic University, Budapest; counselor, Constitutional Court of Hungary, Budapest.

1 Verordnung des Reichspräsidenten zum Schutz von Volk und Staat.

doi: 10.5553/HYIEL/266627012021009001003

reputation exactly because of the *Notverordnung* (Authorization Clause), which made it possible for the executive to restrict and suspend constitutional rights.

Almost ten years thereafter, on 16 February 1942, a couple of months after the Japanese Empire attacked Pearl Harbor, President Franklin D. Roosevelt issued Executive Order 9066, which allowed military leaders to intern Japanese-Americans from the West Coast to concentration camps in the middle of the country, depriving them of all constitutional rights. At the time, the Supreme Court found the measure constitutional. The decision rendered in *Korematsu v United States*[2] upheld the regulation and found that the military urgency of the situation demanded that all citizens of Japanese ancestry be segregated from the West Coast during the war against Japan.

To be fair, in the political climate just after the burn of the Reichstag or the bombing of Pearl Harbor, it may have seemed a wise and popular decision to limit constitutional rights. Such measures most likely met people's expectations: violent demonstrations must be stopped; the war must be won. In hindsight, however, it is clear that short-term solutions may come at a high price.

Today, decades after the restrictions mentioned above, the world has a very different challenge to face. The COVID-19 pandemic resulted in a huge number of infections and deaths, ruined the economy and impaired the mental health of many members of our societies. The situation called for strict restrictions in virtually all countries: the closure of shops, schools and services, the limitation of social interaction and, obviously, the restriction of constitutional rights.

I admit that *special circumstances may require special measures*. This article, however, *attempts to highlight the importance of constitutional rights, also in the time of a pandemic*. Its hypothesis is that constitutional rights are not luxuries one can only afford in peacetime but are much rather at the core of civilization and democracy. History shows that a world without rights may easily turn into a nightmare.

The article first focuses on the Hungarian constitutional basis of state of emergency. Secondly, it analyses the text of the constitution with respect to the limitation of fundamental rights and elaborates on the various interpretations through the lens of the case-law of the Constitutional Court. Finally, the article draws some conclusions.

2. Constitutional Background: The Former Constitution and the Current Fundamental Law

Compared with other constitutional texts, the Hungarian regulation on special legal order is extremely complicated. During the transition, at the roundtable talks the special legal order proved to be a key question. The opposition was in full distrust of the future president, who, according to the expectations at the time, was to be nominated by the Communist party. They were anxious that the Polish scenario, where president Jaruzelski introduced a special legal order and

2 323 U.S. 214 (1944).

Hungarian Yearbook of International Law and European Law 2021 (9) 1
doi: 10.5553/HYIEL/266627012021009001003

intended to break down the transition, would repeat itself. In 1989, the Soviet Army was still stationed in Hungary and there was little knowledge of how the Russian presence would affect the transition. Therefore, the opposition fought for detailed and rigorous rules to govern the special legal order in which the Parliament (and not the President) was to be the key actor.[3]

As a result, the *Constitution stipulated three different special legal orders. (i)* First, the "State of national crisis" (Section 19/B) refers to war under international law: when official armies of countries fight each other. *(ii)* Secondly, the "State of emergency" (Section 19/C) involves a revolution or a civil war when different groups of Hungarian nationals fight each other. *(iii)* Thirdly, natural disasters or industrial accidents result in a "State of danger" [Section 35(1)(i)].

In 1994, a new special legal order emerged. This was the time of the Balkan war between Serbs and Croatians during which Serbian troops, presumably unintentionally, occasionally crossed the Hungarian border causing a threat to locals. As Hungary was not in war with Serbia, a "State of national crisis" was inapplicable. Therefore, a new special legal order was inserted into the Constitution for such purposes: the "Unexpected Attack" (Section 19/E). In such cases, the Government may take measures to respond to the attack.

The fifth one is the "State of Preventive Defense" [Section 35(1)(m)]. It was included in the Constitution as a special legal order in 2004. Before 2003, military service was mandatory for men; they were recruited after secondary school or university to fulfil their service. A political campaign was launched to abolish obligatory military service, and as a result, the Constitution was amended abolishing recruitment into the army during times of peace, *i.e.* when there is no special legal order. The "State of Preventive Defense" involves either the threat of external armed attack or the fulfilment of obligations arising from alliance.

The new Hungarian constitution, the *Fundamental Law* that entered into force in 2012 made very few changes to the regulation of special legal orders; *the very essence of the provisions of the previous Constitution remained unchanged*. Later, in 2016 the Sixth amendment to the Fundamental Law introduced a new special legal order: the "State of Terrorist Threat". Although there has been no terrorist attack in Hungary so far, the Parliament intended to emphasize its commitment to the fight against terrorism.

While the number of special legal orders has risen continuously, the Ninth amendment to the Fundamental Law adopted in 2020 reconsidered special legal orders and reduced their number to three: the "state of war", the "state of emergency" and the "state of disaster". The amendments will enter into force in 2023.

To further complicate matters, there is also a linguistic gap: the internationally used "state of emergency" does not cover all special legal orders. In the following, I still use the term "state of emergency" to encompass all special legal orders, as the article focuses on the restriction of rights irrespective of the situation in question.

3 Csaba Tordai, 'A Társadalmi Szerződéstől az Alkotmánybíróság határozatáig: Kísérletek az államfői tisztség jogi szabályozására', *Politikatudományi Szemle*, 1998/4, pp. 68 and 71.

doi: 10.5553/HYIEL/266627012021009001003

3. Constitutional Provisions Governing the Restriction of Rights

Can a constitution give a blank cheque to the executive in a state of emergency? The recent COVID-19 situation recalled the century-old *Jacobson v Massachusetts*[4] that concerned the question whether a state may make vaccination compulsory during an epidemic. Interestingly, the interpretation of the case varies: certain courts view *Jacobson* as virtually a blank cheque for government actions; others apply standard constitutional doctrines with little heed to the emergency.[5]

Considering the Hungarian legal framework, Article I(3) of the Fundamental Law stipulates that

> "A fundamental right may only be restricted to allow the effective use of another fundamental right or to protect a constitutional value, to the extent absolutely necessary, proportionate to the objective pursued and with full respect for the essential content of that fundamental right."

This provision is for 'ordinary times' and is very much in line with the European Convention on Human Rights on restricting fundamental rights. However, for times of emergency, the Fundamental Law contains a separate provision. Article 54 (1) provides that

> "Under a special legal order, the exercise of fundamental rights – with the exception of the fundamental rights provided for in Articles II and III, and Article XXVIII(2) to (6) – may be suspended or may be restricted beyond the extent specified in Article I(3)."

The key question seems to be *how this latter provision relates to the general rule*. Plain meaning interpretation dictates that Article 54 is a special provision and provides exception from the general rule of Article I(3). Consequently, all fundamental rights that are not mentioned in Article 54 (criminal procedure guarantees, ban of torture, right to life and dignity) can be suspended or restricted more than in 'peacetime'. In other words, the Government is free to introduce any restriction in a state of emergency; even measures that are not connected to the emergency in question. That seems dangerous: too often, policymakers are resorting to law enforcement and national security-oriented measures that not only suppress individual rights unnecessarily but have proven to be ineffective in stopping the spread of the disease and saving lives.[6]

Are there any other interpretations besides the literal one? Absolutely. First, Article R(3) states that

4 197 U.S. 11 (1905).

5 Daniel A. Farber, 'The Long Shadow of Jacobson v. Massachusetts: Epidemics, Fundamental Rights, and the Courts', *San Diego Law Review*, Vol. 57, Issue 1, 2020, p. 833.

6 George J. Annas *et al.*, *Pandemic Preredness*. American Civil Liberties Union, 2008, at www.aclu.org/sites/default/files/pdfs/privacy/pemic_report.pdf.

doi: 10.5553/HYIEL/266627012021009001003

> "The provisions of the Fundamental Law shall be interpreted in accordance with their purposes, the National Avowal contained therein and the achievements of our historic constitution."

Considering the purpose of the provisions of state of emergency, one may conclude that the main goal is to defeat the causes and bring life back to normalcy. There is no need to introduce measures that are unrelated to the extreme situation. Neither is it legitimate to restrict fundamental rights more than it is necessary. One may conclude that necessity and proportionality are required elements of the restriction, also in a state of emergency.

The Fundamental Law also guarantees that Government measures are subject to political and judicial control. The Parliament supervises the activity of the Government and measures do not expire after fifteen days only if the Parliament gives its consent thereto [Article 53(3)]. The activity of the Constitutional Court cannot be restricted [Article 54(2)], which means that the Fundamental Law establishes permanent constitutional review for all legislation, also in a state of emergency.

Secondly, the Fundamental Law stipulates that the detailed regulations of state of emergency are contained in separate laws: the Act on Disaster Management and the Military Act (literally: National Defense Act). Both laws declare that emergency measures must be necessary and proportionate. *Government power is not, and cannot be unlimited and uncontested, even in a state of emergency*.

Arriving at the conclusion that the Fundamental Law does not give absolute power to the Government in a state of emergency, the question arises what the constitutional test for restriction is. Is it the general test Article I(3) of the Fundamental Law prescribes or is it a specific one?

My position is that *a special regulation is necessary only if the general rule is not applicable*; I argue that the general restriction test functions well, even in a state of emergency. At first glance it is obvious that in a state of emergency fundamental rights prevail in a narrower scope (*i.e.* they can be restricted to a greater degree). However, stronger restrictions may also be constitutional according to the general rule. The general rule is not objective: the greater the danger is, the more severe restrictions may become acceptable. The inviolable essence of a fundamental right may vary, depending on the situation at hand. Consequently, if a measure is necessary to face the challenge and it is proportionate to the aim, then it is constitutional, even if it results in a grave restriction. On the contrary, if the measure does not help defeat the causes of the state of emergency or it causes greater damage than it intends to avoid (disproportionate), then the measure is unconstitutional.

4. Case-Law of the Constitutional Court

The Hungarian Constitutional Court has little jurisprudence on COVID-19 legislation. One obvious reason is that little time has passed since the outbreak.

doi: 10.5553/HYIEL/266627012021009001003

Considering the average duration of the procedure, constitutional review takes a couple of months. As emergency measures change quickly, the law in question is easily out of force by the time the review takes place. If the petition is not geared towards a particular decision, the Constitutional Court has no possibility to review 'expired' legal norms.[7]

The other reason for less active review is beyond constitutionalism. The present danger caused by the pandemic is estimated to be great enough to overrule all other purposes, including fundamental rights. It is very tempting for courts (including constitutional courts) not to contribute to the easing of the restrictions, for fear of being accused of a failure to defend the country, whatever 'failure' may mean. Experience suggests that courts are very cautious when challenging an emergency restriction.

Nevertheless, there are cases concerning COVID-19 legislation. *Decision No. 15/2020. (VII. 8.) AB* examined the amendment to the Criminal Code.[8] In Spring 2020, the Parliament adopted an Authorization Act that, among other provisions, amended the Criminal Code. It modified the provision of *'Scaremongering'*: "at times of a special legal order, anyone who expresses a false statement that may hinder the efficiency of the protection can be imprisoned for three years". This provision is invoked when someone falsely states that COVID-19 does not exist; the amendment of the Criminal Code seems to be against conspiracy theories.

Freedom of expression is the most basic political right, as it encourages individuals to participate in public debates. It shapes public opinion and therefore it can be deemed an essential criterion of democracy.[9] Despite the high rank of freedom of expression within the scope of fundamental rights, it is impossible to accept all opinions as equal. Most European countries that have a history of totalitarian regimes are less hesitant to establish content-based restrictions. The rationale behind that is that states are obliged to maintain public order, especially in 'hard times'. However, such a limitation must meet strict criteria. As for the particular case, the decision stated that the law is constitutional only in case two criteria are fulfilled: *(i)* on the one hand, the perpetrator *needs to know at the time of the perpetration that the statement is false* (subjective criteria); and *(ii)* on the other hand, *the information must be capable of hindering the defense against the pandemic* (objective criteria). As a result of the decision, there remained little room to use this provision for scaremongering. The Constitutional Court though

7 Order No. 3413/2020. (XI. 26.) AB refused to review the exceptional provisions on access to information; neither did Order No. 3388/2020. (X. 22.) AB examine the government and a municipality's quarrel over a territory – in both cases the law in question was out of force by the time of the review.

8 Act C of 2012 on the Criminal Code.

9 Péter Smuk, 'The Constitutional Guarantees of Democratic Political Discourses and their Regulation in Central Europe', *in* András Koltay (ed.) *Comparative Perspectives on the Fundamental Freedom of Expression*, Wolters Kluwer, Budapest, 2015, p. 89.

doi: 10.5553/HYIEL/266627012021009001003

it obvious to use the general test to determine the constitutionality of the law in question.[10]

The first time the Constitutional Court reviewed an emergency measure on its merits was *Decision No. 15/2021. (V. 13.) AB*. In this case, the Government introduced a decree that overruled the Information Act: if the pandemic encumbers the authority to the degree that it cannot give access to data within 15 days (as required by the Information Act), then the authority has 45 (in certain cases 90) days to provide the information. The majority opinion concluded that the extension of the time for providing data is a restriction on the access to information, even if the scope of the accessible data is unchanged. The Constitutional Court found that *timing was very important in respect of this fundamental right; as time passes, data may lose their relevance*. The most important part of the decision is the *interpretation of Article 54(1) of the Fundamental Law*: the majority opinion refused the idea that fundamental rights can be entirely restricted in a state of emergency. If it had accepted that all rights not stipulated in Article 54(1) could be suspended, the Constitutional Court would not have reviewed the petition on its merits: freedom of information is a right that can be suspended in a state of emergency. The Constitutional Court relied more heavily on the logical and theoretical interpretation than the plain meaning of the provision. Although the Constitutional Court failed to explicitly declare that the general limitation test of Article I(3) is applicable, the Constitutional Court further evaluated the restriction upon the necessity-proportionality test. The Constitutional Court arrived at the conclusion that *special tasks in times of pandemic may legitimize the longer time to provide the requested data*, but on each occasion, *the authority must give reasons for the delay*.

The question that *Decision No. 23/2021. (VII. 23.) AB* raised is even more interesting. A group of people intended to organize a demonstration in support of rainbow families and against the amendment of the Fundamental Law. Cautious of the pandemic, the demonstrators planned to sit in their own cars (taking care to exercise social distancing) and to raise public attention by blowing their horns and showing posters. However, both the authorities and the courts banned the assembly as according to the emergency measure, no gathering can be organized. For a scholar, *it is quite unclear how a general ban on freedom of assembly can be constitutional*, especially when it is entirely unrelated to the pandemic. The question remains open whether the Government distinguishes between activities, allowing for certain activities while introducing a general ban on others.

5. Conclusion

Scholars of constitutional law unanimously believe that a state of emergency is not a state of extra-constitutionalism. The legalists argue that emergencies must

10 About the decision and the scaremongering-related case-law of the Hungarian Constitutional Court, *see* András Koltay, 'On the Constitutionality of the Punishment of Scaremongering in the Hungarian Legal System', *Hungarian Yearbook of International Law and European Law*, Vol. 9, 2021.

doi: 10.5553/HYIEL/266627012021009001003

be handled by entirely legal responses, though these responses might well be different from those applicable in normal times. Legalists think that this is the only way to preserve constitutionalism and the rule of law.[11] Emergency measures must fit into the framework of the constitution. However, in reality, it is very tempting to broaden these frameworks or to simply overrule the constitution in order to provide greater protection against the present danger. Avoiding danger is in accordance with the expectations of the public, whether the danger entails a violent attack against democracy, an enemy bombing a country or a pandemic causing death and ruining the economy and distressing society. One may say that in such cases the restriction of fundamental rights may be a price that we can afford to pay.

History shows it is wise to resist this temptation. The lack of fundamental rights may easily turn into an abuse of constitutionalism. The crisis sparked by the global lockdown only reinforces this destabilizing scenario, and instability is a fertile ground for totalitarianism.[12] The key question is how legislation can balance between fundamental rights and state security.

Such balancing is extremely difficult on an abstract level. The possible reasons for a state of emergency vary to such an extent that no constitution can provide the specific measures in advance. I find that the guarantee is not in detailed descriptions but in political and constitutional guarantees. A properly functioning parliament and constitutional court provide a greater guarantee than any detailed regulation.

The Hungarian Constitutional Court faced a new challenge of reviewing emergency measures. It is promising that the Constitutional Court interpreted the measures related to the state of emergency in a way that there is no possibility for a total restriction of fundamental rights. Hopefully, the Constitutional Court will continue with that approach and examine emergency measures on the merits.

Evaluating emergency measures during an emergency is always easier in hindsight. Still, the responsibility of the judiciary is to uphold rights and not to defeat the pandemic. Social, economic and medical issues may only provide the context but not the goals for a court.

11 Gábor Mészáros, 'Carl Schmitt in Hungary: Constitutional Crisis in the Shadow of Covid-19', *MTA Law Working Papers*, 2020/17, p. 5.

12 Andrea Cioffi *et al.*, 'COVID-19 Pandemic and Balance of Constitutional Rights', *La Clinica Terapeutica*, Vol. 172, Issue 2, 2021, pp. 119-122.

doi: 10.5553/HYIEL/266627012021009001003

European State Aid Rules in Times of Pandemic

Distorting Competition Between European Airlines?[*]

Mónika Papp[**]

Abstract

The outbreak of the COVID-19 pandemic had an immediate and profound impact on mobility and, more specifically, on air passenger transport: airlines were quickly stranded, and the Member States granted aid to air carriers subject to specific eligibility criteria. The Commission reacted swiftly to challenges posed by the COVID-19 pandemic and adopted its Temporary Framework under which vast amounts could be disbursed to market operators. The most controversial eligibility condition set by the Member States is the holding of a national license. This article's research questions are, first, to explore the conditions under which Member States can grant large amounts of state aid to airlines, and second, to assess whether the requirement to hold a national license is compatible with EU law. By addressing these issues, this article seeks to improve our understanding of EU law's capacity to tackle distortions of competition.

Keywords: state aid, air transport, airlines, COVID-19 pandemic, Ryanair.

1. Introduction

The economic and social damage caused by the COVID-19 pandemic's is widely recognized to be unprecedented. The containment measures adopted to limit the outbreak's effect on citizens' health have had a destructive impact on the economy.

Before the pandemic, the air transport sector had been competitive in Europe, as liberalization had deeply affected the conditions under which air

* As the pandemic and the economic situation change rapidly, I note that this article has been submitted for review at the end of April 2021. It contains information collected until this cut-off date. I am grateful to Dr Francesco De Cecco and the anonymous peer reviewers for their helpful comments.

** Mónika Papp: research fellow, Centre for Social Sciences, Eötvös Loránd Research Network, Budapest; senior lecturer, ELTE Law School, Budapest.

doi: 10.5553/HYIEL/266627012021009001004

carriers compete.[1] The outbreak of the pandemic had an immediate and profound impact on mobility and air transport because the Member States rapidly introduced containment measures. Moreover, entry into several Member States' national territories was prohibited. Most post-virus projections expect demand for flights to remain depressed below pre-virus levels long after the end of the lockdown. Low-cost carriers, whose business model is based on full capacity onboard, low charges and prices, halted most of their fleet as the safety measures introduced gravely limited their profitability. Global airlines ceased most activities due to the significant drop in travel demand: in March and April 2020, the number of flights operated in the European airspace fell by up to 90%.[2] The sector, ravaged by the global lockdown, called for help to alleviate the credit crunch it faced. State aid is the right tool to intervene when the economy is in a situation of crisis, as the Member States may provide financial help to companies to return to viability once the economic conditions normalize.

This article aims to give an overview of the application of state aid rules in the area of air transport, a sector hit particularly severely by the COVID-19 pandemic. The following is not an exhaustive discussion of general state aid rules or crisis measures. Given the scope of this article, it has been narrowed down to focus on selected issues raised by state aid granted to airlines. This article's main questions are, first, to explore the conditions under which Member States grant large amounts of state aid to airlines, and second, to assess whether the requirement to hold a national license is compatible with EU law. By addressing these issues, this article seeks to improve our understanding of the capacity of EU law to tackle distortions of competition. The structure of the article is as follows. First, it outlines state aid rules, identifies their objectives and provides an introduction into the special COVID-19 soft law framework (Sections 2-3). Second, it considers an example of national aid measures introduced to mitigate the effects of the pandemic to airlines (Section 4), followed by a discussion of the General Court's recent judgments on the compatibility of relevant Commission decisions with the Treaty (Section 5). Finally, the article closes with some concluding thoughts (Section 6).

1 On the deregulation of the industry *see* the short summary of Francesco Munoz, 'Lifting the Veil: Covid-19 and the Need to Re-Consider Airline Regulation', *European Papers*, Vol. 5, Issue 1, 2020, pp. 548-550. On state aid issues in the sector, *see also* Filippo Ghersini, 'Overview of State Aid to Particular Sectors: State Aid in the Transport Sector', *in* Alberto Santa Maria (ed.), *Competition and State Aid. An Analysis of the EU Practice*, Wolters Kluwer, Alphen aan den Rijn, 2015, pp. 325-342; Kelyn Bacon (ed.), *European Union Law of State Aid*, Oxford University Press, Oxford, 2013, pp. 307-344.

2 Overview of the state aid rules and public service obligations rules applicable to the air transport sector during the COVID-19 outbreak, at https://ec.europa.eu/competition/state_aid/what_is_new/covid_19.html. Globally, passenger demand fell by 94.3% in April 2020 compared with April 2019; IATA, *Air Passenger Market Analysis (Apr. 2020)*, at www.iata.org/en/iata-repository/publications/economic-reports/air-passenger-monthly-analysis---apr-20202/. *See also* Eurocontrol fresh data to compare the current number of flights to the pre-COVID situation, https://www.eurocontrol.int/Economics/DailyTrafficVariation-States.html?ectl-public.

doi: 10.5553/HYIEL/266627012021009001004

2. A Summary of State Aid Rules

2.1. The Rationale of State Aid Rules in the Treaty

Since state aid is a relatively lesser-known part of EU competition rules, a brief overview is called for to guide the readers into this specific field. Although state aid rules are part of the TFEU Chapter on competition,[3] their aim is not only to prevent distortions of the market, but also to prevent subsidy wars among the Member States.[4] In this context, the TFEU rules on state aid have a fundamental importance in minimizing distortions of competition and trade flows and in ensuring the free movement of capital in the internal market.[5]

Granting a selective advantage to undertakings takes as many different forms as the State can influence the market's functioning: buying or selling goods and services under more favorable conditions than those available on the market, as well as recapitalization, risk finance measures, funding infrastructure or guarantees provided by the State to undertakings, *etc*.

Under Article 107(1) TFEU,

> "Save as otherwise provided in the Treaties, any aid granted by a Member State or through State resources in any form whatsoever which distorts or threatens to distort competition by favoring certain undertakings or the production of certain goods shall, in so far as it affects trade between Member States, be incompatible with the internal market."

As seen above, the definition of prohibited state aid consists of the following five elements: *(i)* it is granted by Member State (imputable to the State) and through State resources (State transfers); *(ii)* it is aid in the meaning that advantage is granted to one or more undertakings; *(iii)* it is selective as it favors 'certain undertakings or the production of certain goods'; *(iv)* it distorts or threatens to distort competition; and *(v)* it affects trade between the Member States. The non-

3 Title VII. (Common rules on competition, taxation and approximation of law) Chapter 1, followed by the tax provisions in Chapter 2.

4 State aid rules have a dual function: to prevent competition from being distorted between undertakings and competition to grant aid between Member States. *See* Jose Luis Buendia Sierra, 'EU State Aid Control: Competition Between Undertakings or Between Member States', *in* Luca Rubini & Jennifer Hawkings (eds.), *'What Shapes the Law? Reflections on the History, Law, Politics and Economics of International and European Subsidy Disciplines'*, European University Institute, Florence, 2016.

5 On the goals of EU state aid control and its development *see* Luca Rubini & Jennifer Hawkins (eds.), *'What Shapes the Law? Reflections on the History, Law, Politics and Economics of International and European Subsidy Disciplines'*, European University Institute, Florence, 2016; Massimo Merola, 'The Forces Shaping State Aid Control in the EU', *in* Rubini & Hawkings (eds.), 2016; Thibaut Kleiner, 'Modernisation of State Aid Policy', *in* Erika Szyszczak (ed.), *'Research Handbook on European State Aid Law'*, Edward Elgar Publishing, Cheltenham, 2011, pp. 1-27; Eugene Stuart & Iana Roginska-Green, *'Sixty Years of EU State Aid Law and Policy'*, Wolters Kluwer, Alphen aan den Rijn, 2018; Juan Jorge Piernas López, *'The Concept of State Aid Under EU Law. From Internal Market to Competition and Beyond'*, Oxford University Press, Oxford, 2016.

doi: 10.5553/HYIEL/266627012021009001004

binding Commission Notice on the notion of state aid provides a helpful starting point to better understand what is covered by Article 107(1).[6]

Under Article 108(3), the European Commission shall be informed of any plan to grant or alter aid.[7] This *ex ante notification obligation enables the Commission to verify whether Article 107(1) conditions are met and whether any Treaty exceptions render the aid compatible with the market*. The Member States shall not put the proposed measure into effect until the Commission's procedure has resulted in a final decision (standstill obligation).[8]

Articles 107(2) and (3) set out exceptions to the prohibition. Article 107(2) exceptions are so-called *ex lege exceptions, where the aid is compatible by law with the Treaty*. Under 107(2)(b), it is compatible with the internal market to grant aid to make good the damage caused by natural disasters or exceptional occurrences. The Commission identified the COVID-19 pandemic as an exceptional occurrence. Under Article 107(2), Member States are under an obligation to notify aid plans to the Commission. The Commission does not have the discretion to authorize the aid. If the aid is granted for the purpose set out in the Treaty (directly linked to it) and is proportionate, it shall be declared compatible with the internal market. 100% of the damage may be rectified, and compensation shall be calculated at the individual company level. Article 107(2) does not require Member States to exclude undertakings in a difficulty from the scope of the aid.[9]

6 On the legal nature of soft law, the CJEU states that a notice, which, being an internal measure adopted by the administration, cannot be regarded as a rule of law, nevertheless forms rules of practice from which the administration may not depart in an individual case without giving reasons which are compatible with the principle of equal treatment. *See*, with regard to the guidelines on state aid, Judgment of 9 June 2011, *Joined Cases C-465/09 P to C-470/09 P Diputación Foral de Vizcaya and others v Commission*, ECLI:EU:C:2011:372, para. 120 (and the case-law cited). On soft law generally *see* Petra Lea Láncos, 'A Hard Core Under the Soft Shell: How Binding is Union Soft Law for Member States', *European Public Law*, Vol. 24, Issue 4, 2018, pp. 755-784; Tihamér Tóth *et al.*, 'Effects of European Soft Law at National Administrative Courts', *Loyola University Chicago International Law Review*, Vol. 14, Issue 1, 2016, pp. 101-131; Oana Stefan, 'COVID-19 Soft Law: Voluminous, Effective, Legitimate? A Research Agenda', *European Papers*, Vol. 5, Issue 1, 2020, pp. 663-670.

7 Within the structure of the European Commission DG COMP is responsible for handling state aid cases. *See* the website of the Commission at https://ec.europa.eu/competition/state_aid/overview/index_en.html.

8 108(3) TFEU. Council Regulation (EU) 2015/1589 of 13 July 2015 laying down detailed rules for the application of Article 108 of the Treaty on the Functioning of the European Union.

9 If a measure is authorized under Article 107(2)(b), the principle of 'one time last time' of the Rescue and Restructuring Guidelines does not apply, since the former type of aid is not "rescue aid, restructuring aid or temporary restructuring support" within the meaning of point 71 of the Rescue and Restructuring Guidelines. Therefore, Member States may compensate under Article 107(2)(b) TFEU the damages directly caused by the COVID-19 outbreak to undertakings that have received aid under the Rescue and Restructuring Guidelines. *E.g.* aid to TAP Air Portugal, the major network airline in Portugal was not granted under the Framework because TAP was already in difficulty on 31 December 2019. Instead, the Rescue and Restructuring Guidelines under Article 107(3)(c) provided the legal basis for the authorization of liquidity support in 2020. France also provided rescue and restructuring aid to Corsair. *See* SA.58125.

doi: 10.5553/HYIEL/266627012021009001004

Nevertheless, if they wish, Member States may exclude such undertakings or a sub-group thereof.[10]

Besides *ex lege* exceptions, under Article 107(3), aid may be declared compatible with the internal market by the European Commission. These are the so-called *discretionary exceptions, where the Commission has the power to define the conditions of compatibility.*[11] COVID-19 aid fits into two categories of Article 107(3). Under Article 107(3)(b) aid to remedy a serious disturbance in the economy of a Member State; under point (c) aid to facilitate the development of certain economic activities or of certain economic areas, where such aid does not adversely affect trading conditions to an extent contrary to the common interest.

For Article 107(3) cases, the Commission has the discretion to declare the aid compatible with the internal market, a discretion which is limited by various secondary acts adopted by the Commission.[12]

Although the Member States used both legal bases to justify their measures, Article 107(3) and the Temporary Framework has also been relied on by the Member States.[13] According to a well-known State aid expert, Phedon Nicolaides, the reason for this is that this measure

> "can be granted both in order to remedy the actual effect of a serious disturbance and to prevent the worsening of the disturbance in the future. In other words, aid can be both 'retrospective' and 'prospective'."[14]

2.2. Special Rules for the Emergency: The Commission Framework

Following the outbreak of the COVID-19 pandemic, the Commission promptly responded in a coordinated way to the challenges posed by the health crisis in order to mitigate its socio-economic effects. Similarly to the global financial and economic crisis, it adopted its soft law document, the so-called Temporary Framework, on the exercise of its discretion concerning the authorization of aid

10 Antonios Bouchagiar, 'State Aid in the Context of the COVID-19 Outbreak, Including the Temporary Framework 2020', *EUI Working Papers*, RSC 2021/03, Robert Schuman Centre for Advanced Studies Florence School of Regulation, p. 54.

11 The Commission enjoys wide discretion under Article 107(3), the exercise of which involves complex economic and social assessments. *See*, to that effect, Judgment of 11 September 2008, *Case C-75/05 P and C-80/05 P, Germany and others v Kronofrance*, ECLI:EU:C:2008:482, para. 59; Judgment of 8 March 2016, *Case C-431/14 P, Greece v Commission*, ECLI:EU:C:2016:145, para. 68.

12 The Commission under Council authorization regularly adopts binding acts limiting its own discretion. The Commission can also adopt non-binding, so called soft law measures. The latter come under different headings and are called notices, frameworks, guidances.

13 Maczkovics pointed out that Article 107(2)(b) "constitutes a straitjacket, requires a solidly documented file and a very strict monitoring in order to avoid any overcompensation." *See* Carole Maczkovics, 'How Flexible Should State Aid Control Be in Times of Crisis?', *European State Aid Law Quarterly*, Vol. 19, Issue 3, 2020, p. 274.

14 Phedon Nicolaides, 'Application of Article 107(2)(b) TFEU to Covid-19 Measures: State Aid to Make Good the Damage Caused by an Exceptional Occurrence', *Journal of European Competition Law & Practice*, Vol. 11, Issue 5-6, 2020, pp. 238-243. "This implies that the exception in Article 107(2)(b) to the prohibition of state aid in Article 107(1) is not useful when the intention of the government is to offer to undertakings enough resources to enable them to implement preventive measures to avoid a further deterioration in their financial situation." *See* p. 239.

doi: 10.5553/HYIEL/266627012021009001004

measures adopted by the Member States.[15] On 20 March 2020, the Commission published its Temporary Framework under Article 107(3)(b).[16] Since then, the Framework has been modified five times.[17]

Considering that the COVID-19 outbreak affects all Member States and that the containment measures taken by Member States impact undertakings, the Commission found that state aid is justified and can be declared compatible with the internal market based on Article 107(3)(b) TFEU, *for a limited period, to remedy the liquidity shortage faced by undertakings* and to ensure that the disruptions caused by the COVID-19 outbreak do not undermine their viability, especially of SMEs.[18] From the beginning, the Commission has foreseen that the overall aid may not exceed EUR 800,000 per undertaking.[19] The aid may be granted in the form of direct grants, tax and payment advantages, or other forms such as repayable advances, guarantees, loans, and equity, provided that the total nominal value of such measures remains below the overall cap per undertaking.[20] A very important condition has been included, under which the aid can be granted only to undertakings not in difficulty on 31 December 2019. This requirement ensures that only viable undertakings receive aid under the Framework. In the first amendment, to preserve employment, the Commission acknowledged that Member States may grant aid in the form of wage subsidies and tax deferrals up to the maximum ceiling. It is permissible for wage subsidies or tax deferrals to be restricted to certain sectors, regions or types of undertakings. In that case, they shall be considered as selective advantages, but the Commission may authorize these under Article 107(3)(b).[21] Furthermore, zero-interest loans and guarantees on loans covering 100% of the risk were introduced into the Framework as compatible with the internal market on the condition of the Commission's approval.

A couple of months later, in May 2020, the Framework was amended for the second time to *include different types of aid, such as recapitalization and subordinated debt*. In the initial text and during the first amendment, the objective had been to reduce the liquidity constraints on undertakings. The prolonged crisis forced the Commission to face companies' insolvency and to authorize aid not only to finance the liquidity shortage, but also the *recapitalization of companies*. Recapitalization m have a significant distortive impact on the market. Therefore, this type of aid was made subject to straightforward entry, exit and remuneration rules, plus compensating measures to prevent market distortions. When

15 Before the Temporary Framework was adopted, only limited aid could be granted to airlines. On this issue *see* European Commission, Guidelines on State Aid to Airports and Airlines (2014).

16 Communication from the Commission Temporary Framework for state aid measures to support the economy in the current COVID-19 outbreak.

17 Until 31 May 2021. The informal consolidated version of the Framework can be found at https://ec.europa.eu/competition/state_aid/what_is_new/TF_informal_consolidated_version_as_amended_28_january_2021_en.pdf.

18 Id. para. 18.

19 The Framework was published in the OJ on 20 March 2020. During the global financial and economic crisis, the Commission set the state aid ceiling in the real economy at 500,000 EUR.

20 Special provisions apply to public guarantee on loans, subsidized interest rates for loans.

21 Framework, para. 42.

doi: 10.5553/HYIEL/266627012021009001004

approving a scheme, the Commission requests the separate notification of individual aid above the threshold of EUR 250 million. In relation to such notifications, the Commission will assess whether existing financing in the market or horizontal measures to cover liquidity needs are insufficient to ensure the viability of the beneficiary; that the selected recapitalization instruments and the conditions attached to them are appropriate to address the beneficiary's serious difficulties; that the aid is proportionate; and that other conditions of the Framework are complied with.[22]

The rules governing recapitalization measures are strict. In order to prevent undue distortions of competition, beneficiaries must not engage in aggressive commercial expansion financed through state aid or must not take excessive risks. If the beneficiary of recapitalization above EUR 250 million is an undertaking with significant market power in at least one of the relevant markets in which it operates, Member States must propose additional measures to preserve effective competition in those markets. In proposing such measures, Member States may in particular offer structural or behavioral commitments foreseen under the EU merger regulation.[23] Beneficiaries receiving a COVID-19 recapitalization measure are prohibited from advertising it for commercial purposes. As long as at least 75% of the COVID-19 recapitalization measures have not been redeemed, beneficiaries other than SMEs shall be prevented from acquiring a more than 10% stake in competitors or other operators in the same line of business, including upstream and downstream operations. State aid shall not be used to cross-subsidize economic activities of integrated undertakings that were in economic difficulties already on 31 December 2019. As long as the COVID-19 recapitalization measures have not been fully redeemed, beneficiaries cannot make dividend payments, nor non-mandatory coupon payments, nor can they buy back shares, other than in relation to the State. Until at least 75% of the COVID-19 recapitalization measures have been redeemed, the remuneration of each member of the beneficiaries' management must not go beyond the fixed part of his/her remuneration effective on 31 December 2019. For persons becoming members of the management on or after the recapitalization, the applicable limit is the fixed remuneration of the members of the management with the same level of responsibility on 31 December 2019. Under no circumstances shall bonuses or other variable or comparable remuneration elements be paid. Andrea Biondi has highlighted how

> "the cumulative effect of all these conditions is particularly burdensome to the point of possibly having a discouraging effect, as companies may prefer to rely on other types of support aid because having the state as a shareholder may make life more difficult."[24]

22 Id. para. 51.

23 Council Regulation (EC) No 139/2004 of 20 January 2004 on the control of concentrations between undertakings (the EC Merger Regulation).

24 Andrea Biondi, 'Governing the Interregnum: State Aid Rules and the COVID-19 Crisis', *King's College London Dickson Poon School of Law Legal Studies Research Paper Series*, Paper No. 2020-48, p. 13.

doi: 10.5553/HYIEL/266627012021009001004

The third amendment, in July 2020, *introduced rules to alleviate the burden of SMEs and modifications to recapitalization conditions*. Under the third modification, aid granted on the basis of Article 107(3)(b) or (c) shall not be conditioned on the relocation of a production activity or of another activity of the beneficiary from another country within the EEA to the territory of the Member State granting the aid. Such a condition would be harmful to the internal market, irrespective of the number of job losses that actually occurred in the initial establishment of the beneficiary in the EEA.[25]

In the fourth amendment, in autumn of 2020, the Commission acknowledged *the need to finance fixed costs not covered by revenues*, up to a maximum of 3 million per undertaking. On 1 February 2021, the fifth amendment took account of the continued economic uncertainty and the fact that government measures restricting economic and social life had been prolonged. One of the most significant modification was the *increase of aid ceilings* from the previous 800,000 EUR per undertaking to 1.8 million EUR. The previous maximum of 3 million EUR was raised to 10 million per undertaking in respect of the fixed cost subsidy. Another major relaxation was the introduction of the conversion of repayable instruments into direct grants. This meant that, for example, *loans previously authorized by the Commission could be transformed into non-repayable direct grants*.[26]

The Commission hesitated to include public policy goals into its Framework, for instance by conditioning its authorization to fulfil higher environmental criteria or to support digitalization. The European Parliament's report admitted that

> "the current state aid principles and practices are mainly defensive in nature, *i.e.* they are designed to avoid competition distortions and do not aim at achieving or facilitating other policy objectives. Though they fulfil the prerequisites for maintaining a level playing field in the European economy, they fail to elevate EU State aid policy beyond its defensive goals."[27]

Before the adoption of the Framework, several stakeholders urged the Commission not to waste the crisis and to adopt green, digital transformation or social conditions for approving state aid.[28] At the end, the Commission did not follow this route in the original text of the Framework and let the Member States freely design their national interventions. The Commission only noted that this possibility is open to Member States, but did not make it a precondition of approval:

25 In effect from 29 June 2020.

26 For a detailed explanation of the crisis rules *see* Bouchagiar 2021.

27 Study Requested by the ECON committee. Jan Van Hove, 'Impact of State Aid on Competition and Competitiveness During the Covid-19 Pandemic: An Early Assessment', European Union, 2020 (Parliament report) p. 18.

28 Some urged the Member States to condition their aid on environmental and societal goals. *See* Julia Anderson *et al.*, 'A Framework for a European Economic Recovery After Covid-19', *Intereconomics*, Vol. 55, Issue 4, 2020, pp. 209-215.

doi: 10.5553/HYIEL/266627012021009001004

"Against this background, the Commission notes that designing national support measures in a way that meets the EU's policy objectives related to green and digital transformation of their economies will allow for a more sustainable long-term growth and promote the transformation to the agreed EU objective of climate neutrality by 2050."[29]

Later on, the amendments sought to strengthen the link between the aid and other EU policies by introducing a condition applicable only to large undertakings to report on how the recapitalization aid received supports their activities in line with EU objectives and national obligations linked to the green and digital transformation, including the EU objective of climate neutrality by 2050.[30]

As long as the COVID-19 recapitalization measures have not been fully redeemed, the beneficiaries, other than SMEs, shall publish information on the use of aid. In particular, this should include information on how their use of the aid received supports their activities in line with EU objectives and national obligations linked to green and digital transformation, including the EU objective of climate neutrality by 2050.[31]

France, for example, conditioned liquidity aid granted to Air France on the fulfilment of national green policy choices.[32] The firm has to curb its emissions and shut down certain domestic routes, thereby redirecting demand towards rail transport.[33]

In the following chapter, the focus will be on *aid granted to airlines*.[34]

3. State Aid Granted to Airlines

Under the given circumstances, most Member States granted state aid to air carriers operating in their territory. A minority of Member States made the aid eligible under uniform criteria. The eligibility criterion determined by a Member State is uniform if it applies without distinction to all affected airlines, for instance by looking at the number of passengers transported in the past, their individual market shares, or the company's contribution to connectivity. The aid in these cases can be implemented in several ways: suspension or deferral of airport taxes, air traffic control charges,[35] government taxes on air travel, or

29 Framework, para. 45 (consolidated text).

30 Id. para. 44.

31 Id. para. 83.

32 *See* SA.57082. The Commission has authorized a guarantee on loans and a shareholder loan of 7 billion EUR to Air France. On the environmental concerns *see* Munoz 2020, pp. 541-548.

33 *See* at www.bfmtv.com/economie/entreprises/air-france-sommee-de-ne-plus-vendre-de-billets-entre-paris-et-une-ville-francaise-situee-a-moins-de-2h30-en-tgv_AN-202004290216.html and www.frontier-economics.com/uk/en/news-and-articles/articles/article-i7377-the-devils-in-the-detail/#.

34 Aid to airports is not discussed in this article.

35 Air Traffic Control (ATC) Charges are levied on aircraft in order to cover the air navigation services provided by the Air Navigation Service Providers over a portion of airspace, generally coincident with national boundaries.

doi: 10.5553/HYIEL/266627012021009001004

through subsidizing public service obligations,[36] or generally subsidizing employment. Up to April 2021, more than 32 measures were taken to support airlines.[37]

3.1. Aid Under Article 107(2)(b) to Make Good Damages Caused by the Pandemic

Several Member States have availed themselves of this opportunity, usually in the form of aid schemes. Italy granted aid to Alitalia, Romania to Blue Air, Greece to Aegean Airlines, Austria to Austrian Airlines, Finland to Finnair in the form of state loan guarantees and hybrid loans, the Netherlands to KLM in the form of guarantees and a subordinated state loan.[38] Alongside the individual aid granted to specific companies, some Member States have also designed schemes to support without distinction airlines operating on their territory. For example, under the Cypriot scheme benefiting 60 airlines, the remuneration level depended on the aircraft's load factor.[39]

3.2. Article 107(3)(b) Measures to Remedy a Serious Disturbance to the Economy

Denmark designed a scheme benefiting all airline servicing scheduled passenger flights in its territory. It was estimated that around 150 airlines are eligible under the Danish scheme.[40] By contrast, France opted for an individual aid measure of 7 billion EUR to support the liquidity shortage of Air France by providing a guarantee on loans and providing a shareholder loan. France conditioned the aid on the fulfilment of national green policies.[41]

Denmark and Sweden provided 1 billion EUR recapitalization aid to SAS.[42] Given the large scale of the aid and SAS's market position, the Commission's approval was granted on several conditions under the Temporary Framework. Bonus payments will be subject to strict limitations, and there is a ban on dividends and share buybacks. Furthermore, a ban on acquisitions and cross-subsidization was applied by the Commission. Likewise, Latvia financed the

36 Public service obligations are imposed on a company by the Member State to provide the services under certain conditions. Usually it serves to connect islands or remote places on the national territory. *See* Regulation (EC) No 1008/2008 of the European Parliament and of the Council of 24 September 2008 on common rules for the operation of air services in the Community. Under Article 16, a Member State may impose a public service obligation in respect of scheduled air services between an airport in the Community and an airport serving a peripheral or development region in its territory or on a thin route to any airport on its territory any such route being considered vital for the economic and social development of the region which the airport serves. That obligation shall be imposed only to the extent necessary to ensure on that route the minimum provision of scheduled air services satisfying fixed standards of continuity, regularity, pricing or minimum capacity, which air carriers would not assume if they were solely considering their commercial interest.

37 *See* at https://ec.europa.eu/competition/state_aid/what_is_new/State_aid_decisions_TF_and_107_2b_107_3b_107_3c.pdf.

38 SA.57116.

39 SA.57691.

40 SA.58157.

41 SA.57082.

42 SA.57543 and SA.58342.

doi: 10.5553/HYIEL/266627012021009001004

recapitalization of Air Baltic, a state-owned enterprise,[43] and the Commission had to ensure that the state receive an appropriate remuneration for the investment. The state-owned Finnair's recapitalization was not made conditional on the above strict conditions because Finnair had no significant market power on the relevant markets; therefore, no additional measure to preserve effective competition was needed.[44] By contrast, the Commission imposed strict requirements to the 1 billion EUR recapitalization of Air France by France.[45] As the company had a significant market position at the airport of Paris-Orly, 18 slots per day were made available to competitors to get the Commission's approval. This condition enables lasting entry and expansion of competing airlines operating at that airport. Besides the above, the usual recapitalization conditions also applied with bans on dividends, share buybacks, limits on the remuneration of management, appropriate remuneration of the State, ban on acquisitions. A special provision was inserted to ensure that the aid does not support the Air France-KLM holding's KLM side. A trustee is appointed to monitor the implementation of the conditions. The Dutch Government subsidized KLM itself with 3.4 billion EUR in loans to reduce night flights at Amsterdam Schiphol by 20% and cut the CEO's bonus payments.[46]

An eye-catching sum of 9 billion EUR was granted to the Lufthansa Group by Germany, which has a significant market position at the Frankfurt and Munich airports. The subsidiary airlines of the Lufthansa Group [Deutsche Lufthansa (Lufthansa), Austrian Airlines, Brussels Airlines and Swiss International Air Lines (Swiss)] are owned by the group's private shareholders. The rescue package of the German Government included EUR 6 billion in recapitalization and a EUR 3 billion loan, in exchange for a 20% government stake in the airline which can be increased to 25% plus one share, in addition to two seats nominated by the Government on the supervisory board. The German Government's approach has been one of safeguarding, notably from hostile takeover attempts, and no conditions on carbon emission targets were attached.[47] The green light given by the Commission was conditional on selling 24 slots per day in the Munich and Frankfurt airports.[48] Recapitalization under the Framework is possible only if the notification contains a credible exit strategy. Should the state's exit be in doubt six years after receiving the recapitalization aid, Germany is also required to re-notify a restructuring plan for Lufthansa, rendering standard state aid terms applicable again. Furthermore, Austria also provided aid to Lufthansa's subsidiary, Austrian Airlines, to keep the company independent within the group, avoid layoffs, and achieve certain climate targets.[49]

43 SA.56943.
44 SA.57410.
45 SA.59913.
46 Steven Truxal, 'State Aid and Air Transport in the Shadow of COVID-19', *Air & Space Law*, Vol. 45, Special Issue, 2020, pp. 72-73.
47 Id. p. 70.
48 SA.57153.
49 Truxal 2020, p. 71.

doi: 10.5553/HYIEL/266627012021009001004

To give a couple of examples for non-discriminatory aid schemes, Hungary granted a wage subsidy under Article 107(3)(b) to employers active in the aviation industry.[50] Denmark[51] and Slovenia[52] granted under a scheme aid to airports and airlines that land in and depart from the Member State territory.

On the other hand, several Member States restricted their aid to airlines holding a national license (flag carriers). The Commission has approved these measures. The approval was either based on Article 107(2)(b) in the French case or on Article 107(3)(b) in the Swedish case.

Ireland did not grant any aid to airline service operators, including Ryanair.

4. Challenges of the Current State Aid Law Framework

4.1. Uneven Distribution of State Aid

Many commentators claimed that although it is open to all the Member States to support their economy *via* State aid, the actual amounts granted were very uneven.[53] Member States with deep pockets naturally have a significant financial capacity to fund their companies. By contrast, severe fiscal constraints in many

50 SA.57767. *Cf.* https://ec.europa.eu/commission/presscorner/detail/en/mex_20_1299. Public support takes the form of exemptions (amounting to up to 23% of the monthly gross salary paid to the employees) from the employers' obligation to pay social security, vocational training and rehabilitation contributions. The scheme is open to employers that are active in the manufacturing of air and spacecraft machinery, repair and maintenance of aircraft and spacecraft, and air passenger transport, provided they have experienced a significant reduction in their business activities due to the coronavirus outbreak in the period of April and May 2020. The scheme aims at alleviating employers' costs and avoiding lay-offs and helping to ensure that employees remain in continuous employment during the period for which the aid is granted. The Commission found that the Hungarian scheme is in line with the conditions set out in the Temporary Framework.

51 SA.59370. *Cf.* https://ec.europa.eu/commission/presscorner/detail/en/mex_20_2252. The scheme is open to all airlines holding a Danish air operator certificate. The support will take the form of direct grants to cover the beneficiaries' wage costs for the staff responsible for certain specific safety-critical functions. The measure is expected to benefit 26 airlines. The aim of the scheme is to support passenger air traffic in Denmark in order to restore the air connectivity within Denmark and to/from Denmark after the coronavirus outbreak. The Commission found that the scheme is in line with the conditions set out in the Temporary Framework.

52 SA.59124. *Cf.* https://ec.europa.eu/commission/presscorner/detail/en/mex_20_2141. The support takes the form of direct grants and will be accessible to all airlines operating routes to/from Slovenia. The level of support per beneficiary depends on the number of passengers carried by the airline and the number of flights. The measure is expected to benefit approximately 20 airlines. The objective of the measure is to re-establish air connectivity to and from Slovenia, with a view to support the recovery of tourism and more broadly the economy of Slovenia which have been negatively affected by the coronavirus outbreak. The Commission found that the Slovenian scheme is in line with the conditions set out in the Temporary Framework.

53 *See* at www.euractiv.com/section/competition/news/germany-gains-most-from-relaxed-eu-state-aid-rules/;Munoz2020, p. 538; Thomas Wilson *et al.*, 'The EC's Third Amendment to the State Aid Temporary Framework', *Kluwer Competition Law Blog*, 7 July 2020, at http://competitionlawblog.kluwercompetitionlaw.com/2020/07/07/the-ecs-third-amendment-to-the-state-aid-temporary-framework/.

doi: 10.5553/HYIEL/266627012021009001004

countries, restrict Member States' choice. Which undertakings should then be rescued?[54]

This is why the *geographical distribution of aid* is so important. The report prepared for the European Parliament on COVID-19 state aid underlined that

> "The airlines and aviation sector stands out as the largest single beneficiary of state aid during the COVID-19 crisis. Almost all these cases provide support to specific companies, and hence, state aid is not provided under a sectoral regime. [...] The high amounts of financial support provided to airlines raise the question of whether the level playing field has been respected. State aid is clearly channeled to national airlines."[55]

On the other hand, *the Commission has weak tools to combat the unequal use of aid by the Member States* and there is a widespread consensus among Member States and around the world that countercyclical massive fiscal support may boost the economy, reverse the crisis and mitigate its effects on the economy and society.[56]

Furthermore, *there is no maximum ceiling beyond which the Member States are prohibited from funding eligible projects under state aid law.* Each intervention should be designed to ensure proportionality of the aid compared to its eligible costs. Like Germany and France, larger Member States grant significant volumes of aid to support companies hit by the pandemic. Meanwhile, countries like Greece or Italy, that is, indebted States have less fiscal space to disburse large sums to their ailing industries. Even if particular state aid cases fulfil all criteria and conditions, the unequal geographical distribution of state aid may be a major cause for market distortion.[57]

As there is no available figure on state aid (authorized and spent) to airlines, I use the general overall COVID-19 state aid spending to show the differences.

The European Parliament's report on state aid stated that

> "State aid is the right policy reaction. State aid measures adopted by the Member States are increasing at a fast pace, both in number and in estimated budgets. Approval by the Commission is based on enhanced principles, in particular the Temporary Framework developed as an answer to deal with the extraordinary circumstances."[58]

On the other hand,

54 *See* Massimo Motta & Martin Peitz, 'State Aid Policies in Response to the Covid-19 Shock: Observations and Guiding Principles', *Intereconomics*, Vol. 55, Issue 4, 2020, pp. 219-222.

55 Parliament report pp. 30-31.

56 *See* at https://ec.europa.eu/info/live-work-travel-eu/coronavirus-response/jobs-and-economy-during-coronavirus-pandemic_en and www.oecd.org/coronavirus/policy-responses/the-territorial-impact-of-covid-19-managing-the-crisis-across-levels-of-government-d3e314e1/.

57 Parliament report, p. 21.

58 Id. p. 6.

doi: 10.5553/HYIEL/266627012021009001004

Figure 1 ***Total COVID-19-related state aid provided by the EU Member States, as % of GDP and in absolute terms (million EUR)***

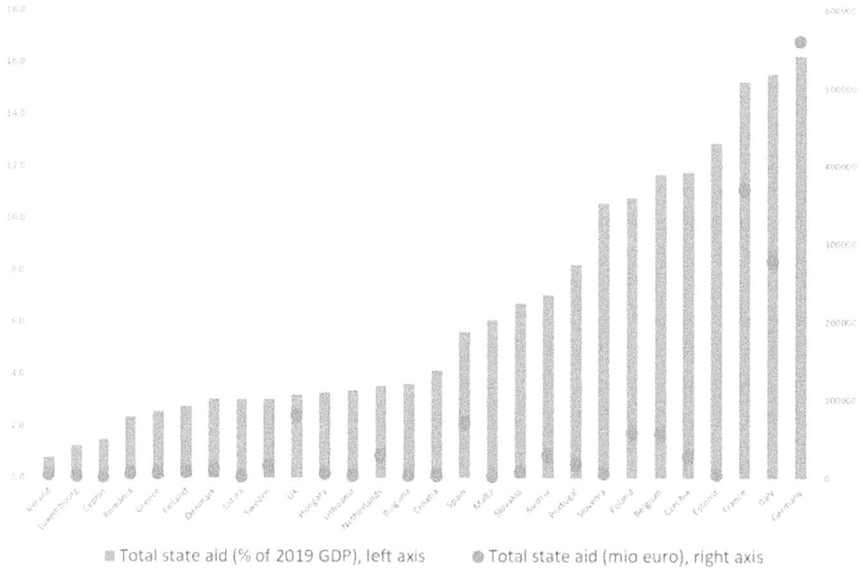

* Id. p. 26. All COVID-19 aid is included in this graph, not only aid given to airlines.

> "total state aid budgets differ substantially across the EU Member States. Moreover, there is no convincing evidence that total state aid is proportional to the economic damage suffered during the first wave of the COVID-19 pandemic. Hence, this raises the question of whether the level playing field is maintained. There is a serious risk that excessive state aid support by some Member States will jeopardize free and fair competition in the EU single market. The only possible compensation would be substantial positive cross-border spill-overs. In other words, state aid provided by one EU Member State could be beneficial to the other EU Member States. Whether this is the case remains to be seen in the future when state aid has actually been provided."[59]

The preliminary figures indicate that *the actual gaps between aid spent by the larger Member States may not be as significant as what they had initially announced.* The Commission has tried to put the differences of nominal amounts in context, partly acknowledging the problem. The Commissioner for Competition conceded that

59 Id.

doi: 10.5553/HYIEL/266627012021009001004

> "not all Member States have the room in their national budgets to provide companies with support. Indeed, the differences in the size of European economies and budgets risk to fragment further the single market."[60]

On the other hand, according to the data of the Commission services, the aid approved does not correspond to the aid paid out. More substantive national schemes have been approved to provide financial leeway to Member States and reduce the administrative burden of notification. On the other hand, these schemes have not been completely exploited by the Member States. According to the end of July 2020 data, the Commission has authorized 2.3 trillion EUR in crisis aid, but the Member States used up much less: only 346 million EUR has actually been spent. Until 30 October, 3 trillion EUR has been approved, more than half is German aid, Italian and French aid account for another 15% each of the total amount, but Spain, for example, only for 5%.[61]

Moreover, it is important to note that under schemes based on non-discriminatory criteria, companies established outside the Member State may also receive aid, such as tax deferrals.[62] Advantages granted to national companies may also have a spill-over effect when the positive economic effects are enjoyed by the entire value chain.

While it is widely acknowledged that the uneven Member State support granted during the crisis may jeopardize the unity of the internal market, state aid law is not the right instrument to tackle this serious problem because it lacks tools to address the roots of the problem.[63] The Commission keeps an eye on the overall state aid spending authorized and notes the difference between the amounts authorized and those actually spent on the economy.

To overcome discrepancies in state aid spending, the Commission made a proposal for the *Solvency Support Instrument*, which would allow equity support to businesses all over Europe, focusing on businesses that are most in need of support as a result of the pandemic. The Instrument would focus on Member States and sectors hardest hit and on those Member States which are least able to offer equity support to businesses. The guarantee provided by the European Investment Bank would help crowd in significant private investment in the equity of companies. The investment supported by these instruments must deliver on the objectives set by the Green Deal and the Digital Agenda.

60 Statement by Executive Vice-President Margrethe Vestager at the press conference on Solvency Support Instrument, 29 May 2020, at https://ec.europa.eu/commission/presscorner/detail/en/STATEMENT_20_973.

61 Speech of Vice-President Margrethe Verstager on State aid at the event organized by the Berliner Gesprächskreis zum Europäischen Beihilfenrecht, 30 October 2020.

62 *E.g.* SA.57691. Cyprus implemented a scheme under which the aid amount depended on the load of the aircraft. *See also* SA.58157. The Danish scheme is open to all airlines servicing scheduled passenger flights in Denmark.

63 According to Maczkovics, "the Commission's approach may thus be seen as too flexible to genuinely preserve the integrity of the internal market and to ensure a level playing field among all economic operators." *See* Maczkovics 2020, p. 279.

doi: 10.5553/HYIEL/266627012021009001004

At the European Council meeting in July 2020, however, EU Heads of State or Government *did not approve the draft EU level instruments, like the solvency support instrument and the strategic investment facility*. Instead, they voted for the Recovery and Resilience Facility designed by the Member States themselves to channel resources to the economy.

The uneven spending rates of different Member States may be corrected in the future by EU instruments such as the Next Generation EU Recovery Instrument, the Recovery and Resilience Facility or the Sure Programme.[64]

4.2. Monitoring Exercise and Transparency

The impact assessment report prepared for the European Parliament highlights some of the changes necessary to ensure a level playing field.

> "The number of cases targeted at individual companies is very limited, with the airline and aviation sector as a notable exception. A limited number of cases are targeted at firms with a specific size."[65]

The report recommended that the Commission enhance the transparency of the case evaluation process and highlighted the need for evaluating the different aid measures in their interconnectedness. "It is recommended that cases be evaluated while taking into account previous cases submitted by the same Member State as well as similar case submitted by other Member States."[66] Furthermore, the report recommended the monitoring of the use of authorized aid. "It is recommended that cases be evaluated while taking into account previous cases submitted by the same Member State as well as similar case submitted by other Member States."[67]

Given the vast number of approvals and the large amounts granted under them, it will be a challenge for the Commission to monitor the implementation of aid schemes and the individual aid measures.[68] As shown above, positive decisions come in the most critical cases with strings, so-called conditions attached to the approval. In some decisions, as indicated above, a trustee has been appointed. Still, in most cases, it is the task of the Member State and the Commission to monitor implementation. *The effectiveness of the Commission's ex post monitoring has been the subject of long-standing criticism by the European Court*

64 *See* the brief overview by Jonatan Echebarria Fernández, 'A Critical Analysis on the European Union's Measures to Overcome the Economic Impact of the COVID-19 Pandemic', *European Papers*, Vol. 5, Issue 3, 2020, pp. 1399-1423.

65 Parliament Report, p. 7.

66 Id.

67 Id. p. 8.

68 *See* in a similar vein: Francisco Costa-Cabral *et al.*, 'EU Competition Law and COVID-19', *TILEC Discussion Paper*, 22 March 2020, available at SSRN, p. 3.

doi: 10.5553/HYIEL/266627012021009001004

of Auditors. Even before the crisis, the European Court of Auditors raised the issue of the lack of robust *ex post* monitoring of state aid cases.[69]

4.3. The External Factor

The European aviation industry is part of the global market, where very different national rules apply.[70] European state aid rules are considered to be very strict compared to other jurisdictions' laws.

One can argue that the relaxation of strict European subsidy rules and the provision of vast amounts of subsidies is not the right approach because *air carriers will not be supported based on their efficiency, but governments will pick winners and losers*. While this argument might hold water, governments, on the other hand, face a real threat of takeovers by private and public undertakings controlled by third states. In the absence of state aid, this threat will materialize because other large economies have provided even more subsidies to companies to bounce back from the crisis. In this regard, the Commission issued an early warning that Member States should tackle this issue.[71]

In 2004, Regulation (EC) No. 868/2004 was adopted. The objective was to protect EU airlines against the subsidization of third-country airlines and unfair pricing practices adopted by the latter when operating on routes to and from the EU. In 2019, the Regulation was repealed, and a new one was adopted. Regulation (EU) No. 2019/712 has a broader scope since it prohibits practices distorting competition, discrimination and subsidies.[72] Besides the air transport sector, the Member States and the Commission tend to react more assertively to distortions created by the global regulatory field. The Commission published its White Paper on levelling the playing field as regards foreign subsidies in July 2020.[73]

69 *Do the Commission's Procedures Ensure Effective Management of State Aid Control?*, European Court of Auditors, Special Report No. 15, 2011; *More Efforts Needed to Raise Awareness of and Enforce Compliance with State Aid Rules in Cohesion Policy*, European Court of Auditors, Special Report No 24, 2016.

70 On the global context *see* Costa-Cabral *et al.* 2020, p. 5. On the global aviation market, its history and regulation *see* Antogoni Lykotrafiti, 'What Does Europe Do About Fair Competition in International Air Transport? A Critique of Recent Actions', *Common Market Law Review*, Vol. 57, Issue 3, 2020, pp. 831-860.

71 Communication from the Commission. Guidance to the Member States concerning foreign direct investment and free movement of capital from third countries, and the protection of Europe's strategic assets, ahead of the application of Regulation (EU) 2019/452 (FDI Screening Regulation) Brussels, 25 March 2020 C(2020) 1981 final. The Parliament report also pointed out that "a more assertive use of State aid policies would align EU state aid policies to the ones implemented by other major economies (*e.g.* US and Japan)." Parliament report, p. 35.

72 Regulation (EU) 2019/712 of the European Parliament and of the Council of 17 April 2019 on safeguarding competition in air transport and repealing Regulation (EC) No 868/2004.

73 COM(2020) 253 final, 17 June 2020. On 5 May 2021 the Commission adopted its proposal based on the White Paper. Proposal for a Regulation of the European Parliament and of the Council on foreign subsidies distorting the internal market. Brussels, 5 May 2021, COM(2021) 223 final.

doi: 10.5553/HYIEL/266627012021009001004

5. The Ryanair Cases and the Issue of Discrimination

Ryanair, the only private company having a substantial share of the European low-cost aviation market, *challenged all Commission decisions authorizing allegedly discriminatory aid measures before the General Court*. Its legal argument is based on several claims: *(i)* first, the violation of the nationality-based discrimination prohibition under Article 18 TFEU and the free provision of services. *(ii)* Second, the violation by the Commission of its obligation to weigh the beneficial effects of the aid against its adverse effects on trading conditions and the maintenance of undistorted competition (the so-called balancing test) or, in case of the French scheme, a manifest error of assessment in the review of the proportionality of the aid. *(iii)* Third, the failure to open a formal investigation procedure despite the fact that the Commission has encountered serious difficulties, and *(iv)* fourth, the failure to state reasons.[74]

Altogether, *Ryanair challenged eleven Commission decisions*, and until now, the General Court has adopted rulings in expedited procedure in nine cases.[75] In the first wave, two Commission decisions, one on the Swedish aid scheme and one on the French aid scheme, were decided by the General Court. Bouchagiar revealed that

> "prior to the COVID-19 outbreak, the Commission seems to have required that aid be non-discriminatory in certain cases. For example, in its communication on aid to the transport sector under Article 107(2)(b) TFEU following the terrorist attacks of 11 September 2001 in the United States, the Commission requested that compensation be paid in a non-discriminatory manner to all airlines in a given Member State. The Commission approved such aid schemes in France and Germany to cover operating losses incurred by airlines, linked to the closure of airspace as a result of the terrorist attacks. Moreover, in the context of the Icelandic volcanic eruption and dust cloud in April 2010, which led to the closure of most of European airspace, the Commission approved an aid scheme in Slovenia covering part of the economic losses of airlines and airports. The Commission noted that the aid was non-discriminatory since it was granted to all air carriers with a valid

74 This article does not deal with the procedural law aspects of the judgments.

75 Until 20 April 2021. Judgment of 17 February 2021, *Case T-238/20, Ryanair v Commission (Sweden)* ECLI:EU:T:2021:91, on appeal under *C-209/21 P;* Judgment of 17 February 2021, *Case T-259/20, Ryanair v Commission (France)*, ECLI:EU:T:2021:92, on appeal under *C-210/21 P*; Judgment of 14 April 2021, *Case T-388/20, Ryanair v Commission (Finnair I, COVID-19)*, ECLI:EU:T:2021:196, on appeal under *C-353/21 P*; Judgment of 14 April 2021, *Case T-378/20, Ryanair v Commission (SAS, Denmark, COVID-19)*, ECLI:EU:T:2021:194, on appeal under *C-321/21 P*; Judgment of 14 April 2021, *Case T-379/20, Ryanair v Commission (SAS Suéde, COVID-19)*, ECLI:EU:T:2021:195, on appeal under *C-320/21 P*; Judgment of 19 May 2021, *Case T-643/20, Ryanair v Commission (KLM; COVID-19)*, ECLI:EU:T:2021:286; Judgment of 19 May 2021, *Case T-628/20, Ryanair v Commission (Espagne; COVID-19)*, ECLI:EU:T:2021:285; Judgment of 19 May 2021, *Case T-465/20, Ryanair v Commission (TAP; COVID-19)*, ECLI:EU:T:284; Judgment of 9 June 2021, *Case T-665/20, Ryanair v Commission (Condor; COVID-19)*, ECLI:EU:T:344.

Hungarian Yearbook of International Law and European Law 2021 (9) 1
doi: 10.5553/HYIEL/266627012021009001004

Slovenian operating license, which were the only companies directly damaged due to the closure of the Slovenian airspace."[76]

Indeed, the CJEU is not bound by the Commission's earlier practice. Hence, *the crucial legal issue is whether a requirement of non-discrimination (based on nationality) can be derived from primary law*. Linked to this, in my opinion, is the role and the freedom of Member States to support their economy. The context in which state aid has to be understood is that state intervention in markets and industrial policy generally is a Member State competence, while transport is a shared competence.[77] Accordingly, it is up to the Member States to design aid measures and set their objectives. At any rate, Member States have limited fiscal capacity to support an entire industry or the entire national economy. Suppose the Member States are bound by the Treaty to provide aid to each air carrier operating on their territory. In that case, they may not have sufficient fiscal capacity to disburse enough support to save each operator. Against this backdrop, the CJEU jurisprudence recognized a long time ago that *there is no entitlement to state aid; companies do not have a right to claim aid from the Member States*.[78]

The General Court directly tackled this argument in the *Danish case* and held that it does not follow from either Article 108(3) or Article 107(2)(b) that Member States are obliged to make good the entire damage, likewise, they cannot be required to grant aid to all of the victims of that damage.[79] In another case, the General Court had to rule on the legality of a loan guarantee granted by Finland to the majority state-owned undertaking, *Finnair*.[80] The aid was approved by the Commission under Article 107(3)(b) to remedy a serious disturbance in the economy. After failing to obtain a loan in the credit market, Finland granted a guarantee to Finnair on a private loan. The Commission approved the aid as justified by mitigating the risk of the company's insolvency due to the sudden erosion of its business, to endure supply chain security and generally due to Finnair's importance for the Finnish economy. Indeed, Finnair is a major air freight and passenger operator in Finland. The General Court held that the guarantee was appropriate to remedy a serious disturbance in the Finnish economy. Ryanair claimed that the Commission failed to balance the beneficial effects of the aid against its adverse effects on trading conditions and the maintenance of undistorted competition. After relying on the textual interpretation of Article 107(3)(b), the General Court rejected this argument. Contrary to Ryanair's claim and the text of 107(3)(c), *the wording of 107(3)(b) does not require the Commission to weigh the positive and negative effects of the aid*

76 Bouchagiar 2021, p. 55.

77 *See* Article 4 TFEU on shared competences and Article 6 on supporting, coordinating and supplementing EU competences.

78 In Judgment of 23 November 2015, *Case T-670/14, Milchindustrie-Verband eV*, ECLI:EU:C:2015:906. The General Court ruled in its order, that it is a matter falling within the sovereignty of the Member State. *See also* Order of 30 May 2018, *Case C-481/17, Yanchev*, ECLI:EU:C:2018:352, para. 22.

79 Judgment of 14 April 2021, *Case T-378/20, Ryanair v Commission*, para. 24.

80 Judgment of 14 April 2021, *Case T-388/20, Ryanair v Commission (Finnair I, COVID-19)*.

measure. For decisions adopted under Article 107(3)(b), the sole condition to be proved by the Commission is the appropriate, necessary and proportionate nature of the aid to remedy the serious disturbance of the economy.

Ryanair's second argument was that the aid is contrary to the general principle of non-discrimination under Article 18 TFEU and to the freedom to provide services. In Ryanair's reasoning, the aid "is a measure of pure economic nationalism."[81] The General Court held that Article 107 is *lex specialis* to Article 18 TFEU because any discrimination on the grounds of nationality within the scope of application of the Treaties is prohibited "without prejudice to any special provisions contained therein."[82] Therefore, the General Court referred back to its reasoning under Article 107. It first noted that individual aid, by definition, benefits only one undertaking, so discrimination is inherent in the individual character of the aid.[83] Under Article 107, the General Court started its reasoning by analyzing the measure's objective and then proceeded to establish whether the two situations are similar in light of the measure's objective. Finland aimed to provide sufficient liquidity to Finnair to maintain its viability and air services. The General Court highlighted that *the main objective was not to preserve Finland's domestic and international air connectivity*. In light of this, the aid provided solely to Finnair was not considered discriminatory. In the General Court's view, the Commission is not obliged to widen the circle of beneficiaries.[84] As to the proportionality of the measure, Ryanair did not challenge the amount of the aid directly. Instead, it claimed that under non-discriminative conditions, each air operator active in Finland should have received aid. The General Court rejected this by reasoning that that would have affected the sufficiency of the resources available to Finnair.

In the *Danish case*, the aid granted by Denmark to SAS and the Commission's approval was subject to judicial review. Ryanair, among others, claimed that the Commission had not taken account of the competitive advantage resulting from the discriminatory nature of the measure. The General Court did not accept this argument either, because it is settled case-law that the advantage procured by

81 Id. para. 78.

82 Id.

83 As opposed to individual aid, aid schemes are any acts on the basis of which, without further implementing measures being required, individual aid awards may be made to undertakings defined within the act in a general and abstract manner and any act on the basis of which aid which is not linked to a specific project may be granted to one or several undertakings for an indefinite period of time and/or for an indefinite amount. Commission Regulation (EU) No 651/2014 of 17 June 2014 declaring certain categories of aid compatible with the internal market in application of Articles 107 and 108 of the Treaty, p. 1. Probably Ryanair's view was that under the proportionality principle, the state should have organized an aid scheme available to any undertaking active in the Finnish air transport sector. Contrary to that argument, under state aid law, there is no obligation on Member States to regulate aid in aid schemes. It is just a choice available to Member States.

84 Id. para. 87. On the other hand, if the measure is declared discriminative, the Member State is under the obligation to widen the circle of beneficiaries or to repeal or modify its conditions.

doi: 10.5553/HYIEL/266627012021009001004

that aid for the recipient does not include any economic benefit the recipient may have enjoyed as a result of exploiting the advantage.[85]

In its earlier decision, the Commission authorized *state aid granted by Sweden* in the form of a loan guarantee scheme to airlines under the Framework and Article 107(3)(b). The Commission concluded that the guarantee is necessary, appropriate and proportionate to remedy a serious disturbance in the Swedish economy. The scheme aims to ensure that the airline which hold a license issued by Sweden and which is important to secure connectivity in Sweden has sufficient liquidity to ensure that the disruptions do not undermine its viability and to preserve the continuity of economic activity. Under Regulation No 1008/2008, a national license is issued to airlines if their principal place of business is in the Member State (in this case Sweden). The financial situation of airlines holding a Swedish license is regularly monitored under the Regulation by the Swedish licensing authority. Ryanair pleaded before the General Court that the Commission's authorization is contrary to Article 18, the prohibition of discrimination on the grounds of nationality. Under CJEU jurisprudence, the Commission cannot declare an aid plan compatible with Article 107 if certain conditions contravene other provisions (including the general principles) of EU law. The General Court considered that Article 107 is a special provision compared to Article 18. Therefore, it examined the argument only from the perspective of Article 107(3)(b). It held that under the said provision, the aid should be viewed from the standpoint of its objective as set by the Member State. The General Court anchored the national eligibility condition in secondary EU law. According to the General Court, the aid is appropriate because it is

> "normal for the Member States concerned to seek to ensure that the airlines eligible for the guarantee have a stable presence, in order for them to be present on Swedish territory to honor the loans granted, so that the State guarantee is used as little as possible."[86]

As to the proportionality of the aid, the General Court pointed out that

> "in order to secure Sweden's connectivity, the double requirement of a Swedish license and air services in Swedish territory through regular flights is the most appropriate for guaranteeing that the presence of an airline on that territory is permanent."[87]

The General Court also assessed the fact that airlines holding a Swedish license were responsible for 98% of the domestic passenger traffic and 84% of the domestic freight transport. The share of national license holders in international

85 Judgment of 21 December 2016, *Case C-164/15 P and C-165/15 P, Commission v Aer Lingus and Ryanair Designated Activity*, ECLI:EU:C:2016:990, para. 92.

86 Judgment of 17 February 2021, *Case T-238/20, Ryanair DAC v Commission*, ECLI:EU:T:2021:91, para. 40.

87 Id. para. 45.

doi: 10.5553/HYIEL/266627012021009001004

passenger air traffic within the EU was 49%. Importantly, it is evident from the judgment that *the proportionality test is not a strict one*. The General Court highlighted that *the Commission is not bound to decide on every alternative measure conceivable* since it is not required to prove positively that no other conceivable hypothetical measure could better achieve the intended objective. Ryanair "cannot ask the Court to require the Commission to take the place of national authorities in that task of normative prospecting in order to examine every alternative measure possible".[88]

In another case, the *aid scheme granted by France* under similar conditions was scrutinized by the General Court. France deferred the payment of civil aviation tax and solidarity tax on condition of holding a national license, and the aid has been held compatible with the internal market under Article 107(2)(b). The General Court held that the national license condition creates an institutional link with the place where the damage suffered arose, and therefore it is appropriate. The General Court linked the requirement of holding the national license to a stable presence on national territory, which the Member States are justified to apply to ensure that the shortfall in tax revenue is as low as possible. For the General Court, the requirement of holding a national license safeguards the administrative and financial stability of beneficiaries in the national territory.

6. Conclusions

This article has explored the ample room available to the Member States to support airlines. The crucial question of how competences are divided between the Member States and the EU helps understand the carefully framed judgments of the General Court. In my view, *the General Court was right to refuse the arguments put forward by Ryanair, but its reasoning is quite timid and hesitant*. A more assertive, strong argumentation would have ensured more clarity in the case-law. Companies under Article 107 do not enjoy entitlement to state aid. The Treaty is based on the following division of competences: Member States may use state aid to intervene in the economy and use this powerful industrial policy tool to further objectives set by themselves. Member States enjoy a margin of discretion to define the conditionality of the aid subject only to binding secondary EU legislation. EU competence is limited to verifying the competition aspects of the intervention, or more precisely, the intervention's appropriateness, necessity and proportionality to achieve the objectives incorporated in Article 107(2) or (3).

The arguments about the breach of the non-discrimination principle, raised by Ryanair, if successful, would have rendered individual aid measure to airlines incompatible with the internal market. This way, the only method to design the aid measure would be through aid schemes reaching and affecting each market

88 Id. para 53. The General Court similarly rejected the argument that the aid measure is contrary to the free provision of services.

doi: 10.5553/HYIEL/266627012021009001004

operator equally. By doing so, the Commission would supplement the Member State competence with its own decision.

That said, there is a seeming tension between the legality of the conditions as illustrated by the General Court judgments and economic reality. The vast amount of aid will probably distort competition at the level of the undertakings on those routes where airlines compete with each other.[89] It is hoped that these distortions will be limited, and the Commission will carefully monitor the fulfilment of the conditions attached to its authorizations in these cases.

89 Generally, academic opinion points into this direction. *See e.g.* Jose Luis Buendia & Angela Dovalo, 'State Aid versus COVID-19: The Commission Adopts a Temporary Framework', *European State Aid Law Quarterly*, Vol. 19, Issue 1, 2020, p. 7.

doi: 10.5553/HYIEL/266627012021009001004

State Aid in the Times of COVID-19 Pandemic

*Katalin Gombos & Anikó Edit Szűcs**

Abstract

COVID-19 caused serious turbulence in the economy worldwide, severely damaging certain industries, while generating extra revenues for others. In order to be able to continue business as usual following the current crises there is a need to provide state aid to sectors and companies which could not have been imaginable previously. The EU has reacted extremely speedily. Under the Temporary Framework issued by the European Commission at the beginning of the pandemic a significant number of state aids has been approved. Although the Temporary Framework was adapted very quickly, the transitional rules ensure that state aids do not interfere with the functioning of the internal market except to the extent a necessary and proportionate. The present article highlights the various legal bases which can be invoked in the present COVID-19 pandemic situation for providing state aid, includes a comprehensive summary of every single state aid notified to the European Commission with respect to the effects of COVID-19 pandemic and presents numerous examples from the practice.

Keywords: temporary framework, competition law, state aid, COVID-19, European Commission.

1. Introduction

On 31 December 2019, the Wuhan Municipal Health Commission (China) reported to the WHO China Country Office cases of pneumonia of unknown cause detected in Wuhan.[1] Late January the Emergency Committee of the WHO discussed the matter and could not reach a decision on whether a "public health emergency of international concern" should be called; it took until 11 March 2020 for the WHO to state that "COVID-19 can be characterized as a pandemic."[2] A little more than a year later, in April 2021 more than 3 million people were confirmed to have died as the result of COVID-19 infection worldwide, while there are more than 140 million confirmed coronavirus cases.[3] Thus, we can

* Katalin Gombos: associate professor of law, National University of Public Service, Budapest; judge, Curia of Hungary, Budapest. Anikó Edit Szűcs: assistant lecturer, National University of Public Service, Budapest; associate, Bird & Bird International Law Firm, Budapest.

1 See at www.who.int/csr/don/05-january-2020-pneumonia-of-unkown-cause-china/en/.

2 See at www.who.int/news/item/27-04-2020-who-timeline---covid-19.

3 See at www.worldometers.info/coronavirus/.

doi: 10.5553/HYIEL/266627012021009001005

safely say that COVID-19 is the gravest health-issue to have been dealt with by the EU from its inception.

The economic impact of the pandemic is extremely significant as well. Various research, analyses and data are available to substantiate this finding, but probably one of the most shocking indicators is the never-before-seen decrease of the economic sentiment indicator (ESI) by more than 30 points in April 2020,[4] which is a negative record since the ESI was introduced in 1985. The ESI is administered by the Directorate General for Economic and Financial Affairs of the European Commission, and it covers the following sectors: industry (40%), services (30%), consumers (20%), retail (5%) and construction (5%).[5] This data tells us that the COVID-19 pandemic has effects for both the overall economy,[6] as well as for specific sectors, these sectors mainly being those most dependent on personal contacts. The study prepared by the Policy Department for Economic, Scientific and Quality of Life Policies Directorate-General for Internal Policies in March 2021 specifies these as "cultural and creative industries and the aerospace industry (due to the decrease in mobility and tourism activities)", also stating that "they are likely to suffer for extended periods from these unprecedented shocks."[7]

Thus, we may conclude that the need for unprecedented forms of state aid and aid provided to sectors earlier almost unimaginable to be eligible for such aid has become imminent. The European Commission was actually not really far behind the WHO: on 19 March 2020 (just 8 days after the WHO declared the COVID-19 situation to be a pandemic) the Commission issued the communication on the Temporary Framework for State aid measures to support the economy in the current COVID-19 outbreak (Temporary Framework).[8]

The state aid measures as laid down in the Temporary Framework do not only include possible ways forward through providing aid to those affected by the COVID-19 outbreak. Namely, the TFEU ab ovo contains provisions which can be invoked to this end: Article 107 (2) and (3).[9] In the following, the authors describe the bricks of this legal framework citing various examples from the practice of the Member States, including an overview of the economic context where the beneficiaries operate.

2. The Economic Context of the Current Situation

The general aim of EU state aid rules is to keep the economic balance between the various EU Member States on one hand, and to ensure fair competition on the

4 See at www.destatis.de/Europa/EN/Topic/COVID-19/COVID-19-article.html.

5 See at https://ec.europa.eu/eurostat/web/products-datasets/-/teibs010.

6 See e.g. Tej Gonza et al., 'Marcora for Europe: How Worker-Buyouts Might Help Save Jobs and Build Resilient Businesses', European State Aid Law Quarterly, Vol. 20, Issue 1, 2021, pp. 61-73.

7 See at www.europarl.europa.eu/RegData/etudes/STUD/2021/662903/IPOL_STU(2021)662903_EN.pdf.

8 See at https://eur-lex.europa.eu/legal-content/EN/TXT/?uri=OJ%3AJOC_2020_091_I_0001.

9 Philipp Werner & Vincent Verouden, EU State Aid Control Law and Economics, Wolters Kluwer, Bedfordshire, 2017, p. 7.

doi: 10.5553/HYIEL/266627012021009001005

market and more generally, the existence of the internal market itself on the other.[10] Since this balance and fair trade can be disrupted not only by intentional actions of a Member State but also by events outside the control of the Governments, it should also be the task of those setting forth state aid rules to make sure that appropriate rules are laid down for exceptional cases where the balance between demand and supply is disturbed.

The COVID-19 pandemic caused exactly such a disturbance: various market sectors are affected through declining demand for fear of becoming infected, while other sectors are faced with the same issue owing to government ordered lockdowns and other restrictions. According to Santander, an international financial services company, wholesale and retail trade, accommodation and food services and transport industries "will face an acute risk of bankruptcy", while 25-35% of companies "would experience a financing shortfall"; losses for EU companies in 2020 are estimated to be "between EUR 720 billion and EUR 1.2 trillion".[11] COVID-19 thus affects multiple layers of the economy: the economic downfall is triggered partially by less people being interested in purchasing a service, the ban on rendering or using certain services, the gradual decline in demand for certain products, and finally, a general economic recession.

As mentioned above, the TFEU already contained various legal bases which could be relied on to provide state aid in the current situation. However given the exceptional nature of the COVID-19 pandemic (resulting in unprecedented and unimaginable restrictions and market turbulence) called for more specific action: the acceptance of the *Temporary Framework*, which is a clear example of how the Commission shaped and amended the aid framework depending on how the economic situation in the EU and the pandemic evolved.

As of 19 March 2020, the Temporary Framework provided for only five types of temporary state aid measures: *(i)* aid in form of direct grants, repayable advances or tax advantages; *(ii)* aid in the form of guarantees on loans; *(iii)* aid in the form of subsidized interest rates for loans; *(iv)* aid in the form of guarantees and loans channeled through credit institutions or other financial institutions; and *(v)* short-term export credit insurance. With amendments adopted on 3 April (aid for COVID-19 relevant research and development; investment aid for testing and upscaling infrastructures; investment aid for the production of COVID-19 relevant products; aid in the form of deferrals of tax and/or of social security contributions; aid in the form of wage subsidies for employees to avoid lay-offs during the COVID-19 outbreak) and on 8 May (recapitalization measures) the current scope of measures was reached, and further amendments shaped the regulatory framework on 29 June and 13 October 2020 and 28 January 2021 that is modified from time to time the detailed rules of relying on the above

10 *See* Michael Flickenschild *et al.*, *Impacts of the COVID-19 Pandemic on EU Industries*, Publications Office of the European Union, 2021, at https://op.europa.eu/en/publication-detail/-/publication/145218e0-a314-11eb-9585-01aa75ed71a1/language-en.

11 *See* at www.santander.com/en/press-room/insights/recovery-plan-and-economic-sectors-most-affected-by-the-covid-crisis.

doi: 10.5553/HYIEL/266627012021009001005

mentioned various measures. Below, the authors discuss the provisions of the Temporary Framework effective from 25 April 2021.[12]

3. Types of State Aid Under the Temporary Framework

3.1. Limited Amounts of Aid

Direct financial aid is considered to be one of *the most intrusive form of aid* which can have a significant effect on the fair market balance of the internal market, and it is thus no wonder that such types of aids are, even where allowed, generally restricted by numerous conditions which must be met additionally. In this case, the preconditions are as follows (all conditions below are to be met):[13] *(i)* the overall aid may not exceed EUR 1.8 million per undertaking; *(ii)* the aid shall be granted based on a scheme with an estimated budget; *(iii)* aid may not be granted to undertakings that were already in difficulty on 31 December 2019; *(iv)* the aid may be granted no later than 31 December 2021; and *(v)* the aid granted to undertakings active in the processing and marketing of agricultural products is conditional upon parameters laid down in the Temporary Framework.

Of course, there are certain exceptions, such as the micro and small enterprises (they must meet less strict preconditions[14]) and aid granted to undertakings in the agricultural, fishery and aquaculture sectors (in which case additional conditions must be met[15]).

Spain introduced an umbrella scheme under the Temporary Framework already in early April 2020 and has had it amended multiple times since then.[16] Among others, the scheme provides for a limited amount of aid for uncovered fixed costs to companies and the self-employed affected by the coronavirus outbreak. The budget for this limited aid was eventually set at EUR 13.65 billion with a maximum aid amount of EUR 225,000 per company active in the primary production of agricultural products, EUR 270,000 per company active in the fishery and aquaculture sector and EUR 1.8 million per company active in all other sectors.

3.2. Aid in the Form of Guarantees on Loans

In order to ensure that there is no undue intervention in the market, several specific preconditions are laid down by the Temporary Framework in its para. 25, among others, those related to guarantee premiums, the overall amount of the loans, the duration of the guarantee, *etc.* The guarantee shall be granted by 31 December 2021 at the latest and (with certain exceptions) may not be granted to undertakings that were already in a difficulty on 31 December 2019. Such

12 *See* at https://ec.europa.eu/competition/state_aid/what_is_new/TF_informal_consolidated_version_as_amended_28_january_2021_en.pdf.
13 Temporary Framework, para. 22.
14 Id. para. 22.c.bis.
15 Id. para. 23.
16 SA.61875.

doi: 10.5553/HYIEL/266627012021009001005

guarantees were provided among others, by Denmark,[17] Finland,[18] France,[19] Germany,[20] Italy,[21] Latvia,[22] Luxembourg[23] and Portugal.[24]

3.3. Aid in the Form of Subsidized Interest Rates for Loans

Very similar preconditions are set forth by para. 27 of the Temporary Framework as in the case of the above-mentioned guarantees, except that instead of guaranteed premiums the credit risk margins are one of the decisive factors. Among others, Germany[25] and Latvia[26] introduced subsidized loan schemes.

The *Latvian* scheme includes an overall budget of EUR 200 million, of which EUR 50 million must be given in the form of a capital injection from the state budget into the state-owned joint stock company and Latvian public development bank Altum, while an additional EUR 150 million will be raised by Altum in the form of loans from an international financial institution (*e.g.* the European Investment Bank) or from the state treasury. The loans are limited to a maximum of three years.

The *German* subsidized interest rate loans are provided either directly by the state-owned development bank KfW together with private banks in a consortium to beneficiaries, or indirectly in the form of risk-sub-participations. These measures are open to all financial intermediaries and their aim is to provide financial means either for investment or working capital needs of the beneficiaries. The duration of the loan is limited to a maximum of six years.

3.4. Aid in the Form of Guarantees and Loans Channeled Through Credit Institutions or Other Financial Institutions

Para. 28 of the Temporary Framework sets forth that

> "aid in the form of guarantees and loans pursuant to section 3.1, section 3.2, section 3.3 and section 3.12 of this Communication may be provided to undertakings facing a sudden liquidity shortage directly or through credit institutions and other financial institutions as financial intermediaries."

If the aid is provided through a financial institution, it

> "should, to the largest extent possible, pass on the advantages of the public guarantee or subsidized interest rates on loans to the final beneficiaries. The financial intermediary must be able to demonstrate that it operates a

17 SA.56708.
18 SA.56809.
19 SA.56709.
20 SA.56787.
21 SA.56690.
22 SA.56722.
23 SA.56805.
24 SA.56755.
25 SA.56714.
26 SA.56722.

doi: 10.5553/HYIEL/266627012021009001005

mechanism that ensures that the advantages are passed on to the largest extent possible to the final beneficiaries in the form of higher volumes of financing, riskier portfolios, lower collateral requirements, lower guarantee premiums or lower interest rates than without such public guarantees or loans."

Among others, the governments of France,[27] Germany,[28] and the UK[29] have employed this type of state aid.

3.5. Short-Term Export Credit Insurance

This type of state aid certainly cannot be called a typical one. The Temporary Framework itself also contains only one single paragraph (para. 32), stating that "there is a lack of sufficient private insurance capacity for short-term export credits in general and that the cover for marketable risks is temporarily unavailable." Thus, *the Commission has temporarily removed all countries from the list of 'marketable risk' countries* under the short-term export-credit communication, enabling Member States to make available public short-term export credit insurances to all countries.[30] That is, all commercial and political risks associated with exports to any country have become eligible for export credit insurance until 31 December 2021.

3.6. Aid for COVID-19 Relevant Research and Development

The COVID-19 pandemic was caused by a novel coronavirus, hence, it is no wonder that related R&D may lawfully be supported by members states (even with a 100% aid intensity in certain cases) provided that the following are obeyed:[31] *(i)* the aid is granted in the form of direct grants, repayable advances or tax advantages by 31 December 2021 at the latest; *(ii)* the aid beneficiary commits to grant non-exclusive licenses under non-discriminatory market conditions to third parties in the EEA; *(iii)* the aid is not granted to undertakings that were already in a difficulty on 31 December 2019.

Many countries have relied on this legal basis. Austria provided a direct grant of *approx.* EUR 840,000 to Apeptico and a direct grant of *approx.* EUR 1.2 million to Panoptes to support R&D projects aiming at assessing the therapeutic potential of two medicinal products developed by these companies for the treatment of coronavirus patients.[32] Belgium has set up an EUR 25 million scheme to support (by means of direct grants and repayable advances) coronavirus related R&D activities in Wallonia[33] and an EUR 4 million direct grant scheme for the Brussels-Capital region.[34] Czechia notified the European

27 SA.56709.
28 SA.56714.
29 SA.5679. and SA.56794.
30 *See* at https://ec.europa.eu/commission/presscorner/detail/en/statement_20_551.
31 Temporary Framework, para. 35.
32 *See* at https://ec.europa.eu/commission/presscorner/detail/en/MEX_20_1276.
33 SA.57173.
34 SA.57057.

doi: 10.5553/HYIEL/266627012021009001005

Commission of an *approx.* EUR 7.3 million scheme to support research and development activities related to the coronavirus outbreak.[35] Estonia set up a EUR 10 million scheme to support research and development by companies affected by the coronavirus outbreak, as well as coronavirus-related research and development.[36] The Hungarian R&D scheme, open to all companies that are capable of engaging in the research and development and/or production of relevant products irrespective of their sector of activity, will take the form of direct grants and has a framework amount of EUR 143 million.[37] The Irish scheme amounting to EUR 200 million also supports the research and development, testing and production of coronavirus-relevant products.[38] Italy has provided EUR 40 million in the form of a direct grant to ReiThera S.r.l., a medium-sized biotechnology company located in the Lazio region, to support its coronavirus related R&D activities.[39] The Luxembourg scheme in the amount of EUR 30 million is open to small, medium-sized and large enterprises of all sectors, with aid to be granted in the form of direct grants to enhance and accelerate research and the production of goods directly relevant to coronavirus.[40] The Maltese scheme is similarly open to everyone and will also take place in the form of direct grants, amounting to a total of EUR 5.3 million.[41] The Polish scheme amounts to a significant PLN 2 billion (*approx.* EUR 449 million) and will be co-financed by the European Structural and Investment Funds.[42]

3.7. Investment Aid for Testing and Upscaling Infrastructures

Infrastructure-related aid under this legal title shall be related to infrastructure necessary for the development, testing and upscaling of COVID-19 relevant products (among others medicinal products, medical devices, hospital and medical equipment, disinfectants, *etc.*). An example is the EUR 80 million Slovak scheme, though it must be mentioned that this amount is not entirely provided based on the currently discussed legal title (investment aid for testing and upscaling infrastructures), but also based on the legal title of COVID-19 relevant research and development. The aid is provided as a direct grant and every company (except for financial institutions) may be eligible. (This scheme is to be co-founded by the European Structural and Investment Funds.[43])

The *most important preconditions* allowing for the use of this type of aid are as follows:[44] *(i)* the aid may be granted in the form of direct grants, tax advantages or repayable advances by 31 December 2021; *(ii)* the investment project shall be

35 SA.57071.
36 *See* at https://ec.europa.eu/commission/presscorner/detail/en/mex_20_2316.
37 *See* at https://ec.europa.eu/commission/presscorner/detail/en/mex_20_1471.
38 *See* at https://ec.europa.eu/commission/presscorner/detail/en/mex_20_995.
39 SA.61774.
40 SA.56954.
41 SA.57075.
42 *See* at https://ec.europa.eu/commission/presscorner/detail/en/mex_20_1132.
43 *See* at https://ec.europa.eu/commission/presscorner/detail/en/mex_20_1338.
44 Temporary Framework, para. 37.

Hungarian Yearbook of International Law and European Law 2021 (9) 1
doi: 10.5553/HYIEL/266627012021009001005

completed within six months after the date of granting the aid; *(iii)* aid intensity shall not exceed 75% of the eligible costs (with certain exceptions); *(iv)* the aid under this measure shall not be combined with other investment aid for the same eligible costs (with certain exceptions); *(v)* the price charged for the services provided by the testing and upscaling infrastructure shall correspond to the market price; *(vi)* the testing and upscaling infrastructures shall be open to several users and access shall be granted on a transparent and non-discriminatory basis; *(vii)* aid may not be granted to undertakings that were already in a difficulty on 31 December 2019.

3.8. Investment Aid for the Production of COVID-19 Relevant Products

This type of aid shall be granted under very similar conditions as aid for testing and upscaling infrastructure, with the difference that aid intensity shall (instead of 75%) not exceed 80% of eligible costs as a general rule. Also, a loss cover guarantee may be granted in addition to the direct grant, tax advantage or repayable advance but as an independent aid measure as well.[45]

Similarly, to the R&D related aid type, investment aid for the production of COVID-19 relevant products was used by many Member States, including Austria,[46] Belgium,[47] Czechia,[48] France,[49] Germany,[50] Hungary,[51] Ireland,[52] Lithuania,[53] Luxembourg,[54] Malta,[55] Poland,[56] Portugal,[57] and Slovenia.[58] It may be observed that in almost all cases, R&D and production-related aid was provided hand in hand. This is not a unique setup: schemes of various Member States usually combine various aid types under the Temporary Framework.

3.9. Aid in the Form of Deferrals of Tax and/or of Social Security Contributions

Denmark introduced a tax deferral scheme to support small and medium-sized enterprises (SMEs) affected by the coronavirus outbreak in January 2021 in the amount of *approx.* EUR 4 million[59] and increased this amount already in March 2021 with *approx.* EUR 34 million.[60] These schemes provide interest-free credit facilities in relation to wage taxes and VAT.

45 Id. para. 39.
46 *See* at https://ec.europa.eu/commission/presscorner/detail/en/mex_20_917.
47 *See* at https://ec.europa.eu/commission/presscorner/detail/en/mex_21_102 and https://ec.europa.eu/commission/presscorner/detail/en/mex_20_1139.
48 SA.56961.
49 SA.57367.
50 SA.57100.
51 *See* at https://ec.europa.eu/commission/presscorner/detail/en/mex_20_1471.
52 *See* at https://ec.europa.eu/commission/presscorner/detail/en/mex_20_995.
53 *See* at https://ec.europa.eu/commission/presscorner/detail/en/mex_20_1831.
54 SA.56954.
55 SA.57204.
56 *See* at https://ec.europa.eu/commission/presscorner/detail/en/mex_20_1132.
57 SA.57035.
58 *See* at https://ec.europa.eu/commission/presscorner/detail/en/mex_20_1483.
59 *See* at https://ec.europa.eu/commission/presscorner/detail/en/mex_21_227.
60 *See* at https://ec.europa.eu/commission/presscorner/detail/en/mex_21_1042.

doi: 10.5553/HYIEL/266627012021009001005

The Lithuanian tax deferral scheme includes tax deferrals and tax-related liquidity measures (payment in instalments of tax arrears, interest free periods, as well as the suspension of tax debt recovery) and is open to businesses affected by the containment measures imposed by the Lithuanian government to limit the spread of the coronavirus. The volume of these measures reaches the amount of *approx*. EUR 156 million.[61]

3.10. Aid in the Form of Wage Subsidies for Employees to Avoid Lay-Offs During the COVID-19 Outbreak

The Temporary Framework sets forth the following *general preconditions for providing aid in the form of wage subsidies*:[62] *(i)* the aid shall be granted only in the form of schemes to undertakings in specific sectors, regions or of a certain size of companies that are particularly affected by the COVID-19 outbreak; *(ii)* the individual aid awards of the wage subsidy scheme are granted no later than 31 December 2021; and *(iii)* the monthly wage subsidy shall not exceed 80% of the monthly gross salary.

Some examples of wage subsidy are those introduced by Hungary, Denmark and Bulgaria. Hungary has introduced an *approx*. EUR 23.5 million wage subsidy scheme in the form of exemptions (amounting to up to 23% of the monthly gross salary paid to the employees) from the employers' obligation to pay social security, vocational training and rehabilitation contributions.[63] The Danish scheme is to support companies that are subject to an operation ban implemented to limit the spread of the coronavirus, that is the scheme is open to companies in all sectors (except financial institutions) and the support is given in the form of direct grants.[64]

Bulgaria has two wage subsidy schemes in place. *(i)* The first scheme is known in Bulgaria as the "60/40" aid scheme: the government covers 60% of an employee's salary (and mandatory social security and healthcare contributions; but this falls under the above-mentioned aid in form of deferrals of tax and/or of social security contributions). *(ii)* The second scheme provides aid in the form of direct grants of *approx*. EUR 150 per beneficiary per month and is open to companies of all sizes and self-employed persons active in the sectors most affected by the coronavirus outbreak: transport, hotels, restaurants and travel agencies. (This scheme will also be co-financed by the European Social Fund.[65])

3.11. Recapitalization Measures

Recapitalization measures[66] were the last to be introduced by the Temporary Framework and thus available only from 8 May 2020. It may be observed, that

61 *See* at https://ec.europa.eu/commission/presscorner/detail/en/mex_21_155.

62 Temporary Framework, para. 43.

63 *See* at https://ec.europa.eu/commission/presscorner/detail/en/mex_20_1299.

64 *See* at https://ec.europa.eu/commission/presscorner/detail/en/mex_20_1882.

65 *See* at https://ec.europa.eu/commission/presscorner/detail/en/mex_20_1359.

66 *See* Antonios Bouchagiar, 'State Aid in the Context of the COVID-19 Outbreak, Including the Temporary Framework 2020', *EUI Working Papers*, RSC 2021/03, Robert Schuman Centre for Advanced Studies Florence School of Regulation, pp. 33-44.

doi: 10.5553/HYIEL/266627012021009001005

this measure is mainly used by governments to aid airlines and generally the air transport sector, which has basically been brought to a halt due to the travel bans and restrictions imposed: *(i)* Germany has contributed to the recapitalization of Deutsche Lufthansa AG (the parent company of Lufthansa Group);[67] *(ii)* SAS (Scandinavian Airlines) was recapitalized by the Danish and Swedish government;[68] *(iii)* Finland has introduced measures to recapitalize Finnair;[69] *(iv)* France has recapitalized Air France;[70] and Latvia has provided recapitalization to Riga International Airport[71] and airBaltic.[72]

Of course, it would not be correct to say that airlines were the only ones receiving recapitalization: *e.g.* Poland has introduced a recapitalization scheme to enable up to EUR 1.65 billion of capital support to SMEs and large enterprises affected by the coronavirus outbreak.[73]

The Temporary Framework sets forth very strict eligibility and entry conditions, defines the possible types of recapitalization measures (which must be either equity instruments or instruments with an equity component), and sets forth rules as to the remuneration and exit of the state. Due to the very high risk of undue distortions of competition, this type of state aid is the one regulated in the most detail in the Temporary Framework.

3.12. Case Study on Hungary

Hungary has notified the Commission on state aid provided within the scope of the Temporary Framework in 22 cases to date, out of which on 14 instances of new schemes were notified, while 8 times the Hungarian government's notification was about increasing already existing schemes.[74] Thus, it is clear that national governments were continuously monitoring the effects of the pandemic on the real economy and the labor market and making necessary adjustments when necessary.

The aggregate amount of the state aid provided by Hungary under the Temporary Framework equals EUR 13.2 billion. By comparison, the country's estimated nominal GDP in 2020 was *approx*. EUR 125 billion.[75] It is clear that the unprecedented crisis triggered an unprecedented amount of state aid as well. Hungary mainly relied on direct grants (Section 3.1 above), but made use of schemes including loans, equity intervention, guarantees, wage subsidies, tax advantages and tax allowances as well.

The aid provided was *generally industry-neutral, with certain exceptions, e.g.* the scheme to support Hungarian agri-food, fisheries and aquaculture, forestry and

67 SA.57153.
68 SA.57543.
69 SA.57410.
70 SA.59913.
71 SA.57756.
72 SA.56943.
73 SA.57055.
74 *See* at https://ec.europa.eu/info/live-work-travel-eu/coronavirus-response/jobs-and-economy-during-coronavirus-pandemic/state-aid-cases/hungary_en.
75 *See* at https://tradingeconomics.com/hungary/gdp.

doi: 10.5553/HYIEL/266627012021009001005

game management (hunting) sectors in the amount of EUR 99 million,[76] the wage subsidy scheme to support the aviation sector in the amount of EUR 23.5 million,[77] and the tax advantage/allowance and direct grant combined scheme targeting the accommodation and food service industry, restaurants and the entertainment and recreation sector (aid amount of EUR 195 million).[78] As mentioned in the Introduction above, these are the sectors which are most dependent on personal contacts: the food, cultural and aerospace industry. Thus, it seems reasonable to introduce schemes specifically for their support, although it may be concluded that these three schemes amount to only less than 3% of the notified state aid provided by Hungary.

4. Aid to Make Good the Damage Caused by Natural Disasters or Exceptional Occurrences [Article 107(2)(b) TFEU]

Given that the Temporary Framework specifically designated the COVID-19 pandemic as exceptional occurrence, under Article 107(2)(b) TFEU Member States may compensate both companies from industrial and commercial sectors severely affected by the consequences of the COVID-19 pandemic and organizers of events cancelled for the same reason, for the damage suffered as a direct result of the pandemic and provided that such compensation is notified to the Commission.[79] Thanks to this provision Member States do not have to verify that the conditions of derogation are fulfilled,[80] making the notification process more simple. Member States must ensure the free, non-discriminatory movement of goods, services, persons and capital when providing state aid.[81] This provision however provides a legal basis only with for compensation provided strictly up to the amount of direct damages, that is, up to the amount of the prospective profit that would be realized through the beneficiary's precisely defined scope of activities if no detrimental effect of the pandemic were present.[82] That is, measures aiming to remedy the general economic downturn caused by COVID-19 events (damage not directly and case-by-case specifically and verifiably related to COVID-19) are not admissible under these grounds.[83]*Member States have invoked this legal basis in numerous cases: (i)* Austria when compensating Austrian

76 SA.57329.

77 SA.57767.

78 SA.59477.

79 Peter Roth QC & Vivien Rose, *European Community Law of Competition*, Oxford University Press, Oxford, 2008, p. 1535.

80 Kelyn Bacon, *European Union Law of State Aid*, Oxford University Press, Oxford, 2013, p. 94.

81 Lennart Ritter & W. David Braun, *European Competition Law: A Practitioner's Guide*, Kluwer Law International, Bedfordshire, 2004, p. 971.

82 Tihamér Tóth, 'Állami támogatások versenyjoga a vírusválság idején', *Európai Tükör*, Vol. 23, Issue 3, 2020, pp. 55-73.

83 Judit Barta, 'Az állami támogatás szerepe és átmeneti szabályozása, valamint a magyar intézkedések a koronavírus-járvány okozta válsághelyzetben', *OPUSCULA CIVILIA* 2020, at https://antk.uni-nke.hu/document/akk-copy-uni-nke-hu/Opuscula_Civilia_2020_Barta_Judit.pdf.

Hungarian Yearbook of International Law and European Law 2021 (9) 1
doi: 10.5553/HYIEL/266627012021009001005

Airlines;[84] *(ii)* Croatia when compensating Croatia Airlines;[85] *(iii)* Czechia to compensate non-profit sport organizations;[86] *(iv)* Denmark with respect to its compensation provided to mink famers;[87] *(v)* Estonia in its scheme established to compensate international ferry operators;[88] *(vi)* Finland when compensating companies in the restaurant industry;[89] *(vii)* France when compensating ski lifts operators;[90] *(viii)* Germany when compensating of companies active in trade fairs and the congress sector;[91] *(ix)* Greece when introducing a scheme to the protect primary residence of vulnerable borrowers;[92] *(x)* Hungary when compensating specifically large companies;[93] *(xi)* Ireland when compensating airport operators;[94] *(xii)* Italy when compensating commercial rail passenger operators;[95] *(xiii)* Lithuania when compensating companies active in the processing of agricultural products in the poultry and eggs sectors;[96] *(xiv)* the Netherlands when compensating zoos;[97] *(xv)* Poland when setting up an aid scheme to compensate airports;[98] *(xvi)* Romania when compensating its regional airport operators;[99] *(xvii)* Slovakia when compensating airport operators;[100] *(xviii)* Slovenia when compensating specifically large companies;[101] *(xix)* Spain when setting up a guarantee scheme to compensate certain self-employed and companies;[102] *(xx)* Sweden when compensating damages caused by cancelled or postponed cultural events;[103] *(xxi)* the UK when compensating companies active in Scotland in the processing of agricultural products in poultry sector.[104]

84 SA.57539.
85 *See* at https://ec.europa.eu/commission/presscorner/detail/en/mex_20_2277.
86 SA.57614.
87 SA.61945.
88 *See* at https://ec.europa.eu/commission/presscorner/detail/en/MEX_20_1331.
89 *See* at https://ec.europa.eu/commission/presscorner/detail/en/MEX_20_970.
90 SA.60949.
91 *See* at https://ec.europa.eu/commission/presscorner/detail/en/mex_21_204.
92 *See* at https://ec.europa.eu/commission/presscorner/detail/en/mex_20_2130.
93 *See* at https://ec.europa.eu/commission/presscorner/detail/en/mex_20_1176.
94 *See* at https://ec.europa.eu/commission/presscorner/detail/en/mex_21_804.
95 SA.59346.
96 *See* at https://ec.europa.eu/commission/presscorner/detail/en/mex_20_1432.
97 *See* at https://ec.europa.eu/commission/presscorner/detail/en/mex_21_581.
98 *See* at https://ec.europa.eu/commission/presscorner/detail/en/mex_20_1771.
99 *See* at https://ec.europa.eu/commission/presscorner/detail/en/mex_20_2191.
100 *See* at https://ec.europa.eu/commission/presscorner/detail/en/mex_20_2529.
101 *See* at https://ec.europa.eu/commission/presscorner/detail/en/mex_20_1230.
102 *See* at https://ec.europa.eu/commission/presscorner/detail/en/mex_20_2191.
103 *See* at https://ec.europa.eu/commission/presscorner/detail/en/mex_20_1831.
104 *See* at https://ec.europa.eu/commission/presscorner/detail/en/mex_20_2507.

doi: 10.5553/HYIEL/266627012021009001005

5. Aid to Promote the Execution of an Important Project of Common European Interest or to Remedy a Serious Disturbance in the Economy of a Member State [Article 107(3)(b) TFEU]

> "This derogation has been used as a basis for a series of decisions and guidelines to deal with state aid to the financial sector and to the "real economy" following the global financial crisis of 2008."[105]

Though measures aiming to remedy the general economic downturn caused by COVID-19 effects are not admissible under Article 107(2)(b) TFEU, such aid may be legitimate under Article 107(3)(b) of the TFEU. Namely, the Temporary Framework specifically refers to this Article and sets forth that

> "state aid is justified and can be declared compatible with the internal market on the basis of Article 107(3)(b) TFEU, for a limited period, to remedy the liquidity shortage faced by undertakings and ensure that the disruptions caused by the COVID-19 outbreak do not undermine their viability, especially of SMEs."[106]

For state aid to be admissible, it has to be notified to the Commission and it has to be proven by the Member State that the measure in question is "necessary, appropriate and proportionate to remedy a serious disturbance in the economy of the Member State concerned."[107]

If one takes a look at the state aids notified by the Member States under this legal title, one may conclude that these projects generally concern a significant amount of aid: *(i)* a Belgian guarantee scheme mobilized EUR 50 billion support for companies affected by the coronavirus outbreak;[108] *(ii)* a French guarantee scheme mobilized up to EUR 20 billion support from private investors for companies affected by the coronavirus outbreak;[109] *(iii)* Italy has set up a guarantee scheme in the amount of EUR 2 billion to support the trade credit insurance market;[110] *(iv)* Germany set up a guarantee scheme in the amount of EUR 840 million to protect consumers and support the travel industry;[111] *(v)* Portugal put in place a top-up insurance scheme in the amount of EUR 500 million to support domestic trade credit;[112] *(vi)* Spain introduced a reinsurance scheme in the amount of EUR 500 million to support the trade credit insurance market.[113]

105 Leigh Hancher *et al.*, *EU State Aids*, Thomson Reuters, London, 2016, p. 141.
106 Temporary Framework, para. 18.
107 Id. para. 19.
108 SA.56819.
109 SA.58639.
110 SA.57937.
111 SA.57741.
112 *See* at https://ec.europa.eu/commission/presscorner/detail/en/mex_21_1542.
113 *See* at https://ec.europa.eu/commission/presscorner/detail/en/mex_20_2335.

doi: 10.5553/HYIEL/266627012021009001005

6. Aid to Facilitate the Development of Certain Economic Activities or of Certain Economic Areas, Where Such Aid Does Not Adversely Affect Trading Conditions to an Extent Contrary to the Common Interest [Article 107(3)(c) TFEU]

The categories listed in Article 107(3) TFEU are so called "aid which may be compatible with the internal market".[114] It comes as no surprise that this legal basis is not a tailor-made one for providing state aid related to the COVID-19 pandemic and accordingly, the authors are aware of only four cases where a Member States invoked this Article: *(i)* Greece when providing aid to protect the primary residence of vulnerable borrowers;[115]*(ii)* the UK when aiding the distribution of free medical grade personal protective equipment;[116] and *(iii)* Portugal when supporting SATA airline[117] and TAP.[118]

7. Comprehensive Summary of Cases Notified to the European Commission with Respect to the Effects of the COVID-19 Pandemic

After analyzing all the 577 state aid cases[119] notified to the European Commission with regard to the COVID-19 pandemic (until 13 June 2021), the following main conclusions may be drawn.[120] Since the country is no longer a member of the EU, the UK was obliged to report the provision of state aid to the European Commission only until 31 December 2020. Accordingly, the figures below contain only the data reported by this date.

More than 80% of the examined state aid cases were reported as to be provided under legal basis Article 107(3)(b) TFEU. In line with the above, this figure does not come as a surprise given that the Temporary Framework specifically puts this legal basis into its focus. In addition, we shouldn't forget that during the financial crisis of 2008 this was the legal basis most heavily relied on. As the Temporary Framework specifically designated the COVID-19 pandemic as an exceptional occurrence, it isn't surprising that state aid provided with reference to Article 107(2)(b) TFEU amounts to the second most commonly cited legal basis. Member States' reliance on Articles 107(3)(c) and 93 is insignificant. State aid cases reported to the European Commission with respect to the COVID-19 pandemic under the various legal bases are shown below in the chart prepared by the authors (see Figure 1).

114 Conor Quigley, *European State Aid Law and Policy*, Oxford and Portland, Oregon, 2015, p. 203.
115 *See* at https://ec.europa.eu/commission/presscorner/detail/en/mex_20_2130.
116 *See* at https://ec.europa.eu/commission/presscorner/detail/en/mex_20_1682.
117 SA.58101.
118 SA.57369.
119 This number includes the amendments made to the already existing state aid schemes. The reason for choosing this methodology is that the notified modifications themselves are to be accounted for as provision of state aid, given that each and every modification resulted in widening the scope of already existing state aid schemes.
120 *See* at https://ec.europa.eu/info/live-work-travel-eu/coronavirus-response/jobs-and-economy-during-coronavirus-pandemic/state-aid-cases_en.

doi: 10.5553/HYIEL/266627012021009001005

Figure 1 Covid-19 related state aid cases

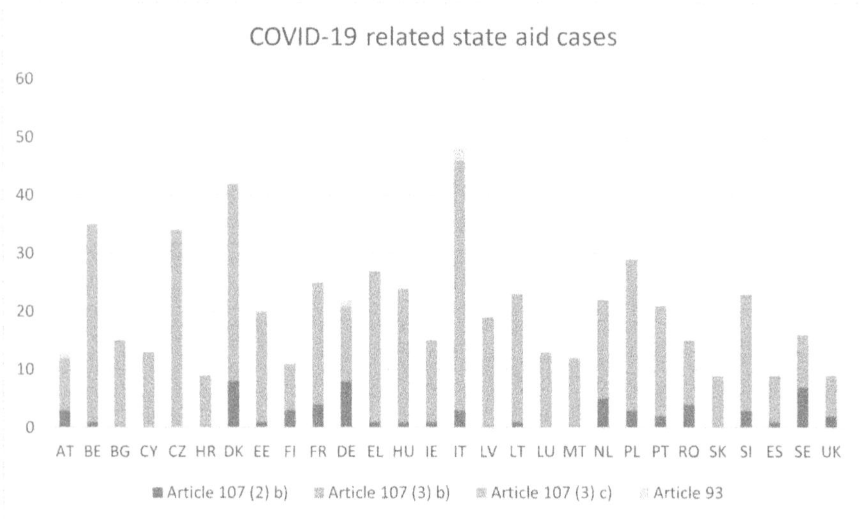

Naturally, what is even more important than the absolute number of reported state aid cases, is the aggregate and individual amount of the provided aid. The total aggregate amount of state aid provided by the Member States with respect to the effects of the COVID-19 pandemic is more than EUR 1.9 trillion, amounting to *approx*. 15% of the total nominal GDP of the EU in 2020.[121] More than half of the total amount of the examined cases were notified by Germany and France, as illustrated by the first chart[122] below (see Figure 2, prepared by the authors). The authors have also prepared another chart showing the state aid notified by the Member States excluding Germany and France, to portray the amounts provided by the rest of the Member States. What is clear is that around 95% of the amounts in question were provided under the legal basis Article 107(3)(b) TFEU. Aid under Article 107(2)(b) TFEU amounts to approx. 2.7%, while aid provided under Articles 93 and 107(3)(c) is insignificant. This is in line with the findings set forth above with respect to the absolute number of the cases notified to the European Commission, thus no disproportion is discernable.

The authors conclude from the second chart that state aid provided by Italy and Romania is quite low compared to their population (and in case of Italy also compared to its nominal GDP), while Austria, Belgium, Czechia and Sweden have notified a considerable amount of state aid compared to their population (see Figure 3).[123]

121 *See* at https://data.worldbank.org/indicator/NY.GDP.MKTP.CD?locations=EU.
122 Given the high numbers involve, the amounts are shown in thousand Euros.
123 *See* at https://ec.europa.eu/eurostat/documents/2995521/11081093/3-10072020-AP-EN.pdf/d2f799bf-4412-05cc-a357-7b49b93615f1.

doi: 10.5553/HYIEL/266627012021009001005

Figure 2 ***Amounts of state aid per country I***

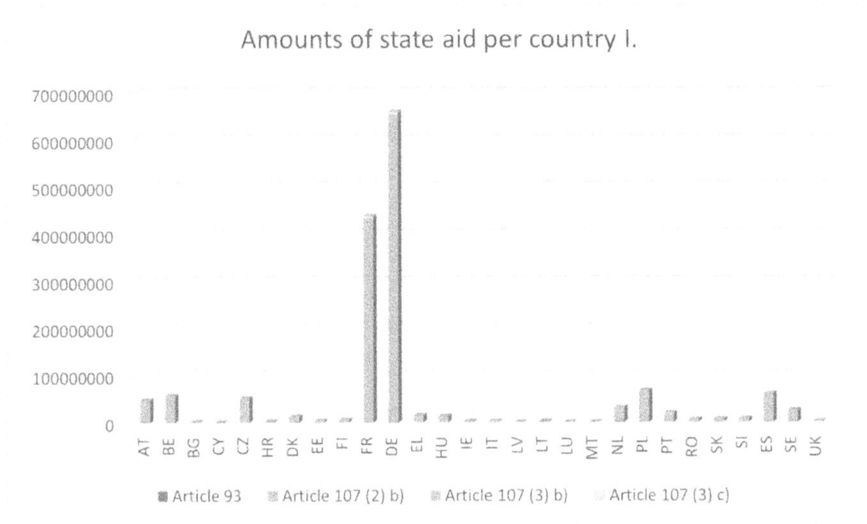

Figure 3 ***Amounts of state aid per country II***

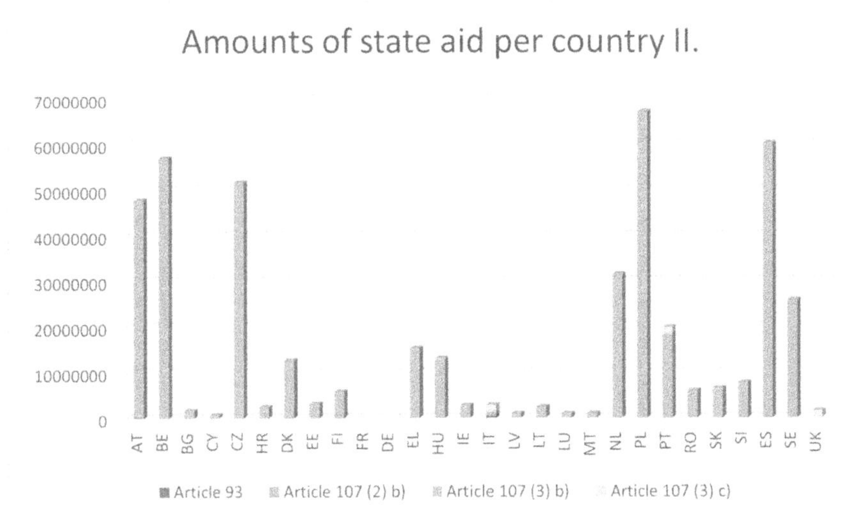

8. Conclusion

Based on the specific cases listed above, the following two conclusions may be drawn. *(i)* The European Commission was quick to issue the Temporary Framework and its amendments in the rapidly changing environment. *(ii)* Given the huge volume of aids provided by the Member States under the legal bases set

doi: 10.5553/HYIEL/266627012021009001005

forth under the Temporary Framework, the rules of the Temporary Framework and the TFEU may be considered flexible enough not to disproportionately restrict the capabilities of the Member States to act speedily and in a flexible manner. The Temporary Framework is the answer to an extraordinary situation. While one cannot predict whether the transitional rules will be used properly in every case, the authors believe that EU state aid rules have proven to be necessary and proportionate in upholding the proper functioning of the internal market. Finally, in case any of the state aid provided is disputed, the CJEU is perfectly placed to rule in such a dispute, just as in the *Ryanair* cases.[124]

124 Judgment of 14 April 2021, *Case T-378/20, Ryanair DAC*, ECLI:EU:T:2021:194; Judgment of 14 April 2021, Case *T-379/20, Ryanair DAC*, ECLI:EU:T:2021:195; and Judgment of 14 April 2021, *Case T-388/20, Ryanair DAC*, ECLI:EU:T:2021:196.

 Hungarian Yearbook of International Law and European Law 2021 (9) 1
doi: 10.5553/HYIEL/266627012021009001005

Support for Families

A Way to Tackle COVID-19 and Its Implications in Hungary

Éva Gellérné Lukács[*]

Abstract

COVID-19 poses a huge challenge for families and children; their exposure to economic, social and mental hardship is considerable and is confirmed by several studies. The pandemic pushes governments to allocate resources to the economy, but it is equally important to invest in the future by supporting families and children. The article outlines general tendencies in the EU and reflects on Hungarian measures in this field. During the first, second and third waves of COVID-19, a wide range of measures were introduced in Hungary. By extending the eligibility periods of family benefits for families with small children (both social insurance contribution-based and universal benefits) approximately 40,000 families (households) were covered. During the first and second COVID-19 waves, not only did the government extend benefit eligibility, but it also announced several new or renewed measures related to cash benefits and housing for families with at least one economically active parent. During the third wave eligibility periods of family benefits have again been extended. On the other hand, the unemployment benefit system remained intact, labor market pitfalls were addressed by providing wage subsidies.

Keywords: family, children, vulnerable groups, social protection, housing benefits, labor market.

1. Introduction

COVID-19 hit Hungary in January 2020. By the end of that month, the 'Operative Corps', jointly led by the Minister of the Interior and the Minister of Human Resources, had been established to coordinate the national response to

* Éva Gellérné Lukács: senior lecturer, ELTE Law School, Budapest; external expert, Kopp Mária Institute for Demography and Families, Budapest.

doi: 10.5553/HYIEL/266627012021009001006

the coronavirus pandemic.[1] Following the WHO's assessment that COVID-19 could be defined as a pandemic on 11 March 2020, the Hungarian government declared a state of emergency on the same day (11 March 2020).[2] It was lifted in mid-June 2020, but an 'Epidemiological alert' remained in place, authorizing the government to uphold restrictions.[3] Strict travel restrictions were imposed at the end of August,[4] and, due to the rapid spread of the virus, the state of emergency was reintroduced in November (still in force probably until autumn).[5] Until April 2021 it meant strict curfew orders, social distancing protocols and the closure of schools and several service providers.[6] Full closure has been lifted gradually from 19 April 2021, but protective measures remained in place, in particular rules that grant access to indoor services only for those who possess a vaccination certificate.[7]

The Hungarian government has passed extraordinary measures to deal with the economic and social impact of the virus during 2020-2021.[8] At the macro level, public expenditure increased by HUF 2,920 billion during 2020, compared with 2019.[9] By the end of December 2020, other general government sector expenditures had surpassed the previous year's level by HUF 2,169 billion (by 56.3%) mainly due to the regulations adopted to reduce the economic impacts of the coronavirus pandemic. Additional costs emerged, among others, as direct costs in the health care sector (vaccinations, public procurement, wage support

1 Government Decision No. 1012/2020. (I. 31.) on the Establishment of the Operative Corps responsible for the Prevention of the Coronavirus Epidemic. The Operative Corps was and continues to be (April 2021) in charge of proposing the necessary medical and epidemiological measures to protect the population and to coordinate the activities of other state bodies. The members of the Operative Corps are the National Chief Medical Officer, directors of the police, the Counterterrorism Centre, the National Ambulance Service, the National Healthcare Service Centre, the National Directorate of Disaster Management, the National Directorate-General for Aliens Policing and the South Pest Central Hospital.

2 Government Decree No. 40/2020. (III. 11.) declaring a state of emergency.

3 Act LVII of 2020 on the Termination of the State of Emergency as of 17 June 2020; Act LVIII of 2020 on the Transitory Rules in Connection with the Termination of the State of Emergency and about the Epidemiological Alert as of 17 June 2020; Government Decree No. 283/2020. (VI. 17.) on the introduction of the Epidemiological Alert.

4 Government Decree No. 407/2020. (VIII. 30.) on the temporary reintroduction of border control; Government Decree No. 408/2020. (VIII. 30.) on travel restrictions during the period of the Epidemiological Alert.

5 Government Decree No. 478/2020. (XI. 3.) declaring a state of emergency.

6 Accommodation and food services sector and indoor sport and entertainment facilities.

7 Government Decree No. 166/2021. (IV. 7.) on extending protective measures; Government Decree No. 60/2021. (II. 12.) on evidencing protection against coronavirus; Government Decree No. 194/2021. (IV. 26.) amending the Government Decrees governing the protection measures to be applied in the event of an emergency, with a view to the third stage of the phasing-out of protection measures.

8 Government Decree No. 140/2020. (IV. 21.) on tax relief to mitigate the negative economic effects of the COVID-19 pandemic within the framework of the Action Plan on Protecting the Economy; Government Decree No. 484/2020. (XI. 10.) on the second wave of measures applicable during the state of emergency. *See* István Balázs *et al.*, 'Veled Uram, de nélküled" – Állam, önkormányzatok, munkáltatók a koronavírus idején', *Magyar Tudomány*, Vol. 82, Issue 5, 2021, pp. 625-634.

9 *See* at www.ksh.hu/gyorstajekoztatok/#/en/document/krm2012.

doi: 10.5553/HYIEL/266627012021009001006

for health care workers), financial support for public service providers, wage subsidies and social assistance benefits. Altogether approximately 67 per cent of the upsurge was related to COVID-19 in 2020.

Several targeted measures were passed to halt the spread of COVID-19, to maintain and restore employment and to support families, in particular families with small children and large families. Eligibility periods of family benefits for families with small children (both social insurance contribution-based and universal benefits) were extended. Level of cash-benefits were raised, and new or renewed measures related to housing of families were introduced. This article seeks to highlight the approach that has been chosen by Hungary in tackling COVID-19, namely, to specifically reinforce support for families instead of cutting them. The article also aims at interconnecting Hungarian measures with strategic EU legal documents that have recently been passed and which strongly encourage Member States to adopt measures to mainstream families and children.

2. Scene Setter – Families, Children and EU Policies

2.1. Societal Challenges of COVID-19

The European Pillar of Social Rights Action Plan,[10] which was adopted on 4 March 2021 to provide for the effective implementation of the European Pillar of Social Rights (Pillar)[11] and which was endorsed by the European Council on 8 May 2021 in the Porto Declaration[12] pinpointed that "Competitive sustainability is at the heart of Europe's social market economy, striving for a sustainable and inclusive growth model that delivers the best for people and the planet."[13] The EU flagship initiative in the social arena is without doubt *the Pillar that sets out 20 key principles for a strong, fair and inclusive Europe*. The right to quality and inclusive education, training and lifelong learning is proclaimed as its first principle. Principle 11 is 'Childcare and support to children' which proclaims children' opportunities to have the right to affordable early childhood education, care of good quality, as well as the right to protection from poverty and the right to specific measures to enhance equal opportunities. These are the cornerstones to create a fair, "stronger and more innovative Europe".[14] *Social Europe is a key concept:*[15] 88% of Europeans said in the Eurobarometer survey that they considered a social Europe to be important to them personally (issues such as

10 *See* at https://op.europa.eu/webpub/empl/european-pillar-of-social-rights/en/.

11 *See* at https://ec.europa.eu/info/strategy/priorities-2019-2024/economy-works-people/jobs-growth-and-investment/european-pillar-social-rights_en.

12 *See* at www.consilium.europa.eu/en/press/press-releases/2021/05/08/the-porto-declaration/.

13 European Pillar of Social Rights Action Plan, p. 3.

14 *Together for Europe's Recovery. Program of the German Presidency*, 1 July to 31 December 2020, at www.eu2020.de/blob/2360248/e0312c50f910931819ab67f630d15b2f/06-30-pdf-programm-en-data.pdf.

15 Catherine Barnard, 'EU Employment Law and the European Social Model: The Past, the Present and the Future', *Current Legal Problems*, Vol. 67, Issue 1, 2014, pp. 199-237.

doi: 10.5553/HYIEL/266627012021009001006

equal opportunities, access to the labor market, fair working conditions and social protection).[16]

The European Council (Social Summit) in Porto welcomed the new EU headline targets for jobs, skills and poverty reduction, namely *(i)* at least 78% of the population aged 20 to 64 should be in employment by 2030; *(ii)* at least 60% of all adults should participate in training every year; and *(iii)* the number of people at risk of poverty or social exclusion should be reduced by at least 15 million by 2030. The European Council also stressed that it is

> "committed to reducing inequalities, defending fair wages, fighting social exclusion and tackling poverty, taking on the objective of fighting child poverty and addressing the risks of exclusion for particularly vulnerable social groups."[17]

The EU and Member States will work hard together to achieve these objectives, and by looking into the future, they are devoted to creating more and better jobs for all within the framework of an inclusive recovery.

The positive approach of the Porto Declaration is essential because Europe's social fabric has been put to a serious test by the COVID-19 pandemic. The achievement of the UN SDG targets is threatened.[18] When COVID-19 hit Europe, governments were forced to introduce mitigating measures which, indeed, were largely similar. A large majority of EU Member States introduced schemes to pay a proportion of the wages of employees who have been at risk of being made redundant, some Member States granted financial support for unemployed people or people on sick leave or for certain societal groups, like the elderly or care-givers.[19]

Emergency measures assisted well the EU Member States to absorb COVID-19 without an irreparable shock on the labor market. According to statistics however, 23 out of 27 EU Member States had lower employment rate in Q4 2020, compared with Q4 2019. After a sharp fall from 73.2% in the fourth quarter of 2019 to 71.7% in the second quarter of 2020, the EU employment rate went up to 72.6% in the fourth quarter of 2020.[20] Not all age groups were affected equally by the COVID-19 crisis. Young people aged 15-24 experienced the largest drop in employment and the greatest increase in labor market slack

16 *Special Eurobarometer 509: Social issues*, March 2021, at https://data.europa.eu/data/datasets/s2266_94_2_509_eng?locale=en.

17 The Porto Declaration, para. 9, at www.consilium.europa.eu/en/press/press-releases/2021/05/08/the-porto-declaration/.

18 *The Likely Impact of COVID-19 on the Achievement of SDG 8*, ILO, 2021, at www.ilo.org/wcmsp5/groups/public/---ed_dialogue/---actrav/documents/publication/wcms_770036.pdf.

19 *Coronavirus Pandemic in the EU – Fundamental Rights Implications*, European Union Agency for Fundamental Rights, 2020, p. 9.

20 *Employment – Quarterly Statistics*, Eurostat, 2021, at https://ec.europa.eu/eurostat/statistics-explained/index.php?title=Employment_-_quarterly_statistics#Employment_overview_in_2020_in_the_EU_and_the_Member_States.

doi: 10.5553/HYIEL/266627012021009001006

during the health crisis when compared with other age groups.[21] Young people and young workers are the most sensitive to changes hence they are usually less experienced career starters, know less and earn less.[22] But at the same time, they are one of the most important age cohorts in many respects, because this is the stage in life when they leave home and start creating their own family life, including having children. Instability and uncertain future prospects can have undesired consequences for them.

In addition to young people, COVID-19 added to the hardship of vulnerable societal groups. Those highly affected by poverty or social exclusion usually include single parents (47.7%), families with multiple children, as well as the Roma and persons with disabilities.[23] The restrictions on work adopted because of COVID-19 adversely affected those who are particularly vulnerable to reductions in income, namely women, single parent families, migrant families, those working in precarious work conditions, and anyone living in, or at risk of, poverty.[24] This in turn has an impact on families and children living in these households.[25]

2.2. EU Strategic Documents during the COVID-19 Pandemic

In the second half of 2020 and in the first quarter of 2021 the EU adopted several strategies and action plans, that are the follow-ups of the Pillar and include measures in the light of COVID-19. The documents envisage intervention areas and foster actions – supported also by EU funds – to make a difference for the life of EU citizens for the period 2020-2025.[26] They always expressly refer to the adverse effects of COVID-19 on families and children and always call for EU and Member State level action to counteract disruptions. These documents were submitted by the European Commission and supported fully by the European Parliament,[27] and also endorsed by the Council. The latter is indeed important hence a considerable part of the implementation of the foreseen actions falls upon the Member States. Issues related to families, children and also initiatives on education and employment fall to a large degree within the competence of the Member States.[28]

21 *Key Figures on the Impact of the COVID-19 Crisis on the Labour Market*, Eurostat, 2021, at https://ec.europa.eu/eurostat/statistics-explained/index.php?title=Key_figures_on_the_impact_of_the_COVID-19_crisis_on_the_labour_market.

22 Daphne Ahrendt *et al.*, *Living, Working and COVID-19*, Eurofound, 2020.

23 *European Semester Thematic Factsheet: Social Inclusion*, European Commission, 18 May 2018, p. 4.

24 Laura Gyeney, 'Mobilitási trendek Európában, különös tekintettel Magyarország helyzetére', *in* Péter Smuk (ed.), *Társadalmi fenntarthatóság*, Ludovika Egyetemi Kiadó, Budapest, p. 1156.

25 *Coronavirus Pandemic in the EU – Fundamental Rights Implications* 2020, p. 19.

26 EU Roma strategic framework for equality, inclusion and participation for 2020-2030, 7 October 2020, COM(2020) 620 final; A Union of equality: EU anti-racism action plan 2020-2025, 18 September 2020, COM(2020) 565 final; Action Plan on Integration and Inclusion (2021-2027), 24 November 2020, COM(2020) 758 final; Union of Equality: Strategy for the Rights of Persons with Disabilities 2021-2030, 3 March 2021, COM(2021) 101 final.

27 EP resolution of 11 March 2021 on children's rights with a view to the EU Strategy on the Rights of the Child, 2021/2523(RSP).

28 *See* Sára Hungler *et al.*, *Az Európai Unió szociális és munkajoga*, ELTE Eötvös, Budapest 2020.

doi: 10.5553/HYIEL/266627012021009001006

Regarding young people, on 20 October 2020 the Council reinforced the *Youth Guarantee, which aims to secure a smooth transition from school to work and support labor market integration.*[29] This has been the follow-up of Council Decision (EU) 2019/1181, and in particular Guideline 6, which called upon Member States

> "to continue to address youth unemployment and the issue of young people not in employment, education or training ('NEETs') through prevention of early school leaving and structural improvement in the school-to-work transition."[30]

The Youth Guarantee recommends Member States to make employment and start-up incentives work, "to use targeted and well-designed employment incentives, such as wage subsidies, recruitment incentives ('bonuses'), reduction of social security contributions, tax credits or disability benefits, and start-up incentives in order *to create good quality opportunities for the sustainable integration of young people into the labor market.*"[31] It was deemed necessary hence the COVID-19 pandemic "is likely to bring back dramatically high youth unemployment and NEET rates."

Almost at the same time, on 25 September 2020 *the European Education Area has been launched*

> "where learning mobility is the norm, where universities can work seamlessly across borders, where it is normal to speak two languages in addition to the mother tongue, where school and higher education diplomas are automatically and mutually recognized, where everyone feels they belong, irrespective of their background and where Europe would become a continent of excellence in education and research."[32]

Clearly, mobility of young students or trainees can also be a tool in mitigating the loss of human capital and in tackling intergenerational transmission of poverty throughout the EU.

Regarding work-life balance, in addition to Directive 2019/1158,[33] on 5 March 2020, *the Commission adopted its Gender Equality Strategy 2020-2025.*[34] It thrives for equal sharing of childcare responsibilities between parents and stresses that the promotion of equality between women and men is a task for the

29 Council Recommendation of 30 October 2020 on A Bridge to Jobs – Reinforcing the Youth Guarantee and replacing the Council Recommendation of 22 April 2013 on establishing a Youth Guarantee (Youth Guarantee).

30 Council Decision (EU) 2019/1181 of 8 July 2019 on guidelines for the employment policies of the Member States.

31 Youth Guarantee, para. 15.

32 Commission communication on achieving the European Education Area by 2025, COM(2020) 625 final.

33 Directive (EU) 2019/1158 of the European Parliament and of the Council of 20 June 2019 on work-life balance for parents and carers and repealing Council Directive 2010/18/EU.

34 A Union of Equality: Gender Equality Strategy 2020-2025, COM(2020) 152 final.

doi: 10.5553/HYIEL/266627012021009001006

EU, in all its activities, required by the Treaties. The COVID-19 pandemic had a disproportionate socio-economic effect on women in this regard: social distancing, working from home, permanent childcare, home-schooling-related duties and domestic work put women under significant pressure from several directions.[35]

Regarding children, on 24 March 2021 the Commission adopted the *first comprehensive EU Strategy on the Rights of the Child for 2021-2024*, as well as a proposal for a Council recommendation establishing a European Child Guarantee. This is highly necessary because 18 million children or 22.2% of children in the EU were growing up at risk of poverty and social exclusion according to Eurostat data from 2019 and this figure is likely to increase due to the socio-economic consequences of COVID-19.[36] One in four children in the EU grows up in vulnerable families that need support to break the cycle of poverty.

> "The increased economic insecurity for many families, with parents risking to lose or actually having lost their jobs, has produced negative consequences for a large number of children, with those from already low-income or socially marginalized families suffering the most."[37]

The protection of children and young people and smooth transition from school to work are issues that are of outstanding importance for European societies. It is imperative that in these areas policy debates in the EU be inclusive and dedicated also to nurture Member States' best practices. Commission President von der Leyen flagged in her speech to the European Parliament, held on 20 January 2021:

> "Change towards a greener, fairer and more inclusive future will entail short-term costs and challenges. That is why it is so important to accompany the change and to help communities and individuals adjust to the new world. This requires keen attention to social issues. The European Pillar of Social Rights should be implemented at EU and Member State level, with due regard for respective competences."[38]

It can't be overlooked, however, that even though the pandemic caused unprecedented economic and social damage by peacetime standards, Europe has long been facing serious societal challenges. The most striking one is demographic ageing which is followed by (or coupled with) economic and social inequalities. Statistics and summaries pinpoint that the number of children in the household has regrettably become a poverty risk. In the EU, compared with a childless

35 Réka Geambașu *et al.*, 'Qualitative Research on Hungarian Mothers' Social Situation and Metal Health During the Time of the COVID-19 Pandemic', *Corvinus Journal of Sociology and Social Policy*, Vol. 11, Issue 2, 2020, pp. 151-155.

36 *Supporting Families and Children Beyond COVID-19 – Social Protection in High-Income Countries*, UNICEF, 2020.

37 *COVID-19 Pandemic Responses*, Council of Europe, Strasbourg, 2020, p. 7.

38 *See* at https://op.europa.eu/webpub/empl/european-pillar-of-social-rights/en/.

doi: 10.5553/HYIEL/266627012021009001006

household with two adults, a two-adult household with two children cost about 40% more.[39] Consequently, it is capable of increasing the risk of poverty, even without COVID-19.

3. The Hungarian Perspective

In Hungary, the years of the 2008-2010 economic crisis hit families the hardest. That time family allowances were cut, family tax credits and housing allowances were abolished, and the paid childcare period was shortened.[40] In 2011, Act CCXI of 2011 on the Protection of Families was passed, the underlying idea of which is that *family and having children should not be a risk of poverty*.[41] Supportive family policies have been a priority in Hungary ever since. An important goal is to achieve a better standard of living for families with children in financial terms than if they had not had children.[42]

In the last decade Hungarian family policy has been newly shaped and it has a remarkable feature: work-related family benefits have become significantly more valuable, the emphasis of support has shifted strongly towards employment-related and wage-related benefits.[43] At the same time the objective goes beyond strict income-replacement, the family support system is of holistic nature, which in addition to the classic cash benefits and benefits in kind also encompasses benefits on a wider horizon, it provides – among other things – considerable housing benefits to buy a home or car acquisition subsidies for large families.[44]

While the proportion of inhabitants born outside the EU has overall increased over recent years,[45] it varies across Member States. It is around 10% or above in Austria, Croatia, Estonia, Germany, Latvia, Luxembourg, Malta, and Sweden, while it is below 3% in Bulgaria, Czechia, Hungary, Poland, Romania, and Slovakia.[46] It means that the target group of Hungarian family policies is rather homogenous in cultural and religious terms.

COVID-19 put the horizontal and intersectoral goals of Hungarian family policy to a test hence the above-mentioned *holistic approach requires considerable*

39 *Child Poverty and Social Exclusion: Investing in Children and Their Well-Being*, The Social Protection Committee, 2014.

40 Tünde Fűrész & Balázs Molnár, 'A családbarát Magyarország építésének első évtizede az Európai Unióban', *Kapocs*, 2020/3-4, pp. 3-11.

41 Act CCXI. of 2011 on the Protection of Families, preamble.

42 Balázs Molnár, 'Foglalkoztatottak gyermekvállalását és gyermeknevelését segítő ellátások Magyarországon', *Munkajog*, 2021/1, pp. 64-71.

43 Zsuzsa Makay, 'Családtámogatás, női munkavállalás', *in* Judit Monostori *et al.* (eds.), *Demográfiai Portré 2018. Jelentés a magyar népesség helyzetéről*, KSH Népességtudományi Kutatóintézet, Budapest, p. 83.

44 Id. p. 71.

45 At the end of 2019, most residence permits in the EU were issued for the following reasons: family (38%), work (17%), asylum (9%), education (1%) and other (32%). *See* Eurostat, Residence Permits Data. *See also* at https://ec.europa.eu/info/strategy/priorities-2019-2024/promoting-our-european-way-life/statistics-migration-europe_en.

46 Action Plan on Integration and Inclusion (2021-2027), 24 November 2020, COM(2020) 758 final, p. 3.

Hungarian Yearbook of International Law and European Law 2021 (9) 1
doi: 10.5553/HYIEL/266627012021009001006

financial resources from the state budget, which however suffered immediate shrinkage due to the pandemic. According to preliminary data, the deficit of the general government sector in 2020 was HUF 3,870 billion, 8.1% of GDP.[47]

Already in May 2020 the Hungarian State Audit Office stressed the importance of maintaining the support of families instead of cutting back benefits:

> "The analysis shows that the significant decline in the number and proportion of people living in poverty between 2010 and 2018 was mainly due to a significant increase in employment and a concomitant decline in unemployment. The loss of jobs due to the epidemic therefore poses a serious risk to maintaining the progress made in reducing poverty. It is therefore appropriate for economic protection measures to give priority to encouraging the retention of jobs and the creation of new ones. *In order to avoid an increase in the proportion of people living in relative poverty, it is justified to continue the priority support for families with children and to gradually introduce a 13-month pension.*"[48]

In 2020 and 2021 extraordinary measures have been introduced in the social protection system to prevent the marginalization of people with low income and/ or who have young children in Hungary. Support of families with children was imperative because "The two most important institutions and scenes for the reproduction of poverty are the education system and the family."[49]

The distortions of the labor market caused by the COVID-19 crisis were addressed by other means, namely tax reliefs and deferrals of social security contributions as well as wage supplement schemes.[50] *No changes were introduced in the unemployment benefit system which corresponds to the long-term target of Hungary*, namely, to support those who are economically active or make all efforts to become employed. This article intends to present the main features of Hungarian crisis management: first the social implications of COVID-19 will be examined, followed by focusing on some distinct aspects of labor market challenges.

47 *See* at www.ksh.hu/gyorstajekoztatok/#/en/document/krm2012.

48 Gyula Pulay & Júlia Szappanos, *A COVID-19 járvány közpénzügyi hatásainak értékelése*, Állami Számvevőszék, Budapest, 2020, p. 8.

49 Andrea Rácz, 'Social Exclusion in Hungary from a Child Perspective', *International Journal of Child, Youth and Family Studies*, Vol. 6, Issue 3, 2015, p. 459.

50 Gyula Pulay *et al.*, *A járványhelyzettel összefüggő gazdaságvédelmi akcióterv munkaerőpiacra gyakorolt hatásai*, Állami Számvevőszék, Budapest, 2020.

doi: 10.5553/HYIEL/266627012021009001006

3.1. Social Implications in Hungary

3.1.1. Family Benefits

Family benefits can be – as a rule – twofold: universal or contribution-based benefits, and both cash and in kind in these baskets.[51] Universal financial transfers are due to basically everyone having children – these mainly aim at decreasing poverty and inequality.[52] On the other hand, according to EU statistics, the vulnerability of children is largely driven by the labor market status of their parents.[53] Contribution-based benefits for economically active parents help these parents to start or continue their professional career and also to raise their children. Labor market activity is important also in avoiding the so-called inactivity trap, namely that the existence and amount of family support is an incentive to stay at home rather than to orient the parents towards the labor market.

In Hungary, parents are entitled to a *monthly family allowance* (35 EUR per month). The family allowance is a universal benefit and paid, as a general rule, until the child reaches 18 years of age. Additionally, families are entitled to child care allowance (GYES), which is granted to all mothers without eligibility testing until the age of three of the child. The amount of the child care benefit is equal to the minimum amount of old-age pension, which is approximately 90 EUR per month.[54] GYET (early childcare supplement) is another benefit, which is the continuation of GYES if the family raises 3 (or more) children and the smallest is under the age of 8. The universal nature of these benefits has not changed in the last decades, however, the personal scope of GYES has been extended to include grandparents in 2001 and a very important material restriction was lifted in 2013.[55] Prior to 2014, mothers were not entitled to take up work during the payment of the GYES, since 2014 they have been able to pursue paid activities and receive the benefit at the same time.

There are *benefits that require preliminary insurance periods* (contribution-based benefits). If the mother has had 365 days of social security coverage within the 2 years before the child was born, baby-care allowance (CSED) is offered for 168 days, amounting to 70% of the salary earned prior to the child was born, whereby no cap applies. CSED is a maternity benefit. CSED is followed by child care allowance (GYED) that is available from the 169th day until the child reaches the age of two: this is already a family benefit. It amounts to 70% of the salary earned prior to the birth of the child but is a capped at 700 EUR / month and is

51 Csaba Dani & Éva Gellérné Lukács, 'Hazai szabályozás uniós kitekintéssel: családok szociális ellátása; öröklési jog az Európai Unióban', *in* Orsolya Szeibert (ed.), *Család, gyermek, vagyon: A joggyakorlat kihívásai. Családjogi tanulmánykötet*, HVG-ORAC, Budapest, 2012, pp. 481-496.

52 *E.g.* the effects of the new Polish benefit. Iga Magda *et al.*, 'The "Family 500+" Child Allowance and Female Labour Supply in Poland', *IBS Working Papers*, 2018/1.

53 *European Semester Thematic Factsheet*, p. 3.

54 Act LXXXIV of 1998 on the Support of Families.

55 Act CCXXIV of 2013 on the Amendment of Certain Legal Acts Relating to the Restructuring of Childcare Benefits, and to the Enlargement of the Benefit of Exemption from the Payment of Social Contribution Tax.

doi: 10.5553/HYIEL/266627012021009001006

indexed annually.[56] It is equally true here that in 2014 the restrictions on engaging in paid activities were lifted. Of course, stay-at-home-motherhood is still an option, but the choice to return to the labor market without losing the benefit lies with the family. As of 1 January 2020, non-retired grandparents may become entitled to child care allowance if they undertake to care for their grandchild. The legal regime thereby *tries to counteract both poverty and the inactivity trap of parents*.

An important innovation has been introduced regarding CSED during COVID-19: from 1 July 2021 the amount of CSED will be increased from 70 per cent of the income to 100 per cent thereof. As a result, the unique situation will evolve that *mothers will earn a higher net income after childbirth than when they were still working*, as no social security contributions are deducted from the CSED, only personal income tax is payable. And if someone spends the childcare period with her fourth child, the amount of CSED is equal to the amount of the previous gross salary. This is a very significant financial support for families during the six months immediately following the birth of a child, as the mother is in a more financially favorable position during this period than when she was still working.[57]

During the first wave of COVID-19, the government *extended the eligibility period of the above-mentioned family benefits*, that would have expired during the emergency period between 1 March and 30 June 2020 for families with small children. Entitlements to GYES and GYET and also GYED were extended until 30 June 2020.[58] According to data collected by the Hungarian State Treasury, over 30,000 families benefitted from the extension of GYES/ GYET.[59] GYES and GYET are paid out to around 180,000 families monthly: with the extension approximately 2 per cent of them and 14 per cent of those already receiving benefits for small children were supported. Around 105,000 families, on average, were receiving the contribution-based benefit GYED, but there is no available data on the number of extensions during the first wave of COVID-19. The author's estimation is that around 10 per cent of child care benefits were due to expire in the period between March and June 2020, *i.e.* the extension likely covered approximately 10,000 families.

Accordingly, about 40,000 families with small children benefitted from the extension of child care allowances during the first wave of COVID-19. *No similar measures were adopted during the second wave*. During the third wave of COVID-19 the extension measures were reintroduced for GYES, GYET and GYED similarly to

56 Both CSED and GYED can be found in Act LXXXIII of 1997 on Mandatory Health Insurance.

57 Molnár 2021, p. 67.

58 Government Decree No. 59/2020. (III. 23.) on extending entitlement to certain maternity and family benefits. The end of extension was declared by Article 71 of Act LVII of 2020 on the Termination of the State of Emergency as of 18 June 2020.

59 Éva Gellérné Lukács, *Social Security in Times of Corona from a Comparative Law Perspective, Country Report: Hungary*, 2021, forthcoming, p. 71.

doi: 10.5553/HYIEL/266627012021009001006

the first wave, reaching out to appr. 9,000 families.[60] The transitory regime in the first and third waves prohibited the overlap of benefits, *i.e.* no other additional benefits or allowances could be claimed by the family during the extended eligibility period.

3.1.2. Housing Benefits

The area of housing, as an important factor of family-planning, has been addressed by unprecedented measures in Hungary over the last decade. Regarding housing, the Hungarian situation is special: the ratio of people who rent their homes is very low in Hungary, *most people aim for home ownership*. A KINCS survey[61] revealed that according to Hungarians in reproductive age the most important factors that influence childbearing are: *(i)* a stable relationship; *(ii)* a secure workplace; *(iii)* an appropriate (own) property.

In 2015 and 2016, the government introduced a housing subsidy scheme for families (CSOK), which is available for purchasing or building a house or flat and also for purchasing and enlarging used properties.[62] Basically the amount of the subsidy depends on the number of children. Families that are raising three or more children, or that undertake to raise at least three children in the future (including the children they already have) may receive a one-off in-cash subsidy of approximately 30,000 EUR for a new house or flat. In addition, they are eligible to another 45,000 EUR residential loan with a state-subsidized interest-rate. Since 2018 the housing allowance covers families with two children as well. An important eligibility condition is that the applicant shall have social insurance coverage prior to the receipt of CSOK. Access to CSOK thereby is connected to legal labor market participation and payment of social security contributions. Every second CSOK contract is concluded by parents who plan on having another child in the future, hence, the birth-promoting effect of CSOK is very significant for Hungary,[63] in addition to the housing market stimulus effect. In the period from January 2016 to December 2020, the number of CSOK disbursed by credit institutions was almost 156 thousand, amounting to HUF 386 billion.[64]

As from 1 July 2019, a new type of an interest-free loan has been made available for married couples where the wife is between the ages of 18 and 40, in an amount of maximum 30,000 EUR. If the couple has a child, repayment will be suspended for 3 years at the time of the birth of the child; while the repayment will be suspended for another 3 years upon the birth of a second child with 30%

60 Government Decree No. 128/2021. (III. 13.) on extension of entitlement of certain health insurance and family benefits related to the care and upbringing of the child as amended by Government Decree No. 155/2021. (III. 27.). Measures were in effect from 8 March 2021 to 7 April 2021.

61 *Intergenerációs kutatás a reprodukciós kort meghaladott idősebb generáció és a reprodukciós korban lévő fiatalok körében*, Kopp Mária Intézet, Budapest, 2019, p. 17.

62 Government Decree No. 16/2016. (II. 10.) on state subsidy for building and purchasing a new flat; Government Decree No. 17/2016. (II. 10.) on subsidy for purchasing and enlarging used flat.

63 Orsolya Béres & Tibor Papházi, 'Családi Otthonteremtési Kedvezményben (CSOK) részesülő családok szocio-demográfiai jellemzői', *Kapocs*, 2019/1-2.

64 *See* at www.ksh.hu/hir_210503.

doi: 10.5553/HYIEL/266627012021009001006

of the outstanding debt released. The entire remaining amount will be released upon the birth of the third child. Regarding already existing (old) mortgages, at the birth of the second child the government will deduct *cca*. 3000 EUR from the mortgages of parents and 9000 EUR at the birth of the third child (and subsequent 3000 EUR in the case of further live births).

The state has further bolstered CSOK during COVID-19. As of 1 January 2021, families building a two-generation house by constructing a separate flat in the attic of the house will be eligible for the full CSOK subsidy amount. The 4 percent levy for purchasing a house/flat will be abolished for CSOK properties. The VAT of newly built houses will be reduced by 22 per cent (from 27 per cent to 5 per cent), and the state will reimburse the remaining 5 per cent VAT for families that purchase their homes through the CSOK housing program. The conditions of the interest-free loan have also been adjusted to the realities of COVID-19. If the wife completed the fortieth or forty-one years of age (which is a condition for the loan) between 18 July 2020 and 10 March 2021, or during the first emergency, the couple remained entitled to the loan until the 30th day after the end of the emergency.[65] Additionally, a moratorium on payments of loans introduced in March 2020 to mitigate the effects of the COVID-19 pandemic had been used by 43 per cent of home loan borrowers by the end of 2020, in about 286,000 cases.

Furthermore, in order to help families living in rural areas the overarching *Hungarian Village Program boosts infrastructural and community investments in the countryside*. The Village Housing Subsidy Program supports the energy efficient housing of families living in the smallest settlements of the country.

Last but not least, in order to improve the housing conditions of families raising children, to encourage the renewal of the domestic housing stock and to whiten the construction sector, *a non-refundable home renovation subsidy* was also introduced during the COVID-19 pandemic, in November 2020.[66]

3.2. Labor Market Challenges in Hungary

3.2.1. General Observations Regarding COVID-19

The European Labor Market faces challenges due to our changing world, which indeed has fed lots of discussion on the jobs of European citizens and growth over the last decade, and also as a follow-up of the Brexit referendum in June 2016.[67]

Digitalization and automation are putting great pressure on the labor market, and this pressure became more visible and tangible with COVID-19. According to statistics, *one-fifth of workers did ICT-based mobile work or telework*

65 *See* at www.portfolio.hu/bank/20201209/tobb-konnyitest-jelentett-be-a-kormany-a-csaladtamogatasoknal-a-koronavirus-miatt-461004.

66 Government Decree No. 518/2020. (XI. 25.) on home renovation support for families with children.

67 Éva Gellérné Lukács, 'Brexit – A Point of Departure for the Future in the Field of the Free Movement of Persons', *ELTE Law Journal*, 2016/1, pp. 141-162; Lilla Nóra Kiss, 'The Optician's Dilemma: Can All These Lenses Be Polished into the Same Frame or Do We Need New Frames, too? BREXIT: Time to Reform EU Citizenship?', *Curentul Juridic*, 2019/2, pp. 21-37.

doi: 10.5553/HYIEL/266627012021009001006

regularly or occasionally already in 2015.[68] While for example in Denmark 38% of the workers did ICT-based or telework, in Italy it was only 8%. These proportions dramatically increased during the pandemic, as both employers and employees needed to adapt to this situation and survive the upcoming period somehow. Two sectors continued to grow (in addition to the health sector), with their net job creation at an even higher level in 2019-2020 compared with 2018-2019: the information and communication technologies (ICT) sector, and the professional, scientific and technical activities sector.[69] In fact, these knowledge-intensive sectors were the sole bastions of job growth across most EU Member States.

This evidences that not all sectors were affected equally by COVID-19. The occupations that revolve around social interaction and which require physical contact evidently suffered more by the lockdown, mostly because in these occupations there are limited options for working from home (teleworking). These are arts, entertainment and recreation, wholesale and retail trade, transport, accommodation and food service activities.[70] Other sectors were hit by different negative developments. These include the circumventing of rights to enforce (unjustified) dismissals,[71] the non-compliance with protective measures such as distance regulations, exposure of increased risk of infection and government-imposed adjustments to working hours, especially in the health sector.[72] Distortion of the labor market is the detrimental result of the pandemic, which can only be partially measured by employment statistics. People who would wish to work more or wish to pursue other occupations (like the ones prior to the COVID-19 but were lost) are statistically 'employed' but obviously their labor market situation has worsened.

In the Hungarian labor market several significant positive changes were seen between 2010 and 2020. In 2010, less than 3.7 million people were employed, while in 2019, more than 4.4 million people.[73] The unemployment rate has fallen from 11.2 per cent to 3.4 per cent over the past decade, and Hungary moved from being the country with the eighth highest unemployment in the EU to the Member State with the fourth lowest rate.[74] The employment rate for men rose from 65.5 per cent to 83.1 per cent.[75] However, perhaps more relevant now is the result that Malta alone was able to increase the level of female employment in the EU to a greater extent than Hungary. The relevant figure expanded from 54.6 per

68 *See* at www.eurofound.europa.eu/news/news-articles/covid-19-could-permanently-change-teleworking-in-europe.

69 *Benchmarking Working Europe 2020. Covid-19 and the World of Work: The Impact of a Pandemic*, ETUI, Brussels, 2020, p. 56.

70 Id. p. 21.

71 Volker Stück, 'Abmahnung und Kündigung im Zusammenhang mit Corona', *Arbeitsrecht Aktuell*, 2021/3, p. 70.

72 *See* at www.economist.com/graphic-detail/2020/11/24/people-are-working-longer-hours-during-the-pandemic.

73 *See* at https://ec.europa.eu/eurostat/databrowser/view/lfsi_emp_a/default/table?lang=en.

74 *See* at https://ec.europa.eu/eurostat/databrowser/view/une_rt_a/default/table?lang=en.

75 *See* at https://ec.europa.eu/eurostat/databrowser/view/LFSI_EMP_A__custom_517061/default/table?lang=en.

doi: 10.5553/HYIEL/266627012021009001006

cent in 2010 to 67.6 per cent in 2019.[76] It is particularly gratifying that by 2019, the employment rate of women aged 25-49 with three or more children had increased from 31.7 per cent to 57.1 per cent compared with 2010.[77]

COVID-19 hit the labor market considerably in 2020: loss of jobs, reduction and suspension of work had to be counteracted by governmental intervention. During the COVID-19 pandemic, tax relief provisions were adopted in the form of payroll tax relief[78]*(i)* for employers in certain sectors, who employed natural persons; *(ii)* for self-employed persons; and *(iii)* for persons working for an undertaking as a member.[79] The economic sectors included, among others, were: the accommodation and food services industry; sports and entertainment services; the production of film, videos and movies; travel agencies; passenger transport; gambling; the production of newspapers and periodicals; and the organization of conferences and other events. Employers, self-employed persons and persons working as members of undertakings were exempt from paying payroll taxes from March to June 2020. During the second wave of the pandemic, the payroll tax relief was re-introduced for the period November 2020 to February 2021 for those same economic sectors.[80] These measures aimed at protecting jobs and to support employers to prevent redundancies.

During the first wave of COVID-19, the wage subsidy program contributed to the retention of nearly 270,000 jobs, but the State Audit Office emphasized:

> "[...] the majority of employers considered the crisis to be temporary and treated it as such; at the cost of significant financial sacrifices, it therefore retained part of the workforce. State aid in this provided assistance. However, with the strengthening of a possible second wave, the decline can no longer be considered temporary, therefore, further redundancy waves may occur."[81]

During the second COVID-19 wave, the so-called sectoral wage subsidy was introduced. The targeted sectors were the tourism and accommodation industries. Until 18 February 2021, employers were able to apply for wage subsidies; the program aimed to protect approximately 130,000 workers.

As a result of these interventions the *employment rate increased* in March 2021 (the first month in which increase was observed compared with previous years), it stood at 72.5 per cent of the economically productive population (15-64 years). It was 0.7% higher compared with the same period in 2020, the average number of employed persons was 4,616,000, which is 41,000

76 *See* at https://ec.europa.eu/eurostat/databrowser/view/LFSI_EMP_A__custom_517061/default/table?lang=en.

77 *10+1 tény a 2010-es években gyermeket szült édesanyákról*, Budapest, 2020, p. 14.

78 Act LII of 2018 on Social Contribution Tax. This is a solidarity tax paid by the employer on top of the employee's wages and is also paid by self-employed persons and members of undertakings.

79 Act LVII of 2020 on the Termination of the State of Emergency, Article 34.

80 Government Decree No. 485/2020. (XI. 10.), Article 5(4).

81 *See* Pulay *et al.* 2020.

doi: 10.5553/HYIEL/266627012021009001006

more than during the same period of the previous year.[82] At the same time, the number of members of Hungarian households working abroad decreased by 39,000. The unemployment rate increased despite these efforts and state interventions: the average number of unemployed persons between January and March 2021 was 215,000, an increase of 42,000 persons compared to the same period in 2020.[83]

COVID-19 also urged protection of one of the most vulnerable groups in the labor market, *young workers*. They have been granted two important benefits recently. From 1 January 2020 onwards, all mothers who are caring for at least four children, or who have cared for four or more children in the past, are fully exempt from paying personal income tax until they retire.[84] Additionally, in 2021, the government announced that from 2022, as the third state after Poland and Croatia, Hungary will introduce a personal income tax exemption for young people under the age of twenty-five.[85] The measure is awaited to increase the rate of young workers while at the same time they will be socially protected hence they will be affiliated with the Hungarian social security system. Social insurance coverage will be important for young workers and couples because at the time of starting a family they will be able to demonstrate the required preliminary insurance periods for housing benefits.

3.2.2. *Importance of Childcare Facilities*

Childcare facilities are generally understood to be caring and educational spaces for children below mandatory schooling age (usually the age of 6). Childcare facilities are part of the social service system or the educational system (or both, it varies between Member States), and they contribute to a very large extent to the employability of mothers and fathers.

In 2002 the Barcelona European Council set objectives with regard to the availability of high quality and affordable childcare facilities for pre-school children, through two targets, *i.e.* 90% of children from age 3 until mandatory school age and 33% of children under 3.[86] In 2018 the Commission assessed in a report to what extent Member States had progressed towards implementing the Barcelona objectives between 2013-2016.[87] The overall rate of children cared for in formal childcare structures, from 3 to the mandatory school-going age increased considerably in the EU between 2011-2016 from 83% to 86.3%. The Commission, in its Gender Equality Strategy 2020-2025 referred to the revision

82 *See* at www.ksh.hu/gyorstajekoztatok/#/hu/document/fog2103.

83 *See* at www.ksh.hu/gyorstajekoztatok/#/hu/document/mun2103.

84 Act CXVII of 1995 on Personal Income Tax, Section 29/D.

85 *See* at https://mandiner.hu/cikk/20210115_orban_viktor.

86 Presidency Conclusions, Barcelona European Council 15-16 March 2002.

87 Commission Report on the development of childcare facilities for young children with a view to increase female labor participation, strike a work-life balance for working parents and bring about sustainable and inclusive growth in Europe (the "Barcelona objectives"), COM(2018) 273 final.

Hungarian Yearbook of International Law and European Law 2021 (9) 1
doi: 10.5553/HYIEL/266627012021009001006

of the Barcelona targets "to ensure further upwards convergence among Member States of early childhood education and care" (ECEC).[88]

The situation of Hungary is peculiar in this respect. On the one hand, increase in the rate of children in formal childcare from age 3 until mandatory school age has been striking in Hungary between 2013-2016, it amounted to 15 percentage points, from 73% to 88%. Full-time childcare (30 hours or more a week) is used most among children attending childcare.[89] In this sense the Hungarian approach is fully aligned with the European target objectives.

As regards *children under the age of 3, Hungarian family policy supports flexibility*. It means that mothers or fathers of small children are given the freedom to have a say in what they judge the best interest of their child before the age of compulsory education. The reinforcement of the family benefit system gives mothers and fathers the choice to stay at home with their small children under the age of 3. On the other hand, overarching reforms were undertaken to increase nursery care options. Over the last decade, Hungary experienced some ups and downs in this area. In 1989, there were 1000 nurseries in Hungary, covering overwhelmingly all demands, however this system was largely dismantled.[90] As a results of reinstalling public day-care nursery now available places are able to cover about 18% of children under the age of 3 and developments are continuous.[91] Additionally, since 2019 those parents who could not find a public nursery place for their children have been entitled to a monthly contribution of 110 EUR to be able to pay the fee of the private nursery.

During the COVID-19 pandemic, public nurseries for children under the age of 3 were partially exempt from closure as opposed to schools for older children. During the first wave all childcare institutions fell under the closure (also nurseries). However, during the second wave and the third wave public day-care nurseries remained open while kindergartens (during the second wave) and schools (both during the second and the third waves) remained closed.[92]

Closely related to ECEC is the provision of full-day education in primary schools. The European Social Partners issued a joint statement on childcare provisions in the EU[93] at the end of 2020 stating that

> "there is also *a shortage of after school hours and holiday childcare in Europe*. This is detrimental for children's well-being and represents a major obstacle to

88 Gender Equality Strategy 2020-2025, p. 12. Early childhood education and care (ECEC) is a key tool.

89 The Barcelona objectives, p. 10.

90 Zsuzsanna Makay, 'Family Support System – Childraising – Employment', *in* Judit Monostori *et al.* (eds.), *Demographic Portrait of Hungary 2015*, Budapest, 2015, p. 68. In 2019, there were 50,000 places and approximately 280,000 children.

91 Id. p. 69. The aim of the Government is to reach 70,000 places until 2022, that would address all demands.

92 Schools were closed between 8 March 2021 and were opened for children aged 6-12 on 19 April 2021 and for children aged 12-18 on 10 May 2021. Public-day care nurseries remained open.

93 *See* at https://lddk.lv/wp-content/uploads/2020/11/13-11-2020_Joint-social-partner-statement-childcare.pdf.

doi: 10.5553/HYIEL/266627012021009001006

> full-time paid work for parents with school age children to remain in employment and increase their working hours, as well as attract more women into the labor market."[94]

In Hungary the possibility of full-day education and care for children under the age of 10 has been a long-standing tradition, but it was made obligatory in 2017.[95] The state is playing a crucial role in the arena of education. In Hungary education is free for every child (primary and secondary schools and also tertiary education if the young adult is in receipt of a state financed scholarship). Free textbooks are granted at the primary and secondary levels of education, as well as free or heavily subsidized meals, that have been continuously provided for families during the closures of the nurseries, kindergartens and schools.

Educational attainment is the output of the socialization process and also one of the most important factors in the determination of adult social status.[96] Full-day childcare facilities enable children to develop their full potential, they assist mothers and fathers to work, while also contributing to the mitigation of differences in the financial status of families.

4. Concluding Thoughts

COVID-19 adversely affected the EU, including Hungary, especially the labor markets and generated challenges at all levels of the social protection system. It is strongly believed that the unprecedented policy responses across the EU have been well-targeted in their scope, direction, and speed of implementation which, in accordance with the Porto Declaration, will result in an inclusive recovery. It is also time to return to issues which were at the center of societal reflections prior to the pandemic (including demographic challenges and struggling social inequalities).

Hungary has in many ways followed similar path in tackling the challenges of the pandemic as the majority of the EU Member States. The wage supplement schemes for sensitive sectors in the labor market is a clear example, the exact volume and effects of which will be measurable at a later stage, especially in the light of the fact that unemployment benefits were not amended throughout COVID-19. The payment of benefits for families in vulnerable situations (families with small children and large families) were also in the focus of tackling COVID. In addition, however, some special measures were introduced that differ from the mainstream. These are particularly related to the housing situation of families and supporting young generations. In 2020-2021 the existing framework of housing benefits has been finetuned, eligibility criteria have been broadened and new types of benefits and subsidies have been introduced. Red tape had constantly been reduced; the entire administrative procedure may now be

94 Id. p. 2.

95 József Mayer & Attila Varga, 'Dilemmák az egész napos iskola nevelési-oktatási programjának bevezethetőségéről (Kritikai észrevételek)', *Új Pedagógiai Szemle*, 2017/1-2, pp. 18-38.

96 Rácz 2015, p. 460.

doi: 10.5553/HYIEL/266627012021009001006

conducted in an electronic manner. Since 2020 mothers of 4 or more children have been exempted from paying personal income tax for their entire lifetime. Young workers until the age of 25 will be granted exemption of paying personal income tax as of 2022. Obviously, these measures are closely related to previous measures, developments must be seen as a genuine continuation of former family policies. Important to note, that the impetus has not been broken by COVID-19, most probably the continuity and reinforcement of the chosen path is of utmost importance now.

Regarding housing benefits, the CSOK, the interest-free loan and the home renovation subsidy are all dependent upon previously performed social insurance periods by the applicants. Access to housing benefits is thereby connected to legal labor market participation and payment of social security contributions beforehand. Housing benefits evidence best that the emphasis of support has been put on employment-related and wage-related benefits, also driven by the notion of avoiding the inactivity trap of parents. The expansion of housing benefits might evolve into a strong incentive for young people and young couples currently living and working in other EU Member States or elsewhere in the world to return to Hungary.

Family policies, family mainstreaming is more important than ever, to battle the reproduction of poverty and to help boys and girls "to pursue their chosen path in life, where they have equal opportunities to thrive and where they can equally participate in and lead our European society".[97] In Hungary, supporting families and children remained a cross-cutting principle throughout the COVID-19, the coronavirus caused no break in this either. Despite the social and economic difficulties caused by the virus, there has been no cutting or termination of benefits, quite on the contrary.

The reinforcement of the family benefit system in Hungary gives mothers and fathers the choice to stay at home with their small children under the age of 3. During the COVID-19 pandemic the extension of the period of entitlement guaranteed financial stability for those who opted for staying at home. On the other hand, childcare facilities for children under the age of 3 (public day-care nurseries) remained open during both the second and the third wave to assist mothers and fathers to remain in employment or even increase their working hours if they decided to pursue their gainful activities during the pandemic.

We can only endorse the summary given in the report of Kopp Mária Institute in 2018 as a compass for the future:

> "The standard of living of those communities and nations is higher, and they are more successful and more likely to establish permanent values, where intergenerational cooperation is strong. In these societies, a promising future, a successful present, and experience appears in both private and community life at the same time. The wisdom of those with a decent career, the impetus and innovation of people in their working ages, the agility of youngsters who want to change their fate and the fate of the community, and

97 Gender Equality Strategy 2020-2025, p. 2.

doi: 10.5553/HYIEL/266627012021009001006

the curiosity of children create values and lay the foundation of the future of the nation together."[98]

98 *Családbarát fordulat 2010-2018*, Emberi Erőforrások Minisztériuma, Budapest, 2018, p. 9.

doi: 10.5553/HYIEL/266627012021009001006

Defining the Common European Way of Life

Exploring the Concept of Europeanness

Lilla Nóra Kiss & Orsolya Johanna Sziebig[*]

Abstract

The article focuses on the interpretation of the European Way of Life and the concept of Europeanness. Ursula von der Leyen determined the Promotion of the European Way of Life as a priority of the 2019-2024 Commission. The purpose behind this was to strengthen European democracy and place the citizens into the center of decision-making. The article examines the role of European identity, European citizenship and those historical-traditional conditions that make our way of life 'common'. The Common European Way of Life may be defined as a value system based on the established legal basis of EU citizenship that can be grasped in the pursuit of common principles and the exercise of rights guaranteed to all EU citizens, limited only under exceptional circumstances and ensuring socio-economic convergence. The article covers general conceptual issues but also focuses on the extraordinary impact of the COVID-19. Lastly, the relevant aspects of enlargement policy are also explored.

Keywords: European identity, Common European Way of Life, coronavirus, European citizenship, Hungary, enlargement policy, Europeanness.

1. Introductory Thoughts

Have we ever considered that we are living our lives relatively simultaneously in all parts of Europe? We start and end our days roughly at the same time, as there is only a three-hour time lag between the westernmost and easternmost points of Europe. Do we have anything else in common in our everyday lives? Is there a common European way of life? If so, what exactly does it mean? What does Europeanness mean? What does the term European identity mean? Is it the same as the European way of life?

Our study revolves around European identity and European values presented in the "Promoting our way of Life" portfolio in December 2019 by Ursula von der Leyen, current President of the European Commission.[1] Vice-President

* Lilla Nóra Kiss: Visiting Scholar at Antonin Scalia Law School, George Mason University, Virginia, US. Orsolya Johanna Sziebig: senior lecturer, University of Szeged.

1 The Commission's Programme for 2020 [COM(2020) 37 final], at https://ec.europa.eu/info/sites/info/files/cwp-2020-publication_en.pdf.

doi: 10.5553/HYIEL/266627012021009001007

Margaritis Schinas is responsible for the portfolio, together with other four key[2] policies.[3] The article presents the concept and definition of the European way of life. It also reflects how the coronavirus affects our way of life, with particular regard to the Member States' restrictive measures.

The EU is unique among international organizations: it can be considered a *sui generis* entity rather than a classical international organization. Its uniqueness lies in the fact that it appears to be a unit from the outside but is an extremely heterogeneous community from the inside. From the inside, we tend amplify the differences among nations within the EU and tend to forget about similarities. If we were to ask a person from a third country, it is unlikely that he would mention sharp differences between individual European nations. Our unity is based in part on our common historical traditions, the unifying and decisive role of the Christian religion, and in part on the respect for democracy and other fundamental values. The article examines the concept of Europeanness and the European way of life from multiple aspects, considering the impact of enlargement policy and COVID-19. Nowadays, enlargement and neighborhood policies are significant EU policy sectors, especially from a Hungarian perspective. Consequently, the Authors analyze *how the newcomers fit into the European way of life*, or *how this concept may change due to the enlargement*, taking into account the role of religion and religious traditions in a common way of life. Do religion or religious traditions constitute compulsory elements of the European way of life? If so, to what extent?

It is evident that in case we accept that core historical, traditional, cultural, political, social, economic and other elements connect us in Europe, we can examine those links and develop a concept for that relationship. Once we have the concept, it is possible to interpret and examine how planned or extraordinary changes [such as the shocking (unexpected) COVID-19 and enlargement policy] affect that definition. In our view, integration could be evaluated from several angles. One way is to analyze the political and economic relationship of the Member States. Another is to see whether Member State citizens, the so-called Union citizens have something in common besides their states' membership status. The former analysis is mainly a general integration-history evaluation that depends on who interprets the process and from what perspective, but it focuses on state-level relations. The latter concentrates on the citizens of the Member States. This perspective is a *novum* that *goes beyond the interpretation of European citizenship but is nevertheless based on it*. The main difference between the two viewpoints is that the European way of life connects the "People of the European Union" without evaluating the interconnectedness of the Member States. We can differentiate between top-down (EU level), and bottom-up (citizens level) approaches. However, to understand the citizens' cultural and traditional

2 These are: migration, security, employment, education.

3 Margaritis Schinas – letter of credence, 2019, at https://ec.europa.eu/commission/commissioners/sites/comm-cwt2019/files/commissioner_mission_letters/president_von_der_leyens_mission_letter_to_margaritis_schinas.pdf.

doi: 10.5553/HYIEL/266627012021009001007

linkages, state-to-state relationships must be understood. Therefore, in a nutshell, the Authors provide some historical remarks in the following.

Generally, the states' political position on the level and form of the European integration has never been genuinely uniform. The differing views were closely tied to the form and extent of cooperation and the states involved. Proposals have also been made several times to move towards a federal[4] Europe, but there has never been a political-social consensus for that concept. Regarding the degree of cooperation, there are numerous examples of differentiated integration in selected areas.[5] It is no coincidence that the concepts related to two- or multi-speed Europe (which have been in place for over thirty years) have also entered the political-legal-social public consciousness. Just as there was no uniform vision of the degree of cooperation in European integration, we can name only *mandatory and additional conceptual elements* regarding Europeanness, European identity and the European Way of Life.

2. The Core of Europeanness – European Way of Life or European Identity?

Before precisely defining the European way of life, the Authors focus on the main historical events that influenced Europeanness. Understanding the roots of European identity and the concepts that shaped European integration is necessary to define the modern vision of a common way of life.

2.1. Historical Remarks

Identity means (self)identity, the full definability of ourselves. Does our European origin belong to the definition of ourselves? In the Authors' view, *common values can be attached to European identity*. Mutual respect for democratic values is one of the essential elements of the afore-mentioned virtues. Under European identity, the Authors mean the shared values of the citizens of the Member States, also referred to EU citizens since the Maastricht Treaty. These values are based on the common socio-cultural worth, historical traditions, and heritage of Europeans.

Nevertheless, the concept[6] of EU citizenship has been on the agenda since the 1970s. The first practical steps were taken after the 1972 Paris Summit,

4 *See e.g.* White Paper on the Future of Europe Reflections and scenarios for the EU27 by 2025 COM(2017) 2025 final.

5 The Single European Act allowed a Member State to opt-out of cooperation and apply a "national provision" to the internal market. The Maastricht Treaty laid down three phases for the implementation of EMU. In addition, the Maastricht Treaty provided for permanent differentiation thanks to a protocol annexed to the Treaty, which enshrined the possibility of opt-outs for the UK and Denmark. Additional measures for multi-speed integration include: the euro area and the Schengen area. The existing Treaties also provide an opportunity for enhanced cooperation.

6 On EU citizenship, *see e.g.* Zsófia Asztalos, '*Az uniós polgárság és a diszkrimináció tilalma*' PhD dissertation, Miskolc, 2009, at http://midra.uni-miskolc.hu/document/5665.

doi: 10.5553/HYIEL/266627012021009001007

according to which a sense of European identity is needed to deepen integration.[7] The European Summit developed the European Identity Declaration at the 1973 Copenhagen Summit. The importance of citizens' involvement was further strengthened at the 1974 Paris Summit. Since then, reference has increasingly been made to Community (EU) citizenship as a *status civitatis*.[8] EU citizenship has rendered the citizens' supranational status a common denominator in terms of content by providing them the same economic and political rights on the legal basis of the citizenship. As a result of its careful, persistent and extensive interpretation of European law, the CJEU now has a wealth of case-law, covering the foundations of EU citizenship.

The Member States can only restrict the free movement rights of EU citizens on the grounds of public interest. The current public health emergency posed by the COVID-19 pandemic is a significant example of public interest that justifies restrictions on free movements. The creation of EU citizenship can be seen as one of the generators of a common sense of identity, which could later serve as grounds for defining, promoting, and protecting the European way of life. Several questions can be raised concerning the new vision of being European. Firstly, what is a common European identity? Is it a simple set of political values or purely the respect for our historical traditions and cultural heritage? The Authors explore the differences between common values and European identity, concentrating on the relevant Treaty provisions and interpretation.

2.2. Common Values as European Identity

In the following, the conceptual elements of European identity are summarized, differentiating among mandatory and optional elements. These elements appear as a part of treaty-law and also as a part of the general concept of Europeanness. The formation of 'individual identity' and 'self-identity' is a result of many factors: origin, family heritage, studies, the socio-economic environment. These all influence a person's definition of himself.

In the past decades, public opinion initially prioritized the citizens' *geographical connection to Europe as a mandatory conceptual element of European identity*. However, Europeanness alone cannot be interpreted as a kind of geographical criterion. The broad idea of Europeanness is also demonstrated by the interpretation of the term 'European state', a requirement for accession to the Council of Europe. In 1994, the Parliamentary Assembly adopted[9] its recommendation on the interpretation of Europeanness. According to the still relevant interpretation, close cultural ties with Europe and adherence to fundamental values may justify accession to the international organization of

7 European Commission, Bulletin of the European Communities, No. 5. 1975, at http://aei.pitt.edu/57736/1/BUL134.pdf.

8 On the development of EU citizenship, *see* Patricia Mindus, *European Citizenship after Brexit, Freedom of Movement and Rights of Residence*, Palgrave Macmillan, 2017, pp. 8-15.

9 Resolution 1247 of the Parliamentary Assembly of the Council of Europe Recommendation (1994).

 Hungarian Yearbook of International Law and European Law 2021 (9) 1
doi: 10.5553/HYIEL/266627012021009001007

new Member States, which would not meet requirement of being European on a purely geographical basis.[10]

The European location raises the question of whether *EU enlargement could be hampered by the geographical borders of the European continent*.[11] For example, even before Turkey became a candidate state to join to the EU, one of the most critical obstacles was that only 3% of its territory is located in Europe. The country was granted candidate status, *i.e.* the integration of EU law into Turkish national law is ongoing, at least, in principle.[12] Interestingly, Turkey was nevertheless admitted to the Council of Europe in 1950 as the thirteenth state.[13] Based on the above, it can be concluded that the European location is not an obligatory condition of becoming a candidate state. However, they can serve as a starting point for defining Europeanness, which can be overridden by adherence to European values, cultural connections, and acceptance of European traditions.[14]

Although the Council of Europe's view will not directly influence the concept of Europeanness for the EU, it highlights the need for a flexible approach. In the Authors' view, instead of adding the European geographical location as a mandatory conceptual element of European identity, *the respect and commitment to European values set out in Article 2 TEU itself is much more expedient*. Article 2 TEU declares that

> "The Union is founded on the values of respect for human dignity, freedom, democracy, equality, the rule of law, and respect for human rights, including the rights of persons belonging to minorities. These values are common to the Member States in a society in which pluralism, non-discrimination, tolerance, justice, solidarity, and equality between women and men prevail."[15]

Does Article 2 TEU provide a legal basis for defining a common European way of life? Article 2 TEU was inserted by the Treaty of Lisbon and over the last decade an intense debate unfolded around the value system established by the provision. Not just the listed values were called into question, but also the EU's limited competences to pursue and enforce them. There is no doubt that Article 2 establishes basic requirements for Member States and for further candidate

10 The Council of Europe has listed Azerbaijan, Armenia and Georgia as countries eligible for cultural relations.

11 Candidates: Northern Macedonia (2004), Turkey (1987), Albania and Serbia (2009), Montenegro (2008). Hungarian Commissioner Olivér Várhelyi is responsible for the European Neighborhood and Enlargement Policy.

12 Tekin Caner, *Debating Turkey in Europe: Identities and Concepts*, De Gruyter, Oldenbourg, 2020, pp. 129-130.

13 A full list of the 47 Member States of the Council of Europe at www.coe.int/en/web/portal/47-members-states.

14 About European values, *see* Oriane Calligaro *et al.*, 'Values in the EU Policies and Discourse. First Assessment', *Les Cahiers du Cevipol*, Vol. 3, Issue 3, 2016, pp. 5-52.

15 Article 2 TEU.

doi: 10.5553/HYIEL/266627012021009001007

countries as well.[16] As a result, "human dignity, freedom, democracy, equality, the rule of law, and respect for human rights, including the rights of persons belonging to minorities" are at the heart of Europeanness, regardless of the surrounding debate.

As an optional (additional) conceptual element of Europeanness, we can mark *the protection of other European values*. These include the European vision of security and safe living environment (*e.g.* a non-terrorist environment or joint action against the spread of the coronavirus pandemic), environmental protection, climate change mitigation, protection of social values, solidarity among states, the right to internet and information, data protection, and the joint protection of additional issues that complement all of these can also be part of our identity.[17] In this context, the Authors would like to highlight the importance of the area of freedom, security and justice (AFSJ) that is built to promote citizens' rights. The shared management of values makes the above concepts an integral part of our way of life. Furthermore, as part of our way of life, they deserve protection. Is it necessary to look for a legal basis at all to determine the conceptual elements of lifestyle? If not, is it common cultural and social circumstances that determine the common way of life?

In order to answer these questions, we may have to go back to the interpretation of the EU's eloquent motto. The *Unitas via Diversitas*, "united in diversity" has been the motto of the EU since 2000. On the one hand, it refers to diversity between the Member States and its citizens, and on the other hand, to common values in addition to these differences, therefore, it refers to the unity which accepts existing differences. It emphasizes *united nature of the peoples*, and *not unification*, that is, the alliance between different states with common values, respecting each others' diversity.

The Authors address the question whether self-identity includes or could include a sense of belonging to a broader political or religious community? The Authors are of the view that the answer is a resounding yes. The EU consists of Christian Member States[18] in general, however, all of these Member States respect the religious freedom and the free practice of religious rights.[19] Therefore, *Christian religious traditions* could be named as additional elements of the concept of our way of life. *Additional, and not compulsory*. The reason behind is that the freedom of choice regarding religious views is laid down in several European and

16 *See* Cristina Fasone *et al.*, 'Revisiting Art. 2 TEU: A True Union of Values?', *European Papers*, Vol. 5, Issue 1, 2020, pp. 255-277; András Jakab & Dimitry Kochenov (eds.), *The Enforcement of EU Law and Values: Ensuring Member State Compliance*, Oxford University Press, Oxford, 2017.

17 With the withdrawal of the UK on 1 February 2020, we are now counting only 27 Member States, which, instead of the previous 516 million citizens, has approx. 450 million citizens. About Brexit legal issues, *see e.g.* Lilla Nóra Kiss, 'Az Európai Unióból való kilépés jogi kérdései', PhD dissertation, Miskolc, 2019, at http://midra.uni-miskolc.hu/document/33257.

18 *See* Jean-Louis Antoine-Grégoire *et al.*, '*Religious Practice and Observance in the EU Member States*', 2013. at www.europarl.europa.eu/RegData/etudes/etudes/join/2013/474399/IPOL-LIBE_ET (2013)474399_EN.pdf.

19 Jonatas E. M. Machado, 'Freedom of Religion: A View from Europe', *Roger Williams University Law Review*, Vol. 10, Issue 2, 2005, pp. 451-535.

doi: 10.5553/HYIEL/266627012021009001007

universal legal documents, conventions and treaties.[20] Therefore, determining religion as an obligatory element of the European way of life would mean the automatic exclusion of those who are not Christians, but agree on all other European values and exercise the rights of European citizenship. These traditions are decisive, rooted deeply in European history. However, the conceptual elements of values, identity and way of life may differ depending on the person, because these concepts are determined by the citizens themselves and not the states. In general, European states are divided from the Church according to the principle of secularization, thus the execution of acts is not influenced by religious beliefs. The states ensure the frames, such the freedom to practice or refrain from practicing religious beliefs. This is very significant in our view, especially when we intend to take into account those candidate states' accession to the EU, which are not Christian (such as Turkey). The religious views as optional elements of the concept of European identity enable Muslim and other religious communities to become a part of the EU without feeling excluded on this ground. European culture (perhaps exactly because of Christian traditions and the respect for diversity) is generally open to accepting different views. Christian heritage and religion have strong roots in Europe. Therefore, Christian values have significant impact on our way of life and religious aspects could be interpreted only as optional conceptual elements of our way of life.

2.3. The Concept of a Common European Way of Life

The next question is whether, for an EU citizen, the broader community is the EU? *Instead of a common European identity, we propose the use 'common European way of life'*, which could be best captured in the exercise of political and economic rights arising from EU law, complemented by a sense of Europeanness, the conscious experience of belonging to the European community ('Family of nations'). The idea of belonging to a certain nation is never expected to be overridden by the idea of Europeanness. This was never an objective of European integration. Thus, for the time being, the feeling of Europeanness is fulfilled by living the common European way of life, of which the exercise of free movement rights is an integral part.

It is apparent that Europe today faces several challenges, both internal and external in nature, environmental and health-related, which require cooperation, obedience, and respect for the views of Union citizens. The promotion of a common European way of life could be interpreted as a bridge among citizens that connect them across Europe while respect their diversity. In the Authors' view, the European way of life is based on the EU's core values and can be grasped by exercising the rights derived from EU citizenship. The EU's core values include "freedom, democracy, and legal certainty, which are an integral part of the European way of life", as set out in the 2017 Comprehensive Report on

20 Id.

doi: 10.5553/HYIEL/266627012021009001007

Citizenship of the Union.[21] Thus, the key to promoting a European way of life may be found if EU citizens can exercise their rights deriving from their status without hindrance. The European Commission has recognized the potential of identifying the common values of its citizens embodied in the promotion of the European way of life. The current Commission's (2019-2024) program addresses European values in several dimensions. One of the core elements of the von der Leyen-led Commission's six-point program announced in 2019 is the initiative entitled "Promoting our European way of life". The aim is to strengthen values (such as the rule of law) on the European stage, through the development of equality, tolerance and social justice in a Union, where the security of citizens is ensured by a rethought immigration and asylum policy, and close cooperation with the neighboring countries.[22] These values also appear in the primary law discussed earlier, highlighting the correlation between the virtues of European integration and guidelines calling for a common European way of life. At a relatively early stage of European integration, it was already apparent that through economic cooperation and later, through free movement, cooperation between European states could be deepened. This could then be accompanied by citizens' rights and protection on a Union (Community) level. The 1974 *Reyners* case also points to the '*economic and social merger*' between European societies. As the Opinion of the Advocate General in *Reyners* declares, "with economic integration must obviously come to the development of legal relations", that is to say, economic integration necessarily entails the development of legal relations.[23] The Authors believe that the concept of the 'European way of life' is a consequence of the above-mentioned economic and legal development.

The concept of a common European way of life may be grasped as follows: *The common European way of life is a value system*, legally based on EU citizenship, which can be defined as the pursuit of common principles and the exercise of rights guaranteed to all EU citizens, limited only in exceptional cases and ensuring socio-economic convergence.[24]

This concept is *necessarily determined by the historical heritage of the Member States* which shaped their national legal systems. This legal heritage is inevitably the value of the EU as the founding treaties refer to the Member States' constitutional traditions.[25] However, this common constitutional and historical heritage is very diverse, complex and heterogeneous. There are significant economic and social differences between the Western European states that founded and joined the EEC at the beginning and the Central and Eastern European states that joined later, in 2004, at the time of the big bang

21 Comprehensive Report on Citizenship of the Union, 2017, p. 12, at https://ec.europa.eu/home-affairs/sites/default/files/what-is-new/news/news/20170124_eu_citizenship_report_2017_en.pdf.

22 Promoting our European way of life, at https://ec.europa.eu/info/strategy/priorities-2019-2024/promoting-our-european-way-life_en.

23 Judgment of 21 June 1974, *Case C-2/74, Reyners*, ECLI:EU:C:1974:68.

24 Authors' definition.

25 Article 6(3) TEU: "[...] as they result from the constitutional traditions common to the Member States, shall constitute general principles of the Union's law."

doi: 10.5553/HYIEL/266627012021009001007

enlargement. Due to their erstwhile participation in the Soviet bloc, these states have many things in common right down to their relatively simultaneous regime changes. There are several conflicting academic positions regarding the division between the West and the East. Still, without attempting to resolve these, it can be said that there are significant differences between states in terms of the civil sector, the foundations of society and their economy.[26] Although, in principle, these differences do not affect the rights deriving from EU citizenship, they may affect the possibility and framework of exercising them, in particular, due to the different financial means of EU citizens. At the same time, the potential political differences among the Member States may create obstacles to the development of a common European identity.

There is a significant difference between the concept of a common European way of life and the idea of a federal Europe. Promoting the way of life include the respect for the diversity of the citizens and therefore it includes "all European ways of life" instead of determining a special list of conditions that makes "a" way of life "European". Historically, in the beginning of European integration, the federal approach was supported by leading politicians creating "Europe", but it soon failed due to deep historical, political and social cleavages. Ever since, the vision of a federal Europe remained a dream for some, but the majority opted out of it. In our view, the realization of a future European federation cannot be predicted today, as all efforts in this direction (suffice to think of the case of the Constitutional Treaty) have failed.[27]

On the other hand, it cannot be ignored that the first steps of European integration after World War II were geared towards creating a federal Europe. In his famous Zurich speech on 19 September 1946, Churchill projected the creation of a regional alliance, the United States of Europe, modelled on the US.[28] Fifty years after the Schuman Declaration, it is still relevant to quote the words of one of the founding fathers of European unity: "European federation indispensable to the preservation of peace."[29] Part of the truth is that initially, a concrete vision of integration based on political foundations emerged. Still, it was mainly the confrontation between Germany and France that made it impossible to complete this vision in addition to the fact that Member States were never fully agree on *raison d'etre* of a political integration within a federal statehood. Following the founding of the Council of Europe in 1949, this led to the launch of cooperation on economic grounds.[30] Later, with the accession of the United Kingdom in 1973

26 Stefan Lehne, *Europe's East-West Divide: Myth or Reality?*, 11 April 2019, at https://carnegieeurope.eu/2019/04/11/europe-s-east-west-divide-myth-or-reality-pub-78847.

27 The ideal of the federation also resurface in a speech by Joschka Fischer, former German Foreign Minister, at Humbolt University (Berlin), '*From Confederacy to Federation – Thoughts on the Finality of European Integration*', 12 May 2000, at https://ec.europa.eu/dorie/fileDownload.do?docId=192161&cardId=192161.

28 Winston Churchill, speech delivered at the University of Zurich, 19 September 1946, at https://rm.coe.int/16806981f3.

29 The Schuman Declaration – 9 May 1950, at https://europa.eu/european-union/about-eu/symbols/europe-day/schuman-declaration_en.

30 Katalin Gombos, *Az Európai Unió jogának alapjai*, Wolters Kluwer, Budapest, 2012, pp. 20-23.

doi: 10.5553/HYIEL/266627012021009001007

to the EC, the confederative visions[31] emerged, counteracting federative aspirations.

It is important to note that *the common European way of life does not aim to realize a European federation*. On the contrary, it provides a shield of shared values common to every Member State, through strengthening citizens' rights without a constitutional legal basis. All of the Member States pledged to accept and protect these rights when they joined the EU.

2.4. The Interpretation of European Identity in the Case of Hungary

Besides the characteristics that they share, each and every Member State has its history and belief about what it means to be European. In the following, the Authors shortly summarize some aspects of the Hungarian approach to Europeanness.

Since the 1990s, European identity has been at the forefront of the attention of the EU and also on the European Commission's agenda. Although, the issue of European identity already emerged in 1973 when the Heads of State and Government decided to find a better understanding of what European identity means.[32] Several comprehensive surveys were conducted not just to find an acceptable meaning but also to measure the Member States' Europeanisation. European identity is a complex term and has several dimensions. In the communication of the European Commission, these dimensions are the following:

> "Multiple social identities and biographical identity, transnational relationships, collective action, standardization and regulation, cultural production, intercultural translation, inclusion/exclusion, structural conditions and opportunity structures and the public sphere and state-regulated institutions."[33]

These characteristics are in line with the approach of the present article and the Authors' understanding of the European way of life. *For Hungary, the modern concept of Europeanisation started in the 1980s*, still within the frames of the erstwhile Soviet system, when the country sought to join in the European discussion. In the economic sphere, Hungary had been balancing between the Council for Mutual Economic Assistance (Comecon) and the EEC and entered into direct communication with the EEC in 1983.[34] Besides being a socialist country,

31 Margaret Thatcher, 'A Family of Nations', *in* Brent F. Nelsen & Alexander C-G. Stubb (eds.), *The European Union*, Palgrave, London, 1994, pp. 45-50.

32 Bulletin of the European Communities, No. 12, 1973, pp. 118-122.

33 The development of European identity/identities: unfinished business. A Policy Review, European Commission. 2012, p. 9, at https://ec.europa.eu/research/social-sciences/pdf/policy_reviews/development-of-european-identity-identities_en.pdf.

34 *See* Pál Germuska, 'Balancing Between the COMECON and the EEC: Hungarian Elite Debates on European Integration During the Long 1970s', *Cold War History*, Vol. 19, Issue 3, 2019, pp. 401-420.

Hungarian Yearbook of International Law and European Law 2021 (9) 1
doi: 10.5553/HYIEL/266627012021009001007

Hungary became a contracting party to the GATT in 1973.[35] To understand how the Eastern European Countries, thus Hungary, interpret the European way of life or European identity, we have to understand the historical background of these states. For more than 40 years (from World War II until the end of the 1980s) the Western and Eastern European blocks were socially separated from each other in every possible way. The regime changes and involvement in European integration meant a reasonable opportunity to "return to Europe". However, both sides realized, the process of European reunification is much more challenging than it first appeared.[36] Finally, in 2004 Hungary became a Member State of the EU and soon benefited from this new position. After restrictions were lifted, an increasing number of Hungarian workers moved to, or provided services in the other Member States. According to the data held by the Hungarian Central Statistical Office, around 5-600 thousand Hungarian nationals moved permanently to other Member States, and another 100 thousand regularly work abroad.[37] Other programs such as the Erasmus scholarship opened the way to study abroad, and EU financial support helped develop the country. For Hungarian nationals, the European way of life is embodied in the free movement and the benefits stemming from the cohesion and structural funds.

3. Concept of the Common Way of Life: Strengthening and Weakening Factors

In the following subchapters, the Authors provide a deeper analyses of particular policy areas that are essential factors influencing the European way of life. Firstly, the importance of direct democracy is highlighted. Then, the future enlargement of the EU and the possible accession of Balkan states are explored. Lastly, as the free movement of EU citizens is an immanent element of the common European way of life, the latter has been dramatically affected by the COVID-19 pandemic. The Authors briefly discuss the effects of the coronavirus on the European way of life.

3.1. The Perspective of Direct Democracy

> "The times of European integration by implicit consent of citizens are over. Europe cannot be technocratic, bureaucratic or even diplomatic. Europe has to be ever more democratic. The role of the European Parliament is essential."[38]

35 Hungary and the WTO, at www.wto.org/english/thewto_e/countries_e/hungary_e.htm.

36 Violette Rey, 'Kelet-Európa után?' (Translated into Hungarian: Barta Györgyi), *Földrajzi Értesítő*, Vol. 42, Issue 1-4, 1993, pp. 244-252.

37 *See* Judit Lakatos, 'Külföldön dolgozó magyarok, Magyarországon dolgozó külföldiek', *Statisztikai Szemle*, Vol. 93, Issue 2, 2015, pp. 93-112.

38 José Manuel Durão Barroso, President of the European Commission, *State of the Union 2012 Address*, Plenary session of the European Parliament, Strasbourg, 12 September 2012, at https://ec.europa.eu/commission/presscorner/detail/en/SPEECH_12_596.

doi: 10.5553/HYIEL/266627012021009001007

In this section, the Authors would like to answer how a sense of community can be achieved if there is only a small window of opportunity to have a say in influencing EU decisions. The answer obviously would be to strengthen the instruments of direct democracy in the EU. In this respect, two more issues can be raised: why and how?

3.1.1. The Tools of Direct Democracy

Generally, the tools of direct democracy were significantly reduced over the last century, as parliaments squeezed out popular decision-making. According to contemporary political views, direct democracy can lead to instability, so the still existing instruments of direct democracy, such as referendums are considered complementary or corrective mechanisms. The question arises whether it is even necessary to introduce the tools of direct democracy in the EU. In order to answer this question, the decision-making process conducted 'above the heads' of European citizens must be addressed. Many European citizens have the feeling that a supranational organization delivers decisions that significantly impact the Member States and citizens' lives without them having any influence on the measures taken. As a result, the instruments of direct democracy in the EU are necessary tools of democratic participation aiming to correct shortcomings of the decision-making process. Policy areas can be identified where these instruments may be beneficial, especially if European citizens widely support them. According to literature, both direct and indirect democracy instruments have a place within the EU framework due to its specific institutional system and unique functioning.[39]

According to surveys, there is growing support for direct democracy in the European sphere, to remedy the lack of trust in decision-making and to reduce the democratic deficit.[40] The creation of EU citizenship alone is the result of "efforts to reduce the democratic deficit". Rights arising from citizenship are also reinforced by the EU Charter of Fundamental Rights. The intention was to codify the rights already enjoyed by citizens of the Union.[41] As a legal status, the Union citizenship is a meaningful, central element of EU law, clarified by the extensive case-law of the CJEU.[42]

Democracy issues are not unknown as the so-called *'democratic deficit'* was often raised in connection with the EU and other historical forms of European integration. In 1972, Richard Corbett, a young British politician, used the term democratic deficit for the first time in history to describe the European

39 Ágnes Tuka, *Az Európai Uniónk színe és fonákja*, Publikon, Pécs, 2009, p. 63.

40 Richard Youngs, *'Getting Europe's Direct Democracy Right'*, Centre for European Policy Studies, 14 November 2018, at https://carnegieeurope.eu/2018/11/15/getting-europe-s-direct-democracy-right-pub-77750.

41 Articles 39-46 of the EU Charter of Fundamental Rights.

42 Imola Schiffner, 'Az Uniós polgársághoz kapcsolódó jogosultságok mint alapjogok az Európai Unióban', *in* Tamás Antal & Tekla Papp (eds.), *Az alapjogvédelem nemzeti, nemzetközi és jogösszehasonlító aspektusai*, Pólay Elemér Alapítvány, Szeged, 2013, pp. 41-55.

doi: 10.5553/HYIEL/266627012021009001007

Parliament's weak legislative powers.[43] Social scientist David Marquand coined the now widely used term to describe the weak democratic legitimacy of the EC's institutions in 1979.[44] *The democratic deficit is a negative, critical term, but its reception was not uniform in literature.* According to the majority position, this phenomenon can be interpreted in two ways: primarily, the democratic nature of the EU's institutional structure is called into question. Secondly, from a socio-psychological point of view, the EU is inherently incapable of reflecting the values of traditional democracy for lack of the necessary structural social preconditions.[45] Democratic deficit has a rich literature; in this context, the Authors do not intend to provide a detailed analysis. In the nineties, Jürgen Habermas argued in connection with transnational democracy "that democratic deficit could only be overcome replacing the technocratic approach by a deeper democratization of European institutions".[46] The TEU also declares that the EU "shall be founded on representative democracy" and "citizens are directly represented" in the European Parliament.[47] Furthermore, it provides the legal basis for the European citizens' initiative.[48]

The tools of direct democracy were integrated into the EU's institutional and decision-making system in a long process and only to a limited extent. However, this is not surprising given the European integration's goals, development and history. In recent decades, the possibility of citizen participation and its impact on decision-making has significantly improved, *via* the European Parliament's increased legislative role, the reform of the electoral system and other solutions.[49] Nowadays, *five forms of direct participation exist in which EU citizens are allowed to express their views* or in some way influence EU decision-making.[50] *(i)* The Maastricht Treaty introduced the right to petition. It provides an opportunity for any citizen of the Union to address the European Parliament on matters falling within the EU's competence.[51] *(ii)* To investigate complaints against EU institutions, bodies, offices and agencies, the European Ombudsman's Office was set up in 1995 and is open to citizens and residents of EU Member States, or to businesses and organizations based in the EU.[52] *(iii)* Thirdly, the

43 Richard Corbett, '*The First Use of the Term "Democratic Deficit"*', 10 October 1977, at http://federalunion.org.uk/the-first-use-of-the-term-democratic-deficit/.

44 David Marquand, *Parliament for Europe*, J. Cape, London, 1979, p. 147.

45 Kübra Dilek Azman, 'The Problem of "Democratic Deficit" in the European Union', *International Journal of Humanities and Social Science*, Vol. 1, Issue 5, 2011, pp. 242-250.

46 Jorge Adriano Lubenow, 'The Paradox of Technocratic Democracy and the Democratic Deficit of European Institutions by Jürgen Habermas', *Aufklärung*, Vol. 2, Issue 2, 2015, pp. 103122.

47 Article 11 TEU.

48 Article 10 TEU.

49 Anna Unger, '*Demokrácia a képviseleten túl: a közvetlen demokrácia intézményrendszere és szerepe az Európai Unió demokratizációjában a demokrácia részvételi elmélete alapján*', PhD Dissertation, ELTE Budapest, 2018.

50 Steven Blockmas & Sophia Russack (eds.), *Direct Democracy in the EU, The Myth of a Citizen's Union*, Rowman & Littlefield International, London, 2018, pp. 9-13.

51 Legal basis: Articles 20, 24, and 227 TFEU and Article 44 of the EU Charter of Fundamental Rights.

52 Article 228 TFEU. *See* legal basis at www.ombudsman.europa.eu/en/legal-basis/treaties/en.

doi: 10.5553/HYIEL/266627012021009001007

European Commission organizes a wide range of consultations on new priorities of existing policies and adopted legislation.[53] *(iv)* Fourthly, aiming at examining the benefits of the EU, the Commission shall conduct regular civil dialogue with the Union's citizens on their experiences of the EU. The advantage of the dialogue is that it is possible to have a personal discussion with policymakers at the announced events.[54] *(v)* Finally, the Citizens' Initiative was introduced, and its recent reform aims to enhance the applicability of this instrument.

3.1.2. The Citizen's Initiative: Reformed but Not Rethought?

The European Citizens' Initiative (ECI) was established in the context of the "failed" Constitutional Treaty, with the urgent support of civil society. Although the Constitutional Treaty did not enter into force, the European Citizens' Initiative has found its way into the Treaty of Lisbon as the latest EU instrument for direct democracy. Since 2012, EU citizens have been entitled to the ECI, which is an excellent opportunity for citizens to make themselves heard on issues of common interest that are important for society and influence rules applicable to them in the future.[55] The aim was laudable, but it could not be achieved because of the overly complex rules governing the initiative, and so, it did not fulfil expectations. The European Commission intended to reform the initiative to make it 'more user-friendly'.[56] The process started in 2015. The new proposal was submitted in 2017, accepted in 2019[57] and entered into force on 1 January 2020. Several problems were identified in connection to the 'old' legislation: the meagre chance of proposing admissible initiatives, as around a third of the registered applications was rejected. Then, it was challenging to obtain statements of support, for example, due to the different reporting requirements applicable in the Member States and the relatively limited impact and debate garnered by European citizens' initiatives.[58]

The general success rate of European citizens' initiative is around 4 per cent, *i.e.* these are the initiatives that were answered by the European Commission. It is important to note that the European Commission is not required to submit a legislative proposal within the initiative's scope. Without going into a detailed analysis of the new and old legislation, we can state that the reform of the European citizens' initiative changed several elements of the procedure, yet its

53 Consultations, at https://ec.europa.eu/info/consultations_en.

54 Public Debates on EU Policies, at https://ec.europa.eu/info/about-european-commission/get-involved/citizens-dialogues_en.

55 The original legal basis was Regulation No 211/2011/EU of the European Parliament and of the Council of 16 February 2011 on the citizens' initiative.

56 State of the Union 2017 — Democracy Package: Reform of Citizens' Initiative and Political Party funding, at https://ec.europa.eu/commission/presscorner/detail/en/IP_17_3187.

57 Regulation 2019/788/EU of the European Parliament and of the Council of 17 April 2019 on the European citizens' initiative.

58 Report on the application of Regulation (EU) No 211/2011 on the citizens' initiative COM(2018) 157 final, p. 2.

doi: 10.5553/HYIEL/266627012021009001007

core characteristics remained the same.[59] Naturally, the initiative is applied in cases where the citizens are interested. In the last ten years, the ECI aimed mainly at common concerns of environmental or animal protection and the rights and legal status of minorities.[60]

In the past months, another successful initiative entitled *"Minority Safepack"*[61] was answered. It "called upon the EU to improve the protection of persons belonging to national and linguistic minorities" and also to "strengthen cultural and linguistic diversity". The organizers collected 1,320,000 statements of support, and they have reached the threshold in 11 Member States.[62] Notwithstanding the considerable support garnered by the ECI, the European Commission still found that existing rules are sufficient for the Member States to support projects that promote the rights of persons belonging to national minorities and their culture; thus, no additional legal act was considered necessary. As usual, the Commission found that the already existing legal norms ensure the required level of protection and legal basis.[63] The Commission's decision is debatable, but it has been so far in the case of any other initiatives as well. As a result, the citizen's initiative is a reformed, but not rethought tool of direct democracy in the EU. *The biggest concern is the Commission's discretion to decide the necessity of proposing new legislation*. In order to strengthen the tools of direct democracy in the EU, the citizens need more power to influence the adoption of EU law, in particular, when the initiative is also supported by the European Parliament.

3.2. The Newcomers of the Balkans – Interconnections Between European Identity and Enlargement Policy

In this subchapter, the Authors will summarize how European identity and the European way of life can be influenced by enlargement policy. The main question is whether the accepted shared values can influence the future enlargement of the EU or whether the accession of new countries will change and dilute Europeanness. To answer the questions raised, the Authors concentrate on the Balkan enlargement.

Enlargement was always significant in the history of European integration and development, since it determined both the territorial extent and the economic power of cooperation. From a market perspective, one may simply summarize the process as a new Member States constituting a new market and

59 A detailed analysis may be found in Katalin Gombos & Orsolya Johanna Sziebig, 'A polgári kezdeményezés mint a közvetlen demokrácia eszköze az Európai Unióban – Jegyzetek az új szabályozás margójára', *Jogtudományi Közlöny*, Vol. 75, Issue 12, 2020, pp. 556-565.

60 *See* Katalin Gombos & Orsolya Johanna Sziebig, 'Az európai uniós környezetvédelmi szabályozás legújabb irányai', *in* Péter Smuk (ed.), *Társadalmi fenntarthatóság*, NKE, Budapest, 2021, pp. 2010-2022.

61 *See* Balázs Tárnok, 'European Citizens' Initiatives for the Protection and Promotion of Rights and Interests of National Minorities – Latest Developments', *Hungarian Yearbook of International Law and European Law*, Vol. 8, 2020, pp. 299-313.

62 Original homepage of the Citizens' Initiative at www.minority-safepack.eu/.

63 Communication from the Commission on the European Citizens' Initiative Minority SafePack – one million signatures for diversity in Europe, 14 January 2021 C(2021) 171 final, pp. 18-21.

doi: 10.5553/HYIEL/266627012021009001007

providing additional labor force.[64] From a cultural-sociological perspective, enlargement is more complex. The different regions of Europe share similarities (*e.g.* the Scandinavian and the Baltic states, Central Europe, Southern Europe, *etc.*) regarding their cultural-social circumstances, but they often share economic and geographic characteristics, too. In order to examine enlargement-related issues from the perspective of Europeanness, the states' cultural and sociological conditions must be considered. As a preliminary observation, the Balkans in general and the Western-Balkan region differ greatly from other European states, perhaps in all of the aspects mentioned above.

Every accession implies the fear of losing national characteristics, and the future possibility of the disintegration of the EU. The Western-Balkan enlargement is a very sensitive issue: understanding historical events, and consequences may provide an objective scope. *From a Hungarian point of view, the integration of the Western-Balkan is a clear national interest*, but why? *(i)* First of all, Hungary is located at the edge of the current map of the EU. Therefore, it constitutes an external border of the EU from the South and North-East, and a border-control state from the Schengen-zone's perspective. As a result, several obligations arise from this position, such as maintaining border control and security as well as cooperating with Frontex. These requirements impose a heavy burden on the public administration executing customs and border control, parallel to police services deployed for related tasks. Border-related issues (such as the permissions to enter the country, the evaluation of asylum seekers' claims) are heavily contested and usually require a complex approach. Moreover, besides the public administrative tasks involved, the financial dimension of maintaining borders, the human resource of providing these services comes at a significant cost for the state. In addition, the treatment of migration issues has been in the focus of political attention since 2015. At the time of COVID-19, the generally sensitive issue of migration gained more awareness. A new dimension of migration occurred due to the healthcare situation of migrants on the one hand and the "free movement of diseases" on the other.[65] *(ii)* Secondly, Hungary lost over two-thirds of its territory and more than half of its population after World War I due to the Treaty of Trianon that formally ended World War I between most of the Allies of World War I and the Kingdom of Hungary. More than a hundred years passed since this tragic event, but its effects and impacts are still tangible. As a result, there are territories beyond the Hungarian borders in every direction inhabited mainly by Hungarians, which are a part of the neighboring states. As a result, the accession of these neighboring states could bridge a century-old gap separating Hungarians from their kin-state. Overcoming this separation was achieved when Romania joined the EU. The same applies not only to Balkan countries but the future accession of Ukraine (Transcarpathia) as well. If Serbia becomes a Member State, more than 200 thousand Hungarians can

64 *See* Szilvia Váradi, *Az Európai Unió bővítésének jogi aspektusai*, Wolters Kluwer, Budapest, 2014.
65 *See* Angeliki Dimitriadi, 'The Future of European Migration and Asylum Policy Post Covid-19', *FEPS Covid Response Papers*, 2020, pp. 1-12.

doi: 10.5553/HYIEL/266627012021009001007

enjoy free movement from Vojvodina to Hungary.[66] Moreover, the accession of neighboring states could strengthen relationships among Hungary and Serbia and Hungary and Ukraine in general. In the current European Commission, the enlargement and neighborhood policy portfolio belongs to the Hungarian Commissioner, Olivér Várhelyi, who is well aware of these states' historical and geographical specificities. The accession of these candidate states would change the *status civitatis* of their citizens automatically into European citizens. *(iii)* Thirdly, but not lastly, enlargement could support the regional development of Eastern Europe by promoting economic relations among these states. Cooperation in border control and public administrative issues could result in burden-sharing. Those states are eligible to apply for candidate statues that fulfill the Copenhagen criteria, laid down during the European Council Summit of Copenhagen in 1993.[67] On the one hand, these include political conditions (such as the respect for European values enshrined in Article 2 TEU) and, on the other hand, a specific level of economic development. From the point of view of the European way of life, we may say that the conditions of the EU's capacity to assimilate and absorb new states is also significant. The European Council declared in 2006 that "the rhythm of the enlargement should be aware of the capacity of the Union to integrate new members".[68] What does this mean? The capacity of the EU is unclear but may refer to the tension among nations that the Authors highlighted in this article. The political conditions for accession include a mutual willingness to live together and cooperate. The financial circumstances of the EU are also of relevance and a decisive component is the EU's institutional capacity. The EU has a complex and unique institution system.[69] Financial aspects include the economic readiness of the EU (and not just the candidates) to allow candidate states to join. Newcomers cost more for the EU than they are able to contribute to the common budget. Some states on the Western-Balkan do not have a stable economy due to the Yugoslavian wars.[70] *(iv)* Finally, the EU's capacity has a social aspect, closely related to our main topic, the European way of life. To be clear, we have to ask whether Western-Balkan citizens are ready to fit into the common European way of life? Not just from a simple economic point of view, but from a social identity aspect. Western-Balkan states' social parameters are radically different from those of the EU Member States and are not uniform across the former Yugoslavian states either. The tension of former conflicts is still tangible between the ex-Yugoslav states. This root of possible future conflicts

66 Tibor Ördögh, *Vajdaság gazdasági és társadalmi jellemzői*, Vajdasági Magyar Doktoranduszok és Kutatók Szervezete, Szabadka, 2017, p. 54.

67 Article 49 TEU. About the accession criteria (Copenhagen), *see* the Glossary at EUR-LEX: https://eur-lex.europa.eu/summary/glossary/accession_criteria_copenhague.html?locale=en.

68 Conseil Europeen – Bruxelles 15-16 June 2006. Conclusions de la Présidence, 54.

69 About the complexity of the EU's institution system, *see* Edward C. Page, 'Bureaucracy and the European Union', *Oxford Scholarship Online*, October 2011 at https://oxford.universitypressscholarship.com/view/10.1093/acprof:oso/9780198280798.001.0001/acprof-9780198280798-chapter-1.

70 Jean-Jacques Mével, 'Les Vingt-Huit s'alarment de l'instabilité dans les Balkans', *Le Figaro International*, 10 March 2017, at www.lefigaro.fr/international/2017/03/10/01003-20170310ARTFIG00254-les-vingt-huit-s-alarment-de-l-instabilite-dans-les-balkans.php.

doi: 10.5553/HYIEL/266627012021009001007

may hinder their accession, in particular, since Croatia will always have the right to veto their accession. Five states are already candidates: Albania, Montenegro, North-Macedonia, Serbia from the Balkan region and Turkey.[71]

The above-mentioned criteria and circumstances determine the enlargement of the EU. *The newcomers are going to impact the existing status quo among the Member States.* The question arises whether the accession presupposes the acceptance of the concept of the European way of life. The concept is elaborated on the grounds of our common values and citizenship status. The answer in the Authors' view is yes. Since accession does not require any resignation from former values of the state or the EU, the concept implicitly strengthens the EU from a democratic perspective. The question is whether the Western-Balkans fit into the EU's framework or not. At this point, *multiple social, cultural and financial issues are still unknown*, so this question cannot be answered yet. The ex-Yugoslav states are extremely heterogenetic nationally, socially and politically.[72]

3.3. How Does COVID-19 Affect the Realization of the European Way of Life?

Generally, the concept and practical implementation of the European way of life are continuously affected by all those events (accessions and withdrawals) and circumstances (economic and / healthcare crises, pandemic) that reach the EU. To put the question into a broader context, promoting the European way of life shows the Commission's commitment towards integration, towards relying on European citizens and building European democracy. European citizenship grants rights directly to citizens *via* the Treaties that provides a pragmatic framework for the institutions. The new concepts – such as in the case of European citizenship – are often filled with content by the practice and later interpreted by the CJEU. Officially, the nation-states have nationals, who are the European citizens, but European citizenship only complements and does not change national citizenship. European citizenship entitles the citizens to live their way of life *via* their political and economic rights. Therefore, by interpreting the elements of citizenship we can discern the substance of our common way of life. European citizenship bridges the gap to the supranational polity without forcing the Member States into a federation.[73] Meanwhile, over last more than one year, the pandemic has showed that some elements of Union citizens' rights may be restricted or temporarily repealed by national legislation.

A consequence of the coronavirus is that *the Member States restricted citizens' mobility rights to prevent the spread of the infection*. The public health emergency temporarily hollows out the concept of the European way of life by restricting the free movement of people. Other freedoms of the single market remained

71 Candidate Countries and Potential Candidates at https://ec.europa.eu/environment/enlarg/candidates.htm.

72 Dusko Sekulic *et al.*, Who Were the Yugoslavs? Failed Sources of a Common Identity in the Former Yugoslavia, *American Sociological Review*, Vol. 59, Issue 1, 1994, pp. 83-97.

73 *See* Lilla Nóra Kiss & Orsolya Johanna Sziebig, 'European Way of Life: Making an Omelette Without Breaking the Eggs?', *Constitutional Discourse blog*, at www.constitutionaldiscourse.com/post/lilla-n%C3%B3ra-kiss-orsolya-johanna-sziebig-european-way-of-life.

doi: 10.5553/HYIEL/266627012021009001007

untouched or still function, such as the free movement of goods. Understandably, some restrictions were introduced due to the health emergency. Seemingly, restrictions hollowed out the mobility freedoms temporarily. In the long run, the restrictions introduced may affect the citizens' rights in general. No one can foresee when citizens are going to travel again. This may only be answered years after the pandemic. At this stage, only predictions can be made. The Authors agreed on some broad ideas as predictions.

First, the concept of the European way of life could be a linkage between the citizens, and by strengthening it, the EU institutions could be brought closer to the citizens. The possible future reform of the ECI within the frames of the Future of the European Union Conference series started on 9 May 2021, can serve as a tool of direct influence while providing answers for questions that matter to the citizens. The series of events under the umbrella of the Conference will contribute to understanding the future trends and directions of EU development. All stakeholders (the EU *via* its institutions and bodies, the Member States, the citizens, NGO-s and civil society organizations, *etc.*) agreed on the proportionate involvement of EU citizens in discussing the future.[74] Thus, citizens are core elements of the discussion on the future of the EU by which the *institutions* established a *quasi* bottom-up process. Obviously, the pandemic affected the citizens' life which needs to be treated later, during and after the Conference-series. The citizens may have a similar experience on the pandemic that could contribute to new policies.

No doubt, *the coronavirus deeply affected the elements of European identity, primarily through the restrictions on free movement in the Schengen Area* and other travel bans. Some programs, such as Erasmus, continued mainly in an online form, thus, the general goals of such initiatives could be reached fully. However, these statements can be formulated not just about the European area, but globally. Hence, COVID-19 greatly influenced everyday life in other countries, other continents as well. The pandemic made us realize the vulnerability of life, nations and the world. Shall we go back to where we were before the coronavirus? – that is the question that the world has to grapple with, even Hungary and the EU. "All countries need to review their strategies now" as Michael J. Ryan, WHO Informal Advisory Group member said.

The coronavirus pandemic showed that *the EU can still function and help Member States, even during such challenging times*. Financially, the EU will distribute EUR 37 billion cohesion money among the Member States. The aim is "to strengthen healthcare systems, as well as support small and medium-sized enterprises, short-term working schemes, and community-based services."[75] The new Coronavirus Response Investment Initiative and Solidarity Fund aims to recover losses incurred due to the coronavirus pandemic and help the Member

74 *See* at https://europa.eu/european-union/conference-future-europe_en.

75 Press release 30 March 2020, COVID-19 – Council adopts measures for immediate release of funds, at https://www.consilium.europa.eu/en/press/press-releases/2020/03/30/covid-19-council-adopts-measures-for-immediate-release-of-funds/.

doi: 10.5553/HYIEL/266627012021009001007

States "strengthen healthcare systems, support SMEs, short-term employment schemes, and community-based services".[76]

Concerns about Hungarian steps taken in response to COVID-19 highlighted that core values, such as democracy and human rights are guiding principles of the EU, even under exceptional circumstances. We will find the answer later to the question, how the coronavirus will influence the European way of life or the future cooperation of Member States. Undoubtedly, the EU and the Member States as well have to reschedule the planned programs and ó strengthen the partnership and mutual acceptance between Member States (regardless of political oppositions) in order to face the crisis.

4. Concluding Remarks

Several factors influence the development of self-identity: family heritage, education, socio-economic environment will primarily affect how a person defines himself. The question is whether this self-definition may include a commitment to a broader community, in our case, the EU? The answer is a definite yes in the framework of the European way of life, our interpretation of European identity. With the words of Ursula von der Leyen: "I want Europeans to build the future of our Union. They should play a leading and active part in setting our priorities and our level of ambition."[77] Being a European citizen cannot and will not replace state citizenship, the most crucial legal connection between countries and their nationals. Nevertheless, it can serve as a source of common identity, based on the shared values of the EU and the Member States, providing significant rights and legal protection for European citizens.

The coronavirus pandemic was a challenge for the international community and the EU as well. All the nations are still in shock, and every day holds new tasks to solve and problems to discuss. The global health emergency is not over, and it is already clear that the world cannot go back to business as usual. The Authors raised some general comments on how the EU has been influenced by COVID-19. Hopefully, these challenging times will show the real strength and future viability of European cooperation, especially with the support of its citizens.

The concept of the European way of life is a special tool that allows the approximation of citizens without any Treaty-change. European way of life shows that there are solutions for bringing the people closer to each other and to the EU. The existing legal basis may be found in European citizenship. Citizenship includes those political and economic rights that are ensured by the EU directly to the citizens. However, some political rights are not considered to be effective, such as the ECI. In order to provide the real opportunities to European citizens, it

76 Legislative measures, at https://data.consilium.europa.eu/doc/document/PE-5-2020-INIT/en/pdf and https://data.consilium.europa.eu/doc/document/PE-6-2020-INIT/en/pdf.

77 Ursula von der Leyen, *A Union that Strives for More. My Agenda for Europe*, Political Guidelines for the next European Commission 2019-2024, p. 19, at https://ec.europa.eu/commission/sites/beta-political/files/political-guidelines-next-commission_en.pdf.

doi: 10.5553/HYIEL/266627012021009001007

is not enough to promote their way of life, but their role in democratic decision-making must also be reinforced within the existing framework. The above-mentioned ECI is an existing legal tool to make the Union citizens' voice heard, but its success rate is relatively low. Thus, we may conclude that European way of life as a common denominator for EU citizens may only be effective if existing mechanisms are rethought, reformed and filled with content.

Europeanness is not just about being born in a European country. It is a fabric of shared values that we all believe in, such as democracy, the protection of fundamental rights and the rule of law. Common values facilitate the exercise of political rights arising from European citizenship, such as the ECI. The future has many attractive paths – from a strengthened confederation to multispeed Europe – for European integration that focuses on the citizens (*e.g.* enlarging Schengen-zone) and respects the diversity as our common heritage. Shall we invite more states to share our values, or remain a centered and robust cooperation of countries that are European in the geographical sense? In the Authors' view, the concept of a common European way of life reflects Europe more a value-based entity, than a simple regional cooperation of European states: a Europe for all, all for one Europe.

doi: 10.5553/HYIEL/266627012021009001007

ANNIVERSARY: COMMEMORATING THE 90TH BIRTHDAY OF FERENC MÁDL, PRESIDENT OF THE REPUBLIC (2000-2005)

Ferenc Mádl, the Hungarian Professor of European Law

*Endre Domaniczky**

Abstract

Living in a country under foreign occupation he became engrossed in the science of private law, and (under the influence and with the support of his masters) he started to study the characteristics of socialist, and later of Western European legal systems. Within the socialist bloc, he became one of the early experts on Common Market law, who, following an unexpected historical event, the 1989 regime change in Hungary, was also able to make practical use of his theoretical knowledge for the benefit of his country. In 2021, on the 90th anniversary of his birth and the 10th anniversary of his death, the article remembers Ferenc Mádl, legal scholar, member of the Hungarian Academy of Sciences, minister in the Antall- and Boross governments, former President of Hungary.

Keywords: Ferenc Mádl, private international law, Central Europe, V4, Hungary.

1. Family Background and Childhood

Ferenc Mádl was born in Bánd, Veszprém County, on 29 January 1931. The erstwhile province of Pannonia, Transdanubia, where his native village was located, had been a part of the Roman Empire for four centuries, uniting significant territories of Europe linguistically, culturally and religiously for the first time. Even with the arrival of the Hungarians the region did not lose its significance: the two neighboring settlements, Veszprém and Székesfehérvár have been important cultural, commercial and administrative centers since the founding of the Hungarian state. It was on the border of the former that the decisive battle between Prince Stephen and leader Koppány took place, as a result of which Hungary confirmed its affiliation with Western Europe and the Roman Church. This decision had both cultural and state organizational consequences. Veszprém, one of the earliest Hungarian Episcopal seats, became "the first citadel of Hungarian legal culture, higher education in law"[1] already in the Árpád-era

* Endre Domaniczky: senior research fellow, Ferenc Mádl Institute of Comparative Law, Budapest.

1 Ferenc Mádl, 'Európa és a magyar jogrendszer', *in* Ferenc Mádl, *Az európai örökség útjain*, Athenaeum, Budapest, 1995, p. 24.

doi: 10.5553/HYIEL/266627012021009001008

since in the 13th century a school providing legal training operated here. "Veszprém – its beauty, history, landscapes speak for themselves", noted Ferenc Mádl as minister, explaining his close affinity to the city. Székesfehérvár, which is also not far from Bánd, was the first center of the Hungarian Kingdom, the coronation city and resting place of many Hungarian kings, the venue of our first parliaments. Among other things, it was also here that the Golden Bull[2] *(Aranybulla)* which can be considered as one of the earliest declarations of human freedom rights, was proclaimed in 1222.

Thus, although the village of Bánd re-founded by German settlers after the Turkish occupation, "never play[ed] a major role in the culture and public life of the nation"[3] before, history was nevertheless alive in the area, it was present in everyday life, as the ruins of a medieval castle standing on its borders suggested.

The Mádl family has lived in the village since the 18th century. Ferenc Mádl's parents were farmers who raised six children: three boys and three girls.[4] In one of his early biographies, Mádl described the financial situation of his parents in detail:

> "I was born ... as a child of poor peasants on both sides ... Before the liberation my parents used to be day-laborers [...] [after 1945 – E. D.] my parents were able to take over the grandparents' small farm of 5-6 acres due to their old age. Until March 1959, they worked as individual farmers there."[5]

Professor Mádl repeatedly emphasized that despite the humble circumstances, his parents provided education for all of their children and all of them graduated. In the twilight of his life, he recalled,

> "It is my parents to whom I owe everything. With their human attitude, moral, religious values, diligence, and undeniable human culture, they gave us, children, a start that has defined our lives. [...] I always remember the cleanliness of my mother [...] no matter how hard life was, we always wore clean clothes, our modest home was always clean. Despite being a peasant, my father was highly educated, so he gave us not only Holy Scripture and other devotional works, but also serious literature. I read Széchenyi, Kossuth at home."[6]

2 *See* the standpoint of István Csekey, a professor of law in Pécs, quoted by Gábor Schweitzer, 'Judgment of Act I of 1946 in Contemporary Public Law Literature', *MTA Law Working Papers*, 2016/14, p. 9. Mádl repeatedly referred to the Golden Bull as an early forerunner of the rule of law, *see e.g.* 'A Ius Commune Europae-től az európai közösségi magánjogig – jogi gondolkodás Magyarországon', *in* Miklós Király (ed.), *Quo vadis Europa? A magyar államfő Európában*, KJK-Kerszöv, Budapest, 2004, pp. 157-163.

3 Zoltán Balog, 'Köszöntő előszó', *in Mádl Ferenc 80*, MPEE, Budapest, 2011, p. 5.

4 'Rólunk is szól a mese. Beszélgetés Mádl Ferenccel', *Magyar Nemzet*, 10 June 2000, p. 25.

5 *Mádl Ferenc önéletrajza*, 22 July 1959, MTAL 68. d. 68/2. Cs.

6 *Magyar Nemzet* 2000, p. 25.

doi: 10.5553/HYIEL/266627012021009001008

Ferenc Mádl attended elementary school in Bánd and Szentkirályszabadja,[7] then, between 1943 and 1951 he studied at the Piarist grammar school in Veszprém. It was the oldest Piarist school in the territory of the country after 1920, having been founded in 1711.[8] The grammar school was not only one of the best schools in Hungary, but also an intellectual center, the impact of which spread far and wide both in space and time. Among others, János Batsányi (1763-1845), the famous poet of the Enlightenment, Gusztáv Wenzel (1812-1891), a law professor of European impact at the University of Pest, the pioneer of teaching comparative legal history in Hungary, and Jenő Cholnoky (1870-1950), the internationally renowned geographer, former president of the Hungarian Geographical Society also studied there. The atmosphere of the school, the excellent teachers had a great influence on the young man, who until his death[9] had a close relationship with his former schoolmates and the Piarist order.[10] Perhaps it is no exaggeration to say that Mádl's worldview, in addition to his parents' house, was largely shaped by the formative years in Veszprém.

Following his excellent matura examination, Ferenc Mádl applied for a place at the University of Pécs.[11] "My father conveyed to me that I should be a lawyer or a priest. [...] He said I had to deal with people, people's affairs."[12]

2. Pécs and Budapest: the Influence of the University Years

Mádl applied to the Law Faculty in Pécs, but he completed only two years of university, because in August 1953 he applied for a transfer to Eötvös Loránd University (ELTE) in Budapest. Despite his difficult financial situation, he was

7 Ferenc Mádl lived here between 1939 and 1945. *See* 'Díszpolgári cím Mádl Ferencnek', *Veszprémi Napló*, 21 August 2006, p. 3.

8 About its history, *see in particular*: András Lichtneckert & Ferenc Tölcséry, *A veszprémi piarista gimnázium története az alapítástól az államosításig 1711-1948*, Veszprém, 2011; Tibor Borián (ed.), *Emlékkönyv a veszprémi Kegyestanítórendi Gimnázium alapításának 275. évfordulójára 1711-1986*, MPDSZ, Budapest, 1986; László Lechner (ed.), *Alma Mater a veszprémi várban*, VPÖD, Veszprém, 2003.

9 He passed away in 2011 while traveling to Veszprém, to the 60th graduating reunion meeting. According to Ferenc Oberfrank, former president of the Hungarian Piarist Student Association: "On Sunday morning, 29 May 2011, Ferenc Mádl left for a graduating reunion meeting of Piarist alumni in Veszprém, but his journey eventually led him to his Creator." *See* at https://hirlevel.mpdsz.piarista.hu/node/93, 03 March 2021.

10 His friendship with József Antall was also partly based on a common feeling of attachment to the school. PM Antall attended the Piarist grammar school in Pest between 1942-1950.

11 Pécs was founded by the Romans in the first century AD and remained one of the most important religious and cultural centers even after the Hungarian conquest. The city is still proud that the first Hungarian university was established here in 1367. However, the university where Mádl enrolled was the successor of Elizabeth University, founded in Pozsony (Bratislava) in 1912, called the University of Pécs since 1951. Due to the border changes after World War I, the University of Pozsony (Bratislava) moved to Budapest in 1919 and then to Pécs in 1923. *See also* Act XXXVI of 1912 on the establishment of the Hungarian Royal Universities in Debrecen and Pozsony (Bratislava); Act XXV of 1921 on the temporary transfer of the University of Pozsony (Bratislava) and the University of Kolozsvár (Cluj-Napoca).

12 *Magyar Nemzet* 2000, p. 25.

doi: 10.5553/HYIEL/266627012021009001008

also an excellent student in Pécs, although ("despite the fact that we had some excellent teachers [...]") university education "was a huge disappointment then".[13] László Sólyom, a later colleague and co-author, who was a fellow-student a few years under him, also confirmed this rapid fall in the standard of education in his memoir.[14]

However, Mádl was rather fortunate, because during the transition period when he was at Pécs University, the old and the new teaching staff still taught together for a while. He was one of the last students to listen to the lectures of József Holub,[15] one of the greatest Hungarian legal historians. He also took the exam at another excellence in Hungarian legal history, Alajos Degré.[16] Finally, it should be mentioned that it was also in Pécs that his scientific interest was sparked, it was recognized, even encouraged there. He wrote his first scholarly work in Pécs in 1953 on administrative law, with which he won first prize in a competition announced by the Faculty of Law.

Although the author was young and inexperienced and the writing still unpublished,[17] Mádl considered it to be his first scholarly work.[18] Even today, the paper can be considered a clear and mature legal study. The system of arguments Mádl's employs in later scientific writings is almost entirely recognizable here; *the comparative legal method, the strong (legal) historical interest, the clarity of questioning and the logical derivation free from detours* all appear in the opus. No wonder one of his opponents wrote the following in his proposal about the young (sophomore) student:

13 Id.

14 "I went to study law without any particular enthusiasm, and a month later I saw that it was a disaster: it was a terrible place where nothing could be gained. [...] We soon saw the fallibility of the teachers. There were those who put on airs, some who did not even do that." *See* 'Hagyni kell történni a sorsot. Interjú Sólyom Lászlóval', *Századvég*, 2004/1, pp. 135-177.

15 József Holub (1885-1962) was a humanist in inhuman world and preserved his civilian values throughout the dictatorship. "He was one of those who could not or did not want to cross the Rubicon of the socialist era." Andor Csizmadia, 'A jogtörténeti oktatás a pécsi tudományegyetemen a két világháború között. Kérészy Zoltán és Holub József munkássága', *in* Tibor Pap (ed.), *Jubileumi tanulmányok II.*, Tankönyvkiadó, Pécs, 1967, p. 125. The parts of his notes from his last, 1950/1951 lectures, on the law of medieval Europe contain statements that still hold true. MTA Könyvtára, MS5205/20.

16 *See more* on the life and work of Alajos Degré: Gábor Béli, 'Degré Alajos, a jogtörténész', *Jura*, 2006/2, pp. 6-13; András Molnár (ed.), *Levéltáros elődeink*, ZML, Zalaegerszeg, 2006. His notes based on the lectures of the 1950/1951 academic year are available again under the editorship of his department's successor, Gábor Béli. Gábor Béli (ed.), *Alajos Degré: Magyar alkotmány- és jogtörténet*, PTE ÁJK – Publikon Kiadó, Pécs, 2010.

17 Ferenc Mádl, *Az államigazgatási alkalmazottak anyagi felelősségének rendezése*, Unpublished.

18 Archives of the HAS node 699/429, Ferenc Mádl's application for an independent postgraduate scholarship, Annex No. 2 (My scientific works and works of scientific nature to date).

doi: 10.5553/HYIEL/266627012021009001008

> "The author of the dissertation has a huge potential for development, and if he continues his studies seriously, a lot can be expected from him. I consider the dissertation[19] to be [...] the most outstanding of all the works."[20]

However, despite his excellent academic results, young Mádl had to leave the university, as he refused to be engaged in political work despite the wishes of the "*hard-liner dean*". Mádl, however, took a firm stand for his conviction although he was aware that retaliation might occur. The fact that the story ended well was only down to luck, as the dean of the Faculty of Law of Eötvös Loránd University at the time, Professor Miklós Világhy, transferred him to Budapest out of turn. Ferenc Mádl's modesty is evidenced by the fact that although he could have benefited from it after the change of regime, he never boasted about this story, he spoke about it[21] only once in his life in a few sentences. The details were reconstructed from archival documents found accidentally.[22]

Mádl was a student at Eötvös Loránd University (ELTE) from 1953 to 1955, where he continued his legal studies with excellent results and graduated "with a diploma with distinction".[23] It became almost immediately clear that he only benefited from the change of university, and here we should not primarily think of the distance between the capital city and the native village or the higher scholarship with which Mádl politely justified his request for transfer.[24] The main gain ("despite the fact that one-party state rhetoric was prevalent here as well"[25] and the purges were also active) was that some old professors still taught there, who were able to maintain their positions in the capital much longer than in the countryside.

Thus, Mádl was able to continue the research he had started in Pécs in close proximity to the greatest, internationally renowned authorities in the field. Géza Marton, professor of Roman law, one of the most outstanding experts in liability, Endre Nizsalovszky, a civil lawyer-turned-*polyhistor* who in addition to law made

19 A total of 42 entries were received from students from different years. In light of this, recognition is even more important.

20 *Opinion of Professor Rezső Hilscher*, 1 June 1953, PTE EL VIII.202.d. 414. Professor Hilscher (1890-1957) was one of the most important Hungarian social politicians. He graduated from the University of Law in Budapest, in 1944, he worked as a lecturer at the Miskolc Law Academy, between 1949 and 1955, he was professor and head of the Department No. 2 of Public Administrative Law (administrative law and financial law). *See* the lecturer's data in the Almanac of the University of Pécs, at https://almanach.pte.hu.

21 *Magyar Nemzet* 2000, p. 25. It reveals Mádl's attitude that he didn't tell the story even when it could have been to his advantage. In 1993, specifically, he averted the inquiry by saying, "Look, I don't want to tell epic stories in retrospect." *See* 'Legyen az oktatás stratégiai ágazat', *in* Mádl 1995, p. 157.

22 The documents related to transfer can be found in two places: in Pécs, in the University Archives and in Budapest, in the Hungarian National Archives. I would like to thank Director István Lengvári and Petra Polyák, director of the archives for their help in searching for the material. For more information on transfer, *see* Endre Domaniczky, *Mádl Ferenc a pécsi jogi karon (a PTE Egyetemi Levéltár iratanyaga alapján)*, forthcoming, 2021.

23 *Mádl Ferenc önéletrajza* 1959.

24 Ferenc Mádl's transfer application dated 28 August 1953, MNL XIX-J-5-a. 214 d. F847 / 855 cs.

25 *Magyar Nemzet* 2000, p. 25.

doi: 10.5553/HYIEL/266627012021009001008

his mark in the field of legal history and literary history, his student association supervisor, Miklós Világhy and later boss, professor Gyula Eörsi taught or assisted him.

In 1955, Mádl as a fourth-year law student (this time with his significantly extended topic) also entered the second national law student associations' conference (TDK)[26] at Eötvös Loránd University, where his lecture attracted a lot of attention and generated intense discussion. His dissertation entitled "The historical formation of the objective liability system" *(Az objektív felelősségi rendszer történelmi kialakulása)* was the result of "extensive source research, careful study of relevant foreign literature"[27] and won first prize at the conference.[28] In fact, this dissertation and this conference made him nationally known and set out the further direction of his research; his extensive, more than half a thousand-page PhD dissertation grew out of this research conducted over nearly ten years.

Although Mádl became a practicing lawyer after graduating, this proved to be only a short detour in his life. "After completing my university studies, I was appointed by the Minister of Justice first as a trainee judge and then as a court secretary at the Budapest District Courts[29] for Districts No. XIX and IV."[30] He worked in Kispest (District No. XIX) in 1955-1956 and in Újpest (District No. IV) in 1956.[31] He dealt with civil affairs in both places,[32] but his scientific work was not neglected either. "I was [p]ursued by the passion of writing, I found it hard to bear when I had blank paper in front of me," he recalled, already a minister, this period.[33]

3. Official and Researcher of the Hungarian Academy of Sciences

In that period, the Main Committee of Law and Political Sciences of the Hungarian Academy of Sciences (HAS) was

26 This competition could be considered the forerunner of the National Conferenceof Scientific Students' Associations (the so-called OTDK). For more information on the history of OTDK, *see* at https://otdk.hu/upload/files/4.%20A_magyar_tudomanyos_diakkori_konferenciak_tortenete_2011.pdf.

27 Iván Szász, 'Második országos jogász diákköri konferencia', *Jogtudományi Közlöny*, May 1955, p. 319.

28 List of Ferenc Mádl's scientific works for the application for an independent postgraduate scholarship, MTAL 429 d. Dossier 699/429.

29 The exact name of the courts at that time, according to Section 2 of 177000/1950. (XII. 10.) IM Decree on the division of the administration of law, was Budapest District Regional Court IV and XV, and Budapest District Regional Court XVIII-XIX.

30 *Mádl Ferenc önéletrajza* 1959.

31 Personal data sheet of Ferenc Mádl dated 29 October 1985, MTAL Personnel Documents 576. d. 6. cs.

32 'Legyen az oktatás stratégiai ágazat', *in* Mádl 1995, pp. 157-158; Ferenc Mádl's application for postgraduate scholarship, 24 November 1959, I /1, MTAL d. 429 699/429 dossier.

33 'Legyen az oktatás stratégiai ágazat', *in* Mádl 1995, p. 157.

doi: 10.5553/HYIEL/266627012021009001008

> "[...] the main organizer and manager of scientific work in the field of political and legal sciences. Its activities include[d] ensuring the systemic arrangement of political and legal sciences, promoting the raising of its standard, organizing comprehensive scientific lectures of fundamental importance, and debates and organizational issues affecting the entire state and legal sciences [...]."[34]

Despite the existing dictatorship, the composition of the Main Committee was shaped by professional considerations. This is why in 1954 the chief legal cadre of the period, Academician Imre Szabó, could write with great pride that "the significant results in our Law and Political Sciences have been achieved in close cooperation between old and new legal scholars."[35]

After graduating, Mádl continued to be in touch with his former teachers, who, in addition to teaching, also participated in research and sometimes in practical legal work.[36] Among them, Academician Endre Nizsalovszky, with whom Mádl, even as a university student came into the closest contact, "even before his release, he was the head of the department at the Budapest Faculty and was one of our best-known private lawyers appreciated abroad as well." The new system could not dispense with his knowledge either, and in the first half of the 1950s Nizsalovszky

> "participated in a wide range and with great zeal [...] in almost every line of our legal life: he was a corresponding member of the Academy of Sciences, member of the Main Committee on Legal Affairs, chairman of the Scientific Council of the Institute of Law and Political Sciences, member of the government committee preparing the civil code [...] "[37]

It was with his help[38] that in May 1956,[39] Mádl was transferred as a "rapporteur-general" from the court to the Office of the HAS.

Initially, he was a "clerk-specialist in Law and Political Sciences and an administrator of international relations at the Department of Social-Historical Sciences"[40] who worked under the direction of the coordinator. His duties also

34 'Az Állam- és Jogtudományi Főbizottság munkájáról', *Jogtudományi Közlöny*, March 1955, p. 184.

35 Imre Szabó, 'Az állam- és jogtudományi kongresszus után', *Szabad Nép*, 6 December 1954, p. 4.

36 *See* 'Jelentés a Politikai Bizottságnak a jogi oktatás és a jogtudomány helyzetéről', 18 February 1954, II /2, *in* Béla Révész, *Iratok az Igazságügyi Minisztérium történetéből 1944–1990*, IM-MHKK, Budapest, Issue 2, 2016, pp. 397-405.

37 The June 1954 proposal of academicians Károly Szladits and Béla Fogarasi for the election of Endre Nizsalovszky as a full member, MTAL Department No. 2 files, 66 d. dossier 9.

38 *Magyar Nemzet* 2000, p. 25; 'Legyen az oktatás stratégiai ágazat', *in* Mádl 1995, pp. 157-158.

39 Questionnaire related to the candidate's dissertation completed on 23 November 1959, MTAL 429 d. 699/429.

40 *Mádl Ferenc önéletrajza* 1959.

doi: 10.5553/HYIEL/266627012021009001008

included editing the Departmental Proceedings[41] and *Acta Juridica*,[42] the "HAS foreign language journal of legal studies".[43]

Mádl enthusiastically threw himself into the organizing work, and although Nizsalovszky was condemned to silence for his activities in the 1956 revolution, Mádl was allowed to remain. Based on the incomplete and partly unsorted documents in the Archives of the HAS, Mádl cultivated good relationships[44] not only with the members of the academic administration but also with actors of scientific life, including his former teachers in Pécs and Budapest.[45]

Meanwhile, he also made progress with his scientific work. He was supported in this field probably not only because of his performance at the workplace, but also because of his previous writings, which had a general resonance in professional circles. Mádl obtained his doctoral degree in 1957, and in 1958, as a contributor to the Institute of Law and Political Sciences, he also engaged in research in an organized way, on a weekly day-off for research, which he was granted for this purpose. And in 1959, as an individual aspirant, he could begin preparing for his next academic degree.

The postgraduate scholarship was under the strict supervision of the HAS at that time. In addition to their academic performance, candidates ranked by family background had to take serious professional and ideological exams and then report regularly on their progress. Their study plan was approved by the Scientific Qualification Committee, and their language and final exams were also decided by the Committee. It appears from Ferenc Mádl's application for admission in the Archives, his study framework and some of his grade sheets, his scientific research carried out diligently since his university years, even in addition to his daily work was highly appreciated by the Scientific Qualification Committee. Moreover, his poor peasant class background was taken into account, as well as the fact that "until the beginning of his university studies [...] he also worked as a manual worker."[46] His high level of language proficiency (he had already taken an advanced language exam in German and English at university

41 The organization and composition of Department No. 2 1958, documents of MTAL No. 2, 68 d, dossier 1.

42 *Mádl Ferenc önéletrajza* 1959.

43 He also highlighted his technical editorial work in his postgraduate scholarship application, 24 November 1959, I/5., MTAL 429. d. 699/429. dossier.

44 The cultivation of acquaintances was also facilitated by performing his duties at work, as part of the postgraduate scholarship affairs of No. 2 passed through his hands and, although he had not yet completed the training himself, *e.g.* he was allowed to be present at the meetings of the postgraduate scholarship committee. However, Mádl, as one of his later colleagues emphasized "[d]id not like the cult of celebrity in the field of science either." László Trócsányi Sr., *Jogászi pályafutásom*, Nagy and Trócsányi Law Office, Budapest, 1995, p. 78, but he helped everyone.

45 *See e.g.* the private letters from Lóránt Rudolf, Alajos Degré or István Szászy and László Trócsányi Sr. written to him in the Archives of the HAS.

46 The opinion of the MSZMP (Hungarian Socialist Workers' Party) organization of the HAS on Ferenc Mádl's application, 26 November 1959, MTAL 429 d. Dossier 699/429. Mádl never kept it secret that "due to the difficult financial situation of my parents, I had already been working constantly during my high school studies. I gave language lessons; [I worked] as an unskilled iron worker [...], as a manager [...], as an unskilled mine worker [...]". *Mádl Ferenc önéletrajza* 1959.

doi: 10.5553/HYIEL/266627012021009001008

and had a good command of Latin[47] since grammar school) was also acknowledged and in view of this, he was exempted from the compulsory language exam.[48]

Mádl was able to start his studies as an independent aspirant, *i.e.* he was expected to continue the research he had already started while working, primarily on his own schedule.[49] His supervisor was Miklós Világhy, who, although temporarily ousted from the leadership of the university after 1956, remained an indispensable factor in legal education and research.

The dissertation was originally entitled "Objective responsibility and its theory. Development history study" *(Az objektív felelősség és elmélete. Fejlődéstörténeti tanulmány)*.[50] Most probably in 1963, just before submission, the title was changed to "Tort responsibility in the history of the development of law and society" *(A deliktuális felelősség a jog és társadalom fejlődésének történetében)*[51] to cover Mádl's research more appropriately. Despite the fact that Mádl was given a day-off for research, due to his workload, he was only able to pass his candidate exams after the deadline was extended. Eventually, his defense was only carried out almost a year after the submission of the dissertation. The chairman of the reading committee was Endre Nizsalovszky, and its members included István Szászy,[52] an excellent international lawyer who was ousted in the early 1950s and banned from university education, similarly to Nizsalovszky. Later, Mádl worked in close scientific cooperation with the Szászy.

The defense was long, but at the end the most outstanding lawyers of the period unanimously proposed that Ferenc Mádl be awarded the degree of candidate. It is worth recalling the comment Gyula Eörsi made, who was Ferenc Mádl's superior at the research institute:

> "[...] now, in fact [...] a scientific ceremony is taking place here. Since this is what it can be called when someone over many years of painstaking, arduous labor creates work which I think everyone agrees, easily clears the hurdle of requirements for a candidate dissertation."[53]

47 It was with such foundation that he began learning French and Russian during his postgraduate scholarship. *See also Magyar Nemzet* 2000, p. 25.

48 *Cf.* Section 3(2)(d) and Section 5(3)(c) of MTE Decree 7269/1950. (XII. 7.) on the implementation of the Law Decree on the regulation of the introduction of the new-system academic degree and its acquisition.

49 *Cf.* Section 3(2) of Decree 41/1959. (X. 3.) Government Decree on aspirant training and academic degrees.

50 Ferenc Mádl's study framework, 13 January 1961, point II, MTAL 429. d. 699/429 dossier.

51 Letter from Sándor Kónya, coordinator, inviting opponents, 14 March 1963, MTAL 429 d. 699/429 dossier.

52 On the role of Nizsalovszky in 1956, *see* Ferenc Mádl, 'Endre Nizsalovszky (1894-1976)', *in* Gábor Hamza (ed.), *Magyar jogtudósok II.*, Professzorok Háza, Budapest, 2001, pp. 129-146. On putting István Szászy aside, *see* László Burián, 'István Szászy (1899-1976)', *in* Hamza (ed.) 2001, pp. 149-168; and Endre Domaniczky, 'Adalékok Szászy István jogászprofesszor 1950-es évekbeli ellehetetlenítéséhez', *Jogtörténeti Szemle*, 2020/3 (forthcoming).

53 Minutes on the discussion of Ferenc Mádl's candidate's dissertation, 5 February 1964, MTAL 429 d. 699/429, p. 9.

doi: 10.5553/HYIEL/266627012021009001008

4. An Examination of European Legal Systems Comes to the Fore

Gyula Eörsi, himself a student of Károly Szladits and Endre Nizsalovszky, who praised Mádl's work with such approval,

> "[...] was the greatest and internationally perhaps the most recognized representative of Hungarian civil law after 1945. [...] he was not simply a scientist. At the Faculty of Law of Eötvös Loránd University, he was an enthusiastic supporter of the civil law students' association, a dedicated talent scout who felt, almost unmistakably, in more and more young people that they are the people of the future."[54]

He also spotted talent in Mádl, who had a part-time job in the civil law department under his supervision at the Institute of Law and Political Sciences of the HAS between 1958 and 1967. Therefore, when

> "Western Europe became interested in Marxist jurisprudence in the early 1960s [...] some students [...] were allowed to travel to study. We were the first, then gradually more and more people could go."[55]

Mádl studied comparative law between 1961 and 1963 in Strasbourg, where, after graduation, he regularly returned to teach for a long time.[56] Moreover, he also attended conferences and went on study visits abroad, and in 1967, he taught and did research in the US. He witnessed the differences between the legal systems of the Western and Eastern Blocs locally and with his own eyes, and he saw the differences in culture and lifestyle as well.

Due to his language skills, professional status and growing international experience, in 1963, *he was appointed to the research groups studying economic integration in Western Europe and Eastern Europe* at the Institute of Law and

54 Tamás Sárközy, 'Aki a tüzet ivóvízzé változtatta (Eörsi Gyula halálára)', *Kritika*, 1992/6, p. 19. For more on Gyula Eörsi, *see e.g.* János Verebics (ed.), *Eörsi Gyula Emlékkönyv 2018*, MKLK, Budapest, 2018.

55 *Magyar Nemzet* 2000, p. 25.

56 Biography of Ferenc Mádl, 19 November 1974, MTAL 429 d. 699/429 dossier. *See also* "[...] the comparative law course in Strasbourg, which lasted two months a year for three years, had to be completed by everyone. [...] And the elders of the institute taught there." 'Hagyni kell történni a sorsot. Interjú Sólyom Lászlóval', *Századvég*, 2004/1, p. 145.

doi: 10.5553/HYIEL/266627012021009001008

Political Sciences of HAS.[57] The former research group was led by Imre Szabó,[58] the latter by Gyula Eörsi, and in both Ferenc Mádl worked together with Géza Herczegh,[59] later a member of the Hungarian Constitutional Court and the ICJ in the Hague. So, even before obtaining the candidate's degree he found his new research topic, in which he was absorbed partly due to his trips and studies abroad and partly due to the tasks received at the research institutes. Although he continued his research within civil law, his interest shifted from sheer private law issues to border areas, private international law, and international trade law.

Studying private international law had significant history in Hungary, but Mádl was not satisfied with the characteristic mechanical analysis. Within a short period of time he not only became an expert on the subject but moving within the Marxist frameworks he was able to shift the focus of his research from the East to the economic integration of Western European states.[60] He managed to achieve his results with *the method of comparative law*, which he had been using and continuously improving since his student years. However, not only the topics and the research method proved to be novel, but also the legal theoretical approach itself, because within the socialist bloc what was considered necessary at that time was to examine economic integration from an economic point of view.[61] In Hungary, however, several of the leading lawyers of the era believed that with the help of East-West comparative law,

> "[...] the '*bourgeois* law' of Europe [...] and its entire set of economic and political values could be beaten and be made to disappear from legal history.

57 Topic sheet for research in 1965, Topic XVIII, title: 'A békés egymás mellett élésnek az ENSZ-szel összefüggő kérdése'. Subtopic: 'A szocialista államok gazdasági együttműködése, a tőkés integráció[s] szervezetek'. Supervisor: Imre Szabó. Progress report on the research carried out in 1965, Topic XXVI, title: 'A szocialista államok gazdasági együttműködése és kapcsolataik a tőkés integrációs szervekkel'. Supervisor: Gyula Eörsi. MTAL Class II, box 170, dossier 6.

58 The duality inherent in the life of Imre Szabó, which also highlights the difficulties of evaluating legal careers during the period of dictatorship, is perhaps best recalled by László Trócsányi Sr. in his *memoir*: "Under the leadership of [Imre Szabó], the institute became an internationally recognized scientific institution, which was frequented by foreign scientists from both the West and the East. [...] On the other hand, there were rumors that in the late 1940s, he was actively involved in the "cleansing work" of the Ministry of Justice and the HAS for the removal of lawyers and academics." Trócsányi Sr. 1995, p. 59.

59 *See* more on the academic career of Géza Herczegh (1928-2010): Gábor Béli *et al.* (eds.), *Emlékkötet Herczegh Géza születésének 90. évfordulója alkalmából*, Publikon, Pécs, 2018; on his personality: Ferenc Mádl, 'Búcsú Herczegh Gézától', *Magyar Szemle*, 2010/3-4, pp. 118-122.

60 According to him, his master, Endre Nizsalovszky, played a decisive role in this recognition: "It was more than twenty years that [...] in his suspension imposed on him, he had been translating and proofreading that many-volumed publication which was then called the encyclopedia of EEC. He involved me in this work [...] This work and his insight into the importance of things to come, his sensibility to new challenges such as EEC law, caused me to 'wander' quite a lot in the law of economic integration toward the West and the East, while sometimes I described what I considered important in this new world of phenomena." *See* Ferenc Mádl, 'Az Európai Gazdasági Közösség és Magyarország', *Jogtudományi Közlemények*, 1988/6, p. 449.

61 *Cf.* Debate on Ferenc Mádl's doctoral dissertation, Iván Meznerics's opponent review, MTAL 429. d. 699/429 dossier; the event calendar of the Czechoslovak Academy of Sciences in 1966, HAS documents of Department No. 9, box 6, dossier 1.

doi: 10.5553/HYIEL/266627012021009001008

> It was the other way round. There were more and more people who fully endorsed these values, and then they became their dream."[62]

Thus, in Hungary, paradoxically thanks to Marxist legal scholars, already during the dictatorship several talented lawyers[63] became immersed in Western professional literature, who, by the time of the regime change, even managed to get professorships and start educating students. Giving priority to topics such as Mádl's new field of research was, of course, motivated not only by legal decisions, but also by changes in the international situation of the country.

> "From the sixties [...], especially towards the end of the '60s, that field became extremely important because Hungary's foreign trade orientation became stronger. That is why the demand for teaching this subject at university arose."[64]

Thus, Mádl started teaching in his former alma mater, ELTE, from 1968, while until 1971, he continued to work full-time in the Office of the HAS. In 1966, representatives of economics and law seceded from Department No. 2 (Department of Social-Historical Sciences), which was previously united, and Ferenc Mádl, the head of the department, became the coordinator of the newly organized Department No. 9. His duties grew in number, his responsibility increased, but he continued his research with even greater enthusiasm. According to the available documents,[65] he participated in almost all the organizational work, while also being present at the various committee meetings. He finally left the Institute of Law and Political Sciences at the end of 1967, "because we had fundamental disagreements that could not be resolved."[66]

5. Becoming Professor from Researcher

Between 1968 and 1971, Mádl gave lectures as an adjunct professor at the university.[67] From 1971 he became a full-time associate professor, and in 1975 he was appointed university professor of law.[68] His knowledge of administration gained at the HAS also proved to be useful at the university, where he worked in the rector's office for six years (1971-1977). From 1971 to 1974, he was head of the International Relations Offices of ELTE, and the vice-rector responsible for international affairs from 1974 to 1977. He worked here to everyone's

62 Ferenc Mádl, 'Európa és a magyar jogrendszer', *in* Mádl 1995, p. 31.

63 One of the centers of talented lawyers was the Institute of Law and Political Sciences of the HAS. *See more* on this period: Trócsányi Sr. 1995, pp. 56-79; 'Hagyni kell történni a sorsot. Interjú Sólyom Lászlóval', *Századvég*, 2004/1, pp. 143-146.

64 'Legyen az oktatás stratégiai ágazat', *in* Mádl 1995, p. 158.

65 *See in particular*: MTAL files of Department, material of boxes 5-9.

66 *Magyar Nemzet* 2000, p. 25. On the termination of the part-time job at the Institute of Law and Political Sciences of the HAS: Change of notification form and note, MTAL 576/6 dossier.

67 Biography of Ferenc Mádl, 19 November 1974, MTAL 429 d. 699/429 dossier.

68 Id.; *ELTE Értesítője 1975/1976*, Budapest, June 1976.

doi: 10.5553/HYIEL/266627012021009001008

satisfaction, so when his term of office expired the University Council awarded him a gold commemorative medal, as Professor Mádl

> "created the organizational conditions for our expanding international relations alongside his high-level teaching and educational work. Perhaps the most sensitive point in university administration is foreign affairs. The preparation and implementation of cooperation agreements with a number of foreign institutions, the benefits of which can be enjoyed above all by our departments are linked with the name of Comrade Mádl. Comrade Mádl, with his usual modesty and willingness, gained authority and general esteem not only in professional circles, but also in public life wherever he represented our institution."[69]

However, Mádl's primary field of work remained teaching and research at the department.[70] There was an entirely new research direction that was founded on the topics of private international law and trade law inherited from the Institute of Law and Political Sciences, followed by the establishment of a new department (Department of Private International Law).[71]

> "[Upon] my proposal a larger department was created for studying and teaching international personal, property, economic and sales law. This is now called the Department of Private International Law. I started working on European integration relatively early. At the time I was also tempted by the dream of European integration, although I did not believe that it would ever be a reality for us. In the late 1950s, articles on the Common Market were more like phraseological writings than scientific papers. I think I have managed to analyze that world objectively and scientifically. [...] At ELTE, with the help of the Common Market we established the European Affairs Center."[72]

– he recalled the years following the change of regime.[73]

Mádl's research on integration continued in parallel with his university teaching, but his relationship with the Academy was not severed either. During this period he maintained close contacts with Endre Nizsalovszky and István Szászy regarding his research topics. The former was one of the opponents of his

69 *ELTE Értesítője 1977/1978*, Budapest, 1978.

70 "He was a professor in the true sense of the word. He laid not simply the curriculum, but also his creed about society and law before his students. He did a great deal for the professional careers of his colleagues who were often decades younger. With his scientific prestige and willingness to cooperate, he created a real professional workshop." Barna Mezey, 'Köszöntő', *in* Miklós Király (ed.), *Fabula de te narratur. Előadások Mádl Ferenc 80. születésnapjára*, ELTE ÁJK, Budapest, 2011.

71 Until 31 December 1986, Section for Private International Law, from 1 January 1987, Department of Private International Law (the head of both was Ferenc Mádl). *ELTE Értesítője 1986/1987 és 1987/1988*, Budapest, 1988, p. 121.

72 *See also* János Martonyi, 'Nélküle másként alakultak volna a dolgok, és mások lennénk mi is', *in Mádl Ferenc 80* 2011, p. 90.

73 'Legyen az oktatás stratégiai ágazat', *in* Mádl 1995, pp. 158-159.

doi: 10.5553/HYIEL/266627012021009001008

doctoral dissertation defended in 1974, the latter was the chairman of the reading committee.[74] He also worked with Szászy on the 1968 draft of the Hungarian Code of Private International Law.[75] The preparation and submission of the doctoral dissertation was supported by all competent bodies (university organizations and academic committees), because they all agreed that Ferenc Mádl's

> "scientific work has gained new impetus since he was awarded the candidate's degree. He has published several books, partly in Hungarian and partly in different foreign languages. His work covers civil law, private international law, and comparative private and trade law. [...] In recent years, his scientific work has been extended to ever wider international fields. He has received multiple invitations [...] to Western countries [...]."[76]

Professor Gyula Eörsi, head of Department No. 9 of the HAS added that

> "in addition to his dissertation, one book of his was published in Hungarian and English, and another booklet of his in German. He has written a large number of studies published in Hungarian and foreign journals. His theoretical contribution to the field of the law of international economic relations is considerable, and on some issues [...] he was the first to publish in Hungary."[77]

The doctoral dissertation itself was novel and relevant in the choice of topic, as unanimously emphasized by its opponents. Beyond describing the rules of the narrower field of his research, civil law, "in order to shed light on the problem", Mádl did not shy away from examining the rules of other areas of law, especially constitutional law, public administrative law, financial law, civil procedural law, international law and labor law.[78] Although it was not specifically stated during the debate of the dissertation, it is clear from the writings of all three

74 The preliminary resolution of the Department No. 9 on Ferenc Mádl's doctoral procedure, undated, MTAL 429 d. 699/429 dossier.

75 Biography of Ferenc Mádl, 19 November 1974, MTAL 429 d. 699/429 dossier, and the recommendation for the initiation of the doctoral procedure issued by the Department of Economics and Law of the HAS on 29 May 1973 – signed by Gyula Eörsi, MTAL 429. d. 699/429 dossier.

76 Opinion of the management of Eötvös Loránd University on Ferenc Mádl's application regarding his doctoral procedure. Preliminary decision of the Subcommittee of Law and Political Sciences of the Scientific Qualification Committee (SQC) on Ferenc Mádl's doctoral application (without date), MTAL 429 d. 699/429 dossier.

77 Preliminary decision of the SQC Subcommittee on Ferenc Mádl's doctoral application (without date), MTAL 429 d. 699/429 dossier.

78 Endre Nizsalovszky's opponent's review on the doctoral dissertation of Ferenc Mádl, MTAL 429 d. 699/429 dossier.

doi: 10.5553/HYIEL/266627012021009001008

opponents[79] that it was considered a bold choice for a research topic. Indeed, although the studies were formally conducted in order to interpret trends in the system of relations and development of the Soviet Economic Zone (CMEA), the work made it clear (and convincingly demonstrated with reference to the jurisprudence) that on the other side of the Iron Curtain a specific form integration evolved, that is beyond capitalist legal systems, driven by economic interests, but also accompanied by active legal development. In his response to the opponents' opinions, Mádl, intentionally or unintentionally, called both formations *equally important* for Hungary. He might have referred to his own insights when he, already a member of the Antall government (the first democratic government after the transition in 1989), said that Western legal systems were "recognized" by more and more people, and it "has been believed by others for a long time, that it is here where the mainstream of Hungarian legal culture continues."[80]

6. From Professor to Public Figure

Ferenc Mádl's scientific career rose even higher after obtaining his doctoral degree. Between 1985 and 1990, he was secretary[81] of the Scientific Qualification Committee of the HAS, which meant that all applications for scientific degrees in Hungary passed through his hands. In 1987, he was elected a corresponding member of the HAS, and in 1993, he became a full member.[82] Owing to his great talent, Ferenc Mádl, professor of law was already at the height of his scientific career at the time of the dictatorship. He loved teaching, was widely published, and his name and work were highly appreciated both at home and abroad.

However, thanks to his research topics and international relations, he saw the political and economic movements of the 1970s and 1980s, as well the changes in the country's situation on the international scene much earlier and in a much more complex way than others.

> "Then came the obvious signs of crisis in the system: economic reforms [...], intensification of East-West cooperation (accession to GATT, the International Monetary Fund, the World Bank [...]), processes of political

79 On the proposal of Gyula Eörsi, chairman of Department No. 9 of MTA, the three opponents invited by the SQC were Endre Nizsalovszky, György Haraszti and Iván Meznerics MTAL 429. d. 699/429 dossier.

80 Ferenc Mádl, 'Európa és a magyar jogrendszer', *in* Mádl 1995, p. 24.

81 *Cf.* Decree 1038/1984. (VIII. 22.) MT on the composition of the SQC and Decree 1106/1990. (VI. 13.) MT on the dismissal of the Secretary of the SQC.

82 According to the 1986 recommendation, Ferenc Mádl "[...] conducts his scientific work at a high level even compared to international research, and with his personality, civic and moral behavior [...] deserves the respect of the world of science and Hungarian society." *See* Vilmos Peschka and Kálmán Kulcsár's recommendation of 2 October 1986 on the issue of corresponding membership, MTAL 429 d. 699/429 dossier. It is worth noting that Academicians Kulcsár and Peschka recommended Mádl as a corresponding member already in 1981. *Magyar Tudomány*, 1981/11-12, pp. 877-878.

doi: 10.5553/HYIEL/266627012021009001008

> liberalization, indebtedness, the desperate endeavor to get out of the vortex, stemming from a recognized alternative of closing up or falling behind. The spirit of '56 has resurrected, the forces of freedom have intensified into a social whirl."[83]

– he summarized succinctly, already as minister; the direction processes were taking in the wake of the crisis signs palpable at the time of submitting his doctoral dissertation. By the second half of the 1980s, "a socio-economic revolution 'broke out' in Hungary unnoticed, a peaceful revolution was spreading everywhere"– he concluded.

Mádl did not take part in the political preparations before the regime change: "[I] remained within the framework of my profession." However, that did not prevent him from talking about the need for change and engagement with the West in a fairly open way in his 1987 academic inaugural address. The speech also appeared in print a year later.[84] In 1989, he too was influenced by events that captivated both the lecturers and students of ELTE. "I watched the negotiations of the Opposition Round Table Talks [in] amazement. It was there that I discovered József Antall, and I immediately saw that he knew what he wanted."[85] Mádl did not know the later prime minister in person, but when Antall called him over the phone,[86] he realized that he could not say no. "I felt it to be my moral duty [...] to assist the much-anticipated transformation with my legal expertise."[87]

By accepting the invitation, a new phase began in his life, lasting more than two decades, during which Ferenc Mádl, the highly respected professor and scientist, became a public figure. What may have motivated his transition into public life, setting his achievements in science aside? Later, Mádl, remembering Prime Minister Antall, clearly defined his own political creed, for the attainment of which he worked until his death:

> "[n]ational liberal thinking, national-folk commitment, Christian-European values and the Atlantic thought, democracy, the rule of law, social market economy, the restoration of the country's sovereignty and a clear commitment to the European heritage."[88]

83 Ferenc Mádl, 'Európa és a magyar jogrendszer', *in* Mádl 1995, p. 31.

84 Mádl 1988, pp. 442-449.

85 Mádl said several times that he followed the events on television, but it is obvious that he could have exchanged ideas personally with some of the people influencing the events, his colleagues and students at the Faculty of Law. Cited from *Magyar Nemzet* 2000, p. 25.

86 Ferenc Mádl, '"Bent vagyunk a fősodorban." Emlékezés Antall Józsefről', *in* Mádl 1995, pp. 11-12. On the background of Antal's request *see e.g.* György O'sváth, *Élettöredékek*, O'sváth Alapítvány, Csenger-Budapest, 2017, pp. 146-147.

87 *Magyar Nemzet* 2000, p. 25.

88 Ferenc Mádl, '"Bent vagyunk a fősodorban." Emlékezés Antall Józsefről', *in* Mádl 1995, p. 12.

doi: 10.5553/HYIEL/266627012021009001008

Words that had been matured over long decades, some of which – however much he had lived in inner emigration,[89] like many of his fellow intellectuals in Hungary – had already been on his mind in his earlier research, and some of which had also appeared, as far as possible, already in his earlier works.[90]

Although he stressed all along that he was above partisan politics, in fact after 1990, whatever his position, he was also a politician, whose performance is well represented by the fact that for two decades he adhered strongly to the values set at the beginning of his political career, and for their representation, he was also able to create majority in the political arena. Furthermore, Mádl did not hide the fact that

> "the rigid concepts of 'right' and 'left' are foreign to me; they of course help orientation in public life. But when it comes to the affairs of the family, the wider community, and the nation, our thoughts and actions must be guided by their interests."

Thus, what may have attracted him to public life was the belief that in the years of transition, he could serve his homeland and the nation, fight for all the values he had witnessed and held dear in the parental home and at school.

7. Minister in the Antall-Government

When he entered public life, Ferenc Mádl first met József Antall, a politician who belonged to the same generation and, perhaps as a result of his Piarist upbringing and his legal studies conducted for four years,[91] was a very like-minded. In a short time, there was a deep human and trusting relationship between him and the Prime Minister, which became even closer before his appointment as Minister of Culture and Education.[92]

89 *Magyar Nemzet* 2000, p. 25.

90 *See e.g.* 'Magyarország első polgári törvénykönyve – az 1959. évi IV. törvény – a polgári jogi kodifikáció történetének tükrében', *Az MTA Társadalmi-Történeti Tudományok Osztályának Közleményei*, January-February 1960, pp. 3-88; *Az Európai Gazdasági Közösség joga*, Akadémiai, Budapest, 1974.

91 József Antall "was [n]ot only a historian. He also studied law for four years. He had great erudition and awareness regarding public law." Ferenc Mádl, '"Bent vagyunk a fősodorban." Emlékezés Antall Józsefről', *in* Mádl 1995, p. 12.

92 "Of course, our [r]elationship has become very deep, not only in the context of cabinet meetings, but also in our personal conversations. [...] We talked a lot especially when it came to taking over the portfolio of culture." Ferenc Mádl, 'Felelősség a kultúráért. Érték és irány – konferencia az antalli örökségről', *Magyar Szemle*, 1996/2, p. 171. It was also clear for the staff that there was a close relationship of trust between these two people: József Antall "found more and more support, a loyal friend and a serious intellectual partner in Ferenc Mádl, although they only got to know each other more closely during the shuffle of the government" – recalled Gyula Kodolányi decades later. Gyula Kodolányi, 'Antall József kormányt alakít – A Hungarian Review interjúja (2. rész)', *Magyar Szemle*, 2015/3-4, p. 9. *See also* György Granasztói, 'Az ellenpélda', *in Mádl Ferenc 80* 2011, p. 36.

doi: 10.5553/HYIEL/266627012021009001008

But before this, Professor *Mádl was first entrusted by Antall to serve as Minister for European Affairs.*[93] At the same time, as a minister without portfolio, he also dealt with science policy,[94] privatization and banking supervision.[95] His portfolio further included

> "relations with European and international organizations. I was a researcher of the field, I gained no small amount of international experience, I consented to the task that I should try to put all this into practice."[96]

From among the different cases he was responsible for, only one example is the diplomatic negotiations over the Danube Dam *Gabčíkovo-Nagymaros* in the administration of which he actively participated as a government commissioner[97] from 1991 to 1993.[98]

In February 1993 *Professor Mádl was appointed minister of Culture and Public Education*. The appointment came as a surprise, yet the Prime Minister had a good eye to assess that Mádl was extremely suitable for the position not only because of his law degree (the preparation of several important laws was taking place at the portfolio at the time), but also thanks to his personal qualities. As expected, Mádl managed the legislative activity of the ministry with appropriate expertise. "As a minister of culture, I was supposed to introduce a new legal basis for the fundamental issues of Hungarian culture and education."[99] As a result, based on the work of the ministry, the Parliament passed the Public Education Act, the Higher Education Act, the Act on the HAS, and the laws on the National Cultural Fund and the National Scientific Research Fund, which formed the basis for the national support of culture and science. Mádl made significant efforts not only to have the draft laws adopted but participated in the preparation of legislation belonging to the ministry in general. Developing the concept of the National Core Curriculum can be considered one of his greatest successes. This concept

> "was not only sharply criticized by the opposition at the time, but there was no consensus among the senior staff of the ministry. When I realized that the

93 Government Decree 1023/1992. (IV. 23.) on establishing an inter-ministerial committee for the coordination of governmental tasks related to European integration.

94 Government Decree 1015/1993. (III. 3.) on certain organizational and supervisory measures related to the reshuffling of the Government; Government Decree 1020/1990. (VII. 17.) on the establishment of the Science Policy Committee and the Science Policy Council. *See more* on his tasks and thoughts related to science policy: 'A tudomány feladatait a tudománynak kell megoldania. Beszélgetés Mádl Ferenccel', *Magyar Tudomány*, 1990/11, pp. 1328-1336.

95 Ferenc Mádl, '"Bent vagyunk a fősodorban." Emlékezés Antall Józsefről', *in* Mádl 1995, p. 12. *See also* Decree 71/1990. (V. 24.) KE.

96 'A tudomány feladatait a tudománynak kell megoldania. Beszélgetés Mádl Ferenccel', *Magyar Tudomány*, 1990/11, p. 1336.

97 'Új miniszterünk: Mádl Ferenc', *Köznevelés*, 1993/9, p. 2.

98 Later, he reviewed the history of the negotiations related to the dam and the annals history of the litigation in a large-scale study. Ferenc Mádl, 'Bős-Nagymaros tegnap és ma', *Magyar Szemle*, 1998/1-2, pp. 7-41.

99 *Magyar Nemzet* 2000, p. 25.

doi: 10.5553/HYIEL/266627012021009001008

> contradictions were irreconcilable, I accomplished the task of writing the Common Core Curriculum *(Nemzeti Alaptanterv)* myself, which was approved by various conciliation forums."

Upon the proposal of Ferenc Mádl, the government also made a decision about the creation of the Eötvös Scholarship of the Hungarian State, which (by state decision, unlike the scientific scholarships based primarily on exchange programs at the time) was aimed at supporting the long-term research of the best Hungarian scientists and candidates abroad.

However, Mádl also *used the position of Minister of Culture to rethink his own opinion on European integration*, based on his decades of scientific work. As early as 1974, during the debate of his doctoral dissertation, it was noticeable that Professor Mádl was speaking about two different phenomena of European integration: *(i)* on the one hand, *unification beginning in an economic field, which is expected to increase;* and *(ii)* on the other hand *the common European traditions* that here in Hungary date back to the first king of the country, St. Stephen. Already during his ministry without a portfolio, he was actively preoccupied with connecting these two lines of thought. At that time, he mentioned several times that the common European heritage[100] and the Hungarian legal culture were determined by European models.[101] As Minister of Culture, he also paid particular attention to building and deepening European relations, from university research and exchange programs to developments in higher education.[102] Following his practical experience as a minister participating in public life, he approached his previous topic from a completely new angle. He summarized his views on the future of European integration in his academic inaugural address titled "The future of culture in European integration" *(A kultúra jövője az európai integrációban)* a few months after having accomplished his ministerial work.[103] In this address, Mádl discussed European integration, starting with economic integration and extending to cultural areas, as not only a possible direction of development, but the only possible way forward of further unification and, indeed, survival.

> "We must realize that Europe is first and foremost a cultural community that has grown out of the past and cannot exist without the cohesive values of its culture [...] the desired and more complete European unity cannot evolve without the cohesive forces of culture [...]."[104]

100 Ferenc Mádl, 'Az európai értékeknek elkötelezve', *in* Mádl 1995, p. 16.

101 Ferenc Mádl, 'Európa és a magyar jogrendszer', *in* Mádl 1995, p. 24.

102 Ferenc Mádl, 'EU (EK) és más külső erőforrások a magyar felsőoktatásban', *in* Mádl 1995, pp. 75-81.

103 Ferenc Mádl, 'A kultúra jövője az európai integrációban', *in* Mádl 1995, pp. 82-105. The material was later published, revised and expanded, *see* Ferenc Mádl, 'A kultúra jövője az európai integrációban', *Magyar Szemle*, 1995/5, pp. 479-500.

104 Ferenc Mádl, 'A kultúra jövője az európai integrációban', *in* Mádl 1995, pp. 82-105.

doi: 10.5553/HYIEL/266627012021009001008

Professor Mádl, examining the provisions of the founding Treaties and the practice of Community institutions, concluded that *cultural goals and values are present in the everyday life of the EU*. One of the findings of his dissertation is that cultural cooperation should be built along a clear strategy; for which he also provides various examples from his ministerial practice. However, his most important finding is that

> "[i]n addition to the national sense of identity [...] what is necessary to make the great European dream come true is the European sense of identity, whose resources are to be found in culture."

8. One of the Creators of Unity Among Hungarian Conservatives

By that time, Mádl had already realized that the idea of a common European heritage was the most important concept and objective not only for Hungary, from which, as a fundamental concept, all elements of his political creed also emanated. He also recognized that all of the moments of his career were connected to it: from the parental home through grammar school and his doctoral dissertation analyzing European integration to the ministerial chair representing the height of his career by that point. Probably, this is why the volume collecting the most important speeches and writings of the period spent in the Antall government was given the title "On the roads of European heritage" *(Az európai örökség útjain)*. The book itself was supposed to be a synopsis and a conclusion, but in fact it can be considered a summary of his thoughts, serving as sources for the most important concepts of the next period.

The support of the first freely elected government was completely devoured by the launch of reforms and the death of its charismatic leader. The two most important tasks, therefore, were to bring the disintegrated camp together and to create a new, joint program. Ferenc Mádl, "[o]ne of the most respected members of the government that fell in '94",[105] played a prominent role in both.

He took part in the organization tasks, because he believed that "without a [c]ivil alternative, the whole regime change is worthless [...]."[106] As a part of this effort and as a candidate of the three opposition parties at the time, MDF, FIDESZ and KDNP, he ran for president. In 1995, "[t]here was no risk in presidential candidacy [...]", he recalled later.[107] What was an even more complex task was to form the Association for Hungarian Civic Cooperation, "which involved an awfully lot of work and responsibility."[108] The association was registered in 1996, and its president was Ferenc Mádl between 1996 and 2000.[109]

105 Viktor Orbán, 'Köszöntő Mádl Ferenc 80. születésnapján', *Magyar Szemle*, 2011/3-4, pp. 4-5.
106 *Magyar Nemzet* 2000, p. 25.
107 Id.
108 Id.
109 *See* at https://mpee.hu.

doi: 10.5553/HYIEL/266627012021009001008

> "I am convinced [...] that the importance of non-governmental organizations is growing worldwide, the role of parties in addressing people is diminishing. [...] There is a need for self-organizing civil groups."[110]

– he later observed, referring to the circumstances of the founding, as already President of the Republic. Not only did he consider non-governmental organizations the framework of organizational work, but thus also the platform for intellectuals' activities, their common thinking. During the operation of the National Circle *(Nemzeti Kör)*,[111] founded in 1994-1995, on György O'sváth's and Ferenc Mádl's initiative,[112] (at least in the 1990s) Mádl undertook both tasks: on the one hand he "tried to bring the fragmented opposition parties closer to each other" and on the other hand, as an early forerunner of today's political think tanks, he was involved in the development of concepts and action plans. Mádl found grassroots organizations and common thinking so important that he also joined another intellectual group[113] after his presidency term, since "[b]oth the harmonizing driving force of our cooperative responsibility is required, and [...] intellectual action is necessary as well."[114]

Mádl participated in establishing the new joint program in two ways: *(i)* in the different circles of common thinking, as we could see above; and *(ii)* as an internationally recognized and respected scientist, an expert on EU integration, continuously developing his topic. The latter line gained more momentum with the aforementioned 1994 keynote speech at the HAS and in the 1995 volume summarizing the ministerial period. By that time the topic had broken out of the narrow scientific framework, since EU accession and framing the country's place and opportunities within the EU was also considered a priority in public debates. That is why it was an important decision that Mádl published his writings on integration in a political periodical called *Magyar Szemle*.[115]

110 *Magyar Nemzet* 2000, p. 25.

111 O'sváth 2017, pp. 167-169. The National Circle was terminated in 2006. 'Megszűnt a Nemzeti Kör', *Heti Válasz*, 28 September 2006, p. 6; 'Közlemény', *Magyar Nemzet*, 17 June 2006, p. 6; 'Nyilatkozat', *Magyar Nemzet*, 26 September 2006, p. 2.

112 O'sváth and Mádl both stated that they founded the National Circle together. *See* O'sváth 2017, p. 167; *Magyar Nemzet* 2000, p. 25.

113 György Granasztói started organizing the National Circle in 2004, Ferenc Mádl only came here at the end of his term of presidency, but the idea originated from him. György Granasztói, 'Előszó', *in* György Granasztói & Ilona Sebestyén (eds.), *Magyarország fordulóban*, Magyar Szemle Alapítvány, Budapest, 2011, p. 5. The National Circle published several volumes of essays over the years (in 2007, and 2011) and after the death of Ferenc Mádl it adopted his name. *See* at https://hirado.hu/2016/08/11/kiemelkedo-es-kiveteles-szemelyisegkent-emlekezeik-meg-a-madl-ferenc-kor-granasztoi-gyorgyrol/#.

114 Ferenc Mádl, 'Előszó', *in* György Granasztói & Gyula Kodolányi (eds.), *Magyarország ma és holnap*, Magyar Szemle Alapítvány, Budapest, 2007, p. 7.

115 *See e.g.* 'Magyarország útja az Európai Unióba', *Magyar Szemle*, 1997/1-2, pp. 7-19; 'Magyarország EU-tagsága: érvek és ellenérvek', *Magyar Szemle*, 1997/5-6, pp. 49-56; Zoltán Csáky, 'Beszélgetés az integrációról Mádl Ferenccel', *Magyar Szemle*, 1998/3-4, pp. 69-74; 'Erkölcsi értékek az európai integrációban', *Magyar Szemle*, 2001/3-4, pp. 7-11.

doi: 10.5553/HYIEL/266627012021009001008

9. The Second President of the Third Republic

After the second term of Árpád Göncz, the first President of the Republic after the transition ended,[116] the former opposition parties now in government since 1998 repeatedly nominated Ferenc Mádl for the position. There were strong arguments in favor of his appointment since

> "Ferenc Mádl is the epitome of the political ideals of the coalition ruling today, an emblematic figure due to the role he played in the politics of the past decade. He was a member of the Antall government, at the beginning of the FIDESZ-MDF coalition, in 1995, he was a joint nominee for President of the Republic, the chairman of the Civil Cooperation, and thus, he has an outstanding role in creating the social coalition behind the present coalition."[117]

It was difficult to convince Professor Mádl of his new candidacy.[118]

> "I had been resisting for a long time, and then [...] I came to the conclusion that maybe it was the task which was not expected and was not desired [...] that gave me more human strength to maintain my integrity in life. I did not think of political bargaining, just to serve where I could offer my help."[119]

One could discuss at length the aims and history of Professor Mádl's presidency from 2000 to 2005, but only the most important aspirations shall be mentioned here. At the heart of Ferenc Mádl's activities were, as it was manifested already at an earlier stage in his political career, the forthcoming accession to the EU and the mapping of the opportunities that would open up for the country and the nation. When he took office, he had been studying the law of European integration for almost four decades. Thanks to his deep knowledge of integration, he was aware not only of the existing rules, but also of the possible directions for the further development, and *he could also foresee the problems which the growing EU was going to face as a result of enlargement*. As a scholar of European law, he also

116 Árpád Göncz (1922-2015) was the President of the Republic of Hungary for two cycles, between 1990-2000. *See more* on his career and presidency: Dae Soon Kim, *Göncz Árpád*, Scolar, Budapest, 2011.

117 János G. Gáspár, 'A magától értetődő meglepetés', *Magyar Szemle*, 2000/7-8.

118 *See e.g.* Viktor Orbán's birthday greeting: "I always thought that it was somehow easier for you to run for president against the odds than for a shoo-in president.". Orbán 2011, p. 6. A decade later, one of his close colleagues, Gáspár Gróh, recalled Mádl's reluctance in a similar way: "There are different stories in political folklore about how he had to be persuaded to run for president in 2000. Only a few remember that he had easily accepted this role five years earlier, that is, he had undertaken a parliamentary contest where an opposition candidate could not succeed against a two-thirds pro-government majority. It was easy to say yes then, as he could be sure he would not be president." Gáspár Gróh, 'Elnök úr kilencven éves lenne... – Mádl Ferenc emlékezete', *Magyar Szemle*, 2020/11-12.

119 *Magyar Nemzet* 2000, p. 25.

doi: 10.5553/HYIEL/266627012021009001008

wanted to express his own opinion on certain issues.[120] Due to the above, his statements about the EU carried much weight both at home and abroad.

It could also be said that Mádl, as President of the Republic, participated in politics on two levels. *(i)* On the one hand, *demonstrating the unity of the nation*, he performed all the duties prescribed for him by the Hungarian constitution and legislation. But he went even further, and here it is worth recalling his speeches analyzing environmental questions or the situation of the Roma among the minorities. *(ii)* On the other hand, *he regularly expressed his views, orally and in writing, on matters relating to the EU*. At such times, however, he spoke not only as president, but also as one of the internationally recognized experts on the subject. His instructions formulated with the usual simplicity were aimed at a wider audience in Hungary: ordinary citizens, as well as Hungarian intellectuals and the political elite. During his long teaching, research and already a decade-long political career, however, Mádl developed a wide network of international contacts. He also expressed his views on the EU in various international fora. At such times, showing an excellent diplomatic sense, he regularly emphasized the historical and cultural parallels between Hungary and (Western) Europe.

Professor Mádl, who ten years earlier argued in favor of the creation of a European community based on a cultural basis instead of pursuing integration based on economic relations, once again, as President of the Republic, took stock of the challenges facing integration. He already summarized these in one of his first speeches[121] as President. One of his main ideas was that in the face of "more distant common perspectives," such as a "federal state, a true European Parliament, a true European president, who is elected, an executive power in true European sense," expectations must also be set in "the other pan of the scale".

> "[This] community shall face its destiny together for better or for worse, in the spirit of mutual trust and shared values. The second is that even the smallest federal state can only be born out of a treaty derived from the power of the people of the member states, we cannot abandon the source of national sovereignty. [...] The third is that as we achieve a higher degree of integration, national cultures shall become richer, we shall make the most of our freedoms [...]."[122]

It is worth specifically mentioning here what he meant as a Hungarian by freedoms and shared values. Mádl understood *the Charter of Fundamental Rights*

120 In this regard, *see* the speeches and writings published in the 2004 volume. Miklós Király (ed.), *Quo vadis Europa? A magyar államfő Európában*, KJK-Kerszöv, Budapest, 2004, pp. 157-163.

121 'Az európai integráció a történelem sodrában: európai és nemzeti perspektívák tegnaptól holnapig. Beszéd az ELTE ÁJK-n tiszteletbeli doktorrá avatásakor', 1 September 2000. Pál Becker (ed.), *A Köztársasági Elnöki Hivatal évkönyve 2000/2001*, KEH, Budapest, 2002, pp. 81-85. It is worth noting here that both *alma maters* conferred the degree of doctor on his former student: he received his diploma in Pécs in 1998 and in Budapest in 2000. On the Pécs proposal, *see* PTE EL VIII.201.b. 274. d. 11-7/1998. Proposal to the meeting of the Senate of JPTE on 14 May 1998, Pécs, 30 April 1998.

122 Becker (ed.) 2002, p. 85.

doi: 10.5553/HYIEL/266627012021009001008

"as the most important part [...] of the future European constitution." This charter will be an epitome of European identity", he emphasized, as "[p]olitical union requires a constitution. Every constitution is based on fundamental principles and moral values." However, such constitution must include the protection of minorities, therefore, as he said as head of state of a country still only a candidate for member status: "[I] think that the Charter should be supplemented first and foremost by a list of minority rights."[123] The *protection of minorities*, which he had already championed as Minister for European Affairs,[124] *was another key idea driving Mádl's presidency*. The topic, which had been continuously emphasized both at home and abroad since his appointment, was given special emphasis by the 2004 Hungarian citizenship referendum.

It shows Mádl's scientific gravitas that he uniformly approached both topics: *integration and minority rights*. With this research method, he shifted minority rights from the level of politics into the realm of science where his proposals received a special weight due to his decades-long professional standing as an expert on international and European law. For this reason, the influence of his speeches delivered at the Permanent Hungarian Conference *(MÁÉRT)* in 2003 and 2004 extended beyond his presidential period, and as a result, had a significant influence on the creation of contemporary citizenship rules.

10. The European Statesman

The success of Mádl's attitude and work is also indicated by the fact that although he acquired the presidential seat as a candidate for the political right, throughout his term he was considered one of the most popular politicians of Hungary.[125] Upon his resignation, his activities were recognized and appreciated by all parliamentary parties and public dignitaries.[126] The campaign launched for his

123 Ferenc Mádl, 'Erkölcsi értékek az európai integrációban', *Magyar Szemle*, 2001/3-4, pp. 7-11.

124 "[E]urope today in our region shall also mean guaranteeing the minority rights of national, ethnic, religious and other minorities. The common Europe, accession to such a Europe, also requires a comprehensive resolution and settlement of national and minority conflicts." Ferenc Mádl, 'Az európai értékeknek elkötelezve', *in* Mádl 1995, pp. 17-18.

125 "[...] Ferenc Mádl was added to the list of politicians in the summer of 2000, and [...] he soon became one of the most popular personalities. He received exceptionally high scores of 63-65 from the public, and to this day he is considered to be among the three most engaging politicians. Mádl remained popular in the following years. Opinions about him were relatively stable between 2001 and 2003: with scores between 60 and 67; he was the first or second most popular public figure. In 2004, his prestige as a politician was also badly affected: his index fell below 60 points. Nevertheless, for the most part, Mádl was at the top of the ranking, as this year [2005 – E.D.] he also led the approval ranking. " *See* 'A köztársaság élén', *168 óra*, 26 May 2005, pp. 26-29.

126 It is worth recalling two leftist opinions here. According to Socialist Speaker of the House, Katalin Szili, Mádl's "example also showed that a personage with clear political values and ties can also be a prestigious president enjoying public confidence." *See* 'Bekezdések az elnökről', *Heti Válasz*, 4 August 2005, p. 14. Gábor Kuncze, the president of the Alliance of Free Democrats (SZDSZ), one of the governing parties at the time, said that Mádl had "acted responsibly, respecting the word and spirit of the constitution all the time. [...] He was a worthy head of state of Hungary." *See* 'Tisztességgel tette a dolgát az államfő', *Magyar Hírlap*, 4 August 2005, p. 5.

doi: 10.5553/HYIEL/266627012021009001008

new candidacy also showed his popularity. Professor Mádl, however, had indicated at the beginning that he would undertake only one term, and he stuck to his decision. "[H]e is really fond of his profession, teaching, jurisprudence. I would like him to spend his time doing what he really wants" – his wife explained why his husband returned to university as professor emeritus.[127]

However, the next half-decade was not spent in retirement either. Although at that time Mádl was dealing primarily as a scholar with EU law[128] and then public law[129] issues, and, occasionally, voiced his opinion on public issues,[130] his prestige of the erstwhile public dignitary made his words especially significant. His ideas continued to receive attention abroad, which is well illustrated by the fact that he was awarded the Wartburg Price in 2007. Having received several distinguished awards from the 1990s onwards,[131] he obtained this prize in recognition of his commitment toward the issues of German-Hungarian relations, the European idea and its implementation. The prize was presented in the Castle of Wartburg where once one of the most popular saints of Europe, St. Elizabeth of the House of Árpád, lived.

In 2010, at the subsequent government shuffle of his former student, Viktor Orbán, it seemed that again he would have to give up the "unengaged peace and quiet"[132] he desired. This is what his excursus written in March 2010 suggested, in which he dealt with, among other things, the structure and content of the new constitution.[133] A year later, at the celebration to mark his 80th birthday the Prime Minister expressly invited him to return to public life: "It is a really difficult one-and-a-half year period we have to face, we need you."[134] However, due to the professor's unexpected death on 29 May 2011 there was no return any more.

127 Dalma Mádl, 'A szeretet diplomatája', *Heti Válasz*, 4 August 2005, p. 16.

128 Here we can only refer to his writings for the general public, published in the columns of *Magyar Szemle*, and his writings and speeches published in the volume titled *Quo vadis Europa?*

129 *See e.g.* one of his last works: Ferenc Mádl, 'A törvények szelleme', *in* Granasztói & Sebestyén (eds.) 2011, pp. 21-25.

130 Mention should be made here of the open letter published during the 2006 government crisis, signed together with several others. *See* 'Gyurcsány Ferenc úrnak, a Magyar Köztársaság miniszterelnökének!', *Magyar Nemzet*, 26 September 2006, p. 1. Otherwise, "he was wary of commenting on daily political events. At the beginning of April, I invited him to a conference on the new constitution, but [...] he rejected its evaluation in front of the media." Péter Farkas Zárug, 'Mádl Ferenc, a státuszférfi', *Demokrata*, 1 June 2011, p. 39.

131 Mention should be made here of the Order of the Legion of Honor of the French Republic (1999), the Jean Monnet Foundation for Europe Gold Medal (2002), the Order of Merit for Jerusalem (2006), MTAL 576/6 dossier, at https://magyarnemzet.hu/archivum/archivum-archivum/jeruzsalemert-erdemrend-madl-ferencnek-es-szili-katalinnak-5749685; https://hvg.hu/kultura/20071017_wartburg_madl_ferenc.

132 The quote comes from the poem *Epilógus*, by one of Mádl's favorite poets, János Arany (1817-1882).

133 Ferenc Mádl, 'A törvények szelleme', *in* Granasztói & Sebestyén (eds.) 2011, pp. 21-25. The study was published only after his death.

134 Orbán 2011, pp. 7-8.

doi: 10.5553/HYIEL/266627012021009001008

11. Summary: "The Story Is Also About Us"

The story is also about us – Ferenc Mádl repeatedly emphasized speaking about European integration. His ideas hold a message not only for his contemporaries and peers but also for later generations. On the one hand, the message lies in his personal fate and life experiences, the way he made value-based decisions from an early age as the ancient heroes he was so familiar with, taking no heed of the possible unpleasant consequences for himself. His moral values were based primarily on his faith; for him, faith and religion were not only experiences on the personal level, but he also considered Christianity with its moral values to be a part of the European cultural heritage. He also regarded the entire era of antiquity, along with its legendary mythology and legal order, which came to an end with Christianity becoming state religion, to form part of this heritage.

While he was speaking about a unified Europe, a shared legal order, and a common European heritage, doing so as a Hungarian jurist, in his writings he referred to Hungarian and European cultural, literary and historical examples side by side. Mádl experienced his Europeanness and Hungarianness at the same time, but from a particular, Central-European perspective, with which not only Hungarians but also other peoples of Central-Europe could identify. Mádl himself was also aware of the uniqueness of this region at the meeting point of the East and the West. That is why he supported the idea of Central-European co-operation (Visegrad Four) even after the EU accession.

During the period of regime change, Professor Mádl was convinced that European integration was not only an old dream that came true, but that the potential for this model of progress was justified by the history of the second half of the 20th century. He made several statements about the way forward, the areas to be improved, but perhaps more importantly, he had important insights into the areas for action and the way to proceed. On the one hand, he believed that the incumbent EU decision-makers should follow the examples of the founding fathers, and on the other hand, regarding integration, he repeatedly quoted a line by the great Hungarian poet, Miklós Radnóti about the "earnestness of 2x2"[135] with which as if he tried to warn us that we should continuously insist on facts and reality. The often fruitless debates characterizing the decade since his death have demonstrated the importance of both ideas.

In light of the above, maybe it is no exaggeration to say that although Ferenc Mádl was a Hungarian professor of European law, his personality and legacy is important not only for Hungarians, but for the peoples of Europe in general, and his spiritual legacy offers noteworthy ideas both for the future of the EU and for Central-European co-operation.

135 Poem by Miklós Radnóti (1909-1944) *Levél a hitveshez* [Letter to my wife].

doi: 10.5553/HYIEL/266627012021009001008

Back to the Future: Ferenc Mádl, The Law of the European Economic Community (1974)

Investment Protection Then and Now

Miklós Király[*]

Abstract

The first part of the article (Sections 1-2) reviews Prof. Ferenc Mádl's magnum opus, published in 1974, emphasizing the importance of the monograph's publication in the communist era. It discusses the unique structure of the volume, which, from the perspective of undertakings and companies, examined the fundamental economic freedoms and EEC competition law in parallel. The second part (Sections 3-5) highlights the issue of investment protection, noting that Mádl's early academic theorem has been vindicated decades later by the case-law of the CJEU, in particular in its SEGRO and Horváth judgment: Provisions ensuring free movement of capital serve to protect foreign investments as well.

Keywords: Ferenc Mádl, investment protection, SEGRO and Horváth, Achmea, BIT.

1. A Monograph on EEC Law – Why and to What End?

In 1974, a major monograph was published on the law of the European Economic Community (EEC).[1] This wouldn't have been all that surprising, had it not been for the book to have been published in Hungary under the Soviet bloc. At that time there were no official ties between the EEC and the Eastern European communist countries, which were trying to build and develop a completely different economic organization in the Soviet hemisphere, known as Comecon.[2]

According to its subtitle, Prof. Mádl's book was devoted to undertakings, economic competition and the role of the state in the process of economic integration. This reflects the unique structure of the monograph (spanning the major aspects of regulating enterprise): on the one hand, the cross-border

* Miklós Király: professor of law, ELTE Law School, Budapest.

1 Ferenc Mádl, *Az Európai Gazdasági Közösség joga*, Akadémiai, Budapest, 1974. The revised English translation of the book was published a few years later: Ferenc Mádl, *The Law of the European Community*, Akadémiai, Budapest, 1978. All the notes refer to the original, Hungarian edition published in 1974, if not indicated otherwise.

2 Council for Mutual Economic Assistance (CMEA), established in January 1949 to facilitate and coordinate the economic development of the eastern European countries belonging to the Soviet bloc.

doi: 10.5553/HYIEL/266627012021009001009

activities of companies under the umbrella of the right to establishment, free movement of capital and protection of foreign investments; and measures having the aim of supporting effective competition within European integration, on the other. Actually, these twin pillars represent two sides of the same coin: the aspects of facilitation and control in the economic law.[3]

Mádl's work offers us a real journey into the past and into the future in many aspects. It is a dig into the past, because it takes us back to an early stage of the EEC, where we can still witness the ongoing formation of the institutions, the legal system and the basic principles of integration. Just like when the Sun begins to radiate in a nascent solar system, the orbits of the planets take shape, and the nebula disappears. The founding fathers of the Communities, Jean Monnet and Walter Hallstein, were still alive or had just passed away, but their thoughts and legacy had a strong impact, which often appear in the book.

"Fabula de te narrator", the tale is also about us, the author wished to write in the introduction to the volume, but censorship struck out this eloquent phrase. Some years later, in the revised English translation of the volume, Ferenc Mádl had the chance to explain his enthusiasm for the subject.

> "Socialist jurisprudence cannot ignore the fact that in one half of Europe – of absolutely vital interest to us – a new system of norms has come into being, a legal system that calls itself European Law or Community law. We cannot ignore the fact that this system has begun to function; that its organizational, legal and procedural institutions have begun to operate [...]."[4]

When the volume was published, a professor from West Germany asked why the author had dealt with such a "completely irrelevant topic" in a communist country. Yet history has proved that the subject was far from being irrelevant or uninteresting. Fifteen years after the monograph was first published, the Soviet systems collapsed in Central and Eastern Europe. By then, a new generation of Hungarian lawyers had the opportunity to learn about the law of the EEC by studying the volume. *The monograph actually sketched the possible future*. Twenty years later, Hungary submitted its application to join the EU. Thirty years later, in 2004, Hungary became a part of integration. By that time, *Ferenc Mádl, as the President of the Republic of Hungary, had authorized the Act of Accession*.

3 The monograph included the following chapters: I. Introduction; II. Forces of production, economic situation [...]; III. Enterprises and economic competition in the pragmatic economic policy of the EEC (premises in principles); IV. General features of the EEC legal system as a structure of economic integration: European Community law and its sources; V. Enterprise in the integration – harmonization of company law; VI. The movement of capital and investments in the integration through the channels of general and EEC Regulation; VII. Economic competition in the integration by an integrated legal structure; VIII. International cartels and monopolies; IX. The state in the economy – public enterprises and economic competition; X. The state in the economy *versus* state immunity; XI. General critical synthesis on the function and institutions of Community Law.

4 Mádl 1978 (English edition), pp. 9-10.

doi: 10.5553/HYIEL/266627012021009001009

There is a great temptation for the reader to continue this mental time travel. Examine the state of the legal institutions presented in the early 1970s, compared to the present situation. This is all the easier because the author chose the most sensitive issues of European economic law with a very sharp eye. The right to establishment and the recognition of foreign companies, the European Company (*Societas Europae*) in *statu nascendi* and its future, the free flow of capital and protection of foreign investments in the EEC, competition law, its instruments and the growing role of the CJEU. Of course, if we wanted to show for each legal institution what had happened in the nearly five decades since the book's publication, we would have to write another major monograph.

2. Free Movement of Capital and the Protection of Foreign Investments

That is why we are now tackling only one issue, the free movement of capital and the protection of foreign investment. Ferenc Mádl rightly referred to the "tact of the legal system" of the Common Market,[5] *i.e.* the fact that the Treaty of Rome (EEC Treaty) did not address the substantive legal protection of foreign investments against expropriation and nationalization of property. This silence is particularly evident when compared with the comprehensive system of protection offered by bilateral investment protection treaties (BITs).[6] Referring to developments that had taken place since, we can add that this difference still exists today, not only with regard to BITs, but also with regard to the founding treaties of the North American Free Trade Area, the NAFTA and the USMCA, which is currently in force.

However, already in 1974, Mádl's monograph noted that although the EEC had not adopted an instrument specifically protecting the investments of natural and legal persons of a Member State against expropriation in another Member State, the very essence of legislation governing undertakings was that freedom of investment must be protected from all discriminatory practices. These include the relevant parts of the Treaty of Rome as main legal bases, *i.e.* Articles 52 to 58 on the establishment of undertakings, Articles 67 to 73 on the free movement of capital (investments), and Articles 132 and 220 on the conditions for non-discriminatory market access for undertakings. In Mádl's view, these provisions, read together, essentially ensured investment protection in a positive sense. This assumption was bold. At the time, the liberalization of capital movements took place step by step and proceeded only very slowly. Any attempt at investment protection presupposed, at the very least, a broad interpretation of the very cautiously worded provisions of the Treaty of Rome.

5 Mádl 1974, pp. 176-178.
6 Id. pp. 171-175.

doi: 10.5553/HYIEL/266627012021009001009

3. The Proof of the Pudding – the SEGRO and Horváth Case

The practical test of this proposition took place several decades later, in a preliminary ruling procedure launched in a Hungarian case, *SEGRO and Horváth*.[7] According to the key provision Article 63 TFEU, all restrictions on the movement of capital between Member States, and between Member States and third countries is prohibited. In Hungary, *the protection of domestic ownership of arable land was a strong priority*. After accession, restrictions were upheld for seven years,[8] which was later extended for another three-year period. Following the expiry of this derogation, the Hungarian Parliament adopted Act CCXII of 2013 on transactions in agricultural and forestry land, laying down various provisions and transitional measures. Section 108(1) of the Act on transitional measures repealing Section 91(1) of the former, 1994 Act, stated that

> "Any right of usufruct or right of use existing on 30 April 2014 and created, for an indefinite period or for a fixed term expiring after 30 April 2014, by a contract between persons who are not close members of the same family shall be extinguished by operation of law on 1 May 2014."

As a result of this provision, *the legally established usufruct rights* of many, including foreigners, who had provided for this in their long-term business plans, *simply evaporated*. Even if it wasn't expropriation proper, it was meant a disenfranchisement of a package of rights *in rem* without compensation. Usufruct is a kind of beneficial ownership. According to Section 5:147 of the Hungarian Civil Code, a person may possess, use, exploit, and collect the proceeds of a property owned by another person by virtue of beneficial ownership. It is no coincidence that an international dispute arose before the ICSID over this provision, with a claim based on the British-Hungarian BIT for the protection of English investors.[9]

The requests for a preliminary ruling were made in proceedings brought, first, by *SEGRO Kft*., and second, by *Günther Horváth*, against decisions deleting rights of usufruct over agricultural land that were held by SEGRO Kft. and Mr Horváth, respectively, from the property register.

According to the judgment of the CJEU in these joined preliminary ruling cases, the national provisions at issue in the main proceedings essentially have the purpose of extinguishing by operation of law previously acquired rights of

7 Judgment of 6 March 2018, *Joined Cases C-52/16 and C-113/16, SEGRO and Horváth*, ECLI:EU:C:2018:157.

8 *See* the Treaty of Accession of the Czech Republic, the Republic of Estonia, the Republic of Cyprus, the Republic of Latvia, the Republic of Lithuania, the Republic of Hungary, the Republic of Malta, the Republic of Poland, the Republic of Slovenia and the Slovak Republic, in particular, its Article 24, providing authorization for transitional measures.

9 *Magyar Farming Company Ltd. Kintyre Kft. and Inícia Zrt. v Hungary*, ICSID Case No. ARB/17/27, Award, 13 November 2019. *See e.g.* János Ede Szilágyi & Tamás Andréka, 'A New Aspect of Cross-Border Acquisition of Agricultural Lands. The Inícia Case Before the ICSID', *Hungarian Yearbook of International Law and European Law*, Vol. 8, 2020, pp. 92-105.

doi: 10.5553/HYIEL/266627012021009001009

usufruct over agricultural land, where the holders of those rights did not satisfy the conditions to which the acquisition of rights of usufruct over agricultural land are henceforth subject under national legislation, and of arranging, consequently, for the deletion of such previously acquired rights from the property registers.[10]

The CJEU declared that, by virtue of its very subject matter, legislation such as that at issue in the main proceedings, which provides for the extinction of rights of usufruct acquired by contract over agricultural land, including those held as a result of exercise of the right to free movement of capital, restricts that freedom on account of that fact alone.[11] Such restrictive measures *may only be permissible if they are justified, on the basis of objective considerations independent of the origin of the capital concerned, by overriding reasons in the public interest and if they observe the principle of proportionality*, a condition which requires them to be appropriate for ensuring the attainment of the objective legitimately pursued and do not to go beyond what is necessary in order for it to be attained.[12]

The Hungarian Government submitted as justification that, inasmuch as the legislation at issue in the main proceedings makes the future acquisition of rights of usufruct over productive land and the preservation of such rights that already exist subject to compliance with the condition that the usufructuary has the status of close family member of the owner of the property concerned, it pursues public interest objectives. Thus, that legislation seeks to limit the ownership of productive land to those persons who work it and to prevent its acquisition for purely speculative purposes. It is also meant to enable it to be farmed by new undertakings, to facilitate the creation of properties of a size that enables viable and competitive agricultural production, and to prevent a fragmentation of agricultural land as well as migration from rural areas and depopulation of the countryside.[13]

However, the CJEU was not persuaded. According to its verdict, the fact that the required family tie exist does not guarantee that the usufructuary farms the land himself and that he has not acquired the right of usufruct at issue for purely speculative purposes. Similarly, it cannot be assumed that a person outside the owner's family who has purchased a usufruct over such land would not be in a position to farm that land himself and that the purchase would necessarily have been made for purely speculative purposes, without any intention to cultivate the land.[14] Other measures with less far-reaching effects than extinguishing the rights *in rem* concerned could have been adopted in order to penalize, from the outset, including any infringements of the applicable exchange control legislation, such as administrative fines.[15]

In sum, according to the CJEU, Article 63 TFEU must be interpreted as precluding national legislation, such as that at issue in the main proceedings, under which rights of usufruct that have previously been created over agricultural

10 *Joined Cases C-52/16 and C-113/16, SEGRO and Horváth*, para. 50.
11 Id. para. 62.
12 Id. para. 76.
13 Id. para. 81.
14 Id. para. 87.
15 Id. para. 106.

Hungarian Yearbook of International Law and European Law 2021 (9) 1
doi: 10.5553/HYIEL/266627012021009001009

land and the holders of which do not have the status of close relation of the owner of that land are extinguished by operation of law and are, consequently, deleted from the property registers. In its ruling, the CJEU made it clear that *the provisions on the free movement of capital also ensure the ownership/usufruct of citizens of another Member State and the protection of their foreign investments*. The theory outlined four decades earlier was validated at the highest level, with the restriction that, in its judgment, the CJEU referred only to the free movement of capital and did not invoke the provisions on freedom of establishment.

4. The EU Charter of Fundamental Rights and the Protection of Property

This line of interpretation was confirmed in the judgment *European Commission v Hungary*.[16] This case was not a reference for a preliminary ruling, but an infringement procedure initiated by the European Commission against Hungary, with strong emphasis on Article 17 of the Charter of Fundamental Rights, in addition to the free movement of capital. According to EU Article 17 of the Charter on the right to property

> "Everyone has the right to own, use, dispose of and bequeath his or her lawfully acquired possessions. No one may be deprived of his or her possessions, except in the public interest and in the cases and under the conditions provided for by law, subject to fair compensation being paid in good time for their loss. The use of property may be regulated by law in so far as is necessary for the general interest."

On those grounds, the Grand Chamber of the CJEU declared that, by adopting Section 108(1) of Act CCXII of 2013 laying down various provisions and transitional measures concerning transactions in agricultural and forestry land and thereby extinguishing, by operation of law, the rights of usufruct over agricultural and forestry land located in Hungary that are held, directly or indirectly, by nationals of other Member States, *Hungary failed to fulfil its obligations under Article 63 TFEU* (on free movement of capital) *in conjunction with Article 17 of the Charter of Fundamental Rights*.[17]

It should be noted, however, that at the time of writing this paper, in April 2021, Section 108 of Act CCXII of 2013 is still in force in Hungary, despite the judgment of the CJEU. More precisely, it still contains the very same provision, which was at the heart of the dispute and according to which

> "[a]ny right of usufruct or right of use existing on 30 April 2014 and created, for an indefinite period or for a fixed term expiring after 30 April 2014, by a contract between persons who are not close members of the same family shall be extinguished by operation of law on 1 May 2014."

16 Judgment of 21 May 2019, *Case C-235/17, Commission v Hungary*, ECLI:EU:C:2019:432.
17 Id. para. 131.

doi: 10.5553/HYIEL/266627012021009001009

This situation may indicate the limits of effective protection of investments under EU law, although some new, fairly complex provisions were added to the paragraph under scrutiny.[18]

5. *Achmea* and the Fall of Bilateral Investment Protection Agreements

It is however worth examining the judgments of the CJEU cited above in a broader context. This, in turn, leads us to the BITs previously concluded between Eastern and Western European countries,[19] which suddenly qualified as international agreements between Member States following the enlargement of the EU in 2004. This new situation has inevitably raised the problematic relationship between investment protection based on bilateral treaties and EU law.[20] Following several relevant cases, the problem culminated in *Achmea*,[21] resulting in a landmark decision.[22]

The CJEU's judgment was based on a dispute between Dutch insurer Achmea B.V. (formerly known as Eureko B.V.) and Slovakia. In 2006, Slovakia partly reversed the earlier liberalization of its health insurance market, thereby prohibiting the distribution of profits generated by Achmea's Slovak insurance activities. In 2008, Achmea brought arbitration proceedings against Slovakia under a BIT[23] for violation of substantive treaty standards. In its final 2012 award, the ad-hoc arbitral tribunal, constituted under the UNCITRAL Rules and seated in Frankfurt, found that Slovakia had violated the BIT and ordered it to pay approximately EUR 22.1 million in damages to Achmea.[24]

In the setting-aside proceedings subsequently initiated by Slovakia before the German courts, Slovakia challenged the arbitral award on jurisdiction. It argued that the arbitral tribunal lacked jurisdiction to hear the claims because the arbitration clause included in Article 8 of the BIT was incompatible with EU law, more specifically Article 18 (non-discrimination and citizenship), Article 267

18 Section 108(4) and (5).

19 The predecessors of these BITs (including the General Economic Treaties and treaties on the payment of compensations due to nationalizations in Central and Eastern European countries) are thoroughly analyzed by Ferenc Mádl in his monographs. *See* Mádl 1974, pp. 171-175. Naturally, the specific consequences of the accession of new Member States to the EU were not foreseeable at that time. The importance of BITs was revisited by Mádl and the author of this article, *see* Ferenc Mádl & Miklós Király, *Külföldi beruházások jogi védelme*, ELTE, Budapest, 1989, pp. 86 and 53-67.

20 Ursula Kriebaum, 'The Fate of Intra-EU BITs from an Investment Law and Public International Law Perspective', *ELTE Law Journal*, 2015/1, pp. 27-35.

21 Judgment of 6 March 2018, *Case C-284/16, Achmea*, ECLI:EU:C:2018:158

22 *See e.g.* Tamás Szabados, 'Az Európai Unió Bíróságának Achmea-döntése. A tagállamok közötti beruházásvédelmi egyezmények választottbírósági kikötéseinek összeegyeztethetetlensége az uniós joggal', *Jogesetek Magyarázata*, Vol. 10, Issue 1, 2019, pp. 29-36; János Martonyi, 'Investor-State Dispute and the Autonomy of EU Law; Battle of Tribunals?' *in* János Martonyi, *Nemzet és Európa, Emlékirat helyett*, Ludovika Egyetemi Kiadó, Budapest, 2021, pp. 105-108.

23 Agreement on encouragement and reciprocal protection of investments between the Kingdom of the Netherlands and the Czech and Slovak Federative Republic ('the BIT'), concluded in 1991.

24 *Case C-284/16, Achmea*, paras. 9-11.

doi: 10.5553/HYIEL/266627012021009001009

(preliminary ruling procedure) and Article 344 (dispute settlement) of the TFEU.[25] In these proceedings, the Higher Regional Court of Frankfurt rejected Slovakia's arguments, finding that the BIT was not incompatible with the aforementioned provisions of the TFEU. However, the German Federal Court of Justice, hearing the case on appeal, referred questions on the compatibility with EU law of the BIT's arbitration clause to the CJEU for a preliminary ruling, at the same time, presenting its view that the arbitration clause was not contrary to the provisions of the TFEU. It is worth recalling the relevant paragraph of Article 8 of the BIT:

> "Each Contracting Party hereby consents to submit a dispute referred to an arbitral tribunal, if the dispute has not been settled amicably within a period of six months from the date either party to the dispute requested amicable settlement."[26]

The CJEU emphasized that, in *Achmea*, apart from the fact that the disputes falling within the jurisdiction of the arbitral tribunal referred to in Article 8 of the BIT may relate to the interpretation of both that agreement and of EU law, the possibility of submitting those disputes to a body that is not part of the judicial system of the EU is provided for by an agreement that was concluded not by the EU but by Member States.[27]

Therefore, Article 8 of the BIT was considered as *calling into question not only the principle of mutual trust between Member States but also the preservation of the particular nature of the law established by the Treaties*, based on the preliminary ruling procedure provided for in Article 267 TFEU, and is therefore not compatible with the principle of sincere cooperation.[28] The other key provision from the point of view of the legal dispute was Article 344 TFEU, according to which Member States undertake not to submit a dispute concerning the interpretation or application of the Treaties to any method of settlement other than those provided for therein.

According to the preliminary ruling delivered by the CJEU, Articles 267 and 344 TFEU must be interpreted as precluding a provision in an international agreement concluded between Member States, such as Article 8 of the Treaty on the encouragement and reciprocal protection of investments between the Kingdom of the Netherlands and the Czech and Slovak Federative Republic, under which an investor from one of those Member States may, in the event of a dispute concerning investments in the other Member State, bring proceedings against the latter Member State before an arbitral tribunal whose jurisdiction that Member State has undertaken to accept.[29] A decision with this content was, in fact, to be expected. The European Commission has long taken the view that

25 Id. paras. 11 and 31.
26 Article 8(2) of the BIT.
27 *Case C-284/16, Achmea*, paras. 45, and 58.
28 Id. paras. 34, and 58.
29 Id. paras. 31, and 60.

doi: 10.5553/HYIEL/266627012021009001009

bilateral investment protection agreements between Member States (intra-EU BITs) are incompatible with EU law and has expressed this view in a number of investment protection disputes.[30]

The judgment created a whole new situation. The net of protection provided by bilateral conventions began to unravel. This was complemented by the fact that most EU Member States have concluded an agreement on the formal denunciation of BITs in 2020.[31] The abolition of BITs will also deprive the Washington Convention[32] of all of its practical significance for investment disputes within the EU. After all, following the CJEU's decision, Member States will hardly submit themselves to the jurisdiction of the ICSID if the investor comes from the EU. Henceforth, investment protection rests with the CJEU and the courts of the Member States; more specifically with the protection offered by EU law and the domestic law of the Member States. And, of course, the main question is whether the Member States' forums will follow the CJEU's previous decisions properly and, where necessary, seek a new preliminary ruling from the CJEU.

The arbitration dispute settlement mechanism guaranteed by the BITs, which provided individuals with the capacity to sue sovereign states before neutral international *fora*, has thus been abolished within the EU. Time will tell how this will affect future investments in the new EU Member States in the long run. Will investors be satisfied with a broad interpretation of the provisions on free movement of capital and the protection afforded by the EU Charter of Fundamental Rights and domestic laws, or will they invest elsewhere?[33] Somewhat surprisingly, investors from third countries have been put in a better position than their counterparts in the EU, because they can still start a procedure offered by ICSID or commercial arbitration, if they feel that their rights have been violated, at least as long as they are not replaced by treaties concluded by the EU under the aegis of the common commercial policy.

Achmea may be justified by the strict application of the provisions of the TFEU and the preservation of the CJEU's monopoly on the interpretation of EU law. It can also be argued that, when it comes to investing within the single

30 *Eureko B.V. v the Slovak Republic*, PCA Case No. 2008-13, Award on Jurisdiction, Arbitrability and Suspension, 26 October 2010; *EURAM v. the Slovak Republic*, PCA Case No. 2010-17, European Commission Observations, 13 October 2011; *Micula v Romania*, ICSID Case No. ARB/05/20, Award, 11 December 2013. *See e.g.* Marcel Szabó, 'Editorial Comments: The Relevance of Foreign Investment Protection in International and EU Law, Foreword to Vol. 8 (2020) of the Hungarian Yearbook of International Law and European Law', *Hungarian Yearbook of International Law and European Law*, Vol. 8, 2020, p. 12.

31 Agreement for the Termination of Bilateral Investment Treaties between the Member States of the European Union, 2020.

32 Convention on the Settlement of Investment Disputes Between States and Nationals of Other States, Washington, 1965. It has established International Centre for Settlement of Investment Disputes (ICSID).

33 Szabó 2020, pp. 13-14, referring to the article by Veronika Korom in the Hungarian Yearbook 2020: Veronika Korom, 'The Impact of the Achmea Ruling on Intra-EU BIT Investment Arbitration. A Hungarian Perspective', *Hungarian Yearbook of International Law and European Law*, Vol. 8, 2020, pp. 53-74. *See also* Szabados 2019, p. 36; Martonyi 2021, p. 108.

doi: 10.5553/HYIEL/266627012021009001009

internal market, because both the investor and the place of investment are tied to it, it is unnecessary to use an external forum to settle investment disputes. At the same time, the denunciation of BITs is a rip in the fabric of a relatively well-functioning global dispute settlement mechanism in the region.

DEVELOPMENTS IN EUROPEAN LAW

The First Ever Ultra Vires Judgment of the German Federal Constitutional Court: PSPP

Will the Barking Dog Bite More Than Once?

Robert Böttner[*]

Abstract

In May 2020, the German Federal Constitutional Court (FCC) delivered its judgment in the PSPP case. At first it seemed that it would be a remake of the Gauweiler/OMT case between the German Court and the CJEU. Shockingly, however, the German FCC decided that not only had the ECB acted ultra vires by failing to duly justify its PSPP decision, but it also found the CJEU to have delivered an incomprehensible and objectively arbitrary judgment by which the German Court was not bound. This case note not only traces the history of the PSPP proceedings, but it also tries to review the heavy criticism that the FCC's verdict has garnered. In the context of European integration and due to the German FCC's authority among supreme courts in Europe, it is a dangerous precedent, that the European Commission tries to curb through infringement proceedings. One can only hope that it will be settled for good and shall remain an unfortunate but singular incident.

Keywords: judicial dialogue, ultra vires, PSPP, German Federal Constitutional Court, infringement procedure.

1. Introduction

In May of last year, a verdict handed down by the German Federal Constitutional Court (*Bundesverfassungsgericht*, German FCC) in Karlsruhe caused a veritable legal earthquake. The Constitutional Court gave its first ever *ultra vires* ruling in matters of European law. The decision made headlines in national and international newspapers alike and before long, internet blogs[1] and scientific journals all across the continent were commenting on the decision.

Against the background of the *OMT/Gauweiler* proceedings, it came as a surprise, albeit not a big one, that the German Constitutional Court actually declared the PSPP program of the European Central Bank (ECB) to be *ultra vires*.

* Robert Böttner: assistant professor of law, University of Erfurt.

1 *See*, among many, the blogposts of *Verfassungsblog*, at https://verfassungsblog.de/.

doi: 10.5553/HYIEL/266627012021009001010

What sent shockwaves through the legal landscape though was the fact that the German FCC held that the CJEU itself had acted *ultra vires* when it upheld the PSPP in its preliminary ruling.

Now that a year has passed and the dust has settled, the judgment and its effects may put into perspective. To this end, the present contribution not only presents and analyses the verdict, but also tries to take stock of the plethora of academic literature already published on this ruling.

2. The Prologue: The OMT/Gauweiler Case

The PSPP judgment was predated by a first procedure on an ECB asset purchase program, the *OMT/Gauweiler* case. As is well known, in September 2012 and following the famous "whatever it takes" statement made by then ECB President Mario Draghi, the ECB's Governing Council adopted the technical features of a program for conducting Outright Monetary Transactions (OMT), aimed at purchasing government bonds of selected Member States if and as long as these Member States simultaneously adhere to the reform measures agreed upon with the European Financial Stability Facility (EFSF) or the European Stability Mechanism (ESM).

In Germany, constitutional complaints were lodged before the German FCC, claiming that the OMT program exceeded the limits of ECB competences conferred upon it by the Treaties. In essence, the claimants held that the ECB was conducting economic policy, which was beyond the scope of its mandate. By order of 14 January 2014,[2] the German FCC suspended the relevant proceedings and referred two questions to the CJEU for a preliminary ruling in accordance with Article 267(1) TFEU. The reference gained considerable attention, not only because of the questions asked, but also and in particular because it was the first ever reference to the CJEU by Germany's highest court.[3]

2 Cases 2 BvR 2728/13 *et al.*, Order of the Second Senate of 14 January 2014, ECLI:DE:BVerfG: 2014:rs20140114.2bvr272813. Most decisions are available in English at the FCC's website at www.bundesverfassungsgericht.de/.

3 *See, inter alia*, Ingolf Pernice, 'A Difficult Partnership between Courts: The First Preliminary Reference by the German Federal Constitutional Court to the CJEU', *Maastricht Journal of European and Comparative Law*, Vol. 21, Issue 1, 2014, pp. 3-13; and Mattias Wendel, 'Exceeding Judicial Competence in the Name of Democracy: The German Federal Constitutional Court's OMT Reference', *European Constitutional Law Review*, Vol. 10, Issue 2, 2014, pp. 263-307.

doi: 10.5553/HYIEL/266627012021009001010

About a year and a half later, the CJEU ruled that a program like OMT (which was never put into place) was in conformity with European law.[4] With the *Gauweiler/OMT* judgment, the CJEU delivered a teleological interpretation of Article 123(1) TFEU and established specific requirements for asset purchase programs in order to avoid prohibited budgetary funding.[5] It underlined, however, that when the ECB purchases government bonds on the secondary market, sufficient safeguards must be established to ensure that the ECB's intervention does not infringe or circumvent the prohibition of monetary financing laid down in Article 123(1) TFEU. Moreover, the measures undertaken in the context of such an asset purchase program must be proportionate to the objectives of monetary policy in accordance with Articles 119(2) and 127(1) TFEU. Finally, any such program must not be designed in a way that would lessen the impetus for Member States to follow a sound budgetary discipline.

Another year later the German FCC handed down its final ruling.[6] It acknowledged the CJEU's judgment and regarded an asset purchasing program in conformity with the German Constitution (meaning that the German *Bundesbank* may participate in the implementation of such a program) if and to the extent that the prerequisites defined by the CJEU are met; *i.e.* if *(i)* purchases are not announced; *(ii)* the volume of the purchases is limited from the outset; *(iii)* there is a minimum period between the issuing of the government bonds and their purchase by the ECB that is defined from the outset and prevents the issuing conditions from being distorted; *(iv)* only government bonds of Member States are purchased that have bond market access enabling the funding of such bonds; *(v)* purchased bonds are held until maturity only in exceptional cases, and 6) purchases are restricted or ceased and purchased bonds are remarketed should

4 Judgment (Grand Chamber) of 16 June 2015, *Case C-62/14, Gauweiler*, ECLI:EU:C:2015:400. *See*, among the many comments, *inter alia*, Georgios Anagnostaras, 'In ECB We Trust... the FCC We Dare! The OMT Preliminary Ruling', *European Law Review*, 2015/5, pp. 744-762; Francesco Martucci, 'La Cour de justice face à la politique monétaire en temps de crise de dettes souveraines: L'arrêt Gauweiler entre droit et marché', *Cahiers de droit européen*, Vol. 51, Issue 2-3, 2015, pp. 493-534; Vestert Borger, 'Outright Monetary Transactions and the Stability Mandate of the ECB: Gauweiler', *Common Market Law Review*, Vol. 53, Issue 1, 2016, pp. 139-196; Takis Tridimas & Napoleon Xanthoulis, 'A Legal Analysis of the Gauweiler Case: Between Monetary Policy and Constitutional Conflict', *Maastricht Journal of European and Comparative Law*, Vol. 23, Issue 1, 2016, pp. 17-39.

5 *Cf.* Patrick Sikora, 'PSPP auf dem Prüfstand: Das Weiss-Urteil des EuGH', *Europäisches Wirtschafts- und Steuerrecht*, 2019/3, p. 141.

6 Cases 2 BvR 2728/13 *et al.*, Judgment of the Second Senate of 21 June 2016, ECLI:DE:BVerfG: 2016:rs20160621.2bvr272813. *See* on this decision, *inter alia*, Sven Kaufmann, 'Le Bundesverfassungsgericht et les limites à la primauté du droit de l'Union. Confrontation ou complémentarité dans l'intégration européenne?', *Revue trimestrielle de droit européen*, Vol. 53, Issue 1, 2017, pp. 59-73; Mehrdad Payandeh, 'The OMT Judgment of the German Federal Constitutional Court: Repositioning the Court Within the European Constitutional Architecture', *European Constitutional Law Review*, Vol. 13, Issue 2, 2017, pp. 400-416; Lorenzo Federico Pace, 'The OMT case, the "intergovernmental drift" of the Eurozone crisis and the (inevitable) rectification of the BVerfG jurisprudence in light of the ECJ's Gauweiler judgment', *Il diritto dell'Unione Europea*, 2017/1, pp. 153-170; Robert Böttner, 'Rechtmäßigkeit des Ankaufs von Staatsanleihen durch die EZB im OMT-Programm', *Zeitschrift für das Juristische Studium*, 2016/6, pp. 776-780.

doi: 10.5553/HYIEL/266627012021009001010

continuing the intervention become unnecessary. The German FCC thus toned down its evaluation of the OMT program as outlined in its reference for a preliminary ruling.[7]

Furthermore, it underlined that the execution of the European integration agenda comes with several drops in influence (Einflussknicke) that may lower the level of the democratic legitimation of European public authorities' acts, for example with regard to the ECB's independence (Article 130 TFEU), but that other strands of legitimation at the supranational level take the particularities of this level into account. However, the *Bundesverfassungsgericht* pointed out that a strict delimitation of competences as enshrined in the principle of conferral (Article 5 TEU) is indispensable for safeguarding the citizens' "right to democracy" that flows from their right to vote [Article 38(1) and (2) of the Basic Law]. It is the task of the German FCC, by way of its *ultra vires review*, to control that acts of the Union do not amount to *de facto* treaty amendments when they transgress the limits of conferred competences, to prevent a violation of the principle of sovereignty of the German people. This is the case when the transgression of competence is "manifest" and "of considerable weight". In its judgment on the banking union, the German FCC added that the assumption of a manifest excess of competence does not presuppose that no different legal opinions are held on this issue. The fact that voices in academic literature, in politics or in the media attest to the harmlessness of a measure does not in principle prevent a finding of an obvious exceeding of competence. "Obvious" exceeding of competence may also be the case if it is the result of a careful and detailed reasoned interpretation.[8]

The German FCC reiterated that the CJEU must be given the opportunity to hand down a preliminary ruling before the national court could determine an *ultra vires* act. In doing so, the German FCC must take into account the Union-specific methods of interpretation that have been developed by the CJEU. It is not the task of the German FCC to replace the interpretation of the CJEU with its own, as long as they are handled in a methodologically correct manner within the usual bounds of legal debate; the CJEU has a "right to tolerance of error" and to judicial development of the law as long as it applies recognized methodological principles and does not proceed in a way that is objectively arbitrary.[9]

7 *Cf.* Sikora 2019, p. 141.

8 *See* Cases 2 BvR 1685/14 *et al.*, Judgment of the Second Senate of 30 July 2019, ECLI:DE:BVerfG:2019:rs20190730.2bvr168514, para. 152 (my translation).

9 *See also* id. para. 151: An exceeding of competences exists "if – when applying established methodological standards – a competence for the contested measure cannot be demonstrated under any legal point of view [...]. In relation to the CJEU, it is also informed by the differences in the mandate to be fulfilled and the standards to be applied by the Federal Constitutional Court on the one hand and the CJEU on the other. In this respect, it must also be taken into account that the CJEU must be granted a certain margin of error [...]. This margin is covered by the mandate conferred in Art. 19(1) second sentence TEU and is only exceeded when an interpretation of the Treaties is not comprehensible and must thus be considered objectively arbitrary."

doi: 10.5553/HYIEL/266627012021009001010

3. The Main Story: The PSPP Proceedings

3.1. Factual (and Legal) Background

Even before the judgment in the *OMT* case was handed down, a new asset purchasing program was established by the ECB: the Public Sector Asset Purchase Program (PSPP) as one of four sub-programs of the extensive Expanded Asset Purchase Program (EAPP) announced by the ECB on 22 January 2015,[10] an instrument of so called "quantitative easing" (QE). Until the end of 2018, a total of around 2.1 trillion euros worth in government bonds was purchased under this program. Of the eligible marketable debt securities, 10% were to be purchased in securities issued by eligible international organizations and multilateral development banks, and 90% were to be purchased in securities issued by eligible central, regional or local governments and recognized agencies or public non-financial corporations. The national central banks' share was 90%, and the remaining 10% were to be purchased by the ECB. The distribution of purchases across jurisdictions was in accordance with the key for subscription of the ECB's capital as referred to in Article 29 of the ESCB Statute.[11] The PSPP was designed within the framework of monetary policy to counteract deflation and increase inflation to the target value of "price stability" (*i.e.* inflation rate below, but close to 2%). This was to serve the underlying monetary policy objective of increasing liquidity on the interbank market and of credit to the euro area economy.[12] In essence, the asset purchase program (*cf.* Article 18.1 of the ESCB Statute) was intended to secure an appropriate monetary policy transmission, which is recognized as a legitimate goal of monetary policy.[13]

Several constitutional complaints were initiated before the German FCC against the PSPP. In essence, the complainants argued that by launching the PSPP the European System of Central Banks violated the prohibition of monetary financing laid down in Article 123 TFEU and the principle of conferral of Article 5 TEU in conjunction with Articles 119 and 127 *et seq.* TFEU. As a result, the German Federal Government and the German *Bundestag* violated the complainants' constitutional rights by not taking the necessary steps to ensure the non-implementation of the PSPP. Moreover, in case of default of government bonds purchased by the national central banks, it is possible that the ESCB decides to share these losses (*cf.* Article 32.4 of the ESCB Statute), which in turn could make the recapitalization of the German National Bank (*Bundesbank*) necessary. As a consequence, the *Bundestag* could be impaired in its right to decide on the national budget on its own authority due to decisions made by third parties. It would amount to a violation of the German constitutional identity

10 ECB Decision (EU) 2015/774 of 4 March 2015 on a secondary markets public sector asset purchase programme (ECB/2015/10), repealed and replaced by ECB Decision (EU) 2020/188 of 3 February 2020 on a secondary markets public sector asset purchase programme (ECB/2020/9).

11 *See* Article 6 of the amended ECB Decision (EU) 2015/774.

12 *See* Recital 4 of the ECB Decision (EU) 2015/774.

13 *See also* the summary of the program by Mark Dawson & Ana Bobić, 'Quantitative Easing at the Court of Justice – Doing Whatever It Takes to Save the Euro: Weiss and Others', *Common Market Law Review*, Vol. 56, Issue 4, 2019, p. 1006.

doi: 10.5553/HYIEL/266627012021009001010

[Article 79(3) of the Basic Law] if such a system of risk sharing was not precluded under primary law.

To be precise, the constitutional complaints only indirectly challenged the PSPP. From the point of view of German constitutional law, they were directed against the Federal Government and the Parliament. Legal standing in the context of constitutional complaints is based on Article 38(1) of the Basic Law,[14] which enshrines the citizens' right to vote in elections to the German *Bundestag*. It guarantees democratic legitimation of public power and aims to protect against measures outside an uninterrupted chain of legitimation. This right to democratic self-determination also applies with regard to European integration and protects against a (manifest and structurally significant) exceeding of competences on the part of the Union and its bodies. If Union bodies act outside the scope of their conferred powers, they act outside the German Act of Assent to the European Treaties conferring these powers upon the Union and are thus not democratically legitimized (*ultra vires*). The Federal Government and the *Bundestag* are required by the principle of democracy to act in accordance with their responsibility for integration and to act towards compliance with the principle of conferred powers. In a nutshell:

> "It is only admissible to challenge acts of secondary or tertiary EU law by means of a constitutional complaint for the purposes of asserting that German constitutional bodies violated their responsibility with regard to European integration (Integrationsverantwortung) either by implementing such acts or, subsequently, by failing to actively take steps to ensure that conformity with the European integration agenda (Integrationsprogramm) is (re-)established."[15]

3.2. The Bundesverfassungsgericht's Reference for a Preliminary Ruling

As in the *OMT* case, the *Bundesverfassungsgericht* decided to submit another set of questions for a preliminary ruling.[16] It is immediately noticeable that the referral (unlike in the *OMT* proceedings, where the FCC rather 'dictated' its findings[17]) is much more fact-oriented and formulated as a balanced request for judicial dialogue.[18]

14 *See* Philip M. Bender, 'Ambivalenz der Offensichtlichkeit: Zugleich Anmerkung zur Entscheidung des BVerfGs vom 5. Mai 2020', *Zeitschrift für europarechtliche Studien*, Vol. 23, Issue 3, 2020, p. 412.

15 Cases 2 BvR 1685/14 *et al.*, Judgment of the Second Senate of 30 July 2019, ECLI:DE:BVerfG:2019:rs20190730.2bvr168514, para. 102.

16 Cases 2 BvR 859/15 *et al.*, Order of the Second Senate of 18 July 2017, ECLI:DE:BVerfG:2017:rs20170718.2bvr085915. *See* in detail Andrej Lang, 'Ultra Vires Review of the ECB's Policy of Quantitative Easing: An Analysis of the German Constitutional Court's Preliminary Reference Order in the PSPP Case', *Common Market Law Review*, Vol. 55, Issue 3, 2018, pp. 923-951.

17 *Cf.* Franz C Mayer, 'Rebels Without a Cause? Zur OMT-Vorlage des Bundesverfassungsgerichts', *Europarecht*, 2014/5, p. 482.

18 Sikora 2019, p. 142; Annelieke Mooij, 'The Weiss Judgment: The Court's Further Clarification of the ECB's Legal Framework', *Maastricht Journal of European and Comparative Law*, Vol. 26, Issue 3, 2019, p. 452; Lang 2018, p. 934.

doi: 10.5553/HYIEL/266627012021009001010

Several aspects justified a new referral. First of all, the German FCC and several experts held that the PSPP is different from the OMT program and therefore, the CJEU did not exhaustively answer the questions surrounding such an asset purchase program. In fact, the OMT was restricted to ESM program States (conditionality, selectivity, parallelism), and additional liquidity in the OMT was to be sterilized through other monetary instruments (which is inherently excluded under quantitative easing).[19] Secondly, from a European law perspective, only the CJEU can rule on the *invalidity* of acts of European institutions, bodies, offices and agencies, either by way of an action for annulment or a preliminary ruling. This holds true even (thirdly) from the perspective of German constitutional law.

The German FCC found that the PSPP violated Article 123(1) TFEU, which prohibits monetary financing from Member State budgets, and exceeded the ECB's monetary policy mandate from Article 127(1) and (2) TFEU as well as Articles 17 *et seq*. of the ESCB Statute because the program's economic policy effects are at least equal to the monetary policy objectives. In essence, the *Bundesverfassungsgericht* argues that *(i)* the program provided not a legal, but a *de facto* certainty regarding the purchase of government bonds by the Eurosystem; *(ii)* it is not possible to ascertain whether a sufficient minimum waiting period elapses between the issuing of the bonds and the purchase on the secondary market, which is necessary fora veritable market price to take shape; *(iii)* all bonds are *de facto* held until maturity, even though this is only allowed as an exception; this would make these sovereign debts irrelevant to the market and thus distort Member States' refinancing conditions; and *(iv)* it is possible, in principle, to purchase bonds with a negative yield at maturity, thereby not only lending money, but effectively also giving money to the issuing State.

Therefore, while formally government bonds are purchased on the secondary market, the PSPP would turn it, in practice, into action with *an equivalent effect to the direct purchase of government bonds from the Member States, thereby undermining the effectiveness of and even circumventing the objectives pursued by Article 123(1) TFEU*. Buyers on the primary market would turn into intermediaries for the ESCB for the direct purchase of government bonds. The FCC concluded that the PSPP is (also) an economic policy instrument. While the ESCB and the ECB have the competence to *support* the general economic policy of the EU, provided that this does not interfere with their primary (monetary policy) objective of maintaining price stability [Article 127(1) TFEU], in the FCC's view *the foreseeability and the volume of the PSPP create economic policy effects that are disproportionate and outweigh their monetary policy character*. Lastly, the FCC holds that the legal framework underlying the PSPP lacks comprehensible reasons that would allow for the close monitoring of the (continued) necessity of the program.

The last question referred to the CJEU concerned *risk sharing within the ESCB*. The Federal Republic of Germany is constitutionally required to ensure the functioning and the financing in the event of insufficient or even negative net equity (institutional liability, Anstaltslast) of its national central bank. The ECB

19 *Cf.* Sikora 2019, p. 140. On the differences *see also* Mooij 2019, p. 460.

doi: 10.5553/HYIEL/266627012021009001010

has argued that no risk sharing applies in respect of securities of national issuers that are purchased by the national central banks (80% of the purchased bonds), a limited risk sharing applies in respect of securities of national issuers that are purchased by the ECB (10% of the purchased bonds), and a full risk sharing in accordance with the relevant capital key applies only in respect of bonds issued by international issuers and purchased under the PSPP (10% of the purchased bonds). The German FCC argued that there is no legal guarantee prohibiting an extension of risk sharing for bonds purchased by national central banks from national issuers. It would amount to a *violation of* Articles 123 and 125 TFEU as well as Article 4(2) TEU and, as a consequence, *Germany's constitutional identity* [Article 79(3) of the Basic Law] if it became necessary to provide recapitalization for the national central banks through budgetary resources to an extent that approval by the German Bundestag would be required, thus affecting the overall budgetary responsibility of the German Parliament.

3.3. Judgment of the CJEU

Another two months later, on 11 December 2018, the CJEU, basically following the AG's opinion,[20] delivered its judgment in the case.[21] First, the CJEU explained that *the PSPP was duly justified.*[22] It argued that, in accordance with its case-law, justification in the sense of Article 296(2) TFEU not only covers the wording of the measure (including the considerations in the published act), but also the context and the whole body of legal rules governing the matter in question.[23] Against this background, the ECB has given sufficient reason for the PSPP in press conferences, minutes of meetings and various publications and reports depicting the economic and monetary background of the measures taken. Moreover, these documents show that the ECB has taken into account the potential side effects and possible impact of PSPP on budgetary decisions of the Member States.[24] Taking into consideration the ECB's primary-law based independence, the CJEU engages in a process-oriented review where the ECB's operational discretion is accompanied by a close review of the procedure and justifications leading to the PSPP.[25]

The CJEU also considers *the PSPP as a measure of monetary policy*. The CJEU reiterates that a measure must be assessed in accordance with the objectives pursued and the instruments used in order to determine whether it is monetary or economic policy. Furthermore, the CJEU underlines that there can be no absolute separation between economic and monetary policies, which was not the intention of the authors of the Treaties.[26] In contrast to the German FCC, the

20 Opinion of Advocate General Wathelet delivered on 4 October 2018, *Case C-493/17, Weiss and others*, ECLI:EU:C:2018:815.
21 Judgment of 11 December 2018 (Grand Chamber), *Case C-493/17, Weiss and others*, ECLI:EU:C:2018:1000.
22 Id. para. 42.
23 Id. para. 33 with further reference.
24 Id. para. 38.
25 Dawson & Bobić 2019, p. 1031.
26 *Case C-493/17, Weiss and others*, para. 60.

doi: 10.5553/HYIEL/266627012021009001010

CJEU holds that even if (economic) effects of a measure were knowingly accepted and definitely foreseeable from the outset, they can still be regarded as "indirect effects" that have no consequences for the characterization of a measure as economic or monetary policy.[27] Otherwise the ESCB would be prevented from using the means that the Treaties provide for the attainment of monetary policy objectives and might even represent and insurmountable obstacle for accomplishing its tasks, especially in times of crises. The AG added in his opinion that "indirect" economic effects that a monetary policy measure can and may produce are not to be confused with "limited", "ancillary" or "marginal" effects.[28] Instead, as the ESCB may support the EU's economic policy, the only limitation on that support is not to undermine the monetary policy objective of maintaining price stability. "Indirect" effects, therefore, can be quite direct, so long as they are not primary. The CJEU also deals in much detail with the question of the PSPP's proportionality[29] and concludes that the program is appropriate to achieve the objective of maintaining price stability and does not manifestly go beyond what is necessary to achieve that objective. The safeguards included in the PSPP (subsidiarity of PSPP within the APP, purchases distributed across all euro area states, limited risk sharing) limit its impact in terms of economic policy and guarantees that the program does not, principally, pursue economic policy objectives.

Concerning the predictability of the ESCB's purchasing practice (thereby rendering the PSPP equivalent to a (prohibited) primary market intervention),[30] the CJEU found that operators cannot know for certain if, when, and to what extent the ESCB would buy government bonds under the PSPP. It held that the constant evaluation and adjustment of the program by the ECB's Governing Council, the subsidiarity to other APP programs, the absence of selectivity, the maximum limits on purchases (which are *no obligation to purchase*), the blackout period (which is monitored by the ESCB's risk management committee in order to ensure the forming of market prices) and the monitored disclosure of information constitute *sufficient guarantees to ensure that government bonds are purchased on the secondary market without these purchases being equivalent to direct purchases* due to certainty on the part of the operators. Constantly evaluating and adjusting the program to what is necessary preserves the temporary nature of the program. The level of predictability is therefore negligible and does not reduce the States' impetus to conduct a sound budgetary policy.[31]

27 Id. paras. 62 *et seq.*; For Dawson & Bobić 2019, p. 1019, "*the most direct effects of the programme are precisely its economic effects*, with a general raising of prices (and therefore a meeting of the inflation target) constituting an *indirect* consequence of a broader easing of economic conditions and the general money supply" (emphasis in the original).

28 *Case C-493/17, AG Opinion*, para. 113.

29 *Case C-493/17, Weiss and others*, paras. 71 *et seq*. For a critical view on the proportionality review *see* Dawson & Bobić 2019, pp. 1022 *et seq*.

30 *Case C-493/17, Weiss and others*, paras. 109 *et seq*.

31 Id. paras. 129 *et seq*.

doi: 10.5553/HYIEL/266627012021009001010

Holding bonds until maturity and/or with a negative yield does not constitute a problem for the Court either.[32] The former is a possibility and is in no way precluded by Article 18 of the ESCB Statute, so long as it meets the objectives of the program in question. On the contrary, the fact that the ESCB has the option of selling purchased bonds at any time helps ensure a sound budgetary policy. As regards the purchase of bonds with a negative yield, the CJEU found that these operations are not excluded by Article 18 of the Statute. It furthermore points out that bonds with a negative yield can be issued only by States whose financial situation is assessed positively by operators in the market. Moreover, the AG argued that excluding bonds with a negative yield from purchases under the PSPP would run counter to the principle of market neutrality.[33]

Finally, the CJEU threw out the final question regarding risk sharing. In line with several written observations submitted in the case, it argues that, *(i)* firstly, there is currently no system of unlimited risk sharing installed by the PSPP Decision. *(ii)* Secondly, there has been a sustained intention on the part of the ECB to strictly limit loss sharing. *(iii)* Thirdly, even if such a system were established, it is uncertain whether recapitalization of national central banks by national budget funds would be necessary. Therefore, in the CJEU's view, the question is hypothetical and thus inadmissible.[34]

All in all, the CJEU's decision did not come as a surprise. The CJEU relied on its previous case-law, especially the *Gauweiler/OMT* decision,[35] and found that *the PSPP does not violate European law*. It confirmed and supported the ECB's wide margin of discretion due to the technical nature of their decisions and its guaranteed independence, resulting in a limited judicial reviewability of its acts. Most authors agreed with the verdict.[36] Some authors criticized that the CJEU rejected the fifth question as inadmissible and considered this as "provoking an

32 Id. paras. 145 *et seq.*

33 *Case C-493/17, AG Opinion*, para. 74.

34 *Case C-493/17, Weiss and others*, paras. 159 *et seq.*

35 In fact, as Corinna Dornacher, 'Schlusskapitel oder Zwischenakt? Anmerkung zum Urteil des EuGH v. 11.12.2018, Rs. C-493/17 (Weiss u. a.)', *Europarecht*, Vol. 54, Issue 5, 2019, p. 547. points out, the CJEU refers no less than 36 times to the *Gauweiler/OMT* case. Mooij 2019, p. 452. points to the fact that the rapporteur (L. Bay Larsen) was the same in both cases.

36 *See*, among others, Sikora 2019; with a critical view on the aspect of the "predictability" of ESCB purchases Peter-Christian Müller-Graff, 'Bank- und Kapitalmarktrecht: Anleihenkaufprogramm der EZB zulässig', *Europäische Zeitschrift für Wirtschaftsrecht*, 2019, pp. 172-173; Dornacher 2019.

doi: 10.5553/HYIEL/266627012021009001010

escalation"[37] and, in view of the CJEU's case-law, this may in fact raise an eyebrow.[38]

3.4. Final Judgment of the Bundesverfassungsgericht

Comments on the CJEU's decision giving prospect on the FCC's final verdict mostly did not expect what happened on 5 May 2020:[39] the German Constitutional Court not only ruled that *the PSPP was ultra vires and thus unconstitutional* (with regard to German law), but it also decided that *the ruling handed down by the CJEU was also an ultra vires act because it was methodologically flawed*.

The FCC, following its earlier case-law and based on the individuals' right to vote, set out to explain that any transfer of competences to the EU must meet democratic standards. This includes that the EU must not have the power to decide on its own competences (no *Kompetenz-Kompetenz*)[40] and the German Parliament must not be deprived of its substantive leeway to take decision and shape policy, especially in the form of its budgetary powers,[41] as this would result in a loss in substance of the sovereign power afforded to German citizens. The Federal Government and the Parliament are called upon to monitor compliance with the European integration agenda and to take the necessary steps to prevent or reverse any transgression of competences and restore accordance of the exercise of public power with their legal bases.

The FCC reiterates that it is the CJEU's task to decide on the validity of Union acts, for otherwise, if national courts could readily invoke this authority, this could undermine the primacy of application of EU law and jeopardize its uniform application. However, the FCC underlines, *national courts must preserve the right to an ultra vires review in order to monitor, in exceptional cases*, that the EU does not adopt a legal interpretation that would amount to an amendment of the Treaties or an expansion of the EU's competences. As *the Member States remain the 'Masters of the Treaties'*, "certain tensions are thus inherent in the design of the EU", which must be resolved "through mutual respect and understanding".[42]

37 Matthias Ruffert, 'Europarecht: Anleihekäufe der EZB: Die massiven Käufe von Staatsanleihen durch das ESZB seit Januar 2015 sind unionsrechtskonform', *Juristische Schulung* 2019, p. 182; Sikora 2019, p. 145; Dornacher 2019, p. 549. refers to it (less dramatically) a "missed opportunity" for judicial dialogue. Mooij 2019, p. 464. agrees with the hypothetical nature of the question, but states that the CJEU could have used the opportunity to provide guidance as to what extent a "silent bailout" under TARGET2 is acceptable.

38 In Judgment of 22 November 1978, *Case C-93/78, Mattheus*, ECLI:EU:C:1978:206, para. 8, and Judgment of 16 July 1992, *Case C-343/90, Lourenço Dias*, ECLI:EU:C:1992:327, para. 18, the CJEU held that it cannot give a ruling on a matter which relates to measures not yet adopted by the Union institutions. In *Gauweiler* (para. 27.); on the other hand, the CJEU admitted hypothetical questions (OMT was in essence only announced in a press release and lacked implementing measures) because these were admissible in the main proceedings before the referring court.

39 Cases 2 BvR 859/15 *et al.*, Judgment of the Second Senate of 5 May 2020, ECLI:DE:BVerfG:2020:rs20200505.2bvr085915.

40 Id. para. 102.

41 Id. para. 103.

42 Id. para. 111.

doi: 10.5553/HYIEL/266627012021009001010

The German FCC goes on to prepare its frontal assault against the CJEU: the methodological standards recognized by the CJEU for the development of the law are based on constitutional legal traditions common to the Member States and the application of the methods and principles by the CJEU cannot and need not completely correspond to the practice of domestic courts. The CJEU is granted a certain margin of error and the FCC must respect the methodologically correct verdict of the CJEU even against weighty arguments. However, *the CJEU exceeds its mandate where "traditional European methods of interpretation" and "general legal principles that are common to the laws of the Member States are manifestly disregarded."* If a decision amounts to a manifest exceeding of competences, it lacks the minimum democratic legitimation required under the German constitution.[43] The interpretation given by the CJEU, the FCC continues, "is simply not comprehensible and thus objectively arbitrary" because it manifestly failed to give consideration to the importance and scope of the principle of proportionality and completely disregarded the effects of the PSPP when determining whether is it monetary or economic policy.[44] This approach by the CJEU "essentially renders meaningless the principle of conferral".[45]

The FCC held that the CJEU *accepted the information given by the ECB as fact without further scrutiny* and without regard to the foreseeable and/or intended economic and fiscal consequences when determining the PSPP's economic or monetary policy nature. In doing so, the CJEU allowed the ESCB to decide autonomously on their own competences. As a result, the FCC continued, the CJEU allows asset purchase programs "even in cases where the purported monetary policy objective is possibly only invoked to disguise what essentially constitutes an economic and fiscal policy agenda." Instead, the CJEU "completely disregarded" the economic policy effects of the PSPP and therefore the proportionality review cannot fulfil its purpose of balancing conflicting interests.[46]

The FCC admitted that the ECB enjoys a margin of appreciation as regards the assessment and appraisal of the consequences of its actions and the weighing of such consequences in relation to the objectives pursued by the asset purchase program. However, the FCC held, the CJEU's interpretation is flawed in that the Contracting Parties did not intend to make an absolute distinction between monetary and economic policy because they belong to two different types of categories of competences (exclusive *versus* supporting). As the ECB and the national central banks enjoy independence, they have a diminished level of democratic legitimation. Therefore, adherence to the limits of conferred competences by the ECB must be subject to full judicial review. Disregarding economic policy effects of a monetary policy measure is incompatible with a restrictive interpretation.[47] This "contradicts the methodological approach taken

43 Id. para. 112.
44 Id. para. 118.
45 Id. para. 123.
46 Id. paras. 136, 138 *et seq.*
47 Id. paras. 141 and 143.

doi: 10.5553/HYIEL/266627012021009001010

by the CJEU in virtually all other areas of EU law", the FCC continued, referring to CJEU case-law concerning, *inter alia*, fundamental rights and fundamental freedoms.[48]

As a consequence of the finding that *the CJEU acted ultra vires*, the FCC found that it cannot rely on the judgment given in the preliminary ruling procedure but instead must conduct its own review to decide on the preliminary questions. The German FCC concluded that due to the lack of sufficient proportionality considerations, the PSPP is neither covered by the monetary policy competence of the ECB [Article 127(1) first sentence TFEU] nor by its merely supporting competence regarding the Member States' economic policies [Article 127(1) second sentence TFEU]. The program must constitute a suitable and necessary means for achieving the aim pursued and the program's monetary policy objective and its economic policy effects must be identified, weighed and balanced against one another. While the FCC held that the PSPP's monetary policy objective is in principle not (yet) objectionable, the ECB manifestly disregarded the principle of proportionality by pursuing that objective unconditionally while ignoring the economic policy effects resulting from the program. More precisely, the ECB failed to show a balancing in its decision and to state the reasons informing such balancing (*Abwägungs- und Darlegungsausfall*).[49] Therefore, the FCC arrived at the conclusion that *the actions of the ECB constitute an ultra vires act*.[50]

On the other hand, the FCC did not strike down the CJEU's finding that *the PSPP does not violate Article 123(1) TFEU*. On the condition that the safeguards established by the CJEU are strictly observed, the PSPP does not circumvent the prohibition of monetary financing.[51] While in the FCC's view the application of some of the criteria give rise to "considerable concerns", an overall balancing leads to the conclusion that *a manifest violation of Article 123(1) TFEU is not ascertainable*. This is not put into question by the purchase under the PSPP of government bonds with a negative yield to maturity.[52] Nevertheless, in order to conduct an effective judicial review of any instruments of the ESCB for which it enjoys broad discretion, sufficient information on the program and its aspects must be given either in advance or *ex post*. If information in advance is not possible without undermining the effectiveness of the PSPP, any relevant information on past operations must be given (so long as this does not provide insights into future operations) in order to meet the requirement under Article 296(2) TFEU that a statement of reasons for any measure (be it *ex ante* or *ex post*) must enable the persons concerned to ascertain the reasons for the measure and to enable the CJEU to exercise its power of review.[53]

As a result of the *ultra vires* finding, the FCC ordered the Federal Government and the Bundestag to take steps seeking to ensure that the ECB conducts a

48 Id. paras. 146 *et seq*.
49 Id. para. 177.
50 Id. paras. 164 *et seq*.
51 Id. paras. 180 *et seq*.
52 In this context, the FCC even agrees with the CJEU's finding on the inadmissibility of the fifth preliminary question on the risk-sharing because it was too hypothetical. *See* Id. paras. 222 *et seq*.
53 Id. para. 189.

doi: 10.5553/HYIEL/266627012021009001010

proportionality assessment in relation to the PSPP within a transitional period of three months. Within that timeframe, *the ECB Governing Council needs to adopt a new decision* that demonstrates in a comprehensible and substantiated manner that the monetary policy objectives pursued by the ECB are not disproportionate to the economic and fiscal policy effects resulting from the program. Following that period, and in the event that the concerns voiced by the FCC are not taken account of, the PSPP would continue to be an *ultra vires* act and would not partake in the precedence of application of EU law (*Anwendungsvorrang*). As a result, the ultra vires act is not to be applied in Germany and has no binding effect in relation to German constitutional bodies, administrative authorities and courts. The Bundesbank would thus no longer be allowed to participate in the implementation and execution of the PSPP, neither by carrying out any further purchases of bonds, nor by contributing to another increase of the monthly purchase volume.[54]

4. Analysis / Comment

It is not quite clear how the German FCC reached its verdict, but sound legal reasoning does not appear to be the main aspect. From the point of view of German constitutional law, the FCC found that the Federal Government and the *Bundestag* violated the constitution because they did not prevent or act against a usurpation of competences on the part of the EU. The FCC rejected those complaints that were directed against the PSPP (and the CJEU's judgment) directly, as those acts are not acts of national public authority and can thus not be subject of a constitutional complaint. Nevertheless, the infringement by the German State bodies was based on the (indirect) finding that the EU (through the ECB and the CJEU) acted outside the scope of its conferred competences (*ultra vires*). However, the German decision was in no way without a (better) alternative. In terms of the cooperative relationship with the CJEU, the German FCC could have obliged the Federal Government and the *Bundesbank* to monitor the risk, to counteract any increase in risk at the European level and, in the event of an overruling, to bring an action for annulment. In (foreseeable) later proceedings, the *ultra vires* card may have been used as *ultima ratio*.[55]

To be clear, the German decision was not the first to declare an act of the Union's institutions inapplicable in the national legal order. The French *Conseil*

54 Id. paras. 232 and 234.
55 *Cf.* Sikora 2019, p. 145.

doi: 10.5553/HYIEL/266627012021009001010

d'État,[56] the Danish *Højesteret*[57] and the Czech *Ústavní soud*[58] already refused to follow certain CJEU judgments. In these cases, however, *the national courts did not replace the CJEU's assessment with their own, as did now the Bundesverfassungsgericht*. The other cases were concerned with the interpretation of national law in light of EU law, whereas the PSPP ruling dealt with the validity of an act taken by the ECB.[59] The German FCC's *ultra vires* ruling carries political and legal dynamite because of the authority of the German FCC among constitutional and supreme courts in Europe and the reservations to European law that other Member States' highest courts had already developed. It has been predicted that this ruling will encourage Eurosceptic states and their highest courts to refuse allegiance to CJEU rulings more easily. This is all the more dangerous because the German FCC did not take recourse to some very specific element of Germany's constitutional identity, but instead to the meta-principle of proportionality, thus opening Pandora's box to making nearly any European act reviewable before a national supreme or constitutional court.[60]

While few authors praised the German FCC's decision as logical, dogmatically convincing, an important red line and by no means surprising,[61] it was criticized by the majority of scholars. It reveals *the 'fundamental paradox' of the EU as a*

56 Conseil d'Etat (Assemblée) of 22 December 1978, Case No. 11604 – *Cohn-Bendit*; *see* on this Gerhard Bebr, 'The Rambling Ghost of "Cohn-Bendit": Acte Claire and the Court of Justice', *Common Market Law Review*, Vol. 20, Issue 3, 1983, pp. 439-472. This case-law has been formally abandoned by the judgment of the Conseil d'État (Assemblée) of 30 October 2009, Case No. 298348 – *Mme Perreux*; *see* on this Claus D. Classen, 'Der Conseil d'État auf Europakurs', *Europarecht*, Vol. 45, Issue 4, 2010, pp. 557-563; and Dominique Ritleng, 'L'arrêt Perreux, ou, La fin de l'exception française', *Revue trimestrielle de droit européen*, 2010/1, p. 223.

57 Danish Supreme Court (*Højesteret*), judgment of 6 December 2016, Case 15/2014 – *Ajos*; *see* Rass Holdgaard *et al.*, 'From Cooperation to Collision: the ECJ's Ajos Ruling and the Danish Supreme Court's Refusal to Comply', *Common Market Law Review*, Vol. 55, Issue 1, 2018, pp. 17-53; Ulla Neergaard & Karsten Engsig Sørensen, 'Activist Infighting Among Courts and Breakdown of Mutual Trust?: The Danish Supreme Court, the CJEU, and the Ajos Case', *Yearbook of European law*, Vol. 36, 2017, pp. 275-313; Mikael Rask Madsen *et al.*, 'Competing Supremacies and Clashing Institutional Rationalities: The Danish Supreme Court's Decision in the Ajos Case and the National Limits of Judicial Cooperation', *European Law Journal*, Vol. 23, Issue 1-2, 2017, pp. 140-150.

58 Czech Constitutional Court (*Ústavní soud*), judgment of 31 January 2012, Case No. Pl. Ús 5/12 – *Landtová*; *see* Jan Komárek, 'Playing with Matches: The Czech Constitutional Court Declares a Judgment of the Court of Justice of the EU Ultra Vires', *European Constitutional Law Review*, Vol. 8, Issue 2, 2012, pp. 323-337; Robert Zbíral, 'Czech Constitutional Court, Judgment of 31 January 2012, Pl. ÚS 5/12. – A Legal Revolution or Negligible Episode?', *Common Market Law Review*, Vol. 49, Issue 4, 2012, pp. 1475-1491.

59 *Cf.* Annegret Engel *et al.*, 'Is this Completely M.A.D.? Three Views on the Ruling of the German FCC on 5th May 2020', *Nordic Journal of European Law*, Vol. 3, Issue 1, 2020, p. 144.

60 Bernhard Wegener, 'Karlsruher Unheil – Das Urteil des Bundesverfassungsgerichts vom 5. Mai 2020 (2 BvR 859/15) in Sachen Staatsanleihekäufe der Europäischen Zentralbank', *Europarecht*, Vol. 55, Issue 4, 2020, p. 354.

61 *See, inter alia*, Michael Pießkalla, 'Das BVerfG-Urteil zum Staatsanleihekaufprogramm der EZB: Eine wichtige rote Line', *Europäische Zeitschrift für Wirtschaftsrecht*, Vol. 31, Issue 12, 2020, pp. 538-542.

doi: 10.5553/HYIEL/266627012021009001010

supranational community with the Member States as 'Masters of the Treaties'.[62] While the EU is founded by and dependent on the will and transfer of powers by the Member States, the CJEU derives from the founding treaties an autonomous legal order that has outgrown classic public international law.[63]

First of all, as regards the content of the judgment, it is interesting to note that the *ultra vires* ruling is not based on the FCC's finding that the PSPP violated the prohibition of monetary financing [Article 123(1) TFEU] or was primarily (and thus illegitimately) an economic policy measure,[64] even though there would be strong arguments that the asset purchase program was indeed a substitute for direct fiscal assistance to indebted States.[65]

Instead, the FCC held that *neither the ECB nor the CJEU sufficiently reviewed the proportionality of the PSPP* because they did not take due account of the economic policy effects of the measure. Hence, the CJEU's interpretation is "simply not comprehensible and thus objectively arbitrary". While this language has been considered too harsh and unfriendly, it is, upon closer inspection, only a logical follow-up on the FCC's *ultra vires* case-law and consequently a dogmatic necessity.[66] The FCC was forced to throw out the CJEU's ruling in order to get to the PSPP Decision. Leaving the irritating language aside, at a substantial level the German FCC insinuates that proportionality arguments can be used for the delimitation of competences. This is one of the greatest flaws of the German judgment.[67]

In accordance with Article 5(2) TEU, the delimitation of competences between the EU and the Member States is based on the principle of conferral. According to this principle, the EU may act only within the limits of the competences conferred upon it by the Member States. Competences not conferred upon the EU in the Treaties remain with the Member States. Proportionality (alongside with subsidiarity), on the other hand, is not a principle that governs the *repartition* of competences, but instead the *exercise* of competences.[68] Only if the EU (or the ECB/ESCB) has a competence under the

62 Classen & Nettesheim, '§ 9. Rechtsquellen des Europäischen Unionsrechts', *in* Oppermann/ Classen/Nettesheim (eds.), *Europarecht*, 8th edn. 2018, para. 8.

63 *Cf., inter alia*, Friedemann Kainer, 'Aus der nationalen Brille: Das PSPP-Urteil des BVerfG', *Europäische Zeitschrift für Wirtschaftsrecht*, Vol. 31, Issue 12, 2020, pp. 533-536.

64 Id. p. 534.

65 *See, inter alia*, Dirk Meyer, Written testimony to the Bundestag's European Affairs Committee on the PSPP judgment, at www.bundestag.de/resource/blob/697480/6a9a51187f089 e80bd6221993926a4de/meyer-data.pdf. *See also* the Memorandum on the ECB's Monetary Policy, signed by former central bankers, October 2019, at www.hanswernersinn.de/dcs/ Memorand-ECB-Monetary-Policy-04102019.pdf.

66 Ulrich Haltern, 'Ultra-vires-Kontrolle im Dienst europäischer Demokratie', *Neue Zeitschrift für Verwaltungsrecht*, 2020/12, p. 821.

67 *Cf.* Kainer 2020, p. 535.

68 *See*, among others, Paul Dermine, 'The Ruling of the Bundesverfassungsgericht in PSPP – An Inquiry into its Repercussions on the Economic and Monetary Union', *European Constitutional Law Review*, Vol. 16, Issue 3, 2020, p. 539; Toni Marzal, 'Making Sense of the Use of Proportionality in the Bundesverfassungsgericht's PSPP Decision', *Revue des affaires européennes*, 2020/2, p. 444; Mattias Wendel, 'Paradoxes of Ultra-Vires Review: A Critical Review of the PSPP Decision and Its Initial Reception', *German Law Journal*, Vol. 21, Issue 5, 2020, p. 985.

doi: 10.5553/HYIEL/266627012021009001010

principle of conferral can proportionality issues lead to the unlawfulness of a measure. In this case, however, the institution would not have acted *ultra vires* (*i.e. outside* its competences) but instead unlawfully, but still *within* their assigned competences. Interestingly, the German FCC explicitly rejected the application of a proportionality assessment for the allocation of competences in the *German* federal system.[69]

It should be stressed in this context that European primary law (in contrast with what the German FCC insinuates) *does* allow the ECB to support the economic policy of the EU, so long as the primary objective of maintaining price stability is guaranteed. In fact, the wording of Article 127(1) TFEU reveals that the ESCB is even obliged to support economic policy as a secondary objective. Moreover, an in accordance with the CJEU's finding, there is hardly any functioning monetary policy without economic effects. Monetary policy conducted by the ECB with (intended or at least accepted) economic effects is thus not *per se* excluded by the Treaties.[70] Therefore, even economic policy *effects* cannot lead to the conclusion that the CJEU has misinterpreted the Treaties. On the contrary, taking the degree of economic policy effects into account when determining whether or not the ECB was competent to act would turn the priorities in Article 127(1) TFEU upside down: The ECB would have to face trade-offs and compromises when conducting their monetary policy, even though the provision just mentioned underlines that economic policy shall be *without prejudice* to the ECB's primary objective of price stability (monetary policy).[71]

Moreover, the CJEU's approach to look at the aims of a measure and the instruments used to pursue these aims in order to delineate economic from monetary policy measures is well in line with the CJEU's established case-law. The CJEU recognizes policy effects but does not consider indirect effects to be decisive for determining the character of a measure. Frankly, the CJEU takes a rather pragmatic (and, of course, Euro-friendly) approach to the likewise pragmatic strategy of the ECB, an approach certainly amenable to criticism. The German FCC, on the other hand, seems to insist on an (unrealistic and artificial[72]) clear-cut separation between economic and monetary policy in order to prevent a "competence creep" on the part of the EU.[73] Even if there were such a clear

69 Case 2 BvG 1/88, Judgment of the Second Senate of 22 May 1990 – BVerfGE 81, 310 (338): "The limits on State intervention in the legal sphere of the individual derived from the principle of the rule of law are not applicable in the federal-state relationship and the repartition of competences. This applies in particular to the principle of proportionality, which has the function of defending individual rights and freedoms. The associated thinking in the categories of freedom and encroachment can neither be applied specifically to the subject-matter competence of the *Land* determined by a competitive relationship between the Federation and the *Land*, nor to delimitations of competence in general." (my translation).

70 *See also* Fabian Amtenbrink & René Repasi, 'The German Federal Constitutional Court's Decision in Weiss: A Contextual Analysis', *European Law Review*, Vol. 45, Issue 6, 2020, p. 760.

71 *Cf.* Phedon Nicolaides, 'An Assessment of the Judgment of the Federal Constitutional Court of Germany on the Public Sector Asset Purchase Programme of the European Central Bank', *Legal Issues of Economic Integration*, Vol. 47, Issue 3, 2020, p. 282.

72 *See, inter alia*, Dermine 2020, p. 535; Engel *et al.* 2020, p. 130.

73 *Cf.* Amtenbrink & Repasi 2020, p. 765.

doi: 10.5553/HYIEL/266627012021009001010

delineation between the two policy fields, classifying a measure as either one or the other negates the fact that it can actually be both. Moreover, the identification of the (economic) costs and the (monetary) benefits (or *vice versa*) of a policy initiative is in itself highly subjective and open to interpretation.[74] This is why, even if one were to accept the new sort of proportionality test that the FCC tried to establish, it would be impossible to comply with:[75] who's to balance economic and monetary policy effects if the Treaties do not tell us what they are supposed to be precisely?

Moreover, in contrast with what the German FCC concludes, the CJEU did not contradict its own case-law. Although the FCC cites a number of CJEU decisions from a wide range of areas, it does not deal with them in substance, but applies a very German understanding of proportionality.[76] In particular, the German FCC refers to a number of areas of CJEU case-law that involve individual rights and their balancing with public interests. This, however, is profoundly different from cases involving the determination of EU and Member State competences.[77] Moreover, it is not true that this form of proportionality assessment is "common to the legal systems of the Member States" as a "recognized method".[78] The Karlsruhe Court overlooks the fact that the principle of proportionality found its way into other national legal systems and, of course, also into the EU legal system partly as a German 'legal transplant' *via* the detour of the CJEU.[79] There, however, they were not adopted blindly as a foreign concept, but formulated within the framework of the respective legal system. This is precisely what the FCC means when it accepts that the CJEU has as its own methods of interpretation (that may differ from the FCC's own standards). In this context, as far as the (EU law) proportionality analysis conducted by the CJEU is concerned, upon closer inspection, it does not seem like the CJEU had incorrectly applied this principle. As Article 5(4) TEU provides, the principle of proportionality requires that the substance and form of EU action not exceed what is necessary to achieve the objectives of the Treaties. When the German FCC finds that a key element in the form of the balancing of conflicting interests (in the meaning of the German "proportionality in the strict sense" or "*Angemessenheit*") is 'missing' from the CJEU's assessment, this is because it is *not* a part of the *European* proportionality principle.[80]

Furthermore, it should be stressed that the CJEU's judgment was rendered by the Grand Chamber, *i.e.* by 15 jurists who, according to Article 253 TFEU, "possess the qualifications required for appointment to the highest judicial offices in their respective countries or who are jurisconsults of recognized competence".

74 *Cf.* Dermine 2020, p. 538.
75 Nicolaides 2020, p. 281.
76 With the same view *see* Engel *et al.* 2020, p. 138.
77 *Cf.* Amtenbrink & Repasi 2020, p. 774.
78 Kainer 2020, p. 535.
79 Marzal 2020, p. 444.
80 *See*, in this respect, *also* Thomas Ackermann, 'Not Mastering the Treaties: The German Federal Constitutional Court's PSPP Judgment', *Common Market Law Review*, Vol. 57, Issue 4, 2020, p. 972; Engel *et al.* 2020, p. 134.

doi: 10.5553/HYIEL/266627012021009001010

If the decision in *Weiss* were indeed "simply incomprehensible and thus objectively arbitrary", there should have been critical voices already in the literature commenting on the CJEU judgment.[81] This holds true even against the German FCC's approach that an obvious *ultra vires* act can exist even if there is no opposing legal opinion on a matter. Overall, the CJEU's limited proportionality test can be understood with good reasons as a necessary expression of judicial self-restraint in the control of an institution that is competent and resolutely independent in highly complex monetary and economic policy contexts.

The German FCC blatantly calls into question the primacy of EU law.[82] In doing so, the FCC's judgment is itself an *ultra vires* act, in essence for two reasons. *(i)* Firstly, even if one were to follow the FCC's approach regarding the principle of proportionality, the German FCC was in breach of European law since it did not give the CJEU a second chance to rule on this very issue.[83] The FCC should have submitted new questions for preliminary ruling allowing the CJEU to clarify its proportionality assessment of the ECB decision.[84] In fact, this would not be unprecedented if one looks, for example, at the judicial dialogue conducted between the CJEU and the Italian *Corte Costituzionale* in the cases of *Taricco*.[85] *(ii)* Secondly, the German FCC ordered the German Government and the *Bundestag* (as institutions in breach of German constitutional law in the course of the proceedings) to ensure that the ECB and German *Bundesbank* redraft the PSPP decision. This is nothing less than an order to interfere with the central banks' guaranteed independence (Article 130 TFEU).[86] In fact, the independence secured by European primary law does not mean that central banks are beyond any legal review. Legal review is indeed necessary to compensate for the lack of democratic legitimacy that independence entails. This is, however, why the CJEU stressed that due to the decreased democratic (input) legitimacy, the central banks need to pay closer attention to the justification of their legal acts. In this context, the Karlsruhe Court should bear in mind that, as a constitutional court, it represents a similar "democratic anomaly" from the point of view of legitimacy as a central bank, whose minimal democratic feedback to the direct representation of the people can only be justified by the function it fulfils.[87]

81 *Cf.* Kainer 2020, p. 536; Franz C. Mayer, 'The Ultra Vires Ruling: Deconstructing the German Federal Constitutional Court's PSPP Decision of 5 May 2020', *European Constitutional Law Review*, Vol. 16, Issue 4, 2021, p. 752.

82 Claude Blumann, 'Quelques enseignements de l'arrêt du Bundesverfassungsgericht du 5 mai 2020 sur les fondamentaux au droit de l'Union européenne', *Revue trimestrielle de droit européen*, 2020, pp. 892 *et seq.*

83 Mayer 2021, p. 756.

84 Hoai-Thu Nguyen & Merijn Chamon, 'The Ultra Vires Decision of the German Constitutional Court', *Hertie School Jacques Delors Centre Policy Paper*, 2020, p. 16; Amtenbrink & Repasi 2020, p. 771; Ackermann 2020, p. 969.

85 *Cf.* Matteo Bonelli, 'The Taricco Saga and the Consolidation of Judicial Dialogue in the European Union', *Maastricht Journal of European and Comparative Law*, Vol. 25, Issue 3, 2018, 357-373.

86 Nguyen & Chamon 2020, p. 16. *Cf. also* Jean-Victor Louis, 'L'indépendance de la Banque centrale européenne', *Revue trimestrielle de droit européen*, 2020, pp. 825 *et seq.*

87 Kainer 2020, p. 536; Böttner 2016, p. 780. *See also Case C-493/17, Weiss and Others, AG Opinion*, para. 117.

doi: 10.5553/HYIEL/266627012021009001010

From the point of view of national constitutional law, the *ius standi* of individuals against EU acts, which has been broadened in recent years, is worthy of criticism. As indicated above, the proceedings are not directed against the acts directly, but are played out *via* the claim that the German constitutional bodies must exercise their responsibility for integration and counteract European acts that are taken outside their competences. This is justified with the right to elect the German *Bundestag* from Article 38 of the Basic Law and the "right to democracy" that follows from this. In the meantime, this right has even been extended to formal aspects of the transfer of powers.[88] As a result of the link between individual voting rights and European integration, *anyone* can lodge a constitutional complaint against virtually *any* transfer of competences to the EU and any use of competences by the EU, even if there is no possible infringement of Germany's constitutional identity.[89] To be clear, this is not to deny that the EU's very construction suffers from a fundamental, maybe even insoluble constitutional and jurisdictional conflict[90] between two equally competent jurisdictions. A national court's 'final say', however, should be restricted to a very narrow set of cases affecting the nation's specific constitutional identity. The above-mentioned dialogue between the CJEU and the Italian Constitutional Court proves that the CJEU is not unwilling to accept this argument on the basis of Article 4(2) TEU.

On the occasion of the order for reference in the *OMT* proceedings, two judges of the FCC expressed considerable doubts about extending the right to vote to a means to challenge EU acts and used strong arguments to justify why, in their view, the constitutional complaints before the FCC should already have been rejected as inadmissible, as a result of which a question for reference would have lacked relevance for a decision.[91] As Justice *Lübbe-Wolff* held, allowing plaintiffs to turn against federal inaction with respect to EU acts goes "beyond the limits of judicial competence under the principles of democracy and separation of powers".[92] The German FCC, Justice *Gerhardt* added, "is not responsible for general constitutional supervision" and an *ultra vires* review [based on Article 38(1) of the Basic Law] opens the door "to a general right to have the laws enforced (*allgemeiner Gesetzesvollziehungsanspruch*)", *i.e.* an *actio popularis*, which the Basic Law does not foresee. It does not fit into the constitutional framework of parliamentary work that, "with the help of the Federal Constitutional Court, an individual may steer the *Bundestag's* right of initiative into a specific direction".[93]

88 Case 2 BvR 739/17, Judgment of the Second Senate of 13 February 2020, ECLI:DE:BVerfG:2020:rs20200213.2bvr073917, on the Agreement on a Unified Patent Court.

89 Wegener 2020, p. 349; Haltern 2020, p. 820. holds that this leads to the constitutional complaint being "wide open as a barn door" and a "de-subjectification of fundamental rights".

90 Taking a different view, Ackermann 2020, p. 968. states instead that the conflict is "inherent in the design of the German constitution". According to Engel *et al.* 2020, p. 133, this specific type of conflict is inherent in the asymmetric distribution of competences in the EMU.

91 *See* Cases 2 BvR 1390/12 *et al.*, Order of the Second Senate of 17 December 2013, ECLI:DE:BVerfG:2013:rs20131217.2bvr139012 – *OMT (reference for preliminary ruling)*, Dissenting Opinions of Justices Lübbe-Wolff and Gerhardt.

92 Dissenting Opinion of Justice Lübbe-Wolff, para. 2.

93 Dissenting Opinion of Justice Gerhardt, paras. 2, 6 and 21.

doi: 10.5553/HYIEL/266627012021009001010

Overall, it is not without irony that the German FCC bases its decision on the eternity clause of Article 79(3) of the Basic Law to oppose European integration and thus the State objective of European integration in Article 23 of the Basic Law. As Justice *Lübbe-Wolff* noted in her dissenting opinion to the judgment in the European Arrest Warrant case:

> "Article 79(3) of the Basic Law, as the constitutional limit of European integration, has rightly been applied with care [...] because the meaning of this provision is to exclude our country relapsing into dictatorship and barbarism, and nothing serves this aim with higher probability than Germany's integration into the European Union."[94]

5. Epilogue

The very same day the ruling was handed down, the ECB "took note" of the German verdict.[95] Only three days after the Karlsruhe judgment, the CJEU released a press statement, underlining first that "departments of the institution never comment on a judgment of a national court", but also reiterating that *"the Court of Justice alone [...] has jurisdiction to rule that an act of an EU institution is contrary to EU law."*[96] This is nothing short of a passive-aggressive confirmation of the now shattered relationship between Karlsruhe and Luxembourg, which used to be a "textbook example of judicial pluralism".[97] In fact, the German FCC's case-law in EU affairs strongly influenced the CJEU and nudged it to develop its own case-law, for example in the area of fundamental rights protection.[98]

The European Commission, on its part, also stressed that EU law has primacy over national law and that rulings of the CJEU are binding on all national courts and that "the final word on EU law is always spoken in Luxembourg. Nowhere else."[99] From the outset, it even considered an infringement procedure against the Federal Republic of Germany. From a legal point of view, this would both be

94 Case 2 BvR 2236/04, Judgment of 18 July 2005, ECLI:DE:BVerfG:2005:rs20050718.2bvr223604 – *European Arrest Warrant*, para. 178 (Dissenting Opinion of Judge Lübbe-Wolff).

95 ECB Press Release of 5 May 2020, at www.ecb.europa.eu/press/pr/date/2020/html/ecb.pr200505~00a09107a9.en.html.

96 CJEU, Press Release No. 58/20 of 8 May 2020. On this press statement *see* the interesting comments by Justin Lindeboom, 'Is the Primacy of EU Law Based on the Equality of the Member States? A Comment on the CJEU's Press Release Following the PSPP Judgment', *German Law Journal*, Vol. 21, Issue 5, 2020, pp. 1032-1044.

97 Niels Petersen, 'Karlsruhe's Lochner Moment? A Rational Choice Perspective on the German Federal Constitutional Court's Relationship to the CJEU After the PSPP Decision', *German Law Journal*, Vol. 21, Issue 5, 2020, p. 998.

98 *Cf.* Amtenbrink & Repasi 2020, p. 770.

99 Statement by Commission President von der Leyen of 10 May 2020, STATEMENT/20/846, at https://ec.europa.eu/commission/presscorner/detail/en/STATEMENT_20_846.

doi: 10.5553/HYIEL/266627012021009001010

possible[100] and not even unprecedented.[101] Regardless of the (political) controversy,[102] however, it may be impossible to rectify this sort of judicial infringement. In effect, the Federal Republic of Germany, through the Federal Government, could not take the necessary measures since it has no control over the independent *Bundesverfassungsgericht* or over the *Bundesbank*.[103] Surprisingly, in early June of this year, the Commission decided to launch an infringement procedure.[104] One can only hope that the dispute will be settled in the preliminary stage, because it does not appear to be promising to the Courts' relationship if the CJEU were to be made the judge in its own case.[105]

As a solution to the underlying judicial conflict, several authors have voiced the idea of a *Union Court of Competence* as a final arbiter.[106] These ideas, in fact, are not new. They have been outlined throughout the years as an approach to tackle the fundamental dilemma of the Union as a supranational compound of sovereign States.[107] Proposals include a separate chamber at the CJEU, a new court as a separate Union institution or a judicial body supplementing the Union legal order. As widespread as the possible institutional designs are the ideas on this court's composition: It should include judges from national supreme courts and the CJEU, but approaches vary as to the size of the bench and the ratio of national and European judges. However, it is questionable if this would be a viable option: considering that the design of European primary law vests the CJEU with this role of final arbiter, doubts remain whether national high courts would renounce their self-given right to have the final say in favor of a different judicial body.[108]

100 *Cf.* Sara Dietz, 'Die gerichtliche Kontrolle der EZB durch den EuGH und das BVerfG – ein Konfliktfall im Verfassungsgerichtsverbund und Eurosystem? Anmerkungen zum PSPP-Verfahren', *Europäische Zeitschrift für Wirtschaftsrecht*, Vol. 30, Issue 22, 2019, p. 933.

101 *See e.g.* Judgment of 9 December 2003, *Case C-129/00, Commission v Italy*, ECLI:EU:C:2003:656; Judgment of 12 November 2009, *Case C-154/08, Commission v Spain*, ECLI:EU:C:2009:695; and Judgment of 4 October 2018, *Case C-416/17, Commission v France (Arcor II)*, ECLI:EU:C:2018:811. *See also* Sara Poli & Roberto Cisotta, 'The German Federal Constitutional Court's Exercise of Ultra Vires Review and the Possibility to Open an Infringement Action for the Commission', *German Law Journal*, Vol. 21, Issue 5, 2020, pp. 1081 *et seq.*

102 *See* the discussion between Ingolf Pernice, 'Sollte die EU-Kommission Deutschland wegen des Karlsruher Ultra-Vires-Urteils verklagen? PRO', *Verfassungsblog*, 16 May 2020, at https://verfassungsblog.de/sollte-die-eu-kommission-deutschland-wegen-des-karlsruher-ultra-vires-urteils-verklagen-pro/ and Christoph Möllers, 'Sollte die EU-Kommission Deutschland wegen des Karlsruher Ultra-Vires-Urteils verklagen? CONTRA', *Verfassungsblog*, 16 May 2020, at https://verfassungsblog.de/sollte-die-eu-kommission-deutschland-wegen-des-karlsruher-ultra-vires-urteils-verklagen-contra/.

103 *Cf.* Nguyen & Chamon 2020, p. 13.

104 Formal notice under Article 258 TFEU of 9 June 2021, INFR(2021) 2114.

105 Benedikt Riedl, 'Die Ultra-vires-Kontrolle als notwendiger Baustein der europäischen Demokratie', *Verfassungsblog*, 12 June 2021, at https://verfassungsblog.de/ultra-vires-pspp/, even considers that the infringement proceedings are inadmissible altogether.

106 *See*, most prominently, Daniel Sarmiento & Joseph H. H. Weiler, 'The EU Judiciary After Weiss: Proposing A New Mixed Chamber of the Court of Justice', *Verfassungsblog*, 2 June 2020, at https://verfassungsblog.de/the-eu-judiciary-after-weiss/; *cf. also* Ackermann 2020, p. 976.

107 *Cf.* Mayer 2021, p. 765. with further references.

108 Id. p. 765.

The practical effects of the case regarding the substance of the German FCC's ruling remained minimal. The *Bundesbank* asked the Governing Council of the ECB to explain its proportionality considerations regarding the PSPP. At its meeting on 3-4 June 2020, the Governing Council presented extensive considerations on proportionality as part of the monetary policy deliberations and made these and the subsequent decision public on 25 June 2020. In addition, at its meeting on 24 June 2020, the Governing Council decided to allow the *Bundesbank* to transmit to the German Government, on condition of confidentiality, documents that reveal the Governing Council's considerations regarding the PSPP since its launch. Meanwhile, the Governing Council adopted a recast of the decision on the asset purchase program which replaced the original PSPP decision.[109] On 2 July 2020, the German *Bundestag* adopted a resolution[110] determining that the ECB has complied with the justification requirement. It has thus fulfilled its overall budgetary responsibility and its responsibility for integration. Nonetheless, upon expiry of the three-month period stipulated in the FCC's judgment, one of the plaintiffs had applied for the issuance of a so-called enforcement order in accordance with section 35 of the Act on the FCC.[111] Unsurprisingly, the FCC found that its judgment has been complied with.[112]

The actual legal dispute has thus been settled, but its implications continue to smolder. The next dark clouds are already gathering on the horizon. In March 2020, the ECB launched the Pandemic Emergency Purchase Program (PEPP),[113] another non-standard monetary policy instrument (such as SMP, OMT, and APP, including PSPP), which covers both private and public sector securities. While PEPP is very similar to the PSPP, some important safeguards that characterized the PSPP are altered or not included in the PEPP (notably purchase limits, allocation of purchases, and eligibility requirements).[114] As expected, a new set of constitutional complaints have been filed against this program in March 2021.[115] The specific characteristics of this program may in fact cross the red lines that the German FCC established before finding an infringement of the prohibition of monetary financing of Article 123 TFEU.[116] On the other hand, the German Federal Government and the *Bundestag* are

109 Decision (EU) 2020/188 of the European Central Bank of 3 February 2020 on a secondary markets public sector asset purchase programme (ECB/2020/9).

110 *See* Parliamentary Paper of the German Bundestag No 19/20621 of 1 July 2020.

111 "The Federal Constitutional Court may specify in its decision who is to execute it; in individual cases it may also specify the method of execution."

112 Case 2 BvR 1651/15 *et al.* – *PSPP (enforcement order)*, Order of 29 April 2021, ECLI:DE:BVerfG:2021:rs20210429.2bvr165115.

113 Decision (EU) 2020/440 of the European Central Bank of 24 March 2020 on a temporary pandemic emergency purchase program (ECB/2020/17).

114 *See* Annamaria Viterbo, 'The PSPP Judgment of the German Federal Constitutional Court: Throwing Sand in the Wheels of the European Central Bank', *European Papers*, Vol. 5, Issue 1, 2020, pp. 677 *et seq*.

115 Case 2 BvR 420/21 – *PEPP*, pending.

116 Sebastian Grund, 'Legal, Compliant and Suitable: The ECB's Pandemic Emergency Purchase Programme (PEPP)', *Hertie School Jacques Delors Centre Policy Brief*, 2020, holds that the PEPP is compatible with the requirements established by the German FCC.

doi: 10.5553/HYIEL/266627012021009001010

forewarned to act in accordance with their responsibility for integration. In response to an enquiry from a Member of Parliament, the Federal Government held that the ECB's Governing Council had conducted a comprehensible proportionality test on the PEPP.[117]

Secondly, constitutional complaints have been initiated against the new Own Resources Decision. On 15 April 2021 the German FCC denied a preliminary injunction (after having issued on 26 March 2021 a so-called 'hanging decision' (*Hängebeschluss*), *i.e.* a form of pre-preliminary injunction before the actual preliminary injunction is decided), which would have barred the German President from signing the Act ratifying the EU's Own Resources Decision, including the 'Corona Reconstruction Fund' (NextGenerationEU).[118] The plaintiffs argue that the Own Resources Decision is an *ultra vires* act because the EU may not incur debt and the decision would create mutual responsibilities among the Member States for their respective liabilities. Upon summary examination, the FCC found that the 2020 Own Resources Decision does not, in any case, violate Article 79(3) of the Basic Law with a high degree of probability. However, the consequence assessment required accordingly shows that the disadvantages that would result from issuing the preliminary injunction clearly outweigh the risk of disadvantages the event of a rejection of the application. The FCC holds that the Own Resources Decision does not affect the overall budgetary responsibility of the *Bundestag*, at least not with a high degree of probability. While this may lead to the conclusion that the FCC will rebut the constitutional complaints as unfounded, it is not impossible that the main proceedings, which are still pending, will reach a different conclusion. In both cases, the German FCC is likely (and, if it wants to hand down an *ultra vires* verdict, obliged) to submit questions to the CJEU for preliminary ruling. These cases may eventually trigger the constitutional crisis that some expected from the PSPP ruling.[119]

Lastly, Poland's relationship to the EU judiciary is becoming increasingly tense. After several referrals by the European Commission to the CJEU and a CJEU ruling on the (lack of) impartiality of the Polish Supreme Court's Disciplinary Chamber[120] (and its continued activity), news got out that the Polish Government has asked the Constitutional Tribunal to decide whether the Polish constitution has primacy over EU law. While it is just another step along the currently difficult road between Poland and the EU,[121] this may well be the beginning of what many considered the most damaging effect of the PSPP

117 *See* Parliamentary Paper of the German Bundestag No 19/22022 of 1 September 2020.

118 2 BvR 547/21, Order of the Second Senate of 15 April 2021, ECLI:DE:BVerfG:2021:rs20210415.2bvr054721 – *Own Resources*. *See* Benedikt Riedl, 'The Own Resources Decision as an Ultra Vires Act or a Violation of Constitutional Identity? An Analysis of Possible Procedural Scenarios', *EU Law Analysis blog*, 14 April 2021, at http://eulawanalysis.blogspot.com/2021/04/the-own-resources-decision-as-ultra.html?m=1.

119 *Cf.* Amtenbrink & Repasi 2020, p. 771.

120 Judgment of 19 November 2019, *Case C-585/18, A.K.*, ECLI:EU:C:2019:982.

121 *See* in this context, Stanisław Biernat, 'How Far Is It from Warsaw to Luxembourg and Karlsruhe: The Impact of the PSPP Judgment on Poland', *German Law Journal*, Vol. 21, Issue 5, 2020, especially p. 1114.

doi: 10.5553/HYIEL/266627012021009001010

judgment, *i.e.* the reception of the judgment as a much appreciated impetus against EU integration by some Member States (and their national constitutional courts), especially Poland and Hungary.[122]

To sum up, it remains unclear why the German FCC decided the way it did. The judgment does not appear to be a logical consequence of the EU's trespassing of well delineated competences. One may only speculate where the relationship between Karlsruhe and Luxembourg took a wrong turn, but the FCC's judgment is clearly out of line. One may even accuse the German FCC of handing down an incomprehensible and arbitrary judgment. Here and there you will hear voices saying that the decision has more to do with individual judges' legal or political opinions than with rational legal arguments. Hopefully, the *ultra vires* judgment will remain a singular incident.

To conclude, one should remember the words of AG *Cruz Villalón* in his opinion in *Gauweiler*:

> "It seems to me an all but impossible task to preserve this Union, as we know it today, if it is to be made subject to an absolute reservation, ill-defined and virtually at the discretion of each of the Member States, which takes the form of a category described as 'constitutional identity'."[123]

122 *See*, among others, Ackermann 2020, p. 974.

123 Opinion of Advocate General Cruz Villalón delivered on 14 January 2015, *Case C-62/14, Gauweiler*, ECLI:EU:C:2015:7, para. 59.

doi: 10.5553/HYIEL/266627012021009001010

The PSPP Judgment of the German Federal Constitutional Court

The Judge's Theatre According to Karlsruhe

Maria Kordeva[*]

Abstract

The PSPP decision of 5 May 2020 rendered by the German Federal Constitutional Court (FCC) does not constitute a break with the earlier jurisprudence of the FCC elaborated since the Lisbon Treaty judgment of 30 June 2009. Even though qualifying the acts of the Union as ultra vires has been likened to a warlike act, one should beware of hasty conclusions and look closely at the analysis of the Second Senate to form a moderate opinion of this decision decried by European and national commentators. Should the PSPP judgment of the Federal Constitutional Court be classified as "much ado about nothing", despite the procedure started by the European Commission, or, on the contrary, will the CJEU in the next months, sanction Germany for its obvious affront to and breach of the principle of the primacy of Union law? The (final?) power grab between the European and national courts remains to be seen. We can criticize the German FCC that it put the fundamental principles of the Union in danger. Yet, it is worth reflecting on the possible encroachment of competences by European institutions, because, in this case, the red line between monetary policy and economic policy is more than thin.

Keywords: German Constitutional Court, basic law, ultra vires, European Central Bank, primacy of Union law.

1. Introduction

Andreas Voßkuhle, the former President of the German Federal Constitutional Court (FCC) of Germany, ended his term of office on 6 June 2020 after twelve years of service.[1] On 5 May 2020, when he publicly pronounced the decision on

* Maria Kordeva: PhD in Public Law (University of Strasburg/University of Constance), lecturer and research associate, Saarland University, Saarbrücken.

1 Elected by the Bundesrat on 25 April 2008, Andreas Voßkuhle was initially Vice-President of the FCC and became, at 46, the youngest President of the FCC on 16 March 2010. The President of the First Senate and Vice-President of the FCC, Stefan Harbarth, is the current President of the *Bundesverfassungsgericht*. The only constitutional judge in office who has a rich political background: member of the *Bundestag* from 2009 to 2018 and elected judge to the FCC by the *Bundestag* on 22 November 2018.

doi: 10.5553/HYIEL/266627012021009001011

the European Central Bank's (ECB) public debt purchase program,[2] Voßkuhle was aware of the wave of incomprehension, annoyance, criticism and even desolation that the sentences he was about to read in the quiet courtroom would trigger in Germany, but also in many EU Member States and even within the European institutions. The President, in his red robe, is used to this kind of public interest. Since the decision of 30 June 2009 on the Lisbon Treaty,[3] this professor of public law at the University of Freiburg im Breisgau has had first hand knowledge of the fact that the position of the German Constitutional Court on European issues is of great interest in both national and European politics. The judgment of the Second Senate of the Court of 5 May 2020 represents a part of a consistent case-law that has climbed to a drastic *crescendo*: an unusual way of celebrating the end of the Voßkuhle era, a dogmatic and political fencing match between a national judge and the European institutions, or merely the logical continuation of the jurisprudential dance of Karlsruhe under the music of the German Basic Law of 23 May 1949?

It is rare that the decision of a national judge is the subject of such a plethora of comments in the general or specialized press: journalists, economists and, naturally, lawyers line up to point out the "unbearable heaviness of the German constitutional judge",[4] to note that the ECB is "put under pressure"[5] or that the FCC has set itself up as the "judge"[6] of the monetary institution whose legitimacy is "undermined".[7] On the face of it, this 237-paragraph decision probably constitutes a violation of EU law. Therefore, the European Commission considered, following the very terse replies to the German FCC by the ECB[8] and the CJEU,[9] the possibility of activating the Article 258 TFEU infringement

2 BVerfG, decision of the Second Senate, 2 BvR 859/15 (PSSP Judgment).

3 BVerfGE 123, 267.

4 Jacques Ziller, 'L'insoutenable pesanteur du juge constitutionnel allemand. À propos de l'arrêt de la deuxième chambre de la Cour constitutionnelle fédérale allemande du 5 mai 2020 concernant le programme PSPP de la Banque Centrale Européenne', *Blogdroiteuropeen Working Paper*, 2020/4, at https://blogdroiteuropeen.files.wordpress.com/2020/05/wp-ziller-bvergg-5-mai-2020.pdf; Among the *plethora* of various comments, *see e.g.* the special issue of *Revue trimestrielle du droit européen* titled 'The ECB, between the Union of Law and Democracy', in particular Diana Urania Galetta & Jacques Ziller, 'Les violations flagrantes et délibérées du droit de l'Union par l'arrêt 'inintelligible' et 'arbitraire' du Bundesverfassungsgericht dans l'affaire *Weiss*', *Revue trimestrielle du droit européen*, Vol. 56, Issue 4, 2020, pp. 855-887; *see also* David Capitant, 'L'arrêt de la Cour de Karlsruhe. Un coup de tonnerre dans un ciel serein?', *Notes du Cerfa, No. 155, Ifri*, October 2020.

5 Éric Albert *et al.*, 'La Banque centrale européenne mise sous pression par la Cour constitutionnelle allemande', *Le Monde*, 6 May 2020.

6 Jean Quatremer, 'La Cour constitutionnelle allemande s'érige en juge de la BCE', *Libération*, 5 May 2020.

7 Adrien Palluet, 'La Cour constitutionnelle allemande sape la légitimité de la BCE', *Courrier international*, 6 May 2020.

8 *See* at www.ecb.europa.eu/press/pr/date/2020/html/ecb.pr200505~00a09107a9.en.html.

9 *See* at https://curia.europa.eu/jcms/upload/docs/application/pdf/2020-05/cp200058fr.pdf.

doi: 10.5553/HYIEL/266627012021009001011

procedure.[10] On 9 June 2021 the Commission finally decided to send letter of formal notice to Germany for breach of fundamental principles of EU law[11] in order to avoid the spread of this kind of decisions to other EU Member States, in particular states such as Hungary and Poland, which are openly Eurosceptic.

The near future will reveal the supposed failings of the German Constitutional Court, now blamed for corrupting the foundations of the EU, for throwing the European idea to the mercy of populists and sovereigntists of all stripes. Andreas Voßkuhle was right: not only the decision of the FCC over which he presides is 'irritating', but when he read it, all the commentators saw red, in the image of the scarlet robes of Karlsruhe judges. However, in view of its previous case-law, was a solution openly favorable to the ECB possible without putting the Basic Law, as interpreted by the German courts, in abeyance? Karlsruhe crossed the threshold of tolerance, but it did not do so without making some important nuances.

The facts are known: more than 1,700 individual constitutional complaints were lodged under Article 93(1), No. 4a of the Basic Law[12] against the failure of the Federal Government and the *Bundestag* to ensure that the decision of the Council of the ECB of 22 January 2015 on the extended asset purchase program and the decision of the ECB of 4 March 2015 on the public sector asset purchase program (PSPP), as amended by the decision of 5 November 2015, as well as the decisions of 16 December 2015, 18 April 2016, 11 January 2017 and 13 December 2017 are complied with, 11 January 2017 and 13 December 2018, be repealed or not implemented, and against the failure of the *Deutsche Bundesbank* to challenge its participation in the ECB's purchase program by bringing an action before the CJEU. Finally, the individual constitutional complaints were directed against the applicability of the Great Chamber judgment of the CJEU of 11 December 2018, which was the answer to the request for a preliminary ruling by the German FCC on 18 July 2017, to the scope of the German Basic Law.[13] Some of the complaints stated that the European Monetary

10 "If the Commission considers that a Member State has failed to fulfil an obligation under the Treaties, it shall deliver a reasoned opinion on the matter after giving the State concerned the opportunity to submit its observations. If the State concerned does not comply with the opinion within the period laid down by the Commission, the latter may bring the matter before the Court of Justice of the European Union." *See* the reply sent on 9 May 2019 by the European Commission President Ursula von der Leyen to the European deputy Sven Giegold, published on her Twitter account, which states that "The Court of Justice in Luxembourg always has the final word on EU law." *See also* "The Commission is currently analyzing in detail the over 100 pages long decision of the German Federal Constitutional Court", at https://twitter.com/sven_giegold/status/1259141585595437056/photo/1.

11 *See* at https://ec.europa.eu/commission/presscorner/detail/en/inf_21_2743. *See* Benedikt Riedl, 'Die Ultra-vires-Kontrolle als notwendiger Baustein der europäischen Demokratie', *Verfassungsblog*, 21 June 2021, at https://verfassungsblog.de/ultra-vires-pspp/.

12 "[...] on constitutional complaints, which may be filed by any person alleging that one of his basic rights or one of his rights under paragraph (4) of Article 20 or under Article 33, 38, 101, 103 or 104 has been infringed by public authority [...]." Basic Law for the Federal Republic of Germany, translated by Christian Tomuschat, David P. Currie, Donald P. Kommers and Raymond Kerr, in cooperation with the Language Service of the German *Bundestag*.

13 Judgment of 11 December 2018, *Case C-493/17, Weiss and others*, ECLI:EU:C:2018:1000.

doi: 10.5553/HYIEL/266627012021009001011

Institute, through the public sector asset purchase program, had exceeded its area of competence by encroaching upon the economic competence of the Member States, but also by violating the prohibition of monetary budgetary financing by central banks and, lastly, by violating the constitutional identity of the Federal Republic of Germany.

Before beginning its controversial analysis, the constitutional judge clarified, by declaring part of the constitutional complaints inadmissible, that a legal act of an EU institution cannot be directly the subject of an individual constitutional complaint (*Verfassungsbeschwerde*), because, according to the FCC's reasoning,

> "acts of institutions, bodies, offices and agencies of the European Union do not constitute 'acts of public authority' within the meaning of Art. 93 (1) No. 4a of the German Basic Law and § 90 (1) of the Federal Constitutional Court Act."[14]

This solution also applies to decisions of the Council of the ECB.[15] With regard to the failure of the Federal Central Bank of Germany to lodge an appeal to contest its participation in the program thus drawn up, the court follows its consistent case-law when finding that the German institution is an authority subordinate to the State administration and cannot be part of the "constitutional bodies" on which a "specific integration obligation" (*spezifische Integrationsverantwortung*) is imposed.[16]

The Second Senate considers the constitutional complaints to be well-founded insofar as they concern the failure of the Federal Government and the *Bundestag* to ensure, by taking appropriate measures, that the ECB does not cross the threshold of the competences conferred on it and ultimately encroach on the economic policy domain of the EU Member States. The FCC's reasoning is based on the fact that the failure of the German federal authorities to act ultimately constitutes an infringement of the principle of the attribution of monetary policy powers. The FCC's reasoning unfolds by highlighting its jurisprudential continuity while moving to a higher stage: *declaring an EU act qualified as ultra vires not binding in Germany*.

It is probably too early to grasp the full extent of the decision handed down on 5 May 2020. A retrospective look at the origins of the German FCC's reasoning (Section 2) could shed light on the controversial elements of its recent judgment (Section 3).

14 PSSP Judgment, para. 93: "[...] Maßnahmen von Organen, Einrichtungen und sonstigen Stellen der Europäischen Union keine Akte öffentlicher Gewalt im Sinne von Art. 93 Abs. 1 Nr. 4a GG und § 90 Abs. 1 BVerfGG sind [...]." BVerfGE 142, 123, 179; decision of 30 July 2019 (2 BvR 1685/14, 2 BvR 2631/14).

15 Id. para. 94.

16 Id. para. 95; *see e.g.* BVerfGE 123, 267, 352 s; BVerfGE 126, 286, 306; BVerfGE 129, 124, 181; BVerfGE 132, 195, 238.

doi: 10.5553/HYIEL/266627012021009001011

2. Freeze Frame or Jurisprudential Continuity in the Service of the German Basic Law: The Political Law according to Karlsruhe

In its decision on the Financial Stability Pact and the Euro Rescue Plan of 19 June 2012,[17] the FCC concluded that Article 23(2) of the Basic Law[18] applied to the procedure for drawing up the Pact and the Euro Rescue Plan. It also stressed the need to preserve the existence of an area of executive responsibility of the federal government (*Kernbereich exekutiver Eigenverantwortung*). On 12 September 2012 the FCC finally declared the creation of a European Stability Mechanism compatible with the German Basic Law under certain conditions: the effective participation (and thus the decision-making power) of the representatives of the German people in these maneuvers to ensure the financial health of the Eurozone must be guaranteed.[19] The broad interpretation of the principle of democracy (*Demokratieprinzip*) and the restrictive understanding of transfers of sovereignty powers under Article 23(1) of the Basic Law[20] are becoming commonplace in the German constitutional jurisprudence.

The principle of democracy, as interpreted by the German FCC,[21] has the function of a barrier to the process of European integration which "finds its limits in the Basic Law"[22] and which serves to demonstrate the possibility of a democratic deficit in the EU (Section 2.1). The integration process is therefore "under the total supervision" of the Karlsruhe judges (Section 2.2).

17 BVerfGE 131, 152.

18 "The *Bundestag* and, through the *Bundesrat*, the *Länder* shall participate in matters concerning the European Union. The Federal Government shall notify the *Bundestag* of such matters comprehensively and as early as possible."

19 BVerfGE 132, 195.

20 "With a view to establishing a united Europe, the Federal Republic of Germany shall participate in the development of the European Union that is committed to democratic, social and federal principles, to the rule of law and to the principle of subsidiarity and that guarantees a level of protection of basic rights essentially comparable to that afforded by this Basic Law. To this end the Federation may transfer sovereign powers by a law with the consent of the Bundesrat. The establishment of the European Union, as well as changes in its treaty foundations and comparable regulations that amend or supplement this Basic Law or make such amendments or supplements possible, shall be subject to paragraphs (2) and (3) of Article 79."

21 Armin von Bogdandy, 'Prinzipien der Rechtsfortbildung im europäischen Rechtsraum. Überlegungen zum Lissabon-Urteil des BVerfG', *Neue Juristische Wochenschrift*, 2010, p. 3 *et seq.*

22 Dieter Grimm, 'Das Grundgesetz als Riegel vor einer Verstaatlichung der Europäischen Union. Zum Lissabon Urteil des Bundesverfassungsgerichts', *in* Dieter Grimm, *Die Zukunft der Verfassung II Auswirkungen und Globalisierung*, Suhrkamp, Berlin, 2012, p. 153: "Der Fortgang der europäischen Integration [...] findet in [dem Grundgesetz] Grenzen".

doi: 10.5553/HYIEL/266627012021009001011

2.1. *The "Democratic Deficit"*[23] *of the EU or the Individual Right to Sufficient Democratic Legitimation of Union Bodies*

The definition of democracy as 'government of the people' does not go beyond the stage of a regime whose primary purpose is domination. It is not an ideal regime in which the people hold all state power and exercise it directly or indirectly. Rather, it is a "principle of organization relating to the holding and exercise of state power", the purpose of which, after all, is no different from that of any other type of regime: to organize people while keeping them in submission.[24]

In the democratic institutional architecture, the parliament occupies a singular place. At the level of the EU, despite the significant strengthening of the competences of the European Parliament, it remains a body whose power is unable to compete effectively with the Commission or the Council, which dominate the institutional landscape. Its direct democratic legitimacy does not correspond to the level of legitimacy of the *Bundestag*,[25] because it does not follow the rule of equal vote (one man – one vote).[26] As long as the principle of democracy does not receive sufficient guarantees at European level, equivalent to those of the national legal system, the EU will continue to be characterized by a

23 BVerfGE 123, 267, 30 June 2009, 364-365: "Ein nach Art. 23 in Verbindung mit Art. 79 Abs. 3 GG nicht hinnehmbares strukturelles Demokratiedefizit läge vor, wenn der Kompetenzumfang, die politische Gestaltungsmacht und der Grad an selbstständiger Willensbildung der Unionsorgane ein der Bundesebene im föderalen Staat entsprechendes (staatsanaloges) Niveau erreichte, weil etwa die für die demokratische Selbstbestimmung wesentlichen Gesetzgebungszuständigkeiten überwiegend auf der Unionsebene ausgeübt werden. Wenn sich im Entwicklungsverlauf der europäischen Integration ein Missverhältnis zwischen Art und Umfang der ausgeübten Hoheitsrechte und dem Maß demokratischer Legitimation einstellt, obliegt es der Bundesrepublik Deutschland aufgrund ihrer Integrationsverantwortung, auf eine Veränderung hinzuwirken und im äußersten Fall sogar ihre weitere Beteiligung an der Europäischen Union zu verweigern." On the influence of the European integration on the democratic principle, see Karl-Peter Sommermann, 'Verfassungsperspektiven für die Demokratie in der erweiterten Europäischen Union: Gefahr der Entdemokratisierung oder Fortentwicklung im Rahmen europäischer Supranationalität?', Die Öffentliche Verwaltung, 2003, p. 1009 et seq.

24 Ernst-Wolfgang Böckenförde, 'Principes de la démocratie, forme politique et forme de gouvernement', *in* Ernst-Wolfgang Böckenförde, *Le droit, l'État et la constitution démocratique. Essais de théorie juridique, politique et constitutionnelle*, LGDJ/Bruylant, Paris/Bruxelles, 2000, p. 278.

25 Martin Morlok & Christina Hientzsch, 'Das Parlament als Zentralorgan der Demokratie', *Juristische Schulung*, 2011, p. 1 *et seq*.

26 Daniel Halberstam & Christoph Möllers, 'The German Constitutional Court says "Ja zu Deutschland!"', *German Law Journal*, Vol. 10, Issue 8, 2009, p. 1247: "[...] the voting mechanisms to the European Parliament do not function according to a strict rule of democratic equality, one (wo)man, one vote. [...] [I]f there is no people, there is no parliament. As there is no European people, the European Parliament is not a real parliament, *i.e.* a popular representation (*Volksvertretung*)."

doi: 10.5553/HYIEL/266627012021009001011

democratic deficit.[27] However, when, in the decision on the Treaty of Lisbon of 30 June 2009,[28] the FCC analyses the characteristics of the "democratic standard", it notes that "the elements of the democratic principle cannot be achieved in the same way within the European Union". The two types of democratic standards lie in the structural differences between the *sui generis* international organization, the EU, and the state constitutional architecture. There is therefore a qualitative difference between these two democratic forms. Indeed, there cannot be a requirement of perfect symmetry between these two legal orders, because "as long as the organization of the competences of the Union" obeys the principle of the express delegation granted by the states following a "procedure of decision-making cooperation respecting the responsibility of state integration" and "as long as a balance between the competences of the EU and those of the states is maintained, the democracy of the EU must and cannot be analogous to the democratic standard of the state".[29]

The core of a democratic regime, which is part of "the common constitutional tradition of the European states", is the right of the people to "freely and equally determine the government and the legislature".[30] But this right cannot be transposed to the institutional level of the EU, because neither the European Parliament nor the Commission has a role equivalent to that of the *Bundestag* or the Federal Government.[31] The "responsibility of the state bodies for sustainable integration" means that the political system of the Federal Republic as well as

27 Stefan Oeter, 'Souveränität und Demokratie als Probleme in der "Verfassungsentwicklung" der Europäischen Union. Fragen aus Verfassungstheorie und Verfassungsgeschichte an die deutsche Debatte um Souveränität, Demokratie und die Verteilung politischer Verantwortung im geeinten Europa', *ZaöRV*, Vol. 55, 1995, p. 661: "The powers of the Parliament are clearly too weak to really respond to the requirements of the principle of democracy and the idea of parliamentary control of legislation and administration" (Die Rechte des Parlaments seien eindeutig zu schwach ausgeprägt, um wirklich den Anforderungen aus dem Demokratieprinzip und dem Gedanken parlamentarischer Kontrolle der Gesetzgebung und Verwaltung gerecht zu werden).

28 BVerfGE 123, 267.

29 BVerfGE 123, 267, 368: "Solange die europäische Zuständigkeitsordnung nach dem Prinzip der begrenzten Einzelermächtigung in kooperativ ausgestalteten Entscheidungsverfahren unter Wahrung der staatliche Integrationsverantwortung besteht und solange eine ausgewogene Balance der Unionszuständigkeiten und der staatlichen Zuständigkeiten erhalten bleibt, kann und muss die Demokratie der Europäischen Union nicht staatsanalog ausgestaltet sein."

30 BVerfGE 123, 267, 366: "[...] die demokratischen Grundsätze in der Europäischen Union nicht in gleicher Weise wie im Grundgesetz verwirklicht werden können [...]"; pp. 367-368: "In einer Demokratie muss das Volk Regierung und Gesetzgebung in freier und gleicher Wahl bestimmen können [...]. Die Europäische Union erkennt diesen demokratischen Kerngedanken als gemeineuropäische Verfassungstradition an [...]."

31 BVerfGE 123, 267, 368: "As a representative body of the peoples in a supranational community [...], it [the Parliament] cannot, and need not, as regards of its composition, comply with the requirements that arise at state level from the equal political right to vote of all citizens. The Commission also as a supranational, special body [...] need not extensively fulfill the conditions of a government that is fully accountable either to Parliament or to the majority decision of the electorate because the Commission itself is not bound by the will of the electorate in a comparable manner."

doi: 10.5553/HYIEL/266627012021009001011

that of the EU must comply with the principles of Article 20(1) and (2) in conjunction with Article 79(3) of the Basic Law.[32]

The FCC's recognition of an individual right to democracy under Article 38(1)[33] paves the way for the FCC to review transfers of sovereign powers to the EU through the prism of constitutional identity.[34] The "unjustified detachment from the scope of Article 38(1), first sentence" is one of the 'procedural peculiarities' of the *Lisbon decision*[35] that recurs in subsequent case-law.[36] The question of whether the Treaty provisions are in conformity with Article 38 does not as such lend itself to criticism. What is problematic is "how Article 38 of the Basic Law is interpreted and applied" by the court.[37] According to the FCC's analysis, the scope of the Article is not limited to the existence of an 'individual guarantee of participation' in the election of members of parliament, but also confers on citizens "the individual right to claim a relationship of legitimacy between those entitled to vote and the public authority of the European Union",[38] an 'individual right to democracy'.[39] The way in which German deputies are elected is used as a justification for developing a complex set of relationships between the voters on the one hand and the power exercised by

32 BVerfGE 123, 267, 356: "A permanent responsibility of integration (*dauerhafte Integrationsverantwortung*) is incumbent upon the German constitutional bodies. In the transfer of sovereign powers and the elaboration of the European decision-making procedures, it is aimed at ensuring that, seen overall, the political system of the Federal Republic of Germany as well as that of the European Union comply with democratic principles within the meaning of Article 20.1 and 20.2 in conjunction with Article 79.3 of the Basic Law"; p. 364: "The constitutional requirements placed by the principle of democracy on the organizational structure and the decision-making procedures of the European Union depend on the extent to which sovereign responsibilities are transferred to the Union and the degree of political independence in the exercise of the sovereign powers transferred."

33 "Members of the German *Bundestag* shall be elected in general, direct, free, equal and secret elections. They shall be representatives of the whole people, not bound by orders or instructions and responsible only to their conscience."

34 Christine Langenfeld, 'La jurisprudence récente de la Cour constitutionnelle allemande relative au droit de l'Union européenne', *Titre VII Les Cahiers du Conseil constitutionnel*, Issue 2, 2019.

35 Christoph Schönberger, 'Die Europäische Union zwischen "Demokratiedefizit" und Bundesstaatsverbot. Anmerkungen zum Lissabon-Urteil des Bundesverfassungsgerichts', *Der Staat*, 2009, p. 539: "Zu den prozessualen Eigenheiten des Lissabon-Urteils gehört die uferlose Entgrenzung des Anwendungsbereichs von Art. 38 Abs. 1 S. 1 GG."

36 BVerfGE 134, 366, 380 *et seq.*; decision of 5 May 2020, paras. 64 and 90.

37 Matthias Jestaedt, 'Warum in die Ferne schweifen, wenn der Massstab liegt so nah? Verfassungshandwerkliche Anfragen an das Lissabon-Urteil des BVerfG', *Der Staat*, 2009, p. 503: "Gegenstand der Kritik ist, *wie* Art. 38 GG ausgelegt und angewendet wird [...]".

38 Schönberger 2009, pp. 539-540: "Der Gewährleistungsgehalt dieser Vorschrift beschränkt sich [...] nicht auf die Individualgarantie der Teilnahme an der Bundestagswahl [...]. Vielmehr leit Art. 38 Abs. 1 S. 1 GG dem deutschen Bürger in der Deutung des Bundesverfassungsgerichts einen umfassenden Individualanspruch auf einen ‚legitimatorischen Zusammenhang zwischen den Wahlberechtigten und der europäischen Hoheitsgewalt'."

39 Matthias Jestaedt, 'Warum in die Ferne schweifen, wenn der Massstab liegt so nah? Verfassungshandwerkliche Anfragen an das Lissabon-Urteil des BVerfG', *Der Staat*, 2009, p. 504 : "[...] individuellen Recht auf Demokratie."

doi: 10.5553/HYIEL/266627012021009001011

the EU on the other. The subjectification[40] of the right to vote in Article 38 makes it possible to set limits on the process of European integration that would go too far and no longer fit into this framework of legitimation. With this reasoning, the German FCC has turned every *quivis ex populo* into a procedural constitutional guardian of European democracy.

The result is not only the demand that the public power of the EU be legitimated in accordance with the canons of the Basic Law. Namely, with Lisbon, it became possible for a citizen who considers that his or her individual right to sufficient legitimation of supranational power is infringed by a 'treaty amendment' to lodge an "individual constitutional complaint against the law ratifying the treaty amendment".[41] Here, the subjectification of this right is all the more astonishing, as it goes against the solutions delivered by the FCC in the national framework. Indeed, a voter cannot rely on Article 38 in order to bring an action before the Karlsruhe Court for a violation of the *Bundestag*'s powers.[42]

The elastic interpretation of Article 38 and its combination with the requirement of legitimacy of the EU's power has only external effects, but still cannot constitute the textual basis for justifying an internal violation of the *Bundestag*'s competences. The political meaning of the decision is clear: in the future, even if the law ratifying a treaty amendment escapes the control of the Constitutional Court thanks to the requirement of "a quorum of one third of the members of the *Bundestag*", it will not be immune to the possibility of an individual constitutional complaint.[43] "The traditional political consensus of the major parliamentary fractions in the field of European issues should not prevent the review by the Constitutional Court."[44]

In order to ensure that the internal system of checks and balances is maintained, the FCC exercises control over the degree of the European integration process, which must remain in conformity with the "eternity clause" enshrined in Article 79(3) of the Basic Law.

40 Martin Nettesheim, 'Ein Individualrecht auf Staatlichkeit? Die Lissabon-Entscheidung des BVerfG', *Neue Juristische Wochenschrift*, 2009, p. 2869, speaks of an "indivisible right posing the requirement of statehood".

41 Schönberger 2009, p. 540: "[...] jeden *quivis ex populo* zum verfassungsprozessualen Hüter der europäischen Demokratie erhebt [...], jede zukünftige Vertragsrevision über den Weg einer Verfassungsbeschwerde gegen das Zustimmungsgesetz [...] unterzogen werden kann."

42 BVerfGE 62, 397, 399, on the early dissolution of the *Bundestag* as a result of Chancellor Helmut Schmidt's clever political game, quoted by Schönberger 2009, p. 541.

43 On the participation of the individual in the development of law and jurisprudence, *see* Johannes Masing, *Mobilisierung des Bürgers für die Durchsetzung des Rechts. Europäische Impulse für eine Revision der Lehre vom subjektiv-öffentlichen Recht*, Duncker & Humblot, Berlin, 1997.

44 Schönberger 2009, p. 541: "Der übliche europapolitische Konsens der großen Bundestagsfraktionen soll die verfassungsgerichtliche Überprüfung nicht hindern." This solution is not "convincing from the point of view of constitutional dogma" and "the political-legal significance of the case-law is obvious" ([s]o wenig das verfassungsdogmatisch überzeugen kann, so offenkundig ist der rechtspolitische Sinne dieser Rechtsprechung).

doi: 10.5553/HYIEL/266627012021009001011

2.2. The European Integration Process under the "Full Supervision of Karlsruhe"[45]

Article 23(1) of the Basic Law provides that in order to contribute to "the development of the European Union", the Federal Republic "may transfer sovereign powers by a law with the consent of the Bundesrat" and that paragraphs 2 and 3 of Article 79 apply to

> "the establishment of the European Union as well as changes in its treaty foundations and comparable regulations that amend or supplement this Basic Law or make such amendments or supplements possible."

The consequence of this article is that any amendment to the "conventional foundations" of the EU must follow the rules of the constitutional revision procedure of the Basic Law and not the ordinary legislative procedure.

Secondly, the "eternity clause" (*Ewigkeitsklausel*), applicable to the European institution, constitutes the material limit that must be respected by the legislator ratifying a treaty or an amendment to existing treaty regulations. If this limit were to be exceeded, the Federal Republic would find itself unable to continue its participation in the European integration process. In this hypothesis, the constituent power of the people would have to be exercised in order to abrogate the current constitution and establish a new one in line with the advanced stage of development of the supranational organization.

For the FCC, in 2009 the process of European integration has reached a stage that cannot be surpassed without violating the 'heart' of the Basic Law, *i.e.* the principles protected by Article 79(3) of the Basic Law. The violation of the constitutional identity codified in Article 79(3) represents, from the perspective of the principle of democracy, an encroachment upon the constituent power of the people. In this respect, the constituent power has not granted the representatives and bodies of the people a mandate to dispose of the identity of the constitution. No constitutional body has been granted the power to amend the fundamental principles of Article 79(3) of the Basic Law.[46]

The application of the "eternity guarantee" to the European integration process is problematic in view of the genesis of the provision and its purpose. It is intended to protect the principles enumerated therein from 'enemies' of the democratic and liberal constitutional system of the Basic Law. The principles enumerated are the following: the division of the Federation into *Länder*, their

45 Christian Calliess, 'Unter Karlsruher Totalaufsicht', *Frankfurter Allgemeine Zeitung*, 27 August 2009, p. 8.

46 BVerfGE 123, 267, 344, or 404: "Without the expressly declared will of the people, elected bodies are not competent to create a new subject for legitimation, or to delegitimize the existing ones." The notion of "constitutional identity" also appears in the decisions of the French Constitutional Council (*Conseil constitutionnel*) without the latter providing satisfactory details. *See e.g.* decision DC No. 2006-540, 27 July 2006, *Loi relative au droit d'auteur et aux droits voisins dans la société de l'information*, para. 19: "Considering, firstly, that the transposition of a directive cannot run counter to a rule or principle inherent in the constitutional identity of France, unless the constituent has agreed to it" (Considérant, en premier lieu, que la transposition d'une directive ne saurait aller à l'encontre d'une règle ou d'un principe inhérent à l'identité constitutionnelle de la France, sauf à ce que le constituant y ait consenti).

doi: 10.5553/HYIEL/266627012021009001011

participation in federal legislation, the principles laid down in Articles 1 and 20 of the Basic Law demonstrate the constituent will of 1949 to ensure a sphere unamenable to amendment in which the constituent elements of a democratic and free order are enshrined. The FCC "fails to demonstrate why the specific problems of the democratic organization of the European Union should trigger the application of the ultimate limitation of the 'eternity clause'".[47]

The Second Senate goes even further and states that *the Federal Republic cannot participate in a European federal state* on the grounds that such a 'creation' would exceed the limits set by the Basic Law. The "eternity clause" is understood by the German Constitutional Court as a guarantee of German "sovereignty":

> "When [...] the threshold of the creation of a federal state and the renunciation of state sovereignty is crossed, which would require the free decision of the people in Germany beyond the present applicability of the Basic Law, the level of democratic requirements should fully correspond to the needs of democratic legitimation of a Union organized according to the state model. [...] An unacceptable democratic deficit under Article 23 in combination with Article 79(3) of the Basic Law would mean that the scope of competences, the political organizational power and the degree of autonomous will formation of the Union's organs have reached a level of federalization comparable to that of a federal state (analogous to a state)."[48]

The FCC stated as early as 2009 that the Basic Law does not allow the transition to a European federal state without a change in the constitutional text. However, "from a constitutional point of view", this analysis becomes "more than doubtful". *(i)* First of all, the question of a European federal state is not on the political agenda. *(ii)* Secondly, the FCC does not offer "any definition of the concept of a federal state", nor does it discuss the importance and functions of a body representing the federated states, alongside the parliament bringing together the representatives of the European people(s).[49]

47 Christoph Schönberger, 'Lisbon in Karlsruhe: Maastricht's Epigones at Sea', *German Law Journal*, Vol. 10, Issue 8, 2009, p. 1208.

48 BVerfGE 123, 267, p. 364-365: "A structural democratic deficit that would be unacceptable pursuant to Article 23 in conjunction with Article 79.3 of the Basic Law would exist if the extent of competences, the political freedom of action and the degree of independent opinion-formation on the part of the institutions of the Union reached a level corresponding to the federal level in a federal state, *i.e.* a level analogous to that of a state [...]. If an imbalance between type and extent of the sovereign powers exercised and the degree of democratic legitimation arises in the course of its responsibility for integration, to endeavor to effect a change, and in the worst case, even to refuse further participation in the European Union."

49 On this argument, *cf.* Schönberger 2009, pp. 556-557, which explains that the Second Senate of the FCC imagines a federal construction "emptied of all substance" (*blutleere Konstruktion*), which is only a "reminiscence of federal state theory" (*Reminiszenzen an die deutsche Bundesstaatstheorie*) of the 19th century. *See* Christoph Schönberger, 'Die Europäische Union als Bund. Zugleich ein Beitrag zur Verabschiebung des Staatenbund-Bundesstaat-Schemas', *Archiv des öffentliches Recht*, 2004, p. 88.

This is the argument that the FCC takes up in its decision of 5 May 2020, while insisting on the "reserved" (*zurückhaltend*) and "Europe-friendly" (*europafreundlich*)[50] nature of the *ultra vires* review it is conducting.

3. The Federal Constitutional Court's Review of the Ultra Vires Decision: On the Edge of Legal Policy

The FCC's review of EU secondary legislation is not a revelation in the judgment of 5 May. The story goes a long way back: the decision on the Maastricht Treaty handed down in 1993 marked the beginning of the controversial review exercised by the German FCC, who ensures that secondary law does not undermine the provisions of primary law (Section 3.1) and in particular the principle of the division of competences between the EU and the Member States (Section 3.2).[51]

3.1. The Duty of the German Federal Authorities to Ensure the Distribution of Powers Attributed to the EU

The Second Senate of the FCC found a violation of Article 38(1) in conjunction with Article 20(1) and (2) in conjunction with Article 79(3) of the Basic Law. This violation consists in the failure of the Federal Government and the *Bundestag* to act to ensure that the measures taken by the ECB in the contested decisions comply with the principle of proportionality (*Grundsatz der Verhältnismäßigkeit*).[52] The German FCC's intellectual sleight of hand consists in finding this violation committed by domestic constitutional bodies. It is not a question of immediately challenging the decisions of the ECB, but of condemning the inaction of the German government and *Bundestag*.

The blow to the European monetary institution comes only at the second phase of the analysis, as a direct consequence of the failure to act. In fact, after having pronounced the violation of the mentioned articles of the Basic Law by the organs of the Federation, the FCC declares that the contested decisions on the purchase of assets represent a

> "qualified, because manifest and structurally significant, exceeding of the competences attributed to the ECB by Article 119, Article 127 ff. TFEU and Article 17 ff. of the Statute of the European System of Central Banks and of the European Central Bank"[53]

by stating that *the decision of the CJEU of 11 December 2018 is no longer "justifiable" (nachvollziehbar) and is therefore rendered ultra vires.*[54] However, in this case, the

50 Para. 112 of the decision.

51 BVerfGE 89, 155 of 12 October 1993; in the same vein: BVerfGE 126, 286, 308 *et seq*.

52 Para. 116 of the decision.

53 "[S]tellt eine qualifizierte, weil offensichtliche und strukturell bedeutsame Überschreitung der EZB in Art. 119, Art. 127 ff. AEUV und Art. 17 ff. ESZB-Satzung zugewiesenen Kompetenzen dar."

54 Id. para. 116.

doi: 10.5553/HYIEL/266627012021009001011

Second Senate does not give a final ruling on the proportionality of the ECB's decisions. After these preliminary remarks, the Second Senate undertakes a lengthy analysis which, despite the violent nature of the result, contains certain nuances that are worthy of the reader's attention.

It is true that the interpretation by the CJEU "binds" (*bindet*) the national authorities, but the content of the delimitation of competences drawn in Luxembourg "is no longer justifiable" (*nicht mehr vertretbar*). The review of the validity or interpretation of a measure taken by EU bodies falls within the jurisdiction of the CJEU, except in those cases in which it is a question of an *"objectively arbitrary interpretation of the Treaties"* (*objektiv willkürlichen Auslegung der Veträge*).[55] The difficulty here is not the reality of an arbitrary interpretation by the CJEU that would disregard the scope of the competences attributed to an institution of the EU, but rather the role of the FCC in declaring this disregard, as it insists, that the judgment of 11 December clearly exceeds the 'mandate' granted to the CJEU under Article 19(1) TFEU, according to which "the Court of Justice of the European Union shall ensure that the law is observed in the interpretation and application of the Treaties". The logical consequence is that the CJEU, by stepping out of its sphere of competence, has issued a judicial decision which is no longer binding on the national authorities, who are exempt from its application.

The *questio diabolica* that draws the conclusion of the existence of an *ultra vires* act is the distinction between the exercise of a monetary or economic policy by the ECB. The red line delimiting the respective competences of the EU and the Member States lies at this level. If the German FCC decides that the preparation and implementation of the asset purchase programs for government securities is not a "monetary policy" (*Währungspolitik*) "exclusively attributed to the ESCB" (*ausschließlich dem ESZB zugewiesene*) in accordance with Article 127 TFEU,[56] but that the measures, taken by a Union body actually involve the exercise of an economic policy (*Wirtschaftspolitik*), a competence which "in principle" (*grundsätzlich*) belongs to the Member States, then it opens the way to declaring that a failure to respect the division of competences entails the expiration of the obligation to apply secondary legislation deemed *ultra vires*. However, the fields of action of monetary and economic policy are not hermetically sealed with

55 Id. para. 118.

56 "[...] The basic tasks to be carried out through the ESCB shall be: to define and implement the monetary policy of the Union [...]."

doi: 10.5553/HYIEL/266627012021009001011

regard to the relevant terms of the TFEU[57] and it is in this sense that the Court of Luxembourg has interpreted the Treaties, in particular by underlining that

> "within the institutional balance established by the provisions set out in Title VIII of the TFEU, in which the independence guaranteed to the ESCB [...] is embedded, the authors of the Treaties did not intend an absolute separation of economic and monetary policy"

and by rejecting the FCC's view that not every effect of an open market operation program which was knowingly accepted and foreseeable with certainty by the ESCB at the time of the establishment of that program should be regarded as an "indirect effect" thereof.[58] The FCC, in turn, dismisses this argument by pointing to the actual effects of the securities purchase program and the lack of an overall assessment in the Luxembourg judgment. By failing to examine whether the ESCB and the ECB were complying with the "monetary policy mandate" (*währungspolitischen Mandats*) granted to them and by failing to carry out a thorough analysis of the proportionality of the measures taken, the CJEU failed, according to the Second Senate, to perform its "corrective function to protect the competences of the Member States". Therefore, from a German perspective, the solution of the CJEU "emptied the principle of limited jurisdiction under Article 5(1), first sentence, and (2) TEU of its substance".[59]

The principle of proportionality, a guiding principle of EU law which has its origins in the legal systems of the Member States, *consists of three elements, three steps which must be followed: the appropriateness, necessity and adequacy of the measure*. The latter satisfies these requirements if it achieves "in a consistent and

57 *See e.g.* Article 119 TFEU: "(1) For the purposes set out in Article 3 of the Treaty on European Union, the activities of the Member States and the Union shall include, as provided in the Treaties, the adoption of an economic policy which is based on the close coordination of Member States' economic policies, on the internal market and on the definition of common objectives, and conducted in accordance with the principle of an open market economy with free competition. (2) Concurrently with the foregoing, and as provided in the Treaties and in accordance with the procedures set out therein, these activities shall include a single currency, the euro, and the definition and conduct of a single monetary policy and exchange-rate policy the primary objective of both of which shall be to maintain price stability and, without prejudice to this objective, to support the general economic policies in the Union, in accordance with the principle of an open market economy with free competition. (3). These activities of the Member States and the Union shall entail compliance with the following guiding principles: stable prices, sound public finances and monetary conditions and a sustainable balance of payments." *See also* Article 120 TFEU: "Member States shall conduct their economic policies with a view to contributing to the achievement of the objectives of the Union [...]"; Article 121 TFEU: "Member States shall regard their economic policies as a matter of common concern and shall coordinate them within the Council [...]."

58 *Case C-493/17, Weiss and others*, paras. 60-61.

59 Id. para. 123; Article 5(1) and 2 TEU: "(1) The limits of Union competences are governed by the principle of conferral. The use of Union competences is governed by the principles of subsidiarity and proportionality. (2) Under the principle of conferral, the Union shall act only within the limits of the competences conferred upon it by the Member States in the Treaties to attain the objectives set out therein. Competences not conferred upon the Union in the Treaties remain with the Member States."

doi: 10.5553/HYIEL/266627012021009001011

systematic manner the objective pursued", which leads the CJEU, according to Karlsruhe, to question the manifestly inadequate nature of the objective pursued and to examine the possibility of taking measures that would have been less intrusive by dispensing with "an examination of proportionality in the strict sense" (*Prüfung der Verhältnismäßigkeit im engeren Sinne*).[60] This interpretation of the principle of proportionality does not allow the CJEU, according to the Senate, to draw the necessary distinction between competences in the field of monetary policy, on the one hand, and in the field of economic policy, on the other, leading it to blur the distribution of these competences between the Union and its Member States. The consequence of the elastic interpretation of the principle of proportionality makes it, in this particular case, "inoperable" (*funktionslos*).[61] However, in the judgment of 11 December 2018, the European Court, after having established the extended competences of the monetary institution, proceeds to examine the proportionality of the contested measures allowing the purchase of assets of public securities in three steps showing successively that "despite the monetary policy measures" the "annual inflation rates of the euro area" are

> "largely below the 2% objective set by the ESCB, which meets the objective pursued by the PSPP: the maintenance of price stability and in view of the foreseeable effects of the PSPP and since it does not appear that the objective pursued by the ESCB could have been achieved by another type of monetary policy measure [...] the PSPP does not go manifestly beyond what is necessary to achieve this objective"

(examination of the appropriateness and necessity of the measure). The public debt purchase program is also "implemented" on a temporary basis in order to achieve the objective pursued and includes mechanisms to prevent and limit the risk of losses to only a part of the securities purchased.[62] The Second Senate notes that these instruments serve the budgetary autonomy of the Member States and thus their budgetary policy, which does not belong to the field of monetary policy controlled by the EU. In view of the solution provided by the CJEU judgment, the Karlsruhe Court logically concludes that, in "this form", the principle of proportionality cannot "fulfil" the "corrective function for the purposes of safeguarding the competences of the Member States".[63] At this point, the FCC begins to deploy its aggressive arsenal in order to deliver the *coup de grâce* to the public debt purchase program:

> "[t]he complete concealment of the economic policy effects of the PSPP, which, with regard to the determination of the ESCB's objectives, is not

60 Para. 126 of the decision, with reference to the jurisprudence of the CJEU, *see e.g.* CJEU, Judgment of 9 September 2010, *Case C-64/08, Engelmann*, ECLI:EU:C:2010:506; Judgment of 16 December 2010, *Case C-137/09, Josemans*, ECLU:EU:C:2010:774

61 Para. 127 of the decision.

62 *Case C-493/17, Weiss and others*, paras. 74 *et seq.*

63 Paras. 132-133 of the decision.

> tenable from a methodological perspective, leads to the proportionality test losing its function, since the appropriateness and necessity of the PSPP, apart from the risk of losses, is not placed in relation to the economic policy effects to the detriment of the Member States' competences, which are not weighed up against the expected benefits."[64]

The minimal control exercised by the Luxembourg judge on the "manifest error of assessment" of the ECB (*offensichtlicher Beurteilungsfehler*) does not allow in any case to probe the disputed measure in depth and to note the possible exceeding of the distribution of competences anchored in the Treaties. This means nothing more than an "erosion of the Member State competences in the field of economic and budgetary policy", as well as a "weakening of the democratic legitimation of the public power exercised by the Eurosystem", the body comprising the ECB and the national central banks that have adopted the euro. Both aspects, erosion and weakening, are incompatible with the German Basic Law.[65]

The FCC argues that it is the close link between the distinction of competences for economic and monetary policy, which constitutes "a fundamental political decision with implications beyond the individual case" (*eine über den Einzelfall hinausgehende politische Grundentscheidung*), and it is the principle of democracy that is undermined by the superficial review of the CJEU. Karlsruhe insists that classifying a measure as a monetary policy measure instead of an economic policy act

> "does not only affect the division of competences between the European Union and the Member States, but also decides on the level of democratic legitimacy and control of the policy area concerned, since monetary policy is transferred [...] to the independent ESCB",

64 Para. 133: "Das völlige Ausblenden der wirtschaftspolitischen Auswirkungen des PSPP, das schon bei der Bestimmung der Zielsetzung des ESZB methodisch nicht nachvollziehbar ist führt dazu, dass die Verhältnismäßigkeitsprüfung ihre Funktion verliert, weil Geeignetheit und Erforderlichkeit des PSPP – von dem Verlustrisiko abgesehen – nicht mit den wirtschaftspolitischen Auswirkungen zulasten der Kompetenzen der Mitgliedstaaten in Beziehung gesetzt und diese nicht mit den erhofften Vorteilen abgewogen wurden"; *see also* para. 136.

65 Id. para. 157; *see also* the constant jurisprudence: BVerfGE 134, 366, 395 *et seq.*; BVerfGE 142, 123, 192 *et seq.*; BVerfGE 146, 216, 250 *et seq.*

doi: 10.5553/HYIEL/266627012021009001011

which is denied state monetary financing[66] under Article 123 TFEU.[67] However, the FCC does not hastily conclude that the mechanism for the purchase of public debt securities circumvents the prohibition contained in Article 123 TFEU[68] by confirming the analysis of the *OMT* decision.[69] Furthermore, an intrusion of the ECB into the economic and budgetary policy of the States could jeopardize its independence. According to the FCC, *de facto* granting such a competence, and leaving the problematic measures (whose sprawling effects extend over a large number of sectors of national political, economic and budgetary life) to the European monetary institution would extinguish any possibility of intervening in the decisions taken. While a change in the delimitation of the areas of action is not excluded, this can only take place following a revision of the Treaty pursuant to Article 48 TEU.[70]

Finally, the FCC transposes here the reasoning it follows with regard to the compatibility of the level of European integration with the German Basic Law: if one wishes to move to a higher stage of integration, it is necessary to leave the current system behind and adopt a new constitutional text allowing for more advanced integration. As with the limits set by the national court in the *Lisbon Treaty decision*, the prospective answer here is a revision of the Treaty to allow for the allocation of economic and budgetary policy issues to the SECB, because the EU must now confine itself to "coordinating state measures" and not take their place. The rigid interpretation by the Second Senate of the principle of the division of competences between the EU and the Member States does not make it possible, in the current jurisprudential configuration, for another mental construction to be made which could validate, in particular, the reasoning of the CJEU. Indeed, it jeopardizes the measures adopted by the ECB and, in general,

66 Para. 159: "Die Zuordnung einer Maßnahme zur Währungs- statt zur Wirtschafts- oder Fiskalpolitik berührt nicht nur die Frage der Kompetenzverteilung zwischen der Europäischen Union und den Mitgliedstaaten; sie entscheidet zugleich über das demokratische Legitimationsniveau und die Kontrolle des entsprechenden Politikbereichs, weil die Währungspolitik [...] dem unabhängigen ESZB übertragen ist", with reference to the Judgment of 9 March 2010, *Case C-518/07, Commission v Germany*, ECLI:EU:C:2010:125. BVerfG, decision of 30 July 2019 (2 BvR 1685/14): "The Europeanisation of national administrative structures and the establishment of independent bodies, offices and agencies of the European Union require a minimum of democratic legitimation and oversight (Art. 23 [1], third sentence in conjunction with Art. 79 [3] and Art. 20 [1] and [2] of the Basic Law)"; para. 181.

67 "Overdraft facilities or any other type of credit facility with the European Central Bank or with the central banks of the Member States (hereinafter referred to as "national central banks") in favor of Union institutions, bodies, offices or agencies, central governments, regional, local or other public authorities, other bodies governed by public law, or public undertakings of Member States shall be prohibited, as shall the purchase directly from them by the European Central Bank or national central banks of debt instruments"; in that respect, *see* Judgment of 16 June 2015, *Case C-62/14, Gauweiler and others*, ECLI:EU:C:2015:400.

68 Para. 213: "Im Ergebnis kann auf der Grundlage des Urteils des Gerichtshofs vom 11. Dezember 2018 [...] eine Umgehung des Verbots monetärer Staatsfinanzierung nicht festgestellt warden"; *see also* para. 214.

69 BVerfGE 142, 123, 228 with reference to *Case C-62/14, Gauweiler and others*, para. 126.

70 "The Treaties may be amended in accordance with an ordinary revision procedure. They may also be amended in accordance with simplified revision procedures [...]."

doi: 10.5553/HYIEL/266627012021009001011

casts the shadow perceived as a weapon of mass destruction over the primacy of the acts of the EU and the jurisdictional competence of the CJEU. Any other interpretation would betray the previous solutions of the German FCC.

3.2. The Effects of the Ultra Vires Review by the Federal Constitutional Court

The integration responsibility (*Integrationsverantwortung*),[71] which in the light of the individual right to democratic legitimation under Article 38(1) in conjunction with Article 20(2) of the Basic Law, obliges federal constitutional bodies to "oppose" the ECB's public debt purchase program (to be "qualified as an *ultra vires* act"), *i.e.* in the event of "manifest and structural infringements by the organs, institutions and other bodies of the European Union".[72] This integration responsibility is the instrument used by the FCC to examine the need for democratic legitimation and to control the European integration process.[73] In this case, the Federal Government and the *Bundestag* are obliged to ensure that a "proportionality review" is carried out by the ECB.

> "The Federal Government and the *Bundestag* must make their legal position known to the ECB or otherwise ensure that a situation in conformity with the Treaties is restored. The qualification of the ECB measure as an *ultra vires* act results in the non-application of the principle of precedence of application of Union law."

The final shot is fired: the act *"is not to be applied in Germany and has no binding effect in relation to German constitutional bodies, administrative authorities and courts"*.[74] Of course, this control is exceptional, because the FCC itself recognizes that it is essential for the smooth running of the European machinery that a certain unity of case-law on the competences of the EU be guaranteed. The FCC therefore confines itself to carrying out a minimal review only if

> "the fact that the act is contrary to the division of competences is manifest and that it is of particular importance with regard to the principle of attribution and the obligation arising from the principle of the rule of law to respect the law."[75]

The review of EU acts results from the failure of the German constitutional bodies to ensure that the division of competences is respected in the preparation of European decisions and only takes place after the preliminary question has been referred to the CJEU.

71 On the concept of integration, *see* Andreas Voßkuhle, 'Artikel 92', *in* Hermann von Magoldt *et al.*, *Grundgesetz Kommentar, 7th Edition*, C.H. Beck, 2018, para. 85a; Andreas Voßkuhle, 'Integration durch Recht – Der Beitrag des Bundesverfassungsgerichts', *JuristenZeitung*, 2016, p. 164 *et seq.*; Claus Dieter Classen, 'Artikel 23', *in* von Magoldt 2018, para. 15.

72 Paras. 229-230.

73 Classen 2018, para. 15.

74 Paras. 232, 233, and 234.

75 BVerfGE 126, 286, 302 *et seq.*

doi: 10.5553/HYIEL/266627012021009001011

The reasoning may offend the reader's sensibilities,[76] but in view of the logical sequence of the decision, which is more than one hundred pages long, it is difficult to imagine any other outcome. The violation of the principle of the division of competences between the EU and the Member States, the (relative) failure to respect the principle of proportionality and the obligation of integration weighing on the German constitutional bodies guided by the principle of (absolute) democracy in its German version seal the fate of the ECB's public debt purchase program. The European Monetary Institute and all the EU's governing bodies are being asked either to explain and justify the measures taken or to engage in hostilities against Germany. If the infringement procedure is brought before the CJEU, *the key to the enigma will be in the hands of the Luxembourg Court, which will have to examine its own case-law. A case-law which, according to its German counterpart, has validated an ultra vires act in violation of the Treaties*. An *abyss* for the CJEU?

The 'drama foretold' in the FCC's *OMT decision*, which did not unravel in 2016, has finally fulfilled the "promise of a confrontation".[77] The setting is the same, but this time heavy artillery is mobilized on both sides. In the specific case of the *PSPP judgment*, the German Parliament neutralized the conflict. A very large political alliance formed of Chancellor Angela Merkel's coalition parties with the Greens and the Liberal Democrats voted on 2 July 2020 to accept the explanation the ECB provided for the public sector purchase program (PSPP). This vote fulfilled the FCC's ruling concerning the proportionality of the measures. The *Bundestag* considered "the ECB's statement to complete a proportionality check as comprehensive" and therefore, sufficient.[78] But that was not the final act in this theatre: in a judgment of 29 April 2021,[79] the Second Senate refused to declare the PSPP decision of 5 May 2020 unenforceable under § 35 of the Act on the Federal Constitutional Court (*Bundesverfassungsgerichts-gesetz*)[80] and indirectly validated the political decision of 2 July 2020 giving the final approval to the public debt asset purchase program. For the Commission, however, the judgment of 29 April 2021 "does not reverse the breaches concerning the principle of primacy of Union law".[81]

76 *See* Franz C. Mayer, 'Auf dem Weg zum Richterfausrecht. Zum PSPP-Urteil des BVerfG', *Verfassungsblog*, 7 May 2020, at https://verfassungsblog.de/auf-dem-weg-zum-richterfaustrecht/, who argues for an infringement procedure as the "civilized" way to resolve the conflict.

77 Philippe Cossalter & Audrey Schlegel, 'La décision OMT de 2016: une ouverture', *RFDA*, 2017/4, p. 811.

78 Antrag der Fraktionen CDU/CSU, SPD, FDP und Bündnis 90/Die Grünen, 1 July 2020, Drucksache 19/20621, at https://dip21.bundestag.de/dip21/btd/19/206/1920621.pdf. The Parliament approves the statement of the ECB resulting of the meeting of 3-4 June 2020: Account of the monetary policy meeting of the Governing Council of the European Central Bank, at www.ecb.europa.eu/press/accounts/2020/html/ecb.mg200625~fd97330d5f.en.html.

79 2 BvR 1651/15, Rn.1-111; *see* Martin Nettesheim, 'Größe und Tragik. Zum Eilbeschluss des Bundesverfassungsgerichts zu 'Next Generation EU'', 21 April 2021, *Verfassungsblog*, at https://verfassungsblog.de/grose-und-tragik/.

80 "The Federal Constitutional Court may specify in its decision who is to execute it; in individual cases it may also specify the method of execution."

81 *See* at https://ec.europa.eu/commission/presscorner/detail/en/inf_21_2743.

doi: 10.5553/HYIEL/266627012021009001011

The Possibility of Using Article 72 TFEU as a Conflict-of-Law Rule

Hungary Seeking Derogation from EU Asylum Law*

*Ágnes Töttős***

Abstract

The purpose of this article is to examine how the CJEU circumscribed the room for maneuver of Member States for safeguarding their internal security and whether the use of and reference to Article 72 TFEU changed over the past years. The starting point of the analysis is the Hungarian asylum infringement case: the article looks back at earlier case-law and identifies how the reference to Article 72 TFEU shifted from considering it an implementation clause to the attempts at using it as a conflict-of-law rule. Although the article finds that the CJEU reduced the scope of possibly using Article 72 TFEU as a conflict-of-law rule and practically excludes its application by the setting high standards for this unique form of application, the article examines some extreme situations from 2020 where it could be validly referred to.

Keywords: Article 72 TFEU, internal security, conflict of law, Common European Asylum System, relocation decisions.

1. Introduction

Article 72 TFEU sets out the important and indisputable rule in the Area of Freedom, Security and Justice (AFSJ) that harmonization in this area shall not affect the exercise of the responsibilities incumbent upon Member States with regard to the maintenance of law and order and the safeguarding of internal security. According to Craig and de Búrca the proposition in Article 72 TFEU

> "has political resonance and is not without substance but does not reflect reality. The AFSJ Title is an area of shared competence. This necessarily means that Member State responsibilities for law and order will be

* The opinions expressed in this article are the author's own and cannot be considered the official standpoint of the Government Office of the Prime Minister of Hungary.

** Ágnes Töttős: senior government counselor, Government Office of the Prime Minister, Budapest.

doi: 10.5553/HYIEL/266627012021009001012

> circumscribed by EU measures. The nature and degree of this circumscription will perforce depend on the particular measure adopted by the EU."[1]

The purpose of this article is to research *how the CJEU circumscribed the room for maneuver of Member States for safeguarding their internal security and whether the use and reference to Article 72 TFEU changed over the past years*. The starting point of the analysis is the most recent case where this Treaty provision was referred to, namely the Hungarian asylum infringement case in which the CJEU declared that Hungary failed to fulfil its obligations in respect of several provisions of EU asylum and migration acquis.[2] Following an introduction to the most recent conclusions of the CJEU, the article looks back at earlier case-law and identifies how the reference to Article 72 TFEU shifted from considering it an implementation clause to the attempts at using it as a conflict-of-law rule. Although the term *conflict of laws* is generally used in the context of private international law, I shall use this term to refer to situations when an EU law provision gives priority to Member State competence over measures enacted by the EU legislature or decision-maker. Having this special nature, Article 72 TFEU was used as an argument in the referred asylum cases in particular by Poland and Hungary and was also referred to as a conflict-of law rule by both the Advocate General and the CJEU.[3]

As the possibility of use of Article 72 TFEU in a different context emerged, it is interesting to examine how the CJEU reacted to the possible disapplication of EU law in extreme situations and how it aimed at fortifying the obligation of implementing EU law even in situations posing threat to internal security. Apart from discussing the CJEU's conclusions, the article also points out that the CJEU could have taken into account further developments that could have resulted in a different evaluation of the situations where conflict of laws was raised. Although the article arrives at the conclusion that the CJEU reduced the scope of possibly using Article 72 TFEU as a conflict-of-law rule and practically excludes its application by setting high standards for this form of unique application, the article examines some extreme situations from 2020 in which it could be validly referred to.

2. The Hungarian Infringement Procedure

In the infringement procedure *C-808/18* the CJEU declared that Hungary had failed to fulfil its obligations under Articles 5, 6(1), 12(1), and 13(1) of Directive

1 Paul Craig & Gráinne de Búrca, *EU Law: Text, Cases and Materials, 6th Edition*, Oxford University Press, Oxford, 2015, p. 976.

2 Judgment of 17 December 2020, *Case C-808/18, European Commission v Hungary*, ECLI:EU:C:2020:1029.

3 *See* Opinion of Advocate General Sharpston delivered on 31 October 2019, *Joined Cases C-715/17, 718/17 and 719/17, Commission v Poland, Commission v Hungary, Commission v Czech Republic*, ECLI:EU:C:2019:917, para. 212. *See also* Judgment of 2 April 2020, *Joined Cases C-715/17, 718/17 and 719/17, Commission v Poland, Commission v Hungary, Commission v Czech Republic*, ECLI:EU:C:2020:257, para. 137.

doi: 10.5553/HYIEL/266627012021009001012

2008/115/EC of the European Parliament and of the Council of 16 December 2008 on common standards and procedures in Member States for returning illegally staying third-country nationals (Return Directive or RD),[4] under Articles 6, 24(3), 43, and 46(5) of Directive 2013/32/EU of the European Parliament and of the Council of 26 June 2013 on common procedures for granting and withdrawing international protection (Asylum Procedures Directive or APD),[5] and under Articles 8, 9 and 11 of Directive 2013/33/EU of the European Parliament and of the Council of 26 June 2013 laying down standards for the reception of applicants for international protection (Reception Conditions Directive or RCD).[6]

The critical conclusions of the CJEU identified four aspects of Hungary's asylum system's non-compliance with EU law. *(i)* Firstly, in providing that applications for international protection from third-country nationals or stateless persons who, arriving from Serbia, wish to access, in its territory, the international protection procedure, may be made only in the transit zones of Röszke and Tompa, while adopting a consistent and generalized administrative practice drastically limiting the number of applicants authorized to enter those transit zones daily. *(ii)* Secondly, in establishing a system of systematic detention of applicants for international protection in the transit zones of Röszke and Tompa, without observing the guarantees provided for in Article 24(3) and Article 43 of the Asylum Procedures Directive and Articles 8, 9 and 11 of the Reception Conditions Directive. *(iii)* Thirdly, in allowing the removal of all third-country nationals staying illegally in its territory, with the exception of those who are suspected of having committed a criminal offence, without observing the procedures and safeguards laid down in Article 5, Article 6(1), Article 12(1) and Article 13(1) of the Return Directive. *(iv)* Finally, in making the exercise by applicants for international protection who fall within the scope of Article 46(5) of APD of their right to remain in its territory subject to conditions contrary to EU law.

2.1. System of Systematic Detention

The CJEU did not accept the reasoning of Hungary that general rules of the Asylum Procedures Directive should apply to the transit zones and not to border procedures as the entirety of the procedure for the examination of asylum applications was conducted there. Furthermore, the placement in transit zones

4 Directive 2008/115/EC of the European Parliament and of the Council of 16 December 2008 on common standards and procedures in Member States for returning illegally staying third-country nationals (Return Directive).

5 Directive 2013/32/EU of the European Parliament and of the Council of 26 June 2013 on common procedures for granting and withdrawing international protection (Asylum Procedures Directive).

6 Directive 2013/33/EU of the European Parliament and of the Council of 26 June 2013 laying down standards for the reception of applicants for international protection (recast) (Reception Conditions Directive).

doi: 10.5553/HYIEL/266627012021009001012

was not considered as detention by Hungary since it was open at the Serbian side.[7] Hungary also claimed that special needs of the applicants are also taken into account.[8] Finally, Hungary also referred to Article 72 TFEU as a provision authorizing it to declare a crisis situation caused by mass immigration and to consequently apply derogating procedural rules in such situations, since the applicable secondary law provisions, namely the Asylum Procedures Directive, have proven insufficient for adequately managing the situation prevailing since the 2015 crisis.[9]

The CJEU dedicated a separate section to examining the legal nature of the placement in the transit zone and in its conclusions reiterated the findings of its judgment of 14 May 2020 in the *joined C-924/19 and C-925/19 PPU* preliminary ruling cases.[10] The CJEU then stated that

> "the detention of an applicant for international protection, within the meaning of that provision, is an autonomous concept of EU law understood as any coercive measure that deprives that applicant of his or her freedom of movement and isolates him or her from the rest of the population, by requiring him or her to remain permanently within a restricted and closed perimeter."[11]

Given the circumstances (length, security tools, space, contacts, *etc.*) of the placement in the Hungarian transit zones the CJEU found that *the placing of applicants for international protection in the transit zones of Röszke and Tompa is no different from a detention regime applied in unlawful manner*, which actually led to the immediate closure of the transit zones by the Hungarian authorities.[12]

In the infringement procedure, the CJEU went further than simply confirming its earlier conclusion on the legal nature of the transit zones, for it also examined the compatibility of this detention with the relevant rules of the APD and the RCD. In its assessment, the CJEU found the *de facto* detention in the transit zone is incompatible with EU law in four aspects.[13] *(i)* First of all, by not accepting the Hungarian argument that the procedures in the transit zones are not border procedures, but regular asylum procedures,[14] the CJEU examined its

7 Judgment of 17 December 2020, *Case C-808/18, Commission v Hungary*, ECLI:EU:C:2020:1029, paras. 138-139.

8 Id. para. 140.

9 Id. para. 141.

10 Judgment of 14 May 2020, *Joined Cases C-924/19 PPU and C-925/19 PPU, Országos Idegenrendészeti Főigazgatóság Dél-alföldi Regionális Igazgatóság and Országos Idegenrendészeti Főigazgatóság*, ECLI:EU:C:2020:367.

11 Id. para. 159.

12 *See* at https://hu.euronews.com/2020/05/21/mar-az-ejjel-elszallitottak-a-tranzitzonakbol-a-menedekkeroket.

13 The fifth ground contended by the Commission, namely that Hungary had infringed Article 2(h) of the Reception Conditions Directive by not transposing the definition of 'detention' properly, was not demonstrated sufficiently in order for the CJEU to accept the Commission's position. *See Case C-808/18, Commission v Hungary*, paras. 210-211.

14 Id. para. 180.

doi: 10.5553/HYIEL/266627012021009001012

compatibility with border procedures set out in Article 43 of APD. The CJEU found that since the procedures entail the entirety of the examination of the applications and throughout the procedure the applicants are kept in the transit zones, this system of detention does not comply with the conditions of the border procedure and therefore the detention is unjustified on the basis of point (c) of the first subparagraph of Article 8(3) of RCD that allows detention to be carried out during the border procedure.[15] *(ii)* Secondly, incompatibility with EU rules was also declared because Hungary infringed Article 24(3) of RCD by not providing adequate support for applicants in need of special procedural guarantees, as it only exempted certain limited categories[16] and those not exempted did not undergo a case-by-case examination by national authorities to ascertain whether they need special procedural guarantees.[17] *(iii)* Thirdly, the CJEU also found that Hungary infringed Article 11(2) of RCD by requiring that all minors above age 14 be placed in the transit zones, thus, not applying detention as a measure of last resort.[18] *(iv)* Fourthly, Hungary also infringed Article 9 of RCD on the grounds that the detention of applicants in the transit zones were not ordered in writing and did not enable the applicants to ascertain the factual and legal grounds of the detention.[19]

2.2. Analysis of the Use of Article 72 TFEU in Case C-808/18

In the judgment, the CJEU dedicated a separate section to examining the possible use of Article 72 TFEU. The examination was carried out when deciding the compatibility of placement in the transit zones with requirements laid down in APD and RCD, but only after the Court found the *de facto* detention in the transit zone incompatible with EU law in four aspects. The CJEU was therefore trying to answer whether the non-compliance could be justified with reference to Article 72 TFEU, as Hungary claimed that

> "Article 72 authorizes Member States to derogate from the EU rules adopted, in accordance with Article 78 TFEU, in the field of asylum, subsidiary protection and temporary protection, where compliance with those rules precludes Member States from adequately managing an emergency situation characterized by arrivals of large numbers of applicants for international protection. It follows, more specifically, in the present case, that the national rules governing the procedures conducted in the transit zones of Röszke and Tompa can derogate from Article 24(3) and Article 43 of Directive 2013/32. "[20]

15 Id. paras. 181-186.

16 Only unaccompanied minors under the age of 14 and those who already held a residence permit in Hungarian territory or who were subject to another detention measure or a measure restricting personal liberty were exempted.

17 *Case C-808/18, Commission v Hungary*, paras. 187-199.

18 Id. paras. 200-203.

19 Id. paras. 204-209.

20 Id. para. 213.

doi: 10.5553/HYIEL/266627012021009001012

While the CJEU acknowledges that it is for Member States to adopt appropriate measures to ensure law and order on their territory and their internal and external security, it also restricts the application of derogations in two ways. *(i)* On the one hand, the CJEU is of the opinion that *such exceptions could only be applied to TFEU Articles that expressly allow derogations* applicable in situations which may affect law and order.[21]

> "It cannot be inferred that the FEU Treaty contains an inherent general exception excluding all measures taken for reasons of law and order or public security from the scope of European Union law. The recognition of the existence of such an exception, regardless of the specific requirements laid down by the Treaty, might impair the binding nature of European Union law and its uniform application."[22]

(ii) On the other hand, the court also emphasizes that *the derogation provided for in Article 72 TFEU must be interpreted strictly*.

> "The scope of the requirements relating to the maintenance of law and order, or national security cannot therefore be determined unilaterally by each Member State, without any oversight by the institutions of the European Union. It is accordingly for the Member State which seeks to take advantage of Article 72 TFEU to prove that it is necessary to have recourse to that derogation in order to exercise its responsibilities in terms of the maintenance of law and order and the safeguarding of internal security."[23]

As the wording of Article 72 TFEU refers to derogations to be allowed with regard to Title V, the CJEU does not dispute (when examining the strict and justified nature of the Hungarian derogation) that all provisions under the Title on the AFSJ, including those based on Article 78 regarding the Common European Asylum Policy, may be subject to derogation. Nevertheless, the CJEU has several concerns as regards the wide Hungarian interpretation of the derogation and comes to the conclusion that *Hungary invoked the risk of threats to public order and internal security of mass arrivals in a general manner*.[24] In its elaboration, the CJEU questions the necessity of such major derogations and states that although Hungary referred to a significant number of offences committed in 2018 linked to illegal migration, it did not specify the impact of these offences on the one hand, and how the derogation was required given such offences, on the other.[25]

It becomes clearly visible in this part of the judgment that the concept of illegal entry and stay could have different interpretations in different areas of EU

21 Articles 36, 45, 52, 65, 72, 346 and 347 TFEU.
22 *Case C-808/18, Commission v Hungary*, para. 214.
23 Id. para. 216.
24 Id. para. 217.
25 Id. para. 218.

doi: 10.5553/HYIEL/266627012021009001012

law[26] and while Hungary considers entries to be illegal based solely on the Schengen *acquis*, the CJEU views it strictly from the perspective of international protection by stating that those arriving as applicants for international protection cannot be regarded as entering or staying illegally.[27] This divergence of legal interpretations also contributed to the conclusions regarding the lack of connection between the evidence provided and the necessity that, according to the CJEU should have been demonstrated.

Even after the CJEU concluded that Hungary's demonstration was not enough for invoking Article 72, the CJEU seems to set out another requirement for the application of derogation, namely the lack of due consideration of the security aspects mentioned in Article 72 TFEU by the European legislators. The CJEU states that the fact that RCD allows for detention and, in case of a significant increase in the number of applicants, both APD and RCD provide for a partial derogation, prove that EU legislature was also careful to take into account extraordinary situations. At any rate, it raises major questions as regards the competences left for the Member States.

Although Article 72 TFEU states that "This Title shall not affect the exercise of the responsibilities incumbent upon Member States with regard to the maintenance of law and order and the safeguarding of internal security", according to the reasoning of the Commission and the CJEU, if the EU law adopted by EU institutions covers the same aspects that Member States would remain responsible for, this should be considered as EU law already providing the maintenance of law and order and the safeguarding of internal security as the CJEU refers to derogations expressly allowed by secondary EU law as provisions serving the same purpose as Article 72 TFEU. This argument, however, raises several concerns. *Article 72 TFEU expressly refers to the exercise of the responsibilities of the Member States* and not the EU. The competence of the Member States is also supported by settled case-law[28] according to which Member States essentially retain the freedom to determine the requirements of public policy and internal security in accordance with their national needs, which can vary from one Member State to another and from one era to another. Should the CJEU's view be followed in the future, it would practically mean that *Member States could no longer decide upon further derogations in accordance with Article 72*

26 *See e.g.* Benedita Menezes Queiroz, *Illegally Staying in the EU: An Analysis of Illegality in EU Migration Law*, Hart Publishing, Oxford, 2018, p. 85.

27 *Case C-808/18, Commission v Hungary*, para. 219.

28 The reasoning was developed by Advocate General Mayras in his Opinion in *van Duyn*, according to which 'Member States have sole power, given the exceptions expressed in certain Community provisions [...], to take measures for the safeguarding of public security within their territory and to decide the circumstances under which that security may be endangered', so that the concept of public security 'remains, at least for the present, national, and this conforms with reality inasmuch as the requirements of public security vary, in time and in space, from one State to another.' Opinion of Advocate General Mayras delivered on 13 November 1974, *Case C-41/74, Van Duyn*, ECLI:EU:C:123, p. 1357. *See also e.g.* Judgment of 10 July 2008, *Case C-33/07, Jipa*, ECLI:EU:C:2008:396, para. 23; Judgment of 13 January 2012, *Case C-430/10, Gaydarov*, ECLI:EU:C:2011:749, para. 32; Judgment of 11 June 2015, *Case C-554/13, Zh. and O.*, ECLI:EU:C:2015:377, para. 48.

doi: 10.5553/HYIEL/266627012021009001012

TFEU thereby limiting Member States or even taking away competence expressly provided to them by Article 72 TFEU.

3. The Different Uses of Article 72 TFEU

3.1. Article 72 TFEU as an Implementation Clause

In earlier cases, the use of Article 72 TFEU focused on the adequate implementation of EU law. On the one hand, the CJEU examined whether Member States act within the margin of discretion provided by secondary law when taking into consideration their national needs in order to maintain law and order. In *Case C-601/15*[29] the CJEU examined whether the detention measure applied in the case of an asylum-seeker in the main proceedings could fall within the grounds for detention mentioned in point (e) of the first subparagraph of Article 8(3) of RCD.[30] The opinion of the Advocate General[31] examining the proportionate nature of the measure applied in the case declared that although the provision at issue does permit interference with the right to liberty and security guaranteed by Article 6 of the Charter of Fundamental Rights, that limitation is justified if it

> "appears necessary in order to allow the Member States, in accordance with the principles referred to in Article 4(2) TEU and Article 72 TFEU, to combat threats to their national security or their public order effectively."[32]

Consequently, when ordering detention based on EU asylum law Member States are allowed to take into account their national security within the discretion that EU law provides as long as the principle of proportionality is kept.

Even in the area of legal migration this room for maneuver was confirmed in *Case C-544/15*.[33] The Advocate General in that case admitted that even though the exact meaning of Article 72 TFEU is not completely clear at first sight, it does point to a difference between public policy and security in free movement law and in immigration law. Nevertheless, both the Advocate General and the CJEU came to the conclusion that the margin of discretion of the German authorities in the case was enough for them to lawfully establish that an Iranian national, previously gaining a degree at a university supported by the Iranian Government and wishing to carry out a research in the field of IT-security, could pose a threat to the Member State's external or internal security.[34]

29 Judgment of 15 February 2016, *Case C-601/15 PPU, N.*, ECLI:EU:C:2016:84.

30 According to point (e) of the first subparagraph of Article 8(3) of RCD an applicant may be detained when protection of national security or public order so requires.

31 View of Advocate General Sharpston delivered on 26 January 2016, *Case C-601/15 PPU, N.*, ECLI:EU:C:2016:85.

32 Id. para. 137.

33 Judgment of 4 April 2017, *Case C-544/15, Fahimian*, ECLI:EU:C:2017:255.

34 Opinion of Advocate General Szpunar delivered on 29 November 2016, *Case C-544/15, Fahimian*, ECLI:EU:C:2016:908, para. 80. *See also Case C-544/15, Fahimian*, para. 50.

doi: 10.5553/HYIEL/266627012021009001012

As regards the implementation of Schengen *acquis*, the proportionality principle limits Member States in two aspects. *(i)* Firstly, as regards the temporary reintroduction of border control at the internal borders, Member States are limited by the specific provisions of the Schengen Borders Code (SBC)[35] both in terms of legal basis and duration. They, nevertheless, have leeway when deciding what constitutes an 'exceptional situation', in the framework of which the principle of proportionality should still be respected. *(ii)* Secondly, the implementation of Schengen *acquis* also has an influence on areas under national law. In *Adil*[36] the CJEU stated that

> "Article 21(a) of Regulation No 562/2006 provides that the abolition of border control at internal borders is not to affect the exercise of police powers by the competent authorities of the Member States under national law, in so far as the exercise of those powers does not have an effect equivalent to border checks; that is also to apply in border areas."[37]

However, it should be noted that even in this case the limitation of police powers was determined with a view not to undermine the efficient implementation of EU law prohibiting the unlawful reintroduction of border control or measures equivalent in nature at internal borders.

3.2. Article 72 TFEU as a Conflict-of-Law Rule: the Relocation Cases

A reference to Article 72 TFEU appeared in a different context when the EU and its Member States faced an exceptional influx of asylum-seekers and the EU reacted to it using a special legal basis for the very first time. Article 78(3) TFEU sets out that

> "in the event of one or more Member States being confronted by an emergency situation characterized by a sudden inflow of nationals of third countries, the Council, on a proposal from the Commission, may adopt provisional measures for the benefit of the Member State(s) concerned."

Two Council decisions[38] (relocation decisions) on Member States relocating asylum-seekers from Greece and Italy were adopted in line with this provision, the second decision setting out compulsory relocation quotas, the annulment of which was requested by the Slovak Republic and Hungary supported by Poland.

35 Regulation (EC) No 562/2006 of the European Parliament and of the Council of 15 March 2006 establishing a Community Code on the rules governing the movement of persons across borders (Schengen Borders Code).

36 Judgment of 19 July 2012, *Case C-278/12 PPU, Adil*, ECLI:EU:C:2012:508.

37 Id. para. 53.

38 Council Decision (EU) 2015/1523 of 14 September 2015 establishing provisional measures in the area of international protection for the benefit of Italy and of Greece; Council Decision (EU) 2015/1601 of 22 September 2015 establishing provisional measures in the area of international protection for the benefit of Italy and Greece.

doi: 10.5553/HYIEL/266627012021009001012

3.2.1. *The First Relocation Case*

In its judgment[39] the CJEU rejected Poland's argument

> "that the contested decision is contrary to the principle of proportionality since it does not allow the Member States to ensure the effective exercise of their responsibilities with regard to the maintenance of law and order and the safeguarding of internal security as required under Article 72 TFEU. The Republic of Poland submits that it is particularly serious given that the contested decision will give rise to significant 'secondary' movements, caused by applicants leaving their host Member State before the latter has been able to rule definitively upon their application for international protection."[40]

The CJEU's reason for rejecting this argument was that Recital 32 of the contested decision states, *inter alia*, that national security and public order should be taken into consideration throughout the relocation procedure, until the transfer of the applicant is implemented. Furthermore, Article 5(7) provides that Member States retain the right to refuse to relocate an applicant only where there are reasonable grounds for regarding him or her as a danger to their national security or public order.[41] The CJEU therefore refers to the content of secondary law as already providing adequate discretion for Member States to exercise their responsibilities set out in Article 72 TFEU.

Nevertheless, the CJEU could not completely exclude that such explicit retention of right to refuse to relocate would be effective enough in case Member States were required to check large numbers of persons within a short period of time. However, even in such extreme cases outlined by Poland, the CJEU is of the view that

> "such practical difficulties are not inherent in the mechanism and must, should they arise, be resolved in the spirit of cooperation and mutual trust between the authorities of the Member States that are beneficiaries of relocation and those of the Member States of relocation. That spirit of cooperation and mutual trust must prevail when the relocation procedure provided for in Article 5 of the contested decision is implemented."[42]

Consequently, even if the specifically provided check would not provide adequate opportunities for Member States to exercise their responsibilities set out in Article 72 TFEU, they should still try to find a practical solution while implementing EU law rather than not implementing it at all.[43]

39 Judgment of 6 September 2017, *Joined Cases C-643/15 and C-647/15, Slovakia v Council and Hungary v Council*, ECLI:EU:C:2017:631.
40 Id. para. 306.
41 Id. paras. 307-308.
42 Id. para. 309.
43 Opinion of Advocate General Bot delivered on 26 July 2017, *Joined Cases C-643/15 and C-647/15, Slovakia v Council and Hungary v Council*, ECLI:EU:C:2017:618, paras. 315-317.

doi: 10.5553/HYIEL/266627012021009001012

3.2.2. *The Second Relocation Case*

By the end of the two-year implementation period most Member States did not or did not completely implement the obligations arising from the two Council Decisions on relocation. The European Commission started infringement procedures against Poland, the Czech Republic and Hungary[44] in which the three Member States put forward a series of arguments which they claim vindicates them for having disapplied Decisions 2015/1523 and 2015/1601. The arguments, *(i)* first, relate to the responsibilities of Member States with regard to the maintenance of law and order and the safeguarding of internal security, arguments derived by the Republic of Poland and Hungary from Article 72 TFEU read in conjunction with Article 4(2) TEU and, *(ii)* secondly, are gleaned by the Czech Republic from the malfunctioning and alleged ineffectiveness of the relocation mechanism provided for under those decisions. These infringement cases raise important questions of EU law, including whether and under what conditions a Member State may rely on Article 72 TFEU to disapply decisions adopted on the basis of Article 78(3) TFEU, the binding nature of which is not disputed.[45] Consequently, the CJEU examined the nature and scope of application of Article 72 TFEU from a broader perspective.

Poland and Hungary referred to the drawbacks of the practical implementation of relocations by other Member States that were later also highlighted by the European Court of Auditors in its special report.[46] The two Member States take the view that, according to their assessment of the risks posed by the possible relocation on their territory of dangerous and extremist persons who may carry out violent acts or acts of a terrorist nature, and the relocation mechanism as it was applied by the Greek and Italian authorities did not enable them to fully guarantee the maintenance of law and order and the safeguarding of internal security. In this connection, they also refer to the many problems encountered in the application of the relocation mechanism as far as it concerns, in particular, establishing with sufficient certainty the identity and origin of applicants for international protection who may be relocated. They claimed that these problems were aggravated by the lack of cooperation on the side of the Greek and Italian authorities in the relocation procedure, in particular, in light of the refusal of those authorities to allow liaison officers from the Member States of relocation to conduct interviews with the applicants concerned before their transfer.[47] Such practical concerns were also highlighted later by the European Court of Auditors, explaining that the relocation decisions had to be adopted quickly in September 2015, before procedures had been established or the necessary structures were in place (to register, transport and accommodate relocation candidates) and it was therefore not clear how to proceed, especially as

44 *Joined Cases C-715/17, 718/17 and 719/17, Commission v Poland, Commission v Hungary, Commission v Czech Republic.*

45 Also noted by the Advocate General in para. 105 of her Opinion.

46 *Asylum, Relocation and Return of Migrants: Time to Step Up Action to Address Disparities between Objectives and Results*, European Court of Auditors, Special Report No 24/2019.

47 *Joined Cases C-715/17, 718/17 and 719/17, Commission v Poland, Commission v Hungary, Commission v Czech Republic*, paras. 135-136.

doi: 10.5553/HYIEL/266627012021009001012

regards performing security checks, and key stakeholders did not agree upon operating protocols[48] until later.[49]

Based on the reasons above, Poland submitted that

> "a Member State can invoke Article 72 in order not to implement an act adopted under Title V of the Treaty each time it considers that there is a risk, even a potential risk, for the maintenance of law and order and the safeguarding of internal security for which it bears responsibility. In that regard, a Member State has a very wide margin of discretion and must only show the plausibility of a risk for the maintenance of law and order and the safeguarding of internal security in order to be able to rely on Article 72 TFEU.'[50]

The Advocate General and the Court used slightly different arguments when rejecting the above-mentioned arguments of Poland and Hungary. AG Sharpston argued that

> "Article 72 TFEU is therefore not – as Poland and Hungary contend – a *conflict of laws rule* that gives priority to Member State competence over measures enacted by the EU legislature or decision-maker; rather, it is a *rule of co-existence*. The competence to act in the specified area remains with the Member State (it has not been transferred to the European Union). Nevertheless, the actions taken must respect the overarching principles that the Member State signed up to when it became a Member State and any relevant rules contained in the Treaties or in EU secondary legislation."[51]

This proposition was supported by two examples given by the Advocate general, namely the *Factortame* litigation and Member States' legislation related to direct taxation. In both examples AG Sharpston pointed to the fact that even in areas of law where the competence to legislate is vested in the Member States, such legislative powers retained must yet still be exercised in consistence with EU law.[52] In this case, it is the Relocation Decisions as well as the entire framework of the Common European Asylum System that prevents Member States from applying Article 72 TFEU as a *carte blanche*.

In its assessment the CJEU reiterated its statement made in the first relocation case, namely, that the Treaty does not contain an inherent general exception excluding all measures taken for reasons of law and order or public security from the scope of EU law as the recognition of the existence of such may impair the binding nature of EU law and its uniform application. Furthermore, it

48 In the summer of 2016 in Greece and at the end of the same year in Italy.

49 European Court of Auditors, Special Report No 24/2019, p. 25.

50 *Joined Cases C-715/17, 718/17 and 719/17, Commission v Poland, Commission v Hungary, Commission v Czech Republic*, para. 137.

51 AG Opinion, *Joined Cases C-715/17, 718/17 and 719/17, Commission v Poland, Commission v Hungary, Commission v Czech Republic*, para. 212.

52 Id. paras. 213-218.

doi: 10.5553/HYIEL/266627012021009001012

once again highlighted that the derogation provided for in Article 72 TFEU must be interpreted strictly, and it is for the Member State which seeks to take advantage of Article 72 TFEU to prove that it is necessary to have recourse to that derogation in order to exercise its responsibilities in terms of the maintenance of law and order and the safeguarding of internal security.[53] Here, the CJEU referred to its settled case-law regarding derogations in other areas of EU law, more specifically the derogation provided for in Articles 346 and 347 TFEU related to the functioning of the internal market being affected by certain measures of the Member States.[54]

It then went on to examine the relationship between the discrepancies of the relocation mechanism and the complete disapplication of the relocation decisions. The CJEU first repeated that the relocation decisions allow the Member States to adequately take into account their responsibilities related to ensuring internal security. Nevertheless, the CJEU points out that the wording of the relocation decisions authorized the competent authorities of the Member State of relocation to rely on *serious reasons or reasonable grounds* relating to the maintenance of their national security or public order *only following a case-by-case investigation of the danger actually or potentially represented by the applicant* for international protection. It follows that the decisions precluded a Member State from peremptorily invoking Article 72 TFEU in that procedure for the sole purposes of general prevention and without establishing any direct relationship with a particular case, in order to justify suspending the implementation of, or even a ceasing to implement its obligations under the relocation decisions.[55] The CJEU highlights that the help of EU agencies was available and additional security interviews could be requested in order to carry out a thorough analysis of each individual case.[56]

Consequently, the CJEU concludes that

> "the mechanism provided for in Article 5(4) and (7) of each of those decisions, including in its specific application as it developed in practice during the periods of application of those decisions, left the Member States of relocation genuine opportunities for protecting their interests relating to public order and internal security in the examination of the individual situation of each applicant for international protection whose relocation was proposed, without prejudicing the objective of those decisions to ensure the effective and swift relocation of a significant number of applicants clearly in

53 *Joined Cases C-715/17, 718/17 and 719/17, Commission v Poland, Commission v Hungary, Commission v Czech Republic*, paras. 143-144 and 147.

54 *See*, to that effect, Judgment of 15 December 2009, *Case C-461/05, Commission v Denmark*, ECLI:EU:C:2009:783, para. 52; Judgment of 4 March 2010, *Case C-38/06, Commission v Portugal*, ECLI:EU:C:2010:108, para. 63.

55 *Joined Cases C-715/17, 718/17 and 719/17, Commission v Poland, Commission v Hungary, Commission v Czech Republic*, para. 160; AG Opinion, *Joined Cases C-715/17, 718/17 and 719/17, Commission v Poland, Commission v Hungary, Commission v Czech Republic*, para. 223.

56 *Joined Cases C-715/17, 718/17 and 719/17, Commission v Poland, Commission v Hungary, Commission v Czech Republic*, para. 166.

doi: 10.5553/HYIEL/266627012021009001012

> need of international protection in order to alleviate the considerable pressure on the Greek and Italian asylum systems."[57]

It is interesting to compare this theoretical statement with what the European Court of Auditors actually found examining the situation first hand:

> "The majority of rejections were justified on public order or national security grounds, in accordance with the Relocation Decisions. However, the explanations given were often generic, without detailed justification of individual cases. The number of rejections was higher for Greece than for Italy owing to the different security profiles of eligible migrants. Greece channeled rejected candidates to the national asylum system, whereas Italy offered them for relocation to another Member State."[58]

It therefore gives the impression that what the way the CJEU approaches the use of the public security clause is a somewhat illusory and in practice even relocating Member States used their discretionary power deviating from the requirements set by the CJEU. Consequently, it rightfully raises the question whether lawful implementation along the required principles could actually have been carried out at all, or is there more in what Poland and Hungary claim regarding the impossibility of enforcing Member State rights related to internal security during the relocation procedures?

4. Conclusions

4.1. The Scope of Interpretation of Article 72 TFEU

Article 72 TFEU reproduces Article 64(1) TEC and Article 33 TEU and now applies to Title V in its entirety.[59] According to Steve Peers, Article 64(1) TEC was not a limitation on EC competence, but rather confirmed that implementation of measures adopted pursuant to previous Title IV "is left to the Member States' authorities, particularly as regards coercive measures" and that *e.g.* Frontex "must therefore continue to be limited to supporting actions of nationals authorities."[60] This interpretation of the present Article 72 TFEU as an implementation rule was also confirmed by earlier EU case-law.

Nevertheless, the relocation cases before the CJEU shed light to a possibly wider scope and interpretation of Article 72 TFEU, read together with Article 4(2) TEU. To varying degrees, the Member States not willing to apply or not applying the relocation decisions adopted in 2015, sought to rely on Article 4(2) TEU read

57 Id. para. 171.

58 European Court of Auditors, Special Report No 24/2019, p. 25.

59 Article 72 TFEU is complemented by Article 276 TFEU, which stipulates that the CJEU has no jurisdiction to review the validity or proportionality of operations carried out by Member States' law enforcement services or the responsibilities exercised by them with regard to the maintenance of law and order and the safeguarding of internal security.

60 Steve Peers, *EU Justice and Home Affairs Law*, Oxford University Press, Oxford, 2006, p. 114.

doi: 10.5553/HYIEL/266627012021009001012

in conjunction with Article 72 TFEU, claiming that these entitled them to disapply the relocation decisions. It is assumed that they did it "to ensure social and cultural cohesion, as well as to avoid potential ethnic and religious conflicts."[61] This use of Article 72 TFEU confirmed Kadelbach's view[62] that the clause is an extension of the identity clause set out in Article 4(2) TEU that embodies two obligations of the EU, the duties to respect national identities and to respect the essential functions of the Member States.

Although the CJEU decisions set out that *the Treaty does not contain an inherent general exception* excluding all measures taken for reasons of law and order or public security from the EU law, by defining specific requirements for the possible use of Article 72 TFEU in conflict of laws situations, it indirectly acknowledged that there is more to this provision than simply being an implementation clause. By examining the reasoning in the relocation cases as well as the infringement case against Hungary, the CJEU actually confirms that Member States have the right to derogate from the requirements of EU law to maintain law and order and protect internal security even if it, with the same momentum, narrows this type of application of Article 72 TFEU by setting certain principles as requirements for such use.

The main principle emphasized by the CJEU is the necessity of disapplying valid EU law. When examining the different sets of proofs submitted by the Member States the CJEU seemed to disregard situations of mass migration and required even more extreme situations to appear with no other options for the Member States but to disregard EU law. At any rate *neither the relocation decisions, nor the limitations of the asylum border procedure could be disregarded by Member States in case of mass influx of migrants and asylum-seekers*.

When evaluating whether there would be a compelling reason for the application of a possible conflict-of-law situation, the CJEU required the taking into account of existing elements of secondary law that already provide some room for maneuver for Member States to protect their internal security. Consequently, the principle of gradation applies, according to which the CJEU expects Member States to first use all measures available within the sphere of EU law to handle challenging situations and to maintain law and order. Thus, the application of Article 72 TFEU as a conflict-of-law rule is only possible in case of their ineffectiveness.

Considering the conclusions above, certain concerns regarding the CJEU's assessment in in *Case C-808/18* may be raised. Firstly, it was clear that the diverging interpretation of what constitutes illegal entry and stay played a major role in the CJEU not finding the number of examples presented by Hungary to be relevant enough to prove the necessity of disapplying EU law. While asylum-

61 Alessandra Silveira, 'We Are All in the Same boat! On the Legal Principle of Solidarity and Its Legal Implications in the Recent CJEU Case Law', *Officalblogunio*, 7 April 2020, at https://officialblogofunio.com/2020/04/07/we-are-all-in-the-same-boat-on-the-legal-principle-of-solidarity-and-its-legal-implications-in-the-recent-cjeu-case-law/.

62 Stefan Kadelbach, *The Law of the European Union and National Security Exceptions of the Member States*, 2018, at www.just.ee/sites/www.just.ee/files/prof._dr._stefan_kadelbach._eesti_vabariigi_pohiseaduse_ja_riigikaitseseaduse_kooskola_analuus.pdf, p. 23.

doi: 10.5553/HYIEL/266627012021009001012

seekers have the right to remain until a specific point of the procedure irrespective of the legal nature of their entry to the country, this should not necessarily be considered equivalent to legal stay. Even if one could argue with this, given that only less than one-third of the applicants[63] are recognized as eligible for international protection, at least after the end of the asylum procedure ending without recognition it should be declared that such entries and stays could not be justified by seeking asylum, and should therefore be considered illegal retrospectively. In case such change in interpretation happens, the CJEU may come to a different conclusion regarding the link between the proof presented by Hungary and the necessity of severe actions.

Another concern follows from the fact that the CJEU *declares the present EU acquis and certain elements of secondary legislation to be appropriate for handing the mass influx of migrants*. It came to this conclusion even though the Commission itself implied the ineffectual nature of the presently valid asylum *acquis* by submitting a number of reform proposals in 2016[64] and then another set of ideas and legislative proposals in 2020.[65] Remarkably, even the EU Commission itself, in its so-called "New Pact on Migration and Asylum"[66] (a bundle of proposals published in September 2020 to reform the current system) copied at least some of Hungary's ideas. For instance, it suggests the introduction of a new screening procedure[67] and a special border procedure.[68] This would mean that border zones like those in Röszke and Tompa will actually have to be established by many Member States.[69],[70] This, at least indirectly refutes the CJEU's declaration that the effective provisions of the Common European Asylum System provide adequate tools for Member States to cope with present challenges of asylum and

63 In January the EU+ recognition rate was 32 % in February 2021, matching the EU+ recognition rate for 2020 overall. In these rates, decisions that granted refugee status and subsidiary protection are considered as positive decisions, while decisions granting national forms of protection are not. *See* at www.easo.europa.eu/latest-asylum-trends.

64 Ágnes Töttős, 'How to Interpret the European Migration Crisis Response with the Help of Science', *in* Zoltán Hautzinger (ed.), *Dynamics and Social Impact of Migration*, Dialóg Campus, Budapest, 2019, pp. 69-81.

65 *See* at https://ec.europa.eu/commission/presscorner/detail/en/ip_20_1706.

66 Communication from the Commission to the European Parliament, the Council, the European Economic and Social Committee and the Committee of the Regions on a New Pact on Migration and Asylum, COM(2020) 609 final.

67 COM(2020) 612 final from the Commission of 23 September 2020 on the 'Proposal for a Regulation of the European Parliament and the Council introducing a screening of third country nationals at the external borders and amending Regulations (EC) No 767/2008, (EU) 2017/2226, (EU) 2018/1240 and (EU) 2019/817'.

68 COM(2020) 611 final from the Commission of the 23 September 2020 on the 'Amended proposal for a Regulation of the European Parliament and of the Council establishing a common procedure for international protection in the Union and repealing Directive 2013/32/EU'.

69 Francesco Maiani, 'A "Fresh Start" or One More Clunker? Dublin and Solidarity in the New Pact', *EU Immigration and Asylum Law and Policy*, 20 October 2020, at https://eumigrationlawblog.eu/a-fresh-start-or-one-more-clunker-dublin-and-solidarity-in-the-new-pact/.

70 Sarah Progin-Theuerkauf, 'Defining the Boundaries of the Future Common European Asylum System with the Help of Hungary?', *European Papers*, Vol. 6, Issue 1, 2021.

doi: 10.5553/HYIEL/266627012021009001012

migration, especially when it comes to maintaining law and order and protecting internal security.

4.2. Future Possible Application of Article 72 TFEU

4.2.1. Conflict-of-Law Rules' Relevance in Schengen Acquis

Stefan Kadelbach refers to the possibility that Article 72 TFEU may provide a justification to introduce internal border controls in exceptional cases even if the requirements of the Schengen Borders Code for a suspension of free movement are not met, provided that the circumstances are of exceptional urgency and the measures remain proportionate and temporary.[71] As there are several internal border sections on which Member States have been upholding reinstated border controls for several years, the question duly arises, whether in these cases it is the conflict-of-law rule nature of Article 72 TFEU that is applied, and why the Commission has not challenged these along the line of the principles set out by the CJEU.

As a result of strategic litigation, the *joined cases C-368/20 NW v Landespolizeidirektion Steiermark*[72] *and C-369/20 NW v Bezirkshauptmannschaft Leibnitz*[73] raise exactly these questions in preliminary ruling procedures before the CJEU.[74] Here, the main legal question before the CJEU is whether the reintroduction of border controls at the internal borders can last for over two years. The answer is very much dependent on whether this limit applies only to a prolonged threat of the same nature or also to the cumulative reintroduction of new measures based on new threats. The cases, nevertheless, once again raise the possible application of Article 72 TFEU, and this time as a conflict-of-law rule even in the realm of Schengen *acquis*. Member States participating in the case, namely Austria, Denmark, France and Germany, generally argue that, within the context of the migration crisis, the current circumstances exceeded the framework of the Schengen Borders Code, and systemic problems in the management of external borders can no longer be resolved through common EU measures applied within a period of two years.[75]

This regulatory gap in EU secondary law therefore justifies a recourse to primary law, although the views of participating Member States differed to a certain extent. Germany argued that the extension of border controls beyond the two-year limit can be grounded directly in primary law, provided that it is necessary and proportionate in light of public safety and order. Meanwhile, other Member States considered the direct applicability of primary law only subordinately, favoring instead an extensive interpretation of the SBC, consistent with the

71 Kadelbach 2018, p. 19.

72 *Case C-368/20, Landespolizeidirektion Steiermark*, request for a preliminary ruling, 5 August 2020.

73 *Case C-369/20, Bezirkshauptmannschaft Leibnitz*, request for a preliminary ruling, 5 August 2020.

74 The joined cases are currently pending before the Grand Chamber of the CJEU, with the Opinion of Advocate General Saugmandsgaard Øe scheduled for 30 September 2021.

75 Pola Cebulak & Marta Morvillo, 'The Guardian is Absent: Legality of Border Controls within Schengen before the European Court of Justice', *Verfassungsblog*, 25 June 2021, at https://verfassungsblog.de/the-guardian-is-absent/.

Hungarian Yearbook of International Law and European Law 2021 (9) 1
doi: 10.5553/HYIEL/266627012021009001012

Treaties.[76] Consequently, it seems that Germany is leaning more towards declaring the conflict-of-law rule nature of Article 72 TFEU, while Austria, Denmark and France rather rely on use it as an interpretation clause.

Not surprisingly, the Commission argues that the absence of secondary law provisions governing border controls exceeding two years is a conscious decision of the EU legislator to limit derogations from free movement to a strictly defined period.[77] Hence, the Member States' responsibilities are already sufficiently taken into account by providing the possibility for derogation but limiting it to two years. Thus, while the Commission does not exclude relying on the national security exception, nevertheless emphasizes that this should be regarded as an *extrema ratio* that requires a higher threshold, similarly to the emergency clause in internal market law (Article 347 TFEU), which is not met by migration control exigencies. Furthermore, Member States cannot unilaterally announce their derogations, but instead must fulfil a necessity requirement subject to judicial review at the EU level.

However, emphasizing strict conditionality does not sound too convincing when voiced the Commission as it failed to require Member States applying excessive internal border controls both to justify the extension and to limit them to two years. On the one hand, it tacitly accepted these vaguely justified and seemingly endless internal border controls, thereby substantiating their application beyond the rules of the SBC, making them seem like "the new normal".[78] The Commission argues that it chose a political rather a legal route and instead of issuing an opinion or a letter of formal notice, it prepared a legislative proposal in 2017 to revise the SBC,[79] not wanting to interfere with the political debates in the Council and Parliament.[80] While in the field of asylum an even more extensive reform and negotiation process has been in process since 2016, which was referred to by Hungary in its asylum infringement case, neither the Commission, nor the CJEU took this substantially into account.

4.2.2. Challenges Brought by the Year 2020

Year 2020 brought two further situations in which the justified use of the conflict-of-law type application of Article 72 TFEU may arise. These are *Turkey's use of migratory pressure for political purposes* in early 2020 and the *global health crisis caused by COVID-19*.

76 Id.

77 Id.

78 Marie De Somer *et al.*, 'Schengen under Pressure: Differentiation or Disintegration?', *EU IDEA Policy Paper*, No. 7, September 2020, p. 3.

79 Proposal for a Regulation of the European Parliament and of the Council amending Regulation (EU) 2016/399 as regards the rules applicable to the temporary reintroduction of border control at internal borders, COM(2017) 0571 final.

80 The negotiations have reached a stalemate and as a result, the Commission set out a new Schengen Strategy in its Communication from the Commission to the European Parliament and the Council, 'A Strategy Towards a Fully Functioning and Resilient Schengen Area' on 2 June 2021.

doi: 10.5553/HYIEL/266627012021009001012

The EU Ministers of Home Affairs met on 4 March 2020, together with the Ministers of the Schengen Associated Countries, for an extraordinary Council meeting to discuss the situation at the EU's external borders with Turkey. In its statement, the Council expressed[81] its solidarity with Greece, Bulgaria and Cyprus and other Member States, which may be similarly affected, including efforts to manage EU's external borders. While the Council acknowledged the increased migratory burden and risks Turkey is facing on its territory and the substantial efforts it has made in hosting 3.7 million migrants and refugees, it strongly rejected Turkey's use of migratory pressure for political purposes as it found the situation at EU's external borders was unacceptable. The EU and its Member States remained determined to effectively protect EU external borders and not to tolerate illegal crossings and human smuggling, since migrants should not be encouraged to endanger their lives by attempting illegal crossings by land or sea. This extreme situation also raised the question whether in the context of such hybrid threats a derogation from existing EU *acquis* could be justified based on the maintenance of law and order and the protection of internal security, for even the Ministers declared that mass illegal migration and migrants themselves were used by Turkey for political purposes.

Not long after this incident another serious threat: the threat to public health appeared as COVID-19 also shook Member States in the spring of 2020. It was obvious that both external and internal border crossings contribute to the spread of the new virus. Even in such a situation the Commission in its Guidance on the implementation of relevant EU provisions in the area of asylum and return procedures and on resettlement[82] failed to recognize that a force majeure situation such as the pandemic could justify derogations beyond those specifically set out in secondary legislation. Consequently, the Commission's Guidance did not allow the suspension of welcoming asylum-seekers and the first procedural step of making an application. It merely referred for instance to the explicit derogation set out in Article 6(5) of the APD that allows Member States to extend the time limit for the registration of applications to ten working days where simultaneous applications by a large number of third-country nationals or stateless persons make it very difficult in practice to respect these time limits.[83]

Based on these two major shocks in 2020 we can conclude that *further derogations in major crisis situations and force majeure situations would be necessary*. The Commission seems to agree with this view, for it proposed a new set of rules in its crisis regulation proposal launched in September 2020.[84] If even the Commission, the initiator of infringement procedures admits that the present set of EU asylum rules are ineffectual in handling the present challenges threatening

81 *See* at www.consilium.europa.eu/en/press/press-releases/2020/03/04/statement-on-the-situation-at-the-eus-external-borders/.

82 Communication from the Commission, *COVID-19: Guidance on the Implementation of Relevant EU Provisions in the Area of Asylum and Return Procedures and on Resettlement*, Brussels, 16 April 2020, C(2020) 2516 final.

83 Id. p. 4.

84 Proposal for a Regulation of the European Parliament and of the Council addressing situations of crisis and force majeure in the field of migration and asylum, COM(2020) 613 final.

doi: 10.5553/HYIEL/266627012021009001012

public security and public health, and if the reforms of the Common European Asylum System can only be adopted as a result of a lengthy legislative procedure, the application of Article 72 TFEU as a conflict-of-law rule could gain justification for the period of these transitional years of reform negotiations. Nevertheless, it seems that not even these unprecedented times of COVID-19 can justify the restriction of entry of asylum-seekers as the European Commission launched another infringement procedure against Hungary on 30 October 2020[85] for requiring a statement of intent for the purpose of lodging an asylum application to be submitted at the Embassy of Hungary in Belgrade or in Kyiv and the approval of the asylum authority before entry could be provided.[86]

4.3. *Further Implications of the Implementation of the Judgment in Case C-808/18 With Regard to Constitutional Autonomy*

Kadelbach also points to the fact that

> "national identity and its emanations into the constitutional structures and essential functions of a state, as legal concepts, presuppose constitutional autonomy so that it is to a considerable extent up to domestic actors and particularly the interpreters of domestic law to whom the task is assigned to define which elements belong to the "fundamental structures" of their respective States. They have retained a margin of discretion in that respect."[87]

Along these lines the constitutional courts of various Member States have claimed the power to declare EU law inapplicable within their respective jurisdictions if they find that such law is either *ultra vires* or that it is in conflict with the core of the Member State's constitutional law.

In February 2021 Hungary's Minister of Justice asked the Constitutional Court for an interpretation of Article E(2) and Section XIV(4) of the Fundamental Law of Hungary.[88] In her request[89] the Minister refers to the judgment of the CJEU in *Case C-808/18*: given that the effectiveness of the EU rules on return is not guaranteed, the implementation of the CJEU judgment may result in non-Hungarian citizens staying in Hungary illegally. Their identity is sometimes unknown, and they remain in Hungary for an indefinite period, thus *de facto*

85 European Commission, *October Infringement Package: Key Decision*, 30 October 2020, at https://ec.europa.eu/commission/presscorner/detail/en/inf_20_1687.

86 On 26 May 2020, the government issued Government Decree 233/2020. (V. 26.) on the rules of the asylum procedure during the state of danger declared for the prevention of human epidemic endangering life and property and causing massive disease outbreaks, and for the protection of the health and lives of Hungarian citizens. It also introduced a new asylum system, the so called 'embassy procedure'. This new system was later included in the Transitional Act, that entered into force on 18 June 2020. The system was first in place until 31 December 2020, with the possibility of extension. The system was extended and is currently in force until 30 June 2021.

87 Kadelbach 2018, pp. 27-28.

88 Case registration number X/00477/2021 (pending).

89 *See* (in Hungarian) at http://public.mkab.hu/dev/dontesek.nsf/0/09e9e8d16d403300c1258695004aef0a/$FILE/X_477_0_2021_ind%C3%ADtv%C3%A1ny_anonim.pdf.

doi: 10.5553/HYIEL/266627012021009001012

becoming part of the country's population. According to the Minister of Justice, as long as effective return is not guaranteed by the EU, compliance with the judgment will lead to population change, which directly affects Hungary's sovereignty enshrined in the Fundamental Law, its historical constitutional identity and its inalienable right to determine its population. In the context of the constitutional problem presented, it is essential that the Constitutional Court interpret Article E(2) and Article XIV(4) of the Fundamental Law to decide whether these provisions mean that Hungary may implement an obligation of the EU which, in the absence of effective European regulation, may lead to foreigner staying illegally in Hungary, de facto becoming a part of the country's population.

The Minister's request also refers to the ruling of the German Federal Constitutional Court of 5 May 2020 with regard to the European Central Bank's Public Sector Asset Purchase Programme (PSPP)[90] that raised *fundamental constitutional questions about the relationship between national law and EU law and between national courts and the EU institutions*. More than 1,700 German citizens filed complaints before the German court alleging the PSPP violated several provisions in the EU's treaties and the German court referred several questions to the CJEU for a preliminary ruling. While in 2018 the CJEU ruled[91] that the PSPP neither exceeded the ECB's mandate nor violated the prohibition of monetary financing, the German Constitutional Court ruled in favor of the complainants. It stated that the German Government and *Bundestag* had violated their rights under Germany's Basic Law by failing to take steps to challenge the fact that the ECB, in its decisions on the adoption and implementation of the PSPP, neither assessed nor substantiated that the measures provided for in those decisions satisfied the principle of proportionality. Consequently, the ECB exceeded its competences. It also stated that the CJEU's review as to whether those decisions satisfied that principle is not comprehensible; to this extent, the judgment was rendered *ultra vires*. For that reason, the German Constitutional Court concluded it was not bound by the CJEU's ruling and must conduct its own review. In turn, the European Commission opened an infringement procedure against Germany over this controversial ruling of the Constitutional Court as it directly challenged the autonomy and primacy of EU law. In the formal notice sent on 9 June 2021 the Commission argues that Germany violated fundamental principles of EU law, in particular the principles of the autonomy, primacy, effectiveness and uniform application of Union law.[92]

Given the developments regarding the relationship between the CJEU and Constitutional Courts, Hungary's Minister of Justice also requests to see if the conclusion of the German Constitutional Court (namely, that the CJEU's 2018 ruling resulted in a structurally significant shift in the system of competences to the detriment of the Member States) could have relevance for the implementation of the CJEU judgment in the Hungarian asylum infringement case.

90 2 BvR 859/15; 2 BvR 980/16; 2 BvR 2006/15; 2 BvR 1651/15.
91 Judgment of 11 December 2018, *Case C-493/17, Weiss and others*, ECLI:EU:C:2018:1000.
92 *See* at https://ec.europa.eu/commission/presscorner/detail/en/inf_21_2743.

doi: 10.5553/HYIEL/266627012021009001012

Whose Interests to Protect?

Judgments in the Annulment Cases Concerning the Amendment of the Posting Directive

*Gábor Kártyás**

Abstract

The directive 96/71/EC on the posting of workers had been in force for over 20 years when its first amendment (Directive 2018/957) came into force on 30 July 2020. The Hungarian and Polish Governments initiated annulment proceedings against the new measure, primarily arguing that as the amendment extended the host state's labor standards ó to posted workers, the directive is no longer compatible with the freedom to provide services (Cases C-620/18 and C-626/18). Although both claims were rejected, the actions contain a number of noteworthy legal arguments (from the perspective of home States), which highlight some of the long-known contradictions of EU legislation on postings. The article summarizes the CJEU's key observations made in the judgments, which are important propositions for further discussion.

Keywords: posting of workers, freedom to provide services, posting directive, remuneration of posted workers, private international law.

1. Introduction

The directive on posting of workers (posting directive)[1] had been in force for over 20 years when its first amendment[2] came into force on 30 July 2020 (amending directive).

Under EU law, *posting* means that a worker who habitually works in one Member State (the home State) temporarily works in another Member State (the host State) to provide services. For example, when a Polish undertaking offering cleaning services has clients in Germany and orders its employees to temporarily perform such services also on the other side of the border. The essence of the posting directive is that although the worker remains subject to the employment law of the home state, the host state's law concerning working conditions

* Gábor Kártyás: associate professor of law, Pázmány Péter Catholic University, Budapest.

1 Directive 96/71/EC of the European Parliament and of the Council (posting directive).

2 Directive 2018/957 of the European Parliament and of the Council of 28 June 2018 amending Directive 96/71/EC concerning the posting of workers in the framework of the provision of services (amending directive).

doi: 10.5553/HYIEL/266627012021009001013

explicitly listed in the directive (that is, the 'hard core'[3] of labor standards) shall apply, if it is more favorable to the worker.[4] An additional requirement is that the posting take place in the framework of the performance of a service contract, intra-corporate posting or temporary agency work.[5] While posted workers make up barely 0.4% of the EU labor market (around 2 million posted workers work in the Member States each year[6]) and therefore have a rather limited impact on the functioning of the EU labor market, this phenomenon attracts significant attention. Since employers may gain a considerable competitive advantage making use of the more favorable domestic labor costs by providing services to the market of another Member State, where local rules would render the service more costly, posting reveals the differences in the level of social protection applicable in the various Member States. Consequently, EU legislation on postings pursues complex aims and ensures not only the freedom to provide cross-border services, but also fair competition among service providers.

The amending directive aims to put more emphasis on the *protection of posted workers*. The new measure introduced the following important changes. It limits the duration of postings to 12 months (which may be extended to 18 months upon the request of the service provider), after which the posted worker will be almost fully covered by the labor law of the host state.[7] The amending directive complements the list of the host State's applicable labor standards with two new elements. *(i)* First, with regard to remuneration, it provides from day one for full equality between posted and local workers in the host Member State as regards all mandatory pay entitlements in the host state's law, while the original directive prescribed only the application of minimum rates of pay. *(ii)* Second, posted workers are now also covered by the host state's standards on allowances or reimbursement of expenditure to cover travel, board and lodging expenses for workers away from home for professional reasons.[8]

However, the debate over the legal status of posted workers did not end with the adoption of the amending directive. The Hungarian and Polish Governments have initiated annulment proceedings against the new measure, primarily arguing that as *the amendment extended the host state's labor standards to posted workers,*

3 Posting directive, Recital (14); COM(2003) 248, p. 5.

4 Before the amendment, the directive covered the following standards: maximum work periods and minimum rest periods; minimum paid annual holidays; the minimum rates of pay, including overtime rates; this point does not apply to supplementary occupational retirement pension schemes; the conditions of hiring-out of workers, in particular the supply of workers by temporary employment undertakings; health, safety and hygiene at work; protective measures with regard to the terms and conditions of employment of pregnant women or women who have recently given birth, of children and of young people; equality of treatment between men and women and other provisions on non-discrimination. *See* posting directive, Article 3(1).

5 Posting directive, Articles 1-2.

6 *Posted workers in the EU*, European Commission Factsheet, 2015.

7 Procedures, formalities and conditions of the conclusion and termination of the employment contract, including non-competition clauses and supplementary occupational retirement pension schemes shall not apply to posted workers, not even after the time limit expires. *See* posting directive as amended Article 3(1a).

8 Posting directive as amended Article 3(1)(c) and (i); Article 3(1a).

doi: 10.5553/HYIEL/266627012021009001013

the directive is no longer compatible with the freedom to provide services.[9] Although both claims were rejected, the actions contain a number of noteworthy legal arguments (from the perspective of home States), which highlight some of the long-known contradictions of EU legislation on postings. The article summarizes the CJEU's key observations made in the judgments, which may be important propositions for further discussion.

2. The Incorrect Choice of Legal Basis: Social Policy or Free Movement of Services?

Hungary and Poland claim that the new directive's legal basis was not correctly chosen. While the directive was adopted based on the provisions relating to the freedom to provide services,[10] considering its purpose and substance, the directive's aim is in fact the protection of workers and should thus have been subject to the chapter on social policy.[11] According to the applications, the fundamental objective of the posting directive is to ensure that workers are afforded equal treatment, in particular as regards remuneration, while the Council has failed to specify which provisions are essential to ensure the genuine development of the freedom to provide services by means of the protection of workers and the prevention of unfair competition.[12]

The CJEU emphasized that the *choice of legal basis for an EU measure must rest on objective factors that are amenable to judicial review;* these include the aim and the content of the measure and the legal framework within which the new rules are situated, considering also the existing legislation that the new law amends. Should the assessment reveal that the measure pursues a twofold purpose or that it has a twofold component and if one of those is identifiable as the main or predominant purpose or component, whereas the other is merely incidental, that measure must be founded on a single legal basis, namely that required by the main or predominant purpose or component.[13]

Following these principles, the CJEU had to examine in detail the objectives and content of the amending (and also the original) directive to decide whether its legal basis was chosen correctly. Such an assessment is all the more important as the possible inconsistency of the posting directive's content and its legal basis

9 Judgment of 8 December 2020, *Case C-620/18, Hungary v European Parliament and Council*, ECLI:EU:C:2020:1001; Judgment of 8 December 2020, *Case C-626/18, Poland v European Parliament and Council*, ECLI:EU:C:2020:1000.

10 Articles 53(1) and 62 TFEU.

11 Article 153(2)(b) TFEU.

12 *Case C-620/18, Hungary*, paras. 28-36; *Case C-626/18, Poland*, paras. 39-40.

13 *Case C-620/18, Hungary*, paras. 38-40; *Case C-626/18, Poland*, paras. 43-44.

doi: 10.5553/HYIEL/266627012021009001013

has been widely debated since its adoption.[14] The development of postings in EU legislation can be described as an ever-changing relationship between the principles of freedom to provide services and of the protection of workers. Therefore, before we turn to the CJEU's assessment of the choice of legal basis, it is worth revisiting how the relationship between these aims evolved and changed over time in the context of the posting of workers.

2.1. 30 Years of Posting in EU Law

As a starting point, posting is indeed closely linked to the freedom to provide cross-border services.[15] This basic economic freedom enables employers to export their home labor standards with their posted workers to host countries. Since lower labor law standards mean lower costs,[16] the posting scenario is a real battlefield of interests of the players' involved.

While the legal background of employment may vary in each Member State, such differences cannot hamper the freedom to provide cross-border services without proper justification, in particular, when such restrictions are discriminatory or not justified by overriding requirements relating to the public interest.[17] However, there were major turns in how EU law addressed posting cases over the last nearly 30 years.

In 1990 the ECJ found no unjustified restriction in the extension of host state labor standards to workers who were posted to their territory in the framework of cross-border service provision. Instead, the famous *Rush Portuguesa* judgment gave the broadest possible authorization for Member States to extend their labor law legislation to posted workers. According to the frequently quoted paragraph of the judgment,

> "Community law does not preclude Member States from extending their legislation, or collective labor agreements entered into by both sides of industry, to any person who is employed, even temporarily, within their territory, no matter in which country the employer is established; nor does

14 *See e.g.* Marco Biagi, 'The 'Posted Workers' EU Directive: From Social Dumping to Social Protectionism', *in* Roger Blanpain (ed.), *Labour Law and Industrial Relations in the European Union*, Kluwer Law International, Hague, 1998, pp. 174-175; Paul Davies, 'Posted Workers: Single Market or Protection of National Labour Law Systems?', *Common Market Law Review*, Vol. 34, Issue 3, 1997, p. 572; Zoltán Bankó, 'Az atipikus foglalkoztatási formákra vonatkozó rendelkezések', *in* György Kiss (ed.), *Az Európai Unió munkajoga*, Osiris, Budapest, 2001, p. 452; Mijke Houwerzijl, 'Towards a More Effective Posting Directive', *in* Roger Blanpain (ed.), *Freedom of Services in the European Union. Labour and Social Security Law: The Bolkestein Initiative*, Kluwer Law International, 2006, pp. 185 and 195; Karl Riesenhuber, *European Employment Law*, Intersentia, Cambridge, 2012, p. 198.

15 Article 56 TFEU.

16 As an illustration, *see e.g.* Eurofound's report on minimum wages in the Member States, ranging from €312/month (Bulgaria) to €2,142/month (Luxemburg). Eurofound, *Minimum Wages in 2020: Annual Review, Minimum Wages in the EU Series*, Publications Office of the European Union, Luxembourg, 2020.

17 Frank Hendrickx, 'The Services Directive and Social Dumping: National Labour Law Under Strain?', *in* Ulla Neergaard *et al.* (eds.), *The Services Directive – Consequences for the Welfare State and the European Social Model*, Djoef Publishing, Copenhagen, 2008, p. 244.

doi: 10.5553/HYIEL/266627012021009001013

> Community law prohibit Member States from enforcing those rules by appropriate means."[18]

30 years on, *it is still a mystery how the CJEU reached this conclusion*. The ruling itself includes no hints as to the basis of this axiom,[19] yet it served as the basis for dealing with posting cases until 1999, the year of the entry into force of the posting directive. Nonetheless, *Rush Portuguesa* could not erase the principles enshrined in primary law (in particular, the prohibition of discrimination and unjustified restrictions), hence, the extension of host state's labor regulation to posted workers was far from unlimited. Moreover, after *Rush Portuguesa* the CJEU seemed to take a step back from its overly 'protective' approach and elaborated a detailed test on the basis of the laconic rules in primary law. The CJEU ruled that even if the application of a given labor law rule to posted workers was not discriminatory and served overriding requirements relating to the public interest (*e.g.* the protection of workers), the measure (*e.g.* the application of host state minimum wage laws) could nevertheless be held an unjustified restriction if it was not objectively necessary or in case it exceeded what was necessary to attain its objectives.[20]

Self-evidently, *Rush Portuguesa divided the Member States*: while some host states adopted their own national legislation defining the rules applicable to posted workers,[21] others (in particular, home States) wanted to revisit the issue and called for the adoption of a new directive.[22] The posting directive was finally enacted after five years of negotiations in 1996. The final text clearly attests that its adoption could not have been possible without a compromise. While Article 3(1) lists all the labor standards that host states shall apply to posted

18 Judgment of 27 March 1990, *Case C-113/89, Rush Portuguesa*, ECLI:EU:C:1990:142, para. 18.

19 Davies 1997, pp. 588-589; Gregor Thüsing, *European Labour Law*, Beck, 2013, p. 161. Sypris found two possible explanations for the Rush Portuguesa axiom: the CJEU considered labor law rules as justified constraints on the freedom to provide services, or it found that such rules are not constraints at all, *e.g.* collective bargaining agreements are exempted from the scope of competition law. Phil Syrpis, *EU Intervention in Domestic Labour Law*, Oxford University Press, Oxford, 2007, pp. 109-110.

20 Paul Davies, 'The Posted Workers Directive and the EC Treaty', *Industrial Law Journal*, Vol. 31. Issue 3, 2002. *See* especially the following cases: Judgment of 25 October 2001, *Case C-49/98, Finalarte*, ECLI:EU:C:2001:564; Judgment of 15 March 2001, *Case C-165/98, Mazzoleni and ISA*, ECLI:EU:C:2001:162; Judgment of 23 November 1999, *Case C-369/96, Arblade*, ECLI:EU:C:1999:575; Judgment of 21 October 2004, *Case C-445/03, Commission v Luxembourg*, ECLI:EU:C:2004:655; Judgment of 19 January 2006, *Case C-244/04, Commission v Germany*, ECLI:EU:C:2006:49.

21 Austria, France and Germany, *see* COM(2003) 458, 7.

22 *See* the Commission's proposal [COM(1991) 230] and its amended version [COM(93) 225]. *See also* Emmanuel Comte, 'Promising More to Give Less: International Disputes Between Core and Periphery around European Posted Labor, 1955-2018', *Labor History*, 2019/2, p. 6.

doi: 10.5553/HYIEL/266627012021009001013

workers, owing to two important derogations it is not an exhaustive list.[23] *(i)* According to the first, Article 3(1-6) shall not prevent the application of terms and conditions of employment which are more favorable to workers.[24] *(ii)* Secondly, Member States may also apply rules concerning other matters than those listed in Article 3(1) (*e.g.* further elements of pay), with reference to public policy, in compliance with the Treaty.[25] As a result, the main question in harmonizing the directive was not which labor standards Member States are obliged to apply to posted workers, but which they are permitted to apply.[26]

However, from 2007 on the Member States' seemingly broad discretion to extend the scope of their applicable labor standards was restricted by the CJEU. In its new line of cases, starting with the famous *Laval* judgment,[27] the CJEU closed all the avenues leading to a more protectionist reading of the directive. As for the first derogation, the CJEU, on the basis of the directive's aim, made it clear that Article 3(7) refers to the home state's law when it permits the application of terms and conditions that are "more favorable to workers". Hence, there is no automatic obligation to apply host state standards solely on the ground that those are more favorable to the employee than the home state standards.[28]

Turning to the second option, the CJEU already ruled before the directive's entry into force that the term public order legislation must be understood as

> "so crucial for the protection of the political, social or economic order in the Member State concerned as to require compliance therewith by all persons present on the national territory of that Member State and all legal relationships within that State."[29]

Later the CJEU added that the *public policy exception is a derogation* from the fundamental principle of freedom to provide services which must be interpreted strictly, and it "may be relied on only if there is a genuine and sufficiently serious

23 Other derogations limit the applicable host state standards, as they enable or oblige Member States to refrain from applying some of their labor standards (minimum paid annual holidays and/or the minimum rates of pay) in certain cases [posting directive, Article 3(2-5)]. Obviously, these rules are less important to Member States, than those which extend the list of applicable rules.

24 Posting directive, Article 3(7).

25 Posting directive, Article 3(10).

26 Eeva Kolehmainen, 'The Directive Concerning the Posting of Workers: Synchronization of the Functions of National Legal Systems', *Comparative Labor Law & Policy Journal*, Vol. 20, Issue 1, 1998, p. 86.

27 Judgment of 18 December 2007, *Case C-341/05, Laval un Partneri*, ECLI:EU:C:2007:809; Judgment of 3 April 2008, *Case C-346/06, Rüffert*, ECLI:EU:C:2008:189; Judgment of 19 June 2008, *Case C-319/06, Commission v Luxembourg*, ECLI:EU:C:2008:350.

28 *Case C-341/05, Laval*, paras. 80-81. Note that the text itself could have been easily interpreted also the other way round. Nonetheless, employers may voluntarily commit themselves to observe those stricter rules in the host state. *See* Claire Kilpatrick, 'Internal Market Architecture and the Accommodation of Labour Rights: As Good as it Gets?', *in* Phil Syrpis (ed.), *The Judiciary, the Legislature and the EU Internal Market*, Cambridge University Press, Cambridge, 2012, p. 233.

29 *Case C-369/96, Arblade*, paras. 30–31.

doi: 10.5553/HYIEL/266627012021009001013

threat to a fundamental interest of society."[30] On these grounds the CJEU ruled that the list in Article 3(1) is not a minimum, but a maximum list: it sets out "an exhaustive list of the matters in respect of which the Member States may give priority to the rules in force in the host Member State".[31] Any other matter may be covered by the host state's law only in case it falls under the strictly interpreted public policy derogation. *Laval* demonstrated that not even the right to bargain collectively or the right to strike would suffice for the use of the public policy clause.[32] *Laval* undoubtedly *reflected a conceptual change* in accepting labor law as a constraint on the freedom to provide services. Seventeen years after *Rush Portuguesa*, the CJEU could not have moved any further from its earlier case-law: the first approach, which took it as evident that host states may apply their own labor law to posted workers, was substituted with the idea of giving priority to the freedom to provide services.[33]

The legislative steps taken after 2008 made only minor adjustments to the *status quo* reached after *Laval*. *(i)* First, instead of effecting a substantive review, the Commission only developed a proposal to facilitate practical implementation, leading to the adoption of the enforcement directive in 2014.[34] However, with these rather detailed rules, neither the Commission nor the Member States took on too much risk, as the enforcement directive does not go beyond codifying the case-law of the CJEU or explaining the obligations already contained in the posting directive. Given the many problems left open beyond these practical issues, it seems that the Member States and EU institutions had wanted to send a political message through the adoption of the enforcement directive (demonstrating that 'something is happening'), rather than focus on its normative content.[35] *(ii)* Second, the Commission's 2016 proposal for a comprehensive review of the posting directive promised substantial progress.[36] Following lengthy debates, by the summer of 2018, 18 and half years after the entry into force of the original directive, the posting directive had finally been recast. However, as appears from the judgments in the annulment cases, the

30 *Case C-319/06, Commission vs. Luxembourg*, paras. 29-33 and 50.

31 Id. para. 26.

32 Catherine Barnard, *EU Employment Law, Fourth Edition*, Oxford University Press, Oxford, 2012, p. 232.

33 Thüsing 2013, p. 158; Kilpatrick 2012, pp. 212-213; Riesenhuber 2012, p. 206; Femke Laagland, 'Member States' Sovereignty in the Socio-Economic Field: Fact or Fiction? The Clash Between the European Business Freedoms and the National Level of Workers' Protection', *European Labour Law Journal*, 2018/1, p. 59.

34 Directive 2014/67/EU of the European Parliament and of the Council of 15 May 2014 on the enforcement of Directive 96/71/EC concerning the posting of workers in the framework of the provision of services and amending Regulation (EU) No 1024/2012 on administrative cooperation through the Internal Market Information System (the IMI Regulation).

35 At the same time, the enforcement directive, by summarizing the case-law, makes it explicitly mandatory in some places to apply certain measures, which were left to the discretion of the Member States before (*e.g.* liability in subcontracting, Article 12). To that extent, therefore, restrictions on posting companies have been tightened.

36 COM(2016) 128 final.

doi: 10.5553/HYIEL/266627012021009001013

fundamental rationale behind posting remains unchanged and some major problems in the law remain unsolved.

Following three major changes in the legal framework relating to posted workers (that is *Rush Portuguesa*, the adoption of the original directive and *Laval*), the relationship (or rather, hierarchy) of the freedom to prove services and the application of host state labor standards is still debated.[37] It seems to be an ever-topical question: which shall take precedent over the other and under what conditions. Naturally, the approach EU law to this issue has always been the result of an actual compromise. The new milestones in this debate are the adoption of the amending directive (which enforces the protection of workers) and the CJEU's decisions in the annulment proceedings confirming that such legislative intervention is not contrary to the freedom to provide services.

2.2. A Free Movement Directive to Protect Workers?

As a starting point of its reasoning, the CJEU emphasized that the EU legislature, when adopting measures to coordinate national rules (which, by reason of their heterogeneity, impede the freedom to provide services between Member States), is also bound to ensure respect for the general interest, pursued by the various Member States, as well as the overarching objectives of the EU, including the requirements pertaining to the promotion of a high level of employment and the guarantee of adequate social protection.[38] Consequently, EU coordination measures must not only have the objective of facilitating the exercise of the freedom to provide services, but also of ensuring, when necessary, the protection of other fundamental interests that may be affected by that freedom.[39] In the case of posting, the directive's aim is not only to guarantee the right to all undertakings to supply transnational services within the internal market by posting workers, but also to protect the rights of those workers. In the CJEU' view, the EU legislature's aim has been to find a fair balance between these concurring interests.[40] As for the content of the new measure, following the aforementioned aims, it offers greater protection for workers than those provided for by the original directive.[41] Namely, the directive aims to ensure that fair competition should not be based on the application, in one and the same Member State, of different terms and conditions of employment, depending on whether or not the employer is established in that Member State.[42]

Undoubtedly, the history of posting in EU law, as detailed above, shows a continuously shifting balance between the economic and social interests involved.

37 *See also* the abandoned Monti II proposal, which would have declared that the exercise of the freedom of establishment and the freedom to provide services on the one hand, and the fundamental right to take collective action, including the right or freedom to strike, on the other, shall mutually respect each other. COM(2012) 130 final, Article 2.

38 Article 9 TFEU.

39 *Case C-620/18, Hungary*, paras. 41-48; *Case C-626/18, Poland*, paras. 51-53.

40 *Case C-620/18, Hungary*, paras. 50-51; *Case C-626/18, Poland*, paras. 55-56; amending directive, Recital 10.

41 *Case C-620/18, Hungary*, para. 57; *Case C-626/18, Poland*, para. 62.

42 *Case C-620/18, Hungary*, para. 60; *Case C-626/18, Poland*, para. 65.

Hungarian Yearbook of International Law and European Law 2021 (9) 1
doi: 10.5553/HYIEL/266627012021009001013

Following the protective approach introduced by the CJEU in *Rush Portuguesa*, legislative intervention pushed for a more liberal regime, where not all labor law provisions could be applied to posted workers. Later, the CJEU's practice changed significantly in favor of the freedom to provide services as opposed to the social aims of the directive (*Laval*). With the amending directive, the legislator stepped in yet again but this time to put more emphasis on the protection of posted workers.[43] Now the CJEU confirmed that while the posting directive and its amendment *mainly target the freedom to provide services*, the legislator could put more emphasis on the social aspect of the posting phenomenon without changing the measure's original legal basis.

However, while the CJEU concluded from the 'context and the aim' of the directive that the legislator was striving for the right balance between the freedom to provide services and the protection of workers, it seems more logical that the real clash of interests lies between the economic interests of home and host states. The EU measures' main aim is rather to reconcile home state undertakings' freedom to provide cross-border services with their counterparts' right in the host states for a fair competition. Taking the perspective of the host states, it is not convincing that their main concern in posting would be to protect the rights of posted workers. As Davies pointed out, the protection of posted workers lies much more in the interest of the home state.[44] Apparently, the CJEU's 'posting practice' spanning thirty years suggests that the legal debates surrounding posting are much more about the Member States' economic interests. It is quite revealing that there is only one case in which a posted worker or his trade union instituted proceedings to protect his rights, demanding that his employer provide him working condition on par with the more favorable law of the host state.[45] Instead, the general starting point of the cases is either a dispute between the posting employer and the recipient of the service, or an action by the authorities of the host state against the posting employer for non-compliance with the host state's administrative provisions or labor standards.

The Advocate General's opinion clearly indicates that the dilemma behind the posting rules is rather a trilemma. Advocate General Campos Sánchez-Bordona argued that the proper balance between the interests of undertakings providing services and the social protection of posted workers must also ensure fair competition between undertakings which had posted the workers, and those established in the Member State of destination.[46] The opinions consistently refer also to this third aim (fair competition between foreign and local competitors) besides the promotion of cross-border provision of services and the protection of

43 Piet Van Nuffel & Sofia Afanasjeva, 'The Posting Workers Directive Revised: Enhancing the Protection of Workers in the Cross-Border Provision of Services', *European Papers*, 2018/3, p. 1405.

44 Davies 2002, p. 302.

45 Judgment of 12 February 2015, *Case C-396/13, Sähköalojen ammattiliitto*, ECLI:EU:C:2015:86.

46 Opinion of Advocate General Campos Sánchez-Bordona delivered on 28 May 2020, *Case C-620/18, Hungary*, paras. 62-63.

doi: 10.5553/HYIEL/266627012021009001013

posted workers.[47] Instead, the CJEU built its reasoning on the dual aim of the directive and on Recital 10 of the amending directive, stating that "ensuring greater protection for workers is necessary to safeguard the freedom to provide, in both the short and the long-term, services on a fair basis".[48] Fair competition appears to be not the consequence but the main idea in the reconciliation of the directive's economic and social aim. Rather, the protection of workers is a side effect of harmonizing the home and host states' economic interests.

Although the judgments confirm that the EU measures adopted to enhance the freedom to provide services must also respect the protection of other affected fundamental interests, such as the protection of workers, it should be pointed out that the new judgments did not change the CJEU's earlier case-law on that matter. The substance of *Laval* remained untouched: the host state's labor standards applicable to posted workers are exhaustively listed in the (amended) posting directive, but this list cannot be broadened in the discretion of the Member States. Instead, it is solely the EU legislator who can offer additional protection to posted workers by adding new elements to this list without restricting unlawfully the freedom to provide services (see also the next Section).[49]

While the above considerations form the backbone of the CJEU's reasoning, it is further enhanced by two additional elements. *(i)* First, *the internal market has significantly changed since the entry into force of the posting directive*, not least due to the successive enlargements of the EU. The CJEU therefore concluded that the EU legislature could take the view that it was necessary to adjust the balance at the heart of the posting directive by strengthening the rights of posted workers in the host state in order to develop a more level playing field for posting undertakings and their counterparts in the host state.[50] *(ii)* Second, the CJEU pointed out that *Article 153 TFEU could not have been the correct legal basis for the directive, for formal reasons*. This Article contains two legal bases for the adoption of measures designed to encourage cooperation between the Member States in social matters and for the adoption of harmonization measures in certain fields falling within the scope of Union social policy Yet neither of these corresponds with the objective to establish the freedom to provide services on a fair basis, and

47 Id. paras. 69 and 108; Opinion of Advocate General Campos Sánchez-Bordona delivered on 28 May 2020, *Case C-626/18, Poland*, para. 72.

48 *Case C-620/18, Hungary*, paras. 51, 107, 122, and 126; *Case C-626/18, Poland*, paras. 56, 90, 104, and 122.

49 The Hungarian action superficially mentioned the problem of posting and fundamental collective labor rights. According to the claim, the directive "excludes the exercise of the freedom to provide services" in connection with the right to strike and the right to bargain collectively. Given that the amending directive does not add any new element to the relationship between economic and collective labor rights, this claim seems to be a misinterpretation of the measure. Not to mention that since *Laval*, economic freedoms have clearly taken precedence over collective labor rights. Therefore, the CJEU briefly confirmed that the exercise of collective labor rights is subject to EU law and the freedom to provide services and rejected this claim. *See Case C-620/18, Hungary*, para. 168.

50 Id. paras. 62 and 64; *Case C-626/18, Poland*, paras. 67 and 69.

doi: 10.5553/HYIEL/266627012021009001013

clearly, the posting directive does not harmonize working conditions.[51] Based on all these considerations, *the CJEU rejected the claim on the incorrect choice of the legal basis*.[52]

Nonetheless, the judgments remain silent on the practical rationale behind the choice of legal basis in 1996. Accordingly, the Council could adopt the directive in co-decision with the Parliament by qualified majority, whereas had it been adopted on the basis of the social chapter, it would have had to act unanimously. It would have been even less feasible to base it on the Social Policy Agreement annexed to TEU, since the acts adopted based on that document did not bind the UK.[53] One may wonder how different the history of posting in EU law would have been if primary law had set the necessary voting rules for adopting measures in these two different fields exactly the other way round.[54]

3. Unlawful Restrictions on the Freedom to Provide Services?

Hungary and Poland argue that the amending directive amounts to an unlawful restriction of the freedom to provide services. More specifically, three provisions stand in the center of the debate. *(i)* First, the amending directive substitutes the term "minimum rates of pay" by "remuneration" and consequently renders all mandatory pay elements in the host state applicable to posted workers. *(ii)* Second, the host state's standards on allowances or reimbursement of expenditure to cover travel, board and lodging expenses for workers away from home for professional reasons shall also apply to posted workers. *(iii)* Third, where postings exceeds 12 months, the posted worker becomes subject to all of the host state's working standards, with some exceptions mentioned in the directive.[55] The claims allege that these new rules are contrary to the freedom to provide services as prescribed by Article 56 TFEU, since they are discriminatory, cannot be justified by overriding reasons in the general interest and constitute an unnecessary and disproportionate restriction.[56] The applicants' reasoning is

51 *Case C-620/18, Hungary*, paras. 66-69.

52 Consequently, the claim that the EU legislature misused its powers by choosing an inappropriate legal basis, was also rejected. Id. para. 84.

53 Davies 1997, p. 572.

54 There is one more dispute around the legal basis of the amending directive. Both actions challenged that the scope of the amending directive extend to the road transport sector once the specific sectoral rules are adopted [amending directive, Article 3(3)]. The claim is based on the fact that the legal basis for the adoption of the amending directive is the free movement of services, while services in the field of transport are covered by a separate legal basis [Articles 58(1) and 91 TFEU]. Previously, in *Dobersberger*, the CJEU did not dispute this argument, but pointed out that services, which are not inherently linked to transport (such as rail catering) can be regulated under the articles on services. *See* Judgment of 19 December 2019, *Case C-16/18, Dobersberger*, ECLI:EU:C:2019:1110, paras. 24-27. Nonetheless, the CJEU could easily overcome the problem by holding that the contested article does not seek to regulate the freedom to provide services in the field of transport, since it is confined to providing a date of application to the sector. *See Case C-620/18, Hungary*, paras. 161-162; *Case C-626/18, Poland*, paras. 146-147.

55 Posting directive as amended Article 3(1)(c) and (i); Article 3(1a).

56 *Case C-620/18, Hungary*, paras. 66-102; *Case C-626/18, Poland*, paras. 72-85.

doi: 10.5553/HYIEL/266627012021009001013

based on the consideration that the protection of posted workers' rights is sufficiently guaranteed by the legislation of the home state, considering that such workers only stay temporarily in the host state. Besides, the amending directive eliminates the lawful competitive advantage of those states in which the level of pay is lower, thus, the new measure distorts competition.

Even if the CJEU stated that the amending (and the original) directive (with the main aim of promoting the freedom to provide services) shall respect fundamental interests such as the protection of workers, it is still questionable how far the directive can go in pursuing such a secondary aim, while still respecting the freedom to provide services. This issue is well known in literature,[57] since the posting directive directly restricts this freedom for the sake of enforcing core labor standards. As a labor law measure, its importance can be highlighted through an overview of the CJEU's case-law concerning the labor law rules as justified restrictions on the freedom to provide services. The least one can say is that all labor rights listed in Article 3(1) shall be applied to posted workers without further evaluating its possible restrictive effect on cross-border services.[58] The CJEU's practice on the application of host minimum wage legislation to posted workers clearly illustrates how the posting directive restricts the freedom to provide services.

Before the posting directive entered into force, in *Mazzoleni*, the CJEU had to decide upon the applicability of the Belgian minimum wage to French posted workers. The Belgian minimum wage was higher than the French, but taken into account also common charges, the French law was more favorable for workers. The CJEU ruled that for the purpose of determining whether the application of the minimum wage rules of the host state is a necessary and proportionate restriction, all relevant factors shall be evaluated, including the level of social security contributions and the impact of taxation.[59] Similarly, in *Portugaia Construções*, the CJEU held that host states may impose their minimum wage legislation to posted workers only if such rules confer a genuine benefit on the workers concerned, significantly increasing their social protection.[60] As such, before the posting directive's entry into force, the CJEU set detailed conditions for the application of host state minimum wage to posted workers. By comparison, according to the original posting directive, minimum rates of pay in the host state applied to posted workers without further conditions.[61] Seen from this perspective, it indeed seems controversial that the directive's legal basis is

57 *See e.g.* the sources referred concerning the debate on the legal base.

58 Barnard 2012, p. 228; Syrpis 2007, p. 124.

59 *Case C-165/98, Mazzoleni*, paras. 36-39.

60 Judgment of 24 January 2002, *Case C-164/99, Portugaia Construções*, ECLI:EU:C:2002:40, paras. 26 and 29.

61 One might agree with Riesenhuber who argues that the most important rule of the directive is the one which makes host state minimum wage applicable to posted workers. Riesenhuber 2012, p. 205.

doi: 10.5553/HYIEL/266627012021009001013

the promotion of the freedom to provide services.[62] As seen above, the CJEU solved this contradiction by stating that while the posting directive provides guarantees for an overarching objective such as the protection of workers, it shall nevertheless be considered a measure to enhance the provision of cross-border services. The annulment cases also revealed that the measures introduced by the amending directive lawfully restrict this basic economic freedom, for the following reasons.

As a starting point, as the Advocate General reminded in his opinion, the case-law of the CJEU on national measures restricting the free provision of transnational services cannot readily be applied to EU measures which are aimed at harmonizing the same. Instead, according to relevant court practice, the EU legislature enjoys a broad discretion in complex areas such as the regulation of the transnational posting of workers. What must be established for annulment is that the legislature made use of that discretion in a way that was manifestly inappropriate when it adjusted the balance of interests struck in the posting directive.[63]

Taking the EU legislature's broad discretion as a starting point, the CJEU built its reasoning around the fact that the amending directive does not eliminate all competition based on costs (not even in the case of long-term postings) therefore, there is still room for competition between undertakings seated in the different Member States.

As the CJEU pointed out, the directive provides that posted workers are entitled to a set of terms and conditions of employment in the host Member State, including the constituent elements of remuneration rendered mandatory in that Member State. Thus, the directive has no effect on other cost components of the undertakings posting the workers, such as the productivity or efficiency of those workers, which are expressly mentioned in Recital 16.[64] The only cost differences that are eliminated by the directive are those listed among the 'hard core' standards in Article 3(1).[65]

The CJEU also emphasized that while the amending directive broadened the list of applicable working conditions of the host State's law (as regards all mandatory pay elements and reimbursement of costs), this still does not entail the application of all the terms and conditions of employment of the host State.[66] *The situation of posted and local workers has not become identical or analogous*.[67] The CJEU found that the posted workers' stay in the host state is temporary and that they are not integrated into the labor market of that state. Consequently, the EU legislature could reasonably consider it appropriate that, for that temporary

62 Jonas Malmberg, 'Posting Post Laval. Nordic Responses', *in* Marie-Ange Moreau (ed.), *Before and After the Economic Crisis. What Implications for the 'European Social Model?*, Edward Elgar Publishing, Cheltenham, 2011, p. 36; Kilpatrick 2012, p. 232.

63 AG Opinion, *Case C-620/18, Hungary*, paras. 107-110. *See also* in *Case C-620/18, Hungary*, para. 112; *Case C-626/18, Poland*, para. 95.

64 *Case C-620/18, Hungary*, para. 128; *Case C-626/18, Poland*, para. 106.

65 *Case C-620/18, Hungary*, para. 141.

66 Id. paras. 148-149.

67 *Case C-626/18, Poland*, para. 111.

doi: 10.5553/HYIEL/266627012021009001013

period, the remuneration to be received by those workers should be the remuneration determined by the mandatory legal provisions of the host Member State, to enable them to meet the cost of living in that Member State.[68] The directive does not proscribe any competition based on costs nor does it declare that competition based on cost differences is unfair.[69]

The CJEU also rejected the claim that the amending directive's provision applying the host State's law almost in its entirety in case of long-term postings is neither necessary nor proportionate. The CJEU referred back to the broad discretion enjoyed by the EU legislature and concluded that no manifest error was committed in taking the view that the consequence of such a long-term posting should be that the personal situation of posted workers should, to an appreciable degree, more closely resemble that of workers employed by undertakings established in the host state. Nonetheless, such rules still distinguish the situation of posted workers from that of workers who have exercised their right to freedom of movement or, more generally, that of workers who reside in that Member State and are employed by undertakings established there.[70]

Undoubtedly, the above reasoning duly reflects the fair compromise struck in the (amended) posting directive, seen from the perspective of the undertakings in the host and the home states. Indeed, the possible advantage of foreign service providers in the host state's market is not limited to cheaper labor: they may also compete with higher productivity or with better trained and more experienced staff. Besides, as pointed out by the Advocate General, the differences in matters of *e.g.* social security and taxation remain in place and, as a general rule, are governed by the laws of the home state.[71] Moreover, an important difference still remains between the legal status of posted and local workers which is (interestingly) not mentioned in the judgments: posted workers do not fall under the scope of the host state's selectively applicable collective agreements, not even in the case of long-term postings.[72] Thus, if the most important pay elements are defined by local or branch level collective agreements, EU law does not close the pay gap between the posted and local workforce. Meanwhile, it was cases involving selectively applicable collective agreements that have been the ones which caused the most tension in the application of the posting directive.[73]

From a labor law point of view, probably the most interesting element in the above reasoning is that the CJEU and also the Advocate General argued that the amending directive constitutes a proportionate restriction on the freedom to

68 Id. paras. 117-118. Poland and Hungary also challenged the new rules on the adding together of different workers' posting periods as regards the calculation of the 12-month time frame. The CJEU however confirmed that this rule is a clear and precise measure to prevent circumventions. *See Case C-620/18, Hungary*, para. 181; and *Case C-626/18, Poland*, paras. 137-138.

69 *Case C-626/18, Poland*, paras. 120-121.

70 *Case C-620/18, Hungary*, paras. 155-156; *Case C-626/18, Poland*, para. 125. As the Advocate General put it, "That provision brings the rules applicable to workers on long-term postings closer to those applicable to local workers, but it does not place those workers on an equal footing because their situations are different." AG Opinion, *Case C-620/18, Hungary*, para. 140.

71 Id. para. 165; AG Opinion, *Case C-626/18, Poland*, paras. 45, 68, 70, and 79.

72 Posting directive as amended Article 3(8).

73 *Case C-341/05, Laval; Case C-346/06, Rüffert.*

doi: 10.5553/HYIEL/266627012021009001013

provide services because the legal status of posted workers remains different from that of the workers employed directly by undertakings in the host state. Nonetheless, one might wonder what rationale lies behind this distinction. The only specific element which could underpin the difference between the legal status of a worker enjoying the right of free movement and a posted worker is that the latter is not subject to the principle of free movement of workers but to the freedom to provide services.[74] Consequently, even in the case of long-term postings, posted workers may lack the legal protection afforded to local workers in the host state, while a worker making use of the right of free movement enjoys the same protection as locals, regardless of the length of the employment.[75] Equal treatment is the fundament of free movement of workers, without this overriding principle this basic freedom would be inoperable in practice.[76] Meanwhile, it is entirely possible that the manner in which a posted worker performs is the same as that of a worker relying on the right of free movement (*e.g.* both of them spend only two months in the host state for a seasonal job). Therefore, the distinction between these groups seems rather formal.

The explanation for such an unconvincing demarcation is that posting is not, in principle, a legal institution based on the legal protection of the worker, but on the freedom to provide services. Apparently, the specific legal situation of the posted worker is nothing more than a compromise between the principle of freedom to provide services and the protectionist ambitions of the host states. The limited applicability of host state law can be well explained by the fact that it partially preserves the competitive advantage of service providers from the home state, while at the same time, providing adequate protection for the market of the host state. The fact that this logic is contradictory from the viewpoint of the worker's legal status seems to be a secondary issue. It is therefore not an exaggeration to say that posting is a legitimate means of discrimination, as it distinguishes between different groups of workers solely for economic reasons.[77]

This is clear, when posting is analyzed not in the light of EU law based on fundamental economic freedoms, but from the aspect of a human rights convention, namely the European Social Charter (ESC). Article 19 ESC provides, *inter alia*, that migrant workers lawfully residing within the Contracting Parties' territories, shall enjoy treatment not less favorable than that of the own nationals of the Contracting Parties in respect of remuneration and other employment and working conditions, membership of trade unions and enjoyment of the benefits of collective bargaining and accommodation. In the Swedish *lex-Laval* case, the

74 *Case C-49/98, Finalarte*, paras. 19-23. This idea was also referred by Advocate General Campos Sánchez-Bordona, *see* the Opinions in *Case C-620/18, Hungary*, para. 164. and *Case C-626/18, Poland*, para. 78

75 Regulation 492/2011/EU of the European Parliament and of the Council of 5 April 2011 on freedom of movement for workers within the Union.

76 Nicola Countouris & Samiel Engblom, 'Protection or Protectionism? A Legal Deconstruction of the Emerging False Dilemma in European Integration', *European Labour Law Journal*, 2015/1, pp. 21-23.

77 Erika Kovács *et al.*, 'Posting of Workers in Croatia and Hungary', *in* Tímea Drinóczi & Mirela Župan (eds.), *Law – Regions – Development*, Pécs-Osijek, 2013, pp. 475-476, and 495.

doi: 10.5553/HYIEL/266627012021009001013

European Committee of Social Rights (ECSR) pointed out that the right to equal treatment of migrant workers shall also apply to posted workers. Although the ECSR acknowledged that there are differences between posted workers and other categories of migrant workers (in terms of length and stability of presence in the territory of the host state, as well as of their relationship with that state), posted workers are workers coming from another state, residing lawfully within the territory of the host state. In this sense, they fall within the scope of application of Article 19 ESC and they have the right, for the period of their stay and work in the host state to receive treatment not less favorable than that of the national workers of the host state in respect of labor standards mentioned in the ESC.[78] From a fundamental rights point of view, therefore, the distinction between a posted worker and a worker making use of the right of free movement has proved to be unfounded.

The amending directive is an important step forward in resolving the problematic distinction between the different types of cross-border working patterns by narrowing the gap between the status of posted (especially long-term posted) and local workers. The remaining differences could well explain that EU measures on posting are not contrary to the freedom to provide services, yet are quite controversial from the perspective of the posted worker. Although the ESC calls for full equality between posted and local workers, under EU law their terms and conditions of employment are only "as close as possible", and the personal situation of posted workers should only to "an appreciable degree more closely resemble" that of local or migrant workers.[79]

4. Other Important Lessons Learnt and Questions Left Open

While it is the amending directive's legal basis and its relationship to the principle of freedom to provide transnational services that lie at the heart of the annulment cases, the applicants also raised some other interesting questions. The CJEU could easily reject these claims, nonetheless they address important issues, which are therefore worth a brief analysis.

4.1. Posting and Private International Law

According to both actions, the amending directive is contrary to the Rome I Regulation,[80] as in case of long-term postings the application of obligations imposed by the legislation of the host Member State is mandatory, irrespective of which law applies to the employment relationship. This claim seems unfounded, as the Rome I Regulation explicitly allows for special rules.[81] Nonetheless, the

78 *No. 85/2012. Swedish Trade Union Confederation (LO) and Swedish Confederation of Professional Employees (TCO) v Sweden*, para. 134.

79 *Case C-620/18, Hungary*, paras. 57 and 155; *Case C-626/18, Poland*, paras. 62 and 110.

80 Regulation 593/2008/EC of the European Parliament and of the Council of 17 June 2008 on the law applicable to contractual obligations (Rome I Regulation).

81 Rome I Regulation, Articles 23 and 9; *Case C-620/18, Hungary*, para. 179; *Case C-626/18, Poland*, paras. 133 and 135.

Hungarian Yearbook of International Law and European Law 2021 (9) 1
doi: 10.5553/HYIEL/266627012021009001013

posting directive (and its amendment) does not entirely coherently fit in the private international law system of the EU and such inconsistencies seem to prevail even after the judgments rendered in the annulment cases.

Under private international law, *the essence of posting is that the worker is temporarily working outside the state where they regularly work.* Thus, the concept has two essential elements: *(i)* first, the place of work differs from where the employee works regularly; and *(ii)* second, working abroad is only temporary. Unlike under the scope of the posting directive, it is not necessary that the posting take place within the framework of transnational services. For example, when the employee attends a two-week long training at the premises of the foreign parent company, travels to another Member State for an international meeting or provides services which by their nature must be performed abroad (*e.g.* tour guide). EU law stipulates that the state where the work is habitually carried out shall not be deemed to have changed if the employee is temporarily working in another state.[82] Temporary work abroad therefore does not change the applicable law to the employment relationship, and the employment remains under the law of the home state (the law of the state where the regular employment takes place). At the same time, the posted worker may also be subject to the so-called imperative rules, which, because of their importance, are crucial for safeguarding the public interests in the host state.[83]

The posting directive prescribes that if the aim of the posting is the provision of a transnational service, although the worker remains subject to the employment law of the home state, the host state's law concerning the working conditions explicitly listed in the directive shall apply, if it is more favorable to the worker. The rules listed here will therefore apply to the posted workers as imperative rules. The posting directive could also be understood as a *lex specialis* to the Rome I Regulation, the latter being the *lex generalis*.[84]

However, it is not clear whether all elements of the directive's 'hard core' list shall qualify as imperative rules. Such overriding mandatory provisions shall be applied irrespective of the law otherwise applicable to the employment relationship. Nevertheless, there is no common ground in labor law literature regarding which norms would fall within this category.[85] For instance Riesenhuber suggests that imperative norms are the ones which are also protected by criminal law sanctions or have a public law character.[86] Daubler (before *Laval*) identified collective autonomy and the protection of labor relations

82 Rome I Regulation, Article 8(2). The Rome Convention (1980) on the law applicable to contractual obligations contained the same principle, *see* Article 6(2)(a).

83 Rome I Regulation, Article 9.

84 COM(2002) 654 final; Florian Schierle, '1996/71/EC: Posting of Workers', *in* Monika Schlacter (ed.), *EU Labour Law: A Commentary*, Wolters Kluwer, 2015, pp. 166 and 178; Herwig Verschueren, 'The European Internal Market and the Competition between Workers', *European Labour Law Journal*, 2015/2, p. 140; Taco van Peijpe, 'Collective Labour Law after Viking, Laval, Rüffert, and Commission v. Luxembourg', *International Journal of Comparative Labour Law and Industrial Relations*, Vol. 25, Issue 2, 2009, p. 101.

85 Davies 1997, p. 596.

86 Riesenhuber 2012, pp. 182-183.

doi: 10.5553/HYIEL/266627012021009001013

as imperative norms.[87] Piir mentioned only possible examples, such as the prohibition to dismiss pregnant women or workers' representatives or certain rules on occupational safety and health. Piir also argued that the labor standards listed in the directive do not necessarily qualify as imperative rules.[88] For example, one may wonder why all the rules on occupational safety and health, paid annual leave or technical rules on secondment of labor should have crucial importance for safeguarding public interests in the host state. As for a further contradiction, while an imperative rule must be applied even where the law otherwise applicable is more favorable to the employee, according to the posting directive, the host state's standards do not apply if the home state's law is more favorable.[89]

While the annulment judgments found the relationship between the Rome I Regulation and the posting directive unproblematic, the CJEU gave no real guidance on how to overcome the mentioned discrepancies. The CJEU only confirmed that Article 9 of the Regulation must be interpreted strictly and concluded laconically that "There is nothing in the documents submitted to the Court to indicate that Article 3(1a) of the amended Directive 96/71 is contrary to such overriding mandatory provisions of law".[90] The question, rather, in case of long-term postings is why nearly all labor law provisions qualify as imperative rules.

4.2. The Nature of the Posting Directive

Some of the claims point to the basic features of the posting directive. The Republic of Poland claims that the substitution of the concept of 'remuneration' with that of 'minimum rates of pay' constitutes a discriminatory restriction on freedom to provide services. This is because the latter provision imposes on service providers an additional financial and administrative burden, the effect of which is to remove the competitive advantage of service providers established in Member States with a lower level of remuneration. In addition, Hungary contests the inaccuracy of the concept of remuneration claiming a violation of legal certainty.

These observations touch upon the legislative technique used in the posting directive, usually referred to as *'partial harmonization'*[91] *or 'coordination'*,[92] meaning that it defines only the legal form and subject of the applicable 'core labor standards' but not their exact content. The directive does not harmonize

87 Wolfgang Däubler, 'Posted Workers and Freedom to Supply Services. Directive 96/71/EC and the German Courts', *Industrial Law Journal*, 1998/3, p. 267.
88 Ragne Piir, 'Safeguarding the Posted Worker. A Private International Law Perspective', *European Labour Law Journal*, 2019/2, pp. 111-113.
89 Posting directive, Article 3(7).
90 *Case C-626/18, Poland*, para. 135.
91 Davies 1997, p. 593.
92 Barnard 2012, p. 221.

doi: 10.5553/HYIEL/266627012021009001013

the core rules,[93] thus, the regulatory competence of the Member States remains untouched.[94] However, this also leads to unending debates over how the labor standards listed shall be interpreted in the various Member States. Having the posting directive in force for over twenty years, only a handful of cases reached the CJEU concerning the interpretation of the elements listed in Article 3(1). To be more precise, solely the meaning of the constituent elements of minimum rates of pay was referred to the CJEU.[95]

In the annulment cases, the CJEU pointed out that if service providers are liable to bear an additional financial and administrative burden, that burden is the consequence of the very nature and objectives of the posting directive, since it is an instrument for the coordination of the laws of the Member States governing the terms and conditions of employment. Moreover, even before the amendment, service providers posting workers were subject concurrently to the rules of their home state and of the host state.[96] The term remuneration can only be determined on the basis of the legal system of the host state, but in itself this does not constitute grounds to claim legal uncertainty.[97] This is a direct consequence of the 'partial harmonization' followed by the posting directive, which in turn does not lead to legal uncertainty if Member States duly comply with their obligations to publish adequate information on their applicable labor standards, which obligation is explicitly required by the posting directive.[98]

Nonetheless, employers can hardly comply with the host state's labor standards if there is no easily accessible information provided by that state. For instance, the term 'minimum paid annual holidays' is not a single number, *e.g.* 24 days annually. The measure of paid annual leave in a Member State may be calculated on the basis of complicated rules concerning the employee's personal status (health, childcare, age, profession, *etc.*), the longevity of the employment relationship, the proportion of the time spent in actual employment over the year, each with different rounding rules. Cross border service providers need to be aware of complex regulations to answer such a simple question as to whether the host or the home state's labor law guarantees more paid leave, and which one shall therefore apply to the posted worker.

Hungary also argued that the directive contains a 'rule on remuneration in substance' by requiring workers to be paid in accordance with the measures in force in the host state, while pay is excluded from the legislative competence of

93 Ruth Nielsen, *EU Labour Law, Second Edition*, Djoef Publishing, Copenhagen, 2013, p. 371. *See also* how such consideration appears also in the CJEU's practice: *Case C-396/13, Sähköalojen ammattiliitto*, paras. 31-32.

94 Which was necessary for the adoption of the directive, after long years of debate. Kolehmainen 1998, p. 73.

95 *Case C-396/13, Sähköalojen ammattiliitto*; Judgment of 7 November 2013, *Case C-522/12, Isbir*, ECLI:EU:C:2013:711.

96 *Case C-626/18, Poland*, paras. 101-103, and 126-127.

97 *Case C-620/18, Hungary*, para. 186.

98 Article 3(1) and (4)-(5). The CJEU expressly referred to this obligation when it rejected Poland's claim that the directive's text gives rise to ambiguity on what standards are applicable in case of long-term postings. The CJEU found the prescription to be clear as all labor standards apply which are not expressly excluded by the directive. *Case C-626/18, Poland*, paras. 128-129.

doi: 10.5553/HYIEL/266627012021009001013

the EU.[99] This plea appears to be unfounded in the light of *Alonso* and the aforementioned 'coordination nature' of the posting directive. The CJEU stated in *Alonso*, that the rationale for the exclusion of pay is that the determination of pay levels at national level falls within the discretion of the social partners and within the competence of the Member States. However, the 'pay' exception cannot be extended to all questions involving any sort of link with pay; otherwise some of the areas falling within the scope of legal harmonization would be deprived of much of their substance.[100] Since the amending directive affects only the scope of mandatory remuneration rules in force in the host state, but does not in any way affect their content or the way in which they are defined, the amending directive cannot, in my view, be annulled by reference to exclusive Member State competences. Nonetheless, the CJEU dismissed this claim on other grounds:[101] since the amending directive was not (and could not have been) adopted on the legal basis of Article 153 TFEU, the exceptions in that Article cannot affect the validity of the directive.[102]

5. Conclusion

The EU is fundamentally a form of economic integration, which has also social objectives.[103] The rules governing posting pose a challenge because it reveals a conflict between Member States' economic and social values and their conflicting interests as to which area should be given priority over the other. Therefore, what eventually becomes EU law on the status of posted workers is the result of a complex political compromise, rather than a dogmatically sound legislation that fits coherently into the system of cross-border employment patterns. Many contradictions and shortcomings may be discovered in the directives which are basically the product of this compromise. The mere concept of the posted worker is a good example, as it cannot be precisely distinguished from other cross-border workers, especially from those making use of their free movement rights. It is reasonable to expect that legislation and CJEU practice continuously adjust the hierarchy of effected interests to strike the right balance between them, considering the changing economic and social context. The basic expectation towards the evolution of EU law is to find an increasingly fair balance between the conflicting interests. One cannot question the CJEU's conclusion in the annulment cases that the main aim of the posting directive is to regulate the freedom to provide services. Nonetheless, in the author's view, the conflicting interests are purely economic in nature (enabling undertakings in the home state to exploit their competitive advantage of lower costs, while ensuring fair

99 Article 153(5) TFEU.

100 Judgment of 13 September 2007, *Case C-307/05, Del Cerro Alonso*, ECLI:EU:C:2007:509, paras. 40-42 and 48.

101 Unlike the Advocate General, who builds on *Alonso* in his opinion. *See Case C-620/18, Hungary*, para. 93.

102 Id. para. 80.

103 Articles 8-10 TFEU.

doi: 10.5553/HYIEL/266627012021009001013

competition with the host state's undertakings), where the protection of the workers is a rather ancillary issue.

doi: 10.5553/HYIEL/266627012021009001013

Applicability of the GDPR on Personal Household Robots*

*Gizem Gültekin Várkonyi***

Abstract

Recent developments in artificial intelligence (AI) and robotics point to a close future collaboration between humans and machines. Even though the use of personal robots is not yet a phenomenon, findings in technical and legal literature highlight several possible risks inherent in the processing of personal data by such robots. This article contributes to the current discussions on the applicability of the GDPR to AI technologies from three aspects: (i) first, it encourages the use of a scenario method to predict possible future legal problems related to new technologies; (ii) second, it analyzes considerations with the support of the relevant case-law and present comparative expert opinions for overcoming the weak points of the GDPR relevant to AI; (iii) and finally, proposals made in the recommendations part aim to contribute to a better application of the GDPR to AI technologies in personal use.

Keywords: artificial intelligence, robots, personal data, GDPR, scenarios.

1. Introduction

Personal service robots have been purchased in growing numbers since 2018 and purchases are expected to grow at least until 2023.[1] Such robots assist people in various tasks, from entertainment to medical care, offering services to make their life easier. Since the beginning of the COVID-19 pandemic, certain healthcare services have been provided to the patients *via* social robots.[2] In Japan, social robots ease elders' loneliness and provide them several health care services.[3] Even though people do not use household social robots (HSR) yet, their undeniably useful personal services may allow them to enter the most intimate area of individuals, to their households.

* This research was supported by the project No. EFOP-3.6.2-16-2017-00007, titled "Aspects on the development of intelligent, sustainable and inclusive society: social, technological, innovation networks in employment and digital economy". The project has been supported by the European Union, co-financed by the European Social Fund and the budget of Hungary.

** Gizem Gültekin Várkonyi: junior research fellow, University of Szeged.

1 https://ifr.org/ifr-press-releases/news/record-2.7-million-robots-work-in-factories-around-the-globe.

2 *See* at https://spectrum.ieee.org/robotics/medical-robots/how-robots-became-essential-workers-in-the-covid19-response.

3 *See* at www.reuters.com/article/us-japan-ageing-robots-widerimage-idUSKBN1H33AB.

doi: 10.5553/HYIEL/266627012021009001014

Increasing engineering knowledge, accessible low-cost hardware coupled with Big Data bring humanity one step closer to the futuristic image of a life with robots. Machine Learning (ML) techniques have been diversifying with the help of the growing volume of easy-to-access data. Data is the lifeblood of robots since it is both the input and the output of algorithmic assessments in robotic brains (algorithm). For personal service robots this is mainly personal data if the goal is to create personal services.

In the EU, it is the GDPR[4] that provides the framework for the lawful collection and processing of personal data from the individuals. Algorithmic assessments based on personal data challenge the applicability of the GDPR since AI overrides the philosophy of technology neutral enshrined in Recital 15 of the GDPR. It requires stricter regulation on processing personal data by AI. The regulation of AI and robotics has often been discussed by the EU Institutions in the last couple of years. A significant part of the recent legal literature generated by the EU Institutions – much in line with the points summarized under the literature review title of this work – show that risks arising from AI technologies, need better regulation. Data protection has always been included in these documents, even though a few works exist that evaluate the risks specific to the right to data protection in AI technologies. Risks regarding the possible invalid consent practices, transparency, difficulties in providing sufficient information on these technologies, and the ethical aspects have been mentioned repeatedly in such works.[5] In order to foresee the challenges faced when designing data protection law of the EU for AI and robotics, this work introduces a scenario method that was constructed on a comprehensive literature analysis specific to AI and the law. The literature review lays down the main hypotheses of the research which are tested through the analysis of the GDPR and the CJEU case-law harmonized with the author's opinions. Expert opinions that were collected by interviews, helped conducting a comparative analysis among four EU MS's and mostly served to support the analysis conducted by the author. Finally, the solutions offered by the article may support the application of the GDPR in the AI technologies.

4 Regulation (EU) 2016/679 of the European Parliament and of the Council of 27 April 2016 on the protection of natural persons with regard to the processing of personal data and on the free movement of such data and repealing Directive 95/46/EC (General Data Protection Regulation, GDPR).

5 White Paper On Artificial Intelligence – A European Approach to Excellence and Trust, COM(2020) 65 final; Communication from the Commission to the European Parliament, the European Council, the Council, the European Economic and Social Committee and the Committee of the Regions, Artificial Intelligence for Europe, SWD (2018) 137 final; *Ethics Guidelines for Trustworthy AI*, High-Level Expert Group on Artificial Intelligence, April 2019; Giovanni Sartor, *The Impact of the General Data Protection Regulation (GDPR) on Artificial Intelligence*, Panel for the Future of Science and Technology; Aimee van Wysenberg, *Artificial Intelligence: From Ethics to Policy*, EPRS Study Panel for the Future of Science and Technology, June 2020.

doi: 10.5553/HYIEL/266627012021009001014

2. Literature Review

An initial note should be made about the terminology used in the entire work. This work uses the term robot interchangeably with AI, since this approach is visible in the technical foundations of the terms, as well as in their relations with law.[6] Robots are specifically chosen, since their physical representativeness in real world make them more intelligent and to be perceived more real.[7] The physical appearance shows significant difference between the social bots and social robots,[8] especially in legal research.[9] *Social robots*, that are able to socially interact with people[10] like another human, might cause more privacy infringements than a social bot. The hardware capabilities of robots, such as sensors, cameras, microphones, and a variety of actuators assist them to collect more data about the real world, including personal data, as it will be discussed below.

2.1. Technical Considerations

The brain of the AI systems, the algorithm is developed with the help of ML techniques that have a crucial impact on collecting and processing (personal) data. Data is actually the lifeblood of robots because a typical ML lifecycle starts with data collection[11] and continues with an endless data evaluation and data generation.

First, the robot's physical advantage, then the humanoid appearance and behavior combined with the natural language interactions causing *Uncanny Valley* encourage people to disclose more personal data to a robot. The term Uncanny Valley was created by the (social) roboticist Masahiro Mori,[12] and was used for

6 Robin R. Murphy, *Introduction to AI Robotics*, MIT Press, Cambridge, US, 2001, p. 248; Xiuquan Li & Hongling Jiang, 'Artificial Intelligence Technology and Engineering Applications', *Applied Computational Electromagnetics Society Journal*, Vol. 32, Issue 5, May 2017, p. 381; *A Definition of AI: Main Capabilities and Scientific Disciplines*, High-Level Expert Group on Artificial Intelligence, April 2019; ISO 8373:2012(en) Robots and Robotic Devices – Vocabulary, para 2.6.

7 Christophe Leroux *et al.*, *Suggestion for a Green Paper on Legal Issues in Robotics*, euRobotics – The European Robotics Coordination Action, 7th Framework Programme, 2012, p. 60.

8 Oliver Korn *et al.*, 'Perspectives on Social Robots: From the Historic Background to an Experts' View on Future Developments', *Proceedings of the 11th PErvasive Technologies Related to Assistive Environments Conference*, PETRA '18, New York, NY, USA: ACM, 2018, p.188; *Draft Motion for a Resolution on Automated Decision-Making Processes: Ensuring Consumer Protection, and Free Movement of Goods and Services*, European Parliament, Committee on the Internal Market and Consumer Protection, 2019/2915(RSP), 21 January 2020, p.3, para D.

9 Carolina Alves de Lima Salge & Nicholas Berente, 'Is That Social Bot Behaving Unethically?', *Commun. ACM*, 60, 2017, p. 30.

10 Terrence Fong *et al.*, 'A Survey of Socially Interactive Robots', *Robotics and Autonomous Systems*, Vol. 42, 2003, p. 145; Eduardo Fosch-Villaronga, *Towards a Legal and Ethical Framework for Personal Care Robots: Analysis of Person Carrier Physical Assistant and Mobile Servant Robots*, Doctoral dissertation, Erasmus Mundus in Law, Science and Technology Consortium, 2017, p. 52; Cynthia Breazeal, *Designing Sociable Robots*, MIT Press, Cambridge, US, 2002.

11 Harini Suresh & John V. Guttag, 'A Framework for Understanding Unintended Consequences of Machine Learning', *ArXiv Preprint ArXiv:1901.10002*, 2019.

12 *The Uncanny Valley: The Original Essay by Masahiro Mori*, translated by Karl F. MacDorman & Norri Kageki, IEEE Spectrum, at https://spectrum.ieee.org/automaton/robotics/humanoids/the-uncanny-valley.

doi: 10.5553/HYIEL/266627012021009001014

the first time in his Japanese publication about forty years ago. Mori made a strong relationship between the human deception and the mathematical functions (when the value x increases, the equivalent y also increases) and conceptualize the deception in the case of robots in a way that, "in climbing toward the goal of making robots appear human, our affinity for them increases until we come to a valley". More precisely, as long as the robots will be designed in a way they look or act like human (f(x)), people will start to have feelings (*e.g.* affection) towards robots (y) and therefore not considering them as machines. As the humanoid design increases, so will the humanoid perception of robots (f(x)=y). Personalization of robots through RL techniques, on the other hand, directly affects people's perception of a (social) robot; the more human the robot is, the user's perception of humanoid companion increases. This kind of perception might manipulate people emotionally, hence, people may even assume that a robot also has emotions deceiving the user.[13] The emotional engagement with robots encourages people to disclose more personal information for functional rewards. When these functional personalized rewards are combined with a humanoid outlook, people tend to engage with robots more, falsely thinking that robots are human, because they act and look like humans.[14] People living with social robots are be required to share personal data if they wish to receive personalized services, however, illusionary perception of the robot in people's minds might raise risks towards the right to data protection. Obviously, more uncanny valley strengthens the trust of people in robots which, in the end, causes even more data disclosure.

In addition to the design factor, and even more significantly, *the nature of the ML techniques which require constant data collection make robots unpredictable data collection by design*. The algorithm then learns to create its own decision-making rules unlikely to the classic programs, where the rules are pre-defined.[15] Once the personal aspects of an individual are evaluated by an algorithm, the output on that individual becomes a new personal data. Even if the collected data is not personal, big data and ML techniques easily turn it to personal data.[16]

The data collection by AI systems is unpredictable, and so is the output of the conducted process on the data. The term *Unpredictable by Design*[17] refers to the fact that robots constantly acquire new data that they feed the algorithm with and generating outputs that are almost impossible to foresee at the beginning of

13 Pauline Kuss & Ronald Leenes, 'The Ghost in the Machine – Emotionally Intelligent Conversational Agents and the Failure to Regulate 'Deception by Design' *SCRIPTed*, Vol. 17, Issue 2, 2020.

14 Anja Richert *et al.*, 'Anthropomorphism in Social Robotics: Empirical Results on Human-Robot Interaction in Hybrid Production Workplaces', *AI & SOCIETY*, Vol. 33, 2018, p. 420.

15 Christian Sandvig *et al.*, 'Automation, Algorithms, and Politics – When the Algorithm Itself Is a Racist: Diagnosing Ethical Harm in the Basic Components of Software', *International Journal of Communication*, Vol. 10, 2016, p. 4978.

16 Michael Veale *et al.*, 'Algorithms That Remember: Model Inversion Attacks and Data Protection Law', *Philosophical Transactions of the Royal Society A: Mathematical, Physical and Engineering Sciences*, Vol. 376, 2018, p. 2.

17 Jason Millar & Ian Kerr, 'Delegation, Relinquishment, and Responsibility: The Prospect of Expert Robots', *in* Ryan Calo *et al.* (eds.), *Robot Law*, Edward Elgar Publishing, Cheltenham, 2016.

doi: 10.5553/HYIEL/266627012021009001014

the whole processing activity. Statistical and mathematical calculations applied on a vast amount of data through the algorithms developed with unsupervised ML have become more complex and more unpredictable.[18] Indeed, such outputs are personal outputs,[19] either being the input personal data or not, since the functionality of the robot is for personal use. Social robots could reach more accurate results of the user's personality over time and with the help of ML techniques that offer more personalized services.[20] Closely related to this concept, these outputs could be used for new purposes that are different from the initial ones[21] or serve to new purposes that the data controller wishes to benefit from.[22] A separate question is whether algorithmically generated personal data fall under the GDPR's scope, and processing personal data by robotic brains is not allowed, unless the data subject gives a (valid) consent.

One of the goals behind the human-AI collaboration is to reduce human involvement with the repetitive and machine-learnable tasks, therefore, to enable robots to act autonomously in real life. Depending on the ML technique used for the development of a social robot, their autonomous nature raises some questions about liability like who is liable in case a robot causes an undesired situation. Even though different discussions on robot liability have already been heard,[23] the situation draws a complex picture of data protection, since there could be many actors involved in data processing, like developers, hardware

18 Woodrow Barfield, 'Liability for Autonomous and Artificially Intelligent Robots', *Paladyn, Journal of Behavioral Robotics*, Vol. 9, Issue 1, 2018, p. 196; Andreas Matthias, 'The Responsibility Gap: Ascribing Responsibility for the Actions of Learning Automata', *Ethics and Information Technology*, Vol. 6, Issue 3, 2004, p. 171; Accompanying the Document Proposal for a Regulation of the European Parliament and of the Council Establishing the Digital Europe Programme for the Period 2021-2027, SWD(2018) 305 final, p. 5; Kaori Ishii, 'Comparative Legal Study on Privacy and Personal Data Protection for Robots Equipped with Artificial Intelligence: Looking at Functional and Technological Aspects', *AI & Society*, Vol. 3, Issue 4, 2019, p. 512.

19 Martijn van Otterlo, 'Gatekeeping Algorithms with Human Ethical Bias: The Ethics of Algorithms in Archives, Libraries and Societty', *ArXiv Preprint ArXiv:1801.01705*, 2018, p. 28.

20 Wu Youyou *et al.*, 'Computer-Based Personality Judgments Are More Accurate than Those Made by Humans', *Proceedings of the National Academy of Sciences*, Vol. 112, Issue 4, 2015, p. 1038; Anthony G. Francis Jr. & Thor Lewis, 'Methods and systems for robot personality development', U.S. Patent 8996 429 B1, 31 March 2015.

21 Guidelines 05/2020 on consent under Regulation 2016/679, European Data Protection Board, 4 May 2020, para. 56.

22 Bart Custers & Helena Uršič, 'Big Data and Data Reuse: A Taxonomy of Data Reuse for Balancing Big Data Benefits and Personal Data Protection', *International Data Privacy Law*, Vol. 6, Issue 1, 2016; Nicola Jentzsch, *Financial Privacy: An International Comparison of Credit Reporting Systems*, Springer, Berlin, 2007, p. 39; Tijmen Wisman, 'Purpose and Function Creep by Design: Transforming the Face of Surveillance Through the Internet of Things', *European Journal of Law and Technology*, Vol. 4, Issue 2, 2013.

23 Gabriel Hallevy, 'The Criminal Liability of Artificial Intelligence Entities-From Science Fiction to Legal Social Control', *Akron Intellectual Property Journal*, Vol. 4, Issue 2, 2010; Peter M. Asaro, 'Robots and Responsibility from a Legal Perspective'. *Proceedings of the IEEE*, Vol. 4, Issue 14, 2007; Susanne Beck, 'The Problem of Ascribing Legal Responsibility in the Case of Robotics', *AI & Society*, Vol. 31, 2016; Robert van den Hoven van Genderen, 'Do We Need New Legal Personhood in the Age of Robots and AI?', *in* Marcelo Corrales *et al.* (eds.), *Robotics, AI and the Future of Law*, Springer, Singapore, 2018; Barfield 2018.

doi: 10.5553/HYIEL/266627012021009001014

providers, or even the users.[24] At this point, it is legitimate to ask, "who is the data controller for an autonomous machine with self-learning capabilities?"[25]

Lastly, the ongoing discussions about the *black-box*[26] algorithms referring to the difficulty in providing explanations on the outputs that the algorithms reach would consist of the final consideration under this title. However, this work does not look into the technical details of the problem, it rather focuses on the effect of the complexity of the technology on average users to perform informed choices based on information provided them.[27] This topic will be later raised under the practical considerations title.

2.2. Legal Considerations

In light of the technical considerations, it is possible to identify the legal problems while examining the application of the GDPR focusing on the consent, purpose limitation, fulfillment of the information obligation and the liability issues.

Initially, as the unpredictable data collection by design concept showed, a social robot placed at the households would be constantly profiling the data subjects. Article 22 GDPR entrusts data subjects the "right to not to be subject to a decision based solely on automated processing, including profiling" unless such a decision is legally permitted, like an explicit consent. In line with Article 7 of the GDPR, the consent should be valid, if it is specific, freely given, informed, and indicated with a clear affirmative action or a statement by which data subject give permission that their data is processed. In order a consent to be considered specific, the purpose(s) of data processing should be clearly defined, and the data subjects shall be informed about these purposes by the data controller. In order a consent to be considered freely given, broadly, data subjects should be provided with a concept leading them to assess the possible risks raised by the data processing activity. Further, data subjects shall be provided sufficient information in line with the rules stipulated in Articles 12 and 13 of the GDPR. Article 12 sets forth the rule on the information to be "concise, transparent, intelligible and easily accessible form, using clear and plain language". Article 13

24 European Parliament Resolution of 16 February 2017 with Recommendations to the Commission on Civil Law Rules on Robotics, 2015/2103(INL); Sartor 2020.

25 Artificial Intelligence, Robotics, Privacy and Data Protection. Room Document for the 38th International Conference of Data Protection and Privacy Commissioners, European Data Protection Supervisor, October 2016, p. 9.

26 Sandra Wachter *et al.*, 'Why a Right to Explanation of Automated Decision-Making Does Not Exist in the General Data Protection Regulation', *International Data Privacy Law*, Vol. 7, 2017, p. 78; Nizan Packin & Yafit Lev-Aretz, 'Learning Algorithms and Discrimination', *in* Woodrow Barfield & Ugo Pagallo (eds.), *Research Handbook on the Law of Artificial Intelligence*, Edward Elgar Publishing, Cheltenham, 2018, p. 5; Ronald Yu & Gabriele Spina Alì, 'What's Inside the Black Box? AI Challenges for Lawyers and Researchers', *Legal Information Management*, Vol. 19, 2019; Oscar Li *et al.*, 'Deep Learning for Case-Based Reasoning through Prototypes: A Neural Network That Explains Its Predictions', *Proceedings of the AAAI Conference on Artificial Intelligence*, 2018, p. xxxii; *AI in the UK: Ready, Willing and Able?*, House of Lords Select Committee on Artificial Intelligence, Report of Session 2017-19, London, 16 April 2018, p. 95.

27 Van Wysenberg 2020.

doi: 10.5553/HYIEL/266627012021009001014

of the GDPR lists the information that shall be provided by data controllers to be able to fulfill their informing obligation such as giving information on the data controller's identity, contact information, purposes, data transfers to third parties, and other similar basic information.

As a result of the new outputs that were unpredictably generated by AI, the probability of using the data in a multi-purpose manner arises. It might not always be possible to simply create a list of clear purposes of data processing, even though a solution could be to ask for a new consent each time there is a new purpose. Once the decision (the output) has been made by the system, the purpose simply was already born, meaning that the data subject is basically not in a position to exercise its right to contest against being subjected to an algorithmic decision making (ADM), but only to give permission to that new purpose. Such re-purposing[28] is a result of the nature of AI but is absolutely not permissible by the GDPR. If there is no specific purpose, there can be no valid consent.[29]

Returning to the Uncanny Valley effect and to the personalization concept, these concepts directly affect the people's free will, because the more humanoid the robot is, the more user's free will is manipulated. This may be an emotional manipulation; hence, people might even assume that a robot can develop emotions towards them,[30] so they interact with the robots without thinking of the privacy borders. For example, this humanoid effect creates a feeling of empathy[31] towards a machine, so the services they benefit from are maximized,[32] which is illusionary in people's minds. Obviously, the more the Uncanny Valley increases the trust of people towards robots, leads to more shared data without a valid consent.[33]

Referring to the explainability concept, this work builds a bridge between the consent and the purpose of limitation principles, and state that pre and/or post

28 Custers & Uršič 2016.

29 *Scientific Foresight Study Ethical Aspects of Cyber-Physical Systems*, European Parliament, Science and Technology Options Assessment Panel, June 2016, pp.7-10. European Parliament Resolution of 12 February 2019 on a Comprehensive European Industrial Policy on Artificial Intelligence and Robotics, 2018/2088(INI), para. 128; Zrinjika Dolic *et al.*, *Robots in Healthcare: A Solution or a Problem?*, Study for the Committee on Environment, Public Health, and Food Safety, Policy Department for Economic, Scientific and Quality of Life Policies, European Parliament, Luxembourg, 2019, p. 8; Giovanni Sartor, *New Aspects and Challenges in Consumer Protection. Digital Services and Artificial Intelligence*, Study for the Committee on Internal Market and Consumer Protection, Policy Department for Economic, Scientific and Quality of Life Policies Directorate-General for Internal Policies, European Parliament, 2020; van Wynsbergh 2020.

30 Kate Darling, '"Who's Johnny?" Anthropomorphic Framing in Human-Robot Interaction, Integration, and Policy', *in* Patrick Lin *et al.* (eds.), *Robot Ethics 2.0*, Oxford University Press, New York, 2017; Robert van den Hoven van Genderen, 'Privacy and Data Protection in the Age of Pervasive Technologies in AI and Robotics', *European Data Protection Law*, Vol. 3, Issue 3, 2017.

31 Fosch-Villaronga 2017, p. 254.

32 Maartje de Graaf, 'An Ethical Evaluation of Human–Robot Relationships', *International Journal of Social Robotics*, Vol. 8, Issue 4, 2016, p. 590.

33 David Leslie, *Understanding Artificial Intelligence Ethics and Safety: A Guide for the Responsible Design and Implementation of AI Systems in the Public Sector*, The Alan Turing Institute, 2019, p. 5.

doi: 10.5553/HYIEL/266627012021009001014

explanations[34] – that are generic to the average user – do not make sense, since the GDPR does not explicitly regulate the information and explanation to be provided to the data subjects in case an ADM is involved.[35] In a digital world where people do not often read or understand the privacy and consent statements that are under dynamic change constantly,[36] giving a valid consent is nothing more than just an imagination. Specific to the AI, where an algorithmic decision carries a certain degree of autonomy, the risk of rendering AI's action becomes unexplainable.[37]

The final topic to be evaluated under this title is an inspiration from the discussions on the possible liability issues in case an autonomous robot causes invalid consent practices. Combining also with the cultural-philosophical narratives that data controllers may carry,[38] it is hard to identify the exact data controllers (also the data processors that are left out of the scope of this work to keep simplicity) that should provide the consent forms and the information to the data subjects will be analyzed in the further sections.

2.3. Practical Considerations

Based on the technical and legal considerations discussed above, there are questions raised about the applicability of the GDPR on HSR from the practical considerations point of view. Besides the technical aspects of AI systems where the possibility of obtaining consent and providing right information about the purposes is reduced, the GDPR, practically, does not oblige the data controllers to ensure the understandability of the information they provide, rather to provide information that is generic to all data subjects.[39] Even though several guidelines build a framework of the concept of the understandable information[40] (meaningful and intelligible information) the term refers to the average data subjects' level of understanding, without requiring a strict analysis on the individual information needs. The data subject specific conditions in terms of

34 Amina Adadi & Mohammed Berrada, 'Peeking Inside the Black-Box: A Survey on Explainable Artificial Intelligence (XAI)', *IEEE Access*, Vol. 6, 2018; Wachter *et al.* 2017.

35 Gizem Gültekin-Várkonyi, 'Operability of the GDPR's Consent Rule in Intelligent Systems: Evaluating the Transparency Rule and the Right to Be Forgotten', *in* Andrés Muñoz *et al.* (eds), *Intelligent Environments*, IOS Press, 2019.

36 Jakub Míšek, 'Consent to Personal Data Processing – The Panacea or the Dead End', *Masaryk University Journal of Law and Technology*, Vol. 8, Issue 1, 2014, p. 76; Bart Custers *et al.*, 'Informed Consent in Social Media Use – The Gap between User Expectations and EU Personal Data Protection Law'. *SCRIPTed: A Journal of Law, Technology and Society*, Vol. 10, 2013, p. 440; Philip Boucher, *Artificial Intelligence: How Does it Work, Why Does it Matter, and What Can We Do about It?*, European Parliamentary Research Service Scientific Foresight Unit, PE 634.421, 2019, p. 15.

37 EP 2017, para. AI.

38 Krisztina Karsai, 'Algorithmic Decision Making and Issues of Criminal Justice – A General Approach', *in* Cristian Dumitru Mihes (ed.), *In Honorem Valentin Mirişan*, Universul Juridic SRL., 2020, pp. 146-161.

39 Tim Miller, 'Explanation in Artificial Intelligence: Insights from the Social Sciences', *Artificial Intelligence*, Vol. 267, 2019, p. 4; Gültekin Várkonyi 2019.

40 Article 29 Working Party, 'Guidelines on Consent under Regulation 2016/679', p. 7; Judgment of 17 July 2014, *Joined Cases C-141/12 and C-372/12, Y.S.*, ECLI:EU:C:2014:2081, para. 57.

doi: 10.5553/HYIEL/266627012021009001014

providing either in case of providing pre or post explanations are left out of the GDPR.[41]

The problem with the *GDPR's unclear statements on providing understandable information to the data subjects* belonging to vulnerable groups (except Article 8 GDPR proclaiming child consent rules) could be raised here as an example. HSR services will most probably be available first to the people who need support with their health or social conditions. One of the results of the Explain project points that 95% accurate decisions may prevail over the importance of the right to explanation in the case of health,[42] meaning that patients might give up their right to explanation in return of receiving a better health care. The elderly might be considered fragile since they could be more open to emotional manipulation and deception.[43] Even though such engagement is desirable and possible,[44] their free will is compromised.[45] People with disabilities is another group that was left out of the understandable information concept, and who might be both in physical and psychological contact with HSR. There is need in informing people that belong to such categories (which the algorithms have already created) with special attention, rather than applying the average user concept to them.

As a result of the previous analysis, *three hypotheses will be further tested* in this work: *(i)* H1: ML techniques enabling AI technologies to perform autonomous decisions, together with profiling, might cause extraction of new data about the data subjects, which is contrary to the principles put forth in the GDPR. *(ii)* H2: Data repurposing, unforeseeable data collection and system functionality, transparency and explainability problems, and complexity in identifying data controllers may cause ineffective consent applications. *(iii)* H3: Unclear legal rules on advanced technologies may hinder the understanding of individuals about the functionality of such technologies; therefore reduces the better enforcement of the legal rules.

3. Methodology

The methodology chosen for testing the hypotheses is the *scenario method* that belongs to the Futures Research Methodology[46] family. Scenarios have been used for forecasting by policy analysis researchers for more than 60 years, with the aim of connecting present issues with the future through cause and effect links.[47] The intention behind the scenarios is to assist policymakers to act now instead of acting later in the emergency cases. A similar goal was already adopted in this

41 Sartor 2020, p. 63.

42 *Project explAIn: Interim report*, Information Commissioner's Office, 2019, p. 15.

43 Tobias Körtner, 'Ethical Challenges in the Use of Social Service Robots for Elderly People', *Zeitschrift für Gerontologie und Geriatrie*, Vol. 4, 2016, p. 305.

44 Panagiotis Tzirakis *et al.*, 'End-to-End Multimodal Emotion Recognition Using Deep Neural Networks', *IEEE Journal of Selected Topics in Signal Processing*, Vol. 11, Issue 8, 2017, p. 1305.

45 EDPB, para 24.

46 Jerome C. Glenn & Theodore J. Gordon, *Futures Research Methodology*, Version 3.0, The Millennium Project; 3.0 edition, 2009, Scenarios section.

47 Id. p. 5.

doi: 10.5553/HYIEL/266627012021009001014

work; to provide some inputs for the EU lawmakers who have been working hard on shaping the future of data protection legislation facing the challenges caused by the AI technologies of today and the future.

Scenario method, together with other forecasting methods, is being practiced in the field of law and technology by many scholars. The Millennium Project,[48] in which all the methodologies have been used for forecasting several issues, including the legal ones, is the most comprehensive work in this sense. Specific to the law and robotics, there are examples of practicing the method in different intersections. It might seem small in quantity, but they give enough background information to understand the applicability of the methods in this field. Dark scenarios designed for helping to identify the impact of AI technologies on data protection,[49] a short scenario questioning and analyzing the liability of robots,[50] scenarios focusing on assessing the ethical and practical aspects of autonomous robots[51] were all created and used for suggesting better policy options for the policymakers. Finally, Ballard and Calo's draft work[52] presented in the WeRobot 2019 conference was the driving force of choosing the present work's methodology, since it was focusing directly on Robolaw with the aim of preventing unintended consequences of future legal problems with the help of a foreword thinking way. Futures research methods could offer efficiency in identifying and raising solutions towards the problems of legal aspects of emerging technologies as proven in the literature.[53]

The scenario constructed in this work is *a result of a comprehensive technical and legal analysis*, as well as based on personal experiences gained from the Sci-Fi and legal literature. Analysis of the scenario firstly considered under personal interpretations in light of the GDPR, the case-law of the CJEU and the literature. Then, with the hope for identifying new interpretations, expert interviews were collected. Such a method is often being used in legal sciences[54] with the same purposes. The interviews were conducted altogether with 15 experts from four EU Member States, specifically, from Finland, Hungary, Italy, and the Netherlands. These countries were chosen based on their geographical representation, meaning that the design of this work chose a sample from the Central and Eastern, Northern, Southern, and Western European States. Furthermore, these countries' rank in the AI readiness Index was considered as

48 *See* at www.millennium-project.org.

49 Pasi Ahonen *et al.*, 'Dark Scenarios BT', *in* David Wright *et al.* (eds.), *Safeguards in a World of Ambient Intelligence*, Springer Netherlands, Dordrecht, 2008.

50 Christina Mulligan, 'Revenge against Robots', *South Carolina Law Review*, Vol. 69, Issue 3, 2018.

51 Henrik Carlsen *et al.*, 'Co-Evolutionary Scenarios for Creative Prototyping of Future Robot Systems for Civil Protection', *Technological Forecasting and Social Change*, Vol. 84, 2014.

52 Stephanie Ballard & Ryan Calo, *Taking Futures Seriously: Forecasting as Method in Robotics Law and Policy*, We Robot 2019 (draft), p. 3.

53 In his work, Minkkinen proposed a new futuristic privacy model shaped by an institutional approach which should be based on the dynamics in understanding the privacy and historical processes. Matti Minkkinen, 'Futures of Privacy Protection: A Framework for Creating Scenarios of Institutional Change', *Futures*, Vol. 73, 2015.

54 Dawn Watkins & Mandy Burton, *Research Methods in Law*, Routledge, London, 2013.

doi: 10.5553/HYIEL/266627012021009001014

the second criteria.[55] Since the GDPR is a regulation and should be applied in every EU MS in the same way, there was no other criteria defined for the sampling method. Choosing the experts (sampling) was based on the following criteria: the Expert has to be working at a law firm or an institution dealing with the interpretation or implementation of the GDPR; they must have a professional interest in AI technologies (*e.g.* published a paper, gave a lecture, analyzed a legal case); and has to accept to be a part of the interview. The questions of the interview were sent to the experts beforehand, leaving some time for the experts to carefully read and pose their questions in lack of clarity.

4. The Scenario: Introduction

This is the future where humans became more dependent on technology. Autonomous cars replaced public transportation and reduced personal cars in traffic; drone delivery replaced the traditional door to door delivery services. Waste disposal robots sweep the streets all day with a smiling face, food and drinks are served at the hands of robo-waiters in cafés. Human beings spend more time developing their personal selves and developing and using technology for their own good.

This is the age of technology in which the cost of hardware and software requirements for producing not just a single robot, but dozens. Most of the people in Europe can easily afford a personal service robot enhanced with several ML techniques. These robots are the so-called *Social Robots* that can enter into social interactions with human users to serve them in different fields, starting from maintaining the home to providing health care services (also in the private home). Depending on their level of AI, these robots can fulfill single to multiple tasks for personal use. For this reason, they are also called as personal household social robots. These multi-purpose robots are very popular since they offer tailor-made services for anyone who opts in sharing their personal life with them. Their humanoid specifications and features make the user feel comfortable during their interactions, which makes it easier for the robots to collect necessary data to develop their algorithms to the personal satisfaction of the user. Companies (the entities producing, selling, and maintaining the robots, and dealing with few problems arising from personal use) behind these robots ensure a high level of security and abide by the strict principle of no-surveillance by third parties and are operating the robots in a safe and trustworthy way. The machines can make highly accurate and bias-free decisions, thanks to the ML research and technology investments made in this field a decade ago.

4.1. Life with a Social Robot at Home

Julia is a successful businessperson in her early forties living alone since she and her husband got divorced two years ago. She has a son whom she meets quite often in a week. Since she works more than a usual after she got divorced, she

55 *See* at www.oxfordinsights.com/government-ai-readiness-index-2020.

doi: 10.5553/HYIEL/266627012021009001014

realized that she could replace some of the repetitive household work with a robot and share her loneliness with it, just like her colleagues did so. She purchased the personal HSR called Robinsan,[56] a Social Robot, whose algorithms run based on and defined by the objective of "maintaining and optimizing the well-being of people". It is able to complete several tasks related to home maintenance and personal care, from cleaning to ordering food, from home security to entertainment, *etc.*, based on the service module the user subscribes. Robinsan's algorithm runs several applications in one central cloud-based database owned and operated by the Company selling it.

Julia evaluated the first month with Robinsan as 'very efficient' due to the robot's high level of performance in completing the tasks she assigned to it. She decided to go on with Robinsan by notifying the Company and upon that, the Company mentioned some of the other functions of the HSR, such as personalized health-care assistance.

A couple of months later, Julia was informed that she has early onset Alzheimer's disease (AD). She already received treatment from her doctor, but she believes in the benefit of a supportive treatment besides the medical one on reducing the AD's effects. Such a supportive treatment can be, for example, daily activities improving her cognitive skills (memory), or herbal tablets based on her physical and psychological needs.[57] She remembers the information given by the Company regarding Robinsan's function as a personal health care assistant and she decides to extend her subscription to the basic personal health-care module which then could be specially tailored to her specific disease. Since it is a matter of her health, she did not much care about all the informative documents and consent papers that the Company made her sign, she took a quick look at them upon purchase.

4.2. Operating the Social Robot

While the installation was on-going, Julia felt exhausted with many interruptions during her interactions with Robinsan, as consent panels were embedded in the installation process to fulfill the Company's relevant obligations. She paid attention to the consent statements several times but did not understand why all these repetitive information (name of the data controller, address, data processing purposes, *etc.*) was presented each time. She also did not understand some of the statements, thinking they were too technical for her. Once Robinsan was updated with the new health-care functionality, she could then start uploading all personal information regarding her health status, by scanning the papers, or by oral introduction. Besides Robinsan collecting data such as pulse, blood pressure, sweat concentration, hemoglobin saturation, *etc.*, through a chip (owned only by the Company) embedded in Julia's arm, it could also analyze

56 This name consists of two words which one of them is robot and the other is 'insan' meaning human in Turkish.

57 The idea of core genomic medicine targeting to deliver personalized medicines and treatments to the patients by analyzing their genomic data (*e.g.* DNA) is based on *Genomics and Genome Editing in the NHS*, House of Common Science and Technology Committee, 2018.

doi: 10.5553/HYIEL/266627012021009001014

physical indicators such as fatigue, happiness, depression, dizziness, *etc.*, *via* Facial Recognition, without needing the chip.

By that time, Robinsan became an important part of Julia's life. She trusted the robot and let it move freely at home without territorial restrictions. She had no fear to share her personal issues with Robinsan since she felt like it was human, due to its humanoid behavior. Whenever Julia felt sad, Robinsan could detect it and cheer her up with several personalized services, such as, playing her favorite song or talking with her. She interacted with Robinsan every day, disclosed her feelings and opinions, and she actually was no longer lonely in this way. She finally decided to approve all the consent statements delivered by the Company and Robinsan's user interface without giving them a further thought.

As part of the health care function, Julia taught the robot to prepare her medicines and bring them every day at a certain time. She also taught Robinsan to order her medication whenever it ran out and to make her recommendations on OTC, holistic herbal medicines if the robot thought those could be helpful for her. Robinsan decides about the additional medication based on Julia's monthly health status evaluation compiled from several resources such as data describing her physiological and emotional status.

Robinsan also prepares personalized memory training exercises based on Julia's own settings. It can present slices of videos and pictures from the events which Julia can decide about and 'teach' the robot. Robinsan could keep records of particular family activities through videos or pictures, which could then be presented in a gamified way to make her engage more with the activity. Robinsan's algorithm chooses the most important moments such as when she is happy, as well as important events such as birthdays, name days, and so on. It could then project the pictures or videos on flat surfaces or displays them on its small touchscreen or using the smartphone Julia has to display them. Besides voice and face recognition and natural language processing, the HSR could analyze mimes and emotions of people, so it could decide on at what confidence interval Julia might remember a certain moment. Julia taught the robot to choose some moments from her daily activities, including when her son visited her. She already asked her son's consent for being part of such recording, and naturally, he did not receive a negative answer. After the recording was finished, Robinsan shared the files with them.

4.3. Problem Statement

After the HSR ordered the second refill for Julia's prescription medication, she opened the delivery box and found her medicines, a box of herbal vitamins, and a leaflet introducing a non-clinical treatment for drug addiction. She discussed the leaflet with her son, since he was the only one who interacted with Robinsan, and who immediately looked for an explanation for the leaflet in Robinsan's operating system. Besides very basic information such as a non-exhaustive list of data Robinsan used for prediction, they found some technical information that they could not understand much. Her son sent an e-mail to the Company requesting an explanation, and the Company responded explaining that personal data might be collected in the course of ordering food, or while preparing for the memory

doi: 10.5553/HYIEL/266627012021009001014

exercise, from both of them (Julia and her son) during their interactions with the HSR. The Company claimed that the information on the decision-making procedure of Robinsan was already explained in an easy-to-understand way to the general public. Furthermore, the Company delivered a report revealing the 85% probability of drug usage by the data subject (in the form of anonymized data).[58] The Company indicated that it was Julia who purchased Robinsan and allowed it to collect data, therefore the means and purposes of data collection were communicated to her. Finally, the Company pointed out the notification which simply informed the users of the risk of having Robinsan at home, generating unpredictable results. The National Supervisory Authority is now preparing for an investigation, with several questions in the case file.

5. Evaluation of the Scenario

5.1. Part I. Case-Law Analysis

Based on the problems stated, first the liability issue will be analyzed in light of the household exemption, then the question of consent and the data controller's information obligations will follow in the course of analysis. Obviously, the main responsibility always belongs to the legal person(s) as a data controller, a different approach is taken into account in this work that is questioning the probability of the partial responsibility of the natural person that is the main user and the data subject. Such a probability was born in light of the existed case-law, that will be presented below. These cases posed the question whether using new technologies for in-house personal purposes should be considered as a household activity. Even though the answer to the question may not always be disputable, the aim here is to make a slight connection between the question of consent and responsibility.

5.1.1. The Household Exemption

The household exemption has its origins in the *Directive 95 aimed of balancing right to privacy against right to data protection* that are interrelated, but also different from each other.[59] The GDPR adopted the same approach as the

58 It should have been mentioned in the scenario, that the robot could process such data to detect other diseases than what the user was introduced about, since it would require the data controller to obtain another consent. Another note should have been made about the data that Robinsan processed to reach to the possible drug addiction outcome, based on the following data: processing the data from the eye pupil (size), eye color, face color (yellow color), sudden changes in the emotional status (mimes and voice, words spoken, also facial indications), dry mouth, shaking body or hands, focusing problems, sweat level (without an additional hardware). Possible use of an external hardware such as a chip that could detect the blood pressure, a real time sweat level, identification of unknown chemicals out of the ordinary chemical components, *etc.* could have been inserted in the text.

59 Raphaël Gellert & Serge Gutwirth, 'The Legal Construction of Privacy and Data Protection', *Computer Law & Security Review*, Vol. 29, 2013, p. 524; Juliane Kokott & Christoph Sobotta, 'The Distinction Between Privacy and Data Protection in the Jurisprudence of the CJEU and the ECtHR', *International Data Privacy Law*, Vol. 3, Issue 4, 2013, p. 228.

doi: 10.5553/HYIEL/266627012021009001014

Directive 95 and exempted the natural persons executing purely personal and household activities as Article 2 (2/c) of the GDPR states. Recital 18 of the GDPR gives some clues on what purely personal or household activity means, that is, activities performed by natural persons and having no connection to a professional or commercial activity. Activities like this could be keeping a phone book or even using social networking tools. In this case, it would be an easy solution to exempt Julia from the application of the GDPR (as a responsible person), for she was just a simple user. However, *if Julia is somehow identified as a data controller, then it is not possible to apply this exemption* in her case since the controllers that provide the means for processing personal data for such activities are subjected to the GDPR. The means for processing were interpreted in several opinions[60] and guidelines,[61] as it could involve the natural persons as data controllers even if it is of the limited application,[62] like sharing other people's personal data online.[63] In the scenario where Robinsan infringes privacy (for the other people), Julia might be considered as a data controller in a very limited case, but still, she has duties in fulfilling her informing obligations and consent requirements as the interpretation in the *Lindqvist* and *Ryneš* cases show.

The *Lindqvist* case[64] was brought before the CJEU in the years when the Internet became accessible for personal use. Mrs Lindqvist established a webpage for a group of friends who knew each other from a parish. The website was operating offline, meaning that it was accessible only by the ones who had the link. While she was keeping some of her colleague's personal data such as names, some sensitive data was also kept on the website such as a colleagues' health condition. Even though Mrs Lindqvist removed this data from the website upon her colleagues' request, the Swedish NSA referred the case to the CJEU seeking an answer to whether such data processing activity falls under the household exemption. The CJEU took the position that the exemption applies only to those actives, which are carried out in the course of private or family life of individuals, "not the case with the processing of personal data consisting in publication on the internet so that those data are made accessible to an indefinite number of people."[65] Further, while she did not notify her friends about the existence of the website, she missed the opportunity to ask for their consent, therefore she was liable in failing to fulfill her information obligations and to obtain consent of her colleagues. In the scenario, if Robinsan would have disclosed the health condition of Julia's son's to someone else, the household exemption never would have been

60 Opinion of the European Data Protection Supervisor on the Commission's Communication on Unleashing the Potential of Cloud Computing in Europe, European Data Protection Supervisor, 16 November 2012.

61 Statement of the Working Party on Current Discussions Regarding the Data Protection Reform Package-Proposals for Amendments Regarding Exemption for Personal or Household Activities, Article 29 Working Party, 2013, p. 5.

62 *Opinion on the Recent Developments on the Internet of Things 8/2014*, Article 29 Working Party, p. 14.

63 *Opinion on Online Social Networking 5/2009*, Article 29 Working Party, p. 7.

64 Judgment of 6 November 2003, *Case C-101/01, Bodil Lindqvist*, ECLI:EU:C:2003:596.

65 Opinion of Advocate General Tizzano delivered on 19 September 2002, *Case C-101/01, Bodil Lindqvist*, para. 47.

doi: 10.5553/HYIEL/266627012021009001014

a question. However, even in the current situation, there is a risk for data to be obtained by others (indefinite number of people), meaning that household exemption should not be applicable.

One may still think that operating a robot at home for personal purposes does not raise liability issues like obtaining consent and fulfilling information obligations. In the *Ryneš* case[66] Mr Ryneš placed a CCTV camera (closed-circuit system to which only the user had access to the data) that helped to identify the people that repeatedly attacked his home, the Czech NSA claimed that he failed to fulfil his obligations as a data controller. The case was referred to the CJEU, which stated that the camera was used for identifying people whose data was processed in an automated meaning and was meanwhile recording a part of the public space. The CJEU did not treat the question whether Mr Ryneš was a data controller but confirmed that he failed to fulfill his information obligations and the consent obtaining requirements. In the scenario, Julia brought the robot home, which could monitor not only her daily routines but also other people entering her home. Moreover, aside from the Company, she was the one who could deploy and access data in Robinsan, taught the robot how to make use of it for her daily memory activities. Further, she has become in a position that allowed her to aware of her son's drug addiction issue, and she might, have visited a doctor to seek a solution for her son based on her legitimate interest, which raises the risk that the data could be accessed by third parties.

In light of the case-law, it is safe to state that if a data controller collects data from public spaces or if there is a potential for the processed data to be accessed by other people, then the processing activity surely does not fall under the category of personal or household purposes. In order to operate a robot, the data controller(s) must fulfill some obligations, such as providing information, obtaining consent, or giving the possibility to the data subjects to withdraw their consent. The space Robinsan was actually used in, is partially public (people entering home) and people under Robinsan's surveillance should have been informed about its operation. On the other hand, Julia, as the main user, is also under surveillance, so first the Company shall inform both Julia and the people entering home and should obtain their consent. Then, Julia shall fulfill at least her information obligations as a potential data controller. The way a valid consent should be obtained and the type of what information that should be presented (to the actual and potential data subjects) will be discussed under the Consent Question.

5.1.2. *The Consent Question*

There is no difference between the natural and legal persons in terms of their liabilities in fulfilling the information obligations and obtaining consent based on the GDPR. The data controller, either a natural person or a legal person, are both bound to follow standard rules related to consent. In the scenario, Robinsan's Company is strictly obliged to inform Julia based on the Articles 12, 13 and 22 of the GDPR, as well as to obtain her consent for operating the robot based on

66 Judgment of 11 December 2014, *Case C-212/13, František Ryneš*, ECLI:EU:C:2014:2428.

doi: 10.5553/HYIEL/266627012021009001014

Article 7 of the GDPR. One may discuss whether the consent would be the right legal basis for operating Robinsan, and the legitimate interest legal basis should be brought up instead. Since Robinsan processes sensitive data (*e.g.* health data) and data based on an ADM, which raise a great risk to the rights of the data subjects, and Robinsan is able to process data for a wider scale of purposes than expected, the legitimate interest may not be appropriate in this case. Based on the daily practices, as well as the fact that no other legal bases could be feasible for processing activity to ADM (*e.g.* processing necessary for the performance of a contract or necessary for compliance with a legal obligation, *etc.*), consent would constitute the best choice for the Company.

Obtaining a valid consent (as well as an explicit consent in the case of processing health data) is mostly about the rules and principles related to providing transparent information, purpose limitation, complying with the conditions of consent and information obligations. There are court interpretations on how the validity of consent could be better ensured in conformity with the rules laid down in the GDPR. For instance, in *Planet49*[67] where an online gaming company that placed two pre-ticked consent boxes enabling cookies to collect personal data from the website visitors' devices, one of the questions referred to the CJEU was about what information the service provider has to give within the scope of the provision of clear and comprehensive information to the user in order to be able to fulfill informing obligations. In the analysis of the case, Advocate General (AG) Szpunar[68] pointed out an important aspect of the cookies which refers to the technical complexity refraining the average internet user from fully understanding how they really function. Moreover, the AG stated in his opinion, that if the data controller does not present sufficient information to the data subjects who already rarely checks the content of the pre-ticked boxes offered online, this puts them in an asymmetrical situation (before the provider).[69] However, the user must be able to assess the consequences of the data processing activity and then give consent; therefore, they should be fully informed before giving their consent. The CJEU, in line with the AG's opinion, further emphasized that the consent text should be presented "with sufficient clarity from a typographical point of view"[70] to ensure that the data subject has considered the consent boxes. Still, the interpretation of the case does not clarify the problem of providing understandable information to each data subject, and in personal basis, as discussed before.

The second issue to be discussed here is related to the question of whom the consent shall be given to, if there are more people involved in data processing than a data controller. It is crystal clear that the Company should have obtained Julia's consent, but what about the people entering her home? Even though Julia

67 Judgment of 1 October 2019, *Case C-673/17, Planet49*, ECLI:EU:C:2019:801.

68 Opinion of Advocate General Szpunar delivered on 21 March 2019, *Case C-673/17, Planet49*, para. 114.

69 Id. para 37. *See also* Orla Lynskey, 'Track[ing] Changes: An Examination of EU Regulation of Online Behavioural Advertising Through a Data Protection Lens', *European Law Review*, Vol. 36, Issue 6, 2011, p. 880.

70 *Case C-673/17, Planet49*, para. 35.

doi: 10.5553/HYIEL/266627012021009001014

is not a joint data controller, and her liabilities as a natural person are milder than the Company's, it is arguable to whom the consent should be given regarding the people entering her home. Should the Company receive even more surveillance power and process people's data, or it should be the user who controls the process? In *Wirtschaftsakademie*[71] a university created a Facebook fan page, and the question was whether it would be the Facebook or the university that should have obtained the consent, despite the university was only a user. The interpretation of the CJEU pointed out that, processing could not have occurred without the prior decision of the university to create and operate a fan page on Facebook,[72] therefore it should have been the university obtaining consent (as a joint data controller). In the *Fashion ID* case, where the company, FashionID, embedded a Facebook like button in its website, and so the same question was referred to the Court and had been analyzed. Even though the FashionID claimed that it had no means of controlling the personal data of the website visitors, the CJEU took the position that it facilitated data collection even though it did not have any control over the data.[73] Therefore the consent should first have been obtained by the Fashion ID since the visitors first consulted the website, which triggered the data processing.[74] Turning back to the scenario, Julia could have at least inform the people about the existence of Robinsan, by providing some basic information, such as the data it might collect and for what purposes, whom the data is being disclosed, the duration of storage, and whom to contact in case they wish to exercise their rights, similarly as Mr Ryneš and Mrs Lindqvist should have done. The information that should have been provided to the potential data subjects and the information the Company should have provided to the data subjects remains vague, due to the complexity of assessment of the functioning of robots. Moreover, there has not been a case yet assessing the concept of the information that should be provided to the data subjects in case an ADM deployed in an embodied machine.

5.2. Part II. Expert Opinions

This section will present the expert opinions that are firstly given as a general evaluation of the questions and the scenario, and subsequently an analysis specific to the questions discussed in Part I. Personal opinions of the experts will be presented with the following quotation form: "Expert from (country X)" and a randomly assigned numeric to differentiate. Country names are abbreviated as follows: Finland "F", Hungary "H", Italy "I", and the Netherlands "N".

As a general evaluation, most of the experts (10 experts in total) said that such a technology referred in the scenario either has already been happening or would surely happen within 20 years. All experts unanimously stated that the GDPR is completely applicable to the scenario, however, regarding the application

71 Judgment of 5 June 2018, *Case C-210/16, Wirtschaftsakademie Schleswig-Holstein*, ECLI:EU:C:2018:388.

72 Id. para. 56.

73 Judgment of 29 July 2019, *Case C-40/17, Fashion ID*, ECLI:EU:C:2019:629, paras. 74-75.

74 Id. para. 102.

doi: 10.5553/HYIEL/266627012021009001014

of the GDPR, Experts H4, H5, and H6 noted that the problems raised in the scenario are already existing ones. This statement somewhat confirms the previously made analyses. Expert H6 added that the GDPR was introduced into the EU's legislation very late, and still without considering the emerging technologies, so this could raise some difficulties in the application. Expert F1 and N4 noted that besides the GDPR, a *lex specialis* could also be applicable to the questions referred to in the scenario. The Expert F1 pointed out that Robinsan was a medical device and there is already relevant legislation[75] (although they have not yet been harmonized in line with the GDPR). Even though the experts agreed on the complete applicability of the GDPR on the scenario, some of them are unsure about the right implementation, since there are lack of practices and interpretation. After a year of collecting the expert opinions, the EC released a draft regulation on AI[76] including new rules on processing data with AI, confirming these statements.

5.2.1. *The Household Exemption and Responsibilities of the User*

Even though divergent opinions were given on the applicability of the household exemption, most of the experts (11 experts) stated that *the exemption was not applicable since there was an automatic data processing activity operated by the robot*. Regarding the liability question, there was significant difference between the approaches of the NSA experts and lawyers. Lawyers were quite clear about that the liability should be shared between the Company and Julia, while the NSA experts approached suspiciously to the operability of this action. For example, Expert H4 stated that the Hungarian NSA probably would not accept this claim in the first place. However, some of the experts (8 experts) agreed on Julia's data controllership and the fact that she should have carried out certain liabilities, like fulfilling the informing obligations. This approach was also divergently adopted by the experts, located even in the same country. While Expert N1 was sure about Julia's data controllership based on the fact that she was the one feeding Robinsan with data and teaching the robot how to evaluate it, Expert N3 did not agree with Julia's data controllership and that she should be on the same liability level as the Company. In Italy and Finland, the possibility for a natural person to become a data controller is almost impossible. In the Netherlands, some of the law offices would consider assigning the controllership also to natural persons in addition to the legal persons. In Hungary, there might be even more diversified approaches; experts independently from their affiliations – would interpret the case differently – the Hungarian NSA or among the lawyers, there would be different approaches to the question. As a result, it can be concluded that the scenario and the question on the household exemption raises complicated interpretation on the probable data controllership of the users of certain

75 Council Directive 93/42/EEC of 14 June 1993 concerning medical devices; Directive 98/79/EC of the European Parliament and of the Council of 27 October 1998 on in vitro diagnostic medical devices. These directives are apparently quite old-dated; since 1990 technology in medical sciences has also been drastically change and these Directives' applicability also could be a question for another research.

76 *See* at https://eur-lex.europa.eu/legal-content/ES/TXT/?uri=COM:2021:206:FIN.

doi: 10.5553/HYIEL/266627012021009001014

emerging technologies and these cases would probably have divergent interpretations at the national courts. It was certain that the data controllers must have fulfilled their information and consent obligations, and the experts were further addressed the question of how these obligations should have been fulfilled.

5.2.2. *Consent and Informing Obligations*

The available literature, as well as the analysis conducted in the Part I, showed that *ensuring the validity of the consent of an HSR user is very difficult, if not impossible*. Almost all the interviewed experts shared the same view that the purpose limitation and transparency of algorithms in robotic brains are among the most difficult issues to ensure from the data protection point of view. They also think that consent alone would not be enough for comprehensive data processing activities, but the other legal bases, such as performance of a contract or legitimate interest rules would constrain the data controller's business logic. Therefore the data controllers would still hold the tendency to use consent as a legal basis, just as it was stated in Part I.

Experts indicated different aspects on the difficulties in obtaining a valid consent, as well as providing concrete information about the purposes on data processing in robotics. Expert I1 stated that the Robinsan's system should have been constrained in a way that only the expected purposes would have been fulfilled, but the Expert would also welcome to receive personal suggestions by Robinsan to make life easier (*e.g.* the robot could 'guess' the users eating habits from the goods in the fridge and suggest some restaurants accordingly). While these suggestions fall far from the exact purposes, the Expert agreed with the fact that putting an exact border on the processing purposes is a difficult task, confirming the impossibility of limiting the purposes. Expert F1 evaluated the consent in the scenario as similar to the practice (where data subjects about all the possible data processing activities as well as the risks arising from processing) of the American companies, and which is not acceptable in Europe. Expert F2 noted that obtaining consent is the pure duty of the company, but the way the company should do this is a difficult question, since using such a robot may have multi-way effects in the real life. The Expert thinks that the user's condition could be a starting point in generating user-specific information, meaning that the information to be provided should be personal, and not generic. The Expert believes that ensuring valid consent is a fiction and the data controllers in Finland are not aware of how invalidly they obtain consent.

The experts also stated that it is hard to clearly identify how the robot user and the company should obtain the data subjects' consent. Expert N1 expressed that while obtaining Julia's consent while being a data subject was purely the liability of the Company, Julia also should have informed the people entering her home about Robinsan. in order to do that, she must have been informed every aspect of Robinsan by the Company, from the operational aspects to the risks. Expert H5 strongly believes that Julia must have obtained other people's consent when they entered her home without an exception, otherwise she should have switched the robot off. Finally, Experts F1, N1, and N3 remarked that there is no rule for ensuring the understandability of the information in the GDPR that data controllers provide to the data subjects. Similar to the analysis made before, the experts referred to the GDPR's general rule on understandability of the information by the average data subjects trespassing the importance of designing a personally tailored information. When patients or elders are the robot users, their health conditions (Expert F2), cultural identity, age, education, (Expert I2), and their vulnerability (Expert H1) must be taken into account when providing information. However, such rule is not directly inserted in the GDPR, and some of the experts share the position that it could be found in the consumer protection law, instead the GDPR.

Finally, the experts were asked to deliver their opinions on the humanoid outlook and behavior of social robots and their influence on data subjects to freely give their consent. All the experts stated that the GDPR cannot prevent data controllers from designing such systems that are encouraging people to disclose more data. Some of the experts (Experts H2, N3, and F2) said that the GDPR should not restrict companies in this sense. Expert H1 added that it might be even a positive aspect if a robot encourages people to include them in their lives since there are many lonely and desperate people in Europe, but they must also be aware of the consequences of their interaction with the robot. Expert H4 does not think that this is related to the GDPR, but to consumer protection (shared view by the Expert N6), in a way that persuasive robots might breach consumer rights. Expert N6 thinks that this question is related to ethics, in addition to consumer protection, and stated that it is a very interesting question to be given further thought. *Uncanny Valley is true, but there is no uniform legal rule preventing it to happen in real life*, if not complicating the essence of the questions raised in this work.

6. Conclusion and Recommendations

This work presented a case-law analysis supported by scenario and interview methods that were used to test hypotheses deriving from comprehensive literature analysis on the applicability of the GDPR on HSR. As a result of the analyses, several practical problems were identified regarding to the consent rule; data subjects do not fully understand the privacy statements and they are not always conscious about the possible consequences of AI technologies, especially HSR. They might share other people's data with robots or could disclose other people's data without being aware of their liability obligations Data controllers operating HSR might not always be able or might not wish to present fully understandable information to their users on the use and risks of HSR.

Technical aspects of AI technologies make it hard for the data controllers to completely comply with the GDPR. Their unpredictable data collection and processing by design may not always make it possible to put very clear statements on purposes the HSR is operating for. However, this should not mean that the data controllers could be exempted from their obligations and responsibilities. Algorithms might generate unpredictable outcomes, but as long as they fall

doi: 10.5553/HYIEL/266627012021009001014

outside of the purpose of the AI system, data controllers must ignore them and not display those purposes to the service of the users. The GDPR cannot prevent robotic companies to produce such robots gaining the trust of people and make them disclose more personal issues. The companies even should not be restrained from doing so since trust may increase the level of the user's treatment. Eligible safeguards specific to this technology should be introduced in the application.

As a result of the analysis above, it can be concluded that complicated cases will be emerging with HSR and their data processing activities within the purpose of serving their users. In order to avoid such these problems, several steps could be taken by the actors involved by either creating or interacting with the robots and further suggestions could be taken into account.

6.1. For Data Controllers

This work proposes a compulsory user education and training program to be prepared by the data controllers about the system usage such as including training for the system's technologic elements, providing tools for personal data management, raising the user's understanding on the possible risks on their right to personal data protection. Further, the trainings should contain several user cases through scenarios and should be shared with the users based on their person-specific case. Data controllers should engage users in the development and testing phase of the robot, or during the course of conducting the DPIA as suggested by Article 29 WP's DPIA opinion in line with Article 35(9) of the GDPR.[77] Pieces of training must be set by the level of user's understanding and this understanding must be verified and proved. Obligatory lifelong training programs should be offered for the people using AI systems so they would be able to catch any new developments within the system and to ensure the full compliance during the lifecycle of the systems. Data controllers should provide these programs by organizing some informative presentations for the other possible data subjects, mainly to the family members of the main user. All training shall be provided free of charge. Trainings should be personalized and the implementing of specific ML techniques for creating user-specific training content could be time and cost-efficient.[78] This way, full user control on the AI system could be ensured. An additional comprehensive internal training program for the company staff could help to raise the awareness of its own staff.

77 Guidelines on Data Protection Impact Assessment (DPIA) and Determining Whether Processing Is "Likely to Result in a High Risk" for the Purposes of Regulation 2016/67, Article 29 Working Party, p. 15, and Article 35(9) GDPR links seeking the data subjects 'views in a "where appropriate" clause, so explaining the cases where it would be appropriate to include the user views in the DPIA could be a good start. Otherwise, introducing a new legal requirement pointing the user views and experiences in a new legislation would be a better idea.

78 For example, the robot could act as an agent to analyze the user's personal informational choices and bring only that information to be read and understand by the user. Even more, the robot could be the cyber representation of the user, acting like the user and represent the user's behavior whenever the user should be informed or request information about the system. *See* Marco Conti & Andrea Passarella, 'The Internet of People: A Human and Data-Centric Paradigm for the Next Generation Internet', *Computer Communications*, Vol. 131, 2018.

doi: 10.5553/HYIEL/266627012021009001014

The second solution to be thought of is to ensure that the information which data controllers deliver to the users is valid and comprehensive. If the information prepared for the users should be specific to their personal conditions (age, gender, education, *etc.*) and personality (mood, behaviors, character, *etc.*), they could use or develop AI-based systems analyzing users' privacy needs and design their systems according to the outcomes reached by these analyses. They could further enhance their legal and ethical compilation with developing and using a personalized AI tool detecting the person-specific information needs. They could also bear in mind the AI tools open for improvement aiming to analyze specific groups of people's data to generate its reasoning itself. When an output is reached by a robot and the data subject wants to find out how that output was reached, real-time explanations with the help of computational models (mainly, RL technique) should permit the data subjects to personalize the explanations could be also useful.[79] Robinsan could be deployed with such an assistant answering the questions in this way, for example, to the question of why did you include the leaflet about drug addiction? Then the answer would be,

> "had the subject sweated less than X ml per day and the blood pressure would be around 120/70, the body would not show sudden trembles, also eye bulb would be around normal size, the subject would not be suggested to solve his drug addiction problem."

Besides, data controllers could use very simple, but effective ways to test their users' knowledge of the systems they offer. For example, after the information phase, a small quiz could pop-up on the user's screen to test the level of understanding of the user. This quiz could include basic questions generated from the given information and there should be no way to skip the test if the user wants to continue using the system. In the same way, there could be set up a certain amount of time for anyone to read the consent statements. If someone skips to check the consent box in, for example, in 5 seconds, this should mean that the user did not read it and would fail to continue with the process. They could also place a button on their websites/services interface, such as the robot's image or use a verbal indication, about preventing data controllers to trade or share their data with third parties. A similar solution is already available in the California Consumer Privacy Act.[80]

6.2. For Users/Data Subjects

The data subjects acting as users of such technologies should be aware of the dark side of the technologies they use and should bear the fact in mind that they have certain liabilities when using these technologies. Regarding the fulfillment of the

79 In their work, Ehsan *et al.* developed an automated rationale generation for providing such explanations based on real human explanations used for training a model. *See* Upol Ehsan *et al.*, 'Automated Rationale Generation: A Technique for Explainable AI and Its Effects on Human Perceptions', *Proceedings of the 24th International Conference on Intelligent User Interfaces*, 2019.
80 CCPA § 1798.135 (1).

doi: 10.5553/HYIEL/266627012021009001014

Figure 1 ***Example warning sign to be placed in the entrance and inside the home.***

consent issue and information obligations, they could place a sign as it is shown in Figure 1. at the entrance and inside their homes warning the visitors of the operation of an HSR. If someone does not wish to be under the surveillance of the robot, the user shall shut it down and shall not put stress on family members and visitors to accept the robot against their will. The sign should be provided by the data controller after the compulsory trainings and should be one of the prerequisites of obtaining the GDPR compliance certificate (mentioned below) for the data controllers.

6.3. For Lawmakers and for the Data Protection Authorities

Bearing in mind the speed of the technological developments and the variety of the available tools, lawmakers could gain from scenarios to better design future-friendly law to avoid unwanted ethical and legal consequences. For the NSAs, some operable solutions could be discussed, ideas coming out from the already existed legislation. The first suggestion is related to operating Article 42 of the GDPR, which calls data controllers to voluntarily have certificates proving their GDPR compliances. The certification includes not only paperwork but also seals and marks for their products and services. It would be a good idea to introduce a compulsory certification system for the companies offering services through personal house robots, unlikely the voluntary certification system as included in the GDPR. *The certification could be established under at least three criteria. (i)* Compulsory user education and training, as mentioned before, to place under the oversight of the NSA in collaboration with the specific national authorities related to the service offered (*e.g.* National Alzheimer Association). *(ii)* Compulsory user and company licenses: without the user license, the user cannot purchase the robot; and without the company license, the company cannot produce the robots. The idea is as simple as it is in the case of driving licenses; people who do not have a driving license cannot drive a car legally. Applying this idea to the personal household robots, users should be designated a specific license to have a personal robot at home. User licenses should be valid for maximum a year and the user must meet certain criteria to renew the license (*e.g.* accomplishment of a new training offered by the company). Such a solution

doi: 10.5553/HYIEL/266627012021009001014

already exists for developers choosing a safeguard plan for themselves against the possible misuse of AI solutions by any user.[81] As for the company licenses, they should be first obtained from the competent authority (*e.g.* EU Agency for Robotics and Artificial Intelligence), from a national institution or from a new authority to be set up (*e.g.* Hungarian Ethics Center[82]). Data controllers that obtained the license could place a seal on their products or services indicating their GDPR compliance. *(iii)* Compulsory insurance system: when the creators and users are found jointly liable or when the liable person cannot be identified because of the robot's autonomous actions, the insurance system should cover the costs of the damaged parties.

Finally, it would be practically useful if the NSAs could broaden their knowledge of emerging technologies and generate more guidelines for the better implementation of the GDPR in this sense. For example, the ICO, in cooperation with the Alan Turing Institute, already published a guideline explaining the decisions made with AI.[83] The NSAs could either benefit from the other NSA's experiences and knowledge, or create their own collaborative works specific to the questions raised in the country in which they operate. Organizing events or being involved in projects focusing on AI and the GDPR surely would guide the NSAs on how to start and provide the necessary technical information that would, in the end, guide the data controllers to understand and implement the GDPR better.

81 *See* at www.licenses.ai.

82 *Hungary's Artificial Intelligence Strategy 2020-2030*, Ministry for Innovation and Technology, May 2020, p. 34.

83 ICO 'Explaining decisions made with AI', 2020.

doi: 10.5553/HYIEL/266627012021009001014

The Sudita Keita Versus Hungary Ruling of the ECtHR and the Right to Private Life of Stateless Persons

A Long Saga Comes to an End*

*Tamás Molnár***

Abstract

In the case of Sudita Keita v Hungary, the ECtHR handed down a key judgment relating to statelessness. In the ruling of 12 May 2020, the ECtHR unanimously found that Hungary's failure to ensure stability of residence for the stateless applicant for roughly 15 years amounted to a violation of his right to respect for private and family life (Article 8 ECHR). This ruling follows in the footsteps of an earlier and similar Strasbourg judgment (Hoti v Croatia), and substantiates the jurisprudential line which provides protection to stateless individuals with unsettled status using the forcefield of Article 8 ECHR. The Sudita Keita case before the ECtHR was the final chapter in a long-lasting saga that had commenced before domestic authorities and courts in Hungary, at various instances, also with the involvement of the Constitutional Court.

Keywords: EctHR, stateless persons, right to private and family life, positive obligations of States, 1954 Convention relating to the Status of Stateless Persons.

1. Introduction

On 12 May 2020, the ECtHR [Fourth Section] delivered a judgment relating to statelessness in the case of *Sudita Keita*.[1] In the ruling, in respect of which request

* The views expressed in this article are solely those of the author and its content does not necessarily represent the views or the position of the EU Agency for Fundamental Rights.

** Tamás Molnár: legal research officer, EU Agency for Fundamental Rights, Vienna; visiting lecturer of international (migration) law, Corvinus University of Budapest.

1 *Sudita Keita v Hungary*, No. 42321/15, 12 May 2020. For other case notes analysing the judgment (upon which the present analysis also draws), *see* Patrícia Cabral, '*Sudita Keita v Hungary* – European Court of Human Rights Decision on the Right to Private Life of Stateless Persons', *Statelessness & Citizenship Review*, Vol. 2, Issue 2, 2020, pp. 324-330; and 'Sudita Keita c. Hungría, de 12 de mayo: apatridia y regularización de situación administrativa', *Revista XDS*, Junio de 2020 (No. 12) [Fundación Cepaim], pp. 57-58.

doi: 10.5553/HYIEL/266627012021009001015

for referral to the Grand Chamber has not been made and has thus become final on 12 August 2020, the ECtHR unanimously found that Hungary's failure to ensure stability of residence for the stateless applicant, Mr Sudita Keita, for roughly 15 years amounted to a violation of Article 8 ECHR, namely his right to respect for private and family life. This ruling follows in the footsteps of an earlier and similar Strasbourg case, the landmark judgment delivered in *Hoti*,[2] and substantiates the jurisprudential line started with the latter, which provides protection to stateless individuals with unsettled status using the forcefield of Article 8 ECHR.

In the case at hand, the litigation before the ECtHR was the final chapter in a long-lasting saga that had commenced before domestic authorities and courts in Hungary, at various instances, also with the involvement of the Constitutional Court (on the intricate procedural history, *see* the Section below).

2. Factual Background and Procedural History – A Long and Tortuous Journey in Brief

The applicant, who was born in Somalia in 1985 to a Nigerian mother and a Somali father, arrived in Hungary in 2002 as a migrant in an irregular situation, without any valid travel documents. Mr Keita soon after applied for asylum, which was rejected by the asylum authority (the then Office of Immigration and Nationality), as was his appeal against the negative asylum decision.[3] As a result, he was then issued an expulsion order in April 2003, which was suspended "until the preconditions for the measure were fulfilled".[4]

Between April 2003 and July 2006, the applicant had no regular legal status in Hungary as his removal was pending; he was without access to health care or employment; nor could he exercise the right to marry since he was unable to produce the documents required under Hungarian law.[5] The Embassy of Nigeria in Budapest refused to recognize him as a Nigerian national and the Hungarian authorities were unable to return him to Somalia due to the ongoing civil war. Owing to these circumstances, later in 2006, he was granted a tolerated status called 'exile' (*befogadott*) under the Hungarian aliens law, with a humanitarian residence permit valid for two years, which entitled him to basic healthcare and employment.[6]

2 *Hoti v Croatia*, No. 63311/14, 26 April 2018. Earlier ECtHR rulings relating to the right to respect for private life in cases of stateless individuals include *e.g. Karassev and Family v Finland*, No. 31414/96, 12 January 1999 and *Kurić and others v Slovenia (GC)*, No. 26828/06, 26 June 2012.
3 *Sudita Keita*, paras. 5 and 7.
4 Id. para. 8.
5 Id. para. 9.
6 Id. paras. 10, 12 and 13.

doi: 10.5553/HYIEL/266627012021009001015

Once the new legislation establishing the national statelessness determination procedure (SDP) entered into force in July 2007,[7] it seems that the Hungarian authorities failed to inform him of his possibility to apply for stateless status, as required by the aforementioned domestic legislation.[8]

In 2008, the Office of Immigration and Nationality reviewed his situation and withdrew his 'exile' (*befogadott*) status, given that no prohibition of *refoulement* existed at that material time regarding Nigeria.[9] Hence, he was once again left without an entitlement to healthcare, employment and marriage, since he had no recognized status or valid documents. A new expulsion order followed in November 2009 (his appeal against it was of no avail) but his removal was yet again suspended.[10]

In September 2010, the applicant initiated his first statelessness determination procedure under Act II of 2007 on the Entry and Stay of Third-Country Nationals (Third-Country National Act). At that time, he possessed a certificate for temporary stay (*ideiglenes tartózkodásra jogosító igazolás*), issued pursuant to the Third-Country Nationals Act, which entitled him to stay temporarily in Hungary pending his removal (the validity of the certificate would expire on 1 October 2010). The competent authority conducting the SDP, *i.e.* the Office of Immigration and Nationality rejected Mr. Keita's application for stateless status in November 2010 on two grounds.[11] *(i)* First, the applicant was unable to prove his real identity due to credibility issues, thus it could not be conclusively proven or substantiated that he was not considered a national by any State under the operation of its laws. *(ii)* Secondly, determining his statelessness was *ex lege* precluded in the absence of his 'lawful stay' in Hungary (as a result of the withdrawal of his 'exile' status), which was, at that time, a precondition under the Third-Country Nationals Act.[12] The applicant appealed the negative administrative decision before the Budapest-Capital Regional Court, which recognized him as stateless in February 2012. However, the Office of Immigration and Nationality initiated the judicial review of this judgment on his recognition as stateless from the Budapest-Capital Court of Appeal. The latter reversed the first instance ruling; and its judgment was later upheld by the Curia

7 *See* Chapter VIII of Act II of 2007 of the Entry and Stay of Third-Country Nationals, coupled with more detailed implementing rules set forth in Chapter VIII of Governmental Decree No. 114/2007. (V. 24.). Both are available *via* the National Database of Legislation (in Hungarian) at www.njt.hu. For more on the Hungarian SDP, *see* Tamás Molnár, 'Statelessness Determination Procedure in Hungary', *Asiel & Migrantenrecht*, Vol. 4, Issue 5-6, 2013, pp. 271-277; and the 'Statelessness Index' in relation to Hungary (under 'Statelessness Determination and Status'), at https://index.statelessness.eu/country/hungary.

8 *Sudita Keita*, para. 11.

9 Id. para. 14.

10 Id. para. 15.

11 This reconstruction of the proceedings relating to his statelessness determination in Hungary is based on Decision No. 6/2015. (II. 25.) AB, Reasoning [1]-[11].

12 *See* its Section 76(1): "Proceedings aimed at the establishment of the statelessness shall be instituted upon an application submitted to the alien police authority by an applicant lawfully staying in the territory of Hungary, which may be submitted by the person seeking recognition as a stateless person (hereinafter referred to as the 'applicant') orally or in writing."

doi: 10.5553/HYIEL/266627012021009001015

of Hungary in December 2013. The main reason given was that *the applicant did not fulfil the precondition of 'lawful stay' in the country as required by national legislation governing the SDP*.

While the proceedings were ongoing before the Curia of Hungary, Mr Keita started a new SDP in December 2012, but this second application was rejected as well. In the judicial review process, the first-instance court (the Budapest-Capital Administrative and Labor Court) requested the Constitutional Court in September 2014 to declare the 'lawful stay' criterion in the Third-Country Nationals Act unconstitutional, for violating provisions relating to the assurance of harmony between Hungarian law and international law [Article Q(2)] and the prohibition of discrimination [Article XV(2)] of the Fundamental Law.[13]

The Constitutional Court accommodated the referring court's request and found, in its *Decision No. 6/2015. (II. 25.) AB*,[14] that *the 'lawful stay' criterion set out in the Third-Country Nationals Act violated Hungary's obligations under the 1954 Statelessness Convention*[15] by unduly narrowing the interpretation of Article 1 of that Convention. As a consequence, this was also found to be in breach of the Fundamental Law, notably Articles Q(2) and B(1), which foresee the assurance of harmony between international law and municipal law and the principle of rule of law, respectively. Hence, the Constitutional Court quashed the 'lawful stay' criterion with legal effect as of 30 September 2015.

In application of the national legislation as adjusted by the foregoing decision of the Constitutional Court, the Budapest-Capital Administrative and Labor Court recognized Mr Keita as a stateless person in October 2015; this decision was then upheld on appeal by the Budapest-Capital Court of Appeal. Once ultimately and irrevocably granted stateless status by virtue of the latter ruling in October 2017, the applicant regained his entitlement to basic healthcare and employment[16] in line with the relevant provisions of the 1954 Statelessness Convention.[17]

3. Arguments of the Parties: the Applicant's and the Government's Position

The *applicant* claimed that the Hungarian authorities' refusal to regularize his status satisfactorily between 2002 and 2017 has gravely prejudiced his human dignity, and more specifically, has resulted in the violation of Article 3 (prohibition of torture and other forms of ill-treatment), Article 5 (right to liberty and security), Article 8 (right to respect for private and family life),[18] Article 13

13 *Sudita Keita*, paras. 18-19; Decision No. 6/2015. (II. 25.) AB, Reasoning [7]-[8], [10].

14 For an analysis of this, *see* Tamás Molnár, 'The Constitutional Court's Decision on the Compatibility of the Hungarian Statelessness Determination Procedure with International Law', *Hungarian Yearbook of International Law and European Law*, Vol. 3, 2015, pp. 593-602.

15 *Convention relating to the Status of Stateless Persons*, New York, 28 September 1954 (360 UNTS 117). The convention was incorporated in the Hungarian legal order by Act II of 2002.

16 He had successfully completed a heavy-machinery operator course back in 2010 with a view to being issued with a work permit. *Sudita Keita*, para. 22.

17 Id. paras. 20-21. *See also* Cabral 2020, p. 326.

18 He has been living together with his Hungarian girlfriend since 2009 in Budapest. Id. para. 22.

doi: 10.5553/HYIEL/266627012021009001015

(right to an effective remedy) and Article 14 (prohibition of discrimination) ECHR.[19] Mr Keita also argued that the Hungarian legal framework was incompatible with the international obligations the country had undertaken, notably the 1954 Statelessness Convention, and prevented recognizing him as stateless or otherwise regularizing his situation. In particular, he argued that for 15 years, he had been deprived of the means of providing for himself, had not been able to access healthcare properly, and was unable to marry.[20]

The *government*, on the other hand, submitted that the applicant's situation had already been resolved due to the afore-mentioned decision of the Constitutional Court and the ensuing judicial proceedings leading to his recognition as a stateless person. The government added that even before these legal developments, the difficulties encountered by the applicant had not represented a "disproportionate burden from the perspective of Article 8" ECHR, hence, they did not amount to a violation of his right to private life protected therein. As the Hungarian submission stressed, the right to private life under Article 8 ECHR cannot, at any rate, be construed as requiring a Contracting Party to grant stateless status to an individual. Finally, it was also submitted that the Hungarian authorities had applied the relevant legislation correctly at all stages of the various procedures.[21]

4. Preliminary Issues

The ECtHR noted that the application was neither manifestly ill-founded, nor inadmissible on any other ground under Article 35 ECHR (*e.g.* the domestic remedies have been duly exhausted as Section 2 above illustrates), hence it was declared admissible.

Despite the multiple legal bases and rights violations relied on by the applicant, the ECtHR, being the "master of the characterization to be given in law to the facts of the case,"[22] considered that the complaint was to be examined under *Article 8 ECHR alone*.[23] In this context, the ECtHR emphasized that, contrary to the Hungarian government's argument, the principal question *was not* whether Mr Keita should have been *granted stateless status*, but rather whether "the Hungarian authorities [...] provided an effective and accessible procedure or the combination of procedures enabling the applicant" to *regularize his status*, "allowing him to lead a normal private life in Hungary".[24] This formulation echoed the main question in *Hoti*.[25]

19 Id. para. 24.
20 Id. paras. 26-27.
21 Id. paras. 28-30.
22 *See Radomilja and others v Croatia (GC)*, Nos. 37685/10 and 22768/12, 20 March 2018, paras. 114 and 126.
23 *Sudita Keita*, para. 24.
24 Id. paras. 32, 36.
25 *See* the similarities with *Hoti*, para. 124.

doi: 10.5553/HYIEL/266627012021009001015

5. Assessment and Findings of the ECtHR

First, the ECtHR recalled extensively the *general principles* flowing from *Hoti*. It reiterated that Article 8 ECHR protects the right to establish and develop interpersonal relationships and can also embrace aspects of a person's social identity, therefore, the social ties between the person and the community in which they live constitute a part of the concept of private life. At the same time, the ECtHR confirmed that the ECHR does not guarantee to non-nationals, including stateless persons, the right to enter or reside in a particular country, since under international law States have the right, subject to their undertaken international obligations, to control the entry, stay and expulsion of non-nationals.[26]

The ECtHR also confirmed that the ECHR cannot be interpreted either as guaranteeing the right to a particular type of residence permit, nor is the ECtHR empowered to decide which legal status should be granted. Yet, the national authorities must offer a solution which allows for the individual concerned to exercise their right to private and family life without obstacles.[27] In certain cases, Article 8 ECHR

> "may involve a positive obligation to ensure an effective enjoyment of the applicant's private and/or family life [which] may be read as imposing on States an obligation to provide an effective and accessible means of protecting [this] right."[28]

Duly protecting private life also requires an accessible domestic remedy, which allows competent authorities to deal with the substance of the complaint under the ECHR and to grant appropriate relief.[29]

When *applying these principles* to the particular case at hand, the ECtHR noted that Mr Keita had been living in Hungary since 2002, where he had established social ties (a long-term relationship with his partner) and successfully completed vocational training, and he did not have a recognized status in any other country, therefore he has undoubtedly enjoyed private life in Hungary. The uncertainty of his legal status in the country for about 15 years, resulting in long periods without access to healthcare and employment, had adverse repercussions on his private life.[30]

The ECtHR underlined that another important element of the case was the applicant's *statelessness*. In this respect, the ECtHR recalled that after the introduction of the SDP in Hungarian law (July 2007), the authorities failed to inform Mr Keita about the possibility to apply for stateless status, despite strong

26 *Sudita Keita*, para. 31, citing *Hoti*, para. 119 (and the quoted case-law therein).
27 Id. citing *Hoti*, para. 121.
28 Id. citing *Hoti*, paras. 122-123.
29 Id. citing *Hoti*, para. 123.
30 Id. citing *Hoti*, para. 126.

doi: 10.5553/HYIEL/266627012021009001015

indications to his lack of any nationality, in particular after the Embassy of Nigeria in Hungary had refused to recognize him as a Nigerian national.[31]

Finally, the ECtHR emphasized that up until the decision of the Constitutional Court (February 2015) removing the 'lawful stay' requirement from the national legislation governing SDP, the requirements under Hungarian law made it *practically impossible for him to be recognized as a stateless person* and "perpetuated a situation of uncertainty".[32] This was in contravention with the principles of the 1954 Statelessness Convention, which, in essence, stipulates that stateless persons should not be imposed requirements that they are unable to fulfil by virtue of their status (Article 6).[33] In addition to the applicant's hardships stemming from the subsequently quashed, unconstitutional pre-condition of 'lawful stay', it took almost two years for the domestic courts to reach a final decision on Mr. Keita's case and ultimately grant him stateless status.

Overall, the *combined effect of the above elements* led the ECtHR to conclude that Hungary had failed to comply with

> "its positive obligation to provide an effective and accessible procedure or a combination of procedures enabling the applicant to have the issue of this status in Hungary determined with due regard to his private-life interests."[34]

Besides finding the violation of Article 8 ECHR, the ECtHR awarded Mr Keita as just satisfaction under Article 41 ECHR 8,000 EUR in non-pecuniary damage (plus taxes) and a reasonable sum covering his costs and expenses.

6. Commentary

To provide insight into the general context, in Europe, there are at least 600,000 stateless people and new cases continue to emerge.[35] Council of Europe member countries undertook obligations to protect stateless persons and uphold their rights as well as to prevent and reduce statelessness in universal and regional conventions they have signed up to.[36]

Sudita Keita follows a new strand of ECtHR case-law relating to statelessness, which started with *Hoti*. Even though stateless individuals have appeared before

31 Id. para. 38.
32 Cabral 2020, p. 328.
33 Id. para. 39; citing *Hoti*, para. 137.
34 Id. paras. 41-42.
35 Viewpoint of 9 June 2008 of the Council of Europe Commissioner for Human Rights, No one should have to be stateless in today's Europe, at www.coe.int/t/commissioner/viewpoints/080609_EN.asp. *See also* The Rights of Stateless Persons must be Protected' – Statement by Thomas Hammarberg, Commissioner for Human Rights of the Council of Europe, at the 4th Council of Europe Conference on Nationality 'Concepts of Nationality in the Globalised World, CommDH/Speech (2010) 13, 17 December 2010 at https://wcd.coe.int/ViewDoc.jsp?id=1722017.
36 *See* these conventions in footnote 53.

doi: 10.5553/HYIEL/266627012021009001015

the ECtHR also in the past (*see e.g.* the *Slivenko*,[37] *Genovese*,[38] *Kurić*, and *Kim*[39] rulings), "their statelessness was at best framed as an additional source of vulnerability, but not as a central issue of their claims."[40] Conversely, both in *Hoti* and *Sudita Keita*, the applicants' statelessness played a crucial role in the legal reasoning the ECtHR put forward.

As a preliminary remark about framing the alleged rights violations in the context of the Convention, it is worth noting that the ECtHR placed the complaint within the perimeters of *Article 8 ECHR solely*. Other alleged rights violations under further invoked ECHR provisions have not been examined, departing from the applicant's characterization under the ECHR, which Cabral considered regrettable.[41] In my view, this was most likely a strategic move by the ECtHR, as proceeding this way was easier for it to follow the line taken in *Hoti* and to situate the case at hand closely within its already established jurisprudence started with the aforementioned leading case.

As regards the nature and content of the *positive obligations* national authorities owe towards (stateless) individuals by virtue of *Article 8 ECHR*, the ECtHR restated the principles set forth earlier in *Hoti*. The elements of this four-pronged 'test' can be summarized as follows: *(i)* assessing the applicant's social ties with the country concerned; *(ii)* establishing that the uncertainty of legal status had adverse repercussions on the applicant' private life; *(iii)* examining whether there was an effective possibility to regularize the person's legal status; and *(iv)* whether any requirement had been imposed that the applicant was unable to fulfil by virtue of their status.[42]

Also, *Sudita Keita* is a good example for regional human rights courts such as the ECtHR engaging with the key international convention on the protection of stateless persons, namely the 1954 Statelessness Convention. As part of the relevant legal framework applicable to the case, the ECtHR enumerated a number of provisions from the 1954 Convention, such as the definition of 'stateless person' [Article 1(1)], the definition of the term 'in the same circumstances' (Article 6), personal status (Article 12), administrative assistance (Article 25), as well as facilitated naturalization of stateless persons (Article 32); then it integrated some of these principles stemming therefrom in its analysis,[43] although the majority of the above provisions have not been unpacked in the subsequent legal reasoning.

37 *Slivenko v Latvia (GC)*, No. 48321/99, 9 October 2003.

38 *Genovese v Malta*, No. 53124/09, 11 January 2012.

39 *Kim v Russia*, No. 44260/13, 17 July 2014.

40 Katja Swider, 'Hoti v Croatia: European Court of Human Rights Landmark Decision on Statelessness', *Citizenship & Statelessness Review*, Vol. 1, Issue 1, 2019, footnote 3; quoting Caia Vlieks, 'Geen (recht op) nationaliteit: De relevantie van artikel 8 EVRM bij de beperking van staatloosheid in Europa', *Nederlands Tijdschrift voor de Mensenrechten*, Vol. 43, Issue 3, 2018, p. 375.

41 Cabral 2020, p. 326.

42 *Sudita Keita*, paras. 33-34, 36, 39.

43 *See also* Cabral 2020, p. 328.

doi: 10.5553/HYIEL/266627012021009001015

In this regard, the *ECtHR gave a remarkable, even progressive interpretation to Article 6* of the 1954 Statelessness Convention. This provision is basically an interpretative one explaining the meaning of the term 'in the same circumstances', which is used throughout the treaty in the context of establishing different levels of protection for 'standards of treatment' enjoyed by identified stateless individuals.[44] Put differently, this provision aims to clarify certain conditions of the enjoyment by stateless persons of various *substantive rights* set out in the 1954 Convention when the corresponding comparator is 'aliens in the same circumstances', and excludes those requirements that stateless individuals are unable to fulfil due to their status (*e.g.* producing evidence of nationality[45]). As such, Article 6 defining the term 'same circumstances' gives precisions to and carves out an exception from the equal treatment obligation between 'aliens' and 'stateless persons', thereby refining the scope of application of certain substantive rights to the latter group. However, the way the ECtHR referred to it went beyond this literal meaning. The ECtHR infused this provision with an additional meaning, making use of it as a *procedural rule*, which prohibits certain requirements imposed in national statelessness determination procedures, such as 'lawful stay,' in respect of those who *seek the recognition* of their stateless status. The ECtHR contended that the former precondition of 'lawful stay' to initiate an SDP in Hungary was contrary to this obligation stemming from the 1954 Convention.[46] Such an interpretation seemingly goes beyond the ordinary meaning of the terms and the grammatical interpretation of Article 6 and expands its horizon, apparently relying on the object and purpose of the 1954 Convention, as set out in particular in its preamble and the Final Act of the diplomatic conference adopting it.[47] The ECtHR thus opted for a more teleological interpretation of the provision,[48] which is not alien to its jurisprudence. The same line of argumentation was also applied in *Hoti*, word for word, without the ECtHR having elucidated the reasons behind the expansion of the protective power of Article 6 of the 1954 Convention to such scenarios.

Finally, Cabral also notes[49] that the ECtHR made, in passing, an unfortunate reference to *de facto* statelessness when asserting that the refusal by the Embassy

44 For an overview of the three different levels of protection offered to stateless people under the 1954 Convention, *see e.g.* Tamás Molnár, 'Remembering the Forgotten: International Legal Regime Protecting the Stateless Persons – Stocktaking and New Tendencies', *US-China Law Review*, Vol. 11, Issue 7, 2014, pp. 832-833.

45 Nehemiah Robinson, *Convention relating to the Status of Stateless Persons: Its History and Interpretation. A Commentary*, Institute of Jewish Affairs, New York 1955; reprinted by UNHCR, Division of International Protection, 1997, p. 19.

46 This confirms that eliminating such an obstacle is not only a domestic constitutional law requirement, but also a pre-requisite of international law (although the former has been deduced also from international obligations).

47 United Nations Conference on the Status of Stateless Persons, held at New York from 13-23 September 1954, Final Act and Convention Relating to the Status of Stateless Persons, E/CONF. 17/5/Rev. 1, at https://undocs.org/pdf?symbol=en/E/CONF.17/5/REV.1.

48 These interpretative methods are, at least partially as concerns the teleological method, codified in Article 31 of the 1969 VCLT.

49 Cabral 2020, p. 328.

doi: 10.5553/HYIEL/266627012021009001015

of Nigeria in Hungary to recognize Mr. Keita as a Nigerian national rendered the applicant '*de facto* stateless'. While I agree with her analysis on why this is a dangerous move towards some disputed and grey zones of international law,[50] I assume that the ECtHR deliberately avoided discussing issues of the declaratory nature of the recognition of statelessness and other matters of legal dogmatics around the 'stateless person' definition under international law.[51] The ECtHR may well have wanted to avoid going into the intricacies of the statelessness determination procedure and the legal effects attached to it, since its aim was not to dwell upon these modalities of a procedural nature and the actual "impossibility for [Mr Keita] to obtain stateless status as such", as already stressed earlier in the judgment. Instead of taking steps in this direction, the legal reasoning stuck to core issues directly linked to Article 8 ECHR, where both substantive law and the ECtHR's purview are the steadiest.

7. Conclusion

It is without a doubt that *Sudita Keita reinforces the protection of stateless individuals in the European legal space*, acknowledging anew statelessness as a relevant, self-standing factor, as well as clearly demonstrating the power of individual petitions under the ECHR to successfully bring unresolved, dragged out cases involving stateless persons to the ECtHR. I fully concur with Cabral who correctly pointed out that "the Court is well positioned to develop regional case-law on the fundamental rights of stateless persons [...] and provide stateless persons with access to the protection afforded by the 1954 Convention."[52] The right to respect for private and family life under Article 8 ECHR is the principal entry point to argue such claims before the ECtHR, which has again shown openness to rely on relevant instruments of international law other than the ECHR.[53] As a result, the new case-law marked by the tandem of *Hoti* and *Sudita Keita* rulings is capable of promoting a human-rights driven interpretation of the (quite dated) international treaty that is the cornerstone of the protection of the

50 On de facto statelessness, *consider e.g.* Alison Harvey, 'Statelessness: the 'de facto' statelessness debate', *Journal of Immigration, Asylum and Nationality Law*, Vol. 24, Issue 3, 2010, pp. 257-264; and Hugh Massey, *UNHCR and de facto statelessness*, LPPR/2010/01 (April 2010), at www.refworld.org/docid/4bbf387d2.html.

51 For a (*quasi-*)authentic detailed explanation, *see* Office of the United Nations High Commissioner for Refugees, *Handbook on Protection of Stateless Persons*, UNHCR, Geneva, June 2014, Part One.

52 Cabral 2020, p. 330.

53 In other statelessness-related cases, the ECtHR not only relied on the 1954 Statelessness Convention, but also referred to the 1961 Convention on the Reduction of Statelessness; the 1997 European Convention on Nationality; and the 2006 Council of Europe Convention on the Avoidance of Statelessness in Relation to State Succession, alongside some materials of the UN International Law Commission, UNHCR as well as other international and regional bodies. *See e.g. Ramadan v Malta*, No. 76136/12, 21 June 2016; and *Kurić and others v Slovenia (GC)*.

doi: 10.5553/HYIEL/266627012021009001015

stateless.[54] This integrated and 'joined-up'[55] approach to human rights, also mobilizing the 1954 Convention is a promising sign of a move towards a more harmonized and inclusive human rights adjudication at the European level, equally helping solidify other areas of international law and strengthening the overall fabric of the legal edifice called 'international legal order'.

Zooming in on the level of the *rights-holders*, *i.e.* the stateless individuals, the ruling displays the power of international law, enforced *via* regional human rights adjudication, to provide at least some – partial – just satisfaction for long-lasting rights denials and violations affecting one of the most vulnerable groups, who often remain 'invisible' and out of sight of official proceedings. Mr Keita is only one of the hundred-something stateless persons who have currently been living in Hungary.[56] For those stateless who have suffered for many years living in a similar legal limbo, on the margins of the society, there now exists a well-established set of judge-made European human rights standards and principles, together with the option of enforcing them before the ECtHR, which can offer effective remedies for such grave interferences with their private life. Time will tell how many of them will step on the same path to seek justice in Strasbourg.

54 Similar to what the UNHCR has been doing in the past decade, in particular in its 2014 Handbook of Protection of Stateless Persons.

55 For this term, *see* the EU Fundamental Rights Agency's toolkit entitled 'Joining up fundamental rights', at https://fra.europa.eu/en/joinedup/home.

56 For the data on stateless population in Hungary, *see*https://index.statelessness.eu/country/hungary, under 'Statelessness Population Data' (last updated: March 2021).

doi: 10.5553/HYIEL/266627012021009001015

The Decision on the Situation in Palestine Issued by Pre-Trial Chamber I of the International Criminal Court

Reflecting on the Legal Merits*

*Rachel Sweers***

Abstract

On 5 February 2021, the Pre-Trial Chamber I of the International Criminal Court (ICC) issued its decision on the Situation in Palestine affirming that its territorial jurisdiction extends to the territories occupied by Israel since 1967, namely Gaza and the West Bank, including East Jerusalem. The Situation was brought before the Chamber by request of the ICC's Prosecutor. Legal issues were addressed in the Majority Decision, as well as in the Partly Dissenting Opinion and Partly Separate Opinion. The procedural history involving the Prosecution Request that seized the Chamber on the Situation in Palestine will be discussed, including a brief analysis of the legal basis for this request. Furthermore, the legal merits of the Situation in Palestine will be compartmentalized into three main pillars in order to analyze step by step how the Chamber reached its conclusion.

Keywords: International Criminal Court, ICC, Palestine, Oslo Accords, jurisdiction.

1. Introduction

On 5 February 2021, Pre-Trial Chamber I (the Chamber) of the International Criminal Court (the ICC or the Court) issued its Decision on the Situation in the State of Palestine (the Decision).[1] The Decision established that the Court's territorial jurisdiction in the Situation in Palestine extends to the territories occupied by Israel since 1967, namely Gaza and the West Bank, including East Jerusalem.[2]

* The views expressed therein are those of the author alone and do not reflect the views of the ICC. This article was written purely to provide an objective summary of the Decision on the Situation in Palestine by the ICC and in no way offers any opinion on the matter.

** Rachel Sweers: legal intern, International Criminal Court, the Hague.

1 *ICC Pre-Trial Chamber I Issues its Decision on the Prosecutor's Request Related to Territorial Jurisdiction over Palestine*, Press Release, (ICC-CPI-20210205-PR1566), 5 February 2021.

2 Id.

doi: 10.5553/HYIEL/266627012021009001016

The Decision was reached by majority of a three-judge panel, with Judge Péter Kovács of Hungary, acting as Presiding Judge, Judge Reine Adélaïde Sophie Alapini-Gansou of Benin and Judge Marc Perrin De Brichambaut of France.[3] Filed alongside the Majority Decision, were a Partly Dissenting Opinion (the Dissent) issued by Judge Péter Kovács and a Partly Separate Opinion (the Separate Opinion) issued by Judge Marc Perrin De Brichambaut. This article will further elaborate on the focal points of the Decision, as well as key legal issues raised in the Dissent and Separate Opinion.

Firstly, the procedural background of the Situation in Palestine, leading up to its referral to the Chamber will be briefly summarized to add context and introduce readers to the matter. The Separate Opinion will be discussed in this section as it is relevant to the legal basis of the Prosecution Request seizing the Chamber. Secondly, this article will delve into the legal merits of the Decision, as well as those contained in the Dissent. This includes an overview of the three main questions (pillars) addressed by the Chamber being: (*i*) is Palestine a State Party to the Rome Statute of the ICC; (*ii*) can Palestine be considered the State on the territory of which the conduct in question occurred;[4] and (*iii*) does the Court's jurisdiction extend to the territories occupied by Israel since 1967, namely Gaza and the West Bank, including East Jerusalem?[5]

2. Procedural History

2.1. The Prosecution Request

The early beginnings of the Situation in Palestine before the ICC unfolded after the State of Palestine lodged its

> "declaration under Article 12(3) of the Rome Statute of the [ICC] thereby accepting the jurisdiction of the Court over alleged crimes "committed in the occupied Palestinian territory, including East Jerusalem" since 13 June 2014."[6]

After accepting the jurisdiction of the Court, Palestine referred the Situation to the Office of the Prosecutor on 22 May 2018.[7] The Prosecutor commenced a preliminary examination into the situation on 16 January 2015 for alleged crimes

3 *See* the website of the ICC, Judges by Judicial Divisions: Pre-Trial Division, at www.icc-cpi.int.

4 Decision on the "Prosecution request pursuant to Article 19(3) for a ruling on the Court's territorial jurisdiction in Palestine" (Majority Decision), 5 February 2021, ICC-01/18-143, para. 1; *see* Presidency, Decision assigning the situation in the State of Palestine to Pre-Trial Chamber I, Annex I, 24 May 2018, ICC-01/18-1-AnxI, p. 39.

5 Id. p. 50.

6 Id. p. 2.

7 Id. para. 3.

doi: 10.5553/HYIEL/266627012021009001016

committed in the occupied Palestinian territory.[8] The Prosecutor found reasonable basis to believe that war crimes have been or are being committed in the West Bank, including East Jerusalem, and the Gaza Strip.[9] Satisfying this precondition, the Chamber was adverted to clarify whether the Court has territorial jurisdiction in the Situation in Palestine. On 22 January 2020, the Prosecution submitted its Request "pursuant to Article 19(3) for a ruling on the Court's territorial jurisdiction in Palestine" to the Chamber.[10] By way of the Prosecution Request, the Prosecutor sought a ruling on "the scope of the Court's territorial jurisdiction in the [S]ituation in Palestine" and requested the Chamber to clarify the territory over which this jurisdiction can be situated.[11] This entailed whether territorial jurisdiction could be exercised over the West Bank, including East Jerusalem and Gaza.[12]

2.2. *Applicable Law of the Request*

The applicable law encompassing the Prosecution Request is therefore Article 19(3) of the Rome Statute which "[allows] [t]he Prosecutor [to] seek a ruling from the Court regarding a question of jurisdiction or admissibility" and allows for those who have referred the situation, in this case, Palestine, as well as victims to "submit observations to the Court."[13]

Flowing from Article 19(3), Palestine, as well as victims, may submit observations to the Court. The Chamber received a number of observations on behalf of various groups of victims which were set out separately in their own paragraph in the Decision.[14] In total, eleven groups of victims' submissions were considered in the Decision. Several *amici curiae* were also invited to submit observations to the Court. The Chamber "address[ed] particular arguments raised by certain *amici curiae* in so far as it considered it necessary to do so for its determination."[15] There were approximately 43 *amici curiae* submissions, from a handful of States, legal commentators, and professors. The *amici curiae* submissions were split into two categories based on the reasons specified in their observations: conditions for the exercise of the Court's jurisdiction *(i)* have not been fulfilled; and *(ii)* have been fulfilled.[16] All observations received equal and

8 Prosecution request pursuant to Article 19(3) for a ruling on the Court's territorial jurisdiction in Palestine (Prosecution Request), 22 January 2020, ICC-01/18-12, together with Public Annex A, ICC-01/18-12-AnxA, para. 1; *see also* Press Release Prosecutor Statement PE Palestine, 16 January 2015.

9 Prosecution Request, para. 2.

10 Id., para. 18.

11 Id., para. 220.

12 Id.

13 Article 19(3) of the Rome Statute: "The Prosecutor may seek a ruling from the Court regarding a question of jurisdiction or admissibility. In proceedings with respect to jurisdiction or admissibility, those who have referred the situation under Article 13, as well as victims, may also submit observations to the Court."

14 Majority Decision, para. 37.

15 Id. para. 49.

16 Id. paras. 51-52.

doi: 10.5553/HYIEL/266627012021009001016

due consideration with the Chamber having "carefully studied the numerous observations submitted [...]".[17]

In order to move forward with the investigation, *the Prosecutor first had to seek guidance on the scope of the 'territory' in the Situation in Palestine*. Article 12(2) of the Rome Statute reiterates that the Court may exercise its jurisdiction if a State Party to the Statute has accepted the jurisdiction of the Court and paragraph (a) further elaborates that it must be "[t]he State on the territory of which the conduct in question occurred [...]".[18] In regard to the question of whether Palestine qualifies as a State, *the primary position taken by the Prosecutor in her request is that Palestine is a 'State' for the purpose of Article 12(2)(a) because Palestine is a State Party to the Rome Statute*.[19] Furthermore, the Prosecutor noted that "[t]he Court need not conduct a different assessment regarding Palestine's Statehood to exercise its jurisdiction in the territory of Palestine."[20]

2.3. The Separate Opinion

This is where the reasoning contained in the Separate Opinion differs from the Majority. While the Separate Opinion agrees with the Majority that Article 19(3) of the Rome Statute is applicable, the Judge arrives at his conclusion in a different manner.[21]

Judge Perrin De Brichambaut distinguishes his current decision from a previous partly dissenting opinion on

> "the question of whether the Court may exercise jurisdiction pursuant to Article 12(2)(a) of the Statute over the alleged deportation of members of the Rohingya people from the Republic of the Union of Myanmar to the People's Republic of Bangladesh" (the 2018 Request).[22]

In the 2018 Request, the Judge noted that Article 19 "applies only once a case has been defined by a warrant of arrest or a summons to appear pursuant to Article 58 of the Statute."[23] In his previous opinion, he noted that there had been

17 Id. para. 49.

18 Article 12(2) of the Rome Statute: "[T]he Court may exercise its jurisdiction if one or more of the following States are Parties to this Statute or have accepted the jurisdiction of the Court in accordance with paragraph 3: (a) The State on the territory of which the conduct in question occurred [...]."

19 Prosecution Request, p. 56; *see also* Majority Decision, para. 89.

20 Prosecution Request, para. 218.

21 Partly Separate Opinion of Judge Perrin De Brichambaut (Separate Opinion), 5 February 2021, ICC-01/18-143-Anx2, para. 1; *see also* Judge Péter Kovács' Partly Dissenting Opinion (Dissent), 5 February 2021, ICC-01/18-143-Anx1, para. 1.

22 Separate Opinion, para. 3.; *Referring to Request under regulation 46(3) of the Regulations of the Court*, Prosecution's Request for a Ruling on Jurisdiction under Article 19(3) of the Statute, 9 April 2018, ICC-RoC46(3)-01/18-1.

23 Id. para. 3; *see also* Request under Regulation 46(3) of the Regulations of the Court, Partially Dissenting Opinion of Judge Marc Perrin de Brichambaut to Decision on the 'Prosecution's Request for a Ruling on Jurisdiction under Article 19(3) of the Statute', 6 September 2018, ICC-RoC46(3)-01/18-37-Anx, para. 10.

doi: 10.5553/HYIEL/266627012021009001016

no indication that the Prosecutor had identified any potential cases at the stage in which the Chamber was seized.[24] He distinguishes the current Situation in Palestine from his previous stance by accepting the applicability of Article 19(3) on the basis that the Prosecutor has identified potential cases in the present situation.[25] This is because, as Judge Perrin De Brichambaut points out, a 'case' must be interpreted in accordance with the relevant stage of proceedings.[26] While there are no cases identified by a warrant of arrest or summons to appear at this stage in the Situation in Palestine, the Judge is of the view that the Prosecution Request has identified potential cases sufficient to meet the criterion of a 'case' as required under Article 19(3) of the Statute.[27]

The Decision also confirms that the principal difference between the previous 2018 Request and the current Prosecution Request in the Situation in Palestine is that for the former, the request was in the initial stages of preliminary examination, while the latter arises out of an investigation "that has, in principle, already been initiated" and that "the Prosecutor has identified potential cases [...]."[28] This brings us to the applicable law and legal merits of the question before the Chamber: whether Palestine can be considered the State on which the conduct in question occurred and furthermore, if said territory comprises the West Bank, including East Jerusalem and the Gaza strip under Article 12(2)(a) of the Statute.[29]

3. The Legal Merits

This Section delves into the legal merits of the Decision as well as the legal issues raised in the accompanying Dissent. The structure of this summary will be formulated around the three identifiable issues in the Decision stemming from the Prosecution Request, while weaving legal arguments from the Dissent in order to offer a more comprehensive view into the approaches employed. The three pillars substantiating the legal merits are as follows: *(i)* Palestine is a State Party to the Statute; *(ii)* Palestine qualifies as the State on the territory of which the conduct in question occurred; and *(iii)* the Court's territorial jurisdiction extends to the territories occupied by Israel since 1967, namely Gaza and the West Bank, including East Jerusalem.

3.1. Palestine as a State Party to the Rome Statute

Recalling the precondition in Article 12(2), States must be Parties to the Rome Statute or have accepted the jurisdiction of the Court in order for the Court to exercise its jurisdiction.[30] The first pillar of the legal merits pertains to whether

24 Separate Opinion, para. 11.
25 Id. para. 11.
26 Id. para. 12.
27 Id.
28 Majority Decision, para. 66.
29 Article 12(2)(a) of the Rome Statute.
30 Id. Article 12(2).

Hungarian Yearbook of International Law and European Law 2021 (9) 1
doi: 10.5553/HYIEL/266627012021009001016

Palestine is a State Party to the Rome Statute. This pillar was adopted unanimously by the Chamber,[31] with the Dissent in agreement that *Palestine is considered a State Party to the Statute*.[32]

3.1.1. *Palestine's Accession*

The Court can rely on the accession procedure and the determination made by the UN General Assembly only to determine whether Palestine can be a 'State' for the purposes of being a State Party to the Statute.[33] The Decision noted that, *regardless of Palestine's status under general international law*, its accession to the Statute followed the correct and ordinary procedure, the effects of which imply that Palestine is a 'State' Party to the Statute.[34] With the confirmation that Palestine is indeed a State Party to the Statute, the Chamber stressed that it would be contradictory to deny the Statute's effects on Palestine.[35] Importantly, so as to avoid any misconceptions, the Chamber elucidated that it was "neither adjudicating a border dispute nor prejudging the question of any future borders".[36] The Dissent sees no reason to "nullify the Palestinian accession" and recapitulates that "Palestine is a State Party, despite its current and peculiar international legal situation" and thus can perform its rights and obligations under the Rome Statute.[37]

3.1.2. *No Determination of Statehood*

The Decision notes that determining that a State qualifies as being a State Party to the Rome Statute does not, however, "require a determination as to whether that entity fulfils the prerequisites of statehood under general international law."[38] The Decision cites jurisprudence from the ICJ where the ICJ refrained from making a determination of whether Kosovo or Palestine were 'States' in its respective advisory opinions.[39] The Decision reiterated that "disputed borders have never prevented a State from becoming a State Party to the Statute and, as such, cannot prevent the Court from exercising its jurisdiction."[40] In the Decision, the Court refrained from determining matters of statehood that would ultimately bind the international community as such a determination is not required for the specific purpose of the proceedings before the Chamber.[41] Furthermore, the Decision acknowledged that *the Chamber is not competent to determine statehood*

31 Majority Decision, p. 60; *see also* Dissent, para. 86.
32 Dissent, para. 86.
33 Majority Decision, para. 108.
34 Id. paras. 102 and 112.
35 Id. para. 102.
36 Id. para. 113.
37 Dissent, para. 267.
38 Majority Decision, para. 93.
39 Id.; *see* ICJ, *Legal Consequences of the Construction of a Wall in the Occupied Palestinian Territory*, Advisory Opinion, 9 July 2004, ICJ Reports 2004, p. 136; *Accordance with International Law of the Unilateral Declaration of Independence in respect of Kosovo*, Advisory Opinion, 22 July 2010, ICJ Reports 2010, p. 403.
40 Majority Decision, para. 115.
41 Id. para. 108.

doi: 10.5553/HYIEL/266627012021009001016

under general international law because the Rome Statute "insulates the Court from making such a determination."[42] The Dissent also stresses that although Palestine is a State Party to the Statute, this "does not mean [Palestine's] "statehood" has been achieved, that the issue of its territory [...] has been settled, or that its "borders" can be conceived as State boundaries."[43]

3.2. The State on the Territory of which the Conduct in Question Occurred

The second pillar focuses on the Decision's confirmation that Palestine is considered "the State on the territory of which the conduct in question occurred" within the meaning of Article 12(2)(a) of the Rome Statute.[44] Here, the Dissent differs from the Majority and the reasoning for this will be discussed below. The Decision confirmed that the word 'State' in Article 12(2)(a) must be interpreted as referring to a "State Party" found in the *chapeau* of Article 12(2) of the Rome Statute.[45]

3.2.1. Reference to the Vienna Convention on the Law of Treaties

In order to answer whether Palestine can be considered "the State on the territory of which the conduct in question occurred", the Chamber referred to the Vienna Convention on the Law of Treaties (VCLT).[46] Specifically, Article 31(1) VCLT outlines methods of interpretation and states that "[a] treaty shall be interpreted in good faith *in accordance with the ordinary meaning* [...] given to the [...] treaty [...] and *in the light of its object and purpose*."[47]

With regards to the phrase 'ordinary meaning' in Article 31(1) VLCT, the Chamber noted that a definition of 'State' is not provided for anywhere in the Statute, Rules of Procedure and Evidence or the Regulations of the Court.[48] Considering the omission of a formal definition of 'State', the Decision noted that the word 'following' used in the *chapeau* of Article 12(2) of the Rome Statute ultimately connects the referenced 'State Parties' in the provision to paragraph (a) being "[t]he State on the territory of which the conduct in question occurred."[49] The Dissent raises the argument that the use of the word 'following' should relate to both limbs of Article 12(2) thereby reaching a different conclusion for this pillar.[50] The Dissent speaks of the importance of the 'two limbs' extracted from Article 12(2) being: *(i)* States which are "Parties to this Statute" and; *(ii)* States which "have accepted the jurisdiction of the Court", and notes that the Decision only relied on the first limb.[51] Furthermore, the Dissent

42 Id.
43 Dissent, para. 267.
44 Id. para. 91.
45 Id. para. 93.
46 Vienna Convention on the Law of Treaties, 23 May 1969, 1155 United Nations Treaty Series 18232.
47 Id. Article 31(1).
48 Majority Decision, para. 92.
49 Id. para. 93.
50 Dissent, para. 57.
51 Id. para. 57.

doi: 10.5553/HYIEL/266627012021009001016

noted that the Decision disregarded the conjunction 'or' between the two limbs and if this had been taken into account, the word 'State' would likely be "understood [...] in its traditional, ordinary meaning" and not just as a 'State Party'.[52] The Decision also referred to the *principle of effectiveness* and the preamble of the Rome Statute to define the territorial parameters of the Court's jurisdiction under Article 12(2)(a).[53] Thus, the Chamber concluded, among other things, that the reference to "[t]he State on the territory of which the conduct in question occurred" in Article 12(2)(a) of the Rome Statute must be interpreted as referring to a State Party to the Statute in light of the object and purpose of the Statute as well as in accordance with the ordinary meaning given to its terms in their context.[54]

3.3. Jurisdiction over the Occupied Territories

This pillar outlines the legal reasoning behind the finding that the Court's jurisdiction extends to the Territories Occupied by Israel since 1967, namely Gaza and the West Bank, including East Jerusalem. The Dissent also differs from the Majority on this pillar. The Dissent stresses the importance of considering relevant rules of international law, such as the Oslo Accords for example, and suggests that the Majority refused to consider these.[55] The Dissent mentions a potential consequence of the Majority's "refusal" being

> "statements and resolutions regarding the legitimate rights of Palestinians, originally adopted in the context of the *people's sovereignty*, are now described in the [...] Decision as elements of *State sovereignty* and are accepted as proof of ownership of a precise territory."[56]

3.3.1. Right to Self-Determination

The Decision notes that the "Palestinian right to self-determination within the Occupied Palestinian Territory has been explicitly recognized by different bodies" such as the ICJ, the UN Security Council, and the UN General Assembly.[57] In defining its territorial jurisdiction, the Court placed emphasis on the right to self-determination based on UN General Assembly resolutions. For instance, the UN General Assembly Resolution 67/19 accorded "non-member observer State status in the [UN]" to Palestine and "[reaffirmed] the right of the Palestinian people to self-determination and to independence in their State of Palestine on the Palestinian territory occupied since 1967."[58] The Chamber noted that it did not have the authority to challenge the validity of Resolution 67/19 and further, that the Resolution cited numerous other "similarly-worded resolutions" including

52 Id. para. 58.
53 Majority Decision, paras. 104-105.
54 Id. para. 109.
55 Dissent, para. 261.
56 Id. para. 279.
57 Majority Decision, para. 121.
58 Id. para. 116; *see* UN General Assembly, Status of Palestine in the United Nations, 29 November 2012, A/RES/67/19, para. 1.

doi: 10.5553/HYIEL/266627012021009001016

relevant UN Security Council Resolutions.[59] One such example cited by the Chamber was the UN General Assembly Resolution A/RES/58/592 which

> "[affirmed] that the status of the Palestinian territory occupied since 1967, including East Jerusalem, remains one of military occupation, and [...] that the Palestinian people have the right to self-determination and to sovereignty over their territory."[60]

In light of above resolutions affirming the right to self-determination cited in the Decision, the Chamber found that *the Court's territorial jurisdiction in the Situation in Palestine extends to the territories occupied by Israel since 1967*, namely Gaza and the West Bank, including East Jerusalem.[61]

The Dissent recognizes that "a general right to self-determination [...] of the Palestinian people, also recognized by the ICJ in its advisory opinion on the Wall [...], is uncontested."[62] However, the Dissent argues that this right is not helpful in determining an existing and recognized legal state-boundary.[63] This can be tied to the fact that the Dissent does not believe the 'State Party' qualification can change the fact of the ambiguity around Palestine's legal borders by stating that "acrobatics with the provisions of the Statute cannot mask legal reality."[64] The Dissent is of the view that Palestine's status as a State may be addressed eventually under the concept of "State for the purposes of the Statute under international law", however, the question of territory remains to be answered.[65] The Dissent also notes several resolutions that contain the same language as the UN General Assembly Resolution 67/19, but it is of the view that this wording "can hardly be interpreted as referring to an already existing, independent and sovereign state."[66] For example, the Dissent emphasizes the use of phrases such as "early realization of self-determination" and "in preparation for independence"[67] which to the Judge signify that Palestine is possibly on a path to achieving this status, henceforth it is not yet a State for the purpose of the proceedings. In the words of the Dissent, "this means that [...] the General Assembly still does not consider Palestine's statehood to be already existing and fully fledged, but rather as an aim to be achieved."[68] The Dissent cannot find

59 Majority Decision, para. 117.

60 Id.; *see* UN General Assembly, Status of the Occupied Palestinian Territory, including East Jerusalem, 6 May 2004, A/RES/58/292, para. 1.

61 Majority Decision, para. 118.

62 Dissent, para. 277.

63 Id.

64 Id. para. 13.

65 Id. para. 244.

66 Id. para. 251.

67 Id. paras. 248 and 250-251; *see e.g.* UN General Assembly, Status of Palestine in the United Nations, 29 November 2012, A/RES/67/19, para. 6; UN General Assembly, Resolution 74/10, 3 December 2019, A/RES/74/10, para. 8; UN General Assembly, Resolution 73/18, 30 November 2018, A/RES/73/18, para. 8; UN General Assembly, Resolution 69/20, 25 November 2014, A/RES/69/20, para. 8; *see also* Annex 2 of the Dissent.

68 Dissent, para. 252.

doi: 10.5553/HYIEL/266627012021009001016

reasons "why a Chamber should accept [...] a statement on the existence of 'the territory of the State' when [...] indicia show that it is premature to speak of a full-fledged 'State' and 'the territory of the State'".[69]

The Dissent further disagrees with the Prosecutor and Majority's reliance on UN General Assembly Resolutions since their legal character is non-binding. The Dissent mentions that "[t]he Prosecutor's primary position and the Majority Decision attribute a decisive effect to the interplay of Resolution 67/19 and the Palestine ICC accession."[70] It further elaborates that reliance on UN resolutions are

> "weakened by the limited legal value of resolutions adopted by the [UN General Assembly], as well as those adopted by the UN SC when it is not "acting under Chapter VII" but under Chapter VI."[71]

Thus, the Judge accentuates the legal value of these UN resolutions as being "soft law documents [...] [which are] nevertheless non-binding."[72] According to the Dissent, the Prosecution Request rightly refrained from stating that a recommendation is binding, however, it failed to distinguish what is binding from what is only a recommendation, suggestion or opinion.[73]

3.3.2. *Interpretation of the Oslo Accords*

The Oslo Accords constitute a set of legal agreements conducted throughout the 1990s between the government of Israel and the Palestinian Liberation Organization.[74] The applicability of the Oslo Accords was explored in the Prosecution Request, the Decision and the Dissent. The Decision briefly addresses the Oslo Accords "for the sake of completeness",[75] whereas the Dissent views the Oslo Accords as having significant importance[76] and provides a detailed interpretation of such. Without going into the legal aspects of the Oslo Accords themselves, this subsection will rather analyze the different ways in which they are interpreted in the Decision and Dissent.

Despite the Oslo Accords regulating Palestine's criminal jurisdiction, the Prosecution Request views the Oslo Accords as not barring the exercise of the Court's jurisdiction for the purposes of the proceedings.[77] The argument that Palestine has limited capacity to delegate its jurisdiction to the Court because it does not have criminal jurisdiction with respect to Israelis or crimes committed in Area C based on the Oslo Accords was noted, however, the Prosecution Request does not consider these limitations to be obstacles of the Court's exercise of

69 Id. para. 10.
70 Id. para. 238.
71 Id. para. 270.
72 Id. para. 6.
73 Id. para. 9.
74 Prosecution Request, para. 63.
75 Majority Decision, para. 124.
76 Dissent, p. 113.
77 Prosecution Request, p. 98.

doi: 10.5553/HYIEL/266627012021009001016

jurisdiction in the present Situation.[78] The Prosecution Request first argues that a separation can be made between *enforcement jurisdiction* and *prescriptive jurisdiction*, with the former regulating compliance with legislation and the latter being the capacity to make laws through legislative, executive or judicial action, including conferring jurisdiction to the ICC.[79] The second argument provided for in the Prosecution Request is that, as a result of Israel's status as an occupying power under international law, the Oslo Accords can be categorized as a "special agreement" within the terms of the Fourth Geneva Conventions and thus cannot "violate peremptory rights nor can they derogate from or deny the rights of 'protected persons' under occupation."[80] Although the Prosecution Request notes that the Oslo Accords limit Palestine's capacity to engage in international relations, they have not precluded it from acceding to a number of multilateral treaties.[81] Moreover, the aforementioned UN General Assembly Resolution 67/19 recognizes Palestine's ability to "accede to treaties bearing the "all States" or "any State" formula."[82] Thus, according to the Prosecution Request, the Oslo Accords appear "not to have affected Palestine's ability to act internationally."[83] This would imply that Palestine has the ability to act internationally, namely the ability to refer a situation to the ICC.

Contained in the Oslo Agreements are a number of clauses limiting the scope of Palestinian jurisdiction.[84] The Decision outlines two arguments with regards to the applicability of the Oslo Agreements to the Situation in Palestine. The first is that Palestine could not have delegated part of its jurisdiction to the Court,[85] however, the Decision rejected the first argument and decided the second argument was applicable being that the Oslo Agreements do not affect the Court's jurisdiction, although some views pointed towards the possibility that the Agreements could affect matters of cooperation with the Court.[86] However, the Chamber did not decide on the matter as it deemed it unnecessary to do so at that specific stage in the proceedings. It therefore does not hold the view that the Oslo Accords have applicability to "a question of jurisdiction in connection with the initiation of an investigation by the Prosecutor arising from the referral of a situation by a State."[87] In other words, *the issues of the Oslo Accords are not pertinent to addressing the question before the Chamber* pertaining to Article 12(2)

78 Id. para. 183.
79 Id. para. 184; Carsten Stahn, 'The ICC, Pre-Existing Jurisdictional Treaty Regimes, and the Limits of the Nemo Dat Quod Non Haber Doctrine', *Vanderbilt Journal of Transnational Law*, Vol. 49, Issue 2, 2016, pp. 450-451; Malcolm N. Shaw, *International Law Eighth Edition*, Cambridge University Press, Cambridge, 2017, p. 483; *see also* Dissent, para. 331.
80 Prosecution Request, para. 186; Dissent, para. 332; *see also* Majority Decision, para. 25.
81 Prosecution Request, para. 184.
82 Id. para. 184; *see* The Office of Legal Affairs of the United Nations, General Assembly, Resolution 67/19 Memorandum, 21 December 2012 (concluding that "Palestine would be able to become party to any treaties that are open to 'any State'"), para. 15.
83 Prosecution Request, para. 184.
84 Majority Decision, para. 125.
85 Id. para. 126.
86 Id.
87 Id. para. 129.

doi: 10.5553/HYIEL/266627012021009001016

(a) of the Rome Statute at this time.[88] The Decision does, however, *leave open the possibility for interested States to raise this issue based on Article 19* of the Rome Statute (covering "[c]hallenges to the jurisdiction of the Court or the admissibility of a case") at a future time.[89]

The Dissent performs a detailed analysis of the Oslo Accords by examining their international legal nature with respect to texts and wording, jurisprudential practice of Israel and Palestine, doctrinal interpretations of their legal nature, and the relevance of the Oslo Accords in answering the main question before the Chamber, to name a few.[90] Judge Kovács takes into consideration specific articles from the Oslo Accords which he believes circumscribe ICC jurisdiction in certain areas, namely Area C. Areas A, B, and C are described as follows: *(i)* Area A refers to populated areas delineated by the Oslo Accords where Palestinians were to acquire control over civil matters with responsibility for internal security and public order;[91]*(ii)* Area B refers to populated areas other than those in Area A, where "'internal security responsibility" was to be transferred to Palestinians "except for issues [...] of permanent status negotiations and of Israel's [...] responsibility for Israelis and borders[92]"'; and *(iii)* Area C covers the West Bank (outside areas A and B) including the settlements over which Israel "retained [...] territorial jurisdiction but [Palestine] was to acquire functional jurisdiction over Palestinians."[93] Interestingly, the Dissent points out that after the COVID-19 outbreak in 2020, the "law regulating health and sanitary issues in areas A and B was that of the Palestinian Authority and area C was under the law of the Israeli authorities."[94]

The Dissent proposes that for areas A and B, the Prosecutor may proceed to investigate, however, to conclude an agreement with Israel in advance would be beneficial in securing optimal conditions for an investigation, if such an investigation does occur in the future.[95] For area C and East-Jerusalem, the Dissent argues that the Prosecutor may *only* proceed to investigate if the "preconditions to the exercise of jurisdiction" under Article 12(3) of the Rome Statute are met, "except under the circumstances described in rule 1(b) of

88 Majority Decision, para. 129.

89 Id.; *see also* Article 19 of the Rome Statute: "Challenges to the jurisdiction of the Court or the admissibility of a case."

90 Dissent, p. 2.

91 Prosecution Request, para. 68; *see* Israeli-Palestinian Interim Agreement on the West Bank and the Gaza Strip (Oslo II), 28 September 1995, UN General Assembly A/51/889, para. 3(a).

92 Id.; *see* Oslo II, para. 3(b).

93 Id.; *see also* Oslo II, para. 3(c).

94 Dissent, para 317.

95 Id. para. 374; *see* Oslo II, Annex IV: Protocol Concerning Legal Affairs, article I (Criminal Jurisdiction), at paragraph 1(a), reads as follows: "The criminal jurisdiction of the Council covers all offenses committed by Palestinians and/or non-Israelis in the Territory, subject to the provisions of this Article. For the purposes of this Annex, 'Territory' means West Bank territory except for Area C which, except for the Settlements and the military locations, will be gradually transferred to the Palestinian side in accordance with this Agreement, and Gaza Strip territory except for the Settlements and the Military Installation Area."

doi: 10.5553/HYIEL/266627012021009001016

Article [I] of Annex IV" of the Oslo Accords.[96] Thus, if a potential investigation concerns Area C and East-Jerusalem, according to the Dissent, the Prosecutor may only proceed if the above-mentioned articles are satisfied. Article 12(3) would entail that the Prosecutor must first gain consent (or in the terms of Article 12(3), "acceptance") of Israel for ICC jurisdiction to be exercised. Article 12(3) states that

> "[i]f the acceptance of a State which is not a Party to this Statute is required under paragraph 2, that State may, by declaration lodged [...] accept the exercise of jurisdiction by the Court with respect to the crime in question [...]."[97]

It is important to note that Israel is not a State Party to the ICC Statute, which is why paragraph (3) of Article 12 would apply.

It has to be noted that a State that is not a State Party to the Statute "[has] no obligations toward the ICC under [the Statute]."[98] Furthermore, should any formal investigation arise post-Decision, the ICC can prosecute individuals for crimes under its Statute, but it cannot prosecute States.[99]

4. Concluding Remarks

As we have seen from the Prosecution Request and subsequent Decision, Dissent, and Separate Opinion, the Situation in Palestine comprises highly complex legal issues. A thorough analysis was conducted by the Chamber regarding the three pillars addressed in this article. The Decision made clear that *the Oslo Accords, although an important aspect of international law, did not influence or impact the present decision* before the Chamber. However, as previously mentioned, the Decision noted that interested States can raise any jurisdictional issues surrounding the Oslo Accords on the basis on Article 19 in the future, leaving this

96 Dissent, para. 374; *see* Oslo II, Annex IV, Article I.1(b): "In addition, the Council has criminal jurisdiction over Palestinians and their visitors who have committed offenses against Palestinians or their visitors in the West Bank and the Gaza Strip in areas outside the Territory, provided that the offense is not related to Israel's security interests."

97 Article 12(3) of the Rome Statute: "If the acceptance of a State which is not a Party to this Statute is required under paragraph 2, that State may, by declaration lodged with the Registrar, accept the exercise of jurisdiction by the Court with respect to the crime in question. The accepting State shall cooperate with the Court without any delay or exception in accordance with Part 9."

98 The International Criminal Court, 'Questions and Answers on the Decision on the International Criminal Court's territorial jurisdiction in the Situation in Palestine' (the ICC Questions and Answers), 15 February 2021, at www.icc-cpi.int/. Please note that this is not an official document. It is intended for public information only.

99 Id.; *see also* Article 1 of the Rome Statute: "[...] [The] [Court] [...] shall have the power to exercise its jurisdiction over persons for the most serious crimes of international concern, as referred to in this Statute [...]."

doi: 10.5553/HYIEL/266627012021009001016

possibility open.[100] It is worth noting that the Decision could have been appealed by the Prosecutor, who had sought the ruling, or by a 'Party' if the conditions under Article 82(1)(a) of the Rome Statute are met.[101] However, no appeal was lodged within the specified time limit, thus, the Decision is definitive and can no longer be appealed as the time limit has passed.

The Chamber's conclusions relate only to the current proceedings before it.[102] If the

> "Prosecutor submits an application for the issuance of a warrant of arrest or summons to appear [...], or if a State or a suspect submits a challenge under [...] the Statute, the Chamber will be in a position to examine further questions of jurisdiction which may arise at that point in time."[103]

The Decision on the Situation in Palestine by the Chamber does not trigger an ICC investigation as this lies with the Prosecutor, however, once the Prosecutor concludes that all elements have been met to open an investigation, which it has done in the Prosecution Request, the Prosecutor has a legal duty to open that investigation.[104] If such an investigation does commence and crimes are proven, individuals can be held liable, no matter what side of the conflict they are on, as the Prosecutor "has a duty to investigate all alleged crimes in a specific situation."[105]

Some participants raised the argument that a ruling on the Court's jurisdiction in the Situation in Palestine would constitute a political decision with political consequences potentially affecting the Court's legitimacy.[106] Importantly, the Chamber responded to these arguments by asserting that

> "by the very nature of the core crimes under the [...] Statute, the facts and situations that are brought before the Court arise from controversial contexts where political issues are sensitive and latent"

and "a judiciary cannot retreat when it is confronted with facts [...] aris[ing] from political situations and/or disputes, but which also trigger legal and juridical issues."[107] The Chamber acknowledged that core crimes under the Statute can often emanate from controversial and political situations, and this reality cannot

100 Majority Decision, para. 129; *see also* Statute, Article 19 ('Challenges to the jurisdiction of the Court or the admissibility of a case').

101 The ICC Questions and Answers; Article 82(1) of the Rome Statute: "Either party may appeal any of the following decisions in accordance with the Rules of Procedure and Evidence: (a) A decision with respect to jurisdiction or admissibility."

102 Majority Decision, para. 131.

103 Id.

104 The ICC Questions and Answers; Article 53(1) of the Rome Statute: "The Prosecutor shall, having evaluated the information made available to him or her, initiate an investigation unless he or she determines that there is no reasonable basis to proceed under this Statute [...]."

105 Id.

106 Majority Decision, para. 53.

107 Id. para. 55.

doi: 10.5553/HYIEL/266627012021009001016

obstruct the Court when legal and juridical issues are triggered,[108] as it is of upmost importance that the ICC have the ability to perform its mandate of prosecuting "persons for the most serious crimes of international concern."[109]

To conclude, the Decision and Dissent unanimously agreed that Palestine is a State Party to the Statute.[110] By majority, the Decision concluded that "Palestine qualifies as "[t]he State on the territory of which the conduct in question occurred" for the purposes of Article 12(2)(a) of the Statute."[111] Finally, the Decision confirmed, by majority, that the Court's territorial jurisdiction extends to the territories occupied by Israel since 1967, namely Gaza and the West Bank, including East Jerusalem.[112]

108 Id.
109 Article 1 of the Rome Statute.
110 Majority Decision, p. 60.
111 Id.
112 Id.

doi: 10.5553/HYIEL/266627012021009001016

The Evolution of Content-Related Offences and Their Investigation During the First 20 Years of the Cybercrime Convention

*Kinga Sorbán**

Abstract

The Convention on Cybercrime otherwise known as the Budapest Convention was a complex, pioneering instrument addressing cross-border computer crimes in the wake of the 21st century. As the first international treaty aiming to tackle new threats emerging from the cyberspace, the Convention signed in 2001 certainly influenced national regulators and law enforcement over many years. Two decades have passed since 2001 and the Internet era has undergone previously unpredictable changes, as web 2.0 services started to thrive. Even though the Convention can be considered a landmark in international legislation, after 20 years one must eventually assess how well it stood the test of time and whether it still has relevance. This article has no smaller goal but to evaluate the evolution of content-related cybercrimes and try to the question whether the Convention is still fit to tackle contemporary issues or rather, is outdated and ready to retire.

Keywords: cybercrime, content-related offence, cyberbullying, privacy, wiretapping.

1. Introduction

The Convention on Cybercrime otherwise known as the Budapest Convention was a complex, pioneering instrument addressing cross-border computer crimes in the wake of the 21st century. As the first international treaty aiming to tackle new threats that emerged from cyberspace, the convention signed in 2001[1] certainly influenced national regulators and law enforcement over many years. 20 years have passed since 2001 and the Internet era has undergone under previously unpredictable changes, as web 2.0 services started to thrive. Web 2.0 was described as an embryo in development by Darcy DiNucci in 1999[2] who envisioned that instead of remaining a static collection of texts and images the

* Kinga Sorbán: junior research fellow, National University of Public Service, Budapest.

1 The Convention was signed on 23 November 2001 and is in force from 1 July 2004.

2 Cristina Aced, *Web 2.0: The Origin of the Word that Has Changed the Way We Understand Public Relations*', International PR 2013 Conference.

doi: 10.5553/HYIEL/266627012021009001017

Internet will be a "transport mechanism, the ether through which interactivity happens."[3]

A couple of years after the signatories adopted the Cybercrime Convention, web 2.0 services started to spread and now we live in an era of abundance in terms of web-based interactive services. There were 361 million Internet users in 2000, now that accounts for two-thirds of the clients of Facebook.[4] The first camera phones appeared around 2000, although around the time the Convention was drafted, it was a high-tech gadget only available to a select few. In our present days, almost everybody has a smartphone or tablet in their bag, with broadband internet access. Facebook was founded in 2004, now it is a social media platform that is among the most important drivers of societal discourse. The notable service YouTube was launched in 2005 when founding member Jawed Karim uploaded his first video entitled "Me in the Zoo".[5] After Google acquired this media service provider in 2006[6] it became the largest global video-sharing platform, with 500 hours of videos being uploaded every minute.[7] Our present days' largest microblogging platform Twitter was launched in 2006. Since then, it has gathered more than 100 million users,[8] among them, politicians and heads of states informing the public.[9]

The Convention received harsh criticism from the very beginning. Jason Wallace for example argued that its wording was too vague, claiming it would trammel civil rights and privacy.[10] Arguing against its signature, Ryan M.F. Baron considered it more of a liability than an asset, raising several concerns including the lack of specific protection for privacy rights[11] and the absence of proper procedural safeguards which allow countries to "use the treaty as a means to enforce government policies".[12] Despite all the criticism it was signed and ratified, and for a long time it remained the sole and most important international tool to tackle computer crime. Several regional and national instruments drew on the Convention, and it also had an impact on the law of the

3 Darcy DiNucci, 'Fragmented Future', *Print Magazine*, Vol. 53, Issue 4, 1999, p. 32, at http://darcyd.com/fragmented_future.pdf.

4 *See* at www.pingdom.com/blog/incredible-growth-of-the-internet-since-2000/#:~:text=There%20were%20only%20361%20million,2000%2C%20in%20the%20entire%20world.

5 Kevin Allocca, *Videocracy*. Bloomsbury, 2018.

6 Andrew Ross Sorkin & Jeremy W. Peters, 'Google to Acquire YouTube for $1.65 Billion', *The New York Times*, 9 October 2006.

7 Hours of Video Uploaded to YouTube Every Minute as of May 2019, at www.statista.com/statistics/259477/hours-of-video-uploaded-to-youtube-every-minute/.

8 Number of monetizable daily active Twitter users (mDAU) worldwide from 1st quarter 2017 to 1st quarter 2021, at www.statista.com/statistics/970920/monetizable-daily-active-twitter-users-worldwide/.

9 *See e.g.* the Twitter account of US President Joe Biden at https://twitter.com/JoeBiden, or of European Commission President Ursula von der Leyen, at https://twitter.com/vonderleyen.

10 Jason Wallace, *Council of Europe Cybercrime Treaty Analysis*, at www.ithell.com/Opinion/CybercrimeTreaty/body-cybercrime-treaty.html.

11 Ryan M.F. Baron, 'A Critique of the International Cybercrime Treaty', *CommLaw Conspectus: Journal of Communications Law and Technology Policy*, Vol. 10, Issue 2, 2002, p. 278.

12 Id. p. 275 and 278.

Hungarian Yearbook of International Law and European Law 2021 (9) 1
doi: 10.5553/HYIEL/266627012021009001017

EU, as the instruments of European cybercrime legislation were worded in accordance with the Cybercrime Convention.

Even though the Convention may be considered a landmark in international legislation, after 20 years one must eventually assess how well it stood the test of time and whether it still has relevance. This article has no smaller goal but to *evaluate the evolution of content-related cybercrimes and try to the question whether the Convention is still fit to tackle contemporary issues or rather, is outdated and ready to retire*. I will proceed in this evaluation by examining the following four key areas of the Convention. *(i)* First, the article will take a look at the Convention's overall structure giving a detailed description of its categorization of cybercrime. This first Section also serves the purpose of determining how content-related cybercrimes fit into the framework established by the Cybercrime Convention. *(ii)* Second, the wording of the Convention will be compared to newly emerged definitions describing the same or similar content-related conducts criminalized. *(iii)* Third, emerging cybercrime trends will be described along with an assessment of whether these new trends fall under the crime categories regulated by the Convention. *(iv)* Last but not least the article will elaborate on the procedural provisions of the Cybercrime Convention that enable the collection of electronic evidence in the online sphere. The Section will articulate concerns that were raised regarding the constitutionality of these procedural provisions putting an emphasis on privacy-based concerns. The final Section of this article makes an attempt to predict the future of cybercrime legislation. In this section I try to describe how the 2nd Additional Protocol to the Convention will affect the current state of play, furthermore, I will formulate some critical remarks with the aim to contribute to scientific and regulatory discourse about cybercrime legislation.

2. The Structure of the Cybercrime Convention

The Convention is a multi-purpose treaty containing substantive criminal law provisions, procedural provisions and elements concerning cross-border procedures, regulating the determination of jurisdiction, and international cooperation. The aim of the Cybercrime Convention is to approximate the State Parties' legal systems in the area of combatting cybercrime. Prior to getting into the assessment of the provisions on content-related crimes it is worth outlining what is meant by cybercrime in general.

2.1. Cybercrime

Despite the fact that cybercrime is a term that appears in the title of the Convention itself, the *notion of cybercrime is not defined nor used in the text*. Instead, many other terms appear in the text to describe information technology-related criminality, such as crimes against the confidentiality of computer systems, computer-related offence and content-related offence. One must therefore first determine whether there is a difference between the concepts of cybercrime, computer crime and computer-related crimes or whether these are

doi: 10.5553/HYIEL/266627012021009001017

interchangeable notions. A publication by the International Telecommunications Union (ITU) argues that these terms cover different concepts, and that 'cybercrime' is a narrower concept than computer crime.[13] It notes that there are considerable difficulties in creating distinctive definitions as there is an abundance of regional and national approaches.

Delving into the scholarly literature on the subject does not alleviate the confusion generated by the diversity of terms. Eoghan Casey refers to computer crime as a limited set of offences that involve a computer such as unauthorized access and software piracy, while defining computer-related crimes as offences that involve a computer indirectly (*e.g.* when evidence can be gathered from a computer).[14] Cybercrime is used by Eoghan Casey as a term to describe offences where a computer network was used to facilitate the offence.[15] A similar definition is applied by Joshua B. Hill and Nancy E. Marion, who refer to cybercrime as acts "that involve criminal uses of the Internet or other networked systems to cause harm".[16] The abovementioned ITU publication shares this concept and covers any illegal behavior committed by means of, or in relation to a computer system or network, including such crimes as illegal possession and offering or distributing information by means of a computer system or network.[17] In its communication the European Commission defines cybercrime as "criminal acts committed using electronic communications networks and information systems or against such networks and systems".[18]

According to Susan W. Brenner the term cybercrime refers to a broader set of offences and includes all kinds of criminal acts that involve information technology.[19] Brenner splits the notion into three subcategories based on the role of the computer in the commission of the act. Target cybercrimes refer to a narrow set of acts where the computer is the object of the crime (such as hacking or malware distribution) while tool cybercrimes include those crimes where the computer or the network is the tool used to commit the crime.[20] I prefer the first approach and consider *cybercrimes to be network-related crimes*. Cybercrimes can be computer crimes (or target crimes) and computer-related crimes (tool crimes) alike if the commission involves a network (either the Internet or a LAN). However, interpreting cybercrime in a narrower sense may not have been the intention of the drafters of the Cybercrime Convention, because adopting this approach would mean that offences without a network element (*e.g.* hacking into a system onsite) are not covered.

13 Marco Gercke, *Understanding Cybercrime: Phenomena, Challenges and Legal Response*, ITU, 2012, p. 11.

14 Eoghan Casey, *Digital Evidence and Computer Crime, Third Edition*, Elsevier, 2011, p. 37.

15 Id. p. 37.

16 Joshua B. Hill & Nancy E. Marion, *Introduction to Cybercrime. Computer Crimes, Laws, and Policing in the 21st Century*, Praeger, 2016, p.10.

17 Gercke 2012, p. 11.

18 Communication from the Commission to the European Parliament, the Council and the Committee of the Regions, *Towards A General Policy on the Fight against Cyber Crime*, COM(2007) 267 final.

19 Susan W. Brenner, *Cybercrime: Criminal Threats from Cyberspace*, Praeger, 2010, p. 39.

20 Id.

doi: 10.5553/HYIEL/266627012021009001017

Despite its widespread use, *cybercrime is not a legally defined term*, as it does not appear in regulatory instruments. Legislators often adopt a typology-related approach to describe what kinds of acts fall under the notion of cybercrime, which is flawed, because there are significant overlaps between the categories. The Cybercrime Convention also adopted a typology-related approach which will be discussed in more detail in the following Section.

2.2. Substantive Provisions of the Cybercrime Convention

According to the Explanatory Report of the Convention,[21] Chapter II which covers substantive criminal issues defines 9 offences grouped into 4 categories. The four categories are the following: *(i)* traditional computer crimes which cover offences against the confidentiality, integrity and availability of computer data and systems, such as illegal access (hacking), data and system interference (malware distribution, DDOS attacks);[22] *(ii)* computer-related offences, such as computer-enabled forgery and fraud;[23] *(iii)* content-related offences;[24] and *(iv)* offences related to infringements of copyright.[25]

The Explanatory Report describes *computer-related offences as ordinary crimes committed through a computer system*[26] and lacks a definition for content-related crimes. This approach may cause problems, because sometimes it is not easy to make clear distinctions between computer-related offences and content-related offences. In fact, content-related offenses are a sub-category of computer-related offences, because acts related to unlawful material in a networked environment always include the use of information technology as a tool.

2.3. Content-Related Offences

The fact that the Cybercrime Convention does not define this term results in a conundrum for all those wishing to identify what acts shall be considered content-related offences. Under the title content-related offences, the Convention regulates only offences related to child sexual abuse material causing a conundrum for researchers, policy analysts and regulators. It is evident that activities concerning child sexual abuse material[27] are indeed content-related offences but it is also clear that the list of content-related offences cannot be narrowed down to simply these activities. The Additional Protocol to the Convention[28] criminalizes the dissemination of racist and xenophobic content on the Internet [such as the dissemination of such material on computer systems

21 Explanatory Report to the Convention on Cybercrime (Explanatory Report), para. 18.
22 Cybercrime Convention, Title 1 – Offences against the confidentiality, integrity and availability of computer data and systems
23 Id. Title 2 – Computer-related offences.
24 Id. Title 3 – Content-related offences.
25 Id. Title 4 – Offences related to infringements of copyright and related rights.
26 Explanatory Report, para. 79.
27 Though the text of the Convention refers to child pornography this term is now outdated as is not capable to reflect the seriousness of the offences. The article therefore will refer to child pornography as child sexual abuse material.
28 Additional Protocol to the Convention on Cybercrime, concerning the criminalization of acts of a racist and xenophobic nature committed through computer systems, ETS No. 189.

doi: 10.5553/HYIEL/266627012021009001017

(classic hate speech), bias-motivated threats, insults, and the denial, gross minimization, approval or justification of genocide or crimes against humanity], expanding the list of content-related offences. Yet even with the Additional Protocol, *the Convention does not cover the full scale of content-related offences*. Three reasons may be identified to justify these deficits of the Convention. *(i)* The first and evident reason is that the drafters of the Convention never strived for completeness, even the Explanatory Report notes, that the Convention was created to set the foundation for the harmonization of cybercrime-legislation and offers only a minimum level of protection. Thus, State Parties are only obliged to criminalize those core offences that are regulated by the Convention, while they are not excluded from adopting a stricter and more detailed regime to tackle cybercrime in their countries. *(ii)* Second, there are some new and malicious activities on the Internet that cannot be regulated globally or regionally. While there is a broad worldwide consensus behind the criminalization of serious acts (*e.g.* the acts related to the creation and dissemination of child sexual abuse material), such a common understanding is missing in the case of several forms of objectionable content. For example: some types of communication amount to criminal offences in certain countries, while they are considered to be protected speech in other countries as they fall under the umbrella of freedom of speech. This is the case with defamation which is punishable in Hungary[29] while criminal defamation was abolished in the United Kingdom by Section 73 of the Coroners and Justice Act 2009. Cultural, social, and governmental specificities can influence whether a certain act is considered punishable by criminal law and since criminal legislation is within the inner core of national sovereignty, it is not easy to develop criminal law on a supranational level. In Europe, the EU never fully harmonized Member State's criminal laws. There are areas where criminal laws were approximated in order to achieve certain policy objectives, mainly for the sake of ensuring the cross-border collection of evidence, to guarantee fair trial[30] and to tackle criminal acts that have cross-border elements,[31] or directly target the institutions of the EU.[32] *(iii)* The third reason is that the Convention was

29 Act C of 2012 on the Criminal Code, Section 226.

30 *See e.g.* Directive 2010/64/EU of the European Parliament and of the Council on the right to interpretation and translation in criminal proceedings; Directive 2012/13/EU of the European Parliament and of the Council on the right to information in criminal proceedings; Directive (EU) 2016/343 of the European Parliament and of the Council on the strengthening of certain aspects of the presumption of innocence and of the right to be present at the trial in criminal proceedings.

31 *See e.g.* Directive 2013/40/EU of the European Parliament and of the Council on attacks against information systems and replacing Council Framework Decision 2005/222/JHA; Directive 2011/92/EU of the European Parliament And Of The Council on combating the sexual abuse and sexual exploitation of children and child pornography, and replacing Council Framework Decision 2004/68/JHA; Directive (EU) 2017/541 of the European Parliament and of the Council on combating terrorism and replacing Council Framework Decision 2002/475/JHA and amending Council Decision 2005/671/JHA.

32 *See e.g.* Convention drawn up on the basis of Article K.3(2)(c) of the Treaty on European Union on the fight against corruption involving officials of the European Communities or officials of Member States of the European Union.

doi: 10.5553/HYIEL/266627012021009001017

adopted in the early 2000s.[33] The drafters could not anticipate all the remarkable achievements that influenced the online industry. We use the Internet to communicate and share content in a way that probably no one could predict. While many people use online communication for working or to stay in touch with friends and family members, some have malicious intent and aim to cause harm. As offenders started to rely on new technologies, the crimes that were originally committed in the physical world such as non-content related crimes (like harassment, stalking or fraud) and content-related crimes (like hate speech and incitement to terrorism) oozed into the virtual space.[34] Besides the evolution of traditional crimes committed in the virtual world, some unforeseen yet harmful conducts gained unprecedented popularity, including image-based abuse (such as revenge pornography) and bullying.

At this point, one may come to the conclusion that it is not possible to formulate an exhaustive list of content-related offences. However, coining a definition and establishing a uniform terminology would be welcomed as it would enable State Parties to draw up their lists of content-related offences on a common foundation. This article considers those acts to be *content-related offences, where a computer or a network is used as a tool to produce, distribute, transmit, procure, possess or store illegal content*. The list of illegal content shall include those materials that are criminalized by international law (such as the Cybercrime Convention) and those materials that are unlawful under national jurisdictions. Although it would be favorable to expand and change the terminology by amending the Convention in order to maintain the clarity of the text, it is not necessary. The Convention has an Explanatory Report and several guidelines which serve the purpose of clarifying certain provisions.

The article has two objectives concerning content-related cybercrimes. *(i)* First, it will introduce how those types of content-related crimes changed which are already criminalized by the Convention. This part of the article will carefully evaluate whether these crimes are sufficiently regulated and will explore the extent to which the current regulatory framework is efficient to tackle these offences. *(ii)* Second, the article will draw attention to newly emerged phenomena, which pose an issue for regulators but are not yet covered by the Convention. Prior to unfolding the previously highlighted issues, one must add, that the Convention shall not be considered a standalone legal instrument. On the contrary, it is but a piece in a very complex system of legislative instruments regulating the cybercrime landscape and should be seen as part of a bigger picture. In order to illustrate the Convention's position within the regulatory landscape, the article will draw up the comprehensive regulatory framework of all

33 The Convention was signed on 23 November 2001 and entered into force on 1 July 2004.

34 Statista reported a significant increase in cyber fraud risk due to the COVID-19 pandemic, at www.statista.com/statistics/1175574/increase-cyber-fraud-coronavirus-outbreak/. The Pew Research Center's survey conducted in the US revealed that roughly four-in-ten Americans have experienced online harassment, *see* at www.pewresearch.org/internet/2021/01/13/the-state-of-online-harassment/. In the UK, 2% of adult hate crimes have an online element, *see* at https://assets.publishing.service.gov.uk/government/uploads/system/uploads/attachment_data/file/811450/Adult_Online_Harms_Report_2019.pdf.

the conducts discussed, elaborating on the most important conventions and supranational legal instruments complementing the Cybercrime Convention.

3. Content-Related Offences in the Cybercrime Convention

According to its Explanatory Report, the language of the Cybercrime Convention was chosen to be technologically neutral in order to futureproof the text.[35] This futureproofing however could not prevent changes to certain notions. The following Section will elaborate on the terms currently used by the Cybercrime Convention and introduce alternatives where it is necessary to update the Convention's wording to keep it relevant.

3.1. Child Sexual Abuse Material

According to the Cybercrime Convention, producing, offering, making available, distributing, transmitting, procuring, and possessing child pornography shall constitute a criminal offence. The Convention consistently uses the term child pornography for child sexual abuse material for which it has received severe criticism. The Convention defines child pornography as

> "pornographic material that visually depicts: *(a)* a minor engaged in sexually explicit conduct; *(b)* a person appearing to be a minor engaged in sexually explicit conduct; *(c)* realistic images representing a minor engaged in sexually explicit conduct."[36]

The Lanzarote Convention on the sexual exploitation of children[37] echoes the criminalization of offences related to child sexual abuse material. The Lanzarote Convention (which also uses the term child pornography) defines the term as follows:

> "child pornography shall mean any material that visually depicts a child engaged in real or simulated sexually explicit conduct or any depiction of a child's sexual organs for primarily sexual purposes."[38]

Several differences can be spotted between the two definitions. First and foremost, the Lanzarote Convention *uses the term 'child' instead of minor*. Furthermore, the Lanzarote Convention only aims to criminalize offences that victimize real children: virtual child pornography and the conduct of adult actors mimicking minors are not addressed, while the Cybercrime Convention also covers material that depicts persons representing or appearing to be minors. As such the two Conventions establish different levels of protection: those States

35 Explanatory Report, para. 36.
36 Cybercrime Convention, Article 9 – Offences related to child pornography.
37 Council of Europe Convention on the Protection of Children against Sexual Exploitation and Sexual Abuse.
38 Lanzarote Convention, Article 20 – Offences concerning child pornography.

doi: 10.5553/HYIEL/266627012021009001017

that did not sign and ratify the Cybercrime Convention have to criminalize a narrower set of conducts. The different levels of protection give rise to merely theoretical debates and do not pose a problem in practice, because the Cybercrime Convention was signed and ratified by all State Parties of the Lanzarote Convention.[39]

Both definitions have *two troublesome elements: the definition of pornographic material and the definition of a minor.*

3.1.1. Sexual Abuse and Pornography

Using the term pornography for describing acts related to the sexual exploitation of children is deemed to be controversial by many, including Allisdair Gillespie as it underplays the significance of the issue.[40] The dictionary definition of pornography states that pornography "is the depiction of erotic behavior (in pictures or writing) intended to cause sexual excitement."[41] Edwards argues that child sexual abuse material cannot be considered erotica as this imagery represent the "rape, abuse and torture of children".[42] The Luxemburg Guidelines on terminology highlights that the term pornography is generally used to describe a commercial product in which consenting adults engage in sexual activity.[43] Danijela Frangež *et al.* highlight that pornography is a commonly used term, which is broadly accepted, trivialized and refers to a type of material that is legal in the majority of the countries of the globe and using the term for material depicting the sexual abuse and exploitation of children may, in fact, legitimize the phenomena.[44]

Adolescents engaging in sexual activities may encounter several new online behaviors that gained popularity since the Convention was adopted. Sexting, meaning the creation and distribution of sexually explicit imagery by text messages or social media have gained popularity among young people in the last couple of years.[45] It would seem illogical and unnecessary to charge teenagers with the creation and dissemination of 'child pornography' yet the Convention does not make a distinction between different kinds of sexual imagery involving

39 *See* the Chart of signatures and ratifications of the Cybercrime Convention at www.coe.int/en/web/conventions/full-list/-/conventions/treaty/185/signatures?p_auth=Ie8q5VWb; and the Chart of signatures and ratifications of the Lanzarote Convention at www.coe.int/en/web/conventions/full-list/-/conventions/treaty/201/signatures.

40 Alisdair A. Gillespie, 'Child Pornography', *Information & Communications Technology Law*, Vol. 27, Issue 1, 2018, p. 31.

41 Merriam-Webster, *Definition of Pornography*, at www.merriam-webster.com/dictionary/pornography.

42 Susan S. M. Edwards, 'Prosecuting 'Child Pornography': Possession and Taking of Indecent Photographs of Children', *Journal of Social Welfare and Family Law*, Vol. 22, Issue 1, 2000, p. 1.

43 Susanna Greijer & Jaap Doek, *Terminology Guidelines for the Protection of Children from Sexual Exploitation and Sexual Abuse*, ECPAT International, Bangkok, 2016, p. 38.

44 Danijela Frangež *et al.*, 'The Importance of Terminology Related to Child Sexual Exploitation', *Journal of Criminal Investigation and Criminology*, Vol. 66, Issue 4, 2015, pp. 291-299.

45 Bruce Y. Lee, 'Here Is How Much Sexting Among Teens Has Increased', *Forbes*, 8 September 2018, at www.forbes.com/sites/brucelee/2018/09/08/here-is-how-much-sexting-among-teens-has-increased/?sh=2dfcb4be36f1.

doi: 10.5553/HYIEL/266627012021009001017

children. It has to be noted that it is not the aim of criminal law to hold persons accountable for conduct that poses little to no danger to society or its members, so to alleviate the concern, a more nuanced wording should be adopted.

A commonly used term in our present days is *child sexual abuse material (CSAM) and child sexual exploitation material (CSEM)*. The latter is used by international police organizations such as Europol,[46] while the former is used by several organizations and private entities including the International Association of Internet Hotlines (INHOPE)[47] and YouTube (Google). The EU also uses the term child pornography, but its Directive on combating the sexual abuse of children clarifies that child pornography consists of images of child sexual abuse.[48] The EU also acknowledged the inadequacy of the term child pornography. The European Parliament started communicating its effort to correct the terminology in its Resolution on Online Child Sexual Abuse in 2015.[49] Either of these terms is acceptable, because they clearly indicate that we are in fact talking of violent, abusive conduct that takes places on a regular basis often with the aim of realizing financial gain. These terms do not cover self-generated, sexually explicit content produced consensually (unless consent is a result of putting pressure on, or coercing children) which helps avoid an unnecessary stigmatization of adolescents.

3.1.2. Minor

While the Cybercrime Convention refers to child sexual abuse material as child pornography, it does not define who should be regarded as a child, instead, it uses the term 'minor'. According to the Cybercrime Convention, *the term minor shall refer to persons under 18 years of age, but State Parties are free to set a lower age limit (but not less than 16 years of age)*.[50] This definition is in accordance with the UN Convention on the Rights of the Child, which uses the same definition, but refers to children. While the two terms appear to be synonymous they are not. The term 'child' shall be perceived as a universal term, referring to all persons under the age of 18 years, while the term 'minor' should be understood as a legal notion. The Luxemburg Guidelines describe minors as persons who have not reached the age of majority.[51] The age of majority is "is the legally defined age at which a person becomes an adult, with all the attendant rights and responsibilities of adulthood."[52] The age of majority is generally set at 18 years, but some exceptions exist. Under some jurisdictions, persons under 18 can become emancipated (*e.g.* by marriage or by obtaining a court order) which means that children can legally

46 *See* at www.europol.europa.eu/crime-areas-and-trends/crime-areas/child-sexual-exploitation.

47 *See* at www.inhope.org/EN.

48 Directive 2011/92/EU of the European Parliament and of The Council on combating the sexual abuse and sexual exploitation of children and child pornography, and replacing Council Framework Decision 2004/68/JHA, Recital (3).

49 European Parliament Resolution of 11 March 2015 on child sexual abuse online, 2015/2564(RSP), para. 12.

50 Cybercrime Convention, Article 9(3).

51 Greijer & Doek 2016, p. 8.

52 Id. p. 6.

doi: 10.5553/HYIEL/266627012021009001017

attain the status of adults. It is generally presumed that minors cannot legally consent to the creation of pornographic material,[53] since they lack sufficient discretion to assess the consequences of their actions. However, the status of being an emancipated minor expressly involves the capability to make certain decisions (such as entering into contracts or managing property) on their own behalf. In the case of emancipated minors, there is clearly a tension between the legal status of a person and the protection offered by the Cybercrime Convention. Being an emancipated minor shall not result in certain persons between the ages of 16 and 18 losing their status as a child and becoming excluded from the protection that international legal instruments provide to children. Thus, it would be strongly recommended for the Cybercrime Convention to use the term 'child' which generally refers to any person under the age of 18 regardless of the legal status. The EU Directive on combating the sexual abuse of children defines and uses the term 'child' and considers any person below the age of 18 years to be a child.[54]

The age-based approach of the Cybercrime Convention may also be challenged. László Dornfeld notes that the biggest problem of the age-based approach is that there is a gap between the age of consent and the protection offered by laws aiming to protect children.[55] The age of consent is 16 years old in the UK, 14 in Germany if both partners are under 18, 15 in France, 12 in Hungary if both partners are under 18.

4. On the Verge of Criminalization: Contemporary Harmful Phenomena on the Internet

There are several recently emerged harmful trends in cyberspace that are not covered by the Convention. National legislations however already started to address these issues, which clearly shows a need for criminalization. Letting these issues be tackled on a national level may result in different levels of protection in State Parties which could deepen the chasm between the substantive criminal laws of states. In this section of the article, two issues will be discussed in greater depth, due to the fact that the EU and the Council of Europe have already made attempts to draw attention to these phenomena: the dissemination of sexual content without consent and cyberbullying. While the former is definitely a content-related issue, the latter not necessarily is. The reason this article discusses cyberbullying among content-related crimes is that cyberbullying is an umbrella term that refers to a wide range of online behavior; some of them can be categorized as content-related crimes.

53 Id.

54 Directive 2011/92/EU of the European Parliament and of The Council on combating the sexual abuse and sexual exploitation of children and child pornography, and replacing Council Framework Decision 2004/68/JHA, Article 2(a).

55 László Dornfeld, 'ICTs and Sexual Exploitation of Children in Europe', *in* Khosrow-Pour Mehdi (ed.), *Encyclopedia of Criminal Activities and the Deep Web*, Hershey, IGI Global, 2020, p. 568.

doi: 10.5553/HYIEL/266627012021009001017

4.1. Dissemination of Sexual Content without Consent

Non-consensual pornography or "revenge porn" as it is called in layman's terms, has become widespread throughout Europe in the 2010s and the phenomenon is surrounded by scandalous events ever since.[56] A British petition in 2020 called for a ban on the biggest pornography video-sharing platform, Pornhub, because the provider allowed the publication of leaked sex tapes and other types of non-consensual sexual imagery, sometimes featuring minors.[57] Clare McGlynn and Erika Rackley consider the dissemination of sexual content without consent[58] to be imagery that violates personal and bodily integrity,[59] dignity and privacy.[60] Even though the personal harms and detrimental societal impacts of the dissemination of such material are severe, legal response to, and the criminalization of creating and distributing such material is inconsistent with approaches varying from country to country. In the United Kingdom, the Criminal Justice and Courts Act enacted a new offence to criminalize disclosing private sexual photographs and films with the intent to cause distress.[61] The French 'Digital Republic Code' modified Section 226-2-1 of the Penal Code which sanctions the taking or recording or transmitting images of sexual nature of a person in a public or private place without consent (226-1) with two years imprisonment and a fine of EUR 60,000.[62] The German Penal Code does not expressly criminalize the unlawful disclosure of sexual images without consent, however, it sanctions the violation of one's personal life by creating and transmitting images unlawfully.[63] In Hungary, the disclosure of sexual images without consent is not an offence, but the Hungarian Criminal Code protects personal data through several broad provisions. The violation of personal data is

56 In 2018 a popular YouTuber named Chrissy Chambers pursued a civil claim against her British ex-boyfriend who had filmed sexual acts they had engaged in and later published these videos widely on the internet. *See* at www.theguardian.com/technology/2018/jan/17/youtube-star-chrissy-chambers-wins-damages-in-landmark-uk-revenge-porn-case. American politician Katie Hill, who had to resign from Congress in November 2019 because her ex-husband had published explicit images of her, which went viral in the global press. *See* at www.wired.com/story/katie-hill-revenge-porn-facebook. Despite these events, porn sites are still reluctant to remove non-consensual sexual imagery, *see* at www.wired.com/story/porn-sites-still-wont-take-down-non-consensual-deepfakes/.

57 Kate Isaacs, 'Pornhub Needs to Change – Or Shut Down', *The Guardian*, 9 March 2020.

58 Clare McGlynn & Erika Rackley, 'Image-Based Sexual Abuse', *Oxford Journal of Legal Studies*, Vol. 37, Issue 3, 2017, p. 535.

59 Id. p. 545.

60 Id. p. 546.

61 Section 33 of the Criminal Justice and Courts Act 2015: "It is an offence for a person to disclose a private sexual photograph or film if the disclosure is made *(a)* without the consent of an individual who appears in the photograph or film, and *(b)* with the intention of causing that individual distress."

62 Codé Penal 226-2-1: "Lorsque les délits prévus aux articles 226-1 et 226-2 portent sur des paroles ou des images présentant un caractère sexuel prises dans un lieu public ou privé, les peines sont portées à deux ans d'emprisonnement et à 60 000 € d'amende."

63 Strafgesetzbuch § 201a(1): "Mit Freiheitsstrafe bis zu zwei Jahren oder mit Geldstrafe wird bestraft, wer 1. von einer anderen Person, die sich in einer Wohnung oder einem gegen Einblick besonders geschützten Raum befindet, unbefugt eine Bildaufnahme herstellt oder überträgt und dadurch den höchstpersönlichen Lebensbereich der abgebildeten Person verletzt [...]."

doi: 10.5553/HYIEL/266627012021009001017

punishable with imprisonment of up to one year.[64] The EU deals with the issue from a privacy perspective. Article 17 of the General Data Protection Regulation (GDPR)[65] ensures that service providers remove personal information upon request, which facilitates the swift removal of sexual content uploaded without consent. However, this privacy-based approach does not offer effective reparation for the victim, nor does it prevent perpetrators from sharing the same images again. Currently, *there aren't any EU legislative instruments to tackle the issue of non-consensual publication of sexual imagery*. The reason for this is that the substantive criminal laws of the Member States are beyond the scope of EU-level harmonization.[66] The Treaty of Lisbon allows for the stronger alignment of national laws in the fields of substantive and procedural criminal laws through the supranational framework of "Judicial Cooperation in Criminal Matters".[67] Still, EU-level harmonization remains limited, "as the Union's competence has been limited to establishing minimum rules concerning the definition of criminal offences and sanctions in the areas of particularly serious crimes with a cross-border dimension."[68] The TFEU lists those offences that are considered particularly serious crimes and as such can be harmonized on an EU level, but the list does not contain content-related offences similar to the non-consensual distribution of sexual imagery.[69] International legal instruments also fail to provide sufficient redress mechanisms. The Istanbul Convention[70] contains several substantive criminal law provisions to criminalize certain forms of violent conduct. It does not mention cyber-related conduct, but any of the behaviors regulated in the discussed sections can be committed in the online sphere. The Cybercrime Convention Committee's (T-CY) mapping study highlights that the Istanbul Convention's explanatory report takes into consideration that threatening behavior may take place in the virtual world (chat rooms, social networking sites, *etc.*).[71] Besides this general remark, the Istanbul Convention does not regulate the dissemination of private images in a separate article and as such, it does not create a straightforward obligation for the State Parties to adopt anti-revenge pornography regulations. The Cybercrime Convention also does not

64 Act C of 2012 on the Criminal Code, Section 219.

65 Regulation (EU) 2016/679 of the European Parliament and of the Council of 27 April 2016 on the protection of natural persons with regard to the processing of personal data and on the free movement of such data and repealing Directive 95/46/EC (General Data Protection Regulation, GDPR).

66 Peter Csonka & Oliver Landwehr, '10 Years after Lisbon. How "Lisbonised" Is the Substantive Criminal Law in the EU?', *Eucrim*, 2019/4, p. 262.

67 Article 82 *et seq*. TFEU.

68 Csonka & Landwehr 2019, p. 262.

69 *See* Article 83 TFEU. These areas of crime are the following: terrorism, trafficking in human beings and sexual exploitation of women and children, illicit drug trafficking, illicit arms trafficking, money laundering, corruption, counterfeiting of means of payment, computer crime and organized crime.

70 Council of Europe Convention on preventing and combating violence against women and domestic violence.

71 Cybercrime Convention Committee (T-CY), *Mapping Study on Cyberviolence*, Strasbourg, 2018. p. 24.

doi: 10.5553/HYIEL/266627012021009001017

address cyber-violence and as such it does not mention the dissemination of non-consensual sexual imagery among content-related crimes. Davin Ryan argues that legislation must focus on setting up a preventive framework, which is coherent and repressive of the behavior.[72] Setting up such a framework could be a new path ahead for the further development of the Cybercrime Convention.

4.2. Cyberbullying

Cyberbullying is a term that is used to describe a complex set of issues including harassing, stalking, threatening behavior, the dissemination of libelous, slandering statements. Enacting anti-bullying legislation is one of the regulatory trends of the 21st century. Several countries (such as Canada and the US) introduced anti-bullying legislation which all have a broader scope than cyberbullying as they aim to put an end to all forms of peer violence. In Canada, the province of Ontario was the first to adopt an anti-bullying law (Accepting Schools Act – 2012) to tackle bullying that takes place in schools or in a learning environment.[73] In the US, several states adopted anti-bullying laws in the 2010s. In 2020 New Jersey introduced the Anti-Bullying Rights Acts, in 2011 Connecticut adopted the Act Concerning the Strengthening of School Bullying Laws, and in 2012 California introduced Seth's Law.[74] Regulatory attention has turned toward cyberbullying in Europe in the last couple of years as well. The United Kingdom doesn't have a dedicated legislative instrument to tackle bullying, but anti-bullying measures can be found in several Acts, including the Protection from Harassment Act (1997) and the Malicious Communications Act (1988) and the Communications Act (2003). Germany employs a similar approach, for instead of regulating cyberbullying as a complex issue, German law deals with conducts that are often categorized as bullying separately.[75] Despite its widespread use, it is not a legally defined term since the phenomenon itself lacks a clear definition. The first definitional attempt identified cyberbullying as traditional bullying taking place in the virtual space. The definition used by P. K. Smith *et al*. defines cyberbullying as "an aggressive intentional act carried out by a group or individual, using electronic forms of contact, repeatedly and over time against a victim who cannot easily defend him or herself."[76] A similar definition was coined by Sameer Hinduja and Justin W. Patchin: according to them, cyberbullying is "willful and repeated harm inflicted through the use of

72 David Ryan, 'European Remedial Coherence in the Regulation of Non-Consensual Disclosure of Sexual Images', *Computer Law and Security Review*, Vol. 34, Issue 5, 2018, p. 1072.

73 Shaheen Shariff, *Sexting and Cyberbullying. Defining the Line for Digitally Empowered Kids*, Cambridge University Press, Cambridge, 2015, p. 133.

74 Id. p. 134.

75 The German Criminal Code *(Strafgesetzbuch)* criminalizes the following conducts: incitement to hatred (Section 130), threatening the commission of a felony (Section 241), insult (Section 185), defamation (Section 186), intentional defamation (Section 187), and violation of intimate privacy by taking photographs (Section 201a).

76 Peter K. Smith *et al*., 'Cyberbullying: Its Nature and Impact in Secondary School Pupils', *Journal of Child Psychology and Psychiatry*, Vol. 49, Issue 4, 2008, p. 376.

doi: 10.5553/HYIEL/266627012021009001017

computers, cell phones, and other electronic devices."[77] Further research pointed out that there are significant differences between cyberbullying and traditional bullying due to the anonymity provided by cyberspace, the distance between the perpetrators and victims and the vast dissemination capacities.[78] Shaheen Shariff points out that the word "bullying" is overused[79] by media, academia and NGOs, thus, it is obsolete and unfit to describe the diversity of the issue. Agreeing with this statement the study will use cyberbullying as an umbrella term with the aim of mapping those acts that are often categorized as bullying in cyberspace and identifying those forms of online bullying that are or could be content-related offences. What is common in all the cited pieces of legislation is that they regulate bullying as a behavior that is conducted by children and adolescents in a school environment. Although bullying is indeed behavior that occurs most often among younger persons it is not exclusively committed in an educational setting. Cyberbullying can also be a form of gender-based violence, since research shows that many women experience bullying at their workplace (in the form of sexist jokes, sexist language, gender stereotypes).[80]

Several forms of cyberbullying can be identified in academic literature: online harassment; online stalking; flaming; exclusion; outing (or in other terms doxing); trickery or phishing;[81] identity theft either in the form of impersonation or in its more harmful form, the sockpuppetry;[82] the nonconsensual dissemination of sexual imagery (such as revenge pornography); unsolicited sexting.

The list above is not exhaustive but can be used to illustrate that *some forms of cyberbullying are content-related*. The repeated dissemination of nonconsensual sexual imagery is definitely content related, because it is almost exclusively realized by the dissemination of unlawful content. Harassment and stalking can be considered content-related in specific cases, when the offender targets the victim through public communication platforms (*e.g.* by posting messages to social media timelines or making threatening abusive comments under posts or videos). Harassing behavior in social media is a serious issue; the Pew Research Centre indicates that the majority of online harassment takes place on social media.[83] The Cybercrime Convention does not regulate the above mentioned

77 Sameer Hinduja & Justin W. Patchin, *Bullying Beyond the Schoolyard: Preventing and Responding to Cyberbullying, Second Edition*, Corwin Press, 2008, p. 5.

78 Anna Costanza Baldry *et al.*, 'Cyberbullying and Cybervictimization', *in* Anna Costanza Baldry *et al.* (eds.), *International Perspectives on Cyberbullying Prevalence, Risk Factors and Interventions*, Palgrave McMillan, 2018, p. 4.

79 Shariff 2015, p. 8.

80 Cybercrime Convention Committee (T-CY), *Mapping Study on Cyberviolence*, Strasbourg, 2018, p. 6.

81 Dorothy L. Espelage *et al.*, 'Cyberbullying in the United States', *in* Baldry *et al.* (eds.) 2018, p. 65.

82 Sockpuppeting is a relatively new term. A sockpuppet is an account developed with an aim to deceive others. *See* Michael Tsikerdekis & Sherali Zeadally, 'Multiple Account Identity Deception Detection in Social Media Using Nonverbal Behavior', *IEEE Transactions on Information Forensics and Security*, Vol. 9, Issue 8, pp. 1311-1321.

83 Pew Research Centre, *The State of Online Harassment*, at www.pewresearch.org/internet/2021/01/13/the-state-of-online-harassment/.

doi: 10.5553/HYIEL/266627012021009001017

content-related conducts under Chapter II, although there are existing examples of regulating the offline form of similar conducts. It must be highlighted that not every behavior considered bullying in nature constitutes a criminal act. In fact, criminal law is on a very far end of the scale and shall only be called upon when all other instruments fail to tackle a certain form of harmful behavior. Distasteful taunts, cruel jokes (even though they are hurtful and cause emotional distress especially to young people whose personalities are not fully evolved) should not be punished by criminal law. Some extreme behaviors such as harassment and stalking are already criminalized by international instruments and national legislation because these are not unique to cyberspace, all of them can be committed through more traditional methods (*e.g.* by speech in front of a large audience, or letters sent *via* postal services). Through these anti-harassment and stalking laws a minimum level of protection is guaranteed, however, owing to their general wording they are unsuitable to reflect the specificities of the virtual forms of these conducts. Therefore, introducing new rules does not seem to be an unnecessary duplication of already existing anti-harassment laws.

5. Procedural Solutions to Tackle Content-Related Offences Online

The Cybercrime Conventions has *a dedicated chapter on procedural provisions in order to aid and enhance the effectiveness of criminal investigations*. Section 2 of the Cybercrime Convention contains procedural provisions which aim to enhance cross border cooperation in evidence gathering while Section 3 deals with the issues concerning jurisdiction which is of paramount importance for the effective investigation of crimes with international elements. Articles 18-21 regulate production orders, the search and seizure of computer-stored data, the collection of traffic data, and the interception of content data (often referred to as wiretapping), respectively. These provisions create an opportunity for the State Parties to oblige private persons and companies such as intermediary service providers to retain and forward data, and to assist law enforcement authorities (LEAs).

5.1. Privacy Issues

As all provisions concern users' personal data and may potentially interfere with the right to private and family life, privacy safeguards are very important. The ECHR protects the right to respect for private and family life in Article 8, whereas private life also includes certain forms of correspondence. The Cybercrime Convention has an article (Article 15) that prescribes the adoption of mechanisms on a domestic level that ensure the adequate protection of human rights, the introduction of judicial or other independent supervision, and the incorporation of the principle of proportionality. A recent survey pointed out that State Parties "are not provided with detailed requirements in terms of protecting fundamental

doi: 10.5553/HYIEL/266627012021009001017

rights and freedoms in the context of data retention."[84] These provisions are too vague as the State Parties were provided with a broad room for maneuver to grant powers to LEAs, without setting limits to the intrusiveness of these powers. It is unclear how the notion of judicial or other independent supervision should be interpreted: should it be connected to the right to an effective remedy, or should it be an authorization preceding the use of such powers? Ryan M.F. Baron draws attention to the fact that the text of the Convention explicitly refers to privacy and "does not specifically state what privacy rights are."[85] The absence of the detailed elaboration of safeguards or competent authorities was a deliberate decision of the drafters of the Cybercrime Convention, as the following reasoning was provided by the explanatory report:

> "the Convention applies to Parties of many different legal systems and cultures [and it is, therefore] not possible to specify in detail the applicable conditions and safeguards for each power and procedure."[86]

Providing effective safeguards with due respect to privacy should be a core consideration, for the right to privacy and LEAs' powers to conduct surveillance or use wiretapping techniques often clash in practice. Several cases found their way to the ECtHR concerning the seizure of computers and data, but also covert investigation techniques such as wiretapping. Thus, there is a pool of judgments that draw attention to the most concerning issues. It has to be noted that the below-mentioned case-law concerns domestic legislation and not the Cybercrime Convention directly. However, such cases demonstrate that State Parties sometimes fail to enact the appropriate safeguards within their respective legal systems, which is a result of

> "the absence of clear guidance on the national transposition of these principles and the identification of 'privacy short-comings' in the actual implementation of the Convention at a national level."[87]

In *Trabajo Rueda*,[88] the ECtHR elaborated on the issue of judicial authorization. The applicant's computer was seized by police in a computer repair shop because the technician noticed that it contained child pornography. The applicant complained that the police obtained the computer without a judicial warrant, thus, the measures interfered with his right to private life and correspondence. The ECtHR examined whether the power to search and seize the applicant's computer was prescribed by law and found that at the time of the commission of the offence, Spain had legal provisions that enabled LEAs to search and seize

84 Data retention in the States Parties to the Budapest Convention on Cybercrime Survey Report 2020 p. 27, at https://rm.coe.int/2088-32-data-retention-report-2020/1680a1f305.

85 Baron 2002, p. 274.

86 Explanatory Report, para. 145.

87 Luca Tosoni, 'Rethinking Privacy in the Council of Europe's Convention on Cybercrime', *Computer Law and Security Review*, Vol. 34, Issue 6, 2018, p. 1208.

88 *Trabajo Rueda v Spain*, No. 32600/12, 30 May 2017.

doi: 10.5553/HYIEL/266627012021009001017

computers.[89] At the time the Cybercrime Convention wasn't yet ratified by Spain,[90] but it is safe to assume that Spanish legislators were drafting their respective national laws with due consideration to the Cybercrime Convention's procedural provisions. The ECtHR found that *the seizure of the computer violated Article 8 ECHR because it was disproportionate to the legitimate aim (to prevent the sexual abuse of children).*[91] The ECtHR also highlighted that judicial authorization is a safeguard, which can be circumvented only in case of a matter of urgency: in this case, such urgency had not been identified.

In *Benedik*,[92] the ECtHR evaluated the preservation of dynamic IP addresses and the way police accessed subscriber information. The case concerned the investigation of a peer-to-peer child pornography distribution network (Razorback) which was monitored by Swiss LEAs. The Swiss police retained several dynamic IP addresses; one of them was linked to the applicant by Slovenian police, whose computer was searched and seized after the internet service provider accessed subscriber information and passed it on to the police. The applicant argued that dynamic IP addresses shall be considered traffic data and as such should only be obtainable with a judicial warrant, which was never issued in the case.[93] Besides the relevant domestic law, the ECtHR examined the 1981 Convention and the Cybercrime Convention as well, which defines "traffic data" as

> "any computer data relating to a communication by means of a computer system, generated by a computer system that formed a part in the chain of communication, indicating the communication's origin, destination, route, time, date, size, duration, or type of underlying service."[94]

The ECtHR emphasized that the rules governing seizure in *Benedik* were foreseeable because the Cybercrime Convention obliges states to introduce measures such as the collection of traffic data and production orders,[95] which the Slovenian Criminal Procedure Act had implemented. However, the ECtHR found that the domestic law that had introduced these measures lacked clarity and "did not offer sufficient safeguards against arbitrary interference"[96] and held that there had been a breach of Article 8 ECHR. *Benedik* well illustrates *what difficulties may arise due to the overly broad rules of the Cybercrime Convention when it comes to safeguards*. Obviously, Article 15 of the Cybercrime Convention laid down the foundations for the protection of certain fundamental rights, yet in the absence

89 Id. para. 38.
90 The applicant was tried and sentenced in 2008, while Spain ratified the Cybercrime Convention two years later in 2010.
91 *Trabajo Rueda*, para. 47.
92 *Benedik v Slovenia*, No. 62357/14, 24 April 2018.
93 Id. para. 15.
94 Id. para. 49.
95 Id. para. 126.
96 Id. para. 132.

doi: 10.5553/HYIEL/266627012021009001017

of clear instructions or guidance on how to implement these measures, many states failed to design a framework for privacy protection.

5.2. The Role of Intermediary Service Providers in Tackling Content-Related Offences
Intermediary service providers such as internet service providers (ISPs), hosting service providers (such as social media platforms like Facebook and video-sharing platforms like YouTube) play an important role in aiding investigations and mitigating the harms caused by perpetrators. Perpetrators using the internet to disseminate and disclose unlawful content must have internet access often provided by an ISP based on subscription. Many of those offences that are committed *via* the publication or dissemination of unlawful content such as the dissemination of child sexual abuse material, hate speech or incitement to terrorism are frequently committed *via* the services of social networking sites such as Facebook, Instagram or YouTube. Intermediary service providers can support the investigative process and the mitigation of harm by various means. On one hand, they can provide traffic and user data to LEAs, or preserve volatile evidence such as stored data. On the other hand, they have tools to remove or block access to illegal content to stop them from being spread. There are several examples of intermediary providers aiding criminal investigations by providing LEAs with user data. Facebook has received a total of 173,592 government requests for user data in the first half of 2020.[97] In 72.8% of these cases the provider produced some sort of data. The majority of these requests were filed in the US (61,528 requests),[98] but the EU Member States also send requests to Facebook. In the first half of 2020 France and Germany filed 11,086[99] and 11,211 requests, respectively.[100] According to the company, these requests usually seek subscriber information such as name, registration data, IP address logs and account content.[101] Subscriber information is considered personal data and as such, procedural rules and safeguards surround the preservation and transfer of such data.[102] When a criminal investigation is conducted in one country but the requested provider is established in another country, the requested data can be obtained through a mutual legal assistance agreement. Acquiring extraterritorially located data is a time-consuming and long procedure[103] and its revision is underway.

The Cybercrime Convention does not have provisions on the blocking, filtering and removal of illegal content, although taking down or restricting access to unlawful

97 *See* at https://transparency.facebook.com/government-data-requests/jan-jun-2020.
98 *See* at https://transparency.fb.com/data/government-data-requests/country/US.
99 *See* at https://transparency.fb.com/data/government-data-requests/country/FR.
100 *See* at https://transparency.fb.com/data/government-data-requests/country/DE.
101 *See* at https://transparency.facebook.com/government-data-requests/jan-jun-2020.
102 *See* at https://transparency.facebook.com/government-data-requests/jan-jun-2020.
103 Council of Europe Cybercrime Convention Committee (T-CY), The Mutual Legal Assistance Provisions of the Budapest Convention on Cybercrime, para. 123.

content is a common practice in the EU.[104] Namely, the intermediary service providers established in any of the Member States must remove any unlawful content reported, otherwise they can be held liable for user-generated content.[105] A well-known domestic example is the German Act to Improve Enforcement of the Law in Social Networks which obliges intermediary service providers including ISPs and social media service providers to remove content that is unlawful under the German Criminal Code.[106]

6. The Future of the Cybercrime Convention

The current problems relating to the text of the Cybercrime Convention mostly stem from issues of terminology. The Convention *lacks the definition of key terms* such as cybercrime and content-related offences, *leaving a broad margin of appreciation for State Parties* to interpret the provisions of the Convention. It would be welcomed to set common foundations by defining core concepts in order to prevent the divergence of legal systems and to establish a uniform level of protection by obliging State Parties to criminalize the most harmful content-related conducts. Although it would be favorable to expand and change the terminology by amending the Convention in order to maintain the clarity of the text, it is not necessary. The Convention has an Explanatory Report and several guidelines which serve the purpose of clarifying certain provisions.

It can be concluded that *the term child pornography is outdated*. On one hand, the term 'pornography' does not reflect the abuse that is suffered by the victims. On the other hand, pornography can be understood as a term that covers sexually explicit images and materials shared among peers. The Cybercrime Convention's aim is to oblige State Parties to criminalize serious crimes such as conduct related to the sexual exploitation of children and not to stigmatize adolescents who are sharing explicit content. These reasons justify the amendment of the wording of the Convention and the introduction of a term that is better suited to grasp the abusive nature of such conduct, such as child sexual abuse material.

Section 2.3 of this article came to the conclusion that the minimum level approach of the Convention cannot really be criticized as *it is difficult to set forth uniform expectations* when the affected countries differ in terms of legal systems and traditions. However, the threshold could be expanded. As it was mentioned in Section 4, several harmful online behaviors emerged in the last couple of years (such as the non-consensual dissemination of sexual imagery or conducts related to cyberbullying), some of which can be categorized as content-related offences.

104 *See* the Comparative Study on Blocking, Filtering and Take-down of Illegal Internet Content prepared by Swiss Institute of Comparative Law, at https://edoc.coe.int/en/internet/7289-pdf-comparative-study-on-blocking-filtering-and-take-down-of-illegal-internet-content-html.

105 Directive 2000/31/EC of the European Parliament and of the Council of 8 June 2000 on certain legal aspects of information society services, in particular electronic commerce, in the Internal Market, Articles 12, 13 and 14.

106 Gesetz zur Verbesserung der Rechtsdurchsetzung in sozialen Netzwerken. § 3. Umgang mit Beschwerden über rechtswidrige Inhalte.

doi: 10.5553/HYIEL/266627012021009001017

In our present days, the list of content-related issues is constantly expanding, and States started to respond to these issues by introducing new laws (*e.g.* the anti-revenge porn laws, and the anti-bullying laws mentioned in Sections 4.1 and 4.2). Thus, the possibility to include some new offences in the Convention would worth considering.

Section 5.1 criticized the Cybercrime Convention due to its broad-brush approach in terms of laying down a framework for the effective protection of human rights. In this section mostly privacy-related issues were discussed. Section 5.2 dealt with the obligations of intermediary service providers, which shall cooperate with LEAs in the signatory states. In this regard, two issues were identified. *(i)* First, extraterritorial data preservation is cumbersome due to the time-consuming mutual legal assistance. *(ii)* Second, the obligations of service providers aim to identify the perpetrator but do not provide for the fate of the illegal content. The swift removal of criminal content is of paramount importance in order to stop the spreading of the content in question.

A partial revision of the text of the Cybercrime Convention is an ongoing process since the drafting of a new additional protocol was announced in 2017.[107] The revisions concern procedural issues that appeared in the last 20 years due to the international nature of cybercrime. Yet they do not concern the terminological issues raised in the previous sections of this study and do not expand the list of substantive provisions. This means that the list of content-related offences will not be expanded in the foreseeable future, leaving the matter of tackling new issues to the domestic legislators. The 2nd Additional Protocol to the Cybercrime Convention will address the issues of language of requests submitted by the LEAs, video conferencing and will hopefully resolve some of the issues that arise in relation to the cross-border collection of electronic evidence.[108] The draft protocol aims to introduce several new measures targeting directly or indirectly service providers that store data that can be used as electronic evidence (such as the IP address, subscriber information, location information, *etc.*).

The *draft of the new Protocol* aims to introduce a new rule about the disclosure of subscriber information.[109] The draft article would enable LEAs to request subscriber information directly from service providers under the jurisdiction of different states. According to the new provisions, such requests may be directly addressed to the service providers instead of requesting assistance from the state in which the provider is established to obtain the necessary information. Parties to the Convention would also be able to request domain name registration information from entities providing domain name services established in another country.[110] The reason behind this provision stems from the fact that the drafters

107 Cybercrime Convention Committee (T-CY), Preparation of a 2nd Additional Protocol to the Budapest Convention on Cybercrime, Strasbourg, 29 November 2017, p. 2.

108 Cybercrime Convention Committee (T-CY), Second Additional Protocol to the Convention on Cybercrime on enhanced co-operation and disclosure of electronic evidence. Draft Protocol version 3 as approved by the T-CY at its 24th Plenary (28 May 2021).

109 Id. Article 7 – Disclosure of subscriber information.

110 Id. Article 6 – Request for domain name registration information.

recognized: "many forms of cybercrime are facilitated by offenders creating and exploiting domains for malicious and illicit purposes."[111] On the one hand these measures are welcomed because they speed up the investigative process which is of paramount importance when the electronically stored evidence is volatile and is deleted by service providers after a certain amount of time. On the other hand, these provisions raise serious privacy concerns echoed by the European Data Protection Board in a statement issued about the draft protocol. The EDPB pointed out that it is

> "essential that EU negotiating parties ensure that the provisions laid down in the additional protocol do comply with the EU *acquis* in the field of data protection in order to ensure its compatibility with EU primary and secondary law."[112]

The EDPB has expressed its concerns regarding the formerly discussed articles of the additional protocol, especially about the transfer of third party data to non-EU State LEAs. The cross-border transfer of electronic evidence has been on the agenda of the EU legislator as well, since 2018 when the European Commission made a proposal on the text of the e-evidence regulation.[113] The proposed regulation includes the introduction of European Production Orders, which would enable Member States to obtain electronic evidence directly from service providers regardless of their place of establishment within the EU.[114] Such production orders can only be issued by a judge, a court, an investigating judge or by another competent authority;[115] furthermore, the issuing of the orders have must comply with strict conditions.[116] The order shall be necessary and proportionate for the purpose of the proceedings and it shall include information such as the relevant provisions of the criminal law of the requesting state. The European Digital Rights (EDRi) association issued a statement in which it characterized the new regulatory trend of accessing data directly from service providers worrisome[117] and called on the Council of Europe "to create a human rights-respecting alternative to dangerous shortcuts." From this aspect, the additional protocol generates some new problems instead of solving the previously mentioned ones. In a world where crime in the online sphere becomes more and more international in nature, and where national LEAs rely on non-

111 Cybercrime Convention Committee (T-CY), Preparation of a 2nd Additional Protocol to the Budapest Convention on Cybercrime, Strasbourg, 2020, p. 32.

112 European Data Protection Board, *Statement 02/2021 on New Draft Provisions of the Second Additional Protocol to the Council of Europe Convention on Cybercrime (Budapest Convention)*, 2021, at https://edpb.europa.eu/sites/edpb/files/files/file1/statement022021onbudapestconvention newprovisions_en.pdf.

113 Proposal for a Regulation of the European Parliament and of the Council on European Production and Preservation Orders for electronic evidence in criminal matters.

114 Id. Chapter 2: European Production Order, European Preservation Order and Certificates.

115 Id. Article 4 – Issuing authority.

116 Id. Article 5 – Conditions for issuing a European Production Order.

117 *See* at https://edri.org/our-work/new-protocol-on-cybercrime-a-recipe-for-human-rights-abuse/.

Hungarian Yearbook of International Law and European Law 2021 (9) 1
doi: 10.5553/HYIEL/266627012021009001017

state party information more than ever, the Additional Protocol's current text seems to be more of a liability than an asset.

doi: 10.5553/HYIEL/266627012021009001017

Is the World Ready to Overcome the Thesis of the Clash of Civilizations?*

*István Lakatos***

Abstract

The article provides a critical overview of the Clash of Civilizations theory by Samuel Huntington, but in this context it also addresses two other important books also aimed at finding the correct answers to the new challenges of the post-Cold War era; Huntington's work was also an answer to their thesis. They are Francis Fukuyama's The End of History and the Last Man, and John Mearsheimer's The Tragedy of Great Power Politics. I argue that neither the Clash of Civilizations nor the End of History theses correctly captures the complexity of our contemporary social and political life, as they are both based on the assumption of the superiority of the West and the inferiority of the Rest.

Keywords: clash of civilizations, end of history, tragedy of great power politics, dignity of difference, clash of ignorance.

"History does not kill. Religion does not rape women; the purity of blood does not destroy buildings and institutions do not fail. Only individuals do those things."[1]

1. Introduction

There are two other important books that must be mentioned in the context of this article, which are aimed at finding the correct answers to the new challenges of the post-Cold War era. Besides *The Clash of Civilizations and the Remaking of World Order* by Samuel Huntington, Francis Fukuyama's *The End of History and the Last Man* became extremely popular and still has a significant impact on public discourse regarding the newly established contemporary political order. The second one, John Mearsheimer's *The Tragedy of Great Power Politics*, is less well known to the public, but still very influential in academic circles. His

* The opinions expressed herein are strictly personal and do not necessarily reflect the position of the Hungarian MFAT.

** István Lakatos: career diplomat, former human rights ambassador of the Ministry of Foreign Affairs and Trade (MFAT) of Hungary, currently senior adviser at the Ministry of Justice, Human and Minority Rights of Montenegro.

1 Giandomenico Picco, Personal Representative of the UN Secretary-General for the Year of Dialogue Among Civilizations (2001). *See* Vesselin Popovski, (2012). '"Dignity of Difference" and Re-evaluation of Western Dominance' *in* Mojtaba Mahdavi & W. Andy Knight (eds.), *Towards 'the Dignity of Difference?' Neither 'End of History' nor 'Clash of Civilizations'*, Routledge, London, 2012, p. 89.

doi: 10.5553/HYIEL/266627012021009001018

argument that in the post-Cold War era other great powers will seek to balance the power of the US, was quoted frequently by researchers.[2]

Following the Yugoslav wars, the dissolution of the USSR, 9/11, the rise of ISIL and the recent refugee/migration crises in Europe focused international attention on Huntington's paradigm. However, Huntington's book is mainly an answer to the work of his former student, Francis Fukuyama, predicting the complete victory of Western democracy and free-market capitalism, in addition, it also includes references to Mearsheimer's thesis. Therefore, this chapter gives a short critical overview of the theses established by the three well-known US scholars; furthermore, by introducing other approaches, it provides more accurate answers to the human rights challenges of this post-Cold War period.

2. The End of History and the Last Man

Fukuyama, in an article published in 1989,[3] and subsequently in a book (1992) entitled *The End of History and the Last Man*,[4] gave a very optimistic analysis of the post-Cold War Era. He claimed that with the demise of the Soviet Union, communism stopped being a challenge to the spread of Western-style liberal democracy, and consequently, democracy would be "the only game in town".[5] According to his paradigm, Western liberal democracy and the free market represent the "acme of human achievement"; after that there is nothing else to achieve anymore.[6] In his book Fukuyama was of the view that the collapse of the Soviet system marked "the end of history as such: that is the end point of mankind's ideological evolution and the universalization of Western liberal democracy as the final form of human government."[7] Fukuyama, and other liberal thinkers, believed that modernization and development would result in Western-style secularism, and "tolerant, rational, pragmatic, progressive, humanistic" societies.[8] According to his vision, in the post-Cold War era Western institutions will gradually increase their influence and "cover the whole world to thereby foster peace and signal the end of historical development".[9] In conclusion,

2 Glen M. E. Duerr, 'Huntington vs. Mearsheimer vs. Fukuyama: Which Post-Cold War Thesis Is More Accurate?', *in* Davide Orsi (ed.), *The 'Clash of Civilizations' 25 Years On. A Multidisciplinary Appraisal*, E-International Relations Publishing, Bristol, 2018, p. 76.

3 Francis Fukuyama, 'The End of History?', *The National Interest*, No. 16, Summer 1989, pp. 3-18.

4 Francis Fukuyama, *The End of History and the Last Man*, Free Press, New York, 1992.

5 Jeffrey Haynes, 'From Huntington to Trump: Twenty-Five Years of the "Clash of Civilizations"', *The Review of Faith & International Affairs*, Vol. 17, Issue 1, 2019, p. 14.

6 Chandra Muzaffar, 'The Clash of Civilizations or Camouflaging Dominance?', *in* Salim Rashid (ed.), *The Clash of Civilizations? Asian Responses'*, The University Press Limited, Dhaka, 1997, p. 99.

7 Fukuyama 1992, p. 217.

8 Riley Quinn, *A Macat Analysis. Samuel P. Huntington's The Clash of Civilizations and the Remaking of World Order'*, Routledge, London, 2017, pp. 38-39.

9 John M. Hobson, 'Deconstructing the Eurocentric Clash of Civilizations: De-Westernizing the West by Acknowledging the Dialogue of Civilizations', *in* Martin Hall & Patrick Taddeus Jackson (eds.), *Civilizational Identity. The Production and Reproduction of "Civilizations" in International Relations*, Palgrave Macmillan, 2007, p. 153.

doi: 10.5553/HYIEL/266627012021009001018

Fukuyama's concept was a Western-centric approach, based on the assumption that, by definition, the West was developed while the Rest was underdeveloped because of its traditional cultures and institutions; the latter to be abandoned by the Rest in order to adopt Western practices.[10] Fukuyama's thesis implies that there is a universal paradigm of development and democracy provided by the West and that both the West and the Rest are monolithic categories. He assumes that there is a "singular path to modernity" and the Rest has no other choice but to follow it. This paradigm implies that the cultures and traditions of non-Western states are not important factors in the whole process.[11]

Fukuyama's paradigm has particularly strong explanatory force for describing the world during the 1990s, when we witnessed the proliferation of democracies and saw more and more states were choosing free market principles. This trend completely changed because of 9/11. The paradigm was also challenged by the rise of China and the resurgence of Russia. However, despite the recent decline in the number of democracies in the world, in 2017, 87 of the 195 measured states were still considered "free".[12] This high number proves that democracy is still considered by many states as the best and final form of human government. Research also underlines that democracy is the best way to prevent interstate wars: democracies do not fight each other. Besides, in the post-Cold War period there is no one distinct ideology (such as the fascism or communism of the past) to compete with liberal democracy and capitalism.[13]

3. The Tragedy of Great Power Politics

In his 2001 book, *The Tragedy of Great Power Politics*,[14] Mearsheimer provides *a neo-realist overview of the international system (offensive realism)*, arguing that the anarchic nature of the international system is responsible for the promotion of aggressive state behavior in international politics, and not necessarily the moral concerns, or the particular characteristics of a given leader. He is of the view that "conflict is a fact of the international system because ultimately the dynamics of great power politics lead to wars over dominance of the system".[15] Mearsheimer argued that states want as much power as they can get and are not interested in maintaining the balance of power.[16] As correctly assessed by Glen M.E. Duerr, Mearsheimer's thesis has not yet been tested for two reasons. *(i)* First, the US is still the principal actor in Europe from a security perspective and Mearsheimer's prediction of the return of great power rivalry in Europe will not happen in the context of such a large presence of US troops. *(ii)* The second, obvious reason is

10 Mojtaba Mahdavi & W. Andy Knight, 'Introduction. Towards 'the Dignity of Difference?' Neither 'End of History' nor 'Clash of Civilizations'', *in* Mahdavi & Knight (eds.) 2012, p. 2.

11 Id. pp. 4-5.

12 Duerr 2018, p. 79.

13 Id. pp. 77-81.

14 John J. Mearsheimer, *The Tragedy of Great Power Politics*, W.W. Norton and Company, New York, 2001.

15 Duerr 2018, pp. 76–77.

16 Mearsheimer 2001, p. 22.

doi: 10.5553/HYIEL/266627012021009001018

that the US is still the sole superpower of the world and so far no other country can outweigh Washington.[17] However, the Russian annexation of Crimea in 2014 and the hostilities between Russia and Ukraine certainly contributed to a wider acceptance of Mearsheimer's thesis. These events could not be foreseen based on Huntington's paradigm, as they were intra-civilizational clashes.[18]

4. The Clash of Civilizations and the Remaking of World Order

Huntington, in his 1993 article in *Foreign Affairs*[19] and later in his book *The Clash of Civilizations and the Remaking of World Order*, predicted that in the post-Cold War period power would be redistributed on the basis of civilizations. Consequently, the major source of conflict would not be ideological or economic, but cultural. It is important to note that *Huntington did not intend this book as a work of social science but rather an interpretation of the evolution of global politics after the Cold War*.[20] Civilization in his understanding was the "highest cultural grouping of people and the broadest level of cultural identity".[21] In his paradigm, it is culture and not the state that is the focal point of war.[22] He is of the view that there was no *lingua franca* among civilizations and that democracy and human rights were Western values, with no real meaning for the Rest.[23] Huntington claims that the "weakness and irrationality" of the Rest is one of the main obstacles to the global spread of Western values and institutions.[24] The term "clash of civilizations" appeared first in a book by Basil Matthews in 1926, entitled *Young Islam on Trek: A Study in the Clash of Civilizations*. However, Huntington borrowed it from Bernard Lewis, who used it in a 1990 paper, published in the *Atlantic Monthly* entitled *The roots of Muslim Rage*.[25]

In his article, Huntington specified eight civilizations (West, Latin America, Africa, Orthodox, Confucian, Islamic, Hindu, Buddhist); he later added Japan to the list in his book and also changed Confucian to Sinic.[26] These civilizations, according to former Harvard professor Peter Katzenstein, are "coherent,

17 Duerr 2018, p. 80.
18 Id. p. 82.
19 Samul P. Huntington, 'The Clash of Civilizations?', *Foreign Affairs*, Summer 1993, pp. 22-49.
20 Haynes 2019, p. 12.
21 Erik Benson, 'Introduction to the Theme Issue: Old Wine in New Skins? Revisiting the "Clash of Civilizations" Thesis', *Christian Scholar's Review*, Vol. 48, Issue 3, 2019, p. 215.
22 Máté Tőzsér, *A Clash of Civilizations or a Clash of Interests? An Analysis Based on the Book "The Clash of Civilizations and the Remaking of World Order" by Samuel P. Huntington*, VDM Verlag, Riga, 2008, p. 3.
23 Davide Orsi, 'The Clash of Civilizations and the Realism in International Political Thought', *in* Orsi (ed.) 2018, p. 11.
24 Mahdavi & Knight 2012, p. 3.
25 Karim H. Karim & Mahmoud Eid, 'Clash of Ignorance', *Global Media Journal – Canadian Edition*, Vol. 5, Issue 1, 2012, p. 18.
26 Samuel P. Huntington, *A civilizációk összecsapása és a világrend átalakulása*, Európa Könyvkiadó, Budapest, 2014, pp. 57-61.

doi: 10.5553/HYIEL/266627012021009001018

consensual, invariant, and equipped with a state-like capacity to act".[27] Huntington predicted that from among the civilizations, Islam and Confucianism would pose a real threat to the West and would in the future clash with Western civilization.[28] In the 1980s, Huntington still thought that Japan would challenge the US economic supremacy. This prophecy became irrelevant in the 1990s when the Japanese economic boom stopped.[29] Huntington's paradigm is very much Western-centric. According to his views, there are three issues which separated the West from other civilizations: *(i)* the ability to maintain its military superiority; *(ii)* the promotion of Western values, like human rights and democracy; and *(iii)* the restriction of the entry of non-Western immigrants and refugees into Western societies.[30] One of the most controversial statements Huntington made was that "Islam has bloody borders". This harsh statement was seen as a prophecy by many in light of the rise of ISIL by neglecting the wider international context and in particular the very low level of inter-state violence in our contemporary world.[31]

5. The Main Elements of the Criticism of the Thesis of The Clash of Civilizations

Many academics criticizing the thesis of *The Clash of Civilizations* point out that *the presentation of the West or of Islam as monolithic entities is a serious misunderstanding of the dynamics of culture*.[32] It is well demonstrated by researchers that both the Western and the Muslim worlds are very much divided based on the shared values and beliefs of the people living there. It is only sufficient to mention the Sunni/Shia division or the heated debates within the EU on human rights issues.[33] Looking at the most important political clashes today, both Russia *versus* the West, and the Korean situation are intra-civilizational conflicts.[34]

Erik Ringmar called *The Clash of Civilizations* an offensive thesis, *i.e.* putting the world population into boxes, calling them civilizations, and stating that people in the same box are the same, but sufficiently different from people in other boxes to clash. He criticized Huntington for not addressing culture in a meaningful way and neglecting the importance of ideas and values in his

27 Peter Joachim Katzenstein, 'A World of Plural and Pluralist Civilizations', *Procedia – Social and Behavioral Sciences*, Vol. 77, 2013, pp. 15-16.

28 Abul Kalam, 'Huntington and the World Order: Systemic Concern or Hegemonic Vision?', *in* Rashid (ed.) 1997, p. 52.

29 Richard Falk, 'Geopolitical Turmoil and Civilizational Pluralism', *in* Fred Dallmayr *et al.* (eds.), *Civilizations and World Order, Geopolitics and Cultural Difference*, Lexington Books, Lanham, p. 9.

30 Haynes 2019, p. 15.

31 Duerr 2018, p. 84.

32 Karim & Eid 2012, p. 9.

33 Haynes 2019, pp. 17-18.

34 Anna Khakee, 'Plus, Ca Change… Civilizations, Political Systems and Power Politics: A Critique of Huntington's 'Clash of Civilizations'', *in* Orsi (ed.) 2018, pp. 88-89.

doi: 10.5553/HYIEL/266627012021009001018

paradigm.[35] Ringmar disagrees with Huntington about the meaning of civilizations, which he thinks do not have a particular content but rather are a "mechanism or a social practice" and not a kind of "supra-culture" as they appear in Huntington's paradigm.[36]

Martin Hall and Patrick Thaddeus Jackson highlight that contrary to Huntington's definition of civilizations as a nation or a society, they are more like an ongoing process. They are never in splendid isolation from each other: inter-civilizational connections are more and more central.[37] Katzenstein also argues that civilizations are pluralistic, and they are generally "characterized by inter-civilizational encounters and trans-civilizational engagements and only rarely by civilizational clashes".[38]

Chris Brown highlights that *civilizations cannot clash; only individuals or groups claiming to represent civilizations can clash*. Systems of ideas cannot clash but also civilizations are unable to authorize people to clash on their behalf.[39] Other academics argue that the overall tendency in our world is moving toward the "fusion" of civilizations, establishing a "common set of expectations" for the vast majority of people in our Planet.[40] Anna Khakee underlines that there are two sets of issues on which Western and non-Western states could clash. The first one could be related to economic competition, weapons proliferation, borders, so issues of power politics, while the second could be on human rights, democracy and institutions, which are related to political systems or regime types. The point is that none of them are civilizational issues *per se*.[41] While Vesselin Popovski admits that civilizations can clash, he claims that this is not because of identity differences, but because they are fighting for "space and power".[42]

Wouter Werner correctly points out that international law is almost completely absent from Huntington's thesis. This is interesting as "international law was born out of such a clash", and for centuries the relationship between the so-called civilized and less civilized world was one of the core issues of international law.[43] International law provides certain criteria for giving full recognition and protection under international law as members of the international community, including civilized peoples. These criteria contain the basic institutions of government and public bureaucracy, organizational capacity for self-defense, published legal code, and adherence to the rule of law, the

35 Erik Ringmar, 'Samuel Huntington and the American Way of War', *in* Orsi (ed.) 2018, p. 26.
36 Id. p. 28.
37 Martin Hall & Patrick Taddeus Jackson, 'Introduction: Civilizations and International Relations Theory', *in* Hall & Jackson (eds.) 2017, pp. 6-7.
38 Katzenstein 2013, p. 18.
39 Chris Brown, 'International Society, Cultural Diversity, and the Clash (or Dialogue) of Civilizations', *in* Dallmayr *et al.* (eds.) 2014, p. 56.
40 Benson 2019, p. 218.
41 Khakee 2018, p. 91.
42 Popovski 2012, p. 90.
43 Wouter Werner, 'The 'Clash of Civilizations' in International Law', *in* Orsi (ed.) 2018, p. 134.

doi: 10.5553/HYIEL/266627012021009001018

capacity to honor contracts in commerce and capital exchange and lastly the recognition of international law and norms.[44]

Mojtaba Mahdavi and W. Andy Knight are of the view that we should speak more about the clash of fundamentalisms than of clash of civilizations to describe the current tensions in our world, where the clash is between two versions of political extremism: a market and a religious fundamentalism. This can be also called "the clash of ignorance".[45] Benjamin R. Barber refers to this phenomenon as Jihad *versus* McWorld. He describes the clash between a "fundamentalist revolt against modernity" and "aggressive materialism". However, he underlines that it was more a clash within a civilization than between civilizations.[46]

Máté Tőzsér argues that in our contemporary world there is no such a thing as clash of civilizations, but what we are witnessing is the clash of interests of states, causing international conflicts. He considers 9/11 as an intra-civilizational provocation by Islamic fundamentalists within the Muslim world, to end the passivity of the rest of Muslim world. Tőzsér supports the "superiority of interests over culture or religion, eventually civilization".[47]

Shireen Hunter also confirms that the real cause of conflicts between the West and Islam is not their civilizational incompatibility, but the balance of power, giving the West greater influence over the fate of the Muslim World, by using different financial and military means.[48] Unfortunately, in this relationship, in the case of a conflictual situation, the ideological and value-oriented goals of the West are always subordinated to security, political, and economic interests. The best example is the lack of interest by the West in fair and open elections if there is a real danger that a pro-Western government would be replaced or weakened.[49] Hunter is also of the view that there are more tensions among Muslim states than between the West and the Islam world.[50] As an important conclusion, he underlines that "the slower pace of secularization in Muslim countries cannot be attributed to Islam's specificity".[51] The less secularized character of most Muslim societies is not because of the special quality of their faith, but due to the social and economic underdevelopment of the region.[52]

44 Brett Bowden & Leonard Seabrooke, 'Global Standards of Market Civilization', *in* Hall & Jackson (eds.) 2017, p. 123.
45 Mahdavi & Knight 2012, p. 12.
46 Benjamin R. Barber, 'Neither 'the Clash of Civilizations' nor 'the End of History', *in* Mahdavi & Knight (eds.) 2012, p. 218.
47 Tőzsér 2008, pp. 28-29.
48 Shireen T. Hunter, *Future of Islam and the West: Clash of Civilizations or Peaceful Coexistence?*, Praeger, Washington DC, 1998, pp. 19-20.
49 Id. p. 24.
50 Id. p. 28.
51 Id. p. 165.
52 Id. p. 166.

doi: 10.5553/HYIEL/266627012021009001018

6. Possible Solutions to Overcome the Flaws of Huntington's Paradigm

Scott Waalkes rightly points out that *peace was beyond Huntington's concern when elaborating his paradigm*. Huntington devotes only a few pages in his book to outlining possible ways to decrease the tensions between civilizations. As noted by Miroslav Volf, this paradigm was "good for fighting, but not for living together in peace".[53] The hermeneutical hospitality Waalkes is offering would mean that committed members of different civilizations would sit together and interpret their sacred texts searching for truth and mutual understanding.[54]

Chiara Bottici and Benoit Challand point out that the clash of civilizations became a successful political myth. Its aim was not to describe the truth but to create it.[55] It is important to note that it is not just a Western myth exported worldwide; it also has its Arab Middle Eastern version. They consider this clash more within, than between civilizations.[56] On the surface, 9/11 turned the idea of the clash of civilizations into a prophecy fulfilled, as the attack of a few extremist terrorists were wrongly considered an attack by Islam on Western civilization. This happened with the help of the other side as well, resulting in the radicalization of Islamic movements, which acted as if the clash between civilizations existed.[57] Bottici and Challand underline that there are no inferior or superior cultures; cultures "must be considered on an equal footing, and not according to what we think is particularly 'civilized'".[58] They highlight that the concept of culture (contrary to the concept of civilizations) went through a process, which liberated it from its original elitist and Eurocentric approach.

The response of the UN to the challenge posed by the clash of civilizations theory was to *designate 2001 a Year of Dialogue among Civilizations*, based on the proposal of Mohammed Khatami, then President of the Islamic Republic of Iran. This initiative was followed in 2005 by the launch of the UN Alliance of Civilizations (UNAOC). These initiatives were complemented by the work of UNESCO and the OIC aimed at organizing actions and programs on the dialogue between civilizations.[59] As noted by Jeffrey Haynes, the role of religion was largely expended at the UN as a consequence of 9/11 and the new institution's name (UNAOC) was a clear response to Huntington's paradigm.[60] Later, in 2017, a Group of Friends was established to support the activities of UNAOC: it included 120 governments and 26 international organizations.[61]

53 Scott Waalkes, 'Beyond the Clash of Civilizations: Hermeneutical Hospitality as a Model for Civilizational Dialogue', *Christian Scholar's Review*, Vol. 48, Issue 3, 2019, p. 237.

54 Id. p. 246.

55 Chiara Bottici & Benoit Challand, *The Myth of the Clash of Civilizations*, Routledge, London, 2012, pp. 2. and 11.

56 Id. p. 50.

57 Id. p. 101.

58 Id. p. 117.

59 Gregoria Bettiza & Fabio Petito, 'Why (Clash of) Civilizations Discourses Just Won't Go Away? Understanding the Civilizational Politics of Our Times', *in* Orsi (ed.) 2018, p. 38.

60 Jeffrey Haynes, 'Huntington's 'Clash of Civilizations' Today: Responses and Developments', *in* Orsi (ed.) 2018, p. 56.

61 Id. p. 57.

doi: 10.5553/HYIEL/266627012021009001018

As a response to the flaws of Huntington's thesis, *many scholars started to use the term "clash of ignorance"* underlining "the value of taking into account the wider historical, intellectual, and religious relationships between societies".[62] This thesis challenges the assumption that civilizations are monolithic entities, which are not interacting with each other, and that they should clash with others. Karim H. Karim and Mahmoud Eid highlight in their article that although there are significant differences and clashes between the West and Islam, there is a remarkable overlap between the two civilizations and good examples in history of their "fruitful engagement".[63] Tőzsér also underlines the importance of "putting emphasis on the similarities and not the differences of each civilization", in order to successfully fight terrorism.[64]

Mahdavi and Knight argue that neither the *Clash of Civilizations*, nor the *End of History* theses capture correctly the "complexity of our contemporary social and political life", as they are both based on the assumption of the superiority of the West and the inferiority of the Rest. They suggest a third way of dialogue and acceptance, the notion of the Dignity of Difference, to overcome the flaws of Fukuyama's universalist paradigm and Huntington's particularist approach.[65] The Dignity of Difference paradigm (which was originally presented by Professor Jonathan Sacks in 2002) is based on the notion that democracy, freedom, and human rights are not exclusively Western ideas; they are a part of all cultures.[66] The supporters of this approach are of the view that as the root causes of radicalism, extremism, and terrorism are diverse, policies to address them should be multiple as well. These policies should respect the Dignity of Difference and should be supportive of multicultural responses.[67] Popovski emphasizes that the most important and successful way to prevent inter-civilizational clashes is to address the economic and political factors of wars, as conflicts are not religious but political and economic in nature. It should be clearly seen that there is no West, there are many 'Wests' and there is no single Rest, or no single Africa or Islam.[68] Popovski underlines that the Dignity of Difference thesis is aimed at mobilizing "action against ignorance, intolerance and violence".[69]

7. Conclusion

The three concepts outlined in this article on the "end of history", the clash of civilizations" and "the tragedy of Great Power Politics" managed to describe certain periods or events during the post Cold-War Era. *Fukuyama's concept was useful in the 1990s*, when everyone thought that with the collapse of the Soviet

62 Karim & Eid 2012, p. 22.
63 Id. p. 7.
64 Tőzsér 2008, p. 39.
65 Mahdavi & Knight 2012, p. 1.
66 Id. p. 13.
67 Id. p. 18.
68 Popovski 2012, pp. 83-84 and 95.
69 Id. p. 92.

doi: 10.5553/HYIEL/266627012021009001018

System, the liberal form of democracy is going to dominate the new world order, without any serious competitors. *Huntington's paradigm became popular with the outbreak of the Yugoslavian War*, as proof that civilizational identity is the main driving force in international relations. Finally, as it was already mentioned, *the Russian annexation of Crimea in 2014 and the hostilities between Russia and Ukraine contributed to the better acceptance of Mearsheimer's thesis*.

However, *none of them was able to provide a comprehensive explanation* for the complexity of our contemporary international landscape. History certainly did not end after the collapse of communism, and as we can see in many countries that the so called "illiberal democracy" became the most popular catchphrase to describe the political philosophy of a given government. More and more researchers made it clear that civilizations cannot clash with each other, there can be confrontation only between people claiming to represent a certain civilization. Besides, civilizations are not monolithic entities, there are serious dividing lines within them. They are in permanent contact with each other and most of their "clashes" are due to different state interests and not to civilizational differences. An interesting survey about the variation in tolerance in 23 Muslim-majority and Western countries also demonstrated that it was more the Islamic political regimes that have a negative effect on social tolerance and not Islam itself.[70] Lastly, despite the significant economic strengthening of China and the more and more "self-confident" foreign policy of Russia, we cannot say at this moment that any of them would become a new sole superpower, replacing the US even in the medium term.

The answer to the question posed in the title of this article should be affirmative, although we can still witness that for many governments it is still more suitable to intensify alleged inter-civilizational clashes or differences in order to remain in power. The best way to overcome civilizational prejudice is education, aimed at combatting ignorance of other cultures. The 'unknown' has frequently been considered a danger in the history of mankind. The international community should finally adopt – at the level of the individual citizens and not only in statements by politicians – human rights and democracy as universal values, which have roots and a place in every culture, and recognize that there are no insurmountable cultural barriers preventing the peaceful cooperation between different peoples in our contemporary world. We have only one world, so our responsibility is exceptional.

70 Scott Milligan *et al.*, 'Assessing Variation in Tolerance in 23 Muslim-Majority and Western Countries', *Canadian Review of Sociology*, Vol. 51, Issue 3, 2014, p. 239.

doi: 10.5553/HYIEL/266627012021009001018

HUNGARIAN STATE PRACTICE

An Institution for a Sustainable Future

The Hungarian Ombudsman for Future Generations

Kinga Debisso & Marcel Szabó[*]

Abstract

The purpose of this article is to give an insight into the process leading up to the establishment of the Hungarian Ombudsman for Future Generations and its tasks: an almost 15-year-old, unique legal institution aiming to protect the interests of future generations. The Ombudsman for Future Generations is an example for the institutionalization of the principle of intergenerational justice. The article aims to introduce the characteristics and strengths of the current institutional design and the structural features that allow for the successful operation of the Ombudsman for Future Generations in Hungary. Following an introduction to the political and historical context in which the institution was established, the article describes in detail the Ombudsman's work, responsibilities, most important functions, elaborating on some examples of its best practices and achievements. Finally, the article touches upon how the example and experiences of the Hungarian institution may be valuable for other countries in Europe and beyond.

Keywords: intergenerational equity, rights of future generations, ombudsman for future generations, Hungary, right to environment.

1. Introduction

Initially, the idea that future generations need institutional protection emerged in the international environmental arena. Promoters of the concept of intergenerational equity advocated for the establishment of a separate institution that can call attention to harmful global processes threatening the well-being of future generations. Under the *aegis* of the UN, it was Malta that first proposed the establishment of a 'guardian for future generations', during the preparations

* Kinga Debisso: political advisor, Ministry of Justice, Budapest. Marcel Szabó: professor of law, Pázmány Péter Catholic University, Budapest; justice, Constitutional Court of Hungary, Budapest.

doi: 10.5553/HYIEL/266627012021009001019

for the 1992 Rio Earth Summit.[1] International efforts to implement the principles of intergenerational equity, however, often seemed insufficient and difficult to put into practice. Many believed that institutional solutions for the protection of the unborn would better work at the state level, where the effects of political decisions regarding the long-term health of the environment are most apparent. For instance, the 2002 New Delhi Declaration of the International Law Association[2] urges not only global, but also national institutionalization of intergenerational equity:

> "The principle of integration reflects the interdependence of social, economic, financial, environmental and human rights aspects of principles and rules of international law relating to sustainable development as well as of the interdependence of the needs of current and future generations of humankind. All levels of governance – global, regional, national, sub-national and local – and all sectors of society should implement the integration principle, which is essential to the achievement of sustainable development. States should strive to resolve apparent conflicts between competing economic, financial, social and environmental considerations, whether through existing institutions or through the establishment of appropriate new institutions."[3]

In 2013, the then UN Secretary General Ban Ki-Moon issued a report entitled "Intergenerational solidarity and the needs of future generations". In this report *the Secretary General highlighted the work of eight national institutions*, from states including Canada, Finland, Hungary, Israel, New Zealand, Wales, Germany and Norway, *as playing a pioneering role in the national implementation of sustainable development and intergenerational solidarity*.[4] At present, out of the eight model institutions named in the 2013 Report, the Hungarian and the Norwegian institutions work in the form of ombudsman offices.[5] While the Hungarian Ombudsman for Future Generations can deal with all the issues concerning the 'interests' of future generations, the Norwegian Ombudsperson for Children can protect the needs of future generations only through the rights of children and

1 *See* the proposal of the Maltese government on setting up a "Guardian for Future Generations", introduced in 1992 at the March preparatory meeting of the first UN Conference on Environment and Development in Rio de Janeiro, at http://193.166.3.2/pub/doc/world/UnitedNations/EnvironConf/PreConfDocs/wg3l8add02. According to para. 16 of the Maltese proposal, "The appointment of an advocate to alert the international community of threats to the well-being of future generations would be the most concrete step in the right direction to safeguard the disadvantaged members of the human species."

2 ILA New Delhi Declaration of Principles of International Law Relating to Sustainable Development, 2 April 2002, UN Doc. A/CONF.199/8, 9 August 2002.

3 Id. paras. 7.1.-7.3.

4 Ban Ki-Moon, *Intergenerational solidarity and the needs of future generations – Report of the Secretary-General*, 5 August 2013, A/68/322 https://sustainabledevelopment.un.org/content/documents/2006future.pdf, paras. 25-31.

5 Gabriele Kucsko-Stadlmayer, *The Spread of the Ombudsman Idea in Europe*, IOI Publications, 2009, pp. 1-3.

doi: 10.5553/HYIEL/266627012021009001019

young people. It is interesting to mention that, independently from their official name, the institutions of the Commissioner for Future Generations in Wales and the Parliamentary Commissioner for the Environment in New Zealand are much more similar to the Hungarian model institution than Norwegian Ombudsperson for Children. In this article we try to introduce how an 'ombudsman-style' institution could effectively protect the rights and interests of future generations.

2. The Way Towards the Establishment of the Office of the Ombudsman for Future Generations in Hungary

The Hungarian Ombudsman institution was born during the democratization process of the late 1980's and early 1990's. The first Ombudsman Act was adopted by the Parliament in 1993,[6] and the first Ombudsmen were elected in 1995.[7] The former Constitution adopted a model of the ombudsman system in which separate Commissioners could be elected for the protection of individual constitutional rights. Although the former Ombudsman Act directly referred to the Commissioner for Civil Rights and the Commissioner for the Rights of National and Ethnic Minorities only, Section 32/B(4) allowed for the election of additional ombudsmen for the protection of other fundamental rights. Applying this Section, in 1995 the Ombudsman for Data Protection, and later, in 2007 the Ombudsman for Future Generations were elected. All the Ombudsmen were nominated by the President of Hungary and subsequently elected by the Parliament for a 6-year term. Before the establishment of the Ombudsman for Future Generations, it was the Commissioner for Civil Rights in Hungary who was responsible for the protection of the right to a healthy environment.

There were a number of factors that resulted in the establishment of the office of the Ombudsman for Future Generations. In May 2000, the Hungarian civil society organization called 'Védegylet – Protect the Future!' initiated the establishment of the institution of the Ombudsman for Future Generations in a draft bill, prepared by László Sólyom, the first president of the Hungarian Constitutional Court (1990-1998) and later President of the Republic (2005-2010). Sólyom drew on the 1993 Ombudsman Act when designing the legal framework of the new institution, and argued for independence, broad competences, and proactivity as the three most vital elements of the proposed institution.

At first, the political sphere was indifferent toward the proposal, and it was uncertain whether any political party would support and take up the cause. In parallel with their advocacy work, therefore, Védegylet launched a public consultation campaign in order to garner further recognition and political legitimacy for the institution. In November 2000, with the cooperation of other Hungarian NGOs, they established the civil committee called 'Representation of Future Generations' (REFUGE) in order to start implementing the content of the

6 Act LIX of 1993 on the Parliamentary Commissioner for Civil Rights.
7 Parliament Decree No. 84/1995. (VII. 6.).

doi: 10.5553/HYIEL/266627012021009001019

bill and to keep the topic on the political agenda.[8] REFUGE had been meant to act as a 'shadow' Ombudsman until the Parliament accepted the original proposal for the establishment of an Ombudsman for Future Generations. Its work focused on cases where the rights of future generations to a healthy environment were seriously infringed and the institution published annual reports about the legal proceedings it had concluded and those, which were still in-progress. REFUGE worked in accordance with the principles and procedural rules laid down in the original draft bill of Védegylet. It is worth mentioning that Védegylet also urged other, foreign NGOs to initiate the institutional protection of future generations in their own states. They even launched a political campaign addressing the EU to set up a European Ombudsman for Future Generations for the effective representation of the interests of the unborn in the transboundary, European context.

Following two failed attempts to submit the bill to the Parliament, a cross-party approval was finally achieved in 2007. Besides the strong societal support, the role of preeminent public figures, including President Sólyom, was indispensable for the successful realization of the proposal. It is often argued that the role of the President in parliamentary democracies is rather modest. While his political leverage may be limited, most parties try to cultivate good relations with the President. More often than not, their endorsement and patronage can go a long way in realizing a particular political project. In Hungary, the continuous support of Sólyom had been imperative for the establishment of the institution by the Parliament. In 2007, Members of Parliament voted almost unanimously for the amendment of the Ombudsman Act. Sándor Fülöp, the first Ombudsman for Future Generations, was nominated by President Sólyom, and was elected by a two-thirds majority in May 2008. Sólyom emphasized that *the Ombudsman is not a law enforcement body but serves as a representative of future generations*:

> "This is why the word 'Guardian' in international law is so fitting. Minors and persons with disabilities have guardians or custodians. Future generations are also unable to defend their rights, and this is what the Ombudsman does on their behalf."[9]

3. The Current Institutional Framework – Following the Adoption of the Fundamental Law

The Fundamental Law (entered into force in 2012) represented a paradigm shift in the Hungarian Ombudsman system, changing the status and constitutional role of the Ombudsman for Future Generations. With 1 January 2012 the independent Ombudsman Offices were merged into one, creating a single new

8 Benedek Jávor, 'Institutional Protection of Succeeding Generations – Ombudsman for Future Generations in Hungary', *in* Joerg Chet Tremmel (ed.), *Handbook of Intergenerational Justice*, Edward Elgar, Cheltenham, 2006, pp. 287-292.

9 László Sólyom, 'A jövő nemzedékek jogai és ezek képviselete a jelenben', *in* Benedek Jávor (ed.), *A jövő nemzedékek jogai*, Védegylet, Budapest, 2000, p. 40.

doi: 10.5553/HYIEL/266627012021009001019

institution: the Office of the Commissioner for Fundamental Rights.[10] Under the new structure, the Commissioner is responsible for the protection of human rights in general, while the two Deputies are entrusted with the protection of the rights of minorities and future generations, respectively. In questions concerning the natural environment and the interests of future generations, the Ombudsman for Future Generations (Deputy Commissioner) has the right to act independently from the Commissioner. This means that although his office is structurally incorporated under the Office of the Commissioner for Fundamental Rights and they may act as Deputy when necessary, his unit is procedurally autonomous in its own area of expertise. This is also reflected in the institution's designation: the Ombudsman for Future Generations (*a jövő nemzedékek szószólója*), an office with the power to carry out activities in its own right.[11] In this regard, the Ombudsman is most similar to institutions that are entrusted with the protection of children's rights,[12] which are either part of the general ombudsman system or function independently of it.[13] The critical question is not necessarily the institutional structure but the legislative background that determines and circumscribes the powers and responsibilities of the Ombudsman.

The tasks of the Ombudsman for Future Generations are laid down in Article 30(3) of the Fundamental Law: the Ombudsman for Future Generations "shall protect the interests of future generations". *The mandate of the Ombudsman for Future Generations extends, at least in principle, to all issues which may, directly or indirectly, affect the interests of future generations*. The economy, education, health care, or state debt are all issues that inevitably affect the living conditions, financial constraints and well-being of future generations, and are subject to institutional protection. The Ombudsman is not barred from taking action in any of the aforementioned areas. Since potentially all legislation may have an impact on future generations, the Ombudsman institution itself had to restrict its scope of action, reflecting on theoretical, scholarly considerations regarding the concept and representation of future generations. Moreover, according to the Ombudsman Act, the Ombudsman may propose the adoption, amendment of

10 According to Gabriele Kucsko-Stadlmayer's classification of various powers, the Hungarian Ombudsman's Office belongs to the institutional 'Human Rights Model', where powers related to fundamental rights protection dominate the mandate of the Ombudsman. Based on the Ombudsman's powers, Kucsko-Stadlmayer differentiates between 'Basic Models', 'Rule of Law Models', and 'Human Rights Models'. The first is characterized by wide investigative powers, while the second's main priority is to monitor the lawful and proper operation of authorities. The protection of fundamental rights is prioritized in the third, Human Rights Model. *See* Gabriele Kucsko-Stadlmayer (ed.), *European Ombudsman-Institutions – A Comparative Legal Analysis Regarding the Multifaceted Realisation of An Idea*, Springer, 2008, pp. 59-66.

11 Section 3(4) of Act CXI of 2011 on the Commissioner for Fundamental Rights.

12 As an example, the European Network of Ombudspersons for Children (ENOC) established in 1997, links 43 offices for children from 34 states in Europe. *See* at http://enoc.eu.

13 For instance, ENOC works together with independent children's rights institutions: children's ombudspersons, commissioners for children, or focal points on children's rights in national human rights institutions or general ombudsman offices. *See* at http://enoc.eu/?page_id=8.

doi: 10.5553/HYIEL/266627012021009001019

legislation on the *rights* of future generations,[14] recognizing that future generations have rights protected by law and the institution of the Ombudsman.

Many states around the world already have an ombudsman-type institution, and a number of these institutions also consider environmental questions. Taking these institutions a step further, their scope of action could be extended to the protection of future generations, drawing inspiration from the Hungarian example. In the light of the current trend of cutting back on bureaucratic structures, expanding existing institutional systems seems to be a more feasible solution than establishing entirely new guardian institutions. It is characteristic of the ombudsmen's work and mandate to be closely tied with that of the Commissioner for Fundamental Rights. This form of cooperation implemented in Hungary has proven to be an effective and common design, making it for a viable option for other institutions to adopt in order to promote the rights and interests of future generations worldwide.

The fact that the Ombudsman for Future Generations works as a Deputy of the Commissioner for Fundamental Rights raises the question whether this new structural arrangement has weakened the institutional protection of future generations. The balance of their cooperation so far, however, indicates that this type of institutional structure could present considerable advantages for the legal protection of both present and future generations.

The Commissioner for Fundamental Rights protects the rights of citizens and other individuals living in the state in accordance with international standards and practice. The Ombudsman for Future Generations, on the other hand, acts not only in cases of concrete impairments of, and threats to private individuals' rights, but may also investigate legal and other matters that have the potential to jeopardize the interests of future generations. The Ombudsman can, in line with the precautionary principle,[15] take action and evaluate decisions in the earliest stages of their development, and take a wide range of measures as necessary, albeit certain measures require the prior approval of the Commissioner (*e.g.* the Ombudsman could turn to the Constitutional Court only *via* the Commissioner).

Cooperation between the Commissioner for Fundamental Rights and the Ombudsman for Future Generations is most critical in areas where *the protection of a specific right is linked to both intergenerational and intragenerational justice*. The right to clean drinking water, for instance, falls under this category of fundamental rights. In Hungary, the improper management of mine pit lakes resulted in the pollution of groundwater and damage to freshwater reservoirs. This can be regarded as an intergenerational issue, which belongs under the jurisdiction of the Ombudsman for Future Generations. The intragenerational

14 Section 3(1)(g) of Act CXI of 2011 on the Commissioner for Fundamental Rights.

15 *See e.g.* Gyula Bándi, 'The Case of the Hungarian Constitutional Court with Environmental Principles – From Non-Derogation to the Precautionary Approach', *Hungarian Yearbook of International Law and European Law*, Vol. 7, 2019, pp. 49-66; Marcel Szabó, 'The Precautionary Principle in the Fundamental Law of Hungary: Judicial Activism or an Inherent Fundamental Principle? An Evaluation of Constitutional Court Decision No. 13/2018. (IX. 4.) AB on the Protection of Groundwater', *Hungarian Yearbook of International Law and European Law*, Vol. 7, 2019, pp. 67-83.

doi: 10.5553/HYIEL/266627012021009001019

aspect of the right to clean drinking water, however, demands the joint action of the Commissioner and the Ombudsman for Future Generations. The example of events that took place in the municipality of Ózd illustrates this well. In the summer of 2013, the municipality closed down a number of public standpipes due to the outstanding debts of some poor families. In this case, the Commissioner and the Ombudsman argued that access to a minimum quantity of drinking water is a human right, which, irrespective of someone's financial capabilities, cannot be violated. In their joint report[16] the Ombudsmen substantiated that in matters concerning water as an environmental resource, there is a concurrent need to protect the rights of both present and future generations. It is interesting to mention that in 2020 the Constitutional Court of Hungary also emphasized that the question of right to water could be an element of the protection of interests of future generations through Article P(1) of the Fundamental Law of Hungary and of the right to a healthy environment through Article XXI(1) of the Fundamental Law.[17]

Another important institutional aspect is that it being a relatively new institution, currently, the processes, functions and activities of the Ombudsman for Future Generations are not overregulated. Meanwhile, the Ombudsman works closely together with the Commissioner, whose activities and processes are strictly regulated.

4. Interests of Future Generations in the Fundamental Law

Besides the general recognition of the right to a healthy environment in Article XXI of the Fundamental Law, including the polluter pays principle,[18] and the prohibition of the transport of pollutant waste into the territory of Hungary for the purpose of disposal,[19] the Fundamental Law complemented the right to a healthy environment with further guarantees. The National Avowal *describes the Hungarian nation as an alliance of past, present and future Hungarians*. This constitutional provision articulates the essence of intergenerational justice: on the one hand, it expresses a commitment to receive the nation's heritage with respect and gratitude, while on the other, it is dedicated to the protection of present conditions for the benefit of coming generations. As Edith Brown Weiss pointed out,

> "in all that we do, we inherently represent not only ourselves but past and future generations. We represent past generations, even while trying to obliterate the past, because we embody what they passed on to us. We represent future generations because the decisions we make today affect the

16 Joint Report No. AJB-5527/2013.

17 Decision No. 3196/2020. (VI. 11.) AB, Reasoning [11].

18 Article XXI(2) of the Fundamental Law.

19 Article XXI(3) of the Fundamental Law.

doi: 10.5553/HYIEL/266627012021009001019

> well-being of all persons who come after us and the integrity and robustness of the planet they will inherit."[20]

The National Avowal further adds that

> "We commit ourselves to promoting and safeguarding our heritage, [...] all man-made and natural assets of the Carpathian Basin. We bear responsibility for our descendants; therefore we shall protect the living conditions of future generations by making prudent use of our material, intellectual and natural resources."

This objective reflects the significance of long-term thinking in governmental decision-making, as well as the unique responsibility to safeguard the natural and cultural heritage of the state for the benefit of present and future generations.[21] Beyond the National Avowal, several other provisions of the Fundamental Law refer explicitly to the protection of the interests of future generations. For instance, Article 38 on the property of the state sets out that the

> "management and protection of national assets shall aim at serving the public interest, meeting common needs and preserving natural resources, as well as at taking into account the needs of future generations."

The Fundamental Law contains a unique provision in Article P,[22] enshrining the concept of the *'common heritage of the nation'*. This Article provides a powerful constitutional mandate to the Ombudsman for Future Generations to take action for the benefit of future generations and for the protection of the natural and cultural resources of Hungary. Generally speaking, the Fundamental Law entrusted the Deputy Commissioner with the protection of the interests of future generations, while the Act on the Ombudsman refers to the rights of future generations as the object of protection.

The concept 'common heritage of the nation' can be linked to the notions of the 'common heritage of mankind' and the 'common concern of humanity', already in use in international law. The 'common heritage of mankind' prescribes the protection of humanity's common cultural heritage and certain natural objects, including the seabed, the Moon and celestial bodies. The concept holds that these places and natural objects cannot become the sovereign part of any one state, and that the benefits originating from the use of their resources must be

20 Edith Brown Weiss, 'Intergenerational Fairness and Rights of Future Generations', *Intergenerational Justice*, Vol. 2, Issue 3, 2002, p. 1.

21 Oxford Martin Commission, *Now for the Long Term – Report of the Oxford Martin Commission for Future Generations*, Oxford University Press, Oxford, 2013, p. 10; *National Policies & International Instruments to Protect the Rights of Future Generations*, World Future Council, 2010, pp. 2-3.

22 "Natural resources, in particular arable land, forests and the reserves of water; biodiversity, in particular native plant and animal species; and cultural artefacts, shall form the common heritage of the nation, it shall be the obligation of the State and everyone to protect and maintain them, and to preserve them for future generations."

doi: 10.5553/HYIEL/266627012021009001019

distributed equally and fairly among all nations of the world. The notion of mankind necessarily comprises not only present generations but also the unborn:

> "If history does not end, mankind will have an eternal value [...] present generations are merely the managers of the common heritage; – they are accountable to future generations for their management."[23]

The UN Framework Convention on Climate Change[24] and the UN Convention on Biological Diversity[25] refer to biodiversity[26] and the climate as forming part of the common concern of humanity. This legal concept makes the nation's irrecoverable natural heritage the subject of state concern, allowing for legitimate legal intervention for the protection of these invaluable assets. The concept common heritage of the nation is the concretization of these two international concepts.[27] Article P requires that the *natural resources and cultural assets that form part of the national heritage be maintained, preserved and protected for the benefit of future generations*.

Several environmental principles and concepts are incorporated into this Article of the Fundamental Law, including *the principle of non-retrogression or non-derogation*[28] [as the Constitutional Court adopted it in its *Decision No. 28/1994. (V. 20.) AB*], the concept of sustainable development, intergenerational equity, the precautionary principle, the principle of integration, and the principle of participation. With this provision a hypothetical legacy is bestowed upon future generations. In practice, therefore, the exact boundaries of the notion of intergenerational justice can only be determined if they are linked with the hypothetical concept of heritage. The concept of the common heritage of the nation outlines the obligation to preserve the state's natural and cultural resources for future generations in no worse condition than in which these had been received. Based on this principle, the protection of future generations in the

23 René-Jean Dupuy & Daniel Vignes (eds.), *A Handbook on the New Law of the Sea, Volume 1*, Martinus Nijhoff Publishers, 1991, p. 584.

24 *See* the Preamble of the UN Framework Convention on Climate Change, para. 1.

25 *See* the Preamble of the UN Convention on Biological Diversity, para 3.

26 It is worth noting that Hungary is part of the Pannonian biogeographical region of Europe, 80% of which can be found in the territory of Hungary. The fact that the Carpathian basin is home to biological values that are unique and endemic to the region justifies the concept of 'the common heritage of the nation', and calls for the establishment of a special legal system capable of its protection for the benefit of future generations.

27 The consequences of biodiversity loss and climatic changes pose a real and, without direct and meaningful state intervention, inevitable threat to the well-being of present and future generations. Ensuring the long-term protection of environmental resources requires long-term thinking and a concrete obligation of the state to act. Through the protection of the environmental resources to secure the biological foundations of the Hungarian nation, as well as through the safeguarding of Hungarian culture, Article P of the Fundamental Law aims to preserve humanity's one tiny mosaic, the Hungarian population.

28 The generally accepted term is 'non-retrogression', *see e.g.* John. C. Jeffries Jr. & Daryl J. Levinson, 'The Non-Retrogression Principle in Constitutional Law', *California Law Review*, Vol. 86, Issue 6, 1998, pp. 1211-1249. By contrast, in Hungary the term 'non-derogation' is the commonly used one.

doi: 10.5553/HYIEL/266627012021009001019

Fundamental Law can also be understood as a horizontal principle, a structural premise: a principle that should have bearing on every political and societal decision made.[29] Article P provides a powerful constitutional mandate to the Ombudsman for Future Generations to take action in this respect.

Article P established a direct link between the environment, the interests of future generations, and some fundamental constitutional rights, including the right to physical and mental health, and the right to a healthy environment. This strong interrelationship between the aforementioned rights was first established by the Constitutional Court, which has an exclusive mandate to provide an authoritative interpretation of the Fundamental Law and the former constitution. In its *Decision No. 28/1994. (V. 20.) AB*, the Constitutional Court elucidated the right to a healthy environment as a distinct fundamental right, which can be best described as an "independent and autonomous institutional protection."[30] It implies the State's obligation to provide adequate legal and institutional guarantees for the protection of the environment with such safeguards being elevated to the level of fundamental rights.[31] Furthermore, *Decision No. 28/1994. (V. 20.) AB* established the requirement of an environmental *status quo* and set out that the right to a healthy environment encompasses the duty of the state to ensure that the level of environmental protection is not reduced *(principle of non-retrogression or non-derogation)*. This principle can only be overruled if another fundamental right or constitutional principle would otherwise be violated. This means that the state is not allowed to withdraw or repeal any legally mandated rights or privileges that were already provided for the purpose of environment protection, unless it is strictly necessary for implementing another competing human right or constitutional principle.[32]

The Constitutional Court further argued that the level of protection of the right to a healthy environment is not arbitrary: it cannot be determined by the state alone. To maintain the achieved level of protection, the state cannot retreat from the preventive measures towards protection through sanctions. It may deviate from the above obligation only in case of inevitable necessity and only in line with the principle of proportionality. The Constitutional Court emphasized that the obligation to maintain the established level of protection also stems from the state's duty to protect the natural foundations of human life and to

29 In this regard it is worth referring to the fundamental message of Pope Francis's Encyclical Letter *Laudato Si*, which argues that our central task is to answer the ontological question of what meaning can be attributed to our earthly existence. This task cannot be fulfilled if the future of our children and grandchildren is compromised. This ethical standard is also implied in Article P of the Fundamental Law. *See* the Encyclical Letter *Laudato Si'* of the Holy Father Francis on Care for Our Common Home, Vatican Press, 2015, at http://w2.vatican.va/content/dam/francesco/pdf/encyclicals/documents/papa-francesco_20150524_enciclica-laudato-si_en.pdf.

30 Decision No. 28/1994. (V. 20.) AB, ABH 1994, 138, available in English at http://public.mkab.hu/dev/dontesek.nsf/0/bd7d0855c0550a5bc1257ada0052749c/$FILE/en_0028_1994.pdf.

31 *See* Balázs Majtényi & Gábor Győri, 'A Right Without a Subject? The Right to a Healthy Environment in the Hungarian Constitution and the Practice of the Hungarian Constitutional Court', *Fundamentum*, Vol. 12, Issue 5, 2008, p. 27.

32 Decision No. 28/1994. (V. 20.) AB, ABH 1994, 134.

doi: 10.5553/HYIEL/266627012021009001019

develop the institutions that manage the finite resources, since environmental damage is often irreversible. The Decision established that the state's duty in relation to the institutional and objective protection of human life ensures the protection of human life in general, including the life and well-being of future generations. All this requires that, compared to other rights, the protection of the right to a healthy environment by legislative instruments be particularly strict.[33]

In its more recent jurisprudence, the Constitutional Court aimed to enforce the non-retrogression (non-derogation) principle in a consistent manner.[34] In *Decision No. 16/2015. (VI. 5.) AB*, the Constitutional Court linked the National Avowal, Article P and Article XXI of the Fundamental Law to interpret the intrinsic meaning of environmental protection as the duty of the state and its citizens. Elements of this duty include ensuring the protection, maintenance, and preservation of environmental resources for future generations. Accordingly, the state's duty towards protecting the environment gained emphasis and independent regulation in Article P. In addition, the Fundamental Law extends the scope of subjects who are obliged to protect the natural environment. While the former Constitution underlined only the state's obligations in the field of environmental protection, the Fundamental Law underlines that this is everyone's duty, including civil society actors and citizens.[35] The Constitutional Court argued that environmental and economic considerations are necessarily in competition, because the implementation of environmental protection requires certain forms of self-restriction from the state, which cannot be expected from profit-oriented organizations. The Constitutional Court also stated that the inadequate protection of the natural environment could result in long-term negative externalities, social costs, and harm that are incompatible with the state's obligation to preserve natural resources and cultural assets for future generations. It could also violate the right to a healthy environment enshrined in Article XXI of the Fundamental Law. Moreover, the decision emphasized that changes in the institutional system of nature protection could, in themselves, result in a lower level of environmental protection, in case specific amendments to applicable legal provisions are not made.[36]

According to the logic of the Constitutional Court, *the concept of the environment is not limited to the natural environment*. It encompasses our physical surroundings in general, both natural and man-made.[37] Consequently, the non-retrogression (non-derogation) principle applies not only to nature preservation, but also to the protection of the built environment.[38] *Decision No. 3104/2017. (V. 8.) AB* extended the *ratione materiae* of the non-derogation principle to national monuments as well, which form the most valuable part of the built environment.

33 Id. 140.

34 Majtényi & Győri 2008, p. 34.

35 Decision No. 16/2015. (VI. 5.) AB, Reasoning [92].

36 Id. Reasoning [110].

37 László Fodor, 'A környezethez való jog dogmatikája', *Miskolci Jogi Szemle*, Vol. 2, Issue 1, 2007, p. 16.

38 Zsolt Balogh & Barnabás Hajas, 'Rights and Freedoms', *in* Lóránt Csink *et al.* (eds.), *The Basic Law of Hungary – A First Commentary*, Clarus Press, Dublin, 2012, p. 95.

doi: 10.5553/HYIEL/266627012021009001019

According to the Constitutional Court, when it comes to listed buildings, the withdrawal of legal protection requires specific justification. This means that, in a constitutional sense, national monuments fall under the non-retrogression (non-derogation) principle established in relation to the right to a healthy environment.[39] The above reasoning of the Constitutional Court supports the view of the Ombudsman for Future Generations, according to which the non-retrogression (non-derogation) principle intrinsically requires that natural and cultural assets listed under Article P be preserved under conditions similar to those applicable to natural resources.[40] Thus, in the past few years *the Hungarian Constitutional Court developed a uniquely strong concept of the constitutional protection for the common heritage of the nation and future generations.*

5. The Powers of the Hungarian Ombudsman for Future Generations

The framework of functions of the Ombudsman for Future Generations is laid down in Article 30(3) of the Fundamental Law. Pursuant to the Fundamental Law, the Ombudsman for Future Generations *"shall protect the interests of future generations"*. At the time of its establishment, the mandate of the Ombudsman was primarily geared towards the protection of the right to a healthy environment, leaving the institution with a narrower focus and authority.[41] However, from 2012, the mandate of the Ombudsman for Future Generations is not restricted to the enforcement of this right only. Institutional protection is extended to all fundamental rights which can, directly or indirectly, affect the interests of future generations. Since the Fundamental Law considers the protection of the common heritage of the nation to be part of the interest of future generations, the Ombudsman can undertake action in all questions that concern the nation's common heritage. This way, the Fundamental Law provides real power to the Ombudsman, for in practice, nearly all decisions can be considered to have an impact on the interests of the unborn. The economy, education, health care, or state debt are all issues that inevitably affect the conditions, financial burden, and wellbeing of future generations, and are therefore in need of institutional protection. Hence, according to Article P, consideration for future generations should become a part of every decision taken by the Hungarian legislature and enforcement bodies. There are no conceptual obstacles to prevent the Ombudsman from taking action in any of the aforementioned questions. However, acting upon such a broad interpretation of its mandate will only be possible after the institution's further consolidation in the Hungarian political and institutional system.

39 Decision No. 3104/2017. (V. 8.) AB, Reasoning [40].

40 *See, inter alia*, the statement of the Ombudsman for Future Generations entitled "National Parks as safeguards of natural and cultural values for future generations" (in Hungarian), issued on 16 December 2014 at www.ajbh.hu/documents/10180/12318/Nemzeti_Park_JNBH_%C3%A1ll%C3%A1sfoglal%C3%A1s.pdf/05d1d19b-18f6-4154-bf55-3fa8b8d0a349.

41 Section 27/B(1) of Act LIX of 1993 on the Parliamentary Commissioner for Civil Rights.

doi: 10.5553/HYIEL/266627012021009001019

One of the most powerful features of the Office of the Commissioner for Fundamental Rights is its publicity and transparent operation. As Ewa Letowska, former Ombudsman and Constitutional Judge from Poland, noted: "For the ombudsman the measure of success was by no means whether she won or lost before the Tribunal, her success was in raising general interest in the problem."[42] Every year, the Commissioner and the two Ombudsmen report on and prepare a statistical analysis of the cases and petitions they handled. These reports serve as important indicators of environmental policy-making and are highly relevant for the future work of the Office. The complaints are grouped into categories reflecting the lack, abuse, or violation of laws in certain environmental matters. This, on the one hand, can point to systemic anomalies of the judicial regime in environmental matters, while on the other, it can ensure that the public's view on environmental issues is better reflected in environmental governance.[43]

Pursuant to the new Act on the Ombudsman adopted in 2011,[44] the Ombudsman for Future Generations can draw the attention of the Commissioner, other affected institutions, and the public to any suspected infringement of the interests of future generations.[45] This direct channel to the public can help influence the public perception of risks and long-term consequences. In order to enhance the efficiency of its work, the Ombudsman can use various communication tools, including patronage of noble causes, operation of an official Facebook page,[46] and extensive media coverage that can reach wide segments of the population. A successful example for the latter was raising public awareness for air quality standards through the Ombudsman's cooperation with civil society organizations, governmental bodies, and local municipalities.

According to the Ombudsman Act, only the Commissioner for Fundamental Rights has the right to carry out investigations (based on *ex officio* proceedings, public complaints or individual petitions), but the Ombudsman for Future Generations can also initiate and partake in the inspections.[47] If an investigation initiated by the Ombudsman is rejected by the Commissioner, the Commissioner must note the refusal and provide an explanation for it in his annual Parliamentary report. This provides an important safeguard mechanism for *ex officio* proceedings of the Ombudsman for Future Generations. Reflecting the excellent professional and institutional relationship between the Ombudsman

42 Excerpt from the lecture of Ewa Letowska, former Polish Ombudsman and Constitutional Judge, entitled "Constitutional doubles: the interplay between ombudsmen and constitutional courts in the protection of human rights" held at Central European University in September 2012, cited by Attila Lápossy, 'Közvetve és közvetlenül: az alapvető jogok biztosának indítványozási jogköre az alkotmánybíráskodás és alapjogvédelem szemszögéből', *Kodifikáció és Közigazgatás*, Vol. 5, Issue 1, 2012, p. 39.

43 The annual reports (in Hungarian) can be found at the official website of the Commissioner, at www.ajbh.hu/eves-beszamolok.

44 Act CXI of 2011 on the Commissioner for Fundamental Rights.

45 Id. Section 3(1)(a).

46 *See* at www.facebook.com/J%C3%B6v%C5%91-Nemzed%C3%A9kek-Sz%C3%B3sz%C3%B3l%C3%B3ja-885959088173953/?fref=ts.

47 Section 3(1)(c)-(d) of Act CXI of 2011 on the Commissioner for Fundamental Rights.

Hungarian Yearbook of International Law and European Law 2021 (9) 1
doi: 10.5553/HYIEL/266627012021009001019

and the Commissioner, the Commissioner never rejected any investigations initiated by the Ombudsman.

Should the Commissioner and the Ombudsman for Future Generations find an instance of maladministration, they issue a *joint report*. The joint reports present the results of the investigation, reveal the noted maladministration, and if necessary, formulate general or specific recommendations to remedy the harm done. Reports of the Commissioner for Fundamental Rights and the Ombudsman for Future Generations are not binding upon the Parliament nor the Government or any other addressee. However, when an infringement constitutes the violation of the Fundamental Law, *i.e.* the adopted regulation is not only harmful to the interests of future generations but also constitutes a breach of the Fundamental Law, the Ombudsman for Future Generations may turn to the Commissioner for Fundamental Rights to propose the submission of a petition to the Constitutional Court, requesting the annulment of the legal provision in question.[48] Joint reports are especially important when the remedy of the cases concerned can ensure the realization of both intergenerational and intragenerational justice. In 2020, the Ombudsman and the Commissioner published 13 joint reports that concerned, in particular, the issue of noise pollution, waste management, air quality control and damage to the environment.[49]

The Ombudsman for Future Generations can issue non-binding statements and make proposals to any public authority, including the Government. Besides revealing instances of maladministration in individual cases, the Ombudsman's proposals provide an opportunity to highlight policy developments that threaten the protection of the current state of the environment, jeopardizing the interests of future generations. For instance, in 2015 the Ombudsman for Future Generations called upon the Government to save one of the last habitats of a critically endangered endemic mammal, the mole-rat.[50] This species is on the brink of extinction, with an estimated number of about 400 individuals left in the wild. Mole-rats are only known to inhabit three regions: one in northern Serbia, one in Hungary and one on the border of the two countries. In line with the recommendation of the Ombudsman, the competent National Park Directorate issued a proposal to designate the biggest Hungarian reservation area of the species as a so-called 'protected natural area with national significance'. The case provided an opportunity for the Ombudsman to disseminate scientific information and concepts about the general role of biological diversity for human

48 *See e.g.* Decision No. 14/2020. (VII. 6.) AB, in which the Constitutional Court stated that several elements of the 2017 amendment of the Act on Forests is unconstitutional. The case was initiated by the Commissioner for Fundamental Rights, in agreement with the Ombudsman.

49 Joint Reports No. 540/2019, 94/2020, 385/2020, 642/2020, 669/2020, 1025/2020, 1026/2020, 1073/2020, 1100/2020, 1365/2020, 1371/2020, 2037/2020, 4642/2020. All the Joint Reports are available (in Hungarian) at the website of the Office of the Commissioner for Fundamental Rights.

50 *See* the Statement of the Ombudsman for Future Generations on the conservation of the highly protected mole-rat for future generations (in Hungarian) at www.ajbh.hu/documents/10180/1957691/D%C3%A9lvid%C3%A9ki+f%C3%B6ldikutya+%C3%A1ll%C3%A1sfoglal%C3%A1s/53ba0e75-dfdb-440a-ac8a-ed6373932906.

doi: 10.5553/HYIEL/266627012021009001019

and non-human life on Earth and helped strengthen the social reception of these concepts. In 2016, the Ombudsman issued proposals for the protection of the soil,[51] in which he made recommendations to stop the qualitative and quantitative deterioration of soil and urged the Government to create a national strategy for soil protection. The Ombudsman aims to develop its proposals relying on the latest nationally and internationally available scientific findings and positions. The Ombudsman (together with the Commissioner) also called the attention of the lawmaker to the importance of the protection of groundwater in 2021.[52] Groundwater is an element of the 'common heritage of the nation' under Article P of the Fundamental Law, and for this reason it is the obligation of the Hungarian State and everyone to protect, maintain and preserve it for future generations, as it flows from the 'public trust'[53] doctrine.

6. Beyond the Powers – Why is the Role of the Ombudsman of Future Generations so Important?

Early warnings are one of the most effective tools in the hands of the Ombudsman: the Ombudsman can draw the attention of the public and decision-makers to the potential dangers that a planned investment poses to the cultural and natural heritage of the state. If the Ombudsman receives enough support from the public, this may have a significant impact on the implementation or the repeal of the planned activity. Early warnings are, in effect, the practical application of the precautionary principle. An apt example of how early warnings change the public's, and through that, the Government's perception about a planned investment, is from 2013. The local Government of Budapest prepared plans to build a mobile dam on the northern side of the Danube. This section of the riverbank is covered with alluvial gallery forests and is one of the ecologically most sensitive areas of the river. Through press releases, public events and consultations, as well as with the continuous support of a number of civil society organizations, the Ombudsman was able to call attention to the potential loss of valuable forest coverage that would have resulted from the construction of the mobile dam system. The Ombudsman asserted that the removal of trees from this area would not be necessary as other technological solutions could more effectively solve the question of flood protection.[54]

The Ombudsman for Future Generations also *could monitor all the legislative proposals*, to make sure that these bills do not pose a severe or irreversible risk to the environment and harm the interests of future generations. The Ombudsman,

51 *See* at www.ajbh.hu/documents/10180/2762244/talaj_allasfoglalas_vegleges_melleklet_nelkul.pdf/bb275681-70f8-9cdb-e886-aeb5d52b9ac9.

52 *See* the joint statement of the Commissioner and the Ombudsman on World Water Day (in Hungarian), at www.ajbh.hu/-/az-alapveto-jogok-biztosa-es-a-jovo-nemzedekek-szoszoloja-kozos-kozlemenye-a-viz-vilagnapja-alkalmabol.

53 *See e.g.* Katalin Sulyok, 'The Public Trust Doctrine, the Non-Derogation Principle and the Protection of Future Generations: the Hungarian Constitutional Court's Review of the Forest Act', *Hungarian Yearbook of International Law and European Law*, Vol. 9, 2021.

54 *2013 Annual Report of the Commissioner for Fundamental Rights*, AJBH, 2014, pp. 274-275.

doi: 10.5553/HYIEL/266627012021009001019

through the Commissioner for Fundamental Rights, can deliver his opinion on draft laws, long-term land-use planning and development policies, as well as other initiatives that directly influence the quality of life of future generations.[55] In case the Commissioner's opinion is not taken into account by the legislature, the draft can later be challenged before the Constitutional Court.

The Ombudsman for Future Generations may recommend that new legislation be drafted or existing laws affecting the *rights* of future generations be amended. Based on this mandate, the Ombudsman can successfully represent the rights and ecological interests in the process of national and local law-making. For example, in 2016, the Ombudsman for Future Generations initiated the "Seedling-Sibling" nationwide tree-planting campaign,[56] which builds on long-standing national traditions, and on other international models adopted for instance in Wales.[57] The goal of the Seedling-Sibling project was to celebrate the birth of every newborn in the country by planting a seedling of a native tree species in the birthplace of the child. The project would have served a number of goals and has both symbolic meaning and ecological significance. While the Parliament did not accept the draft resolution of the Ombudsman for Future Generations, in 2020 the Government officially announced that 10 trees will be planted for every baby born.

In connection with its afore-mentioned powers, the Ombudsman for Future Generations also has *the right to speak before the respective committees of the Parliament*. On many occasions, it is the competent committees themselves who ask the Ombudsman to speak to the legislative process relating to the rights and interests of future generations. This is a very powerful instrument, since decisions on the adoption or amendment of laws are made within the framework of the parliamentary commissions. Through active lobbying and promoting proposed amendments that take the interests of future generations into consideration, the Ombudsman can steer legislation in a new, more environmentally friendly direction. When in 2017, a major amendment to the forest law was put on the Parliament's agenda that emphasized the economic functions of forests rather than their role in environmental conservation, the Ombudsman expressed its position in a number of parliamentary committee meetings. He argued that forests are the most complex terrestrial ecological systems receiving the highest level of constitutional protection (afforded to elements of the national heritage under Article P of the Fundamental Law), and that he was convinced that the bill is unconstitutional. Following the adoption of the bill in its original form, the Ombudsman asked the Commissioner for Fundamental Rights to turn to the Constitutional Court (*see* Section 7 below).[58]

55 Section 2(2) of Act CXI of 2011 on the Commissioner for Fundamental Rights.

56 *See* the recommendation of the Ombudsman for Future Generations (in Hungarian) at www.ajbh.hu/documents/10180/2584047/Fatestv%C3%A9r+Program_OGY+hat%C3%A1rozat-javaslat.pdf/ad71d370-4c13-4ff7-9cc9-b47ee5d160a3.

57 For more information on the Welsh "Plant!" program, *see* at https://sizeofwales.org.uk/about-us/plant-scheme/.

58 Decision No. 14/2020. (VII. 6.) AB.

doi: 10.5553/HYIEL/266627012021009001019

7. The Legal Relationship between the Ombudsman and the Constitutional Court

The Ombudsman for Future Generations and the Constitutional Court have a multi-faceted relationship. As outlined above, the Ombudsman often refers to the decisions of the Constitutional Court for normative guidance. In general, presenting the Constitutional Court's practice constitutes a central part of the Ombudsman's individual proposals and joint reports, providing a critical foundation for the Ombudsman's assessment of questions relating to fundamental rights.

The Ombudsman for Future Generations turned to the Constitutional Court in several cases *via* the Commissioner for Fundamental Rights to contribute to the protection of Hungary's natural resources. For example, in *Decision No. 14/2020. (VII. 6.) AB* the Constitutional Court stated that several elements of the 2017 amendment of the Act on Forests are unconstitutional. The case was initiated by the Commissioner for Fundamental Rights, in agreement with the Ombudsman for Future Generations. The Constitutional Court fully agreed with the petition that the amendment to the Forest Act primarily served the interests of forest owners by overshadowing key environmental considerations.[59]

The Ombudsman for Future Generations also assists the Constitutional Court by filing *amicus curiae* briefs. *Amici curiae* may help the Constitutional Court develop its interpretation regarding the environmental provisions of the Fundamental Law. The Ombudsman can act as a guardian for future generations representing their long-term interests and influencing the decisions of the Constitutional Court by providing important legal interpretations and reasoning. In a landmark decision taken in 2015, the Constitutional Court annulled certain clauses of an Act, which had not been promulgated at the time. The clauses in question would have made it possible for government-run authorities, whose primary responsibility was not environmental protection, to take over the management of nature conservation areas from the national park directorates. Following an extensive investigation, the Ombudsman for Future Generations issued an independent statement entitled 'National Parks as safeguards of natural and cultural values for future generations'.[60] His statement concluded that pursuant to the Fundamental Law, the protection and maintenance of biodiversity, and its preservation for future generations was, among others, the obligation of the state, which responsibility is best fulfilled by the existing national park directorates. The Ombudsman highlighted that the land management activities of national parks are characterized by the highest standards of preservation, stemming from their primary task to protect the natural environment. Deviating from this arrangement, therefore, would be

59 About the decision *see e.g.* Sulyok 2021; Attila Pánovics: 'Decision No. 14/2020. (VII. 6.) of the Hungarian Constitutional Court on the Protection of Forests', *Hungarian Yearbook of International Law and European Law*, Vol. 9, 2021.

60 "National Parks as safeguards of natural and cultural values for future generations", Statement of the Ombudsman for Future Generations (in Hungarian), issued on 16 December 2014, p. 2.

doi: 10.5553/HYIEL/266627012021009001019

unconstitutional.[61] This statement influenced the decision of the Constitutional Court, which referred to the Ombudsman's brief as a persuasive source on the constitutional protection of the environment.

Besides *amici curiae*, based on Section 57(3) of the Act on the Constitutional Court, the Constitutional Court has the right to invite state bodies and authorities to make a declaration, send documents or give an opinion in pending cases. In 2017 the Hungarian Constitutional Court took a huge step towards the general recognition of the protection of the interests of future generations in the Hungarian legal system in a posterior norm control case initiated by Members of the Parliament. In this case, the Constitutional Court had to evaluate whether the privatization of certain Natura 2000 sites without sufficient environmental guarantees may be considered a violation of the core obligation of the state under the Fundamental Law to preserve natural resources, including biodiversity. Applying Section 57(3) of the Act on the Constitutional Court, this was the very first case when *the Constitutional Court invited the Ombudsman to submit his detailed opinion*.[62] In its landmark decision, the Constitutional Court stated that

> the core obligation to protect biodiversity as the UN Convention on Biological Diversity (ratified by 196 parties, including Hungary) prescribes, is a peremptory norm of general international law accepted and recognized by the international community of States as a whole from which no derogation is permitted.[63]

Through the Commissioner, the Ombudsman can initiate constitutional court proceedings in cases, where it is reasonable to believe that a national or local piece of legislation is in violation of the Fundamental Law or an international agreement. Similarly, the Ombudsman can recommend that the Commissioner request an interpretation of a provision of the Fundamental Law from the Constitutional Court.[64] It should be noted, that in case the Commissioner rejects the recommendation, he must note and provide reasoned justification for the refusal in his annual report to the Parliament.[65] This provision is an important guarantee for the success of the Ombudsman's new initiatives.

61 Id.

62 In 2018 the Constitutional Court invited the Ombudsman again to submit his opinion in a preliminary norm control case, in which the President of Hungary stated that an adopted but not yet promulgated Act on groundwater is unconstitutional; *see* Decision No. 13/2018. (IX. 4.) AB. About the Decision, *see e.g.* Marcel Szabó, 'The Precautionary Principle in the Fundamental Law of Hungary – Judicial Activism or an Inherent Fundamental Principle? An Evaluation of Constitutional Court Decision No. 13/2018. (IX. 4.) AB on the Protection of Groundwater', *Hungarian Yearbook of International Law and European Law*, Vol. 7, 2019, pp. 67-83; Gábor Kecskés, 'The Hungarian Constitutional Court's Decision on the Protection of Groundwater – Decision No. 13/2018. (IX. 4.) AB of the Constitutional Court of Hungary', *Hungarian Yearbook of International Law and European Law*, Vol. 8, 2020, pp. 371-382.

63 Decision No. 28/2017. (X. 25.) AB, Reasoning [38].

64 Sections 2(3) and 3(1)(e) of Act CXI of 2011 on the Commissioner for Fundamental Rights.

65 Id. Section 3(3).

doi: 10.5553/HYIEL/266627012021009001019

8. The Ombudsman at International Level

On the basis of his special responsibility in promoting the needs of the unborn, the Hungarian Ombudsman for Future Generations wished to contribute to a closer cooperation between these national institutions. To this end, he initiated, together with the other institutions for future generations, the establishment of an international network that could enhance the concept of sustainable development and intergenerational solidarity on a global level. As a first step, the Ombudsman aimed to bring together representatives of the eight institutions as well as a number of international scholars and NGOs to lay down the theoretical and practical foundations of implementing intergenerational justice. The first meeting, which was entitled "Model Institutions for a Sustainable Future" after the reference made in the former UN Secretary General Ban Ki-Moon's report, was held in the Hungarian Parliament in April 2014. As a part of this conference, the participants adopted the Budapest Memorandum,[66] which aims to spread tested institutional solutions and best practices worldwide. The Memorandum was signed by representatives of 44 institutions.[67] With the aim to formalize and further enhance their future cooperation, participants also agreed to establish the Network of Institutions for Future Generations.[68]

9. Concluding Remarks

There is a general agreement among scholars that the institutional representation of future generations should not be uniform across different countries and regions. It is argued that such efforts must be tailored to the specific characteristics of the intergenerational issues at hand, and to the cultural and legal specificities of each country.[69] The effectiveness of the institutional representation of future generations depends on a large number of factors, only one of which is the institutional framework. This framework can be filled with substance on the basis of the perspectives, available tools, and opportunities for cooperation between individual representatives. The model institutions that enjoy the most freedom to interpret their own mandate are usually Ombudsman institutions. Therefore, in the case of this establishment, it is particularly important how the holder of the office interprets the norms regulating its

66 Budapest Memorandum adopted at the Conference of Model Institutions for a Sustainable Future held in Budapest, 24-26 April 2014, at www.ajbh.hu/documents/14315/121663/Budapest_Memorandum.pdf/29f4b867-0afa-4d15-b3c4-4383ad732f73.

67 The proposal for such a memorandum also gained support from the UN Secretary General Ban Ki-moon, who addressed the aforementioned conference and called upon the participants to deliver "a powerful message to all countries about the need to create effective institutions that will maintain a robust focus on our common future."

68 The official page of the network is available at http://futureroundtable.org/en/web/network-of-institutions-for-future-generations/welcome.

69 Boldizsár Nagy, 'Speaking Without a Voice', *in* Emmanuel Agius & Salvino Busuttil (eds.), *Future Generations and International Law*, Earthscan, 1998, p. 62.

doi: 10.5553/HYIEL/266627012021009001019

powers, and how it makes use of the opportunities afforded to it.[70] So far, all Ombudsmen for Future Generations sought to take advantage of the broad spectrum of opportunities, exploiting the potential in this unique institution. They truly aspired "to make human responsibility felt in all [areas] of state and civil life, with respect to the conservation of natural values [...] for the sake of protecting the next generations."[71]

One of the most important guarantees of the Ombudsman for Future Generations' success is the support and participation of the public in its activities. Environmental concerns raised by the Ombudsman are often met with a strong response from the public, urging decision-makers to re-think the problem and potential solutions. It is important to point out, however, that the intensity of the public response is in direct connection with the amplification of the Ombudsman's message by the media. Since long-term thinking is not a typical feature of the press, it is difficult to publicize issues concerning the interests of the unborn. It is mostly issues that have a day-to-day relevance that are taken up by the media. In cases, where no acute event draws attention to the importance of a cause, the biggest supporter of the Ombudsman is the scientific sphere. If the Ombudsman wants to prove that certain decisions and processes cause permanent damage to the environment, it is much easier to achieve progress, if the Ombudsman works in close cooperation with the Hungarian Academy of Sciences and professional NGOs. Supported with sufficient scientific evidence, it is harder for the political sphere to disregard the assertions of the Ombudsman.

The change in the institutional set-up of the Office of the Commissioner for Fundamental Rights in 2012 resulted in a number of positive changes. With the adoption of the Fundamental Law, the constitutional powers of the institution were widened considerably. The Fundamental Law entrusted the Ombudsman for Future Generations with protecting the interests of future generations, while the Ombudsman Act refers to the rights of future generations as the object of protection. Cooperation with the Commissioner for Fundamental Rights is critical in a number of cases, when the given problem only partially concerns the protection of future generations. Coordinated, joint action can therefore be valuable, or may even become an important source of legal protection. In accordance with the precautionary principle, the Ombudsman for Future Generations frequently relies on early warnings and presents its position in the earliest stages of a potentially unlawful activity, when the Commissioner is not yet entitled to act.

The example of the Hungarian Ombudsman for Future Generations shows that while the protection of future generations could potentially affect all policies, their representation cannot be effectively expanded to all fields of legislation and governance. No national institution for the protection of future

70 Bernadette Somody, 'Jogállami paradoxon – A sikeres ombudsmani jogvédelem sajátosságai', *in* Éva Heizerné Hegedűs (ed.), *Az ombudsman intézménye és az emberi jogok védelme Magyarországon*, OBH, Budapest, 2008, pp. 101-106.

71 *See* the Comprehensive Summary of the Parliamentary Commissioner for Future Generations of Hungary, at http://jno.hu/en/pdf/Comprehensive_Summary_2009.pdf.

doi: 10.5553/HYIEL/266627012021009001019

generations will ever be mandated to act as a branch of power taking action on behalf of future generations. Therefore, the activities of future generation institutions should mainly focus on the 'conservation of options' as Brown Weiss put it. That is to say, they must concentrate their efforts on helping maintain the quality of the environment and the ecology to the degree possible, acting for the preservation of biodiversity, clean air, soil, water and other natural resources.

doi: 10.5553/HYIEL/266627012021009001019

The Public Trust Doctrine, the Non-Derogation Principle and the Protection of Future Generations

The Hungarian Constitutional Court's Review of the Forest Act*

*Katalin Sulyok***

Abstract

This article analyzes the doctrinal findings of the Hungarian Constitutional Court with respect to the constitutional protection afforded to future generations in the Fundamental Law. It focuses on Decision No. 14/2020. (VII. 6.) AB in which the Constitutional Court abolished an amendment to the Forest Act for infringing the right to a healthy environment and the environmental interests of future generations as enshrined in Article P of the Fundamental Law. On this occasion, the Constitutional Court for the first time explicitly recognized that Article P embodies the public trust doctrine; and stressed that it confers fiduciary duties on the State to act as a trustee over the natural heritage of the nation for the benefit of future generations, which limits the executive's discretion to exploit and regulate such resources. This article puts the Hungarian constitutional public trust in a comparative perspective by exploring the origins, role and functioning of similar constitutional public trust provisions in other jurisdictions. This is followed by setting out the normative principles derived by the Hungarian Constitutional Court in its previous practice from Article P, such as the non-derogation principle, the principle of inter-generational equity, the imperative of long-term planning, economical use of resources and the precautionary principle. The article then sets out the legal bases featured in the ex post constitutional challenge brought against the amendment of the Forest Act by the Ombudsman, and the Constitutional Court's reasoning. It concludes with offering some wider lessons for the judicial enforcement of long-term environmental goals vis-á-vis short-term economic private interests.

Keywords: public trust, non-derogation, Article P, Constitutional Court of Hungary, future generations.

* The views expressed in this article are solely of the author's and do not necessarily resemble the position of the institution she works for.

** Katalin Sulyok: senior lecturer, ELTE Law School, Budapest; chief legal advisor, Office of the Hungarian Ombudsman for Future Generations, Budapest.

doi: 10.5553/HYIEL/266627012021009001020

1. Introduction

On 9 June 2020, the Hungarian Constitutional Court has struck down an amendment to the Forest Act in its *Decision No. 14/2020. (VII. 6.) AB* for infringing the right to a healthy environment and the provision stipulating an obligation to protect the forests for future generations. The Constitutional Court has also acknowledged that the latter provision creates a constitutional public trust, which confers fiduciary duties on the government to act as a trustee over the natural and cultural heritage of the nation for the benefit of future generations, and which therefore limits its discretion to exploit, manage, and regulate the use of such resources.

By adopting a broader scope, this study not only comments on the doctrinal aspects of this recent decision, but also explores the origins, role and functioning of similar constitutional public trust provisions in other jurisdictions. Section 2 will first provide an overview of the wider landscape of public trust provisions in foreign jurisdictions with a brief commentary on how this doctrine has been interpreted by domestic judicial bodies in resolving environmental conflicts. This will be followed by setting out the normative principles derived by the Hungarian Constitutional Court in its previous practice from the right to a healthy environment as well as Article P, the public trust provision of the Hungarian Fundamental Law. Section 3 will then address in detail the facts of the case and the legal bases featured in the *ex post* constitutional challenge brought against the amendment by the Ombudsman. The article will also assess the Constitutional Court's reasoning in finding the amendment to the Forest Act unconstitutional. It will conclude in Section 4 by offering some wider lessons for the judicial enforcement of long-term environmental goals *vis-á-vis* short-term economic private interests.

2. A Constitutional Public Trust Doctrine in Hungary: Normative Requirements Flowing From the Imperative to Protect the Interests of Future Generations

As a welcome development, provisions relating to environmental protection have become the norm in the constitutions of countries around the world.[1] The exact formulation and wording of such provisions vary to a great extent. While environmental human rights and provisions on sustainable development appear to be the most common formulations, there is an emerging trend of enshrining public trust provisions in national constitutions.[2] The Hungarian Fundamental Law, adopted in 2011, is the only European jurisdiction that contains such a

1 James R. May & Erin Daly, *Global Environmental Constitutionalism*, Cambridge University Press, Cambridge, 2015, for the wide acceptance of human rights to the environment in national constitutions *see* HRC 'Report of the Special Rapporteur on the Issue of Human Rights Obligations Relating to the Enjoyment of a Safe, Clean, Healthy and Sustainable Environment: Right to a Healthy Environment: Good Practices' (30 December 2019) UN Doc A/HRC/43/53.

2 May & Daly 2015, p. 267.

doi: 10.5553/HYIEL/266627012021009001020

provision in its Article P. Before delving into the normative content of this public trust provision in the practice of the Hungarian Constitutional Court, a brief overview is due on the origins, structure, and the various normative contents derived from this doctrine in other jurisdictions.

2.1. The Public Trust Doctrine in Constitutions and Laws of Various Jurisdictions

The *public trust doctrine* imposes fiduciary duties on States to preserve their natural resources as trust assets for the benefit of present and future generations. Having its roots in ancient Roman law[3] and English common-law,[4] public trust provisions now appear in the constitutions of several States in Africa, Asia and South America, more specifically Tanzania, Uganda, Ethiopia, Papua New Guinea, Ghana, Swaziland, Bhutan, Kenya, Brazil and Ecuador.[5] In Europe, only Hungary has adopted a public trust provision in its constitution. In Sri Lanka, courts have read the doctrine into the Constitution since the beginning of the 1990s.[6] In North America, several States of the US incorporated such provisions in their constitutions,[7] besides deriving it from common-law,[8] and having it enshrined in certain statutory laws, while Canada discerned trust obligations from common-law.[9] In India, the doctrine is regarded to be part of common-law,[10] while in the Philippines it was gleaned from the constitutionally enshrined right to a healthy environment.[11] South Africa enacted several statutes that codify public trust obligations.[12] The doctrine's wide recognition on the international arena has led some to suggest that *the doctrine became a general principle of international law*.[13]

At its core, *the public trust doctrine imposes fiduciary duties on the trustee, i.e.* the government, which therefore has an obligation to manage the trust's assets

3 The Institutes of Justinian declared that "the following things are by natural law common to all – the air, running water, the sea, and consequently the seashore." *Institutes of Justinian, Book II on the Law of Things, Title I of the Different Kinds of Things*, p. 1 (translated into English by J.B. Moyle, Oxford, 1913).

4 Alexandra B. Klass, 'Modern Public Trust Principles: Recognizing Rights and Integrating Standards', *Notre Dame Law Review*, Vol. 82, Issue 2, 2006, p. 702.

5 Michael C. Blumm & Rachel D Guthrie, 'Internationalizing the Public Trust Doctrine: Natural Law and Constitutional and Statutory Approaches to Fulfilling the Saxion Vision', *UCD Law Review*, Vol. 45, 2011, p. 783.

6 Dinesha Samararatne, *Public Trust Doctrine the Sri Lankan Version*, International Centre for Ethnic Studies 2010, p. 26.

7 *E.g.* State constitutions of Hawaii, Pennsylvania, North Dakota, Montana, Alaska, and Texas have trust-like provisions.

8 Robin Kundis Craig, 'A Comparative Guide to the Western States' Public Trust Doctrines: Public Values, Private Rights, and the Evolution Toward an Ecological Public Trust', *Ecology Law Quarterly*, Vol. 37, Issue 1, 2010, p. 58.

9 Blumm & Guthrie 2011, pp. 801-802.

10 Id. p. 760. A leading case is the Supreme Court of India's decision in *M.C. Mehta v Kamal Nath*, (1997) 1. SCC 388.

11 Id. p. 771.

12 Elmarie Van der Schyff, 'Unpacking the Public Trust Doctrine: A Journey into Foreign Territory', *PER: Potchefstroomse Elektroniese Regsblad*, Vol. 13, Issue 41, 2010, p. 122.

13 Blumm & Guthrie 2011, p. 750; Catherine Redgwell, 'Principles and Emerging Norms in International Law Intra- and Inter-Generational Equity', *in* Kevin R. Gray *et al.* (eds.), *The Oxford Handbook on International Climate Change Law*, Oxford University Press, Oxford, 2016.

doi: 10.5553/HYIEL/266627012021009001020

for the beneficiaries of the trust, typically the public and future generations. Traditional trust law concerns the management of financial assets and defines certain obligations for the trustee owed to present and future beneficiaries of the trust.[14] By way of analogy, rules applicable to financial trusts are invoked in relation to public trusts as well.[15] Such obligations traditionally include a duty to protect the assets from damage, and to prevent waste to the trust assets.[16] As a consequence, in a public trust context, fiduciary obligations entail that a public trustee cannot allow the trust assets to "fall into ruin on his watch",[17] and the trustee should exercise supervision over the assets concerned.[18]

We may witness a wide range of obligations conferred upon sovereign trustees across respective jurisdictions in relation to managing natural resources and ecosystems. Essentially, *the doctrine imposes limitations on State policies regarding the use, exploitation and transfer of ownership over the trust assets*. The scope of constitutional public trust provisions varies across the different States, yet they tend to be widely defined.[19]

The following list of domestic court decisions showcases the doctrine's diverse possible contents applied in the context of protecting ecosystems and managing natural resources. US courts discerned from the doctrine a restraint on the State's ability to alienate trust assets.[20] The Pennsylvania Supreme Court used the public trust provision enshrined in the State constitution to ban hydraulic fracking.[21] In California, courts relied on it to prevent a private landowner from filling a tideland, which was regarded as a trust asset, as filling the area would have threatened the ecological integrity of an important habitat.[22] Similarly, in the famous *Mono Lake* case, the California Supreme Court compelled an agency to reconsider the allocation of the water of Mono Lake, in order to protect the stability of the fragile ecosystem dependent upon the lake, even to the detriment of the City of Los Angeles, which drew a significant amount of water from the tributaries of Mono Lake to satisfy its increasing water demand.[23]

Sri Lankan courts employed the doctrine to put a limit on the government's discretionary power, when they suspected that the divestiture of public land did

14 *Kelsey Cascadia Rose Juliana et al. v United States of America, et al.*, No. 6:15-cv-1517, No. 6:15-cv-01517-TC (D. Or. Nov. 10, 2016).
15 Mary Christina Wood, 'Advancing the Sovereign Trust of Government to Safeguard the Environment for Present and Future Generations (Part II): Instilling a Fiduciary Obligation in Governance', *Environmental Law*, Vol. 39, Issue 1, 2009, pp. 94-96.
16 Id. pp. 94-95.
17 *United States v White Mountain Apache Tribe*, 537 U.S. 465, 475 (2002). *See* in more detail Mary Christina Wood & Dan Galpern, 'Atmospheric Recovery Litigation: Making the Fossil Fuel Industry Pay to Restore a Viable Climate System', *Environmental Law*, Vol. 45, Issue 2, 2015, pp. 282-283.
18 Id.
19 Blumm & Guthrie 2011, p. 748.
20 Craig 2010, p. 69; *Illinois Central Railroad Co. v Illinois*, 146 U.S. 387, 460 (1892); *Scott v Chicago Park District*, 360 N.E.2d 773 (Ill. 1977).
21 *Robinson Township et al. v Commonwealth of Pennsylvania*, 147 A.3d 536 (Pa. 2016).
22 California Supreme Court's decision in *Marks v Whitney*, 491 P.2d 374, 378 (Cal. 1971).
23 *Mono Lake*, 658 P.2d 709, 711 (Cal. 1983).

doi: 10.5553/HYIEL/266627012021009001020

not serve the "public good".[24] The courts also emphasized that conservation measures should be guided by "a long term view of such [assets] being conserved for intergenerational use".[25] The doctrine may require agencies to adopt particular management measures to protect the trust's assets.[26] The Louisiana Court of Appeals ordered a state agency to reduce the level of organic matters in a lake in order to improve its ecological health.[27] In the Philippines, the public trust doctrine served as an action-forcing tool compelling governmental measures to restore the trust assets. In *Manila Bay*, the Supreme Court of the Philippines relied on the doctrine to order the government agency to take various actions, such as constructing a sewage treatment facility, restocking indigenous fish species and fostering environmental education of local people.[28]

2.2. *Future Generations and the Public Trust Doctrine in the Hungarian Fundamental Law*

The Hungarian Constitution as revised in 1989 already stipulated a right to a healthy environment, which has been later included in the new Fundamental Law as well in Article XXI.[29] In addition, the Fundamental Law also enshrines Article P, which creates an idiosyncratic heritage concept, the *'common heritage of the nation'*, and confers an obligation on the State and everyone to preserve the assets of that heritage for posterity. Article P provides that

> "all natural resources, including arable land, forests and water resources, as well as biological diversity, in particular native plant and animal species together with cultural heritage shall comprise the nation's common heritage; the responsibility to protect, maintain and preserve such a heritage for future generations lies with the State and every individual."

Ever since the late 1990s, the Hungarian Constitutional Court has been particularly active in affording in its interpretations the right to a healthy environment a normative 'bite' and has struck down several laws on the basis of infringing the right to a healthy environment. Since 2015, when the first environmental case was brought to the Constitutional Court under the Fundamental Law, the Constitutional Court also interpreted Article P as a normative rule as opposed to a mere symbolic obligation on the part of the State. This resulted in an extensive environmental case-law, rich in normative principles

24 Samararatne 2010, p. 27, citing decision in case *De Silva v Atukorale* [1993] 1. Sri. L.R. 283.

25 *Watte Gedara Wijebanda v Conservator General of Forests and others*, cited by Samararatne 2010, p. 33.

26 Wood 2009, p. 115.

27 *Lake Bistineau Preservation Society, Inc. v Wildlife & Fisheries Commission*, 895 So 2d 821, 191.

28 *Metropolitan Manila Development Authority v Concerned Residents of Manila Bay*, G. R. Nos. 171947-48, 574 S.C.R.A. 661 (S.C., Dec. 18, 2008).

29 "Article XXI(1) Hungary shall recognize and implement the right of all to a healthy environment. (2) Any environmental damage shall as a priority be rectified at source in accordance with the relevant legislation and the principle that the polluter shall pay. (3) It is prohibited to import waste to Hungary for the purpose of disposal."

doi: 10.5553/HYIEL/266627012021009001020

derived from Article XXI and Article P. These principles have supplied the basis of the *Forest decision*. Hence, before turning to discussing this particular decision, we shall briefly recall the doctrinal principles governing the constitutional protection of the environment under the Fundamental Law.

2.3. Intergenerational Equity in Article P of the Fundamental Law

The Constitutional Court has emphasized that Article P stipulates objective and substantive obligations for the State in terms of preserving the natural capital and cultural heritage for future generations.[30] In particular, the Constitutional Court opined that the decline in biodiversity is contrary to Article P,[31] and stressed that bequeathing the common heritage of the nation in a deteriorated state to later generations would in fact hollow out the government's obligations under Article P.[32] Echoing *the pillars of intergenerational equity* in international law, as articulated by Edith Brown Weiss in her seminal book,[33] the Constitutional Court stipulated three basic duties owed by present generations towards posterity: *(i)* the conservation of options; *(ii)* the conservation of quality of resources; and *(iii)* the conservation of access to such resources. In the Constitutional Court's reading, this ensures that present stakeholders' decisions do not create path dependencies for future generations. The Constitutional Court also articulated that natural resources could be freely exploited by present generations as long as they respect the equitable needs of future generations.[34] In an *ex ante* constitutional review proceedings concerning whether the act allowing increased water withdrawals for households from groundwater resources was in conformity with Article P and Article XXI, the Constitutional Court invoked the duty to conserve the quality of resources and opined that present generations "must aim to pass down the natural environment to future generations in a no less favorable state in which it was received".[35] As a result, it declared a provision to be contrary to Article P, which did not provide adequate protection against polluting finite groundwater resources.[36]

In essence, Article P imposes limits on the discretion of the sovereign to utilize natural resources.[37] As the Constitutional Court noted in its *Forest decision*,

> "the State shall act as a sovereign trustee and shall manage natural and cultural heritage entrusted to its care for the benefit of the trust's beneficiaries, *i.e.* future generations. This means that it can only allow the exhaustion of such resources for present generations until it does not

30 Decision No. 28/2017. (X. 25.) AB, Reasoning [32]; Decision No. 17/2018. (X. 10.) AB, Reasoning [85].

31 Decision No. 28/2017. (X. 25.) AB, Reasoning [74].

32 Id. Reasoning [32].

33 Edith Brown Weiss, *In Fairness to Future Generations: International Law, Common Patrimony, and Intergenerational Equity*, The United Nations University and Transnational Publishers, 1988.

34 Decision No. 28/2017. (X. 25.) AB, Reasoning [33].

35 Decision No. 13/2018. (IX. 4.) AB, Reasoning [71].

36 Id. Reasoning [72].

37 Decision No. 28/2017. (X. 25.) AB, Reasoning [43].

doi: 10.5553/HYIEL/266627012021009001020

threaten the long-term existence of the natural and cultural assets that are worthy of being protected on account of their inherent values."[38]

2.4. The Non-Derogation Principle in Hungarian Constitutional Doctrine

Ever since the first major environmental decision of the Constitutional Court in 1994, the most significant normative requirement flowing from the right to a healthy environment has been the *non-derogation principle*.[39] According to this doctrinal principle, the legislature cannot go below the level of statutory protection existing in the environmental law sector unless it is strictly necessary for realizing a competing human right or constitutional goal and the measure is proportionate to that aim.[40] The principle has been interpreted as a substantive criterion requiring the maintenance of the efficiency of legislative protection across procedural, institutional and substantive laws.[41] In other words, the legislature has no discretion to lower the stringency of environmental protection measures that exist under laws in force at any given time. The requirement has been upheld under the Fundamental Law as well under the right to a health environment,[42] and importantly, the Constitutional Court has read this principle into Article P as well.[43] The principle has been functioning as a strict normative criterion, leading the Constitutional Court to quash several acts that were found to be in contravention of the non-derogation principle.[44]

2.5. Prevention and Precaution

Under the *preventive action principle*, the State must not impair the natural environment or enact legislative measures that would cause irreversible environmental harm,[45] and also has a positive duty to prevent such damage through adopting relevant measures and legislative acts.[46] The Constitutional Court has also read the precautionary principle into the guarantees flowing from the Fundamental Law.[47] In line with the principle, the legislature bears the burden of proving with a high level of certainty, on the basis of uncertain scientific evidence, that a particular measure will not deteriorate the state of the

38 Decision No. 14/2020. (VII. 6.) AB, Reasoning [22].

39 For an overview of the early environmental decisions of the Constitutional Court and an evaluation of the role of the principle in the Constitutional Court's case-law, *see* Gyula Bándi, 'The Case of the Hungarian Constitutional Court with Environmental Principles – From Non-Derogation to the Precautionary Approach', *Hungarian Yearbook of International and European Law*, Vol. 7, 2019, pp. 49-66.

40 Decision No. 28/1994. (V. 20.) AB.

41 Decision No. 17/2018. (X. 10.) AB, Reasoning [97].

42 Decision No. 16/2015. (VI. 5.) AB.

43 Decision No. 3104/2017. (V. 8.) AB, Reasoning [40].

44 Decisions No. 28/1994. (V. 20.) AB, 16/2015. (VI. 5.) AB, 13/2018. (IX. 4.) AB, 17/2018. (X. 10.) AB, 4/2020. (VII. 6.) AB.

45 Decision No. 13/2018. (IX. 4.) AB, Reasoning [62].

46 Decision No. 28/2017. (X. 25.) AB, Reasoning [44].

47 In more details *see* Marcel Szabó, 'The Precautionary Principle in the Fundamental Law of Hungary', *Hungarian Yearbook of International and European Law*, Vol. 7, 2019, pp. 67-83.

natural environment.[48] Even tolerating the risks of such an impairment runs counter to the State's obligation flowing from Article XXI and Article P.[49] Such an interpretation of the duties of the public trustee squares well with international trends, signaling that courts increasingly use the public trust doctrine as a vehicle to establish precautionary fiduciary obligations for the sovereign trustees.[50]

2.6. The Imperatives of Long-Term Planning and the Economical Use of Natural Resources

As a further requirement under Article P, the Constitutional Court stressed that in order to respect the long-term needs of future generations, the legislature in its decision-making processes "must engage in long-term planning over several governmental cycles."[51] The constitutional mandate to protect the common heritage of the nation must be translated into "cross-sectoral policies and long-term strategies as well as into concrete legislative measures implementing them".[52]

Moreover, the State must utilize natural resources in an economical manner and must also incentivize such use by private actors through adopting appropriate legislative measures. The piece of legislation, which did not prevent private persons from a wasteful use of groundwater resources was found to be in breach of Article P.[53]

3. The Ex Post Constitutional Review of the Forest Act: Facts of the Case, Legal Grounds, and the Constitutional Court's Reasoning

The most recent environmental decision of the Constitutional Court regarding the constitutionality of the 2017 Amendment to the Forest Act is worth closer examination for doctrinal reasons as well as considering its transformative impact on the reach and depth of environmental protective tools in the forestry industry in Hungary. In essence, the Constitutional Court's *ex ante* constitutional review decision successfully restored important powers of the public authority to prescribe mandatory limits on logging by private land-owners and forest managers, which powers were significantly curtailed by the 2017 Amendment of the Forest Act.[54]

48 Decision No. 28/2017. (X. 25.) AB, Reasoning [75].
49 Decision No. 16/2015. (VI. 5.) AB, Reasoning [110].
50 For a more detailed discussion, *see* Katalin Sulyok, 'Scientific Uncertainty as A Key Obstacle to Efficient Legal Protection of the Environmental Interests of Future Generations', *in* Marie-Claire Cordonier Segger *et al.* (eds.), *Intergenerational Justice in Sustainable Development Treaty Implementation*, Cambridge University Press, Cambridge, 2021, pp. 295-314.
51 Decision No. 28/2017. (X. 25.) AB, Reasoning [34].
52 Id. Reasoning [45].
53 Decision No. 13/2018. (IX. 4.) AB, Reasoning [71].
54 The piece of legislation subject to constitutional review was the 2017 Amendment of the Forest Act as accepted in Act LVI of 2017, which modified the Act XXXVII of 2009 on forests and forestry (Forest Act).

doi: 10.5553/HYIEL/266627012021009001020

3.1. Factual Background and the Legal Grounds for the Constitutional Challenge

The *ex post* review proceedings were initiated by the Hungarian Commissioner for Fundamental Rights together with his deputy, the Ombudsman for Future Generations. The Commissioner is granted with the power under relevant laws to challenge acts before the Constitutional Court that are believed to run counter to constitutional safeguards; in this instance, the right to a healthy environment and the protection of interests of future generations as guaranteed under Article P. Notably, *Hungary is among the very few countries in the world, which have a dedicated spokesperson to represent and advocate for the environmental interests of future generations*.[55]

Prior to passing the 2017 Amendment, several attempts were made to amend the Forest Act on account of the lobby of private forest managers, which were all ultimately abandoned due to concerns for environmental protection goals voiced by civil society organizations and the Ombudsman for Future Generations. The 2017 Amendment was nevertheless adopted despite the opposition of green NGOs and the public statements of the Ombudsman for Future Generations.

The petition submitted to the Constitutional Court outlined several concerns in relation to breaches of the right to a healthy environment and Article P on account of the substantial modifications of the 2017 Amendment. The overarching concern lay in the fact that the Amendment appeared to foster the financial interests of private land-owners and forest managers by narrowing down the possibilities of state authorities to intervene and impose temporal and spatial restrictions on for-profit logging. The new rules of the Amendment relaxed previous statutory safeguards for the environment to such an extent that allowed private interests to prevail over environmental protection goals in several respects. In particular, the Commissioner and its Deputy pointed out seven main reasons to argue that the Amendment breaches the non-derogation principle as flowing from Article P and Article XXI of the Fundamental Law.[56] *(i)* First, the Amendment narrowed down the spatial scope in which the forestry authority could impose limitations on logging in forests under Natura 2000 protection, by restricting the applicability of Natura 2000 rules as envisaged by the Habitats Directive[57] and the relevant domestic transposing legislation, only to a portion of Natura 2000 forests. In particular, protective limitation under the Amendment could only be imposed with respect to Natura 2000 forests representing priority forest habitats, if they were designated as Natura 2000 sites for the habitat they

55 For an overview of existing national institutions articulating and safeguarding the needs of posterity *see* Cordonier Segger *et al.* 2021. For a recent summary on the legal mandate and activities of the Hungarian Ombudsman for Future Generations, *see e.g.* Gyula Bándi, 'Interests of Future Generations, Environmental Protection and the Fundamental Law', *Journal of Agricultural and Environmental Law*, Vol. 15, Issue 29, 2020, pp. 7-22; Kinga Debisso & Marcel Szabó, 'An Institution for a Sustainable Future: The Hungarian Ombudsman for Future Generations', *Hungarian Yearbook of International Law and European Law*, Vol. 9, 2021.

56 The Ombudsman's petition (in Hungarian) is available on the Constitutional Court's website at http://public.mkab.hu/dev/dontesek.nsf/0/e7ebea823ab5fcd4c1258392005f8646/$FILE/II_201_0_2019_ind%C3%ADtv%C3%A1ny_anonim.pdf.

57 Council Directive 92/43/EEC of 21 May 1992 on the conservation of natural habitats and of wild fauna and flora.

doi: 10.5553/HYIEL/266627012021009001020

represented, and not on account of Natura 2000 species present in the area. Furthermore, Natura 2000 restrictions were applicable, in contrast with the previously applicable legal rules, only with respect to forests categorized as 'natural' forests, but not to those where the combination of species present was slightly altered by human intervention or the presence of invasive species. This markedly reduced the spatial scope of forests, where rules flowing from the Habitats Directive could actually be applied, and hence where competent state authorities could unilaterally impose, on their own motion, limitations on logging for environmental protection purposes. *(ii)* Second, the amended rules required the explicit consent of the private landowner or forest manager to designate their forests for nature conservation purposes, even if the respective forest habitat has already been declared protected in a decree of the local authority. The purpose to which a particular forest has been designated under the Forest Act is of utmost importance in the domestic legal regime governing forestry activities, since it is the purpose that defines the aims that can be legitimately pursued by the forest management activity in a given forest. Hence, environmental safeguards will not be fully applicable in forests under nature conservation measures, if the area cannot be designated for the purpose of nature conservation. Importantly, prior to the Amendment, the local authority could initiate such a designation in an *ex officio* procedure with respect to protected forests. *(iii)* Third, the Amendment also enabled the designation of protected forests for economic uses, contrary to the previous clear prohibition to designate protected forests for such a secondary purpose once they had been designated primarily for nature conservation purposes. Pursuant to the Amendment, only strictly protected forests that make up 80% of all protected forests cannot be designated for economic purposes. By contrast, previously applicable rules ensured that for-profit logging could not be pursued in protected forests: a ban that has effectively been removed by the Amendment. In addition, pursuant to the Amendment, any limitations on logging in protected forests designated for secondary economic use could only be imposed by the forestry authority if the respective private forest owner explicitly consented to such a limitation. By contrast, under the previous rules, such limitations could be imposed unilaterally by the authorities. *(iv)* Fourth, the petition voiced concerns in relation to a new rule which made it possible to designate protected and Natura 2000 forests for primarily flood protection and military defense purposes, which had priority over the nature conservation purposes of such forests. This amendment conferred wider powers on the flood protection authority as well as the Ministry of Defense to order the felling of trees in protected forests with reference to military and flood security interests. *(v)* Fifth, the Amendment broadened the scope of exceptions under the prohibition of clearance of forests and included forests designated primarily for Natura 2000, nature conservation, or public use purposes. Under the Amendment, the clearance is only prohibited in such forests if they are fully owned by the State, opening the possibility of clearance on all privately owned forests. *(vi)* Sixth, the complaint of the Commissioner also related to narrowing down the temporal and spatial scope in which the authorities could restrict logging activity. Specifically, the new rules reduced the minimum volume of dead

doi: 10.5553/HYIEL/266627012021009001020

wood that ought to be left in the forests, and the minimum number of trees left standing after logging. Furthermore, it mandated universally applicable periods in which temporary bans on logging could be introduced for nature conservation purposes, *e.g.* to preserve the nesting place of protected birds in the area. The Amendment also universally capped the spatial scope of imposing limitations on logging due to the presence of protected species in 50 meters. Previously, the authorities enjoyed discretion to set the time period and the spatial scope of restrictions as they deemed fit under the specific circumstances. The Commissioner and the Ombudsman pointed out that the time period set in law by the Amendment did not have a scientific foundation as it did not match the nesting period of several bird species. Another problematic point lay in the fact that any restrictions going beyond the maximum limits as set in law, could only be imposed by the authority based on an agreement concluded with the private landowner. *(vii)* Seventh, the Amendment abolished the requirement for forest managers to obtain a permit from the environmental authority as a condition for pursuing any activities during restriction periods. It only required a unilateral, *ex post* notification of the manager to the forestry authority. Such a modification not only excluded the environmental authority from the decision-making process but also enabled taking any protective intervention only after the activity concerned had already begun.

3.2. The Constitutional Court's Reasoning

The significant implications of the Amendment for nature conservation, as well as for the possibilities of private forest owners is aptly signaled by the fact that the Constitutional Court received a large number of *amicus* briefs. Specifically, from the Hungarian branches of the World Wildlife Fund, Friends of the Earth and Birdlife International, the National Council for Agriculture and the Association of Private Forest Owners. The Constitutional Court also sought the positions of relevant ministries, the Pro Silva forestry NGO, the National Council for Sustainable Development, which is the advisory body of the Parliament, and the National Committee for Environmental Protection, the advisory body of the government.

The Constitutional Court agreed with all but one challenge and found unconstitutional the derogation from previously applicable levels of statutory protection with respect to all accounts, expect for the one concerning the possibility to designate protected forests primarily for military and flood protection purposes.[58] In all other respects, the Constitutional Court agreed with the Ombudsman's petition that *the Amendment lowered the level of stringency* with which public authorities could unilaterally intervene in order to enforce environmental protection goals and interests, without meeting the legitimate aim and proportionality requirements. The Constitutional Court therefore quashed the challenged provisions of the 2017 Amendment.

58 In this latter respect, the Constitutional Court found a derogation from previously applicable statutory protection, yet it found it to be proportionate to the legitimate aims pursued, and thus, declared it to be in conformity with the Fundamental Law.

doi: 10.5553/HYIEL/266627012021009001020

The point of departure for the Constitutional Court's inquiry was the constitutional public trust provision of the Fundamental Law. *The Constitutional Court explicitly declared for the first time* that Article P shall be regarded as a *constitutional manifestation of the public trust doctrine*, which embodies an emerging rule of international law.[59] The Constitutional Court stressed that Article P posits natural and cultural heritage "as having inherent value, which is worthy of protection even against the (momentary financial) interests of present stakeholders for the benefit of future generations, which are not subjects of rights."[60]

The Constitutional Court also underlined the special significance that forests bear among the assets of the national heritage to be preserved for posterity. Due to the numerous ecosystem services[61] forests provide "they shall be protected and maintained for the public interest", which imposes obligations on private forest owners, managers and any other forest users as well.[62] Accordingly,

> "the unfettered discretion of forest owners and managers in exploiting the forests' resources shall be replaced by a constitutional obligation of responsible, sustainable management, and to use of forests in a way, which accommodates the interests of future generations."[63]

Under Hungarian constitutional law doctrine, in order to find a breach of the non-derogation principle, the Constitutional Court must first establish *whether the efficiency of statutory protection has decreased*. If this requirement is met based on a comparative assessment of the substantive, procedural and institutional legal guarantees as provided under the previous laws and those in force at the relevant time, the Constitutional Court may proceed to the second step of its analysis. The second arm of the review comprises *a legitimate aim and proportionality analysis*, under which a particular amendment is found to be unconstitutional if the Constitutional Court establishes either the lack of competing human rights that may justify a derogation from the obligation to protect the common heritage of the nation, or the unnecessary and disproportionate nature of such a measure.

As to the first arm of the review, the Constitutional Court agreed with the petition of the Ombudsman and found a retrogression from previously mandated environmental protection standards with respect to all provisions complained of. Under the second arm of the review, the Constitutional Court investigated whether private landowners and forest managers' right to property and their freedom to conduct business may serve as a legitimate aim justifying the Amendment's provisions narrowing the scope of environmental protection measures. The right to property and the freedom of business are guaranteed

59 Decision No. 14/2020. (VI. 9.) AB, Reasoning [22].
60 Id. Reasoning [35].
61 For the concept of ecosystem services *see* Robert Costanza *et. al.*, 'The value of the world's ecosystem services and natural capital', *Nature*, Vol. 387, 1987, pp. 253-260.
62 Decision No. 14/2020. (VI. 9.) AB, Reasoning [23].
63 Id.

doi: 10.5553/HYIEL/266627012021009001020

under Article XII and XIII of the Fundamental Law, and hence in principle may justify limitations on environmental rights and obligations under Hungarian constitutional law doctrine.

The Constitutional Court *generally accepted that these competing rights may serve as legitimate aims* to curtail the extent to which logging may be limited for environmental protection purposes. *Yet it firmly announced that the restrictions set forth by the Amendment are disproportionate*. To reach this conclusion, it attached great weight to the unequally stronger bargaining position granted by the Amendment to private landowners and forest managers *vis-à-vis* state authorities.[64] As mentioned above, mandating unilateral restrictions on logging for environmental protection purposes have been precluded by the Amendment in many instances, as state authorities could only impose such restrictive measures in excess of those mandated by law if the private forest owners or managers explicitly consented to such restrictions, which is highly unlikely with a view to the considerable level of profits foregone by decreasing the extent of logging.

In justifying its conclusion regarding *the appropriate balance between the rights and accompanying economic interests of present stakeholders* on the one hand, *and the interests of future constituencies* on the other hand, the Constitutional Court relied on its previous finding regarding the special significance of the principles included in the Parliament's long-term strategies. The Constitutional Court cited the 2016-2030 National Strategy of Forests, which clearly stipulates that "legal regulation of forestry shall serve the goal that the people use and exploit forests in a sustainable way".[65] From this statement, the Constitutional Court inferred "that monetary interests of forest owners and managers cannot prevail over the imperative of preserving the forest for future generations."[66]

4. Some Lessons Learnt Regarding the Judicial Protection of Long-term Public Interests Vis-à-vis Short-Term Individual Interests

What remains to be addressed in levelling this case commentary is to draw some wider lessons for the judicial enforcement of long-term environmental goals in the face of competing financial interests and sometimes even rival human rights guarantees. Some of the reasoning techniques applied by the Constitutional Court in the *Forest decision* may be operationalized under different constitutional and legal settings as well in resolving inherent and pervasive conflicts between economic and environmental policies. The forthcoming remarks therefore seek to highlight some judicial tools that may prove to be useful in legally articulating the interests of posterity, and in enforcing such interests with a normative force, even though they are often couched in vague and symbolic terms. The *Forest decision* bespeaks of judicial strategies enabling the Constitutional Court to carve

64 *See e.g.* Id. Reasoning [77]-[85], [135] and [161]-[167].
65 Id. Reasoning [31].
66 Id.

doi: 10.5553/HYIEL/266627012021009001020

out certain terrains from the policy choices that are otherwise at the disposal of incumbent political and economic stakeholders.

4.1. Non-Derogation Principle: Restraints on the Present to Preserve Assets for the Future

It is apparent from the Constitutional Court's analysis that under the Hungarian constitutional doctrine, *the non-derogation principle marks the red line of unconstitutional environmentally harmful (economic) policies*. As seen above, this principle also forms an inseverable part of the public trust provision enshrined in Article P and is conducive to a strict judicial overview of any legislative changes seeking to relax regulatory standards in the field of environmental law. This test enables the Constitutional Court to focus its review on the efficiency of environmental safeguards, turning abstract legal constructions, such as the efficacy of powers conferred on environmental authorities, into the object of the right to environment, the preservation of which lies at the core of obligations imposed on the sovereign trustee. The non-derogation principle functions as a strict and substantive test, as the efficiency of tools vested in environmental authorities is measured in light of actual realities rather than theoretical possibilities. Such a reading of the principle is capable of singling out those regulatory reforms, which on paper leave room for enforcing nature conservation goals, yet in practice render such interventions highly unlikely. In the material case, the non-derogation principle has led the Constitutional Court to find that the legislature cannot replace direct and *ex officio* interventions of authorities with measures conditioned upon the consent of the adversely affected forest owner. Notably, nothing in the Amendment precluded the imposition of environmental restrictions, the new rules only drastically reduced such an outcome.

In light of the more than 30-year-long jurisprudence of the Constitutional Court, the non-derogation principle strikes as a particularly efficient way of preserving the legal safeguards of environmental assets, which have been under constant pressure and challenge, *inter alia*, by the lobby of industrial interests groups, the ever increasing need for resource extraction and the expansion of anthropogenic land use, the restructuring of competent governmental authorities, and the abolition of environmental licensing requirements under the aegis of eliminating unnecessary bureaucratic hurdles. It comes as no surprise that the principle can be seen as imposing the perhaps most tangible limits under Article P, delineating what the sovereign is allowed to do with its natural and cultural heritage in complying with its public trust obligation. Under Hungarian constitutional doctrine, the interests of posterity are captured as an obligation of present stakeholders not to deteriorate the quality of the heritage to be passed onto their descendants.

Yet, the non-derogation principle remains a unique conceptualization of the right to a healthy environment and the public trust doctrine both on the international landscape of environmental human rights protection and with respect to constitutional safeguards for the environment, albeit the idea embodied in the principle is not alien to general international human rights law

doi: 10.5553/HYIEL/266627012021009001020

and international investment and trade law.[67] The principle has been also included in Article 17 of the Global Pact for the Environment as the principle on non-regression,[68] an ambitious proposal drafted by the *Club des juristes*, aspiring to be a binding international environmental treaty.[69]

4.2. Imposing Limits on the Right to Property under the Public Trust Doctrine

Humanity by now has reached a point where environmental conflicts present themselves as marked intergenerational problems. Our fundamental detrimental impact on the Earth's resources and the functionality of its systems turn environmental challenges to zero-sum games between present and future generations. Such distributional dilemmas will ultimately permeate and shape constitutional legal doctrine as well. Any judicial attempt at striking a fair balance between utilizing natural resources in the present and the preservation of access to such resources for the future gives rise to a need for organizing principles guiding the reconciliation of conflicting human rights claims. It appears that courts may resolve such tensions by either setting a hierarchy between the fundamental rights of contemporaries, as the Hungarian Constitutional Court did in its *Forest decision*, or by extending the temporal scope of individual freedoms of future rights holders, as the German *Bundesverfassungsgericht* did in its recent climate law decision.[70] Common to both approaches is that they seek to level the playing field for claims raised in the name of, or for the benefit of, future constituencies.

The most frequent rival to environmental protection goals, which is couched as a fundamental rights claim, lies in private ownership. Individual property rights, which form the very basis of our economies, often inhibit and sometimes even preclude mandating strict protective measures for common resources, such as clean air, water, biodiversity and natural ecosystems. Calling for a critical evaluation of how property rights could be reconciled with much needed respect for the public interest both in intra-generational and inter-generational contexts appears to be timely.[71] Judicial bodies have long faced dilemmas of discerning limits on the exercise of individual freedoms if those impair the rights of others or the public interest.

The wording of the Fundamental Law envisages certain constraints on the owners' freedom by stressing that property entails social responsibility.[72] But how to detect socially irresponsible forms of using one's own property? The

67 Michel Prieur, 'Non-regression', *in* Yann Aguila & Jorge Vinuales (eds.), *Global Pact for the Environment: Legal Foundations*, C-EENRG Report, 2019-1, p. 144.

68 Article 17 reads as follows: "The Parties and their sub-national entities refrain from allowing activities or adopting norms that have the effect of reducing the global level of environmental protection guaranteed by current law."

69 For more details on the initiative, which is currently ongoing, *see* https://globalpactenvironment.org/en/.

70 Decision of 24 March 2021 – 1 BvR 2656/18.

71 For a scholarly proposal on how to *"make property law ecologically responsive"*, *see* Péter D. Szigeti, 'A Sketch of Ecological Property: Toward A Law of Biogeochemical Cycles', *Environmental Law Review*, Vol. 51, Issue 1, 2021, pp. 41-87.

72 Article XII of the Fundamental Law.

doi: 10.5553/HYIEL/266627012021009001020

Constitutional Court based its inquiry on the public trust doctrine, by emphasizing that Article P compels the legislature to allow the *exercise of property rights only to the extent that it does not jeopardize the long-term viability of the natural and cultural heritage*.[73] The Constitutional Court went on to find that the unlimited freedom of forest owners and managers shall be replaced by the requirement of pursuing sustainable forestry.[74] The public trust doctrine was also interpreted as entailing an obligation for the lawmaker to account for the interests of both future and present generations in designing laws governing the use of the common heritage of the nation.[75]

4.3. Giving Normative Weight to Non-Binding Long-Term Strategies

The key obstacle to accounting and advocating for the environmental needs of future (and present) generations usually lies not in the lack of a proper scientific understanding of the risks or the absence of agreed overarching goals or principles. The latter are frequently set out in non-binding political statements on the domestic and the international level as well. Rather, the problem lies in watering down ambitious long-term strategic goals in binding laws and regulations.

Against this background, a third respect in which the Constitutional Court's reasoning may potentially serve as a source of inspiration for other jurisdictions is the way in which it *gave a normative reading to the otherwise non-binding political strategy adopted by the legislature*. Such long-term sectoral policy documents can provide particular apt foundations for judicial findings, because they reflect the necessary political and scientific consensus on the measures deemed necessary to protect legitimate interests of the future in a particular sector. Put differently, long-term policy strategies of the legislature provide courts with objective, non-arbitrary benchmarks to articulate and identify what lies in the interests of future generations.

To conclude this assessment of the Hungarian constitutional public trust doctrine, it is worth pointing out that the *Forest decision* of the Hungarian Constitutional Court can be seen as a success of environmental protection goals over short-term policies – yet altogether it is a bittersweet victory. Somewhat paradoxically, the very existence of the decision signals the greatest weakness of the functioning of the public trust doctrine as enshrined in Article P of the Fundamental Law. Namely, that a public trust provision can only reach its full potential, and fulfil the ideals it aspires to, if embraced by the sovereign trustee, *i.e.* the government and the legislature, and not (only) by judicial bodies. The ultimate role of the public trust doctrine lies in appealing to the ethical sense of obligations of governmental stakeholders to guide decisions taken at all levels of the executive and the legislative branch.[76] Only if the fiduciary obligations under the constitutional public trust doctrine are taken seriously by political

73 Decision No. 14/2020. (VI. 9.) AB, Reasoning [22].
74 Id. Reasoning [23].
75 Id. Reasoning [22].
76 Wood 2009, p. 103.

doi: 10.5553/HYIEL/266627012021009001020

stakeholders of the present can this constitutional imperative efficiently guard against sliding back on, and diluting stringent environmental protection measures for the sake of securing short-term profits at the expense of the natural capital and heritage.

doi: 10.5553/HYIEL/266627012021009001020

CASE NOTES

The Hungarian Constitutional Court's Decision on the Protection of Forests

Decision No. 14/2020. (VII. 6.) AB of the Constitutional Court of Hungary

Attila Pánovics[*]

Abstract

In its decision delivered on 15 June 2020, the Hungarian Constitutional Court stated that several provisions of the 2017 amendment of the Act XXXVII of 2009 on Forest, Forest Protection and Forest Management are unconstitutional. The case was also an opportunity for the Constitutional Court to adopt another milestone decision on the interpretation and application of the environment-related provisions of the Fundamental Law and the "non-derogation principle". The progressive decision of the Constitutional Court entrusts the Hungarian State with trustee duties. The present Case Note is an analysis of Decision No. 14/2020. (VII. 6.) AB of the Constitutional Court.

Keywords: public trust, non-derogation, Constitutional Court of Hungary, Article P, future generations.

1. Legal Background

In 2017 the Hungarian Parliament adopted Act LVI of 2017 on the amendment of Act XXXVII of 2009 on Forest, Forest Protection and Forest Management (Forest Act). According to the explanatory memorandum,[1] the aim of the amendment was to find a balance between the right to a healthy environment and the right to property. In reality, the amendment considerably weakened the achieved level of protection, tried to maximize the economic value of forest land areas, and prioritized mainly economic interest over nature conservation in forest management.

* Attila Pánovics: senior lecturer, University of Pécs.

1 *See* T/14461, available in Hungarian, at www.parlament.hu/irom40/14461/14461.pdf.

doi: 10.5553/HYIEL/266627012021009001021

The proceedings of the Constitutional Court were initiated by the Commissioner for Fundamental Rights,[2] based on a complaint submitted by environmental NGOs.[3] Before adopting its decision, the Constitutional Court had requested the Minister of Agriculture, the Minister of the Interior, the Minister of Defense, the National Council for Sustainable Development, the National Council for Environmental Protection, and the Pro Silva Hungaria Association. The environmental NGOs, the Hungarian Chamber of Agriculture (HCA/NAK), the National Agricultural Research and Innovation Center (NARIC/NAIK) and the Hungarian Association of Agricultural Machinery Manufacturers (MEGOSZ) filed *amicus curiae* briefings.

The *right to a healthy environment* was incorporated into the Hungarian Constitution in 1990. The Constitutional Court of Hungary then ruled that the State must not allow the already achieved level of environmental policy, legislation and conservation decline.[4] This was the declaration of the famous *'non-derogation principle'* in *Decision No. 28/1994. (V. 20.) AB*. The right to a healthy environment, enshrined in the Fundamental Law, has a substantial element, namely that a specific level of protection, once achieved, should not be decreased. This prohibition of stepping back from the achieved level of protection is not an absolute ban; it shall be enforced in accordance with its function in the course of the protection of fundamental rights.

In 2011 the Hungarian Parliament established a direct link between environmental protection, the interests of future generations, and human rights at the constitutional level by stating that "agricultural land, forests and reserves of water, biodiversity, in particular native plant and animal species, as well as cultural assets are part of the nation's common heritage", and declared that "the State and everyone" is obliged to protect, maintain, and preserve them for future generations.[5] This provision provides a *non-exhaustive list of the elements of common heritage of the nation*, thereby allowing for the extension of the list by further elements.

Under Article 38(1) of the Fundamental Law the property of the State and local governments shall be considered national assets, and the management and protection of national assets shall aim at serving public interests, meeting common needs and preserving natural resources, as well as taking into account the needs of future generations. In the present case, the Constitutional Court also reinforced its jurisprudence that in every case when the rules governing the

2 Under Article 24(2) of the Fundamental Law, the Commissioner for Fundamental Rights has the right to turn to the Constitutional Court in cases where there is a strong belief that a national or local piece of legislation is in violation of the Fundamental Law. The Deputy Commissioner for Future Generations can only propose that the General Commissioner for Fundamental Rights turn to the Constitutional Court.

3 World Wildlife Fund (WWF) Hungary, BirdLife Hungary (MME – the Hungarian Ornithological and Nature Conservation Society) and the National Society of Conservationists (MTVSZ – Friends of the Earth Hungary).

4 László Sólyom & Georg Brunner, *Constitutional Judiciary in a New Democracy. The Hungarian Constitutional Court*, Michigan University Press, Ann Arbor, 2000, pp. 24-25, and 298-305.

5 *See* Article P of the Fundamental Law.

doi: 10.5553/HYIEL/266627012021009001021

protection of the environment are amended, the principles of prevention and precaution should be taken into account, since the failure to protect the nature and the environment may induce irreversible processes.[6]

2. The Importance of Forest Protection

Forests form an essential part of the unique natural heritage of Hungary; therefore, the responsible management of forests is of primary importance.[7] Based on the data taken from the National Forest Inventory, more than 22% of the total area of Hungary (approximately 2 million hectares of land) is covered by forest lands, including forests as well as forest roads and other areas serving forest management practices but actually not covered by trees.[8]

In recent decades, the social (public welfare) function and the environmental role of forests have increased.[9] Therefore, the proportion of forest areas designated for protective purposes has increased,[10] and there are further 70 so-called 'forest reserves' in the country. Forest operations in these reserves are limited to buffer zones, which surround the core zones where no traditional operation is conducted whatsoever.[11] All protected forests are also included in the coherent Natura 2000 ecological network of special areas of conservation to which various protection measures under Union law apply.[12]

Forests provide important ecosystem services to society like fresh air, and they have value as an exploitable reservoir of timber and fuel, as a source of food, as a habitat rich in wildlife, and as a major reservoir of biodiversity. In addition, the forestry sector is a carbon sink because of the huge carbon uptake of forests, thanks to ongoing afforestation efforts and sustainable forest management.[13] Hungary is located in an area gravely vulnerable to the consequences of climate change and logging is one of the major contributors of greenhouse gas emissions.

Planned forest management has a long history in Hungary. After the political transition about 40% of Hungarian forests were privatized. In 2009 the Forest Act closed the transition related to the ownership structure, emphasized the importance of sustainable forest management, provided more opportunities for

6 Decision No. 14/2020. (VII. 6.) AB, Reasoning [38].

7 Id. Reasoning [24].

8 Forest is basically defined as land spanning more than 0.5 hectares with trees higher than 5 meters and a canopy of over more than 30%, or trees able to reach these thresholds *in situ*; *see* Tamás Tobisch & Péter Kottek (eds.), *Global Forest Resources Assessment 2020, Report (Hungary)*, Rome, 2020, p. 9.

9 It was in 1939, when an area, part of the Great Forest of Debrecen, was declared protected in Hungary for the first time.

10 In Hungary, forests in protected natural areas must always be state-owned forests, and the proportion of these forests was more than 18% in 2018.

11 *National Inventory Report for 1985-2018*, Hungarian Meteorological Service, Unit of National Emissions Inventories, 2020, p. 484.

12 All Natura 2000 site types (Birds Directive Sites and Habitats Directive sites) can be found on the European Environment Agency's Natura 2000 Network Viewer, at https://natura2000.eea.europa.eu/.

13 *National Inventory Report for 1985-2018*, p. 10.

doi: 10.5553/HYIEL/266627012021009001021

members of the public to participate in forest planning, and introduced the quantitative definition of naturalness as a qualitative parameter of forest management.[14] The Forest Act also created a legal basis for transitioning from clear-cutting and the shelterwood system to selection, in addition, the interest in close-to-nature forestry has also been introduced into the forest management practice.

The duty of forest planning is performed in the framework of district forest management planning. Forest management planning activities cover the entire forest area of Hungary. The plans are normally drafted for a period of 10 years covering all of the country's forest land areas,[15] forming the basis for managing forests legally and sustainably, in harmony with societal interests, and with a view to economic and ecological balance. Each forest manager receives his or her forest management plan, which describes his or her rights and responsibilities.

A long-term, future-oriented perspective is crucial in forest management. In Hungary, an unfavorable overall conservation status of forests is largely due to excessive human destruction (*e.g.* deforestation, removal of dead trees which provide food and shelter for forest-dependent species), and the introduction of invasive non-native species associated with forest degradation processes, ultimately displacing native species, thereby completely altering the original forest landscape.[16] The Constitutional Court underlined in its decision that, according to Article P(1) of the Fundamental Law, *the State manages as a kind of trustee for future generations the natural and cultural assets* entrusted to it and belonging to the common heritage of the nation.[17] Therefore, the right of the present generations to use and exploit these resources is not unlimited. These rights shall only be of such extent that does not jeopardize either the natural values themselves. These values must be protected individually or through the safeguarding of the interests of future generations. This general standard *can be considered as a part of newly established and consolidated universal customary law*,[18] and it is also applicable to the constitutional review of the rules governing forests, as natural values that form part of the nation's common heritage according to Article P(1) of the Fundamental Law.

3. Weighing of Competing Interests

The common heritage status of forests imposes responsibilities on forest owners (including the Hungarian State), forest managers and recreational users alike.

14 Forestry-related Databases of the Hungarian Forestry Directorate, 8 October 2013, p. 3.
15 About one tenth of the forest area is subject to forest management planning each year.
16 Bálint Dobi & Annamária Holes (eds.), *State of the Environment in Hungary*, Herman Ottó Institute Nonprofit Ltd., Budapest, 2020, at www.hermanottointezet.hu/sites/default/files/mka_2020_digi_en_jav.pdf, p. 56.
17 The idea of using the public trust doctrine to influence the management of public resources is not new in other States. *See e.g.* John Meyer, 'Using the Public Trust Doctrine to Ensure the National Forests Protect the Public from Climate Change', *Hastings Environmental Law Journal*, Vol. 16, Issue 1, 2010, p. 198.
18 Decision No. 14/2020. (VII. 6.) AB, Reasoning [22].

doi: 10.5553/HYIEL/266627012021009001021

Based on Article P of the Fundamental Law, all these parties must follow the rules of sustainable forest management. The amendment changed the definition of the Natura 2000 protection purpose due to which a significant part of the forest areas classified as such have lost their Natura 2000 protection purpose, making the assertion of economic considerations to the maximum extent the sole purpose of forest management. The Constitutional Court found it to be in conflict with the Fundamental Law and annulled those provisions that allowed the designation of an economic purpose in respect of forests in protected natural areas.[19]

Natura 2000 areas are of EU significance and any damage to these areas may result in an infringement procedure at Union level. The Constitutional Court pointed out that the very reason an area belongs to the Natura 2000 network is because species of plants and animals in need of special protection live there. Natura 2000 areas can also be farming territories where (in the interest of protecting the species of plants and animals living there) agricultural activity can only be performed under significant restrictions to comply with specific environmental protection and nature conservation rules. Where, in the light of the best scientific knowledge in the field, there is reasonable doubt that human activity will not have adverse effects on the conservation of habitats and protected species, that activity cannot be authorized.[20]

The Constitutional Court therefore held that *the right of private forest owners to property shall not justify the prioritization of economic interests against the protection of natural values* and that forest managers do not have a constitutionally protected right to obtain, in the forests bearing natural values, additional rights of economic management to the detriment of the enforcement of nature conservation. The Constitutional Court therefore annulled the relevant provisions of the 2017 amendment concerning Natura 2000 areas.[21]

According to the reasoning of the decision, the Constitutional Court had declared in several earlier decisions that the right to property is a fundamental right guaranteed by the Fundamental Law,[22] which may only be restricted in exceptional cases in such circumstances and manner as stipulated by an act. The state is obliged to set up a system of guarantees that renders the right to property operational. While a restriction of the right to property may be necessary in the public interest, such a restriction shall require reasonable grounds. Following its earlier practice, the Constitutional Court expressed that the possibility for

19 Id. Reasoning [50].

20 *See e.g.* Judgment of 7 September 2004, *Case C-127/02, Waddenvereniging and Vogelbeschermingsvereniging*, ECLI:EU:C:2004:482, para. 44; Judgment of 8 November 2016, *C-243/15, Lesoochranárske zoskupenie VLK*. ECLI:EU:C:2016:838, para. 66; Judgment of 17 April 2018, *C-441/17, Commission v Poland (Białowieża Forest)*. ECLI:EU:C:2018:255, para. 117. Those judgments concerned Article 6 of the Habitats Directive in so far as it establishes that a plan or project not directly connected with or necessary for the management of a Natura 2000 site but likely to have significant effect on that site can be authorized only to the extent that the competent authority has satisfied itself that the plan or project will not adversely affect the integrity of that site.

21 Decision No. 14/2020. (VII. 6.) AB, Reasoning [66].

22 Article XIII of the Fundamental Law.

doi: 10.5553/HYIEL/266627012021009001021

constitutional review regarding the restriction of the right to property (compared with other fundamental rights) is relatively narrow, since the Constitutional Court shall not examine whether the restriction was inevitably necessary but focuses only on whether it is justifiable by the public interest.

The Constitutional Court also annulled the relevant provisions of the 2017 amendment that made the registration of the protection purpose of protected natural areas of local significance subject to the prior consent of the forest manager. It also annulled certain rules on leaving seed-trees or dead trees in the forest.[23] Nevertheless, certain amendments were not declared to be unconstitutional, such as with regard to changing the order of the protection purpose of certain forests, according to which flood protection and national defense purposes precede the purpose of nature conservation.[24]

The decision also reflected the public sensitivity and general opposition to the forestry practices of clear-cutting. The Constitutional Court also annulled legal provisions which essentially made the practice clear-cutting widespread in state-owned forests.[25] It was found that clear-cutting causes extremely severe and irreversible damage to the ecosystem, which, in the case of state-owned forests, cannot by substantiated by any opposing fundamental right or constitutional value; therefore, such practice cannot be constitutionally justified.[26]

To mitigate the unnecessary burden of forest owners and forest managers, the Constitutional Court also annulled the provisions that introduced a notification obligation to the forestry authority to replace the previous procedure of obtaining nature conservation permits to allow activities in forests in protected natural areas. Prior permissions not only provide authorities with information but are capable of directly influencing the living conditions of future generations as well. Rules establishing posterior control by the authority instead of the process of issuing preliminary permissions introduced with the purpose of decreasing the level of bureaucracy is a step-back compared to the level of protection already achieved; therefore, it is contrary to the Fundamental Law. It is worth noting that this was the reason why four members of the Constitutional Court[27] attached dissenting opinions to the decision. They argued that the distinction between permission and notification is unconstitutional, since there is no difference in their legal effects, and they highlighted the importance of public trust in the administration.[28]

23 Decision No. 14/2020. (VII. 6.) AB, Reasoning [81]-[83] and [154].

24 Id. Reasoning [98]-[106].

25 Clear-cutting or clear-felling is a logging practice: the removal of most or all trees from an area chosen for harvesting. In some areas clear-cutting can be an appropriate harvest method for certain tree species, because new seedlings need direct sunlight to grow quickly.

26 Decision No. 14/2020. (VII. 6.) AB, Reasoning [130]-[132].

27 Justices Tünde Handó, Béla Pokol, Mária Szívós and András Varga Zs.

28 Decision No. 14/2020. (VII. 6.) AB, Reasoning [196]-[204].

doi: 10.5553/HYIEL/266627012021009001021

4. Conclusions

The decision confirms that while a bit hesitant in certain other issues, the Constitutional Court is still relatively active in interpreting cases in connection with the right to a healthy environment and other environment-related provisions of the Fundamental Law, and is widening its approach to cover even more aspects than its earlier case-law.[29] This case also demonstrates that the Deputy Commissioner, together with the Commissioner for Fundamental Rights is a strong advocate for combining the representation of the interests of future generations with the protection of national heritage as established in the Fundamental Law.[30] In my opinion, the decision also stresses the importance of public participation in environmental matters and the role of environmental NGOs.

The sustainability of the natural support systems of society and the quality of the human environment takes priority over economic growth,[31] and the public interest of nature conservation prevails over the private interests of forest owners and managers. I agree with the Constitutional Court that *economic interests cannot have automatic precedence over environmental interests:* the interests of forest owners and forest managers do not have primacy over nature conservation interests.

The decision of the Constitutional Court reinforced its settled case-law,[32] emphasizing that it is the primary obligation of the State, laid down in the Fundamental law, to regulate forest protection and forest management by also taking into account the interests of present and future generations, for the purpose of protecting the environment.[33] In response to scientific findings, public concerns and advanced forest management practices, the decision clearly implies that those in charge are obliged to ensure that the natural heritage is preserved for future generations, and allows the forestry and nature conservation authorities to prescribe, in all forests, the implementation of measures necessary for the protection of the particular natural values of the forest concerned.

29 Gyula Bándi, 'Interests of Future Generations, Environmental Protection and the Fundamental Law', *Journal of Agricultural and Environmental Law*, Vol. 15, Issue 29, 2020, p. 17.

30 *Guarding Our Future: How to Include Future Generations in Policy Making*, World Future Council Foundation, March 2019, p. 9.

31 László Sólyom 'Governing for Sustainability', *Asia Europe Journal*, Vol. 6, Issue 2, 2008, p. 188.

32 *See e.g.* Decision No. 3068/2013. (III. 14.) AB, Decision No. 16/2015. (VI. 15.) AB, Decision No. 3223/2017. (IX. 25.) AB, Decision No. 27/2017. (X. 25.) AB, Decision No. 3292/2017. (XI. 20.) AB, Decision No. 28/2017. (X. 25.) AB, and Decision No. 13/2018. (IX. 4.) AB.

33 Decision No. 14/2020. (VII. 6.) AB, Reasoning [22].

doi: 10.5553/HYIEL/266627012021009001021

The Constitutional Court of Hungary on the Borderlines of Blasphemy

A Note on Two Recent Cases

Balázs Schanda[*]

Abstract

Blasphemy used to be a criminal offence in traditional legal systems. Although offending the transcendent is not criminalized in most Western legal systems, free speech must respect the dignity of others. Religious conviction constitutes an inherent part of dignity. The protection against hate speech offending the dignity of members i.e. of religious communities may include criminal sanctions in extreme cases. The new Civil Code of Hungary (2013) enables the bringing of a civil lawsuit for hate speech. After years of litigation the first two cases where litigants claimed their dignity violated by offensive images have reached the Constitutional Court. The Constitutional Court guaranteed protection of religious identity on the one hand, on the other hand, it upheld the freedom of political speech even when using a religious symbol. Degrading religion offends all members of the religious community, criticism of the religiosity of public actors, however, is protected by the freedom of speech.

Keywords: blasphemy, freedom of speech, protection of dignity, protection of religion, Hungary.

1. The Prohibition of Blasphemy

Once upon a time even swearwords were more elaborate. When it comes to abusive language people related differently to blasphemy and to the uncouth or sometimes obscene speech targeted at God, the saints, and all things holy. Traditional legal systems used to criminalize blasphemy and, even if they did not always exercise the right of punishment, it was considered a capital offence, one of the most serious of crimes. The law was rooted in the Bible, as the Ten Commandments clearly state: "Thou shalt not take the name of the Lord thy God in vain; for the Lord will not hold him guiltless that taketh his name in vain." (Exodus 20:7)

* Balázs Schanda: professor of law, Pázmány Péter Catholic University, Budapest; justice, Constitutional Court of Hungary, Budapest.

doi: 10.5553/HYIEL/266627012021009001022

Prior to the communist takeover (1948) blasphemy was a criminal offence in Hungary. As the first Criminal Code (Act V of 1878, the so-called *Csemegi Code*) stated in its Section 190:

> "Any person who, in the manner specified in Section 171, causes a public scandal by way of abusive words aimed at God or who forcefully prevents or disturbs a religious ceremony acknowledged by the State shall be considered to have committed a misdemeanor and will be punished by imprisonment for up to one year and the imposition of a fine up to one thousand forints. Attempts thereat are also punishable."

Although causing a public scandal is a provable fact, *i.e.* blasphemy in itself was not a crime, the object of the protection in the Criminal Code was, in line with the traditional approach to blasphemy, supernatural: God Himself. The title of the chapter also indicates that the legislator wishes to protect not only the freedom to practice religion, but also the religion itself ("Crimes and misdemeanors against religion and the free practice thereof").

Blasphemy was not reinserted into the Hungarian Criminal Code following the collapse of the communist regime and it has been decriminalized in most Western legal systems, *e.g.* in 2008 in the United Kingdom, in 2017 in Denmark, in 2019 in Greece, *etc.* Decriminalization of blasphemy has made the carefully balanced jurisprudence of the ECtHR on margin of appreciation concerning offensive expression somewhat obsolete.[1]

2. The Protection of Religious Sensitivity and Sacred Objects

2.1. Criminal Law and Religious Conviction

Most contemporary legal systems do not offer God any protection. However, they do protect human dignity, which, for someone who believes in God, is inseparable from faith.[2] *Profanity and blasphemy are forms of verbal abuse* against believers and as regards its effects, it is considered similar to the desecration of an object with spiritual reverence. The question is whether the freedom of religion and the protection of the dignity/religious feelings of others can be a legal basis to restrict the freedom of others to voice their opinions, and what tools the State has at its disposal for promoting peace in society. The 2015 terrorist attack on the headquarters of the satirical weekly Charlie Hebdo in Paris has shown that

1 András Koltay, 'Az Emberi Jogok Európai Bírósága és a blaszfémia mint a szólásszabadság korlátja', *Iustum Aequum Salutare*, Vol. 13, Issue 1, 2017, pp. 175-189.

2 Bernát Török, 'Can Religions or Religious People be Protected against Blasphemy?', *in* András Koltay (ed.), *Media Freedom Regulation in the New Media World*, CompLex Wolters Kluwer, Budapest, 2014, pp. 509-531.

doi: 10.5553/HYIEL/266627012021009001022

finding the right balance between the protection of competing rights is an ongoing challenge.[3]

Today, criminal law approaches the problem not from the aspect of God, but from the personal side: by criminalizing any conduct that hinders the freedom of practicing religion through violence or threats (Section 215 of Act C of 2012), it protects not religion, but the freedom of worship; by making hate speech illegal, it protects human dignity. The law on misdemeanors also protects the objects of religious devotion and those used for religious rites, and criminalizes any public scandals caused in places for worship (Section 188 of Act II of 2012). Contemporary legislation treats the issue not through the concept of blasphemy, but rather the protection of religious feelings and sensitivities: the object of protection is not the transcendent, but a particularly sensitive part of human dignity. Although the freedom of expression occupies a prominent place amongst fundamental rights, it may be justified to impose certain restrictions to ensure the protection of human dignity. In this case, it is not freedom of religion, but human dignity that is concurring with the freedom of speech (abuse and contempt in themselves do not restrict the freedom of the persons involved to practice their religion). Human dignity is seriously violated if religious beliefs are subjected to verbal or pictorial aggression. Dignity is also violated if the aggression is aimed not at the person, but at the person's religion or an object that the person holds sacred.

2.2. Civil Law and Religious Conviction

In Hungary, the effective law aims at the protection of the religious feelings of citizens, to safeguard their dignity. Considering that the criminal persecution of hate speech crimes has proven to be ineffective and recognizing that criminal sanctions should be reserved to the most outrageous cases,[4] the new Civil Code of Hungary (Act V of 2013) opened the possibility of bringing a civil lawsuit for violations of dignity:

> "Any member of the community may enforce his personality rights within a thirty-day term of preclusion from the occurrence of a legal injury that was committed with great publicity in relation to some essential trait of his personality, his belonging to the Hungarian nation or some national, ethnic, racial or religious community, and is grossly offensive to the community or unduly insulting in its manner of expression. With the exception of relinquishing the material gain obtained through the violation of rights, any member of the community may enforce any sanctions of the violation of personality rights."[5]

3 Jeroen Temperman & András Koltay (eds.), *Blasphemy and Freedom of Expression: Comparative, Theoretical and Historical Reflections after the Charlie Hebdo Massacre*, Cambridge University Press, Cambridge, 2017.

4 Following Decision No. 30/1992. (V. 26.) AB, the Constitutional Court adopted a liberal approach to the freedom of speech limiting the possibility of criminal sanctions for hate speech to the most excessive cases.

5 Section 2:54(5) of the Civil Code.

doi: 10.5553/HYIEL/266627012021009001022

Civil litigation is possible if someone (a member of a certain group) is seriously offended. Although freedom of expression occupies a prominent place amongst fundamental rights, it may be justified to impose certain restrictions for the protection of human dignity. In this case, it is not freedom of religion, but *human dignity that is competing with the freedom of speech*. Freedom of religion is in fact not curtailed by being offended, but human dignity suffers a serious violation if religious beliefs of an individual are subjected to verbal or pictorial aggression. The same holds true when aggression is not aimed at the person, but at the person's religion or an object that the person holds sacred.

It must be noted that the Fundamental Law itself in its section guaranteeing free speech provides for the protection of dignity *against* free speech on a constitutional level (through criminal law or civil law provisions):

> "The right to freedom of expression may not be exercised with the aim of violating the dignity of the Hungarian nation or of any national, ethnic, racial or religious community. Persons belonging to such communities shall be entitled to enforce their claims in court against the expression of an opinion which violates their community, invoking the violation of their human dignity, as provided for by an Act."[6]

3. Recent Decisions of the Constitutional Court of Hungary on Offending Religion Sentiment

Early 2021 the Constitutional Court decided two remarkable cases. The cases had in common that litigants saw their dignity violated by offensive images and filing a civil lawsuit relying on the above mentioned new instrument of the Civil Code. In both cases, the petitioners were Catholic individuals who started litigating before the lower courts and continued litigation until the third instance. Since they did not receive remedy at the Curia of Hungary, they filed constitutional complaints.

3.1. Provoking Performance

The reason for one of the lawsuits was a performance held in front of the embassy of Poland in Budapest. An activist dressed as a Catholic bishop distributed abortion pills as the communion.[7] The petitioners claimed to be offended by the performance mocking the most holy sacrament of their belief. The demonstrators protested against the tightening of the Polish abortion law and its support by the Catholic Church. During the demonstration the performance imitated the Eucharist that was placed by an activist on the tongue of the other two participants, uttering the words "Body of Christ". The white pill was held in a bag labelled 'abortion pill'. The performance was later published on the internet for the general public to view. In their action, the plaintiffs asked the

6 Article IX(5) of the Fundamental Law of Hungary.

7 Decision No. 7/2021. (II. 19.) AB, Reasoning [34]. Images from the performance can be seen at https://images.app.goo.gl/yiv6yqfDRwuBPsY69.

doi: 10.5553/HYIEL/266627012021009001022

court to declare that through their actions, the defendants violated their human dignity and their right to practice their religion freely, owing to the plaintiffs affiliation with the Catholic religious community, which is an essential feature of their personality. The Budapest-Capital Regional Court acting on first instance dismissed the action, the second instance regional court quashed the first instance judgment. Finally, the Curia of Hungary, in its judgment closing the review proceedings, upheld the judgment of first instance and quashed the regional courts' decision. The plaintiffs then turned to the Constitutional Court. In their petition, they asked that it annul and declare the judgment of the Curia of Hungary contrary to the Fundamental Law, as they considered the first instance court's and the Curia of Hungary's judgments to be contrary to the provisions of the Fundamental Law stating that the exercise of the freedom of expression should not be aimed at offending the dignity of others or a religious community. The Constitutional Court found that the judgments delivered by the Curia of Hungary and the Budapest-Capital Regional Court in the subject-matter of offending the Catholic community were in conflict with the Fundamental Law and, therefore, annulled them.

In its decision, the Constitutional Court found that the challenged judgments acknowledged that the petitioners had been offended as a religious community. At the same time, they accepted the offensive communication as constitutionally protected speech, without examining the content of the opinion of the specific conduct actually complained of or its contribution to the discussion of public affairs. Consequently, the courts hearing the case could not have examined with due diligence whether or not the communication at issue was intended to offend the community concerned. With respect to the offensive communication, the courts stated that members of the religious community were offended by the provocation but had to tolerate this like public figures have to tolerate critique. The Curia of Hungary stated that the dignity of the petitioners' religious community was in fact undermined by the demonstrators' exercise of freedom of expression, but the members of the religious community have to endure this as a consequence of the public statements of the Church on abortion. The Constitutional Court found in its unanimous decision that the challenged court decisions were in conflict with the Fundamental Law and therefore annulled them. This opens up the possibility for a new court procedure that is to find a new balance between competing rights. Offending a community would not raise a constitutional issue but *offending the dignity of (the members of) a community can set limits to free speech*.[8]

3.2. Political Caricature – or Ridiculing the Nativity Scene?

The Constitutional Court also ruled on the case of the HVG weekly's cover page from Christmas 2014 that depicted a redesigned version of the painting 'Adoration of the Shepherds' by Gerard Von Honthorst.[9] The faces of the original characters were replaced by the faces of leading politicians, and the image of the

8 Id. in particular, Reasoning [29].

9 The original of the painting (1622) can be seen in the Wallraf Richartz Museum in Cologne.

doi: 10.5553/HYIEL/266627012021009001022

infant Jesus was replaced by a pile of gold coins.[10] The petitioner claimed that the picture offended the Catholic community. After having lost at all court instances she filed a constitutional complaint arguing that her human dignity and freedom of religion were violated. She claimed that her fundamental right to have the symbols and liturgy of her religion respected, and to practice her religion in an undisturbed manner in the community space was violated because the Curia of Hungary and the proceeding courts have accepted without criticism the defendant's argument that the communication complained of was aimed at criticizing the politicians concerned and had no anti-religious purpose. The petitioner therefore turned to the Constitutional Court seeking that it declares the Curia of Hungary's judgment in conflict with the Fundamental Law. Although the figures pictured in the caricature are not portrayed in a degrading way, the cover page can still offend Christians. Yet this provocation remains limited. It can be noted that this type of caricature is only comes through as long as the Christian symbolism is understood.

According to the decision of the Constitutional Court, the courts acting in the main proceedings recognized correctly that the pivotal issue to be assessed was the purpose of the communication, as a question of primary importance. Examining the front page in question, the Curia of Hungary stated, on the one hand, that it was not aimed at offending Christians, and it did not convey a negative value judgment about believers. Figures in the picture were not displayed in a degrading manner. The Constitutional Court identified the specific political opinion conveyed by the authors. The *form of expression of this political opinion was not found to be arbitrary or unjustified* in relation to the content of the opinion.[11] The Christian symbolism in this case was a carrying agent of the message but the target was the attitude of the political elite. The Constitutional Court rejected the constitutional complaint with nine votes to five. Justices authoring dissenting opinions argued that the image amounted to an infringement of the dignity of believers, neglecting the commitment of the Fundamental Law to the Christian legacy.

Representatives of religious communities (*e.g.* bishops) when entering the public discourse have to bear criticism like all other parties to public debates. The central difference between the two cases is not that in one case politicians were targeted, whereas in the other it was (Polish) bishops. The central difference is much rather that mocking the Eucharist is much more offensive than the non-degrading portrayal of the figures of the nativity scene. Mocking the Eucharist offends also fellow believers, whereas the cover page primarily targeted politicians. The basic message of the cases is that freedom of expression deserves protection as long as it does not jeopardize the human dignity of others. A dignity

10 Decision No. 6/2021. (II. 19.) AB, Reasoning [26]. The controversial image can be found at https://images.app.goo.gl/zHr7utGJMvLa67UR7.

11 The case summaries in English (also used in the present note) are available at https://hunconcourt.hu/kozlemeny/the-expression-of-opinion-is-free-the-dividing-line-is-the-protection-of-human-dignity.

doi: 10.5553/HYIEL/266627012021009001022

of the community and the dignity of members of the community seem to be interlinked.

According to Article R(4) of the Fundamental Law of Hungary "[t]he protection of the constitutional identity and Christian culture of Hungary shall be an obligation of every organ of the State." The Fundamental Law does not commit the Hungarian State to Christian religion or even to Christian culture in general and provides for the freedom of religion and belief in respect of all faiths. This way the state is neutral with regard to religion, but it expressly orders the protection of the culture of Hungary as a Christian culture. The aim of the constitutional legislator was undoubtedly to afford the identity of the nation a stronger emphasis and protection. Furthermore, the Fundamental Law's preamble refers to the 'Christian heritage' of the nation. Religions (the dignity of people of various faiths) deserve equal protection, in does not make a difference if the target of provocation belongs to a religious minority or a mainstream religion. The cultural tradition of the country enjoys constitutional protection, but paradoxically it is this cultural background that makes it possible that the public is able to understand the message of a provocation.

4. Conclusion

The protection of the dignity of members of a faith community can be a legitimate reason to set limitations to free speech. Critical expression can also have or target religious content, in particular when discussing public affairs. On the one hand, the target of criticism must be scrutinized. If religion itself is the target, critical expression may also hit those who have not been party to the public discourse and beyond a certain limit the members of a faith community do not have to tolerate provocations. Offending them cannot be considered a legitimate collateral damage of public debate. On the other hand, public figures (including representatives of religious communities) have to bear criticism, even if criticism relates to their religious conviction.

doi: 10.5553/HYIEL/266627012021009001022

The Afterlife of the Relocation of Judicial Cases

Ágnes Czine[*]

Abstract

The requirement of an independent and impartial tribunal established by law is set out in Article 6(1) ECHR and Article XXVIII(1) of the Fundamental Law of Hungary. The elements of the definition of the right to a fair trial are closely tied to the requirement of judicial independence, impartiality and a court established by law. These guarantees' purpose is to ensure that the applicant receive a judgment that is not prejudged by other branches of power, such as the influence of the executive, or the arbitrariness of the judiciary. This important human and fundamental rights requirement is monitored by bodies dedicated to the protection of democratic institutions. According to the laws of Hungary, lawsuits may be transferred to another court by the National Office for the Judiciary in order to reduce the workload. This solution has received strong international attention and scrutiny. Although these are actually not in force, they still have repercussions, which must be dealt with by the Constitutional Court. This article seeks to provide insight into the constitutional afterlife of this system of reallocation.

Keywords: right to a lawful judge, National Judicial Council, relocation of judicial cases, reasonable time, length of proceedings.

1. Introduction: A Historical Overview

The legal institution of transferring a case in order to avoid lengthy procedures was established by Act CLXXXIII of 2010 on the amendment of certain laws for the efficient operation of courts and the acceleration of court proceedings which introduced by law from 7 January 2011. Pursuant to this Act, the Act on the Organization and Administration of Courts (Court Organization Act), the 1952 Act on the Code of Civil Procedure and the 1998 Act on Criminal Proceedings were amended. As a general rule, Section 33/A of the Court Organization Act provided that

> "The Supreme Court shall have powers to reassign – in exceptional cases, upon recommendation by the President of the National Council of Justice certain cases from the court of original jurisdiction to another court of analogous jurisdiction, if providing a reasonable timeframe for hearing the case or a group of specific cases assigned to the court cannot be ensured

* Ágnes Czine: justice, Constitutional Court of Hungary, Budapest; associate professor of law, and acting rector, Károli Gáspár University of the Reformed Church, Budapest.

Hungarian Yearbook of International Law and European Law 2021 (9) 1
doi: 10.5553/HYIEL/266627012021009001023

> otherwise due to the irregular and disproportionate workload of the court, and if having additional cases assigned will not burden the court affected beyond reason."

It is interesting to mention that at that time, the President of the Supreme Court was the President of the National Council of Justice. The 1998 Act on Criminal Proceedings[1] and the 1952 Act on the Code of Civil Procedure[2] were also amended in accordance with the amendment of the Court Organization Act to provide for the possible reallocation of cases.

On 1 January 2012, the Fundamental Law of Hungary entered into force, and the National Office for the Judiciary (NOJ) and the National Judicial Council (NJC) started operation.[3] Rules on the transfer of cases were changed and a new level of regulation appeared governing the transfer of cases, notably the Transitional Provisions of the Fundamental Law that also contained rules to this effect:

> "In the interest of the enforcement of the fundamental right to a court decision within a reasonable time guaranteed by Article XXVIII(1) of the Fundamental Law, and until a balanced distribution of caseload between the courts has been achieved, the President of the National Office for the Judiciary may designate a court other than the court of general competence but with the same jurisdiction to adjudicate any case."[4]

A significant change compared with the previously mentioned rules is that here, it is no longer the President of the Supreme Court who may decide on the reallocation, but the President of the NOJ. The elaboration of the relevant regulation was also improved, with the regulations issued by the President of the NJC and the President of the NOJ defining the detailed rules of reallocation.[5] However, by its *Decision No. 45/2012. (XII. 29.) AB*, the Constitutional Court annulled the rules of the Fundamental Law's Transitional Provisions governing

1 Section 20/A of Act XIX of 1998 on Criminal Proceedings: "The Supreme Court shall have powers to reassign – upon a recommendation by the President of the National Council of Justice – certain cases from the court of original jurisdiction to another court of analogous jurisdiction, if providing a reasonable timeframe for hearing the case cannot be ensured otherwise due to the irregular workload of the court, and if having additional cases assigned will not burden the court affected beyond reason."

2 Section 47(1) of the Act III of 1952 on the Code of Civil Procedure: "The Supreme Court shall have powers to reassign – on a recommendation by the President of the National Council of Justice – certain cases from the court of original jurisdiction to another court of analogous jurisdiction, if providing a reasonable timeframe for hearing the case or a group of specific cases assigned to the court cannot be ensured otherwise due to the irregular and disproportionate workload of the court, and if having additional cases assigned will not burden the court affected beyond reason."

3 About the Hungarian self-governing system of the judiciary, *see e.g.* https://birosag.hu/en/national-office-judiciary.

4 Transitional Provisions of the Fundamental Law, Article 11(3).

5 *See* (in Hungarian) Decision No. 36/2012. (VIII. 17.) OBT.

doi: 10.5553/HYIEL/266627012021009001023

the transfer of cases with retroactive effect to 31 December 2011.[6] The Constitutional Court also annulled the provisions on the transfer of cases laid down in the Court Organization Act and the 1998 Act on Criminal Proceedings with its *Decision No. 36/2013. (XII. 5.) AB*.[7]

Following the two decisions of the Constitutional Court, on 25 March 2013, the Parliament adopted the Fourth Amendment to the Fundamental Law, which elevated to the constitutional level the President of the NOJ's power to transfer a case.[8] According to the newly adopted Article 27(4) of the Fundamental Law,

> "To give effect to the fundamental right to a court decision taken within a reasonable time and to balance the workload across courts, the President of the National Office for the Judiciary may appoint, in the way defined by cardinal Act, a court other than a court of general competence but with the same powers to hear particular cases defined by cardinal Act."

These rules governing jurisdiction were thereby reinforced, for up until then, they were only included in the Transitional Provisions of the Fundamental Law and regulated as a temporary, extraordinary measure. Yet as of 2013, *the possibility of reallocation was incorporated into the main text of the Fundamental Law*. The amendment of the Fundamental Law also meant that *the Constitutional Court had no power to review (and annul) the rules concerning the reallocation of cases*, since the Constitutional Court only has jurisdiction to review the Fundamental Law of Hungary for procedural reasons. According to Article 24(5) of the Fundamental Law of Hungary,

> "The Constitutional Court may review the Fundamental Law or the amendment of the Fundamental Law only in relation to the procedural requirements laid down in the Fundamental Law for making and promulgating it."

These provisions of the Fourth Amendment to the Fundamental Law garnered an unfavorable international response already in the drafting phase. The European Commission expressed its serious concerns on the Fourth Amendment and asked that the constitution-maker take into account the relevant opinion of the Venice Commission.[9] *The Venice Commission strongly criticized the broad power of the President of the NOJ to transfer cases from one court to another based on the vague criterion of "adjudicating cases within a reasonable time"*. It emphasized the importance of the "right to a lawful judge" and stressed that the problems caused by the extraordinary and disproportionate workload of individual courts must be resolved by less intrusive means. These may include, in particular: ensuring adequate number of judges and court staff, redistribution of jurisdiction, or

6 Decision No. 45/2012. (XII. 29.) AB.
7 Decision No. 36/2013. (XII. 5.) AB.
8 Article 27(4) of the Fundamental Law of Hungary.
9 *See* at https://ec.europa.eu/commission/presscorner/detail/en/IP_13_327.

doi: 10.5553/HYIEL/266627012021009001023

relocating judges on a voluntary basis. The Venice Commission pointed out that this kind of reallocation system should not be applicable in its entirety, even if it is completely objective. The panel also recalled that the Hungarian Constitutional Court had already reviewed the case transfer system and had not found the earlier law to be in line with the Constitution in force at the time. Nevertheless, the Parliament had reintroduced the transfer of cases as a part of the Transitional Provisions of the Fundamental Law. In the Venice Commission's view, if a transfer is a temporary solution, it must rely on objective criteria, both as regards the selection of cases and the designation of the host court.[10]

The power of the President of the NOJ to reallocate cases has also triggered an intense debate in the legal literature. This debate not only centered on the theoretical approach to the right to a lawful judge, but also revolved around specific, factual data. The original, proclaimed purpose of the power to reallocate cases was to redistribute the court burden proportionately, in order to enforce the principle of disposing of cases within a reasonable time. Contemporary analyses have shown that this power has not lived up to expectations because the number of cases to be reallocated was negligible compared to the tremendous volume of cases handled in those years.[11]

Károly Zaicsek arrived at the conclusion that

> "the volume of cases to be transferred is not justified in light of the extraordinary and disproportionate workload of the court seized, which would have provided a legal basis for removing the parties from a lawful judge. While the principles underlying the transfer of cases provide guidance for deciding what situations may be classified as constituting an extraordinary and disproportionate workload, these principles are nevertheless not stipulated in procedural law."[12]

Finally, in order to meet international expectations, *the Parliament adopted the Fifth Amendment to the Fundamental Law*,[13] which *abolished the power of the President of the NOJ to transfer cases*. The Amendment entered into force on 1 October 2013 and *does not contain a retroactive provision regarding the previously reassigned cases*.

10 CDL-AD (2012) 020-e, Opinion adopted by the Venice Commission at its 92nd Plenary Session (Venice, 12-13 October 2012), at www.venice.coe.int/webforms/documents/?pdf=CDL-AD(2012)020-e.

11 László Örkényi, 'Arányos ügyteher elosztás az igazságszolgáltatásban – elvek és teendők', *Debreceni Jogi Műhely*, 2012/1, pp. 13-36.

12 Károly Zaicsek, 'Törvényes bíróhoz való jog az ügyáthelyezés jogintézményének tükrében', *in* István Varga (ed.), *Codificatio processualis civilis. Studia in honorem Németh János II.*, ELTE Eötvös, Budapest, 2013, p. 537 (translation by the Author of this article).

13 Article 7(1) of the Fifth Amendment of the Fundamental Law, repealing Article 27(4) of the Fundamental Law.

doi: 10.5553/HYIEL/266627012021009001023

2. The Right to a Lawful Judge

The central constitutional and international law issue of the case reallocation solution presented earlier and the legal dispute unfolding around it was the protection of the right to a lawful judge. The Hungarian regulation of this right does not differ from the applicable European requirements in its essence. In Article XXVIII(1) of the Fundamental Law, the right to a lawful judge as a part of the right to a fair trial is based on the principles elaborated by the ECtHR. Therefore, let us first consider the essence of the system of principles developed by the ECtHR.

According to the case-law of the ECtHR, under Article 6(1) ECHR, the court must in all cases be *"established by law"*. The term is based on the rule of law, which forms an integral part of the system of legal protection established by the ECHR and its Additional Protocols.[14] According to the Article 6(1) ECHR, "law" means not only legislation governing the establishment and jurisdiction of judicial bodies,[15] but also any provision of domestic law the breach of which would render irregular the participation of one or more judges in a case.[16] Examples for such provisions are those governing the independence of members of the judicial panel, the length of their term of office, their impartiality and the existence of procedural guarantees.[17] In other words, the term "established by law" refers not only to the legal basis for the existence of the court, but also to the fact that the court must comply with it in all cases.[18] In principle, a breach by a court of the provisions of domestic law relating to the establishment and jurisdiction of judicial bodies also violates Article 6(1) ECHR. The ECtHR may therefore assess whether national legal provisions have complied with this requirement. Nevertheless, in view of the general principle that it is primarily for the national courts to interpret domestic law, the ECtHR has stated in several judgments that it may not call into question the interpretation of national courts unless there has been a manifest breach of national law.[19]

The practice of the ECtHR can therefore be summarized as follows: the selection of the trial judge and the principles and other legal aspects of the case allocation system must always be verifiable. Otherwise, national regulation may give the appearance of a lack of independence and impartiality and that it does not ensure the foreseeability and certainty that is necessary for a court to qualify as a court "established by law". The ECtHR also emphasized that the above procedural errors could not be remedied by a subsequent appeal or review.[20]

14 *Jorgic v Germany*, No. 74613/01, 12 July 2007, para. 64
15 *Lavents v Latvia*, No. 58442/00, 28 November 2002, para. 114.
16 *Gorguiladze v Georgia*, No. 4313/04, 20 October 2009, paras. 20 and 68; *Pandjikidze and others v Georgia*, No. 30323/02, 27 October 2009, para. 104.
17 *Coeme and others v Belgium*, No. 32492/96 and 4 others, 22 June 2000; *Gurov v Moldova*, No. 36455/02, 11 July 2006, para. 36.
18 *Sokurenko and Strygun v Ukraine*, No. 29458/04 and 29465/04, 20 July 2006, para. 24; *Buscarini v San Marino (dec.)*, No. 31657/96, 4 May 2000.
19 *See Coeme and others*, para 98; *Lavents*, para. 114.
20 *Miracle Europe Kft. v Hungary*, No. 57774/13, 12 June 2016, paras. 45-52 and 63.

doi: 10.5553/HYIEL/266627012021009001023

Hungarian legal thinking was significantly influenced by the German legal approach, so it is worth looking at the relevant practice of the German Federal Constitutional Court *(Bundesverfassungsgericht)*. In the German legal system, the establishment of new courts clearly falls within the competence of the legislature, since it enforces one of the elements of the right to a lawful judge through regulation by law. The executive also has some power to decide on the organization of the judiciary, *i.e.* it can set up or suspend judicial bodies, but such measures must not be case-specific, but must be governed by general organizational considerations. These requirements were summarized as a prohibition of arbitrariness by the German Federal Constitutional Court.[21]

According to the consistent practice of the Hungarian Constitutional Court, the requirement of the right to a lawful judge includes a judicial forum *(judge) acting in a specific case in accordance with the general rules of competence and jurisdiction established in procedural laws*. This constitutional principle is enshrined in the Court Organization Act, foreseeing among the principles of the Act that no one may be deprived of his or her legal judge.[22] A judge established by law is a judge designated on the basis of a pre-established order of division of cases in a court with jurisdiction in accordance with the rules of procedure.[23] The order of case allocation is established by the president of the court in the previous year in order to ensure objectivity and impersonality, to exclude arbitrariness, which may be changed in the current year only in the interests of service or for important reasons affecting the operation of the court.[24] It follows that the assignment of case to a judge can only be constitutionally made on the basis of objective rules determined in advance.[25]

It follows from the above, that the principles applied by the Constitutional Court are based on internationally accepted standards and necessarily led the body to declare *the power of the President of NOJ to transfer cases as unconstitutional*, since it violates to the rights to a lawful judge. In the words of Nóra Balogh-Békési, this led to the abolition of a complete legal institution enshrined in the Fundamental Law. Although a more proportionate distribution of cases within the judiciary is a legitimate goal, the way it was implemented did not stand the test of constitutionality and time.[26]

3. Cases from the Afterlife of Relocation of Cases

The Parliament therefore extinguished the unlawful power of the President of the NOJ to reallocate cases from the Hungarian legal system. In accordance with

21 András Osztovits, 'A törvényes bíróhoz való jog a német szövetségi és az osztrák alkotmánybíróságok gyakorlatában', *Jogtudományi Közlöny*, Vol. 60, Issue 10, 2005, p. 422.
22 Section 8(1) of the Court Organization Act.
23 Id. Section 8(2).
24 Id. Section 9(1).
25 Decision No. 36/2013. (XII. 5.) AB, Reasoning [32]; Decision No. 3272/2018. (VII. 20.) AB.
26 Nóra Balogh-Békési, 'A bírói hatalmi ág az Alaptörvény rendszerében', *Iustum Aequum Salutare*, Vol. 12, Issue 4, 2016, p. 12.

doi: 10.5553/HYIEL/266627012021009001023

international principles, the rules of jurisdiction are regulated by law and the assignment of cases also takes place on the basis of an objective system of case allocation. However, a dilemma arose in cases that were "diverted" by power of the President of the NOJ. Where should those cases that were diverted" from the lawful judge continue?

Two approaches are possible. *(i)* One approach, retroactive or *ex tunc*, is that, as a result of the annulment of a power, the case should be treated as if it had not been "diverted", as if that administrative power had not originally existed. Thus, the case in question should be reallocated to the court where it should have been disposed of under the general rules of jurisdiction. However, this would require a legislative provision that would bring some of the "hijacked" cases back within the scope of the general rules, amounting to an intervention in court proceedings by another branch of government. *(ii)* According to the other view, the consequence of the abolition of this reallocation power is that the proceeding court must be designated in accordance with the general rules in force. In this case, it should be taken into account that the case was already pending before a court (*ex nunc* approach). Fewer than a dozen such cases have reached the Constitutional Court, from among which I would like to present two examples.

3.1. Order No. 3272/2018. (VII. 20.) AB

In the case underlying the constitutional complaint, the prosecutor's office filed the indictment with the Budapest-Capital Regional Court. Upon the initiative of the President of the Court, the President of the NOJ appointed the Szolnok Regional Court to conduct the proceedings after seeking the opinion of the Prosecutor General and the President of the Curia of Hungary. In view of the annulment decision of the Constitutional Court,[27] the Szolnok Regional Court found that it had no jurisdiction in the criminal proceedings pending before it and referred the case to the Budapest-Capital Regional Court. The Budapest-Capital Regional Court also declared that it had no jurisdiction due to priority because the case was already pending at another court, so the Szolnok General Court referred the case to the Curia of Hungary for designation.

The Curia of Hungary re-appointed the Szolnok Regional Court to conduct the first-instance proceedings on the basis of the "ordinary provisions of the Criminal Proceedings Act". According to Section 20(3) of the Act on Criminal Proceedings, "[t]he acting court shall also be designated by the Curia of Hungary if the conditions for determining jurisdiction cannot be established." Section 17(2), (4)-(6) also regulated how the question of jurisdiction shall be decided. The reasoning of the Curia of Hungary's order emphasized that the criminal proceedings conducted by the Szolnok Regional Court could not be disregarded when making the decision on the issue of jurisdiction, and thus, this procedure provides a basis for applying the precautionary principle. It also emphasized that the proceedings of the Szolnok Regional Court were not affected by *Decision No. 36/2013. (XII. 5.) AB*, so the lawsuit was not unconstitutional in itself. The petitioner appealed to the Constitutional Court against order of the

27 Decision No. 36/2013. (XII. 5.) AB, which annulled Sections 62-63 of the Court Organization Act.

 Hungarian Yearbook of International Law and European Law 2021 (9) 1
doi: 10.5553/HYIEL/266627012021009001023

Curia of Hungary. In its decision,[28] the Constitutional Court also emphasized that *the re-appointment of the Szolnok Regional Court, as emphasized in the decision of the Curia of Hungary, was based on the "ordinary" provisions of the Act on Criminal Proceedings*. During the proceedings at first instance, a judge appointed in accordance with the pre-established order of division of cases proceeded as designated court in accordance with the rules of competence and jurisdiction specified in the Act on Criminal Proceedings. The Constitutional Court therefore dismissed the complaint on the basis that there was no conflict with the Fundamental Law that significantly affected the judicial decision, nor did the case raise constitutional law issues of fundamental importance.

3.2. Order No. 3310/2020. (VII. 24.) AB

In the case related to the constitutional complaint, the Kecskemét Regional Court acted as the court of first instance. In the course of the proceedings, the Kecskemét Regional Court, taking into account *Decision No. 36/2013. (XII. 5.) AB*, established that it had no jurisdiction and referred the case to the Budapest-Capital Regional Court. The Budapest-Capital Regional Court also found that it had no jurisdiction and transferred the case to the Curia of Hungary. The Curia of Hungary finally appointed the Kecskemét Regional Court to conduct the proceedings.

In the statement of reasons of the order rendered by the Curia of Hungary, it emphasized that *Decision No. 36/2013. (XII. 5.) AB* did not affect the validity of judicial decisions made on the basis of the unconstitutional reallocation provision, if the proceedings were otherwise fair. Referring to the uniformly followed jurisprudence,[29] the Curia of Hungary also pointed out that in criminal proceedings pending at the time of the entry into force of a new law, procedural acts implemented under the previous law remain valid even where these differ from the new legislation. It also stressed that under the previous Act on Criminal Proceedings,[30] following the commencement of a trial, lack of jurisdiction can only be taken into account in two cases: *(i)* if the adjudication of the case exceeds the jurisdiction of the court; or *(ii)* another court has exclusive jurisdiction over it. As none of these statutory grounds for exclusion existed in the present case, *the Curia of Hungary found that the jurisdiction of the Kecskemét Regional Court had been fixed at the beginning of the trial and designated this court to continue the proceedings*. The petitioner appealed to the Constitutional Court primarily for violation of the right to a lawful judge. The Constitutional Court emphasized that the re-appointment of the Kecskemét Regional Court, as stated by the Curia of Hungary in its decision, was based on the former Act on Criminal Proceedings. Although the same court had been appointed, the designation of the jurisdiction of the court of first instance and, consequently, the court competent for conducting the procedure of first instance, was not based on an earlier decision of the President of NOJ. Instead, the Kecskemét Regional Court was appointed in accordance with

28 *See* Decision No. 3272/2018. (VII. 20.) AB.

29 *See* BH 2004.455.

30 *See* Act XIX of 1998 on the Criminal Proceedings, Sections 308(1) and 17(5)-(6).

doi: 10.5553/HYIEL/266627012021009001023

the rules of jurisdiction enshrined in the previous Act on Criminal Proceedings that were not affected by *Decision No. 36/2013. (XII. 5.) AB*, and a new judge was appointed in accordance with the pre-established order of case distribution of this court. Again, the Constitutional Court dismissed the complaint on the basis that there was no conflict with the Fundamental Law that significantly affected the judicial decision, nor did the case raise constitutional law issues of fundamental importance.

4. Conclusions

What is the conclusion that may be drawn from these examples? The competence in the cases did not change by virtue of the fact that the right of the President of the NOJ to transfer the case was declared unconstitutional by the Constitutional Court and the Parliament abolished the rules establishing this competence. This is because the general and 'ordinary' rules of jurisdiction have fixed proceedings that are already in progress.

It appears that, in the end, the same courts were involved in these cases as those appointed by the President of NJO, so nothing changed. However, this is not the case. Based on the case-law of the ECtHR, the term "established by law" in Article 6 ECHR is intended to ensure that "in a democratic society the judiciary does not depend on the discretion of the executive power but is governed by laws of Parliament."[31] In countries with codified law, the organization of the judiciary cannot be left to the discretion of the judicial authorities, although this does not mean that the courts do not have some leeway in interpreting the relevant domestic law.[32]

In the light of all these principles, the situation in the present case is in fact different from when the President of the NOJ exercised her power of transfer, because the final word on jurisdiction was not spoken by an administrative body but by the judicial system itself – and not on the basis of the former reallocation rules. Jurisdiction was determined based on general laws adopted in accordance with the requirements of international law and consistent domestic judicial practice.

In my view, the right to a lawful judge rests on two important pillars. *(i)* One is *legislation governing the establishment of courts, the determination of their jurisdiction, basic operating conditions, as well as the independence and impartiality of a judge*. This pillar is based on internationally accepted principles and structured similarly in any democratic society. *(ii)* The other pillar is *the order of case distribution*, in respect of which *ad hoc* influence exercised from outside the organization, primarily by the executive power, must be excluded. In this matter, therefore, the judicial system itself must be the one to have the final word, as illustrated by the examples in this article. Meanwhile, objectivity in case distribution based on uniform principles must be ensured internally, too. The

31 *Zand v Austria (ECommHR dec.)*, No. 7360/76, 16 May 1977.

32 *Coeme and others*, para. 98; *Savino and others v Italy*, No. 17214/05, 20329/05 and 42113/04, 28 April 2009, para. 94; *Fruni v Slovakia*, No. 8014/07, 21 June 2011, paras. 21 and 134.

Hungarian Yearbook of International Law and European Law 2021 (9) 1
doi: 10.5553/HYIEL/266627012021009001023

international debate concerning the reallocation power of the NOJ's President and the legislative process following it have provided a number of important lessons in this regard.

doi: 10.5553/HYIEL/266627012021009001023

Can a Two-Tailed Dog Be Allowed Into the Polling Booth?

The Case of Magyar Kétfarkú Kutya Párt Versus Hungary Before the ECtHR

János Tamás Papp[*]

Abstract

The Hungarian satirical Two-Tailed Dog Party (Magyar Kétfarkú Kutya Párt – MKKP) applied to the ECtHR as a result of the decisions rendered by the Hungarian National Electoral Commission, the Curia of Hungary and the Constitutional Court, who ruled that a mobile application developed by the party allowing anonymous users to share their invalid votes violated Hungarian election law. By 16 votes to 1, the Grand Chamber of the ECtHR ruled that the Hungarian authorities had violated the Article of the ECHR on freedom of expression. According to the ECtHR's reasoning, the severe uncertainties about the possible consequences of the legal provisions applied by the domestic authorities went beyond what is permissible under Article 10(2) ECHR. The ECtHR has ruled that a judicial interpretation of a law's rules does not inherently violate the requirement that laws be written in such a way that the legal implications are predictable. However, since the national law in this case provided for a case-by-case limitation on the expression of an opinion on voting, electoral bodies and national courts that interpreted and enforced these rules enjoyed an excessive amount of discretion. In conclusion, the ECtHR found that legislation restricting freedom of expression must be treated more strictly in connection with electoral procedures: it must not be in any way misleading or inconsistent.

Keywords: freedom of speech, elections, ECtHR, democracy, secrecy of votes.

1. The Facts of the Case

Hungary held a referendum on the EU's migrant relocation scheme on 2 October 2016. During the referendum campaign, several opposition parties had called on voters to vote in such a way that their ballots would be invalidated to protest of the referendum. The Hungarian Two-Tailed Dog Party (*Magyar Kétfarkú Kutya Párt*, MKKP), a registered political party that did not meet the

* János Tamás Papp: PhD candidate, research fellow, Pázmány Péter Catholic University, Budapest; media specialist, Institute for Media Studies of the Media Council of the National Media and Infocommunications Authority, Budapest.

doi: 10.5553/HYIEL/266627012021009001024

legislative threshold for parliamentary representation and expresses its political views primarily through satire and satirical material, considered the referendum initiative misleading and disrespectful of direct democracy mechanisms. In order to express its political opinion, the applicant party had made a mobile phone application called 'the cast-an-invalid-vote app' available to voters, where they could upload and exchange photos of their ballots with the public, as well as add suggestions about why they cast their ballots in the way they did. Users could upload and exchange photos anonymously, which was one of the app's key features. Because of the application's hashing technique, neither MKKP nor the developer could access the users' personal information. A total of 3,894 images were posted on the day of the referendum.

A private citizen filed a complaint about the application with Hungary's National Election Commission on 29 September 2016. According to the Commission,[1] the application of MKKP had violated the rules of electoral fairness, voting confidentiality, and the proper exercise of rights. In the eyes of the public, the application had the potential to discredit the role of electoral bodies and tallying systems, according to the Commission. The Commission issued a cease-and-desist notice to the respondent political party. It concluded, among other items, that photographing ballot papers may have resulted in election fraud. The use of the mobile application, according to the Commission, violated the principles of election fairness, voting confidentiality, and exercising rights in accordance with their purpose, in violation of Hungary's Fundamental Law and the National Election Procedure Act.[2]

The applicant then petitioned the Curia of Hungary *(Kúria)* for judicial review of the ruling. The Curia of Hungary upheld the Commission's ruling on the violation of the principle of the proper exercise of rights on 10 October 2016.[3] It was determined that a ban on photos and publishing would not infringe on voters' freedom of speech because they were free to express their views by voting and sharing how they voted with others.[4] The remainder of the Commission's decision on election confidentiality and discrediting the role of electoral bodies was reversed by the Curia of Hungary. The conventional approach to the role and use of paper ballots in a voting system was central to the Curia of Hungary's case for considering a breach of this principle (*i.e.* only for the purposes of casting a secret vote). Sharing the results of the vote verbally, in writing, or on social media, according to the Curia of Hungary, was in line with the intended purpose of paper ballots. However, taking and sharing a picture of a paper ballot *via* a mobile application to express a political opinion was incompatible with this traditional position.[5] According to the Curia of Hungary,

1 118/2016. NVB decision.
2 Id.
3 Case No. Kvk.VI.37.942/2016/2.
4 Id. para. 16.
5 Id. para. 25.

doi: 10.5553/HYIEL/266627012021009001024

> "The conduct that calls on voters to photograph and publish the ballot paper of the national referendum through an application created for this purpose is contrary to the principle of the right to vote."[6]

MKKP filed a complaint with Hungary's Constitutional Court, alleging that their constitutional right to freedom of speech had been violated. The Constitutional Court rejected the constitutional complaint, arguing that the petitioner had only created the medium, the surface where these opinions could appear, but that in itself does not mean that the petitioner himself expressed an opinion.[7] The Constitutional Court shared the Curia of Hungary's view that the case concerns the freedom of expression of voters, however, according to the Constitutional Court, this does not mean that the petitioner's right to express an opinion was also the subject of court proceedings.[8] The petitioner therefore referred only to an indirect violation of his freedom of expression, namely that the alleged restriction of the freedom of expression of voters also infringed his freedom of expression. Thus, the Constitutional Court rejected the petitioner's request that its activities would fall within the scope of freedom of expression.[9] Following these domestic procedures, MKKP filed a complaint with the ECtHR.

2. The Judgments of the ECtHR

The case was initially assigned to the ECtHR's Fourth Section. The Chamber found that punishing MKKP for offering a means of dissemination from which others would impart and obtain information infringed MKKP's right to freedom of speech under Article 10 ECHR. Furthermore, the Chamber found that the Government of Hungary violated the invoked right by failing to specify which interest the ban served under Article 10(2). As a result, the Chamber unanimously decided that the intervention could not be deemed to be pursuing a valid goal under Article 10(2) ECHR, and thus that Article 10 ECHR had been violated. The ECtHR cited the Grand Chamber's *Öztürk* case,[10] emphasizing that freedom of speech requires the freedom to transmit information, as any limitation on these media inevitably interferes with the right to communicate and learn information. *The Hungarian Government*, according to the Chamber, *was unable to identify a valid goal* recognized by the ECHR in relation to Article 10 that would have justified limiting the MKKP's right to express an opinion. In light of the finding of a breach of the ECHR, the Chamber decided not to look into the merits of the legislation because the MKKP's domestic conviction was plainly

6 Id. para. 28.
7 Decision No. 3226/2016. (XI. 14.) AB.
8 Id. Reasoning [26].
9 Id. Reasoning [29].
10 *Öztürk v Turkey (GC)*, No. 22479/93, 28 September 1999.

doi: 10.5553/HYIEL/266627012021009001024

wrongful enough.[11] Following the decision of the Chamber, the Hungarian government requested the referral of the case to the Grand Chamber.[12]

The Grand Chamber stated that the MKKP had been penalized for providing a means of transmission enabling others to impart and receive information. It considered that providing a forum for others to express their opinions in the form of posting ballot photographs constituted conduct in the exercise of the MKKP's right to freedom of expression.[13] It also underlined, that the parties agree that the domestic authorities' actions infringed on the MKKP's right to freedom of speech.[14]

The Grand Chamber considered the Government's preliminary claim that the claimant had not exhausted all domestic remedies, since the MKKP should have asked the Constitutional Court to find the applied legislation unconstitutional within the scope of normative regulation instead of referring to the unconstitutional judgment. The Grand Chamber rejected this point, holding that the applicants' political communication was restricted by the *incorrect application of standards, since these allowed for an overly broad leeway in the case*. As a result, the MKKP filed a 'genuine' constitutional complaint (stating that the judgment of the Curia of Hungary was unconstitutional), which can be used to address those issues. As a result, in this regard the Government's argument was rejected by the Grand Chamber.[15]

The Grand Chamber found that the smartphone application was created to allow users to share their comments and photographs using information technology in the case at hand. The Grand Chamber judgment went into great detail on whether MKKP's right to freedom of speech had been restricted and whether the intervention was legal. The ECtHR stated that the existence of an interference with MKKP's freedom of speech was not disputed by the parties and was further confirmed by the Grand Chamber.[16] It then went on to say that in the present case, the cell phone application has a communicative meaning and therefore constitutes speech on a matter of public concern, as covered by Article 10 ECHR. Furthermore, the Grand Chamber was satisfied that what the applicant political party was condemned for in this case was precisely the provision of means of transmission for others to impart and receive information, as specified by Article 10 ECHR.[17] According to the ECtHR, *the use of the application was an expression of political speech and a conscious activity of citizens*.[18]

The Grand Chamber then had to decide whether the intervention was justified under Article 10 ECHR, that is, whether it was *(i)* prescribed by law; *(ii)* served a legitimate aim; and *(iii)* was necessary in a democratic society. The

11 *Magyar Kétfarkú Kutya Párt v Hungary*, No. 201/17, 23 January 2018. The case was decided by the Fourth Section of the ECtHR.
12 *Magyar Kétfarkú Kutya Párt v Hungary (GC)*, No. 201/17, 20 January 2020, para. 65.
13 Id. para. 66.
14 Id. para. 85.
15 Id. para. 89.
16 Id. para. 85.
17 Id. para. 87.
18 Id. para. 74.

doi: 10.5553/HYIEL/266627012021009001024

ECtHR ruled that it is not up to them to express a view on the appropriateness of the methods chosen by the legislature, but to determine whether the application of it to the claimant was in violation of the ECHR.[19] In determining whether the fine had a legitimate goal, the Grand Chamber looked first at the Government's claim that the fine was intended to ensure the orderly operation of the voting process and the correct use of ballot papers. The Government had refused to show any other real rights of 'others' that may have been harmed by the anonymous publishing of imagery of marked or spoiled ballots, according to the ECtHR. Furthermore, they did not demonstrate any resulting defect in the voting process that would make a restriction of the application's use necessary. The Grand Chamber emphasized that the phrase prescribed by law in the second paragraph of Article 10 not only includes the presence of a legal basis in domestic law, but also establishes standards for the quality of law.[20] The ECtHR provided a comprehensive review of this last point. The Grand Chamber's evaluation began with the premise that the concept of legal quality necessitates, as a corollary of the foreseeability test, that the legislation be consistent with the rule of law; this means that adequate protections against arbitrary intervention by public authorities must exist in domestic law.

The key problem in this case, according to the Grand Chamber, was *whether the legal justification for interfering with MKKP's freedom of speech was adequately foreseen*, and therefore whether the interference was 'prescribed by law'. Or in other words, whether the *MKKP could be expected to anticipate under the law that publishing an application for sharing anonymous images would breach the Electoral Procedure Act.*[21] The Grand Chamber stated in this regard that neither the National Election Commission nor the Curia of Hungary agreed on the relevant principles.[22]

The ECtHR believes that a situation requiring judicial interpretation of legally enacted standards would not necessarily violate the requirement that the law be framed in sufficiently specific terms. The fact remains, however, that the domestic regulatory structure used in this case allowed for a case-by-case restriction of voting-related expressive behavior, giving electoral bodies and domestic courts broad latitude in interpreting and applying the rules.[23] In light of this, the Grand Chamber concluded that the legislation gave electoral bodies an especially broad margin of discretion in interpreting the legal obligation of good faith and proper exercise of rights. Simultaneously, predictability is particularly relevant when the state limits a political party's activity in connection with an election or referendum.[24]

The decision was accompanied by a dissenting opinion from Russian Judge Dimitry Dedov, who believes that an application that encourages the casting of an

19 Id. para. 96.
20 Id. para. 93.
21 Id. para. 102.
22 Id. paras. 105-107.
23 Id. para. 111.
24 Id. paras. 113-114.

doi: 10.5553/HYIEL/266627012021009001024

invalid vote is an act of contempt for the referendum. According to the judge, the applicant should have predicted the authorities' reaction in this case.

3. Comments

The central question in this case is whether the MKKP knew or should have known that its actions would violate the existing electoral rules in the absence of a binding provision of domestic legislation explicitly regulating the taking of ballot photographs and anonymously uploading those photographs to a mobile application for dissemination while voting was in progress.

The current case *was the first where national authorities applied the concept of the fair exercise of the right to photograph and share ballot papers*. Although the interpretation of the law was predictable in and of itself, the predictability of the law is especially relevant when a political party's freedom of speech is limited during elections or referendums, according to the ECtHR.

The Grand Chamber used this opportunity to directly incorporate two innovative elements presented by this case into the ECtHR's case-law: *(i) the publishing of ballot images*, and *(ii) the operation of a smartphone application* allowing voters to upload a picture of their invalid ballot papers. Indeed, the ECtHR confirmed that a photograph of a ballot paper comes under the freedom of expression protection related to photograph publishing.[25]

The ECtHR made it clear that the fact that this case happened during election season and involved a political party played a significant role in the decision. While these clarifications seem helpful, it is unfortunate that the Grand Chamber failed to mention that political parties that operate a mobile application *are not only protected by freedom of speech, but also have a duty to ensure that contact through the mobile application is respectful towards the referendums*, which are important democratic mechanisms. Given that this was the ECtHR's first time dealing with this type of problem, a more balanced general approach would have been preferable. The Grand Chamber described the incitement to vote as invalid, and the questioning of the seriousness of the referendum as an expression of opinion,.

Following this judgment, it's unclear whether the Grand Chamber would have reached a different conclusion if the foreseeability of the legal basis limiting a political party's freedom of speech had not been a primary concern. Indeed, had the case not been about elections or had the applicable provisions been more elaborate, the duties of the mobile application would have been set forth in more detail in the reasoning judgment.

The ECtHR ruled that a judicial interpretation of a law does not inherently violate the requirement that laws be written in such a way that the legal implications are predictable. However, since the national law in this case provided for a case-by-case restriction on the expression of an opinion on voting, the

25 The Grand Chamber cited *Von Hannover v Germany (No. 2.) (GC)*, No. 40660/08 and 60641/08, 7 February 2012, para. 103; and *Ashby Donald and others v France*, No. 36769/08, 10 January 2013, para. 34. *See* Id. para. 86.

electoral bodies and national courts that interpreted and enforced it had an excessive amount of discretion. The ECtHR claims that differing interpretations of the Electoral Procedure Act, as well as national authorities' and courts' exclusive interpretation powers have increased the threat to freedom of speech. Unfortunately, it impossible to draw far-reaching conclusions from the ECtHR's judgment for future cases, as a really specific decision was made here. Therefore, we do not know how to classify a mobile application with other functions or photos taken in different contexts in polling booths.

As the dissenting opinion points out, the case also highlights concerns surrounding political campaigns on election day, with the goal of actively influencing voter opinion, as well as potential disdain for the democratic institution of a referendum through the use of invalid votes. As Judge Dedov wrote

> "the MKKP sought to influence voters to invalidate their ballot papers. This is not a case about punishment for taking ballot photographs, [...] it is a case about showing disrespect for the democratic decision-making process."[26]

I have to agree with the above, because the essence of the matter was not the issue of taking photographs of ballot papers, but the assessment of whether democratic processes where influenced this way. Unfortunately, however, the Grand Chamber judgment did not deal with this issue in sufficient detail, which, in my opinion, leaves an important question unanswered. The issue of respect for democratic institutions merits more rigorous consideration.

The consequence of the case was *a proposed amendment to the Hungarian Electoral Procedure Act*, which would have allowed the taking of a 'private' image of a ballot paper without compromising the secrecy of the ballot. According to the explanation attached to the statute, the amendment was required as a result of this decision, which specified that taking a private picture of the ballot paper does not breach the vote's secrecy. In the end, this proposal *was removed from the final text of the amendment* to the law, but still, it should be noted that no such conclusion can be drawn from the ECtHR judgment. In connection with the amendment, facilitating vote buying was also raised as a counter-argument, however, when someone waives the secrecy of their vote, this does not violate the principle of secret ballot. The State must ensure the conditions under which the vote can be cast secretly. Based on this, *e.g.* the polling station or the envelope guarantees the principle of secrecy, but their use by voters is not obligatory.[27] Under the current regulations it is possible to take a photograph of the ballot paper for one's own personal use. However, if anyone gives compensation for this vote, it violates the purity of the election.

In conclusion, the judgment further clarifies the ECtHR's case-law on predictability. It points out that legislation restricting freedom of expression

26 Id. Dissenting opinion of Judge Dedov, para. 10.

27 Gábor Kurunczi, 'A választójog', *in* László Trócsányi *et al.* (eds.), *Bevezetés az alkotmányjogba – Az Alaptörvény és Magyarország alkotmányos intézményei*, HVG-ORAC, Budapest, 2019, p. 167.

doi: 10.5553/HYIEL/266627012021009001024

must be treated more strictly in connection with electoral procedures, stating that it must not be in any way misleading or controversial. In the present case, the ECtHR also pointed out that there was a difference of opinion even between the judicial forums within a Member State, so that it is clear that the rules restricting freedom of expression are not entirely clear. *The conclusion of the Grand Chamber* is surely to be welcomed, as it reaffirms the notion that *political speech can only be restricted within a very narrow range*.

doi: 10.5553/HYIEL/266627012021009001024

CONFERENCE REPORTS

Conference on the Bindingness of EU Soft Law

Report on the 'Conference on the Bindingness of EU Soft Law' Organized by Pázmány Péter Catholic University, 9 April 2021, Budapest[*]

Vivien Köböl-Benda[**]

Abstract

The online 'Conference on the bindingness of EU soft law' was organized by the Ereky Public Law Research Center at Pázmány Péter Catholic University (Hungary), the Universidad de Castilla-La Mancha (Spain), and the Portsmouth Law School (United Kingdom) on 9 April 2021. The presentations described EU soft law instruments' legal effect on EU institutions and the Member States. The soft law instruments of different policy fields were also examined, including the analysis of the language of EU soft law.

Keywords: conference report, soft law, Pázmány Péter Catholic University, bindingness, Grimaldi.

There is no doubt about the existence of soft law norms in international law, especially in particular fields like environmental law. Nevertheless, the legal status, potential normativity and added value of these non-binding instruments are widely disputed. Some authors criticize these tools referring to a danger of relativizing normativity,[1] which process can lead to the destabilization of the international legal system.[2] However, others focus on the advantages offered by soft law norms, such as their flexibility and suitability in regulating uncertain and rapidly changing situations. Moreover, legally non-binding tools may facilitate agreement between international actors, especially those states whose

* The preparation of this conference report was supported by the ÚNKP-20-3-II-PPKE-34 New National Excellence Program of the Ministry for Innovation and Technology from the Source of the National Research, Development and Innovation Fund.

** Vivien Köböl-Benda: PhD student, Pázmány Péter Catholic University, Budapest.

1 About the danger of the so-called 'relative normativity', *see* Prosper Weil, 'Towards Relative Normativity in International Law?', *The American Journal of International Law*, Vol. 77, Issue 3, 1983, pp. 413-442.

2 The soft law instruments' negative or harmful effect on the legal certainty is a frequent argument against the use of these tools. *See e.g.* László Blutman, 'In the Trap of a Legal Metaphor: International Soft Law', *International and Comparative Law Quarterly*, Vol. 59, Issue 3, 2010, pp. 605-624.

doi: 10.5553/HYIEL/266627012021009001025

sovereignty could be affected by the agreement.[3] Sometimes it is argued that these instruments have an inherited legal potential, and they are interim steps between hard law norms and legally non-binding political statements.[4]

While soft law is a timely and popular topic of international law, the use of soft law norms in the EU is also emerging and on the one hand, shows similarities with the features of international soft law, on the other hand, it can be concluded that the EU's soft law displays it owns trends and characteristics. All this was reflected in the presentations of the 'Conference on the bindingness of EU soft law'. The online conference was organized by the Ereky Public Law Research Center of the Pázmány Péter Catholic University (Hungary), the Universidad de Castilla-La Mancha (Spain), and the Portsmouth Law School (the UK) on 9 April 2021.

The increasing use of EU soft law is undeniable and according to soft law literature, may be categorized based on its different functions. According to this system, EU soft law norms can be considered as tools of providing information ('pre-law'); as interpretative instruments ('law-plus'), or as orientating norms ('para-law').[5] The conference sought to take a step further in the investigation of EU soft law: it raised the issue of the potential bindingness of the EU soft law norm and also identifies the different forms of legal effects. Takis Tridimas[6] stated in his keynote speech that the concept of bindingness is relative in the light of several aspects. For instance, the CJEU only considers bindingness in a formal normative sense, without taking into account the societal context, the norm's impact on behavior. This approach is restricted, since it defines bindingness by referring to specific process requirements, such as jurisdiction, causes of action, or remedies. Rejecting the use of a binary concept, Tridimas suggests considering bindingness as a continuum. This approach leads to a categorization system with four elements: soft law proper; hard soft law (*e.g.* recommendations, guidelines); soft hard law (*e.g.* Charter principles); hard law.

Using only the binary concept and contrasting hard law and soft law, without taking into consideration the different (sometimes even legal) effects of soft law, or the interaction and co-existence between the norms is outdated. This concept is increasingly recognized in EU soft law research and adapting this non-binary approach could also be advantageous in international law research. Wolfgang

3 About the advantages of the international soft law, *see e.g.* Kenneth W. Abbott & Duncan Snidal, 'Hard and Soft Law in International Governance', *International Organization*, Vol. 54, Issue 3, 2000, pp. 421-456.

4 *See e.g.* Andrew T. Guzman & Timothy L. Meyer, 'International Soft Law', *Journal of Legal Analysis*, Vol. 2, Issue 1, 2010, pp. 171-225.

5 This categorization is used by several authors, *e.g.* Petra Lea Láncos, 'Az uniós soft law kutatásának főbb eredményei és aktuális kihívásai', *Iustum Aequum Salutare*, Vol. 14, Issue 4, 2018, pp. 55-68; Emilia Korkea-Aho, 'EU Soft Law in Domestic Legal Systems: Flexibility and Diversity Guaranteed?' *Maastricht Journal of European and Comparative Law*, Vol. 16, Issue 3, 2009, pp. 158-161; Linda A. J. Senden, 'Soft Law and Its Implications for Institutional Balance in the EC', *Utrecht Law Review*, Vol. 1, Issue 2, 2005, pp. 79-99.

6 Title of the presentation: "The evolution of EU soft law".

doi: 10.5553/HYIEL/266627012021009001025

Weiß[7] analyzed EU soft law as an increasingly significant governance tool that may improve the implementation and enforcement of EU law at different levels: at the supranational level of the EU (implemented by EU institutions)and at the domestic level (implemented by national authorities). Soft law is present in all phases of regulation and implementation, serving as a tool to prepare legislation or as an instrument of interpretation, and it can help the implementation of other norms. At the domestic level, soft law can promote uniform and consistent implementation of EU law. According to the speaker, these considerations highlight the link between bindingness and legal effect because the different levels or the type of competence can affect the degree of the bindingness. The various degrees of bindingness can come from the different functions of soft law measures, as it was demonstrated by Luis Arroyo.[8] Legal effect may arise in four ways. *(i)* One is in soft law's interpretative function, which can also have genuine legal effect, *e.g.* if it defines the scope of interpretation. Besides serving as an ordinary interpretative tool, it can have a qualified effect, *e.g.* when authorities must consider the soft law norm in the course of their interpretation. *(ii)* Secondly, soft law can trigger subsequent annulment for instance, if its content is incorporated into hard law or recognized by the CJEU or in case of the above mentioned situations where authorities must take soft law take into account. *(iii)* Thirdly, in certain scenarios, soft law can be linked to compensation, *e.g.* in case of an infringement of legitimate expectations. *(iv)* Finally, even if it lacks legally binding force, soft law may have an internal punitive effect, *e.g.* in the field of administration, in the context of the principle of hierarchy.

Legal effect and bindingness are not only graduated but demonstrate a special dynamic characteristic as well. Law is traditionally aimed at regulating social relations, Napoleon Xanthoulis emphasized, referring to concepts developed by Sigmund Freud.[9] In this concept, the law represses desires and exists because of this repression at the same time, which indicates that law was mandatory from the very beginning of human civilization. However, this situation has changed, and regulation is much subtler today, giving rise to hybrid modes of governance and regulation. An example for such a hybrid model is the EU's structure and its instruments which can cause direct but indirect legal effects too. Thus, legal effect shall not be considered a static and one-dimensional phenomenon, because it can flow through multiple acts, *e.g.* a soft law act as a recommendation can trigger the legal effect of another provision, *e.g.* acts of national authorities. So, at the time of the adoption of a certain act, its potential legal effect cannot be predicted. Addressing this dynamic approach can have the benefit of measuring the actual effect of soft law, by taking into account its function and effect.

Besides dealing with the concept of bindingness and its graduation, several speakers identified main areas where EU soft law is dominant, illustrating the

7 Title of the presentation: "Reconsidering the legal effect of EU soft law in national implementation: Bindingness by private response?".

8 Title of the presentation: "Beyond bindingness: a typology of soft law legal effects".

9 Title of the presentation: "From soft law to bindingness".

doi: 10.5553/HYIEL/266627012021009001025

theoretical approaches with practical examples of soft law instruments. However, it must be highlighted that the speakers also revealed possible problems relating to the use of soft law in particular fields and proposed solutions as well. One of these fields is the area of state aid, where soft law acts, such as guidelines, recommendations, communications, notices are abundant and show particular legal effects in two ways, as Verena Rosic[10] explained. These soft law instruments can have a legal effect through enforcement, *e.g.* when the European Commission's decision is based on soft law. Moreover, they have legal effect, if the Member States voluntarily follow them to avoid the negative consequences. The second area is environmental protection, where, according to Verena Rosic, soft law can also have normative importance, in an informative and preparatory manner or a steering manner. The former includes the promotion of negotiations or the enhancement of better implementation, while the latter can provide practical help in implementation, especially in the case of framework measures, which are common in EU environmental protection. The third and perhaps most challenging areas is public health, in particular during the current COVID-19 pandemic.

Corina Andone and Florin Coman-Kund[11] drew attention to the emerging use of soft law instruments (mostly adopted by the Commission) enacted in an attempt to deal with the pandemic. It involved the 'hardening' of some soft law instruments, which causes legitimacy problems, the potential imbalance between its adoption form, namely, that while the norm is adopted as soft law, its actual substance may be driven by the intention of 'hardening'. In fact, this can exacerbate legal uncertainty and institutional imbalance. However, soft law measures are designed to provide quick answers to rapidly changing situations and benefit voluntary coordination. Oana Stefan[12] also analyzed soft law instruments adopted in response to the COVID-19 pandemic and specifies further fields where they can have a significant impact, such as the area of state aid and antitrust law, the use of technology in the fight against the pandemic, or the background of safe re-opening. She also recalled that soft law tools are used by the Commission during a crisis, such as the financial crisis or the H1N1 pandemic.

The fourth area discussed was the field of the EU telecommunication law. Emanuel Kollman[13] pointed out that while the regulatory framework is defined by EU law, implementation is carried out by independent National Regulatory Agencies (NRAs). This raises the challenge of harmonization; therefore, the Commission adopts soft law instruments, recommendations, guidelines, or notices. Finally, Robert Böttner[14] discussed the financial market supervision,

10 Title of the presentation: "EU soft law: Validity, normativity and "bindingness" reviewed".

11 Title of the presentation: "Persuasive rather than 'binding' EU soft law? An argumentative perspective on the European Commission's soft law instruments in times of crisis".

12 Title of the presentation: "EU soft law in the time of coronavirus".

13 Title of the presentation: "Hard Rules for Soft Law. The case of European Union telecommunications law".

14 Title of the presentation: "The comply-or-explain mechanism in the European Supervisory Authorities, or: Does Meroni allow nudging?".

doi: 10.5553/HYIEL/266627012021009001025

where four agencies[15] issue guidelines and recommendations. There is a particular mechanism, the so-called 'comply or explain' mechanism, which is linked to these instruments, based on related funding regulations. This mechanism entails that the national authorities should aim to comply with the documents or if they don't, they must give reasons to the supervisory authority concerned. Moreover, 'naming and shaming' may also arise if they do not comply, since agencies make public their findings public.

The blurring lines as illustrated by the above-mentioned examples require the application of interdisciplinary research methods, such as combining legal and linguistic research methods. Namely, the language of norms says a great deal about their legal nature. Regarding the Commission's soft law COVID-specific recommendations and guidelines, Corina Andone and Florin Coman-Kund pointed out that their language is similar to that of hard law, and they outlined four argumentative aspects,[16] of which the proper design is related to language. According to this, the soft law instruments' language should be in accordance with their legal nature. Danai Ionescu and Mariolina Eliantonio[17] analyzed the language of the guidance documents of four directives.[18] The guidance documents of these hard law instruments are soft law at first sight. In line with that the speakers raised the question, why do national authorities aim to comply with them if they do not show legally binding traits? The answer may be found in their language, since Ionescu and Eliantonio revealed that most of the language use contained 'strong' words ('must', 'shall'), *e.g.* the definitions. This indicates strong obligations and does not provide a margin for choice. Furthermore, the examined documents also used 'moderate' language ('should'), for example, demonstrating good practices. The lowest rate is assigned to documents using 'weak' language ('can', 'could'), *e.g.* mentioning additional examples.[19] They added that sometimes strong language can be accompanied by moderate language like in the case of procedural recommendations. This means alternative (moral, social, or political) types of bindingness, that can be as strong as legal bindingness, and these blurring lines could raise legitimacy concerns and democratic problems. Eljalill Tauschinsky and Petra Láncos[20] applied a computer-based technique to cluster the language of directive-like recommendations (DLRs) in English, German and Spanish language. The DLRs are formally soft law instruments but they are worded as directives, which are hard law norms. Their research divided the non-

15 The European Banking Authority (EBA); the European Securities and Markets Authority (ESMA); the European Insurance and Occupational Pensions Authority (EIOPA); the European Systemic Risk Board (ESRB) – together the European System of Financial Supervision.

16 Content; design; effectiveness; and soundness.

17 Title of the presentation: "Words Are Stones: Constructing Bindingness Through Language in EU Environmental Soft Law".

18 The Environmental Impact Assessment (EIA) Directive (85/337/EEC); the Strategic Environmental Assessment (SEA) Directive (2001/42/EC); the Habitats Directive (92/43/EEC); and the Birds Directive (2009/147/EC).

19 According to the speakers' presentation the overall results of the 26 guidances' and over 4500 statements' analysis was the following: strong: 48%; moderate: 31%; weak: 21%.

20 Title of the presentation: "Verbal markers of 'softness' in EU law? A computer-based analysis to delimit soft law and hard law focusing on directive-like recommendations".

doi: 10.5553/HYIEL/266627012021009001025

lemmatized and lemmatized[21] results; the non-lemmatized version is important because the hortatory or mandatory forms of a word can be manifested in various forms. The non-lemmatized results showed that DLRs use directive-like terms ('shall', 'ensure', 'shall apply') and weaker terms such as 'invite' and 'encourage'. While the non-lemmatized versions provided more or less identical same results in the three language versions analyzed, the lemmatized results revealed differences, in particular in English. In light of the language-focused presentation, it can be concluded that this kind of analysis is essential to examine specific soft law instruments that use strong or moderate words and terms that are normally typical of hard law. However, the several versions in line with the EU's official language can be a challenge in such research.

Finally, one of the most interesting aspects of EU soft law is the position of the CJEU. We know that the CJEU refrains from using the term soft law, but the essence of the relevant case-law is decisive. Wolfgang Weiß recalled *Grimaldi*,[22] where the CJEU observed that national courts must take into account EU soft law. However, the CJEU's approach is not unequivocal because in the most recent cases, *e.g.* in *Expedia*[23] the CJEU stated that the Member State's national authorities are not legally required to do this. Takis Tridimas illustrated the issue of uncertainty by referring to the source of authority in *Chyrsostomides*,[24] in which the CJEU declared that the Euro Group is not an EU body, and it does not possess the power of decision-making and its decisions are not subject of review and cannot give rise to EU liability. Tridimas underlined, while the Treaties did not establish the Euro Group, Protocol No. 14[25] requires that certain tasks be carried out by the Euro Group, which may be a point of conflict. Verena Rosic added that in the area of environmental protection, the framework norms' implementation is supported by the Commission's guidance. Sometimes the interpretation of hard law can lead to different results. In these cases, the Commission's guidance has priority and even the CJEU takes them into consideration.

In conclusion, the presentations took a step beyond the binary concept of soft law and hard law, putting the focus on the legal effect in the context of the several functions of EU soft law instruments. The conference's main merit was the illustration of the function and specific legal effect of these instruments in certain areas of EU law, such as the field of state aid, environmental protection, telecommunications law, the European System of Financial Supervision, and public health, in particular during the COVID-19 pandemic. The presentations also drew attention to the blurring lines between hard and soft law and presented legal and linguistic analyses, drawing attention to the fact that the context and wording of these documents can be decisive in eliciting legal effect. The

21 Lemmatizing means reducing a word's different forms and after this use one single form.

22 Judgment of 13 December 1989, *Case C-322/88, Grimaldi*, ECLI:EU:C:1989:646.

23 Judgment of 13 December 2012, *Case C-226/11, Expedia*, ECLI:EU:C:2012:795.

24 Judgment of 16 December 2020, *Joined Cases C-597/18 P, C-598/18 P, C-603/18 P, and C-604/18 P, Council v Chrysostomides & Co. and others, Council v Bourdouvali and others, Chrysostomides & Co. and others v Council, Bourdoouvali and others v Council*, ECLI:EU:C:2020:1028.

25 *See* Protocol No. 14 on the Euro Group.

doi: 10.5553/HYIEL/266627012021009001025

conference also mentioned the CJEU's (not fully unequivocal) approach to EU soft law. The presentations also revealed that the Commission is likely to use soft law instruments, for example where the hard law is only framework-like, or in the course of harmonization or in the field of crisis management. The speakers also highlighted the possible dangers and issues of the hardening tendency of EU soft law. Finally, they also identified the further areas of research. The main findings of the conference are not only significant for EU law, for overcoming the outdated binary approach may be beneficial in international law as well.

Hungarian Yearbook of International Law and European Law 2021 (9) 1
doi: 10.5553/HYIEL/266627012021009001025

Marie-Claire Cordonier Segger et al. (eds.), Intergenerational Justice in Sustainable Development Treaty Implementation. Advancing Future Generations Rights Through National Institutions (Book Review)

Cambridge University Press, Cambridge, 2021, 870 p, ISBN 978-1-10848-802-0[*]

Tejas Rao[**]

> *"Carbon emissions to the atmosphere, pollution of the water resources, testing of nuclear weapons, surreptitious disposal of nuclear waste, deforestation, endangering of fauna and flora, uncontrolled disposal of industrial waste and depletion of the Earth's resources are proceeding at an ever-increasing rate. This is regardless of the fact that the damage already done has been so great that it has even caused significant climate change in our time, which will increase exponentially if preventive action is not taken immediately. If such operations are continued even at the present rate, the environment will, in the next decade or two, have deteriorated to levels which will not be able to support the global population as we now know it."*[1]

In his afterword to this volume, H.E. Justice C.G. Weeramantry, a standard-bearer for the clarion call to action in sustainable development and intergenerational justice, speaks to the urgency of the environmental problem we face on our blue and green planet. Justice Weeramantry's legacy is best reflected by this Afterword. As his final piece of writing published posthumously, it draws the attention of the reader to the central issue this volume seeks to tackle. In short, this volume seeks to ascertain how the lives and identities of future

* The author wishes to thank the JN Tata Endowment for the Higher Education of Indians and the ERM Group of Companies (India), without whose support the opportunity to review this book would not have arisen.

** Tejas Rao, B.A., LL.B. (Hons.), LL.M. (Cantab.), associate fellow, Centre for International Sustainable Development Law (CISDL), Montreal, Canada.

1 Marie-Claire Cordonier Segger *et al.* (eds.), *Intergenerational Justice in Sustainable Development Treaty Implementation. Advancing Future Generations Rights Through National Institutions*, Cambridge University Press, Cambridge, 2021, p. 793.

doi: 10.5553/HYIEL/266627012021009001026

generations will be impacted by the place given to intergenerational equity in law and policy.[2]

In linguistics, studies have investigated whether the academic community is using the right language: calling it climate change, and not a climate crisis.[3] The question this debate asks is if the vocabulary we use is enough to explain the urgency with which these issues need consideration, and solutions. It seeks to investigate if the current definitional force given to the environmental challenge is adequate to prepare the present generation for the suffering and harm that is likely to inflict upon future generations if the *status quo* continues.

Despite my own optimism, in reading this volume, published in the series *Treaty Implementation for Sustainable Development*, it was this debate that played out in the background. This series of books addresses this need and provides a serious contribution to ongoing global debates by conducting a detailed analysis of how myriad new treaty regimes that cover the future's most pressing concerns can be made to work in practice.[4] Admittedly, this is a lofty ambition. Previous volumes have tackled this challenge by focusing on specific regimes, for example, the Cartagena Protocol,[5] International Aviation[6] and International Criminal Justice.[7] However, the most recent editions have seen a turn in the series, with a view to the future, with one volume on children's rights and sustainable development,[8] and now, this seminal volume on intergenerational justice.

This volume in particular, surveys current commitments to sustainable development, analyzing innovative policies, practices and procedures to promote respect for intergenerational justice. Expert contributors provide serious scholarly and practical discussions of the theoretical, institutional and legal considerations inherent in intergenerational justice on the local, national, regional and global scale. They investigate treaty commitments related to intergenerational equity, explore linkages between regimes, and offer insights from diverse experiences of national future generations' institutions.

Conducting a study utilizing this approach is not new for any of the editors of the volume. In both theory and practice, each of them embody the spirit that the intergenerational perspective necessitates. A survey of their accomplishments and academic positions evidence this.

Professor Cordonier Segger is the Leverhulme Visiting Professor at the University of Cambridge, and Full Professor of Law at the University of Waterloo,

2 Id. p. 15.

3 Larissa Jaskulsky & Richard Besel, 'Words That (Don't) Matter: An Exploratory Study of Four Climate Change Names in Environmental Discourse', *Applied Environmental Education & Communication*, Vol. 12, Issue 1, 2013, pp. 38-45.

4 Cordonier Segger *et al.* (eds.) 2021, p. iii.

5 Marie-Claire Cordonier Segger *et al.* (eds.), *Legal Aspects of Implementing the Cartagena Protocol on Biosafety*, Cambridge University Press, Cambridge, 2014.

6 Armand L.C. de Mestral *et al.* (eds.), *Sustainable Development, International Aviation, and Treaty Implementation*, Cambridge University Press, Cambridge, 2018.

7 Sébastien Jodoin & Marie-Claire Cordonier Segger (eds.), *Sustainable Development, International Criminal Justice, and Treaty Implementation*, Cambridge University Press, Cambridge, 2013.

8 Claire Fenton-Glynn (ed.), *Children's Rights and Sustainable Development. Interpreting the UNCRC for Future Generations*, Cambridge University Press, Cambridge, 2019.

doi: 10.5553/HYIEL/266627012021009001026

Canada. She is also laureate of the 2020 H.E. Judge C. G. Weeramantry International Justice Award and advises countries and international organizations on treaty commitments on climate change, biodiversity, trade, investment and other Sustainable Development Goals. Professor Szabó is a Full Professor at Pázmány Péter Catholic University in Budapest, and since 2016, also serves as Justice at the Constitutional Court of Hungary. In addition, between 2012 and 2016, he was the Deputy Commissioner for Fundamental Rights and Ombudsman for Future Generations in Hungary. Together with Professor Cordonier Segger, he sits on the International Commission for the unique UNESCO-Voices of Future Generations project, which aims to empower children's voices in shaping their futures. Professor Harrington is the Fulbright Canada Research Chair in Global Governance at the Balsillie School of International Affairs in Waterloo, Canada, and has written extensively on the interpretation of sustainable development goals. With the numerous contributing authors, they use their expertise to offer insight from their experiences and paint a holistic picture of what intergenerational justice in alignment with the sustainable development goals should look like. All three editors of this volume are leaders at the Centre for International Sustainable Development Law (CISDL), an independent international legal research institute integrating environment, human rights and economy through legal scholarship and empowerment.

This experience is perceptible in the introductory text of the volume, which provides the reader with the lens through which to look at the chapters that follow. The editors say,

> "The implementation of intergenerational equity and justice commitments is complex, not least owing to the abstract nature of the State obligations laid down in treaty law, but also because of the multiplicity of areas which intergenerational justice touches upon, ranging from environmental, social and economic sustainability to questions of demographical trends, public participation, fiduciary duties and the contours of a common heritage for humanity."[9]

From this premise, the promise of the volume emerges. To the reader, it offers a sweeping, cross-cutting, multidisciplinary look at what intergenerational justice means in substance. Here, the structure of the volume deserves much commendation. Instead of delving straight into these interdisciplinary challenges, the volume first paints a picture of what obligations exist upon the State under the *lex lata*, using the extensive experience of the Hungarian Ombudsman for Future Generations as a principal case-study. Once this is outlined, the volume proceeds to examine challenges, before proceeding to specific law, policy, and economic innovations necessary to achieve intergenerational justice. The future trends highlighted provide four useful frameworks by which to examine whether progress is made in achieving intergenerational equity – with two pressing sustainable development challenges: climate change and access to water, and two

9 Cordonier Segger *et al.* (eds.) 2021, p. 3.

doi: 10.5553/HYIEL/266627012021009001026

conceptual frameworks, both of which have merit, and call for an adaptation of how law is made today.

What is also particularly appreciable, and is a novel contribution to existing literature, is how comparative insight is offered: it is not exclusively focused on the Global North, but provides space, in particular, for the rights of indigenous peoples, written by authors belonging to the indigenous community. This is particularly of relevance as critical international legal studies are gaining a prominent place in scholarship and offering perspectives from these groups leading to contextual learning. Given geographical, cultural, social, political, economic variance, it is impossible to transplant solutions (especially ones that call for innovation of this kind) from region to region. This volume makes that apparent. Moreover, the national case-studies are not theoretical, but linked to the realpolitik. In choosing to focus on national institutions, contributing authors had the opportunity to present the challenges they face and see in the field.

It is perhaps this, then, that is my only bone of contention with the volume and presents its one drawback. Despite the wealth of viewpoints on display, it does not present perspectives from two of the most highly populated countries in the world: China, and India. The chapter on lessons from Asia seeks to offer some comparison, but does not account adequately, in this reader's view, for the systemic economic differences that exist across the continent – which invariably, presents unique challenges to each of these countries for the future. Even if these were not included, it would have been relevant for the book to examine how population explosion and the resource crunch links to issues of intergenerational equity, a debate to which passing references are made throughout, but no explicit link is drawn.

This is, however, a minor flaw. In its contribution to existing literature on intergenerational justice, it is unparalleled, and sets the stage for a conversation that cries out for more ears. As a young lawyer and international law researcher, it has, in many ways, revealed to me, the promise of public international law, which detractors seem to confine to its limits. It has reinvigorated my sense of purpose in advocating for advancing the sustainable development goals, while being cognizant of the critiques that exist about its limitations. All in all, I have no hesitation in recommending that this book be read by as many people as it can reach from young students trying to decide the causes they want to champion, to established lawyers working in private law, there are takeaways for everybody. It becomes clear at the conclusion of the volume that this is an effort that calls upon every member of the community. Borrowing from Jona David and Tyra Sioni, UNESCO Voices of Future Generations Child Authors and Trust for Sustainable Living Medallists,

> "For a real chance of global sustainability and justice, we need present generations of leaders, experts, and practitioners to make a deep commitment to help transform all the inefficient, wasteful, destructive systems by which we currently live."[10]

10 Id. p. xxxvii.

doi: 10.5553/HYIEL/266627012021009001026

With increased confidence, I can now say that the linguists were right – we do not, in our every day communication of the climate crisis or the development challenge, use the right vocabulary to convey the devastating impact natural and man-made events are having on livelihoods. This volume gives us a chance to use a new wealth and depth of vocabulary to confront the challenge head-on and so, with optimism, I look forward to the conversations and action that will surround actors who seek to engage with its mission.

doi: 10.5553/HYIEL/266627012021009001026

Viktor Luszcz, European Court Procedure: A Practical Guide (Book Review)

Bloomsbury-Hart, Oxford, 2020, 730 p, ISBN 978-1-50990-091-6

Petra Lea Láncos[*]

The lead author of the book, Viktor Luszcz is attorney at law and partner at Danubia Legal – Luszcz Law Firm. He is Vice President of the European Patent Office's Board of Appeal, former President of the Hungarian Intellectual Property Office and former *référendaire* of the CJEU. Viktor Luszcz and his co-authors Martin Farley, Viktor Bottka, Alexandre Geulette, Vivien Terrien and Milan Kristof have a combined experience of 70 years working as *référendaires* at the EU Courts or as officials of the European Commission Legal Service. The book, *European Court Procedure: A Practical Guide* published by Hart is a gap-filling and comprehensive work, indispensable for anyone interested in litigation before the CJEU.

The book is structured into five parts. Part 1 is an introduction to the enforcement of EU law and the judicial system of the EU, such as the CJEU's powers and organizational structure, the Courts' main formations, governing principles and the specific roles of the staff and members of the Courts. Part 2 discusses the enforcement of EU law against Member States and private parties through infringement proceedings and claims before national courts based on EU law. In addition, preliminary rulings are also discussed as avenues to determine the correct interpretation of EU law in the context of national judicial proceedings. Remedies against EU acts are presented in Part 3, including actions for annulment, failure to act, damages and other procedures. Part 4 provides an overview of the procedure before the Court of Justice and General Court, introducing their relevant rules of procedure, the applicable case-law on procedural issues and the elements of applications. Finally, Part 5 covers 'Incidental and Ancillary Procedural Issues', such as obtaining documents held by EU institutions to build the case, the treatment of evidence and confidential information, seeking interim relief and useful information on the important subject of interventions, among others.

A comprehensive work on EU court practice, the book provides important clarifications and definitions for EU procedural law concepts, while also bringing examples from CJEU practice to illustrate notions and procedural exigencies. Requirements concerning admissibility and standing are clearly laid out in respect of the different procedures, helping legal practitioners make sense of the applicable rules of procedure and the relevant case-law to bring successful actions.

* Petra Lea Láncos: associate professor of law, Pázmány Péter Catholic University, Budapest.

doi: 10.5553/HYIEL/266627012021009001027

Perhaps the most exciting part of the book is the subchapter on 'How to Construct Pleas in Law?', which promises "a simple and efficient method of drafting pleas in law",[1] proposing a clear structure and the following of certain substantive drafting requirements. In particular, this subchapter repeatedly refers back to the fact that submissions will be translated into French (the working language of the EU Courts). Indeed, this element of multilingualism may be foreign to attorneys or even referring national courts used to the typically monolingual context of domestic proceedings. Instead, they must contend with the issue of not only presenting their pleadings or questions in a comprehensible form in their own language but employ certain strategies to ensure that their submission will be properly translated and then considered in another language. In fact, as the authors imply, a part of the responsibility for the clarity of pleadings in the target language lies with the drafter of the submission in the original language. The authors therefore encourage the use of proper and precise terminology in the pleadings. This means that to the degree possible, the terms of EU legislation and case-law should be applied, since these already have their multilingual equivalences in the EU terminological databases (*e.g.* the CuriaTerm developed by the lawyer-linguists of the Directorate-General for Multilingualism and the terminologists from the Projects and Terminological Coordination Unit of the CJEU; the database has now been migrated to IATE, the EU's standardized terminology database). Besides suggesting that applications be kept brief (allowing for speedier translations into French and other official languages, and in turn, allowing for the Court to deal with the case swiftly), the authors encourage that the wording of the briefs be as clear and concise as possible. They encourage the use of short, straightforward sentences, avoiding synonyms and explaining any and all technical terms that are specific to the national legal system in order to forego confusion or mistranslations. Yet, as clearly set forth in the case-law: in the balancing act between clarity, brevity and elaborateness,

> "it is for the applicant and its lawyer to set out the factual and legal grounds on which the action is based and not for the Court to do their work by trying to locate and identify, from all the evidence to which the application makes general reference, the information which may support the claims formulated in the application."[2]

The book, long time coming, is highly topical, bringing the reader up to date on the latest developments in EU court procedure: it integrates not only the General Court's 2015 Rules of Procedure, but also the new Practice Rules of the General Court of 2018, as well as the most recent CJEU Practice Directions of the 2020. As Judge Marc van der Woude, President of the General Court writing the foreword to the book notes: the authors

1 Viktor Luszcz, *European Court Procedure: A Practical Guide*, Hart Publishing, 2020, p. 443 *et seq*.
2 Order of 29 November 1993, *Case T-56/92, Koelman v Commission*, ECLI:EU:T:1993:105, para 23.

doi: 10.5553/HYIEL/266627012021009001027

> "have conducted a near-unrivalled work of research, based on the raw material of EU procedures that is the case-law, by analyzing thousands of decisions, with a particular focus on those adopted since the new structure governing litigation before the EU courts was adopted. More than just another theoretical study, this book really is a practical and useful tool."[3]

The book is a must have for all agents and attorneys appearing before the EU Courts, referring national judges, legal scholars and professors researching and teaching EU law and finally, law students interested in broadening their knowledge of EU litigation.

3 Luszcz 2020, p. vi.

Hungarian Yearbook of International Law and European Law 2021 (9) 1
doi: 10.5553/HYIEL/266627012021009001027

Tamás Molnár, The Interplay Between the EU's Return Acquis and International Law (Book Review)

Edward Elgar, Cheltenham, 2021, 272 p, ISBN 978-1-83910-522-7*

*Izabella Majcher***

Tamás Molnár is a legal research officer in matters concerning asylum, migration, and borders at the EU Agency for Fundamental Rights (FRA) in Vienna. He is also a visiting lecturer in international migration law at the Corvinus University of Budapest, Hungary. Molnár has widely published in the fields of international law, EU law, and statelessness law. Among the several positions he has held, he was also the head of the Migration unit, Department of EU cooperation, Ministry of the Interior of Hungary (2010-14). Additionally, he holds memberships in several organizations, such as the European Society of International Law (ESIL), the American Society of International Law (ASIL), the International Law Association (ILA) Hungarian Branch, the *Société française pour le droit international* (SFDI), the Italian Society of International Law (SIDI), the *Fédération internationale de droit européen* (FIDE), and the European Law Institute (ELI).

The book *The Interplay Between the EU's Return Acquis and International Law* is dedicated to the return (expulsion) of migrants in an irregular situation under EU law. In particular, it examines the interactions between EU and international law in the field of the return or expulsion of migrants. On the one hand, it assesses how the EU's return acquis is inspired by, and integrates, international migration and human rights law, and on the other hand, it examines how this body of EU law has shaped international law-making pertaining to the removal of non-nationals. By exploring the question of return from the perspective of interactions between the two legal orders, the book offers unique analyses and reflections.

The author first explores the relationship between EU and international law from the internal (inward-looking) perspective of the EU legal order. Does EU law in the area of return policies reflect international law? The key focus is on the EU Return Directive, which is the main EU instrument regulating return, removal, pre-removal detention, and entry ban.[1] Molnár's nuanced analysis leads him to

* The views expressed in this book review are those of the author and do not necessarily reflect the position of ECRE.

** Izabella Majcher: senior legal officer, European Council of Refugees and Exiles (ECRE), Brussels.

1 Directive 2008/115/EC of the European Parliament and of the Council of 16 December 2008 on Common Standards and Procedures in Member States for Returning Illegally Staying Third-Country Nationals.

doi: 10.5553/HYIEL/266627012021009001028

the conclusion that the EU's legislative and judiciary institutions have adopted divergent approaches to international human rights law in shaping and interpreting the Return Directive. From a legislative perspective, the text of the Return Directive makes several references to international (UN Convention on the Rights of the Child and Geneva Refugee Convention) and regional (ECHR) human rights conventions as well as standards (Council of Europe's Twenty Guidelines on Forced Return). Likewise, some international human rights norms are reflected in the text of the Directive, including the principle of *non-refoulement*, the best interests of the child, the right to family life, and adequate conditions of detention.[2] On the other hand, from a judicial perspective, the autonomy of EU law prevails. The CJEU exhibits a strong autonomy-driven approach, rarely relying on international law (including the case-law of the ECtHR) to interpret the Return Directive. However, as Molnár points out, although the CJEU has generally formally disregarded international human rights norms, it still considered some of these norms to be general principles of EU law.[3]

The Return Directive is in the process of being recast. The recast proposal presented by the European Commission in September 2018 significantly reduces safeguards for returnees.[4] Key changes include restrictions on the suspensive effect of appeal against return, additional ground justifying immigration detention, restriction on granting a so-called voluntary departure period, and additional conditions for imposing a re-entry ban.[5] If the recast is adopted, as Molnár argues, the CJEU may need to change its approach towards the interpretation of the Return Directive and begin relying on external legal standards beyond EU legislation to uphold standards and safeguards protecting returnees' rights.[6]

The second part of the analysis probes the interactions between the two normative orders from the external (outward-looking) perspective of the EU's engagement with international law. It investigates how the EU has attempted to shape the development of international law in the field of return of migrants. Molnár takes three examples of such an engagement to demonstrate variable levels of contribution by the EU. *(i)* First, in its contribution to the work of the UN International Law Commission (ILC) on the Draft Articles on the Expulsion of Aliens,[7] the EU generally adhered to its commitment to "progressively develop international law", as per Article 3(5) TEU. It sought to ensure that the ILC take the Return Directive and CJEU case-law into consideration to the extent possible.

2 Tamás Molnár, *The Interplay Between the EU's Return Acquis and International Law*, Edward Elgar, Cheltenham, 2021, pp. 88-89.

3 Id. pp. 101-103, 121, and 123.

4 European Commission, Proposal for a Directive of the European Parliament and of the Council on Common Standards and Procedures in Member States for Returning Illegally Staying Third-Country Nationals (Recast), COM(2018) 634 final.

5 For an analysis of the recast proposal, *see* Izabella Majcher & Tineke Strik, 'Legislating without Evidence: The Recast of the EU Return Directive', *European Journal of Migration and Law*, Vol. 23, Issue 2, 2021, pp. 103-126.

6 Molnár 2021, pp. 123-124.

7 International Law Commission, Draft Articles on Expulsion of Aliens, A/CN.4/L.832, 30 May 2014.

doi: 10.5553/HYIEL/266627012021009001028

While some of the EU's proposals tried to prevent the ILC Draft Articles from offering stronger protection than the level guaranteed under the Directive (*e.g.* qualification of detention of children under the same conditions as adults as cruel, inhuman or degrading treatment; or automatic suspensive effect of appeal), most EU proposals sought to strengthen protective safeguards (*e.g.* inclusion of sexual orientation as a ground for non-discrimination, limitation on grounds justifying detention, judicial review of the lawfulness of detention, consideration of the health status of the person, written return decision, or preference for voluntary departure over forced return).[8] *(ii)* Secondly, the EU's engagement in two other codification processes exhibited a conservative approach that aimed at upholding and promoting its values and interests, as per the first limb of Article 3(5) TEU. In the process of developing the Global Compact for Migration (GCM),[9] the EU's position centered on restating existing international standards and settled principles, with the aim of shielding its own migration *acquis*.[10] In particular, the EU attempted to prevent the endorsement of a ban on the detention of migrant children[11] and generally focused on the readmission commitments of destination countries at the expense of human rights safeguards in the return process.[12] A similar conservative approach was followed in the context of the Council of Europe's standard-setting activities in the area of immigration detention [see the (Draft) European Rules on the Administrative Detention of Migrants]. The EU expressed its opposition to a codification of new rules which were not yet embedded in EU law and may prejudice ongoing EU negotiations (*i.e.* the reform of the Common European Asylum System) and the future development of EU law in that field (notably the recast of the Return Directive). In a nutshell, the EU wanted to prevent EU Member States from being subject to more stringent rules on immigration detention than under EU law. Hence, it sought to maintain the status quo and block the adoption of more protective detention standards.[13] It was primarily the EU's position that caused the process of codification of pan-European immigration detention standards to be put on hold.[14]

As Molnár argues, this restrictive approach satisfies only the first limb of Article 3(5) TEU, which commits the EU in its relations with the wider world to "uphold and promote its values and interests." It has failed to live up to its commitment to "develop international law," as articulated in the second limb of the same provision. Molnár explains the conflicting approaches by reference to

8 For a more detailed account, *see* Tamás Molnár, 'EU Migration Law Shaping International Migration Law in the Field of Expulsion of Aliens: The Case of the ILC Draft Articles', *Hungarian Journal of Legal Studies*, Vol. 58, Issue 3, 2017, pp. 237-260.

9 Global Compact for Safe, Orderly and Regular Migration, A/RES/73/195, 19 December 2018.

10 Molnár 2021, pp. 191-192 and 218.

11 Izabella Majcher, 'Immigration Detention under the Global Compacts in the Light of Refugee and Human Rights Law Standards', *International Migration*, Vol. 57, Issue 6, 2019, pp. 96-97.

12 For a more detailed account, *see* Tamás Molnár, 'The EU Shaping the Global Compact for Safe, Orderly and Regular Migration: The Glass Half Full or Half Empty?', *International Journal of Law in Context*, Vol. 16, Issue 3, 2020, pp. 321-338.

13 Molnár 2021, pp. 209-211, and 218.

14 Majcher & Strik 2021, p. 126.

doi: 10.5553/HYIEL/266627012021009001028

the shift in the EU's position on the question of return following the so-called refugee crisis of 2015-2016.[15] Indeed, to deal with the "crisis," the EU focused on the number of returns at the expense of potential improvement in other areas, such as the functioning of asylum systems and the fair distribution of protection seekers across the EU Member States. The EU adopted more restrictive policy lines and soft-law guidance, culminating in the proposal for the recast of the Return Directive mentioned above. *(iii)* Finally, beyond the EU's involvement in international standard-setting processes, Molnár observes that the expanding network of EU readmission agreements and arrangements has the potential to covertly influence the treaty-making practice of other countries in the area of readmission.[16] Under the EU readmission agreements and arrangements, non-EU countries are obliged to cooperate in identification procedures and readmit their nationals or other non-nationals who transited their territory before entering the EU. Non-EU countries are encouraged to conclude similar agreements with other countries to send back non-nationals readmitted from the EU. As Molnár argues, the EU's focus on readmission cooperation has most likely influenced the treaty-making practices of non-EU countries, but it's unfeasible to gather evidence on its actual impact. A recent review of the implementation of the GCM within the region falling under the UN Economic Commission for Europe (UNECE) appears to demonstrate such an impact. One country, indicating the readmission agreements concluded with nearly all the EU Member States, stressed the challenge it faced in concluding readmission agreements with countries of origin. Further, two other countries that already have readmission agreements with the EU in place highlighted that they also have readmission agreements with other non-EU countries and are in the process of concluding more such agreements with other countries.[17] The readmission agreements do not guarantee that the recipient country will effectively admit the readmitted person to its asylum procedure, which may result in chain *refoulement* and is a prime example of the externalization of refugee protection and migration management by the EU.

In conclusion, as Molnár puts it,

> "[the] EU seeks to have an impact on international law, from which it claims normative independence (autonomy), but which simultaneously forms an integral part of its legal order [...] and which the EU is internally (constitutionally) committed to respect."[18]

15 Molnár 2021, p. 223.

16 Id. pp. 215-216, and 218.

17 Izabella Majcher, 'Implementation of GCM Objective 21 in the UNECE Region: Selective Interpretation of the Return, Readmission, and Reintegration Commitments', *Refugee Law Initiative*, 20 May 2021, at https://rli.blogs.sas.ac.uk/2021/05/20/implementation-of-gcm-objective-21-in-the-unece-region-selective-interpretation-of-the-return-readmission-and-reintegration-commitments/.

18 Molnár 2021, p. 223.

Hungarian Yearbook of International Law and European Law 2021 (9) 1
doi: 10.5553/HYIEL/266627012021009001028

By exploring the question of return from the perspective of a multifaceted relationship between EU and international law, the book proves to be a unique contribution to the existing literature in the field. It enriches the literature devoted to both the EU and international legal orders. From the EU law perspective, it has the potential to influence a broader debate about the place of the EU within the international legal order by offering significant insights into this field from both a constitutional perspective and the point of view of the substantive area of migration law. The book will be a useful read for legal scholars and practitioners, as well as postgraduate students who wish to deepen their understanding of the links between these two legal orders. It will also be instructive for academics and lawyers dealing with the expulsion of migrants in an irregular situation. This book is timely and relevant as the negotiations on the recast Return Directive are ongoing and an overriding objective of the EU's new Pact on Migration and Asylum[19] is to increase the number of returns. In light of the risk of reducing protective safeguards in various pieces of EU secondary legislation, the book is a timely reminder of international human rights return-related norms and standards applicable to all EU Member States.

19 European Commission, Communication from the Commission to the European Parliament, the European Economic and Social Committee and the Committee of the Regions on a New Pact on Migration and Asylum, COM(2020) 609 final.

doi: 10.5553/HYIEL/266627012021009001028

Katalin Sulyok, Science and Judicial Reasoning. The Legitimacy of International Environmental Adjudication (Book Review)

Cambridge University Press, Cambridge, 2020, xxxii + 398 p, ISBN 978-1-108-48966-9

Lukasz Gruszczynski[*]

In 2012 Australia was the first country in the world to introduce a new law (dubbed a 'plain packaging law') which set certain restrictions on the color, size and format of the packaging of tobacco products and established rules applicable to the appearance of brand, company and variant names on packages. It also prohibited the use of any trademarks or other marks on retail packaging except for the brand and business or company name, which however could only be placed in a specific area and be displayed in a standardized font. In addition, the size of the health warning was increased to 75% of the front and 100% of a back surface of the package.[1] The law was clearly of an experimental character and was aimed at minimizing the attractiveness of packaging in order to reduce the prevalence of tobacco use among Australians. Since then, similar regulations have been adopted in other countries. Not surprisingly, the Australian measure was contested in the different legal venues. One of the proceedings was instituted in the World Trade Organization (WTO), where several Members claimed that the plain packaging law violated various provisions of the TRIPS Agreement: a treaty that sets minimum standards for the protection of intellectual property rights. In this context, they argued in particular that the law constituted an unjustifiable restriction on the use of the trademark (in this case, that of tobacco companies) in the context of trade.

One of the issues that the WTO panel, and later the Appellate Body,[2] had to decide was whether there was sufficient justification behind the Australian measure (in essence this was a mixed question of law and fact). In the course of the proceeding, the panel therefore had to deal with very complex scientific issues relating to the effectiveness of the plain packaging requirement. It was clear to everyone involved that that the outcome of the dispute depended on how the

* Lukasz Gruszczynski: associate professor of law, Kozminski University, Warsaw; research fellow, Centre for Social Sciences, Institute for Legal Studies, Budapest.

1 Tobacco Plain Packaging Act 2011, No. 148, 2011, An Act to discourage the use of tobacco products, and for related purposes.

2 *See e.g.* Appellate Body Reports, *Australia — Certain Measures Concerning Trademarks, Geographical Indications and Other Plain Packaging Requirements Applicable to Tobacco Products and Packaging*, WT/DS435/AB/R WT/DS441/AB/R, 9 June 2020. Note that technically speaking the dispute was decided by the several panels, each of them dealing with the complaints of specific WTO Member.

doi: 10.5553/HYIEL/266627012021009001029

panel would assess this aspect. Should it perform a *de novo* review of the scientific basis behind the national measure? Or perhaps grant the defendant a certain level of deference? Did it need to consult scientific experts? If so, how should the questions be formulated? And how 'binding' are the experts' opinions?

The book by Katalin Sulyok is precisely about these kinds of dilemmas. The author is a senior lecturer at the Department of International law at ELTE Law School, Budapest. Although she works as a legal researcher, she also has a background in biology (BA), a fact which proved to be very helpful in writing her interdisciplinary monograph. The book as such is a revised version of the doctoral dissertation she defended in 2018 at ELTE Law School. It is worth noting that her thesis was awarded the prestigious 2019 Henry Wheaton Prize[3] as a part of the J.B. Scott competition organized by *Institut de Droit international.*

The book itself is a dense 398-page text, composed of 11 chapters which are grouped into three Parts. The first Part introduces the Readers to the subject, by generally discussing three challenges that emerge when judges engage with science in international environmental adjudications. These include in particular: epistemic (*i.e.* competing cognitive authorities of science and law), doctrinal (*i.e.* structural differences between law and natural sciences), and legitimacy challenges (stemming from the complex relationship between scientific expertise and judicial decisions which can be regarded as legitimate).

Against this background, the second Part identifies four different techniques used by international courts and tribunals for engaging with science (*i.e.* ways in which scientific arguments are handled in the judicial processes) and analyses their use before the selected judicial fora. In particular, the author distinguishes between: *(i)* framing science-intensive disputes and adjusting the level of science entering the judicial inquiry; *(ii)* scientific fact-finding, in particular through the use of experts and expert opinions; *(iii)* causal inquiries; and *(iv)* the standard of review applied to scientific claims. Each chapter in this part is dedicated to one specific court or a group of similar courts/tribunals, and each examines the relevant practice against the above-mentioned taxonomy of judicial techniques. The courts/tribunals analyzed in the book include the ICJ; tribunals in inter-state environmental arbitration; regional human rights courts (such as the ECtHR and IACtHR); WTO panels and the Appellate Body; international investment tribunals; and the ITLOS.

The last Part of the book provides a comparative analysis of these judicial practices. In this context, the author examines the existing differences and similarities in the treatment of science and scientific evidence in the adjudicatory processes, and assesses the advantages and trade-offs connected with each of the four techniques identified above.

The scope of the book has been well thought out. Sulyok correctly limits her analysis to legal adjudication and excludes various diplomatic forms of dispute settlement. This limitation is not only justified (*e.g.* because of the differences

3 Gabriella Szamek, 'The 2019 Henry Wheaton Prize. An Introduction to Katalin Sulyok's Award-Winning PhD Dissertation', *Hungarian Yearbook of International Law and European Law*, Vol. 8, 2020, pp. 412-416.

that exist between these two types of mechanisms) but also desirable as it allows for creating a common platform that can subsequently be used to compare the relevant judicial practices. By the same token, domestic courts are excluded from the scope of the examination. Although they also deal with similar problems [think *e.g.* about the US Supreme Court in the famous *Stenberg v Carhart (Carhart I)*[4] and *Gonzales v Carhart* (*Carhart II*) cases[5]], such courts operate in the specific legal frameworks established under the respective national legal systems, which are very different from international legal settings. The same reason stands behind the omission of the CJEU.[6] It is true that the CJEU is frequently confronted with science-intensive disputes. At the same time however, one has to recognize that it is a unique institution that is located somewhere between the domestic and international levels. The institutional and legal structure in which the CJEU operates has a profound impact on its approach and makes it an uneasy point of reference for comparison with traditional international courts and tribunals.[7]

Despite the title of the book, its scope is not strictly limited to environmental cases. Actually, this category is understood by the author broadly and includes all disputes with an environmental component, as well as those which relate to public health.[8] Such an approach allows the author to look at a diverse (yet sufficiently similar) catalogue of cases that come from different fields of international law (*e.g.* human rights, international trade, investment protection), and draw parallels and identify existing differences. The inclusion of health-related disputes should also be welcomed. In practice, international courts and tribunals rarely distinguish between these two categories of cases and uniformly apply the same judicial techniques to science and scientific evidence (*e.g.* by framing disputes in specific ways, applying a deferential standard of review, using external experts, *etc.*). Ignoring this jurisprudence only because it relates to public health rather than the environment as narrowly conceptualized would definitely be a mistake.

The book fits well in the literature on the subject. While the topic of the interaction between science and law (including adjudication) is not new,[9] Sulyok skillfully builds on the existing scholarship, ultimately producing an original account of the various practices developed by international courts/tribunals.

4 *Stenberg v Carhart*, 530 U.S. 914 (2000).

5 *Gonzales v Carhart*, 550 U.S. 124 (2007).

6 Katalin Sulyok, *Science and Judicial Reasoning. The Legitimacy of International Environmental Adjudication*, Cambridge University Press, Cambridge, 2020, p. 17.

7 For details *see* Patrycja Dąbrowska-Kłosińska, 'Risk, Precaution and Scientific Complexity before the Court of Justice of the European Union', *in* Lukasz Gruszczynski & Wouter W. Werner (eds.), *Deference in International Courts and Tribunals: Standard of Review and Margin of Appreciation*, Oxford University Press, Oxford, 2014, pp. 192-208.

8 Sulyok, 2020, p. 16.

9 *See e.g.* Sheila Jasanoff, *The Fifth Branch. Science Advisers as Policymakers*, Harvard University Press, New Haven, 1998; Kenneth R. Foster & Peter W. Huber, *Judging Science. Scientific Knowledge and the Federal Courts*, MIT Press, Cambridge, MA, 1999; Stephen Breyer, 'Science in the Courtroom', *Issues in Science and Technology*, Vol. 16, Issue 4, 2000, pp. 52-56; Robin Feldman, *The Role of Science in Law*, Oxford University Press, Oxford, 2009.

doi: 10.5553/HYIEL/266627012021009001029

There are at least three aspects that distinguish this title from other works currently available on the market. First, the taxonomy of the judicial techniques plausibly arranges the different approaches used to interact with the scientific aspects of a dispute, providing at the same time an analytical framework against which the practices of the various courts/tribunals can be assessed.[10] While specific techniques have been already discussed in the literature, to my knowledge Sulyok is the first to arrange them systematically and explain their mutual relationship. Second, the book genuinely compares different judicial practices. This analysis exposes the considerable differences that exist between courts/tribunals, with some of them embracing science and others limiting the scope of their examination to judicial issues. Sulyok also enquires into the reasons behind these differences and investigates whether there is a process of cross-learning between the different tribunals.[11] This is a very laborious task; one that is avoided by most researchers as it requires a minute examination of the vast case-law scattered across different fields of international law. A typical research approach in the field is most often to concentrate on one specific aspect[12] or to discuss one of the techniques.[13] Probably the two books that are the most similar to Sulyok's work are the monographs by Jacqueline Peel and Caroline Foster.[14] Of course, an obvious element that distinguishes her book is that it's more up-to-date. This is important, for the last decade has been very rich in science-intensive legal disputes decided in different fora.[15] Peel and Foster were therefore forced to make certain predictions, while Sulyok was able to verify them by looking at actual judicial practices. But the reviewed monograph is also broader in its scope and takes a different perspective. Rather than choosing landmark decisions as case studies (Peel & Foster) or discussing international risk regulation in general (Peel), Sulyok undertakes a systematic review of the entire relevant jurisprudence

10 *See* Sulyok, 2020, pp. 43-63.

11 Id., particularly Chapter 9.

12 *See e.g.* Lukasz Gruszczynski, *Regulating Health and Environmental Risks Under WTO Law: A Critical Analysis of the SPS Agreement*, Oxford University Press, Oxford, 2010; Valentina Vadi, *Public Health in International Investment Law and Arbitration*, Routledge, Abingdon, 2013; Malgosia Fitzmaurice, *Whaling and International Law*, Cambridge University Press, Cambridge, 2015.

13 *See e.g.* Andrew Legg, *The Margin of Appreciation in International Human Rights Law: Deference and Proportionality*, Oxford University Press, Oxford, 2012; Gruszczynski & Werner (eds.) 2014; Mónika Ambrus *et al.*, *The Role of 'Experts' in International and European Decision-Making Processes. Advisors, Decision Makers or Irrelevant Actors?*, Cambridge University Press, Cambridge, 2014.

14 Jacqueline Peel, *Science and Risk Regulation in International Law*, Cambridge University Press, Cambridge, 2010; Caroline E. Foster, *Science and the Precautionary Principle in International Courts and Tribunals. Expert Evidence, Burden of Proof and Finality*, Cambridge University Press, Cambridge, 2011.

15 *See e.g.* ICJ, *Whaling in the Antarctica (Australia v Japan: New Zealand intervening)*, Judgment, 31 March 2014, ICJ Reports 226; ITLOS, *Request for an advisory opinion submitted by the Sub-Regional Fisheries Commission (SRCF), Advisory Opinion*, Case No. 21, 2 April 2015; *Philip Morris Brands Sarl, Philip Morris Products SA and Abal Hermanos SA v Oriental Republic of Uruguay*, ICSID Case No. ARB/10/7, Award, 8 July 2016; Panel Reports, *Australia – Certain Measures Concerning Trademarks, Geographical Indications and Other Plain Packaging Requirements Applicable to Tobacco Products and Packaging*, WT/DS435/R, WTDS441/R, WT/DS458/R, WT/DS467/R, 28 June 2018; ECtHR, *Cordella and Other v Italy*, Nos. 54414/13, and 54264/15, 24 January 2019.

doi: 10.5553/HYIEL/266627012021009001029

(also in the area of human rights law), which makes it possible to present a more complete picture of the relevant developments in field of international law. Third, Sulyok's book includes insightful postulates as to the ways in which scientifically untrained judges can craft persuasive reasoning to justify their choices between competing, and often ambiguous, scientific or science-based arguments offered by the parties or experts in environmental disputes. This also guarantees that the book will remain relevant in the years to come.

I have no doubt that this is a must read for anyone interested in the multifaceted interactions between law and science, and the legal mechanisms used to adjudicate complex disputes with scientific or technological elements.

doi: 10.5553/HYIEL/266627012021009001029

Tamás Szabados, Economic Sanctions in EU Private International Law (Book Review)

Hart Publishing, Oxford, 2020, 280 p, ISBN 978-1-509-93351-8

*Susanne Gössl**

The author of this book, Tamás Szabados, LL.M. (UCL), PhD (ELTE) is associate professor of law at ELTE Law School, Budapest, and one of the founding members of the EAPIL Young EU Private International Law Research Network.[1]

Economic Sanctions are one of those 'repeat players' in international politics. They have become an important instrument of EU foreign policies.[2] States or State Unions can impose penalties against another State, a political group or certain individuals for political and sometimes social issues. Such penalties can be trade embargos or barriers or (perhaps more important today than in the past) restrictions on financial transactions. While these sanctions usually come from International Public Law, they affect international trade, and, thus, become a matter of private international law (PIL). The book is one of the first comprehensive works that scrutinizes the issue of Economic Sanctions from the PIL perspective in EU Private International Law.

While Economic Sanctions have frequently been used as one of the typical examples where public law enters into the domain of PIL, and scholars from international law or international politics have thoroughly discussed issues regarding that topic, a comprehensive study from the PIL point of view in the English language literature had been missing – until now. Szabados undertook the task to write a book with a special focus on the PIL matters. As economic sanctions from the PIL perspective usually become relevant in the areas of international contract law and international tort law, the phenomenon had to be studied not from the mere national but a European perspective, in particular, from the perspective of the Rome I and Rome II regulation.

While this topic and an analysis from the point of view of EU PIL would already have been enough to focus on, Szabados broadens his perspective in a truly European way by adding a comparative view. He analyses the relevant rules and their application and discussion in scholarship and case-law from different national angles, especially the German, English/Welsh, Dutch and French perspective. The result is a well-written, multi-dimensional and entertaining book that shows a deep knowledge of European and comparative PIL that will certainly be of interest for everyone working or writing in that area.

The book starts with an introduction to clarify the core concepts of the book, especially, of course, 'economic sanctions' and the author's general approach to

* Susanne Gössl: professor of law, Christian Albrechts University, Kiel.

1 *See* at https://eapil.org/eapil-activities/young-eu-private-international-law-research-network/.

2 *See e.g.* the EU Sanctions Map at https://sanctionsmap.eu/#/main.

doi: 10.5553/HYIEL/266627012021009001030

PIL.[3] For a scholar from the realm of PIL Chapter 2 about the legal framework for imposing economic sanctions is a very interesting read, as it goes more into detail than usual PIL articles do. Furthermore, and maybe more importantly, Szabados takes a stand in the question of how PIL must be understood and how the EU uses this field of law. At this point, already one of the main topics of the book unfolds: Szabados repeatedly comes back to the notion of an allegedly 'neutral' PIL and shows that this neutrality is only a starting point in theoretical thinking but, as he puts it, is a "fading" notion.[4] He could have been even bolder in his statement. Even though today it is generally recognized that PIL is neither 'neutral' nor 'apolitical' and never has been so, in several academic works this idea is still present. Szabados gives a short introduction into the political nature of PIL and its connection and interplay with substantive law and domestic values, with special regard to the EU and her foreign policy aims. That helps prepare the groundwork for the following discussion and how that idea must be refuted. Szabados, in that regard, is a bit timid, as he only hesitantly and carefully does strides away from the neutrality idea. But maybe he does not need to be bolder, as economic sanctions work as a self-explanatory example to show how political PIL can be. Economic sanctions are usually regarded as overriding mandatory law. These rules have been regarded from the beginning the exception to the 'neutral' PIL and, obviously, their enforcement or non-enforcement is always a result of a political decision.

Another recurrent theme of the book is the EU law's focus on coherence and legal certainty as the main values of EU PIL. Coherence is usually discussed with regard to EU substantive private law. Szabados innovatively also brings PIL and EU external relations law together under one roof and looks at coherence between economic sanctions as instruments of foreign policy and PIL as a supposedly 'apolitical' instrument. The book demonstrates through various examples that a common and coherent EU foreign policy approach (particularly in respect of foreign sanctions) is lacking. Therefore, coherence and legal certainty on the PIL level will more often than not, not be achieved – reflecting a general problem all over the EU.

A part of this argument forms the third key element of the book. Referring to national case-law and national articles, Szabados shows that in different jurisdictions questions regarding the implementation of economic sanctions are treated very differently. As a consequence, the outcome of a case depends highly on the court where the case is brought, even though those courts might apply the same harmonized PIL rules.

Szabados weaves together these three elements. On the theoretical level, he describes several highly controversial issues related to overriding mandatory law that have been discussed in the literature for the last 200 years and have gotten new fuel since Article 9 Rome I Regulation has been in force. The book unfolds a rich spectrum of general knowledge and comparative analysis. These questions

3 Tamás Szabados, *Economic Sanctions in EU Private International Law*, Hart Publishing, 2020, *see* the Introduction, and Chapters 2-3.

4 Id. p. 149.

doi: 10.5553/HYIEL/266627012021009001030

involve the functioning of overriding mandatory provisions in relation to the general law applicable, *i.e.* whether public law rules apply as part of the applicable law (*lex cause* theory or *Einheitsanknüpfung*) or as a different statute (*Sonderanknüpfungstheorie*) or a combination of both (*Kumulationslehre*) and how far the Rome I Regulation can be the relevant instrument to determine their application.[5] Furthermore, Szabados describes the discussion whether overriding mandatory provisions foreign to the *lex fori* and *lex causae* will be applied as a different statute or can become relevant on the substantive law level within the application of the *lex fori* (especially *via* the so-called theory of local data or *Datumstheorie*). Unclear is also the treatment of overriding mandatory provisions of the *lex causae* (part of the *lex contractus* or not?).[6]

Szabados approaches these questions first from an academic point of view. He analyses Article 9 Rome I Regulation in depth from a historical-comparative-functional perspective, referring to Dutch, German, English/Welsh, French, Swiss and other case-law and scholarship. Afterwards, he analyses the concrete case-law on these questions, focusing primarily on French, German and English/Welsh court decisions and the reception of those decisions in the afore-mentioned jurisdictions. Here he elaborates on the finding (and one of the key topics of the book), namely: the high diversity in how Member States treat economic sanctions, therefore coming to different conclusions even though courts deal with the same facts and apply harmonized PIL rules. Szabados includes the famous *Nikiforidis* judgment[7] of the CJEU regarding the interpretation of Article 9 Rome I and derives from this judgment and the embedding of Article 9 how to treat overriding mandatory provisions in EU PIL. Nevertheless, a recurring conclusion is the inadequacy of the current legal situation. To substantiate this view, he arrives at the same findings regarding 'blocking statutes', *i.e.* provisions that prohibit the application of a foreign economic sanction and can lead to a "conflict of overriding mandatory provisions."[8] Finally, he also invokes a topic connected with economic sanctions but often neglected in the academic debate: the treatment of choice-of-court and arbitration agreements having the purpose to avoid a certain *lex fori* and, thereby, certain overriding mandatory provisions. The result is a very diverse picture which nevertheless can be connected by the three above-mentioned recurring elements. Szabados shows deep understanding of PIL and EU law and an impressive knowledge of scholarship from all over Europe. A small point of critique: he could be bolder in drawing his concrete conclusions. Demonstrating as he does, that he knows how to play on the PIL methodology keyboard in a masterful way, and given his deep understanding of the issue, clearer suggestions or legislative proposals would have been highly desirable.

To conclude: we need more books like this, particularly in languages accessible to many of us all over Europe. European PIL still has the big flaw that it is applied by national courts in their respective languages, and, consequently,

5 Id. p. 39 *et seq.*

6 Id. p. 59 *et seq.*

7 Judgment of 18 October 2016, *Case C-135/15, Nikiforidis*, ECLI:EU:C:2016:774.

8 Szabados 2020, p. 155 *et seq.*

doi: 10.5553/HYIEL/266627012021009001030

academic discussions very often center on national decisions and are limited to the native tongues of the respective academics. Access to case-law and literature from different Member States is still scarce, even though several projects try to bridge that gap.[9] Hopefully, in the future there will be more books like this one, promoting a truly European discussion, *i.e.* a thorough academic discussion based on academic articles and cases from different jurisdictions. For a European PIL scholar, this book is a must-read; and for those who want to become an EU scholar, hopefully a great model on how to succeed.

9 *E.g.* databases such as unalex, at www.unalex.eu/ and lynxlex at www.contentieux-international.net/358_p_12967/base-lynxlex.html.

doi: 10.5553/HYIEL/266627012021009001030

www.ingramcontent.com/pod-product-compliance
Ingram Content Group UK Ltd.
Pitfield, Milton Keynes, MK11 3LW, UK
UKHW051027041026
15470UKWH00015B/1600

9 789462 362543